THE ROUTLEDGE HANDBOOK OF THE ETHICS OF CONSENT

While the importance of consent has been discussed widely over the last few decades, interest in its study has received renewed attention in recent years, particularly regarding medical treatment, clinical research and sexual acts. *The Routledge Handbook of the Ethics of Consent* is an outstanding reference source to this exciting subject and the first collection of its kind. Comprising over thirty chapters by a team of international contributors, the *Handbook* is divided into five main parts:

- General questions
- Normative ethics
- Legal theory
- Medical ethics
- Political philosophy.

Within these sections central issues, debates and problems are examined, including: the nature and normative importance of consent, paternalism, exploitation and coercion, privacy, sexual consent, consent and criminal law, informed consent, organ donation, clinical research, and consent theory of political obligation and authority.

The Routledge Handbook of the Ethics of Consent is essential reading for students and researchers in moral theory, applied ethics, medical ethics, philosophy of law and political philosophy. This volume will also be very useful for those in related fields, such as political science, law, medicine and social science.

Andreas Müller is Assistant Professor for Ethics at the University of Bern, Switzerland. Before that, he was a postdoctoral researcher at the Centre for Advanced Study in Bioethics at the University of Münster, Germany. He is currently preparing a monograph on the normative relevance of consent.

Peter Schaber is Professor for Applied Ethics at the Centre for Ethics, University of Zurich, Switzerland. He was previously lecturer at the Universities of Göttingen and Hannover, Germany. He is an editor of *Moral Philosophy and Politics* and a member of the executive board of the Society for Applied Philosophy.

Routledge Handbooks in Applied Ethics

Applied ethics is one of the largest and most diverse fields in philosophy and is closely related to many other disciplines across the humanities, sciences and social sciences. *Routledge Handbooks in Applied Ethics* are state-of-the-art surveys of important and emerging topics in applied ethics, providing accessible yet thorough assessments of key fields, themes, thinkers, and recent developments in research.

All chapters for each volume are specially commissioned, and written by leading scholars in the field. Carefully edited and organized, *Routledge Handbooks in Applied Ethics* provide indispensable reference tools for students and researchers seeking a comprehensive overview of new and exciting topics in applied ethics and related disciplines. They are also valuable teaching resources as accompaniments to textbooks, anthologies, and research-orientated publications.

Available

The Routledge Handbook of Global Ethics
Edited by Darrel Moellendorf and Heather Widdows

The Routledge Handbook of Food Ethics
Edited by Mary Rawlinson

The Routledge Handbook of Neuroethics
Edited by Syd Johnson and Karen S. Rommelfanger

The Routledge Handbook of the Ethics of Discrimination
Edited by Kasper Lippert-Rasmussen

Forthcoming

The Routledge Handbook of the Philosophy of Paternalism
Edited by Kalle Grill and Jason Hanna

The Routledge Handbook of Ethics and Public Policy
Edited by Annabelle Lever and Andrei Poama

For more information on this series, please visit www.routledge.com/Routledge-Handbooks-in-Applied-Ethics/book-series/RHAE

THE ROUTLEDGE HANDBOOK OF THE ETHICS OF CONSENT

Edited by Andreas Müller and Peter Schaber

Routledge
Taylor & Francis Group
LONDON AND NEW YORK

First published 2018 by Routledge

2 Park Square, Milton Park, Abingdon, Oxon, OX14 4RN
605 Third Avenue, New York, NY 10017

Routledge is an imprint of the Taylor & Francis Group, an informa business

First issued in paperback 2020

British Library Cataloguing-in-Publication Data
A catalogue record for this book is available from the British Library

Library of Congress Cataloging-in-Publication Data
A catalog record has been requested for this book

ISBN: 978-1-138-85554-0 (hbk)
ISBN: 978-0-367-73433-6 (pbk)

Typeset in Bembo
by Sunrise Setting Ltd, Brixham, UK

CONTENTS

CONTRIBUTORS

Johann S. Ach is Head of the Centre for Bioethics and Academic Coordinator of the Centre for Advanced Study in Bioethics at the University of Münster, Germany.

David Archard is Professor of Philosophy at Queen's University Belfast. He has written extensively in applied ethics and political and moral philosophy, especially on the subject of children's rights, the family and the state. His books include *Procreation and Parenthood: The Ethics of Bearing and Rearing Children* (2010); *The Family: A Liberal Defence* (2010), *Reading Onora O'Neill* (2013) and the 3rd edition of *Children, Rights and Childhood* (2015).

Vera Bergelson is a Professor of Law and Robert E. Knowlton Scholar at Rutgers University School of Law, USA. Professor Bergelson specializes in criminal law theory. She has written about consent, provocation, self-defense, necessity, strict liability, and victimless crime.

Brian H. Bix is the Frederick W. Thomas Professor of Law and Philosophy, University of Minnesota, USA. He writes in the areas of Jurisprudence, Contract Law, and Family Law. His publications include *Jurisprudence: Theory and Context* (7th edn, 2015) and *Contract Law: Rules, Theory and Context* (2012).

Emma C. Bullock is Assistant Professor of Philosophy and Research Associate at the Centre for Ethics and Law in Biomedicine (CELAB), at Central European University, Budapest, Hungary. Her primary research interests are in medical ethics, normative ethics, and epistemology, especially in relation to issues surrounding the value of autonomy and justified paternalism.

Bart Custers is Associate Professor and Head of Research at eLaw, the Center for Law and Digital Technologies at Leiden University, the Netherlands. His research interests are privacy, consent and profiling.

Francien Dechesne works as a researcher at Leiden University Law School's Center for Law and Digital Technologies (eLaw), the Netherlands. She has a background in formal methods in computer science and in ethics and information technology.

Michelle Madden Dempsey is a Professor of Law at Villanova University Charles Widger School of Law outside of Philadelphia, USA. She is a former criminal prosecutor, specializing in violence against women. Presently she serves as an editor of *Criminal Law & Philosophy* (Springer).

Anna Deplazes-Zemp is a senior researcher at the Center for Ethics at the University of Zurich, Switzerland. Her research focuses on the ethics of biotechnology, research ethics and environmental ethics.

Tom Dougherty is a University Lecturer in Philosophy at the University of Cambridge, UK and a Fellow of Trinity Hall. He researches moral philosophy. He has written several articles on the ethics of consent, and is currently writing a monograph on the topic.

William A. Edmundson is Regents' Professor of Law and Philosophy at Georgia State University in Atlanta, USA. His most recent book is *John Rawls: Reticent Socialist* (2017).

David Estlund is the Lombardo Family Professor of Humanities and Philosophy at Brown University, USA. He is the author of *Democratic Authority: A Philosophical Framework* (2008) and editor of *The Oxford Handbook of Political Philosophy* (2012).

Nir Eyal is Associate Professor of Global Health and Population at the Harvard T.H. Chan School of Public Health, USA. His work focuses on bioethics. He co-edits Oxford UP's series "Population-Level Bioethics". His work outside bioethics surrounds egalitarian and consequentialist theory.

Thomas Gutmann holds the Chair for Civil Law, Philosophy of Law and Medical Law in the Faculty of Law, University of Münster, Germany, and is Director of the University's Centre for Advanced Study in Bioethics.

Tatjana Hörnle holds the Chair for Criminal Law, Criminal Procedure, Legal Philosophy, and Comparative Criminal Law in the Faculty of Law, Humboldt University of Berlin, Germany. She is member of the Berlin-Brandenburg Academy of Sciences.

Heidi M. Hurd is the Ross and Helen Workman Chair in Law, Professor of Philosophy, and Co-Director of the Program in Law and Philosophy at the University of Illinois, USA. She is a scholar and teacher in the areas of criminal law, torts, environmental law and ethics, political theory, moral philosophy, and general jurisprudence.

John Kleinig is Professor Emeritus of Philosophy in the Department of Criminal Justice at John Jay College of Criminal Justice and the PhD Program in Philosophy at the Graduate Center, CUNY, USA and Adjunct Professor of Philosophy, School of Humanities and Social Science, Charles Sturt University, Australia. His main philosophical interests are in moral, social, and political philosophy.

George Klosko is Henry L. and Grace Doherty Professor of Politics at the University of Virginia, USA. He works in both normative political philosophy and the history of political theory. Recent books include *The Transformation of American Liberalism* (2017) and *The Oxford Handbook of the History of Political Philosophy* (2011), which he edited.

Felix Koch is a Lecturer in Philosophy at the Free University Berlin, Germany. His main research areas are ethics and political philosophy.

Daniel Lee is Assistant Professor of Political Science at the University of California, Berkeley, USA. He is the author of *Popular Sovereignty in Early Modern Constitutional Thought* (2016).

Neil C. Manson is a Senior Lecturer in Philosophy at Lancaster University, UK. He is the author, with Onora O'Neill, of *Rethinking Informed Consent in Bioethics* (2007). He is currently working on a range of topics to do with the fundamental nature of permissive consent.

Terrance McConnell is Professor Emeritus, Department of Philosophy, University of North Carolina at Greensboro, USA. He is the author of *Gratitude* (1993), *Moral Issues in Health Care* (2nd edn, 1997), and *Inalienable Rights* (2000), as well as numerous articles on ethical theory and biomedical ethics.

Andreas Müller is Assistant Professor for Ethics at the University of Bern, Switzerland. Before that, he was a postdoctoral researcher at the Centre for Advanced Study in Bioethics at the University of Münster, Germany. He is currently preparing a monograph on the normative relevance of consent.

Collin O'Neil is Assistant Professor of Philosophy at Lehman College, City University of New York, USA. He has written articles on deception, trust, and other topics in applied ethics, and is co-editor (with S. Matthew Liao) of *Current Controversies in Bioethics* (2017).

Tom O'Shea is a moral and political philosopher whose research focuses on freedom in history, theory, and practice. His latest work develops a civic republican approach to medical ethics, the philosophy of disability, and mental capacity law. He was recently appointed Senior Lecturer in Philosophy at the University of Roehampton, UK.

Wolter Pieters is Associate Professor of Cyber Risk in the Faculty of Technology, Policy and Management at Delft University of Technology, the Netherlands. He has a background in computer science and philosophy of technology, and a PhD in information security.

Ben Saunders is Associate Professor in the department of Politics and International Relations at the University of Southampton, UK. His research interests and teaching include the ethics of public policy, such as organ donation, reproductive technology, and state regulation of food and drugs.

Peter Schaber is Professor for Applied Ethics at the Centre for Ethics, University of Zurich, Switzerland. He was previously lecturer at the Universities of Göttingen and Hannover, Germany. He is an editor of *Moral Philosophy and Politics* and member of the executive board of the Society for Applied Philosophy.

Bart Schermer is an Associate Professor at eLaw, the Center for Law and Digital Technologies at Leiden University, the Netherlands. He is also a partner at the consultancy firm Considerati, where he advises multinationals and governments on privacy and data protection.

Hubert Schnüriger is a Postdoctoral Fellow in the department of Arts, Media and Philosophy at the University of Basel, Switzerland. His main areas of research are normative ethics in general, philosophy of law, the concept of rights, supererogation and moral demandingness.

Alex Tuckness is Professor of Political Science and Philosophy at Iowa State University, USA. His research focuses on the history of political philosophy and applications to contemporary questions.

Simone van der Hof is full Professor of Law and Digital Technologies and Head of the Center for Law and Digital Technologies (eLaw) at Leiden University, the Netherlands. Her research interests are digital child rights, privacy and cybercrime.

Tom Walker is Senior Lecturer in Ethics at Queen's University Belfast. His research centers on ethical questions raised by both chronic illness and public health interventions. He has a particular interest in the role of autonomy in both these areas.

Anthony Wrigley is Senior Lecturer in Ethics at Keele University, UK. His research focuses on philosophical issues in bioethics and the margins of life. He has special interest in issues of harms, personhood, vulnerability, and proxy consent.

Gideon Yaffe is Professor of Law and Professor of Philosophy and Psychology at Yale Law School, USA. He is the author of books and articles concerned with how philosophy of mind, action, psychology and neuroscience bear on criminal law.

Matt Zwolinski is Professor of Philosophy at the University of San Diego, USA and director of USD's Center for Ethics, Economics, and Public Policy. His publications deal with issues of exploitation, sweatshop labor, price gouging, libertarian theory, and the basic-income guarantee.

ACKNOWLEDGEMENTS

We are grateful to Fabio Briante, Gabrielle Coakeley, Claire Plassard, Stefan Riedener and Rebecca Shillabeer for their help in preparing this volume.

THE ETHICS OF CONSENT

An introduction

Andreas Müller and Peter Schaber

Consent plays an important role in our life. It does so by affecting both our moral and our legal rights and obligations. For instance, consent often makes acts morally permissible that would be impermissible without consent. Actions of various kinds may only be done to competent adults if and because they consented to them – medical treatment, clinical research, and sexual acts are the most common examples. In those cases, as well as in many others, the affected person's consent not only makes a difference to whether or not the action is morally acceptable, it is also required for it to be legally permissible. Many legal codes, as well as the World Medical Association's Declaration of Geneva, the modern version of the Hippocratic Oath, require physicians to respect a patient's decision to give or withhold their consent to a procedure, even if the patient does not follow the physician's recommendation. Similarly, the laws and regulations of many countries allow medical and other research on human subjects only if the research subject's informed consent has been obtained beforehand. If the subject is incapable of giving it, the informed consent of an authorized proxy must be sought. This requirement is also included in the Declaration of Helsinki, the World Medical Association's principles for human subject research. But the moral and legal relevance of consent extends far beyond the medical sphere. Most importantly, non-consensual sex, whether it is violently imposed or not, is now widely acknowledged to be a serious moral wrong and constitutes a criminal offence in many jurisdictions. Beyond that, the moral and legal condemnation of many types of assault and battery can be reversed or mitigated by the victim's consent.

Due to the importance of consent in all of these areas, the interest in its study has increased over the last decades. Especially in medical ethics, the concept of (informed) consent has been discussed extensively. Much of that discussion has focused on the conditions a person's factual consent has to meet in order to be morally effective, as well as on why the patient's or research subject's consent is so important in the first place. Because whether or not an act constitutes a punishable crime often depends on whether it was performed with the victim's consent, legal scholars have taken a great interest in defining what exactly it means for a person to have given her consent to a particular action. At least since Hobbes, the concept of consent is also of central importance in political philosophy, where it has played a crucial role in theories of political obligations and the authority of the state.

Until recently, inquiries into the nature and normative importance of consent have focused on its role in a particular context, such as medical ethics or political philosophy. Many of the more specific questions that arise from the role of consent in those contexts and that have often been discussed for decades, if not centuries, are still the subject of controversial discussions, discussions that are often reignited or reshaped by the progress of medicine, new technologies, or social developments. Today, however, some authors have also begun to approach the topic of consent from a more general perspective. Indeed, many of the most fundamental questions about consent have only just received the philosophical attention they deserve. One hope for future research is that the various debates concerning consent, those in different areas of scholarship as well as those on different levels of abstraction, can learn from each other, both about the various problems and challenges raised by that complex concept and about potential solutions, and thereby inspire progress towards a more comprehensive understanding of the ethics of consent in all its facets.

The present volume includes contributions by philosophers, legal scholars, and political theorists on a wide range of topics related to consent. Its 32 chapters are grouped into five parts. The chapters in Part I address a number of general questions concerning consent. The chapters in Part II explore the moral relevance of consent and its relations to other issues in normative ethics. The chapters in Part III discuss the importance of consent for various topics in legal theory. The chapters in Part IV are concerned with the importance of consent in several areas of medical ethics. The chapters in Part V discuss the role of consent in political philosophy.

General questions

Our conception of the normative importance of consent has changed over time. Daniel Lee (Chapter 1) sheds light on the history of the idea of consent and the important role it has come to play in modern moral and political philosophy. He also presents some of the modern criticism which that role has attracted. Hubert Schnüriger (Chapter 2) addresses the question of what it means to give consent. He distinguishes two major answers to that question, the mental view and the performative view, and discusses the main arguments put forward in favor of them. Many authors think that there is an important parallel between consenting and promising. In particular, they suggest that, like the obligation that is created by promising, the normative effect of consent can be explained as the result of exercising a normative power. Felix Koch (Chapter 3) explains the concept of normative power and discusses whether the ability to consent should be thought of as such a power. Heidi Hurd (Chapter 4) surveys various accounts of the normative effects that are brought about by consent. In particular, she distinguishes between accounts that take consent to constrain the liberty of the person giving the consent and accounts that take consent to enhance the liberty of the person receiving it. One normative effect that is often attributed to consent is that it ensures that the consenter is not wronged by the consented-to act. Peter Schaber (Chapter 5) explores the relationship between valid consent, permissibility, and the wronging of a person. He discusses the role of the consenter's interests and her autonomy in that relationship and what its proper understanding entails for the limits of what we can effectively consent to. Each instance of effective consent, however, is restricted in its scope, too: it affects the normative status of some (potential) actions, but not that of others. Neil Manson (Chapter 6) introduces this idea of the normative scope of an act of consent, distinguishes it from the act's intentional content, and discusses what determines that scope.

Consent is required for some actions to be morally or legally permissible, but not for others. Terrance McConnell (Chapter 7) asks when a person's consent to an action is required and when it isn't. He argues that this depends on whether some right of that person is implicated by the action. Even when it is required, however, consent is only effective if it meets certain procedural constraints of validity: it has to be voluntary, informed, and decisionally competent. Emma Bullock (Chapter 8) examines these requirements and argues that their strength is context-dependent and that meeting them might not always be sufficient for an act of consent to be effective. Many authors assume that what is normatively relevant about consent is not just what a person actually consents to, but also what she would have consented to in a certain hypothetical situation. Gideon Yaffe (Chapter 9) deals with such hypothetical consent and addresses a major puzzle about how it can be morally effective. Another extension of the standard conception of consent concerns the question of who can consent. It has been argued that, in several practical contexts, the consent of certain groups, rather than individual people, is required. Anna Deplazes-Zemp (Chapter 10) presents such contexts and distinguishes three interpretations of what is meant by group consent in those contexts.

Normative ethics

Consent can make a difference to what we are morally obligated to do and refrain from doing. Andreas Müller (Chapter 11) discusses whose obligations are affected by a person's consent, which moral obligations are sensitive to consent, and why consent can ensure that those moral obligations are not breached by an action. One popular understanding of the moral relevance of consent emphasizes the relation between consent and autonomy. Tom Walker (Chapter 12) discusses two ways of understanding that relation. According to the first, an act of consent makes a moral difference only if it is autonomous. According to the second, acting without someone's consent would be wrong because it would fail to respect another's autonomy. A paradigmatic way of failing to respect a person's autonomy is paternalism. John Kleinig (Chapter 13) focuses on the case of so-called hard paternalism, in which a person's refusal to consent is overridden for reasons of benevolence. He offers an account of what is problematic about such behavior and why certain exceptions could nevertheless be justified. Another way to wrong another person is to exploit them by taking advantage of their vulnerability or their weaknesses. Matt Zwolinksi (Chapter 14) discusses whether such exploitative interactions are necessarily non-consensual. He argues that this need not be the case, and that the lack of valid consent alone does not entail that an interaction is wrongfully exploitative, either. One reason why a person's consent might be invalid is that she has been deceived into giving it. Tom Dougherty (Chapter 15) discusses when and why deception invalidates consent and distinguishes between "duty-first" and "awareness-first" approaches to answering these questions. One of the areas in which consent is widely considered to be especially important is sex. David Archard (Chapter 16) critically examines the orthodox liberal view on this issue, according to which non-consensual sex is impermissible and consensual sex permissible, and discusses prostitution and incest as two problem cases for the latter part of this view.

Legal theory

The maxim *volenti non fit injuria* is a well-known doctrine according to which someone who has consented to an action cannot claim to have been wronged by it. Michelle Madden Dempsey (Chapter 17) outlines the maxim's history and addresses several issues concerning the scope of its application. She also discusses what normative force the *volenti* maxim has and why it bears that force. Vera Bergelson (Chapter 18) discusses the moral limits of what we can authorize by giving our consent, focusing on consent to pain. She surveys various rationales for invalidating consent to serious physical harm and questions whether they are also applicable to pain that is not accompanied by such harm. If someone is coerced into consenting to an action, that consent is invalid because it has not been given voluntarily. Thomas Gutmann (Chapter 19) discusses this condition of the validity of consent. He proposes a normative conception of voluntariness, which explicates coercion not in psychological terms, but in terms of a proposed rights violation.

Brian Bix (Chapter 20) shows how the notion of consent that is at the core of modern contract law differs from the consent that is involved in many other transactions. He also addresses the tension between the difficulty of ascertaining valid consent and the importance of the predictable enforceability of contracts in modern commercial life. There is a growing consensus that the legal assessment of sexual acts should focus on consent. Tatjana Hörnle (Chapter 21) outlines the reasons for this approach and their source in the right to sexual autonomy. She also addresses a challenge for the adequate (re-)formulation of criminal laws, as well as the circumstances that render consent to sex legally invalid and the *mens rea* requirements in the area of sexual offences. Bart Custers and his colleagues (Chapter 22) address the central role that consent plays in privacy and personal data protection legislation. They highlight various issues related to limitations of communication and decision making, which inhibit the effectiveness of consent requirements for protecting privacy.

Medical ethics

The requirement of informed consent is one of the cornerstones of modern medical ethics. Tom O'Shea (Chapter 23) traces the role of consent in the history of medical ethics, looking at ancient Greece, medieval Europe, the Middle East, and the development in Western law and ethics from the early modern period onwards. He also addresses the development of the social and intellectual infrastructure that supports modern medical consent. Nir Eyal (Chapter 24) deals with the scope and the force of the modern informed consent requirement. He also discusses the various grounds that have been proposed for it and argues that the complexity of these grounds makes the status of the requirement less clear than it is often taken to be. Johann Ach (Chapter 25) focusses on a particular aspect of the informed consent requirement for medical treatment: the physician's obligation to disclose all relevant information to the patient. Ach shows how the scope and the content of that obligation depend on the kind of justification that is endorsed for the requirement. Collin O'Neil (Chapter 26) addresses several central issues concerning the role of consent in clinical research. In particular, he discusses when consent to such research is necessary and what conditions it has to meet in order to be valid, and compares moralized and non-moralized accounts of the latter. A special case in medical ethics is organ donation, since the removal of a healthy organ for transplantation constitutes neither treatment of nor research on the donor. Such a donation is usually assumed to require the consent of the donor or their next of kin. Ben Saunders (Chapter 27) examines this requirement, as well as the different systems for registering as an organ donor. He also addresses the consent of the recipients and their relatives. The question of what to do when a person is incapable of giving consent can arise for medical treatment, too. In that case, we often ask other people to consent on their behalf. Anthony Wrigley (Chapter 28) discusses the grounds of such consent for others, as well as the different standards that can guide a proxy's decision to give or withhold consent.

Political philosophy

In the history of political thought, the concept of consent has been at the core of many theories of political obligation and the authority of the state. Alex Tuckness (Chapter 29) examines its role in the work of Thomas Hobbes, John Locke, David Hume, and John Stuart Mill. He surveys their answers to five questions: whose consent is required, when is consent relevant, what renders it invalid, what is the source of its normative force, and what are its effects. However, the historically dominant idea that the consent of the governed provides the best explanation of their political obligations faces the problem that most people have never actually given such consent. George Klosko (Chapter 30) presents this problem and critically discusses various attempts to solve it. David Estlund (Chapter 31) suggests that, similar to the way in which consent can be nullified if it fails to meet certain standards of validity, the lack of actual consent to political authority can be nullified if the people in question are morally required to consent. He then addresses the "bypass objection" to this idea of "normative consent", as he calls it, as well as its relation to various kinds of voluntarism. William A. Edmundson (Chapter 32) raises the question of whether a citizen's consent to the state's demands could be valid if she was raised to believe in being bound to that state. He argues that the proposal that such consent can be valid if the citizen would freely consent to such an education leads to a dilemma: either early education must be radically reformed, or we must acknowledge that the state's authority can ultimately not rest on consent alone.

PART I

General questions

1

HISTORICAL PERSPECTIVES ON THE ETHICS OF CONSENT

Daniel Lee

My goal is to provide brief historical perspectives of the idea of consent in the moral, social, and political thought in the West. It is not intended to be comprehensive, but rather only to survey some of the major texts, themes, and interpretive problems to be explored in this volume. While acknowledging the limitations necessary to such a broad discussion as this, I nevertheless hope this chapter will convey points both of continuity as well as discontinuity in the understanding and valuation of consent over time in various philosophical and political traditions.

1.1 Consent in Antiquity

It is tempting to suppose that consent must have always enjoyed a privileged place in the history of moral, social, and political thought. That conventional wisdom, however, bears little relation to the historical reality of ancient ethics, where consent played a relatively minor role. Indeed, ethics in Antiquity, understood as the practical science of the good, operated on the cardinal principle that notions of value and virtue could not be determined simply by the human will, or even the concord of human wills, but only by something beyond human powers – whether in the divine or in nature.

It is true that writers in Antiquity made the occasional appeal to consent as a potential source of justification. The Greek physician, Hippocrates (c.450–c.380 B.C.E.), for example, is believed to have introduced informed consent in framing the moral boundaries of the doctor–patient relationship (Dalla-Vorgia et al. 2001: 60). Plato (c.429–c.347 B.C.E.), to take another well-known example, formulated a theory of political obligation based on a strict notion of "tacit" consent in the *Crito*, a dialogue depicting the final days of the condemned Socrates. Given the opportunity to escape, Socrates refuses and quietly accepts his fate. Socrates' reasoning relies on the principle that "when one has come to an agreement that is just with someone . . . one should fulfill it", including agreements that bind individuals under the obligation to obey the law (Plato 1997: 44 [*Crito* 49e]). Socrates, Plato conjectures, voluntarily entered into such an agreement, not by any formal oath or express contract, but simply by enjoying without complaint the many advantages of living in Athens. Socrates "could have gone away", but he chose to remain and live as a citizen (Plato 1997: 46 [*Crito* 52e]). In so doing, Socrates, it is thought, voluntarily consented to take up the burdens of citizenship, including the solemn obligation to obey the law – even laws requiring his death.

What must be stressed, however, is the skepticism, even disdain, for the suggestion, advanced by sophists, that social and political institutions, and the duties they define, could be simply the product of consent, just like any commercial transaction in the marketplace. To Plato and many thinkers of Antiquity, there was something base and ignoble about grounding ethical matters upon consent, just as if it were the product of haggling, as in a bargain or barter.

It is thus remarkable that, given this background, consent gradually begins to take on special importance in the history of ideas, so much so that one of the most celebrated moral philosophers of Antiquity, Cicero (104–43 B.C.E.), specifies "consent" as one of the hallmarks defining a well-ordered society (Cicero 1988: 64 [*De Re Publica* 1.39]). This shift in the evaluation of consent occurs, I argue, for a very practical reason – to facilitate commerce and exchange between the diverse peoples of Antiquity, where, in the absence of shared customs and values, consent between parties engaging in some commercial transaction, hoping to reach a bargain, becomes the only reliable marker to validate a binding obligation.

One important source documenting this shift is to be found in the history of classical Roman law, the cornerstone of Western legal science. Roman law, like many other ancient legal systems, originated as a closed system, based on formal customs exclusively applicable to free Roman citizens. Because of this narrow scope of application, the legal remedies and rights of Roman law remained inaccessible to the foreigner, or *peregrinus*, who, legally speaking, was "rightless and dutiless" in the eyes of the Roman lawyer (Jolowicz & Nicholas 1972: 102). One of the practical consequences of this arrangement was the near-impossibility for Roman citizens to engage in legal or commercial relations with foreigners.

At first, this presented no real difficulty for Romans in the early history of the Republic, where commerce was largely contained within the city walls of Rome. But as Rome grew to become, in effect, a multinational empire and the major military and economic power in the ancient Mediterranean world, the archaic Roman law felt like an obstacle hindering commerce, rather than a catalyst enabling it. The acknowledged need for a pragmatic solution, to address the increasing diversity of the Mediterranean economy, rapidly led to a period of creative jurisprudence in the later Republic, introduced via Praetorian edicts, which gradually removed the traditional barriers legally excluding foreigners and made it easier for legal parties, whether of Roman citizenship or not, to engage in commerce.

Among the most important principles introduced into Roman law by the Praetors was the principle of consent, a doctrine that would become vitally important to the Roman theory of contract [*pactum*]. Ulpian, the Roman authority first cited in the title, *De Pactis*, in the *Digest of Justinian*, declares that the Latin word, *pactum*, like the word for "peace" [*pax*], is derived from the more generic notion of "agreement" or "bargain" [*pactio*]. He explains the common feature of all such *pactiones* is "the consent of two or more parties concerning the same thing" (D.2.14.1.2; cp. 50.12.3). Because the function of consent is to "collect" and "gather" [*convenire*] together many wills and unify them as one, the act of consent is to be called *conventio* [literally, a "coming-together"]. So central is the function of consent that Ulpian feels confident in making an even stronger doctrinal claim: "Unless there is consent", there can be no contractual obligation (D.2.14.1.3).

This evolution in ancient contract law illustrates not only how consent came to play a central role in the ancient social imagination, but also a more general trend in Antiquity, once famously observed by Sir Henry Sumner Maine, whereby ancient law proceeds "from status to contract" (Maine 1885). Still, despite the elevation of the importance and practical value of consent, it made little difference to various categories of persons in Antiquity, such as women, minors, and especially slaves, whose legal status effectively handicapped their ability to express consent without some form of representation or legal fiction. An underage *paterfamilias*, though technically the head of the household and empowered with the legal status *sui iuris*, nevertheless could not legally express consent without the intermediating agency of a legal guardian. So, while the principle of consent may have been theoretically recognized in the ancient world, it misses one key element that is vital to the appraisal of consent in modernity – that is, a genuine respect for the moral autonomy and equality of individuals as consenting agents.

1.2 Consent in medieval thought

The history of ethics often overlooks the Middle Ages as a period critical to the notion of consent. One reason for this exclusion can be traced to nineteenth-century historical scholarship of medievalists such as Guizot, Carlyle, and Gierke, who assumed that medieval references to consent specifically meant *collective* consent, mediated through representative bodies such as parliaments, estates, or ecclesiastical councils, rather than *individual* consent. This characterization of medieval Europe as a "collectivist" or "corporative" anti-liberal culture reflected long-settled patterns of collective decision-making, especially in the Church where canons "were established by universal consent" [*universali consensu*] (Tierney 1982: 16).

Yet, while norms of collective or communal consent were central to medieval thought and practice, it is inaccurate to treat the Middle Ages as wholly antagonistic to individual consent. We can observe this in the feudal contract, so central to the socioeconomic organization and land distribution of medieval Europe. What is so exceptional about the solemn, quasi-ritualistic feudal oath binding a lord to his vassal was its intimately personal nature: The exchange of rights and duties between lord and vassal was an unmediated transaction, requiring the formal expression of consent between individuals (Bloch 1961: 145–62, 219–30; Berman 1983: 298–9, 304–7). The moral force of individual consent was further reflected in the various sources forming the medieval *ius commune*, the shared legal system of Roman and canon law that would become the foundation for Western legal science. There is perhaps no better illustration of this principle than in the canon law of Gratian's *Decretum*, where, in a radical shift, individual consent becomes central to the law of marriage. Citing Isidore of Seville, Gratian declares that only "consent makes marriage" (Gratian 1584: C.27, qu.2); everything else is secondary. And Thomas Aquinas' *Summa Theologiae* (1988: S.T. II-I, §15), one of the great documents of Scholastic theology and philosophy, evinces a genuine concern for the authenticity of individual consent when he identifies consent as a capacity exclusive to the rational nature of man.

Consent also performed a vital social and political function in medieval societies, especially in the institutional context of monarchical government, which, revealingly, pictured the relationship between the king and his kingdom as a symbiotic relationship connecting the head of a living being to the rest of its body (e.g., Kantorowicz 1985: 216). Bound in this way, kings were by no means absolute and "exempt from the laws" [*legibus soluti*], but strictly limited in their ability to govern unilaterally, especially regarding legislation and taxation (Pennington 1993: 113–16). Understood to be more suzerains than sovereigns of the body politic, kings were customarily obligated to seek not only the counsel, but, more importantly, the collective consent of the "great men", lords both lay and spiritual, of their realms, assembled in such bodies as the Estates General of France and the *Reichstag* of the Holy Roman Empire. While this did not translate into liberal democracy, it did at least introduce the constitutional norm requiring royal government by consent of the governed.

Securing communal consent of magnates was particularly important in medieval English thought, where Parliament's consent-granting function was reinforced in the Roman-law text appended by clerks in Chancery to Parliamentary writs declaring the purpose for such assemblies: *Quod omnes tangit ab omnibus approbetur* (Post 1964: 163–240). Henry de Bracton (c.1210–c.1268), the medieval jurist cited with approval by John Milton and John Locke, would identify these "counts and barons" of the king's Parliamentary *curia* as the "king's partners" [*socii regis*] and treat their collective *consilium* as one of the principal limitations upon a potentially tyrannical royal will (Bracton 1915: 110). Nearly two centuries later, the English chief justice Sir John Fortescue (c.1395–c.1477) would highlight Parliamentary consent as the key feature distinguishing the English monarchy from all other monarchies, such as the French, where the king is able to "change the laws of his kingdom at pleasure . . . and also impose on [subjects] tallages and other burdens without consulting them" (Fortescue 1997: 17). In England, by contrast, the monarch governs only by "such [laws] as [the people] assent to" (Fortescue 1997: 83).

Some of the most important contributions to medieval theories of consent are to be found in theories concerning the ecclesiastical government of the medieval Church. Officially, the Church was classified as a monarchy, with supreme authority vested in the Pope, as Christ's sole representative on earth. The extreme version of this theory appeared in the 1302 Bull of Boniface VIII, *Unam Sanctam*, which outlined the so-called "hierocratic" theory of Papal plenitude of power, elevating the Papacy to a position theoretically unaccountable to any human authority (Black 1992: 44). It was against this background that medieval theologians and jurists crafted an alternative theory specifically designed to target the hierocratic theory by relocating the source of political legitimacy in the consent of the community.

The most important theorist of consent in this controversy was Marsilius of Padua, whose critique, developed in his treatise *Defensor Pacis*, involved a careful appeal to the anti-clerical notion that coercive powers of temporal government are derived entirely from popular consent, not from the episcopacy acting as the sole intermediaries distributing all powers exercised on earth. For Marsilius, all such temporal powers actually originate in political communities, which he designates "the human legislator", since they are the sole origin of temporal lawful authority. Only by consent of "the people or the whole body of citizens, or the weightier [*valentior*] part thereof" can it be possible for governments to be legitimately established and laws to be enacted (Marsilius of Padua 2001: 45).

In this way, Marsilius developed a theory that positioned communal consent as the foundation for political legitimacy in medieval constitutional thought. For this reason, commentators have sometimes seen Marsilius as a key progenitor of the modern social contract tradition. But Marsilius' theory had a more direct influence in the most important constitutional crisis of the Middle Ages – that is, the Great Schism in the medieval Church, which produced two (and briefly three) competing Popes with claims to the throne of St. Peter. Who decides which claimant has the best title to the Papacy? Marsilius' answer is that such supreme decision-making powers in the Church belong ultimately to the *concilium*, the universal council of the Church.

Through this doctrine, known generally as "Conciliarism", consent emerges as the governing principle even for the Church. The doctrine is best summarized in the decree *Sacrosancta*, published by the Council of Constance in 1415 as the theoretical justification for Conciliar authority to end the Great Schism. Jean Gerson, the Parisian theologian who was one of the principal authors of the decree, summarized the basic tenets of the theory: God intends the Church to be governed through conciliar bodies. Power, thus, descends from God, first to the whole membership of the Church as one mystical body represented in council, and then, only secondarily, to prelates commissioned to serve the Church. Since the power of all prelates, including the Pope, derives ultimately from this general community of the faithful [*universitas fidelium*], any executive decision or action made by a prelate without consent of the community is to be treated as unauthorized and without force.

Consent of the whole [*universi*] body of the Church, as represented in Council, becomes therefore the unique source of Papal legitimacy, just as it was for kingly legitimacy. And it is upon this basis that Conciliarists introduce the formulation that, while the Pope may be greater than any single member of the Church [*maior singuli*], he nevertheless remains subordinate to the whole Church as one body [*minor universi*]. The German canonist and cardinal Nicholas of Cusa, writing in the years after the enactment of *Sacrosancta*, formalizes the principle of consent in his treatise *De Concordantia Catholica*, where he writes that "the binding force of every law consists in . . . consent" (Cusa 1991: 101). In Church and State alike, he writes, "it should be the aim of the ruler to establish laws by agreement . . . of the council" and "decide each matter by consent" (Cusa 1991: 248–9). By positioning consent as the foundation of a general theory of political legitimacy, the Conciliarists adumbrated the basic insight of modern social contract theory.

1.3 Consent in modern thought

John Neville Figgis once described *Sacrosancta* as the "most revolutionary official document in the history of the world" (Figgis 1956: 31), and commentators, following Figgis, have tried to retrace, along various pathways, the intellectual legacy of Conciliarism, as the starting point of a trajectory of thought originating in Constance and concluding with the Revolution of 1688 (Laski 1936; Tierney 1955; Oakley 1962; Skinner 1978; Black 1988; Nederman 1990; Oakley 2003). This can be seen, for example, in the Protestant Reformation, where the appeal to common consent was a typical formulation used in designing a Reformed model of ecclesiastical government such as in Hooker and Calvin. Nor was this exclusive strictly to Protestant thought, as Jesuit theorists, such as Vitoria, Suarez, and Parsons, would locate the origins of authority in a voluntary consensual act transferring natural rights of individuals to government authorities (Höpfl 2004).

Perhaps most striking, however, was the stubborn persistence of the medieval constitutional norm requiring monarchs to secure the consent of the community, assembled in Estates and Parliaments, to enact new taxation and legislation, a trope that would remain vital to the constitutional thought of writers as diverse as Claude de Seyssel, Sir Thomas Smith, and François Hotman (Franklin 1973; Skinner 1978). Most notably, the requirement for the formal expression of such institutionalized popular consent would become central to the radical logic of resistance that would emerge in the context of religious warfare. The author of the *Vindiciae Contra Tyrannos* (1578), perhaps the most notorious treatise justifying the permissibility of armed resistance to kings, pays special attention to consent: Since it is by consent that the community confers their common power upon kings, it is by a similar act of consent that the community can, in principle, revoke that same power.

Such arguments locating a residual or "ephoral" right of resistance in consent-granting assemblies as a remedy of last resort against tyrannical princes fueled the flames of civil war, especially in sixteenth-century France. But they also raised deep skepticism about the moral force of consent in royal politics. The first theorist to challenge directly the consent theory emerging from medieval institutional practice was the French jurist and philosopher Jean Bodin (c.1530–1596). Famous for his analysis of sovereignty, Bodin challenged the constitutional norm that law is always the product of consent between a sovereign prince and a subject (Bodin 1586: 86). The consent of subjects, though perhaps a nice additive, is nevertheless inessential to the validity of legislation.

Bodin's argument is motivated by the tendency to confuse "law" for "contract". His argument is based on the rule that obligations of all types – whether legal, contractual, and (one may reasonably extrapolate) political – can be dissolved only in the same manner in which they were created. The source of this principle is to be found in the *Digest* (D.50.17.35), which Bodin cites in a key expository passage delineating the relationship between sovereignty and law. There, he observes, as a general legal principle, the mutuality of contractual obligations [*mutua obligatio*]: Contracts are "mutual, which reciprocally bindeth both parties, so that the one partie may not start therefrom, to the prejudice, or without the consent of the other" [*mutuo consensu*] (Bodin 1606: 93; Bodin 1586: 87; Gaius 1946: 3.173–5). The principle is meant to apply not only to legal relations between private persons, but also to relations in which a sovereign is a party, such that even sovereigns are prohibited from unilaterally absolving themselves of contractual obligations that they have freely accepted. It is only fair and "agree[able] vnto naturall equitie" that contracts entered into by the mutual consent of all parties, including sovereigns, should be amended or dissolved again by mutual consent (Bodin 1606: 107, citing D.2.14.1).

But laws [*leges*] are different. At least one party remains "free" or "exempt" [*solutus*] from the binding force of the enacted law, which is the sovereign authority – as the "author" of the laws (C.1.14.12.5). It is for this reason that Bodin invokes the famous doctrine of Roman law in formulating his own definition of sovereignty: *Princeps legibus solutus* (Bodin 1586: 85, citing D.1.3.31). Since the sovereign does not need anybody's consent or permission to make law and to bind subjects under legal obligation, neither does the sovereign need, by parity of reason, anybody's consent to *unmake* law, to release subjects from the bond of legal obligation. Indeed, this is precisely why Bodin explicitly insists that law can be made and unmade *without consent* (Bodin 1586: 153; Bodin 1606: 159; Lee forthcoming).

Bodin's analysis of law and sovereignty became one of the first formal expressions of what legal theorists now call the "command theory of law" (Austin 1995; Hart 1994). By eliminating the need for "common" or popular consent in matters of legislation, Bodin highlights what he believes to be the superfluity of consent-granting bodies, such as parliaments and estates, in legislation. What matters here is not so much the consent of subjects, but the legislative will of the sovereign authority.

One criticism of Bodin's theory is that it presupposes the existence of states without explaining the origin of states. Because he doesn't explain this, Bodin's theory came under scrutiny, first of all, from the German jurist Johannes Althusius, who was perhaps the first to fuse together Bodin's theory of sovereign authority with a general theory of consent. Sovereignty is activated only when "all members [of the state are] joined together" as one body (Althusius 1932: 91). But individuals can only join together "by explicit or tacit agreement" [*qua pacto expresso, vel tacito*] in the sharing and cultivation of a common social life (Althusius 1932: 15). In this way, sovereignty and consent are made to be not only compatible with each other, but mutually constitutive.

This line of reasoning, investigating the pre-social natural origins of the sovereign state in the free choices of individuals, serves as one of the key starting points of the modern social contract tradition. Perhaps the first in this tradition is the Dutch jurist and philosopher Hugo Grotius (1583–1645), who plays a crucial role in the revival of consent theory, especially in explaining the origin of private property. Grotius states that, in the state of nature, there was no private property. The whole world was instead, at first, held without division "by a right common to all men" (Grotius 2005: 420). So how did humanity make the transition from common property to private property? Grotius' answer was through an original act of collective consent, "from a certain Compact and Agreement, either expressly, as by a Division; or else tacitly, as by Seizure. For as soon as living in common was no longer approved of, all Men were supposed, and ought to be supposed to have consented, that each should appropriate to himself, by Right of first Possession" (Grotius 2005: 426–7).

Observe that the consenting parties are pre-social individuals, without regard to arbitrary socially defined differences in rank or status. Any individual naturally possesses the capacity to give her consent to designate something as properly her own. Just as private property, then, emerges from consent, so too, Grotius suggests, does the state emerge from a prior "covenant binding upon all of its parts . . . formed by a general agreement for the sake of the common good" (Grotius 2006: 36). Republics and even certain limited monarchies are, in this way, said to be states "originally established by the full and free Consent of the People" (Grotius 2005: 293). Likewise, law – especially what Grotius calls the "primary law of nations" – is thought to derive from "the common consent of mankind", and, following Chrysippus, Demosthenes, and Plato, Grotius states that all law "rests upon the mutual agreement and the will of individuals" (Grotius 2006: 25, 40). Grotius' ultimate purpose in his major works, however, concerns the origin and scope of obligations binding states in their relations with other states, especially in times of war. Even here, Grotius insists upon the consensual origins of obligatory ties between states.

What is perhaps most controversial in Grotius' theory is the extent to which he is willing to use consent to justify obligations that may be detrimental to the interest of the consenting party. There is no better illustration of this strategy than in his notorious statement that, just as "it is lawful for any Man to engage himself as a Slave to whom he pleases", it is similarly "lawful for a People that are at their own Disposal [*sui juris*], to deliver up themselves to any one or more Persons, and transfer the Right of governing them upon him or them, without reserving any Share of that right to themselves" (Grotius 2005: 261). In theory, all rights can be alienated irrevocably, so that a free individual could, if he so wished, voluntarily consent to enslave himself under the power of an absolute master, even an absolute prince. Nor does it matter *why* anybody would want to consent to such self-enslavement (Grotius 2005: 262). Whatever the reason may be for someone to give up their rights, Grotius' point is that it is entirely within the scope of one's rights to do so.

What is crucial to note, however, is that this extreme case of voluntary self-enslavement represents only a theoretical possibility. It does not mean that enjoying the advantages of life in society with others *requires* the voluntary surrender of *all* rights. Indeed, as Richard Tuck once put it, "interpretive charity requires that we assume that all [rights] were not *in fact* renounced", even if "all our rights *could* be renounced" in principle (Tuck 1979: 80, citing Quine 1960: 59).

But such interpretive charity is not enough to satisfy Grotius' critics, who see Grotius as much too willing to "barter [. . .] away" individual rights, as if they were vendible commodities (Grotius 2005: 285). The celebrated social contract theorist Jean-Jacques Rousseau (1712–1778), for example, targets Grotius' doctrine of consensual self-enslavement and rejects it as "vain . . . contradictory" and "incompatible with the nature of man" (Rousseau 1997: 45–6). Indeed, Rousseau's own doctrine of inalienable rights is formulated largely in response to what he sees as a disturbing consequence of the Grotian analysis of consent, one that can potentially be used to legitimize through consent all sorts of unnatural and morally unjustifiable institutions such as slavery and absolute monarchy.

While the Grotian analysis of consent would find its detractors, it also found adherents, especially in England, where theories of individual consent first began to take shape. The greatest English heir to this Grotian analysis of consent was Thomas Hobbes, the philosopher for whom consent not only acknowledged the natural equality of individuals but also made possible the sovereign state. Consent performs a critically important function in Hobbes' theory. Not only is it the conduit through which naturally free and equal, rights-holding men in nature knit themselves together as a Hobbesian state, or "commonwealth", for reasons of rational self-interest, it is also the means by which individuals tie themselves under a general bond of obligation owed to an absolute sovereign authority who is thereby authorized to act on their behalf for the sake of preserving peace.

One critical point in Hobbes' theory of consent is the strictly individualistic character of the consent necessary to constitute a sovereign state. As Hobbes puts it, "a Multitude of men, are made One [civil] Person, when they are by one man, or one Person, Represented, so that it be done with the consent of every one of that Multitude in particular" (Hobbes 1991: 114). Unlike earlier medieval political theories of consent, which typically relied on some form of corporative or communal consent expressed through representative consent-granting bodies, such as estates, parliaments, or councils, Hobbes explicitly insists that the authorizing consent necessary to create a sovereign state must originate from each individual who is to be *subject* to that state. It is precisely this Hobbesian insistence upon the *individual* consent of naturally free and equal, rights-bearing men that – for many commentators – places Hobbes at the beginning of the modern liberal tradition of political philosophy (Kavka 1988).

What complicates this liberal interpretation of Hobbes, however, is his notoriously broad understanding of voluntary consent. While consent, for Hobbes, can certainly be signified expressly by "words spoken" (Hobbes 1991: 120), so too can consent be identified simply "by inference" whether as "the consequence of Silence" or even as "the consequence of Actions . . . [or] the Forbearing an Action", all of which may be sufficient to indicate "the will of the Contractor" (Hobbes 1991: 94). In this way, inferring consent through such notionally "free" actions of individuals functions as a vitally important device in Hobbes' theory, to show how an authoritarian vision of the sovereign state, even a state ruled under the *de facto* power of a usurping conqueror, could still be regarded as a state established technically "by the consent of the People" (Hobbes 1991: 121; Hoekstra 2004).

Inferred consent was a powerful device, enabling Hobbes to show why modern states, into which individuals are born, should still be regarded as legitimate regimes based on consent just as much as the very first primitive state in Antiquity, formed by an express covenant created by naturally free individuals. For Hobbes, actions speak far louder than words when it comes to consent and they reveal the deliberative chain of reasoning that pushes one's will to act. So, he argues, submission to another, even submission secured through fear, threats, or sheer coercion so as to "avoid the present stroke of death" or some other perceived harm, always counts as a valid form of consent resulting from rational calculation. This analysis of consent applies just as much to the person who submits to the highway robber and pays his ransom for fear of his life, as it does to the subject who submits to the sovereign and obeys the sovereign's law for fear of criminal penalties, whether capital or otherwise.

Hobbes goes one step further to say that even states forced under the *de facto* authority of a usurping conqueror – a commonwealth "by acquisition", as he put it – could still be regarded as a regime based on consent, so long as the conquered subject does not resist. Writing in the context of civil war and swift constitutional change with the regicide of Charles I and the establishment of the Commonwealth, Hobbes is particularly keen to show how even the usurping order could still be regarded as a government based on consent.

There is, however, an important limitation to Hobbes' consent theory, which is that one cannot consent "not to defend [one] selfe from force, by force" (Hobbes 1991: 98). Such contracts are, by default, "voyd". Readers of Hobbes have highlighted the significance of this condition. Even with Hobbes, very early in the modern social contract tradition, there is yet a concern, albeit a minimal one in Hobbes' case, about the sort of things to which one may licitly consent.

That concern becomes much more prominent in later consent theorists, who begin, like Hobbes, from the starting point of the natural equality and natural rights of individuals and, yet, insist upon strict limitations on consent, especially upon actions that potentially involve risk, harm, or some other self-inflicted disadvantage. One of the most celebrated examples of this strategy of reasoning is to be found in John Locke (1632–1704), whose contract theory specifies the primary purpose of civil government to be in the "secure Enjoyment of their Properties" (Locke 1988: 331). Such government, designed to protect property rights, requires individuals who are "by Nature, all free, equal, and independent" to "be put out of this Estate, and subjected to the Political Power of another" (Locke 1988: 330). This can only be done, Locke argues, by individual consent, which, as Locke famously argues, can take the form of a "tacit consent" simply when one "hath Possession, or Enjoyment, of any part of the Dominions of any Government" (Locke 1988: 348). But even though individual consent is the foundation of civil government, it aims narrowly at a particular goal, of limited government. Anything more is illegitimate, a "power without right": Seeing that humans are the "workmanship" of God, Locke argues each is bound under natural law to preserve himself and each other. We cannot, therefore, consent to put ourselves in a condition that would be self-destructive, such as slavery or absolute monarchy. Any act of consent that would reflexively alter or undermine one's autonomy and higher-order capacity to consent in the first place deserves, at the very least, careful scrutiny.

1.4 The modern critique of a consent-based ethics

The idea of consent has come to enjoy a privileged position in modern moral and political reasoning. Nevertheless, it is worth highlighting, as a concluding thought, the modern skepticism that has grown alongside the modern theory of consent. And so I want to conclude this chapter by briefly sketching out several prominent criticisms of a consent-based ethics and politics.

One criticism raises the point that theories of consent only rely on a fictive, theoretically crafted *hypothetical* consent, such as the consent of anarchical individuals in a conjectural primeval state of nature or that of self-interested persons deciding whether or not to consent behind an imagined veil of ignorance, rather than the *actual* consent of real, living, flesh-and-blood individuals. The problem, according to this criticism, is that a worrisome gap may emerge between the consent of real people and the hypothetical consent of the imaginary people who stand in for us. This criticism applies to influential moral theories such as Scanlon's contractualism, which imagines moral principles "that no one could reasonably reject as a basis for informed, unforced, general agreement", or Gauthier's contractarianism, which imagines morality as a contracted agreement reached by individuals motivated, not by passion, but by rational self-interest (Scanlon 1998: 153; Gauthier 1986).

This is especially problematic in the social contract tradition. As the Scottish Enlightenment philosopher David Hume (1711–1776) once observed, more often than not it is the case that political authority is established by "usurpation or conquest, or both, without any pretence of a fair consent, or voluntary subjection of the people" (Hume 1994: 189–90). In his view, then, consent "very seldom . . . and almost never" serves as the "just foundation of government" (Hume 1994: 192). Given the practical difficulties of securing the consent of every individual in a modern state on every question of law or policy affecting citizens, modern political theorists have instead tried to devise schemes of representation whereby the need to seek the consent of all would be minimized or, at least, restricted, such as in a plebiscite on constitutional matters of fundamental importance to the state (e.g., Tuck 2016). Another response, championed by political libertarians, bites the bullet by insisting that collective actions of the state ultimately can and should be treated as reducible to the choices of free individuals (Buchanan & Tullock 1962).

Another criticism, often associated with the German philosopher Hegel, concerns the reduction of ethical and political life, and the values associated with membership of a community, to a potentially arbitrary act of will, what Hegel designates by the German term *Willkür.* The problem with the privileging of consent is that it potentially treats "membership, authority, and obligation as though they were optional. Individuals may choose to enter into the state, or they may not; they may legislate some set of institutions for the state, or they may not; they may recognize the authority of the state and assume certain obligations, or they may not" (Patten 1999: 111). But such things, according to the Hegelian view, are not optional and not subject to one's choice and consent, as consent theories suggest. This is particularly important in Hegel's theory of obligations, which derive *not* from an anterior act of consent, but are constituted by the social roles carved out in any ethical and political community (Hardimon 1994a, 1994b).

A third influential criticism, associated with the Marxist tradition and also developed in recent theoretical scholarship on gender, deals with the potentially exploitative nature of consent and targets the assumption that consent is a genuinely free and authentically voluntary act of the individual. On this view, what may superficially appear to be a free expression of consent really isn't free at all, and that is because the ideology that exploits the language of consent, as a transaction among free persons, works by masking deep material inequalities and asymmetries of power. This is particularly problematic in the classical Marxist theory of historical materialism, which positions the working class of modern industrial societies in a desperate condition of unending dependence upon the property-owning class. The Marxist diagnosis explains why workers willingly accept this dehumanizing material inequality and humiliating disempowerment. It is because they are falsely made to believe their condition is the equitable result of free consent, when in fact it is, in the Marxist view, a subtle coercion. Indeed, such consent is nothing more than what the Marxist philosopher Antonio Gramsci has called an inauthentic "manufactured consent", representing the complete ideological "hegemony" of the ruling classes. This doubt about the value and authenticity of consent has, consequently, exposed some important problems in the philosophical foundations of such traditions of thought as libertarianism (e.g., Cohen 1995).

1.5 Conclusion

My remit in this chapter has been to offer some historical perspectives on the ethics of consent, and so I end by asking whether the growing skepticism of the value of consent in normative reasoning is symptomatic exclusively of modernity. The answer, I think, has to be "no". The intellectual history of consent in moral and political thought is usually presented as a series of innovative stages that progressively widen the moral field in which consent can be invoked. But it is worth remembering that the starting point of this trajectory in Antiquity was one of skepticism and doubt. It is, I feel, a position that we have never really left.

References

Althusius, J. (1932) *Politica Methodice Digesta*. Ed. C. Friedrich. Cambridge, MA: Harvard University Press.

Aquinas, T. (1988) *St. Thomas Aquinas on Politics and Ethics*. New York: Norton.

Austin, J. (1995) *Province of Jurisprudence Determined*. Ed. W. Rumble. Cambridge: Cambridge University Press.

Berman, H. (1983) *Law and Revolution: The Formation of the Western Legal Tradition*. Cambridge, MA: Harvard University Press.

Black, A. (1988) "Conciliar Movement," in J.H. Burns (ed.), *Cambridge History of Medieval Political Thought*. Cambridge: Cambridge University Press.

Black, A. (1992) *Political Thought in Europe, 1250–1450*. Cambridge: Cambridge University Press.

Bloch, M. (1961) *Feudal Society: Volume 1. The Growth of Ties of Dependence*. Trans. L.A. Mayon. Chicago: University of Chicago Press.

Bodin, J. (1586) *De Republica Libri VI*. Paris: Jacques Du Puys.
Bodin, J. (1606) *Six Bookes on a Commonweale*. London: Impensis G. Bishop.
Bracton, H. (1915) *Bracton de Legibus et Consuetudinibus Angliae*. Vol. 2. Ed. G. Woodbine and S. Thorne. New Haven: Yale University Press.
Buchanan, J. and G. Tullock (1962) *Calculus of Consent*. Ann Arbor: University of Michigan Press.
Cicero (1988) *De Re Publica*. Trans. C. Walker Keyes. Loeb Classical Library. Cambridge, MA: Harvard University Press.
Cohen, G.A. (1995) *Self-Ownership, Freedom, and Equality*. Cambridge: Cambridge University Press.
Cusa, N. (1991) *The Catholic Concordance*. Ed. P. Sigmund. Cambridge: Cambridge University Press.
D. (1998) *The Digest of Justinian*. Vol. 4. Ed. A. Watson. Philadelphia: University of Pennsylvania Press. [Standard Mommsen citations]
Dalla-Vorgia, P. et al. (2001) "Is Consent in Medicine a Concept Only of Modern Times?" *Journal of Medical Ethics* 27(1): 59–61.
Figgis, J.N. (1956) *Studies of Political Thought from Gerson to Grotius, 1414–1625*. Cambridge: Cambridge University Press.
Fortescue, J. (1997) *On the Laws and Governance of England*. Ed. S. Lockwood. Cambridge: Cambridge University Press.
Franklin, J. (1973) *Jean Bodin and the Rise of Absolutist Theory*. Cambridge: Cambridge University Press.
Gaius (1946) *Institutes of Gaius*. Ed. F. De Zulueta. Oxford: Clarendon Press.
Gauthier, D. (1986) *Morals By Agreement*. Oxford: Oxford University Press.
Gratian. (1584) *Decretum Gratiani*. Lyon, France.
Grotius, H. (2006) *Commentary on the Law of Prize and Booty*. Ed. M.J. van Ittersum. Indianapolis: Liberty Fund. [*De Jure Praedae Commentarius*]
Grotius, H. (2005) *Rights of War and Peace*. Ed. R. Tuck. Indianapolis: Liberty Fund.
Hardimon, M. (1994a) *Hegel's Social Philosophy: The Project of Reconciliation*. Cambridge: Cambridge University Press.
Hardimon, M. (1994b) "Role Obligations," *Journal of Philosophy* 91: 333–63.
Hart, H.L.A. (1994) *Concept of Law*. Oxford: Clarendon Press.
Hobbes, T. (1991) *Leviathan*. Ed. R. Tuck. Cambridge: Cambridge University Press.
Hoekstra, K. (2004) "*De Facto* Turn in Hobbes's Political Philosophy," in T. Sorell and L. Foisneau (eds.), *Leviathan After 350 Years*, pp. 33–74. Oxford: Oxford University Press.
Höpfl, H. (2004) *Jesuit Political Thought: The Society of Jesus and the State, c.1540–1630*. Cambridge: Cambridge University Press.
Hume, D. (1994) *Hume: Political Essays*. Ed. K. Haakonssen. Cambridge: Cambridge University Press.
Jolowicz, H.F. and B. Nicholas (1972) *Historical Introduction to the Study of Roman Law*. Third Edition. Cambridge: Cambridge University Press.
Kantorowicz, E.H. (1985) *King's Two Bodies*. Princeton: Princeton University Press.
Kavka, G. (1988) "Some Neglected Liberal Aspects of Hobbes's Philosophy," *Hobbes Studies* 1(1): 89–108.
Laski, H. (1936) "Political Theory in the Later Middle Ages," Vol. 8, *The Close of the Middle Ages*, in C.W. Previté-Orton and Z.N. Brooke (eds.), *Cambridge Medieval History*, pp. 620–45. Cambridge: Cambridge University Press.
Lee, D. (forthcoming) "Unmaking Law: Jean Bodin on Law, Equity, and Legal Change," in *History of Political Thought*.
Locke, J. (1988) *Two Treatises of Government*. Ed. P. Laslett. Cambridge: Cambridge University Press.
Maine, H.S. (1885) *Ancient Law*. Tenth Edition. London: John Murray.
Marsilius of Padua (2001) *Defensor Pacis*. Trans. A. Gewirth. New York: Columbia University Press.
Nederman, C. (1990) "Conciliarism and Constitutionalism: Jean Gerson and Medieval Political Thought," *History of European Ideas* 12: 189–209.
Oakley, F. (1962) "On the Road from Constance to 1688: The Political Thought of John Major and George Buchanan," *Journal of British Studies* 1(2): 1–31.
Oakley, F. (2003) *Conciliarist Tradition: Constitutionalism in the Catholic Church, 1300–1870*. Oxford: Oxford University Press.
Patten, A. (1999) *Hegel's Idea of Freedom*. Oxford: Oxford University Press.
Pennington, K. (1993) *Prince and the Law*. Berkeley: University of California Press.
Plato (1997) *Complete Works*. Ed. J. Cooper. Indianapolis: Hackett Publishing.
Post, G. (1964) *Studies in Medieval Legal Thought: Public Law and the State, 1100–1322*. Princeton: Princeton University Press.

Quine, W.V.O. (1960) *Word and Object*. Cambridge: MIT Press.
Rousseau, J.-J. (1997) *Social Contract and Other Later Political Writings*. Ed. and Trans. V. Gourevitch. Cambridge: Cambridge University Press.
Scanlon, T.M. (1998) *What We Owe To Each Other*. Cambridge, MA: Harvard University Press.
Skinner, Q.R.D. (1978) *Foundations of Modern Political Thought*. Vol. 2. Cambridge: Cambridge University Press.
Tierney, B. (1955) *Foundations of the Conciliar Theory: The Contribution of the Medieval Canonists from Gratian to the Great Schism*. Cambridge: Cambridge University Press.
Tierney, B. (1982) *Religion, Law and the Growth of Constitutional Thought, 1150–1650*. Cambridge: Cambridge University Press.
Tuck, R. (1979) *Natural Rights Theories*. Cambridge: Cambridge University Press.
Tuck, R. (2016) *Sleeping Sovereign: The Invention of Modern Democracy*. Cambridge: Cambridge University Press.

Related topics

Ch.30 Consent theory of political obligation

2
WHAT IS CONSENT?

Hubert Schnüriger

Consent works as a criterion of legitimacy, deeply pervading social life, making actions and practices permitted that would otherwise be forbidden. What constitutes consent is, however, contested. This issue often figures as a question of the ontology of consent. Two main positions can be distinguished. What may be called the Mental View takes the term 'consent' to refer to a particular mental state or mental action of the consenting agent. According to this understanding, consent is given *foro interno*. In contrast, the second main position, often called the Performative View, conceives of consent as a public act. There is no consent without communication according to this position. Thus, consent is given *foro externo*. Clearly distinguishing these two understandings of consent is of crucial importance in order to prevent conceptual confusions and, in consequence, distortions in substantial normative questions (see e.g. Westen 2004).

The Mental View and the Performative View are introduced in more detail in the first two sections of this chapter. Rather than structuring the debate on the ontology of consent by distinguishing between these two main views, some authors distinguish between three main views. The third view is, then, introduced as the Hybrid View, supposedly combining the core elements of both the Mental View and the Performative View. It will be argued that this threefold distinction only makes sense against the background of a narrow understanding of the Performative View that is hardly ever, if at all, seriously defended. The last section further explores the two main views by investigating what may turn out to be hard cases for each of them.

Before introducing and discussing the two main views, a few clarifications are in order. First, it is often argued that whether consent should be understood as a mental state or a public action depends on the function it is supposed to fulfill (e.g. Bergelson 2014). As the opening remark reveals, consent is here taken to function as a deontic transformer in the sense that it can make actions permitted that would otherwise be forbidden. Alternatively, consent is also often taken to bear on the consent-receiver's responsibility or blameworthiness. Through this lens, the question would not (primarily) be whether a particular act is forbidden because it is performed without the required consent but whether the agent performing it is culpable or blameworthy for performing it without consent. This function is sometimes called the exculpatory function. It is often emphasized by scholars focusing on criminal law (e.g. Feinberg 1986; Westen 2004).

Second, consent can be understood as an intersubjective undertaking or transaction between two agents (e.g. Miller & Wertheimer 2010). It proves helpful to further qualify this transaction in terms of Wesley Newcomb Hohfeld's famous conceptual framework (1913). A consent transaction first implies a so-called claim–duty relationship between two agents. The consenting agent has a claim right against another agent that this other agent performs a particular act or refrains from performing it. She may e.g. have the property right that the other person does not use her car. The other agent has the correlative duty owed to her not to use the car. A consent transaction secondly implies that the consenting agent has the power to waive her claim right and, thus, to release the other agent from his duty. By exercising her power, she changes the deontic landscape (see Hohfeld 1913: 44f). The car owner in the example has the power to permit the other person to use her car by releasing him from his duty owed to her not to use her car. Consenting to another's action is, thus, best understood as a particular means of performing a normative power over another's duty (see Koch, this volume, Chapter 3).

Third, since the transformation of the deontic landscape belongs to the concept of consent itself, it is necessary to build preconditions of validity into it. Three main conditions of validity are commonly distinguished (see Bullock, this volume, Chapter 8). One, the consent-giver must be competent. She must have the mental capacities to understand what she is doing. Furthermore, she must be informed and, finally, she must consent voluntarily. If one of these conditions is not met, the agent cannot validly consent. The debate on the ontology of consent is best understood as a debate on valid consent.

Fourth, even though consent in the sense of valid consent necessarily changes the deontic landscape since it releases an agent from a duty owed to the consenting agent, it is an open question whether that means that the consented-to action is permitted, all things considered. The fact that the consent-giver releases the other agent from a duty owed to her does not necessarily imply that there cannot be other considerations making the performance of the act in question wrong, all things considered. As it is sometimes put, an agent performing a consented-to action does not wrong the consenting agent, but it is an open question whether he nevertheless commits a wrong (see Walker, this volume, Chapter 12).

Finally, 'consent' is here treated as a moral concept. Yet the main arguments and positions can, *mutatis mutandis*, be applied to legal contexts as well. Indeed, some of the arguments discussed below have originally been put forward in discussing the legal concept of consent.

2.1 The Mental View

According to the Mental View, the term 'consent' refers to a particular mental state (Hurd 1996: 125; Alexander 1996: 165f; 2014: 104; Dressler 1998: 424; Husak 2006: 277). This view also figures as 'the Subjective' or as 'the Attitudinal View'. The mental state of an agent consenting to another's action has been characterized in different ways. A first suggestion analyses consent in terms of desire (Westen 2004: 32). Arguably, this suggestion is in line with conceptions that, referring to the etymological roots of 'consent' in the Latin verb *consentire*, take 'consent' to mean 'being of a like mind' (Siegler 1968: 258) or to be 'concurring in mind and spirit' (Dressler 1998: 424). However, these latter conceptions seem quite narrow. Proponents of what may be called a desire-conception usually agree that consent can be given with a broad spectrum of attitudes towards the act in question, ranging from an unconditional welcoming state of mind as it fulfils the consent-giver's deepest wishes, over plain indifference, to all kinds of aversions. They maintain that it is compatible with this broad range of attitudes as it must not be understood as an unconditional desire. It may just be the lesser evil and, that way, be conditional on the circumstances (Westen 2004: 29ff).

Critics of the desire-conception of consent object that it fails to do justice to situations in which an agent desires something without consenting to it: A person may desire to have sexual intercourse with another person without giving her consent to it as the other person may be married (Hurd 1996: 126) or because the former believes in celibacy before marriage (McGregor 2005: 121, 126). Trying to argue that examples of this kind just show that the desire not to have sex under the given circumstances is stronger than the general desire to have sex misses its mark according to this objection. These examples are supposed to show that giving or withholding consent cannot be reconstructed as a desire because it implies an active element. It must be under the agent's control (Ferzan 2006: 204f). Consent must, according to this objection, be understood as an exercise of the will and, that way, as a choice (Hurd 1996: 125; Alexander 1996: 165). This raises the question of whether consent conceived of as a choice is best understood as a particular mental state, as its proponents do, or whether it should be understood as a mental act (see den Hartogh 2011: 301; Tadros 2016: 205). Doubts about calling what may seem essentially an act-of-will approach a 'Mental State View' will be set aside in what follows and 'consent' taken to refer to a conscious and deliberate stance towards what is consented to that has been brought about by an exercise of the will. Two versions of a choice model of consent can be distinguished.

Heidi Hurd famously contends that the consent-giver consents to another's action by choosing it. She takes that to imply that the consent-giver intends the other's action (1996: 126f). This immediately raises the question of how one can intend another's action. Hurd tackles this problem by maintaining that intending another's action is to intend a state of affairs in which this action occurs. Intending others' actions is "[. . .] to intend to allow or enable those actions by means of some act or omission of one's own" (Hurd 1996: 130). This proposal is problematically unspecific. Undoubtedly, the colloquial term 'consent' can be understood as implying that the consent-giver facilitates or enables what she consents to. That may range from 'facilitating' in the sense of 'not resisting' over 'approving of' and 'going along with' to 'permitting' and 'positively promoting'. Yet the meaning of consent functioning as a deontic transformer must be specified in a narrower way. Otherwise, it would not be possible to distinguish between what has been called the core notion of consent and its secondary meanings (Kleinig 2010: 5): For example, it would be impossible to distinguish between the fiancée consenting to the marriage and her parents approving of it (Kleinig 1982: 96ff).

The second version of a choice model gives the mental state of the consent-giver a determinate form by taking the other's action's deontic status rather than the action itself as the object of the choice (Alexander 1996: 166; see also Beauchamp 2010: 57). She has the mental state of waiving her right that the consented-to act not be performed and permits it that way (Alexander 2014: 107f; see also Sherwin 1996: 217; critically Westen 2004: 31ff). The mental state of consenting corresponds in this model directly to the fundamental normative function of consent.

The Mental View does not deny that consent is normally signaled or communicated as doing so gives evidence that the agent consents (Hurd 1996: 125; Alexander 2014: 105). Yet it insists that consent must be distinguished from its communication. But why should that be so?

Proponents of the Mental View commonly argue that it leads to an extensionally adequate identification of tokens of consent in cases in which an agent has a consenting mental state but fails to communicate it. A typical example of this kind imagines a foreigner who intends to communicate consent to another's request for sex but, due to her poor language skills, mistakenly communicates non-consent (Alexander 2014: 105). A more radical case is represented by a competent agent physically unable to communicate consent. For example, a mute quadriplegic may have a consenting mental state towards having sex with another person although she is not able to communicate it (Hurd 1996: 137). The Mental View maintains that consent occurs in cases of this kind even though it is not or not adequately communicated. Consequently, the other person would not wrong the quadriplegic when having sexual intercourse with her. The

Mental View does not deny that the other person would be blameworthy or culpable when having sex with her as he cannot know that he received her consent; quite the contrary. But it insists that he would not violate a right of hers as she has a consenting mental state. *A fortiori*, he would not wrong her (Alexander 2014: 103).

A second line of argument in favor of the Mental View tries to systematically justify why the communication of consent does not form part of the concept of consent itself. It does so by emphasizing the pivotal role consent plays in contemporary ethics. The requirement of consent, it is commonly said, expresses the normative relevance of the individuals' own stances on acts or practices that concern them. Proponents of the Mental View contend that the prominent role consent plays reflects the value of autonomy (Hurd 1996: 124; Alexander 1996: 165; Dressler 1998: 424). This contention, however, is not unique to them but also widely held among proponents of the Performative View (e.g. Sherwin 1996: 210ff; see also Beauchamp 2010: 57ff and Walker, this volume, Chapter 12). Consequently, proponents of the Mental View must not only argue that consent mirrors the value of autonomy. They must argue that it only reflects the value of autonomy adequately when it is conceived of as a mental state. The sole argument to be found in the literature trying to discharge this burden of proof is Hurd's: "If autonomy resides in the ability to will the alteration of moral rights and duties, and if consent is normatively significant precisely because it constitutes an expression of autonomy, then it must be the case that to consent is to exercise the will. That is, it must be the case that consent constitutes a subjective mental state" (Hurd 1996: 124f, Fn. omitted; see also Alexander 1996: 165).

This argument has quite strong implications. Consent is just one way in which an agent can autonomously shape her deontic surroundings. Promising is another, as Hurd herself writes (1996: 124). Whereas an agent consenting to another's action thereby releases him from a duty owed to her, an agent giving a promise to another agent binds herself to him. She incurs a duty owed to him and gives him a (claim-)right against her. It is widely held that a promise must explicitly be given to and accepted by the other agent. Promising always takes two, as the saying goes. That makes it difficult to conceive of promises as mental states or mental actions. Proponents of the Mental View of consent can, of course, bite the bullet and, in quite a revisionist manner, maintain that promises are given *foro interno* as well. The alternative is to deny that the argument applies to promises – but then it would have to be substantially complemented and refined (for a suggestion of the direction such an argument could take, see Alexander et al. 2016: 657). Furthermore, and more specifically, proponents of the latter strategy would have to make intelligible how a Performative View of promises can be coherently combined with a Mental View of consent. It has been argued that this proves highly difficult (Dougherty 2015: 234ff).

A much more fundamental objection questions directly the crucial assumption of the argument that only mental states or acts deserve to be called expressions of autonomy. As has been alluded to above, proponents of the Performative View often explicitly agree with the proponents of the Mental View that consent's crucial role is due to the normative relevance of the individuals' autonomous will and their own stance on things that concern them. They may even agree that being autonomous is in the most basic sense a property of the will. Nevertheless, they insist on the distinction between the *raison d'être* of the normative function of public tokens of consent and tokens of consent themselves. According to this understanding, agents have the normative power to shape their deontic surroundings by performing an openly accessible act token of consent because it is valuable that agents should be able to do so if they want. Performing a public act token of consent can hence be understood as an expression of autonomy even if it is agreed on that only the will can be autonomous in the strict sense of the word.

2.2 The Performative View

The main alternative to the Mental View takes 'consent' to refer to public actions (Raz 1986: 81; Feinberg 1986: 173ff; Sherwin 1996: 209; Archard 1998: 4; Brett 1998: 69; Schulhofer 1998: 271; McGregor 2005: 124f; Beyleveld & Brownsword 2007: 188ff; Owens 2012: 165; Dougherty 2015: 244ff; Healey 2015: 357ff; see also Manson 2016: 3325ff). It has been defended under different names, all of them expressing the difference between understanding consent as a mental state on the one hand and understanding consent as a public act on the other hand. The most popular as well as the most helpful term to capture the distinguishing characteristic of this alternative view is 'Performative Action View' or, for short, 'Performative View'. It refers to the work of the speech act theorist John L. Austin. Austin introduced the concept of a performative speech act in order to argue that utterances do not only describe or report a state of affairs but that they can also bring about the very state of affairs the words uttered refer to. A helpful device in order to distinguish performative speech acts understood in this way from other speech acts consists in inserting 'hereby'. For example, by uttering 'I (hereby) name this ship the *Queen Elizabeth*' one does not assert, express or report that one is naming the ship *Queen Elizabeth* or that one has already named it so mentally, but one christens it by uttering these very words (1975: 117). In a similar vein, an agent consents to something by performing an openly accessible act token of consent. A patient consents, for instance, to an operation when she says to the surgeon: "I (hereby) consent to the operation" or when she signs a patient consent form. There is no consent before the utterance or before the signing.

Even though the concept of a performative act owes a lot to the theory of speech acts, the Performative View is not committed to holding that consent must necessarily be given in a verbal way. Nodding, handing over the key to someone who has asked whether he can use one's bicycle or taking a seat in the hairdresser's chair can all count as instances of consent. Crucially, both verbal as well as non-verbal forms of consent presuppose implicit or explicit rules that determine what public behavior counts as a token of consent. They presuppose conventions.

It has been mentioned at the outset that the literature on the ontology of consent is divided on how to conceive of the Performative View exactly. What may be called a strictly conventionalist or narrow understanding of the Performative View takes consent to occur when an agent behaves in a way that conventionally counts as an act token of consent no matter whether she believes she is consenting (Wertheimer 2003: 144; see also Healey 2015: 354). Authors subscribing to this narrow understanding of the Performative View tend to complement it with the introduction of a third concept of consent, calling it the 'Hybrid View'. The Hybrid View of consent is supposed to combine this narrow understanding of the Performative View with the Mental View by holding that consent occurs only when a conventional act token of consent is performed with the respective mental state. Both having a consenting state of mind and performing a public act of consent are, then, supposed to be necessary but not individually sufficient for constituting consent. Yet they are jointly sufficient in combination (Wertheimer 2003: 144; Healey 2015: 354).

This tripartite classification proves problematic, though. It presupposes an understanding of the Performative View that has hardly ever been defended. Scholars representing themselves as proponents of the Performative View normally contend that consent must be performed intentionally and, in this sense, with a consenting mental state (e.g. Archard 1998: 4ff; McGregor 2005: 126, 131; Owens 2012: 165; Dougherty 2015: 229; see also Malm 1996: 147f; Sherwin 1996: 219). A famous exception to this is Wertheimer (2003: 148), although he seems to have changed his position later (see Miller & Wertheimer 2010: 85). His reason for defending a narrow conception of the Performative View will briefly be discussed in the last section. It suffices for the moment to emphasize that the Hybrid View conforms *cum grano salis* to the Performative View as it is commonly understood by its proponents. Their understanding of the Performative View is supported by two quite general considerations. First, it builds on the general view that actions can be distinguished from mere behavior by their intentional structure. To say of someone that she consents to another's action means accordingly that she does so intentionally. Still, it is not obvious what exactly this intentionality- condition amounts to. Whereas some proponents of the Performative View take it to imply that an agent performing a token of consent must have the intention to do so and, thus, the intention to waive her right that the consented-to act not be performed (e.g. Sherwin 1996: 219f), others prefer the weaker understanding that it only implies that the consenting agent must know that she performs what conventionally counts as a token of consent (e.g. Archard 1998: 6). She must not have the intention to release the other person from her duty. This weaker understanding allows the insincere performance of a public token of consent to be classified as an instance of consent. Second, its proponents' own understanding of the Performative View fits better with the commonly accepted conditions for valid consent. The consenting agent is supposed to be competent and informed. She is, in other words, supposed to know what she is doing.

The Performative View has been justified in several ways. Its advocates also rely prominently on the argument of extensional adequacy. On the one hand, they directly question their opponents' intuitions. In the case of the foreigner who wants to accept another's request for sex but mistakenly communicates non-acceptance, the Performative View can agree that the foreigner has a consenting mental state. However, it classifies this mental state as the intention to consent. In the case of the mute quadriplegic, it is highly doubtful that she can even intend to consent. Knowing that she will not be able to communicate consent it seems more plausible to argue that she can at best desire to have sexual intercourse with the other person even though she knows that this will never occur in a consensual way. On the other hand, proponents of the Performative View have come up with cases that are supposed to show that communication of consent does not just fill an epistemic gap but forms a constitutive part of consent itself. An example of this kind of case is an agent pondering on a request of her neighbor who wants to use her parking lot for a few days. She inwardly grants him the permission to use it and mentions that to her friend without (explicitly) authorizing him to communicate this to the neighbor. As it happens, her friend runs into the neighbor and tells him of the decision to grant him the permission. Proponents of the Performative View contend that it would be wrong of the neighbor to use the parking lot in consequence and that he would have to wait for the owner to communicate the decision to him (Owens 2012: 169f; see also Wertheimer 2003: 146). Again, proponents of the Mental View will most probably take the example to show that consent has indeed occurred.

As it seems, the argument of extensional adequacy leads to a stalemate based on contradictory intuitions. What the Mental View conceives of as a difference between consent and its public communication, the Performative View takes to be a difference between the intention to consent and an actual occurrence of consent.

A prominent further argument in favor of the Performative View states that reasons must be accessible to the agent whose reasons they are. Loosely following Alan Wertheimer's proposal, it can be conceived of as an argument based on two premises. The first one states that an agent's consent functions as a deontic transformer because it changes the other agent's reasons for action. The second premise contends that the mental states of one agent cannot, on their own, change another agent's reasons for action. That is taken to lead to the conclusion that consent must be understood as an openly accessible token of consent (Wertheimer 2003: 146). The first premise will not be questioned here, even though it is less trivial than it might seem at first sight (see for this Dempsey 2013: 19ff; Manson 2016: 3227ff). The second premise presupposes that reasons must be accessible to the agent whose reasons they are in order to determine the deontic status of his actions. This assumption is not self-evident. It is not implausible to argue that an agent can have reasons for actions he has no immediate access to (Raz 1990: 178ff). A surgeon wondering whether he should perform surgery on a patient may have a good reason to perform it if she has a small but dangerous tumor even if he has no possibility of diagnosing it given his technical facilities. According to this understanding, the fact that she has a tumor speaks in favor of the operation quite independently from his awareness of the tumor. The argument from the public accessibility of reasons rests thus on a contestable metaethical premise.

Arguably, the most natural reason why the Performative View may seem nearly self-evident to its defenders consists in the genuinely intersubjective character of consent (Kleinig 2010: 5; Sherwin 1996: 216). In addition, it has been emphasized that the agent to whose action the consent is given is normally not just passively reacting to the consent-giver's consent. At least in paradigmatic cases, he actively seeks the other's consent, as he would commit a wrong without having it (Manson & O'Neill 2007: 72). He asks for the other's consent in order to get her permission and he must be able to rely on her consent (Beyleveld & Brownsword 2007: 187ff). Thus, the consent transaction would seem incomplete without communication. Against this background, the Mental View may also seem counterintuitively arbitrary, since it allows for consent to be given and revoked too easily, and in a way that leaves it unnoticed by the agent asking himself whether he is allowed to perform a particular act (Malm 1996: 150). This line of reasoning proves less conclusive than its proponents sometimes seem to assume. Defenders of the Mental View happily agree that consent has a genuinely intersubjective character without drawing the same conclusion. They can even agree that an agent needing another's consent must make sure that the other indeed consented. Otherwise, he would act in an unjustifiable and even culpable way. Proponents of the Mental View may suspect that this line of reasoning seems primarily plausible to their opponents because they conflate the function of consent as a deontic transformer with the question of culpability, arguing that communication is decisive for the latter but not for the former (see Alexander 2014: 104ff; Alexander et al. 2016; for a rejection of this explanation see Healey 2015: 356, 362).

A more fundamental argument in favor of the Performative View holds that consent's particular function in practical reasoning and its value is only adequately grasped if it is conceived of as a public action (Dougherty 2015; Healey 2015). The meaning of the interactions and relations between the consent-giver and the consent-receiver and, in consequence, their value depend according to this line of reasoning on whether both agents can assume that it is a consensual interaction. This condition implies, at the very least, that the interacting agents must not only be able to believe that consent has been given. They must also be able to reliably believe that the other party believes that consent has been given. In other words, they must be able to presuppose common belief or public knowledge that consent occurs. This argument may be spelled out in different ways. Maintaining that consent has its place in a moral framework that attributes agents normative control over what agents may do to (and with) each other, Richard Healey argues that agents can only relate to each other as agents having moral control over the relevant sphere if they give the presence or absence of consent an explicit and adequate role in their deliberations. And that implies that they must be able to reliably believe whether consent has been given, withheld or revoked (2015: 359). Only if consent is understood as a public act can it capture what it means to mutually recognize each other as autonomous agents having control over crucial parts of their own life. In a similar vein, Tom Dougherty emphasizes that a consent-seeking agent can only guide his behavior by respect for the other's consent and, therefore, by respect for her when consent is given publicly (2015: 246f; similarly Manson 2016: 3330). He complements this basic line of argument with the further thought that consent changes the way agents can hold each other accountable. Only if consent is conceived of as necessarily given publicly can an agent be held accountable for acting without consent by the agent whose consent is required (2015: 245). This further contention in particular will likely provoke the already familiar objection of conflating the legitimizing deontic function of consent with its exculpatory function. With regard to the general line of argument, proponents of the Mental View may suspect that it undercuts another fundamental distinction. They might insist on the difference between the moral value of a moral action and its legitimacy, suspecting that justifying the Performative View by invoking the value of public consent in the way outlined compounds these two dimensions.

2.3 Difficult cases

As the sections above make evident, both the Mental View and the Performative View have to come to terms with two characteristics. On the one hand, the requirement of consent is commonly thought to ensure that the consent-giver's own stance on crucial questions that concern her is taken seriously and that she can shape her deontic surroundings intentionally. On the other hand, consent is genuinely intersubjective. Only a consent transaction in which both interacting partners understand what is consented to can count as a complete and successful consent transaction. That, in turn, allows for many ways a consent transaction may prove to be defective even in cases where the criteria of valid consent mentioned at the outset are met.

It is instructive to ask as a last step how the Mental View and the Performative View cope with the most important forms of defects in the communication of consent, although these forms pose a more fundamental challenge to the latter.

The Mental View has on the face of it a smooth way to handle defective consent transactions, since it strictly distinguishes between consent and the communication of consent. Accordingly, flaws in the communication of consent such as misunderstandings are external to it. They only bear on the blameworthiness of an agent performing an action he needs another's consent to and not on the action's deontic status. Separating consent from its communication comes, however, at a price. An agent who thinks to violate another's right because he justifiably thinks to act without her consent might be blameworthy, but he does not wrong her according to this approach when she has, unbeknownst to him, waived her right (Alexander 2014: 103), even though he displays the utmost disrespect for her. That is all the more problematic if the requirement of consent is about respecting people's autonomy, as its main supporters maintain. Furthermore, an agent who insincerely signals consent to another person without indeed consenting mentally would be wronged by the latter when he acts on the supposed consent (Manson 2016: 3323).

Defective consent transactions prove naturally more delicate for the Performative View as the communication of consent forms a constitutive part of the very concept of consent itself (Sherwin 1996: 210ff): The tokens of consent itself are defective or infelicitous (see Austin 1975: 13ff). It is an open question how best to treat them. Proponents of the Performative View might adhere to a strict reading according to which an act only counts as a token of consent when both interacting partners indeed identify it as a token of consent and understand what it refers to. Such a reading clearly distinguishes the question of what successful consent consists in from the question of how to cope with infelicitous tokens of consent and goes hand in hand with emphasizing the distinction between acting wrongly and being responsible for doing so. It seems to suggest itself primarily in the case of the moral concept of consent. More formalized contexts such as the law often explicitly address the danger of misunderstandings and stipulate what kinds of infelicitous tokens of consent nevertheless count as tokens of consent. Still, it is up for discussion whether this distinction is not too rigorous even for the concept of moral consent.

On the one hand, the strict understanding does not allow for failures of uptake. On principle, a successful communication of something implies that it is understood adequately by all the parties involved. But it seems counter-intuitive to condition consent on it being recognized as such by the consent-receiver. An agent may carefully perform what conventionally counts as a token of consent and the consent-receiver may nevertheless accidently or carelessly fail to notice it. A car owner leaving a written note at her neighbor's place that he may use her car seems to consent to him using her car even though he may fail to see the note (see Manson 2016: 3330). Furthermore, and more fundamentally, conditioning consent on its uptake would threaten to subvert the very point of the publicity condition discussed in the last section as the consent-giver would have to have access to the other's mental state in order to know whether she herself has given consent or not (Healey 2015: 360 Fn).

On the other hand, the intentionality condition raises the converse suspicion that it unduly privileges the supposed consent-giver's point of view by giving it the status of a necessary condition. It too threatens to subvert the arguments brought forward on behalf of the Performative View. Primarily two kinds of situations seem problematic.

A notorious example of the first kind of situation is a patient not paying attention to her surgeon's explications and signing a consent form to a dangerous and difficult intervention without intending to consent to this very intervention. She may be under the impression that the surgeon suggests a less invasive one. Importantly, the patient is not only competent, but she has also all the relevant information available. It is due to her negligence that she tokens consent to a particular intervention without intending to do so. This kind of case motivated Alan Wertheimer in his 2003 monograph to suggest a narrow, conventionalist conception of the Performative View and to abdicate the condition that the consenting agent must do so with a particular mental state *tout court* (2003: 148). To be sure, this understanding must not completely deny that the requirement of consent mirrors the moral relevance of the consenting agent's own stance. It does deny, however, that an agent's actual mental state should work as a criterion for the identification of tokens of consent. It has been mentioned already that this remains a solitary position so far even though other proponents of the Performative View sometimes also emphasize the need to give epistemic considerations a role in determining when consent is morally valid (e.g. Dougherty 2015: 249).

A less radical view is to build into the concept of consent conditions of the consent-giver's responsibility for successful consent transactions, that way allowing for certain forms of unintended consent. An agent performing what conventionally counts as a token of moral consent indeed consents according to this suggestion if the mismatch between the public meaning of her action and her mental state is due to her own carelessness. Adjustments of this kind have explicitly been suggested with a view to the concept of consent in the law (Beyleveld & Brownsword 2007: 193f). Proponents of the Performative View are more explicit when it comes to cases of insincere consent. The main reason why some proponents of the Performative View deny that a token of consent must be performed with the intention to consent is exactly that they insist that an agent who only feigns to intend to release another person from his duty by performing what conventionally counts as a token of consent should be held to have consented thereby.

So far, it has implicitly been presupposed that the conventional meaning of act tokens of consent is undisputed. The second kind of situation raising suspicion that the Performative View unduly favors the consent-giver's standpoint is that in which the meaning of the public action is at stake. On the one hand, a consent transaction may be infelicitous due to differing interpretations of a particular public action. This problem is amplified by the fact that consent may not only be given in verbal ways. It is, for example, notoriously contested whether there are social conventions that justify someone to take another's behavior as an implicit consent to sex. On the other hand, the precise content and scope of a given token of consent may be referentially opaque (see McGregor 2005: 135ff). If a car owner consents to another person using her car in a case of need, it is not at all obvious what she indeed consents to as it is not evident what exactly counts as 'a case of need'. The Performative View seems to imply that it is the consent-giver's understanding of whether she consents or not and what she consents to that is decisive. This implication is indeed often justified by invoking the burden of proof. It is the consent-receiver who has a moral duty to make sure that the consenting agent indeed understands what is at stake. Only then can he honestly and reasonably believe that she consents (Beyleveld & Brownsword 2007: 192f). He has this duty as he is seeking her permission. A consequence of this understanding of the terms of consent seems to be that the agent seeking consent must not rely on contested and referentially opaque social conventions or speech acts when there is a possibility to further clarify the terms of consent (Archard 1997: 278; Brett 1998: 80). It is, however, a substantial and contested question how far this responsibility reaches and what it needs to live up to it. That may depend on the normative area and the goods or harms at stake. Consent to sexual relations could have to meet different criteria than consent to surgery or to using one's car.[1]

Note

1 Many thanks for helpful comments to Tom Dougherty, Richard Healey, Angelika Krebs, Andreas Müller, Jan Müller, Peter Schaber and Susanne Schmetkamp.

References

Alexander, L. (1996) "The Moral Magic of Consent (II)," *Legal Theory* 2(2): 165–74.
Alexander, L. (2014) "The Ontology of Consent," *Analytic Philosophy* 55(1): 102–13.
Alexander, L., H. Hurd and P. Westen (2016) "Consent Does Not Require Communication: A Reply to Dougherty," *Law and Philosophy* 35(6): 655–60, doi: 10.1007/s10982-016-9267-z.
Archard, D. (1997) "A Nod's as Good as a Wink. Consent, Convention, and Reasonable Belief," *Legal Theory* 3(3): 273–90.
Archard, D. (1998) *Sexual Consent*. Oxford: Westview Press.
Austin, J.L. (1975) *How to Do Things With Words*. Second Edition. Cambridge, MA: Harvard University Press.
Beauchamp, T.L. (2010) "Consent and Autonomy," in F.G. Miller and A. Wertheimer (ed.), *The Ethics of Consent. Theory and Practice*. Oxford, New York: Oxford University Press, pp. 55–78.
Bergelson, V. (2014) "The Meaning of Consent," *Ohio State Journal of Criminal Law* 12(1): 171–80.
Beyleveld, D. and R. Brownsword (2007) *Consent in the Law*. Oxford: Hart.
Brett, N. (1998) "Sexual Offenses and Consent," *The Canadian Journal of Law and Jurisprudence* 11(1): 69–88.
Dempsey, M.M. (2013) "Victimless Conduct and the *Volenti* Maxim: How Consent Works," *Criminal Law and Philosophy* 7(1): 11–27.
den Hartogh, G. (2011) "Can Consent be Presumed?" *Journal of Applied Philosophy* 28(3): 295–307.
Dougherty, T. (2015) "Yes Means Yes: Consent as Communication," *Philosophy & Public Affairs* 43(3): 224–53.
Dressler, J. (1998) "Where We Have Been, and Where We Might Be Going: Some Cautionary Reflections on Rape Law Reform," *Cleveland State Law Review* 46(3): 409–42.
Feinberg, J. (1986) *Harm to Self*. New York, Oxford: Oxford University Press.
Ferzan, K.K. (2006) "Clarifying Consent: Peter Westen's The Logic of Consent," *Law and Philosophy* 25(2): 193–217.

Healey, R. (2015) "The Ontology of Consent: A Reply to Alexander," *Analytic Philosophy* 56(4): 354–63.
Hohfeld, W.N. (1913) "Some Fundamental Legal Conceptions as Applied in Judicial Reasoning," *The Yale Law Journal* 23(1): 16–59.
Hurd, H.M. (1996) "The Moral Magic of Consent (I)," *Legal Theory* 2(2): 121–46.
Husak, D. (2006) "The Complete Guide to Consent to Sex: Alan Wertheimer's *Consent to Sexual Relations*," *Law and Philosophy* 25(2): 267–87.
Kleinig, J. (1982) "The Ethics of Consent," *Canadian Journal of Philosophy*, Supplementary Volume VIII: 91–118.
Kleinig, J. (2010) "The Nature of Consent," in F.G. Miller and A. Wertheimer (ed.), *The Ethics of Consent. Theory and Practice*. Oxford, New York: Oxford University Press, pp. 3–24.
Malm, H.M. (1996) "The Ontological Status of Consent and Its Implications for the Law on Rape," *Legal Theory* 2(2): 147–64.
Manson, N.C. (2016) "Permissive Consent: A Robust Reason-Changing Account," *Philosophical Studies* 173(12): 3317–34, doi: 10.1007/s11098-016-0665-8.
Manson, N.C. and O. O'Neill (2007) *Rethinking Informed Consent in Bioethics*. Cambridge: Cambridge University Press.
McGregor, J. (2005) *Is it Rape? On Acquaintance Rape and Taking Women's Consent Seriously*. Aldershot: Ashgate.
Miller, F.G. and A. Wertheimer (2010) "Preface to a Theory of Consent Transactions: Beyond Valid Consent," in F.G. Miller and A. Wertheimer (ed.), *The Ethics of Consent. Theory and Practice*. Oxford, New York: Oxford University Press, pp. 79–105.
Owens, D. (2012) *Shaping the Normative Landscape*. Oxford: Oxford University Press.
Raz, J. (1986) *The Morality of Freedom*. Oxford, New York: Clarendon Press.
Raz, J. (1990) *Practical Reason and Norms*. Princeton: Princeton University Press.
Schulhofer, S.J. (1998) *Unwanted Sex. The Culture of Intimidation and the Failure of Law*. Cambridge, MA: Harvard University Press.
Sherwin, E. (1996) "Infelicitous Sex," *Legal Theory* 2(3): 209–31.
Siegler, F. (1968) "Plamenatz on Consent and Obligation," *The Philosophical Quarterly* 18(72): 256–61.
Tadros, V. (2016) *Wrongs and Crimes*. Oxford: Oxford University Press.
Wertheimer, A. (2003) *Consent to Sexual Relations*. Cambridge, NY: Cambridge University Press.
Westen, P. (2004) *The Logic of Consent. The Diversity and Deceptiveness of Consent as a Defense to Criminal Conduct*. Aldershot: Ashgate.

Related topics

Ch.3 Consent as a normative power
Ch.4 The normative force of consent
Ch.8 Valid consent
Ch.12 Consent and autonomy

3

CONSENT AS A NORMATIVE POWER

Felix Koch

3.1 Introduction

Acts of consent effect changes in the normative situations of both their authors and their addressees. For instance, an act of consent may bring about that a certain previously impermissible action or activity becomes permissible. Yet it can appear mysterious how consent accomplishes this, since it seems that the giving of consent need not change anything about the inherent desirability of the actions and activities whose normative status it nevertheless affects. This is perhaps especially salient if we conceive of consent as a communicative act, which need not be accompanied by any desire or intention that the consented-to action or activity take place. What could explain how acts that do not change the non-normative situation in any extensive way can have such far-reaching normative consequences?

The way in which consent seems to effect significant normative changes by comparatively minimal means has led many authors to compare consent to promising. A promise, too, can bring about far-reaching changes in both the promisor's and the promisee's normative situations through a simple declaration. Perhaps the same type of explanation is available for both kinds of phenomena. This article considers one such candidate explanation, which interprets promising and consenting, along with other kinds of normatively consequential communicative acts, as exercises of what is often called normative power. Normative power accounts have long been among the main contenders for explaining the normative effects of promising, but they have received somewhat less attention in the context of debates about consent.

Sections 3.2 and 3.3 of this chapter are devoted to explaining the concept of normative power, starting with the more specific case of legal power and then turning to generalizations and refinements of that concept aimed to make it applicable outside the legal sphere. Section 3.4 relies on this explanation to ask whether the ability to consent should be thought of as a normative power, and section 3.5 considers some further implications.

3.2 Normative powers: what they are

Normative power is a certain type of agential ability. As a first pass, it can be characterized as an agent's ability to bring about normative changes in the world *in a particular way*. That agents are able to bring about normative changes in the world in *some* way or other, and to do so intentionally, is not a contentious claim: many things that we are able to do have normative consequences because they affect non-normative features of the world, and the normative situation partly depends on those non-normative features. But not all ways of changing the normative situation are exercises of normative power in the sense at issue here. The main burden of a more precise explanation of the concept of normative power thus lies in spelling out the qualifier "in a particular way".

Some of the most familiar instances of normative power are found in the legal sphere. Since they are in the first instance abilities specifically to affect the legal situation (that is, the normative situation concerning legal norms), and since they are themselves created by the law, they are known as legal powers. Consider the authority to appoint someone to an office. This is an ability, conferred by law, to bring about a change in the appointee's legal position, by investing her with certain legal rights and obligations (and perhaps also with other so-called Hohfeldian incidents, such as powers, liabilities, and immunities). The authority to appoint is thus a legal power. Similarly for many other legal acts: being able to perform them presupposes various legal powers. These include, for example, powers of legislation and adjudication, as well as the power to make a will or to enter into a contract.

The canonical early analyses of normative powers were analyses of legal powers.[1] The concept of normative power was first generalized to non-legal contexts in writings by Joseph Raz (1972, 1975) and has since acquired wide currency (Wellman 1995, 1997; Watson 2009; Owens 2012; Westlund 2013).[2] A paradigmatic instance of non-legal normative power is the power to promise. It seems that the ability to make promises is an ability to change one's own and others' (non-legal) normative situation in distinctive respects: the making of a promise places the promisor under an obligation to do as promised, and it also confers a claim right (to performance) and a power (of release) on the promisee. These normative effects seem to be brought about simply through an act of communication (perhaps coupled with acceptance), rather than by altering the properties of the promised act in more significant ways that might explain its becoming obligatory – for example, by making it the case that some harm would eventuate if the act were omitted.[3]

Again, that people should be able to bring about changes regarding their own and others' rights and obligations in some way or other is hardly remarkable. All that is needed to account for this broad ability is the observation that deontic facts about rights and obligations often depend on non-normative facts, and that agents can change those non-normative facts through their actions. For instance, there may be a general obligation to do something if one has intentionally invited others to rely on one's doing it, and if they will as a result be worse off if one fails to do it than they would have been if one had not invited them so to rely. If there is any particular interest in the idea of normative power, it must be because the way in which the normative situation is changed through the exercise of such powers is more direct than in the case just given, and does not rest on comparable changes to the non-normative situation.

This takes us back to the proviso introduced at the beginning of this section by the placeholder phrase "in a particular way". Among philosophers who believe that the exercise of normative power is a distinctive phenomenon, we find a number of proposals about how to spell out this proviso. Among the most developed of these are ones by Joseph Raz, David Enoch, and David Owens.[4]

Raz (1972) suggests that a first step toward capturing the distinctiveness of normative power is to require that the normative effects brought about through exercises of normative power should be related to the acts constituting such exercises in a specific way: they must be the "results" of such acts rather than just "consequences" of them.[5] If I do something that leads you to make a promise, I have in a certain sense brought it about that you are now obligated to do as you promised. But your obligation is merely a consequence of my action. The very same action on my part could have failed to bring about the obligation, since it could have failed to bring about your promise. Not so with respect to the relation between your act of promising and your obligation: the obligation is related to the act of promising as a result, insofar as performing that very act could not have failed to bring the obligation into existence.[6]

While this requirement succeeds at distinguishing exercises of normative power from many other ways of influencing the normative situation, it does not by itself suffice to demarcate an intuitively plausible concept of normative power. If I intentionally wrong someone, I thereby incur new obligations toward that person: to apologize, compensate them, or make amends in some other way. In terms of the distinction just highlighted, those new obligations are "results" rather than merely "consequences" of my action. My action does not contingently cause their existence, but is part of some type of non-causal explanation of their existence. Nevertheless, we may not want to say that we have a normative power to create duties to apologize and to compensate. This suggests that further refinement is needed to arrive at a satisfactory characterization of normative power.

Raz proposes that a second necessary condition for an act's counting as an exercise of normative power is that the explanation of why the act affects the normative situation in the relevant way must be of a special sort. As he suggests, "it is the nature of the reasons justifying the norm [e.g., the obligation created by a promise] which determines whether acts affecting its existence or application are power exercising acts" (1972: 95). Some obligations are justified or explained by reference to the desirable consequences of people's discharging them, that is to say, the desirability of the actions required by them. In the terminology used by Raz, the justification of such obligations is "content-dependent". Other obligations are justified instead by the fact that they "ought to be respected as created and regulated by human action", which makes their justification "content-independent" (Raz 1972: 95; Raz 2009: 210–1).[7] For example, if promises are exercises of normative power, then the obligation created by a promise does not rest on the independent desirability of the promised act. Promissory obligations are instead "justified by the justification of the general norm that promises (. . .) ought to be respected; they are not justified by giving reasons for the desirability of each obligatory act in its particular circumstances" (Raz 1972: 98). Unlike, say, an obligation to help someone in danger because one is the nearest person around – an obligation one may have intentionally taken on by placing oneself there – a promissory obligation not only happens to be created by human action but is binding precisely because it was so created, rather than being binding because of the consequences of discharging it.[8]

More recent accounts of what normative power consists in are found in work by David Owens and by David Enoch, among others.[9] Owens (2012: 4) writes that in exercising a normative power, "I change what someone is obliged to do by intentionally communicating the intention of hereby so doing". He contrasts obligations resulting from exercises of normative power, in which "the speaker must present himself as intending (. . .) to change the normative situation by means of this very communication", with "obligations [which] may be unintended side effects of what we do, and no part of our plan of action" (2012: 5). Thus, in contrast with Raz's account, it is not part of Owens' definition (though it is part of his fuller account, on which more below) that normative power be justified or explained in any particular way.

Enoch (2014) offers an analysis of a phenomenon that he calls "robust reason-giving", which he suggests is the kind of thing that possessing a normative power allows one to do. Robust reason-giving takes place when an agent A succeeds in realizing a set of intentions whose content is as follows: "(i) A intends to give B a reason to ϕ, and A communicates this intention to B; (ii) A intends B to recognize this intention; (iii) A intends B's given reason to ϕ to depend in an appropriate way on B's recognition of A's communicated intention to give B a reason to ϕ" (Enoch 2014: 7–8; cf. also Enoch 2011).[10] In order for robust reason-giving to take place, these intentions must succeed and they must do so partly because of the existence of an independent "general" reason that B has – namely, a reason to ϕ if the intentions in (i) through (iii) are in place. For instance, A's request that B should ϕ will succeed only if its addressee has a general reason to comply with A's requests. To assert that such a general reason exists then seems equivalent to ascribing to A the normative power to make (successful) requests.

Owens' and Enoch's definitions are less committal than Raz's concerning the justification (or the conditions of existence) of normative power. For that reason they fail to rule out as exercises of normative power certain cases that are plausibly excluded by Raz's definition with its built-in reference to the value of such powers. Some person A may be able to change what some person B is obligated to do, simply by intentionally communicating the intention of hereby so doing, where the explanation of her ability to do so is that C has publicly threatened to kill D unless B complies with A's communication. Should we say that A now has normative power? Are normative powers the kinds of things that can be created through coercive threats? Intuitively, the full explanation of B's obligation in this type of case seems to be of the wrong kind for regarding that obligation as created through the exercise of a normative power, although on Owens' account we might so regard it. A similar worry arises for Enoch's characterization of robust reason-giving. It seems that some further constraint is needed on the type of "general reason" that must be in place in order for the realization of the intentions in (i)–(iii) to constitute a case of robust reason-giving. In a case like the one just described, where the "general reason" consists simply in some adverse consequences that would follow from B's not ϕ-ing under conditions in which A's non-normative intentions are realized, we would hesitate to classify the realization of A's normative intentions – the normative change brought about by A's communication – as resulting from the exercise of a distinctive kind of agential ability.

There would be little point in discussing these alternatives if they merely concerned the definition of a philosophical term of art. The interest in the concept of normative power, if any, is that its features help illuminate a certain shared structure of normative explanation underlying a number of familiar phenomena. Before I turn in section 3.4 to the question of whether the concept of normative power is useful for understanding the phenomenon of consent in particular, I will first briefly consider what could entitle us to believe that people do in fact possess normative powers, i.e., that the concept is sometimes instantiated.

3.3 Normative powers: what explains them

Legal powers are a special case of normative powers. What makes them specifically legal powers is not only that their normative consequences are specifically legal consequences, but also that their existence is explained by reference specifically to legal rules. By contrast, normative powers that are not legal powers have normative effects that are not legal effects, and their explanation – or a demonstration of their existence – will have to appeal to something other than legal rules. Take again the case of promising. When a person promises to ϕ, she thereby places herself under a (non-legal) obligation to ϕ. But what explains her ability to do so? What makes it the case that she has this power?

We have seen that the demarcation of a sufficiently distinctive concept of normative power already requires us to say something about what explains the possession of such powers. On Enoch's account, there must be a "general reason" (and we might add: of a suitable kind) that is instantiated by the reason created through an instance of robust reason-giving. Depending on the case, this general reason will be a reason to do what one has promised, or to do as requested, or to do as one was ordered. But Enoch does not offer any details as to what such a reason may consist in. More generally, we can say that, in order for someone to have a normative power, there has to be some true normative principle that assigns the relevant kind of normative role to power-exercising acts. But what explains the truth of such principles? The answers that have been offered to this question are broadly of two types, one appealing to the value of normative power and the other to its constitutive role in moral autonomy.

A first type of answer is elaborated by Raz and Owens. Raz (1977) supposes that what establishes the existence of some particular normative power is that it is valuable that people should possess that power. For instance, the existence of the power to place oneself under obligations through promising is established by pointing to the fact that the possession and exercise of that power allow people to establish and maintain valuable kinds of special relationships with others. The power to promise is explained by the fact that "it is desirable to make it possible for people to bind themselves and give rights to others if they so wish" (Raz 1972: 101). Similarly, Owens (2012) holds that a normative power exists only if it is non-instrumentally good for us that the existence (or absence) of certain obligations should depend on our exercising such a power. When this condition is met, we can be said to have a "normative interest" that is served by our possessing that power. On Owens' view, the existence of such an interest is not sufficient to show that we do in fact have the requisite power. A further necessary (and jointly sufficient) condition is that there is an established social practice of recognizing the power in question (2012: 9–10).

A second type of answer to the question of what grounds or explains normative powers has been offered by Seana Shiffrin, and related proposals are found in Thomson (1992), Hurd (1996), and Chang (2013). In the context of a discussion of promising, Shiffrin (2008: 500–2) asks what could explain the "moral power" that underlies "the generation of morally significant relations merely through the expression of the will to do so", and she argues that this power "flows (. . .) naturally from a plausible understanding of a meaningful right of autonomy". We may be entitled to assume that Shiffrin believes that this "right of autonomy" is of value to us, but this further assumption is not invoked by her to explain why we have such moral powers. Rather, "[t]he idea that an agent can intentionally form an obligation through the exercise and expression of her will alone (and not by first transforming the state of affairs around her) comes part and parcel with any plausible conception of an autonomous agent"(Shiffrin 2008: 500). Insofar as we think of ourselves and others as autonomous agents, we are thereby committed to ascribing to them promissory powers (and that is to say, to believing the relevant normative principle).

A discussion by Gary Watson straddles the two types of answer just outlined. Watson agrees with Raz and Owens that the value of normative powers, and our corresponding interest in having them, plays a role in explaining them. Thus, promises bind partly because of the "value of being in a position to bind oneself by making assurances" (Watson 2009: 164). Yet, in Watson's view, this is insufficient grounds for being entitled to believe that we have such powers. What needs to be added for a satisfactory explanation is that the relevant powers are "integral to our conception of our moral standing (. . .) as autonomous beings" in such a way that the normative principles that entail their existence pass a contractualist test, being principles that no one could reasonably reject (Watson 2009: 164–5). Considerations of value and considerations of moral autonomy are two necessary and jointly sufficient components of a justification of normative power.

3.4 Is consent a normative power?

A number of authors have taken the view that acts of consent are exercises of normative power. We can call this the normative power view of consent, or the normative power view for short.

Writers on consent who have endorsed this view either at length or in passing include Thomson (1992), Wellman (1995, 1997), Wertheimer (2000), Shiffrin (2008), Watson (2009), Owens (2012), Dempsey (2013), Enoch (2014), Dougherty (2015), and Manson (2016). Are they right in thinking that we exercise a normative power when we give our valid consent? And if they are, does this help us answer any of the questions surrounding consent, or contribute to settling any of the disputes over the nature and explanation of consent?

Before looking at some considerations in favor of the normative power view, consider first the question of whether the effects of consent are of the right sort for them to result from the exercise of normative power. It seems that they are. There is broad agreement among philosophers that at least core cases of valid consent have the effect of creating permissions. Consent makes otherwise (*pro tanto*) prohibited acts (*pro tanto*) permitted, removing the wrongfulness (in the relevant respect) of acts that would otherwise constitute wrongings (Thomson 1992: 348; Westen 2004; Shiffrin 2008: 501; Watson 2009: 160; Owens 2012; Dougherty 2015; Manson 2016; Schaber 2016). This may be because to consent is to waive a claim-right (Thomson 1992: 350; Wellman 1997: 21; Owens 2012; Schaber 2016), or because consent removes certain reasons against an action (Wellman 1995: 66), or because consent permits its recipient to exclude certain reasons from deliberation (Dempsey 2013).

Beyond permission-creating acts, it may be that some acts that give rise to obligations or liabilities for those who perform them – and perhaps also to claim rights, liberties, or powers – also qualify as acts of consent. Weale (1978: 68), Thomson (1992: 352), Raz (1986: 82), and Simmons (2010: 305) are among those who endorse some version of such a broader conception of consent. For instance, perhaps one can consent to being bound by the terms of a contract (thus incurring an obligation), or consent to deferring to another person's decisions (thus conferring on them a normative power and incurring a corresponding liability), or consent to assuming a certain office (thus acquiring a range of corresponding rights and obligations). And by consenting to a duty-imposing act on the part of some other person one may not only be permitting that person to perform the act but first enabling her to do so, thus giving her a normative power. For example, by consenting to take B as her spouse, A does not simply make it permissible for the officiating party C to impose spousal duties on her by declaring A and B married, but rather she first confers on C the normative power to do so, and thereby incurs a corresponding liability. All these putative normative effects of consent seem to be of the right sort to make consent a candidate for a normative power. But is it one?

On the broader view of consent just outlined, some acts of consent – for instance, those in which one consents to being bound by the terms of an agreement – may simply *be* cases of promising. If promising, in turn, is an exercise of normative power, it follows that consent is at least sometimes an exercise of normative power. Yet for the general purpose of assessing the normative power view of consent, it may be useful to remain neutral, as between this broader conception of consent (which may best capture the extension of "consent" in everyday parlance) and the narrower, more regimented conception – shared by a number of philosophers – that limits consent to the creation of permissions.

A number of considerations speak in favor of the normative power view. One is that it allows a unified explanatory treatment of different normative phenomena that seem to play structurally similar roles in our practical lives and our practical reasoning. Like promising, the giving of consent is presented as an expression of the intention, sometimes successful, to bring about a relatively important normative change through the performance of an act that is itself relatively trivial. Both promising and consenting, and perhaps other types of acts as well, can plausibly be regarded as involving "the generation of morally significant relations merely through the expression of the will to do so" (Shiffrin 2008: 500). To say that they can be plausibly so regarded is not to say that all agree in regarding them thus. Those who think of consent as a mental attitude may be especially reluctant to stress the analogy between consenting and promising, as will those who, like Scanlon (1998), aim to explain the normative effects of promising without recourse to the idea of normative power.

A second consideration in favor of a normative power view of consent is that it allows us to account for the unity of the phenomenon of consent itself. Suppose we were to think of consent not as an exercise of normative power, attended by the generic normative consequences of that exercise – say, permissibility – but instead as a class of acts that have broadly similar non-normative features and similar normative consequences, but whose normative consequences are explicable in light of general normative principles which themselves contain no reference to the value or autonomy-constituting role of a power of consent. The burden of any such approach would be to explain why the consent-constituting acts or attitudes should have the same kinds of normative implications across such a large variety of otherwise quite heterogeneous kinds of situations. Shouldn't we expect the normative import of the relevant acts or attitudes to be highly variable depending on the specific circumstances, if that import is not one that they have simply *qua* exercises of consent?

Third, acts of consent can plausibly be thought to meet Raz's two necessary and jointly sufficient conditions for counting as exercises of normative power. Regarding the first condition, it seems plausible – although, again, not trivial – that consent changes the normative situation not by causing some state of affairs that has the requisite normative import, but rather by normatively resulting in such a state of affairs, by grounding or partly constituting it. In giving our consent, we (and the recipients) are not simply hoping that we will succeed in contingently changing the non-normative facts in such a way as to make the consented-to act normatively innocuous. Rather, we give and receive consent in the belief that that is all it takes to ensure the intended normative effect.

Regarding Raz's second condition, the content-independence of justification, the matter is less clear. Some accounts of consent, especially some of those that conceive of consent as a mental attitude, are most naturally interpreted as holding that the normative result of A's consenting – say, that B is now permitted to ϕ – is explained by the difference consent makes to the value or desirability of B's ϕ-ing. On such accounts, the normative difference made by consent is not content-independent, and thus consent would not be a normative power in the relatively specific sense discussed above. At the same time, many accounts of consent do explain its normative results in a way that meets the condition of content-independence. Consent renders actions permissible, on those accounts, independently of any difference it may make to the value of those actions. This is consistent with acknowledging that consent may make various sorts of difference to the desirability of actions.[11] One of the attractions of the normative power view is that it allows us to clearly distinguish between these contingent normative effects of acts amounting to consent, on the one hand, and their content-independent normative results *qua* acts of consent, on the other.

Fourth, like other putative normative powers, our ability to consent is one that we have reason to value. As Owens (2012) has argued, the ability to issue permissions, and to do so independently of whether we desire the performance of the act we thereby permit, is an integral component of many of our valuable relationships with intimates as well as with strangers. We thus have "permissive interests" (Owens 2012: 172–82; for similar considerations see also Raz 1986: 86–8). And Dougherty (2015: 244) has highlighted the ways in which consent enables intimacy and the shared use of property and facilitates interaction. It is also plausible, as Shiffrin (2008) and Ripstein (2009) do among others, to regard the ability to consent as a central aspect of our self-conception as autonomous agents, whether or not we believe this kind of autonomy to be valuable. Thus, if the possession of normative powers can be established in one of the ways discussed earlier, the normative power view of consent would allow us to explain why we are able to bring about the normative effects we do in giving our consent.

While consent thus seems in many respects to fit into the mold of a normative power, some may also see reasons to be wary of the normative power view. I will mention two main concerns here.

The first concern, already broached above, is that the normative power view of consent is unlikely to be neutral vis-à-vis one of the most contested questions regarding the nature of consent – namely whether the normative effects of consent-giving result (at least partly) from the performance of some communicative or expressive act, or rather from the presence of a suitable mental state or attitude.[12] The normative power view naturally aligns with a performative or communicative conception of consent. On the accounts of normative power canvassed in section 3.3 above, exercises of normative power consist in intentional acts and, what is more, in acts that communicate the intention to affect the normative situation in the relevant way. To view consent as a normative power is therefore to emphasize the agential aspect of consent, the fact that it is an ability that persons exercise when they intend to bring about certain normative results. But the mental attitude that does all the normative work according to attitudinal theories of consent need not be, and perhaps is not most naturally, thought of as an intentional act, or as resulting from an intentional act. It may be that one could develop an attitudinal conception of consent that embraces the model of normative power, on the basis of a suitably adapted conception either of the relevant mental attitude or of the valuable ability in question. But on the face of it, the attitudinal theory and the normative power view do not seem to be well matched. Whatever reasons there are for accepting some form of an attitudinal theory are thus likely to be at the same time reasons against the normative power view. Of course, the reverse holds as well.

A second concern rests on the observation that consent may be given through actions undertaken for reasons that are quite independent of its normative effects. For example, it may be that we consent to being subject to the rules of a public transportation system simply by entering a subway station in the knowledge that those rules apply to all those who enter (cf. Raz 1986: 83–4). But is it true that entering a subway station is an exercise of normative power? That seems doubtful. Whatever the explanation of the fact that entering a subway station has this normative result, it does not seem to rest on the desirability of persons being able to bring about this normative result in this fashion. More plausibly, the explanation is content-dependent: it turns on the fact that conformity with those rules on the part of those located in the station is on the whole desirable. This species of consent thus does not conform to the characteristic pattern of explanation by which we demarcated exercises of normative power. If consent encompasses cases like the one just described, the normative power view seems inadequate as a general characterization of consent.

If one or both of these concerns turned out to be well placed, this would not entail that the normative power view of consent is on the whole misguided. Rather it would restrict the scope of that view. It is hardly far-fetched to think that the term "consent", as used in our complex and heterogeneous moral and legal practices, denotes more than just one single normative phenomenon, and that it may require disambiguation in contexts where we are looking for a detailed account. There may be a number of different ways in which we can change our normative situation, all bearing some resemblance to each other but subject to different kinds of explanation. The normative power view may help us isolate one of those ways even if it does not explain all of them.

3.5 Further questions

Accepting a normative power view of consent, or of one species of consent, leaves us with a number of further questions.

One set of questions concerns the implications of this view for on-going debates about the nature of consent: how it is instantiated, what kinds of acts can be consented to, under what conditions consent is valid or effective, and what it could mean to speak of hypothetical, presumed, tacit, and implied consent. The goal of this article has been to sketch the normative power view in general outline rather than to apply it to these substantive issues. We can suspect that the normative power view will be neutral with regard to some of those questions, and that it will favor or exclude certain answers with respect to others. One example of the second sort has been the issue of the "ontology of consent" addressed in the previous section. But, concerning a number of other issues, the details of a normative power account of consent will simply be answerable to the results of substantive normative reflection about consent. Normative powers have boundaries and possession conditions, which we discover either by thinking about the value of these powers or by thinking about their specific role in our self-conception as autonomous agents.[13]

This, then, is a second set of questions arising with respect to a normative powers account, concerning not its conceptual implications but rather its normative implications and the constraints imposed on it by first-order normative judgments. In this respect, the normative power view supplies a framework for thinking about the role that consent plays in our lives, by thinking about what could justify taking the normative situation to be sensitive to specific kinds of communication in systematic ways. This inquiry points in two interrelated directions. On the one side, we want to find out which values or self-conceptions are served by the power to consent. On the other side, we want to know what exactly the power to consent is a power to do, who has it, and to what constraints its exercise is subject. These two lines of inquiry are interrelated, and no strict priority can be assigned to either. The value of the normative power to consent has to guide our reflection about the content of this power, and vice versa.

In carrying out these more detailed investigations, it may prove useful to relate the power of consent back to the Hohfeldian context of legal incidents. Doing so alerts us to the fact that the question of whether we have the power to bring about a certain result – say, to create a permission – is distinct from the question of whether we are at liberty to use or refrain from using that power, or whether we are under an obligation to use or refrain from using it in certain ways. Thinking about consent in the context of the Hohfeldian framework also reminds us that powers are correlated with liabilities. To the extent that we and others have the power to make otherwise impermissible acts permissible, all of us are also under corresponding liabilities to have some of our obligations taken away or annulled at the say-so of others. These liabilities may be of interest in their own right, most saliently when it comes to explaining the existence of the correlative normative power. In thinking about the value of the power to consent, we should consider the possibility that it consists not just in its benefit to the power-holder but also in the way it serves the interests of those who are under corresponding liabilities.[14] In these ways, there is reason to think that the normative power view can be fruitful for understanding what our ability to consent amounts to and what its grounds are.[15]

Notes

1 The most influential discussion is by Hohfeld (1913), and a detailed earlier account is found in Bentham (1970). For a summary of the latter, see Hart (1972). Other accounts of legal power (sometimes also referred to as "legal competence") are found in twentieth-century legal theorists such as Salmond

(1902), Pound (1959), Kelsen (1945, 1967), and Hart (1997). For recent overviews, see Halpin (1996), Essert (2015), and Kurki (2017).

2 The term "normative power" already occurs in Von Wright (1963), where it seems to denote a similar phenomenon. But one cannot be quite sure, as the presentation is overly abstract and contains no reference to the earlier treatments by authors such as Hohfeld and Kelsen. Arguably, the concept of normative power was also developed, contemporaneously with Hohfeld's influential work, in Reinach (2012).

3 To be sure, promises often generate reliance, and the violation of the corresponding expectations may be a harm that could explain the obligation to perform. But this does not seem to be a necessary aspect of all promises. A more sophisticated attempt to explain the bindingness of promises by recourse to the value of assurance can be found in Scanlon (1998: 295–327). For an overview of the difficulties encountered by this approach, see Heuer (2012) and Pratt (2013), and for a "hybrid" account that combines elements of Scanlon's proposal with elements of an explanation in terms of normative power, see Kolodny & Wallace (2003). For criticisms of the normative power approach to explaining promissory obligation, see Pratt (2007).

4 There are others. For instance, MacCormick (2008: 97) holds that "acts of exercising [normative] power are acts which necessarily and intrinsically *invoke* the [power-conferring] rule in some way". And Wellman (1997: 93), who uses the terminology of "ethical power" or "moral power", holds that such a power consists in "the ethical ability to perform some act that has specific ethical consequences and that is normally performed in order to bring about some such consequences".

5 This terminology, and the conceptual distinction, is adopted by Raz from Kenny (1975). Raz's own gloss on this distinction is that the exercise of a normative power affects the normative situation "normatively and not causally" (1972: 94). As a number of writers have remarked, the distinction here is reminiscent of the distinction between the illocutionary and the perlocutionary effects of speech acts (cf. Weale 1978). Readers are invited to consider the import of this parallel, and whether the result of the exercise of a normative power may simply be identical with the illocutionary effect of the speech act whereby that power is exercised.

6 Essert (2015) makes the plausible suggestion that the "results in" relation invoked here is a type of grounding relation.

7 The term was originally introduced by Hart (1958) as part of an explanation of the concept of obligation. According to him, a reason for action is "content-independent" when it "[functions] as a reason independently of the nature or character of the actions to be done" (Hart 1982: 254). On the challenges of explaining what content-independence amounts to, see Markwick (2000) and Sciaraffa (2009).

8 To say that the obligation does not derive from the consequences of the act of discharging it is not to say that the obligation is independent of the act's value. On one reading, the condition of content-independence does not require dispensing with the idea that reasons for action derive from the value or desirability of the relevant actions, and some recent accounts of normative power that resemble Raz's in other respects do not embrace this implication. For instance, Edmundson (2010: 184), while retaining the terminology of content-independence, takes exercises of "moral power" to "[impart] to another action a value that it would not otherwise have, and which might easily have been imparted to an action of a wholly unrelated kind". Cf. also Wellman (1995, 1997).

9 Explanations along broadly Razian lines are also found, for instance, in Estlund (2009) and Edmundson (2010). Another account is offered by Chang (2013), who adopts the term in the context of an avowedly meta-normative explanatory project. Her explanandum is the normative significance of personal commitments, rather than the nature of interpersonal transactions such as promises, orders, requests, or communications of consent.

10 As stated, the conditions are meant to capture only the specific cases of requests and authoritative directives. If the account is to be made to work as an account of promissory reasons, which after all are created by an agent for herself, the first, fourth, and sixth occurrences of "B" in the schema will have to be replaced by "A". Adapting Enoch's account to explain the phenomenon of consent would require yet more far-reaching modifications.

11 Not only may consent, understood as the exercise of a normative power, have consequences – as opposed to direct normative results – that make the consented-to action less undesirable, it may also give rise to reasons against an action, or remove reasons in favor of it. Think, for instance, of a case where A accepts B's bet that A will not ϕ without C's consent. A then has a (financial) reason to ϕ that is removed when C consents to A's ϕ-ing. The fact that an action has been consented to may also give rise to reasons against that action: for example, if performing the action under those circumstances would contribute to fostering a manipulative habit in the consenting party.

12 For defenses of the latter view, see Alexander (1996), Hurd (1996), and Westen (2004). For a recent critical discussion, see Healey (2015).

13 Thus, to say that their justification is content-independent does not entail that it is entirely content-insensitive. This point is emphasized by Raz (2009) and Watson (2009), among others.

14 Here we should be careful not to say that the *existence* of the liability explains the existence of the power, since both consist in one and the same normative state of affairs. The relation between Hohfeldian legal correlatives is not a relation of grounding or explanation but one of identity. But this does not bar us from thinking independently about the respective value of two legal correlatives.

15 For valuable comments on an earlier draft of this chapter, I am grateful to Jan Gertken, Andreas Müller, and Daniel Viehoff.

References

Alexander, L. (1996) "The Moral Magic of Consent (II)," *Legal Theory* 2: 165–74.

Bentham, J. (1970) *Of Laws in General*. London: The Athlone Press.

Chang, R. (2013) "Commitments, Reasons, and the Will," in R. Shafer-Landau (ed.), *Oxford Studies in Metaethics*, Vol. 8. Oxford: Oxford University Press.

Dempsey, M. (2013) "Victimless Conduct and the *Volenti* Maxim: How Consent Works," *Criminal Law and Philosophy* 7: 11–27.

Dougherty, T. (2015) "Yes Means Yes: Consent as Communication," *Philosophy & Public Affairs* 43(3): 224–53.

Edmundson, W.A. (2010) "Political Authority, Moral Powers and the Intrinsic Value of Obedience," *Oxford Journal of Legal Studies* 30(1): 179–91.

Enoch, D. (2011) "Giving Practical Reasons," *Philosophers' Imprint* 11(4): 1–21.

Enoch, D. (2014) "Authority and Reason-Giving," *Philosophy and Phenomenological Research* 89: 296–332.

Essert, C. (2015) "Legal Powers in Private Law," *Legal Theory* 21(3–4): 136–55.

Estlund, D. (2009) *Democratic Authority*. Princeton: Princeton University Press.

Halpin, A. (1996) "The Concept of a Legal Power," *Oxford Journal of Legal Studies* 16(1): 129–52.

Hart, H.L.A. (1958) "Legal and Moral Obligation", in A.I. Melden (ed.), *Essays in Moral Philosophy*. Seattle: University of Washington Press, 82–107.

Hart, H.L.A. (1972) "Bentham on Legal Powers," *Yale Law Journal* 81(5): 799–822.

Hart, H.L.A. (1982) "Commands and Authoritative Legal Reasons," in H.L.A. Hart (ed.), *Essays on Bentham: Jurisprudence and Political Philosophy*. New York: Oxford Press.

Hart, H.L.A. (1997) *The Concept of Law*. Oxford: Oxford University Press.

Healey, R. (2015) "The Ontology of Consent. A Reply to Alexander: The Ontology of Consent," *Analytic Philosophy* 56(4): 354–63.

Heuer, U. (2012) "Promising," *Philosophy Compass* 7(12): 832–51.

Hohfeld, W.N. (1913) "Some Fundamental Legal Conceptions," *The Yale Law Journal* 23: 16–59.

Hurd, H.M. (1996) "The Moral Magic of Consent (I)," *Legal Theory* 2: 121–46.

Kelsen, H. (1945) *General Theory of Law and State*. Cambridge, MA: Harvard University Press.

Kelsen, H. (1967) *Pure Theory of Law*. Berkeley: University of California Press.

Kenny, A. (1975) *Will, Freedom and Power*. New York: Barnes & Noble.

Kolodny, N. and R.J. Wallace (2003) "Promises and Practices Revisited," *Philosophy and Public Affairs* 31(2):119–54.

Kurki, V. (2017) "Legal Competence and Legal Power," in M. McBride (ed.), *New Essays on the Nature of Rights*. Oxford: Hart Publishing, 31–48.

MacCormick, N. (2008) *H.L.A. Hart*. Stanford: Stanford University Press.

Manson, N. (2016) "Permissive Consent: A Robust Reason-Changing Account," *Philosophical Studies* 173: 3317–34.

Markwick, P. (2000) "Law and Content-Independent Reasons," *Oxford Journal of Legal Studies* 20(4): 579–96.

Owens, D. (2012) *Shaping the Normative Landscape*. Oxford: Oxford University Press.

Pound, R. (1959) *Jurisprudence*. New Jersey: The Lawbook Exchange.

Pratt, M.G. (2007) "Promises, Contracts and Voluntary Obligations," *Law and Philosophy* 26(6): 531–74.

Pratt, M. (2013) "Promises and Perlocutions," in M. Matravers (ed.) *Scanlon and Contractualism*, London: Frank Cass.

Raz, J. (1972) "Voluntary Obligations and Normative Powers," *Proceedings of the Aristotelian Society* 46: 79–102.
Raz, J. (1975) *Practical Reason and Norms*. Oxford: Oxford University Press.
Raz, J. (1977) "Promises and Obligations," in P. Hacker and J. Raz (eds.) *Law, Morality, and Society*. Oxford: Oxford University Press.
Raz, J. (1986) *The Morality of Freedom*. Oxford: Oxford University Press.
Raz, J. (2009) "Reasoning with Rules," in J. Raz (ed.), *Between Authority and Interpretation*. Oxford: Oxford University Press.
Reinach, A. (2012) *The Apriori Foundations of the Civil Law*. Heusenstamm: Ontos Verlag.
Ripstein, A. (2009) *Force and Freedom*. Cambridge, MA: Harvard University Press.
Salmond, J.W. (1902) *Jurisprudence: Or the Theory of the Law*. London: Stevens and Hayens.
Scanlon, T. (1998) *What We Owe to Each Other*. Cambridge, MA: Harvard University Press.
Schaber, P. (2016) "Kann eine Handlung, in die eingewilligt wurde, moralisch falsch sein?" *Zeitschrift für philosophische Forschung* 70(4): 477–92.
Sciaraffa, S. (2009) "On Content-Independent Reasons: It's Not in the Name," *Law and Philosophy* 28(3): 233–60.
Shiffrin, S.V. (2008) "Promising, Intimate Relationships, and Conventionalism," *The Philosophical Review* 117(4): 481–524.
Simmons, A.J. (2010) "Political Obligation and Consent," in F.G. Miller and A. Wertheimer (ed.), *The Ethics of Consent. Theory and Practice*. Oxford: Oxford University Press, 305–28.
Thomson, J.J. (1992) *The Realm of Rights*. Cambridge, MA: Harvard University Press.
Von Wright, G.H. (1963) *Norm and Action: A Logical Enquiry*. London: Routledge & Kegan Paul.
Watson, G. (2009) "Promises, Reasons, and Normative Powers," in D. Sobel and S. Wall (ed.), *Reasons for Action*. Cambridge: Cambridge University Press.
Weale, A. (1978) "Consent," *Political Studies* 27: 65–77.
Wellman, C. (1995) *Real Rights*. Oxford: Oxford University Press.
Wellman, C. (1997) *An Approach to Rights*. Dordrecht: Kluwer Academic Publishers.
Wertheimer, A. (2000) "What Is Consent? And Is It Important?" *Buffalo Criminal Law Review* 3: 557–83.
Westen, P.K. (2004) "Some Common Confusions About Consent in Rape Cases," *Ohio State Journal of Criminal Law* 2: 332–59.
Westlund, A.C. (2013) "Deference as a Normative Power," *Philosophical Studies* 166: 455–74.

Further reading

An influential exposition of the concept of normative power is provided in Raz (1975), and a useful recent discussion of the concept of legal powers is found in Essert (2015). For an exemplary attempt to account for the normative effects of one type of putatively power-exercising act – promising – in a way that does not rely on the concept of normative power, see Scanlon (1998). Heuer (2012) offers a critical survey of the debate over the normative power approach to explaining promissory obligation, which is suggestive of corresponding options regarding the explanation of consent-based permission. Some recent substantive accounts of consent as a normative power are found in Dempsey (2013), Dougherty (2015), and Owens (2012: 164–86).

Related topics

Ch.5 Consent and wronging a person
Ch.11 Moral obligations and consent

4

THE NORMATIVE FORCE OF CONSENT

Heidi M. Hurd

To be an autonomous moral agent is to have the ability to create and dispel rights and duties. To respect persons as autonomous is thus to recognize them as the givers and takers of permissions and obligations—it is to conceive of them as very powerful moral magicians. By recognizing their capacity for self-legislation—for the creation and dissolution of rules that uniquely concern them—one gives meaning to the historic philosophical claim that persons are free inasmuch as they will their own moral laws. One very powerful means by which persons will their own moral laws—by which they alter the moral landscape for themselves and for others—is by granting or withholding consent to other's actions.

In this contribution, I shall construct a menu of ways in which consent might be thought to have this kind of normative force. While consequentialists can and must have some account of the role of consent in practical reasoning,[1] the most interesting (and in my view, the most compelling) analyses of the normative force of consent presuppose a deontological morality in which at least some obligations are categorical. The entries on the menu that I shall canvass thus explore ways in which consent may work to alter such categorical obligations—both the obligations of the person to whom consent is granted, and the obligations of the person who gives the consent. As I shall make clear, on some accounts, consent adds obligations and is thus liberty-limiting, while, on other accounts, consent subtracts obligations, and is thus liberty-enhancing.[2]

Readers are free to reject various entries on this menu as not to their philosophical taste (indeed, I shall reject some myself in passing, although my reasons for so doing will hardly be sufficient to dispose of them altogether). Some may find one or more of my alternative accounts of the normative force of consent to be too costly, committing them to contentious claims about the nature of consent, the conditions for its validity, the nature of moral obligations, the possibility of moral dilemmas, the kinship of consent with other normative powers, and so forth. Those, like me, who are a bit philosophically gluttonous, may find that most of these accounts are not only fully compatible with one another, but also compelling within certain domains, leaving one with an abundance of means by which to account for why expressions of consent will do moral work in a wide variety of circumstances. But whether readers are gluttonous or spartan in their moral appetites, they should find within the following taxonomy a conception of consent that captures their core convictions about how and why consent can function as a moral game-changer.

4.1 Liberty-limiting conceptions of consent

Many assume that consent enhances liberty by altering *others'* obligations in ways that expand the size of their morally legitimate choice set.[3] When one gives consent to others' actions, one substitutes permissions or agent-relative prerogatives for negative obligations, making it possible for them to do things that were not possible in the absence of consent. In section 4.2 I shall take up five variations of this claim that consent alters the obligations of others in ways that expand their opportunities. Before I come to this understanding of consent, however, let me begin in this section by canvassing two conceptions of the normative force of consent that focus on ways in which consent might alter, not the obligations of the person to whom consent is given, but rather, the obligations of the person who grants consent. As shall become clear, I am not, myself, a fan of these particular conceptions of the normative force of consent. But inasmuch as my goal is to taxonomize the various ways in which theorists *might* conceptualize the moral magic of consent, I include them here. Those who are tempted by one of these accounts can then determine whether they are up to the task of defending all of the necessary presuppositions and philosophical implications that attend that position.

We often better understand claims about rights, duties, permissions, and prerogatives when we translate them into the language now commonly employed to unpack the nature of the practical reasoning that is required in given choice situations (Green 1990).[4] As I work through the ways in which consent may function to alter the morality of one's own and others' actions, it may thus be useful to understand, in each case, the manner in which consent is thought to affect the reasons for action that determine what morally can or must be chosen. I shall thus seek to do this translational work as I go, coupling accounts about the various ways in which consent may alter obligations—one's own or others'—with claims about how consent thereby affects the (objective) reasons for action that are the appropriate objects of an agent's practical reasoning. Indirectly, such an analysis will thereby reveal the sorts of reasons upon which an agent subjectively ought to dwell, and about which she therefore ought to collect available evidence.

4.1.1 Consent as the basis of an obligation not to enforce a right or prosecute a wrong

It is common practice to sign so-called "consent forms" when seeking to pursue activities that might ultimately prove disappointing or even injurious. One might think that these sorts of forms capture in an explicit way what is implicitly going on when one grants consent to another's actions. One might think, that is, that consent alters the rights of the person who grants it, instead of expanding the rights of the person to whom it is granted. To give consent on this interpretation is effectively to create a new obligation on *one's own* part not to complain about a later disappointment or injury, even if that injury counts as a kind of wrong that would otherwise give rise to a moral or legal claim against the injurer.

On this view, consent is rights-constricting rather than rights-expanding. It curtails one's own later actions by creating an exclusionary reason that bars one from acting on first-order reasons for asserting rights to redress. It constitutes the creation of an obligation not to seek repair or pursue punitive action, even if what one thereafter suffers indeed counts as an injustice that would otherwise permit demands for corrective and/or retributive justice.

As should be clear, then, on this view consent is simply a species of promising. To consent to another's action is to promise him that one will not seek redress for any complaints to which his action gives rise. It is a promise to hold him morally and legally harmless in the event that a harm happens. One does not give him a new content-*dependent* first-order reason to do the action in question, for one's consent (promise) does not make that action any more or less wise on the merits. The act itself is made no more right than it was prior to one's consent; it does not, in Peter Schaber's words,[5] change the deontic properties of the act itself.

One might think that the correlativity thesis entails that if one creates an obligation, one also creates a right; and therefore, that consent not only generates a duty on the part of the person who gave it not to enforce secondary rights of repair, but also a right on the part of the person to whom consent was given not to provide compensation in the event that a harm ensues. But the correlativity thesis is not axiomatic. Many believe that one can have duties to do things to which others have no rights.[6] And if this is the case, then it is possible that consent could simply bind the one who grants it (by foreclosing after-the-fact complaints) while leaving intact the *ex ante* rights and duties of the person to whom consent is given. On this view, the person to whom one has given consent may retain his secondary obligation to redress any wrong he does, despite one's having forfeited one's own ability to complain of that wrong. If consent functions in this manner, it constrains one's own liberty without expanding that of the person to whom one's consent is given.

Many may find this account of consent attractive, for by conceiving of consent as a species of promising, it has the virtue of philosophical parsimony. If promising has normative force and consent is a species of promising, then consent shares in the normative force that has traditionally been assigned to promising. Yet there are at least three reasons to be wary of this account of the normative force of consent.

First, for reasons that I have spelled out elsewhere but that I cannot rehearse here, I am prepared to defend the (non-standard) view that promising itself has no normative force (Hurd 2017). When persons rely on a promise to their detriment, their reliance interests provide reasons to do what one promised; but the promise itself provides no reasons, in and of itself, to perform as promised. On the other hand, consent is indeed morally magical. While some have charged me with inconsistency in asserting both of these claims, I take there to be sound moral reasons why we can now alter the morality of others' contemporaneous actions while we cannot now change the morality of our own future actions. But I shall leave this debate for another day. Suffice it to say here that to conceive of consent as a species of promising commits one, in my view, to the much more difficult project of defending why one should not do what the balance of reasons, all things considered, dictates in the future, simply because of what one has said in the past.

Second, it is but a quick slide down a slippery slope to move from the claim that consent constitutes a promise not to complain of any wrongdoing to the claim that consent and assumption-of-risk are not merely cousins, but identical twins. For, on this view, one who explicitly agrees to assume a known future risk is on the same footing, and for the same reason, as one who consents to another's contemporaneous action. Both have taken ownership of the consequences of another's acts or omissions by effectively promising not to complain of those consequences. This might not seem problematic, but here's the rub. Many think that there is no means of cabining claims of assumption-of-risk to circumstances in which they function as explicit promissory waivers of future moral or legal liability. Many believe that it is equally valid to think that persons assume the risks of others' activities when they knowingly and voluntarily encounter them, despite having made no promise to do so. After all, what does a promise add to an actor's knowledge about, and voluntary willingness to accept, risks that she considers to be outweighed by the benefits of an activity? Of course, once one takes this step, the slope is positively greased, and one slides very quickly into having to explain why the woman who wears a low-cut red dress into a bar isn't assuming the risk of forcible sex, or the driver who ventures out for milk on New Year's Eve isn't assuming the risk of being hit by a drunk driver. Inasmuch as the concept of assumption-of-risk quickly invites a tangle of confusions, any theory of consent that suggests that it is of a piece with assumption-of-risk is a theory that will also be vulnerable to those confusions. On pain of having to solve all of the problems raised by the notion of assumption-of-risk, I, for one, am anxious to analyze consent in a manner that does not make it a pea in assumption-of-risk's pod.

Finally, if one's consent does not make another's action right—if that action is right or wrong independent of one's consent—then what could be good about giving consent to it? If the action is independently wrong, why would it be good to promise not to complain about it? And if the action is independently permitted, what moral good is one's promise not to complain about it? The fundamental problem with this account is that in our daily activities consent appears to affect the morality of *others'* actions, rather than simply the morality of our own later actions. When one consents to intercourse, one is not simply promising not to complain of a rape, one is making it not a rape at all. When one consents to a friend's borrowing a hammer, one is not simply promising not to complain about a theft, one is making it not a theft at all. To unpack consent as a promise not to complain about the wrongfulness of another's action is not to capture the fact that, in many cases, consent makes that action not a wrong at all.

4.1.2 Consent as a form of estoppel

A second account that locates the normative force of consent in its liberty-constraining effects on the person who grants it abandons the claim that consent is a special case of promising. It appeals instead to the intuition that sometimes we are simply estopped from complaining about others' deeds—not because we promised not to complain about them, and not because they are not genuine harms, but because we, at least in part, culpably brought them upon ourselves, and are thus justly hoisted upon our own petards. We have hands too dirty to complain about the hands of others. We were contributorily responsible for what befell us. Others are entitled to say that "it does not lie in your mouth" to voice a complaint about your injuries, given your own culpable contributions to them.

One can certainly construct cases in which consent appears culpable, and in such cases it is unsurprising that we are not moved by subsequent claims of wrongdoing on the part of the person who provided the consent. While we might think that Armin Meiwes, the self-confessed German cannibal, did grave wrong to 43-year-old Bernd Brandes, when he chopped him up and ate him over the course of a couple of weeks, it is hard to think that Brandes did not ask for it when he advertised to be the victim of such cannibalism and himself participated in the amputation, butter-frying, and consumption of various of his body parts. One might say in his case that his consent normatively functioned to estop him from complaining about the harms done to him, even as it did nothing to reduce the wrongfulness of those harms.

We can also imagine a case in which no actual consent is given, but in which another is culpably induced to believe that consent is present. When she relies on her false belief, it is tempting to say that the burden of her mistake should lie with the one who culpably induced it. In short, others should be entitled to rely on the notion that "yes" means "yes", and anyone who insists otherwise, *ex post*, is estopped from complaint.

While consent can certainly give rise to powerful intuitions of estoppel, and while Hollywood exploits "what goes around, comes around" scenarios in ways that reveal our innate sense of satisfaction when people get as good as they give, most instances in which consent does normative work are not aptly analyzed as estoppel cases. When one kindly consents to a friend borrowing one's car, it is not the case that the normative force of one's kindness is best analyzed by thinking that one cannot complain about the loss of the car because one has brought it on oneself in a way that makes that loss an instance of divine justice. Rather, the taking is not a wrong at all, let alone one that needs to be distributed according to a principle that seeks the most culpable contributor and finds it in the lender. Whatever mileage we might get out of intuitive notions of estoppel in cases in which consent appears to function as a culpable contribution to a wrong, it is essential to look elsewhere for an account of consent that explains its normative force within our daily interactions and transactions.

4.2 Consent as means of dissolving obligations on the part of others

Let us now turn to accounts that construe consent as liberty-enhancing by virtue of its claimed ability to convert others' negative obligations into positive permissions. It appears that there are at least six possible ways in which consent can affect existing obligations. In some cases, consent is morally transformative. It thoroughly eliminates all obligations, indeed, all reasons for action, that constitute moral barriers to another's conduct. It thus morally cleanses that conduct—making it right when it would otherwise be wrong. In other cases, consent does significant moral work, but the permissions it provides remain stained. As I shall explain, the stains, in such cases, may derive from one or more of five possible sources.

4.2.1 Consent as a morally transformative permission

First, in the clearest of cases, consent is morally transformative, because it removes the only existing moral barrier to an action, and thus effectively makes an action right when it would otherwise be wrong. When it functions in this manner it makes all the moral difference; it literally reverses the morality of a deed. It negates the only existing obligation not to do an act—making permissible what was otherwise prohibited; making right what was otherwise wrong. Thus, for example, consent can, by itself, turn a battery into a handshake; a sexual assault into a kiss; a trespass into a dinner party; a theft into a gift; and the commercial appropriation of a name and likeness into a biography. Moral magic.[7]

If one conceives of deontological obligations as a source of second-order exclusionary reasons not to act on certain existing first-order consequentialist reasons, then, for example, one might think of consent as vitiating the second-order reason that bars one from considering an action that is prohibited absent consent. Upon their expression of mutual consent, for example, one is free to act on the balance of first-order reasons for action, and thus to cross the threshold of a couple's home so as to enjoy their hospitality for an evening. Their consent to one's doing what would otherwise constitute a rights-invasion does not add a new first-order reason to join them for the evening[8] (although their affirmative request that one join them would add such a reason, and very often expressions of consent do double-duty by also embodying invitations or expressions of affirmative desire), but it does remove any claim that one has done them a wrong in entering onto their property.

4.2.2 Consent as a stained permission

In many cases, however, consent is not morally transformative by itself. It does not make all the difference between an act being wrong or right, lamentable or laudable. It is not morally cleansing. By removing a particular obligation, it gives another a permission to do an act that remains, in some sense, morally condemnable.[9] When consent operates in this second manner, it grants another "a right to do wrong". It conveys a "stained permission", for the act done remains, on some basis, morally objectionable, but the consent defeats any rights on the part of the consenting party for the actor not to do what is otherwise still, in some sense, immoral. There appear to be at least five ways in which consent might generate a "stained permission". Let us consider these in turn.

4.2.2.1 When consent vitiates one but not all obligations

First, in a case in which multiple obligations conspire to prohibit a person from performing a given action, another's consent to that action may release the person from one such obligation, but not from the others. Put differently, consent might vitiate one exclusionary reason that one would otherwise have for not pursuing a given action, but it might leave intact other such exclusionary reasons. In such a case, consent does not make the action justified, all things considered—indeed, it does not make it deontologically non-wrongful, for other reasons categorically exclude one from pursuing the benefits of the action. Consent simply functions to remove the basis upon which the action would otherwise also be wrongful to the consenting person. Thus, when a married woman agrees to adulterous sex with her lover, her consent vitiates any claim of rape, but it does not morally transform or cleanse her lover's actions altogether, for they remain adulterous and arguably, then, wrongful to her husband. Her consent thus conveys a "stained permission"—a right to do a deed that remains a wrong, albeit not a wrong *to her*.

Such a stained permission does not do all the work that is needed to make an action all-things-considered-permissible. It thus does not, by itself, count as a robust permission. But one can only put one's pants on one leg at a time. Where a permission eliminates one wrong, it does significant moral work, even if other permissions are required to eliminate all sources of wrongfulness. In that limited sense, consent is importantly transformative. When the woman's consent is secure, no rape transpires; what is left is adultery. And that is surely of lesser moral significance. Consent alone has done the work to transmute a very serious wrong into one that is much less serious. Moral magic.

4.2.2.2 When consent licenses consequentially prohibited actions

Second, there may be cases in which no other deontological obligation binds the actor save the obligation to secure consent before proceeding. Nevertheless, the balance of relevant first-order reasons that weigh in favor of and against the action makes the action in question consequentially unjustified. In such a case, consent releases the actor from any deontological obligation not to act; but the permission afforded by her consent creates a kind of agent-relative prerogative to do an act that still ought not to be done, because it does more harm than good or is otherwise consequentially ill-advised. In such a case, consent provides a stained permission, for we can condemn the act even as it cannot be declared a rights-violation of any sort, and hence, cannot be thought to do wrong to anyone.

Consider, for example, the case of a woman who seeks ever more aggressive and extensive plastic surgery. Suppose that, by any objective measure, the procedures she now demands of her surgeon are ones that will not enhance her appearance or her health; indeed, suppose that they risk long-term adverse health consequences (e.g., an increased risk of various kinds of cancer). Suppose also that her plastic surgeon has warned her of these risks and used all manner of persuasion to convince her that further augmentation of various features will make her look more comic than appealing. Nevertheless, it seems that her consent makes further surgical alterations permissible on the surgeon's part. Since a permission conveys a right, the surgeon cannot be thought to violate her rights when he does what she asks—even as we might retain a sense that he did something not only regrettable, but condemnable, when he made a profit at the expense of her (objective) well-being. If the ethics of his profession gave him exclusionary reasons to refuse service under the circumstances, then, like the adulterous lover, we might think that there were other obligations that compelled him to turn away her business. But even if no other exclusionary reasons applied, so that the choice came down to a balance of first-order reasons, we might think that he got that balance wrong. Her consent to the surgery insulated him from any claim that he violated her rights; but we might still think that, all things considered, he did something condemnable by proceeding with a consensual surgery that imposed more costs than benefits. In short, we might think that her consent gave him a permission that was stained by the unfortunate consequences of his choice.

One might think such a case a ripe invitation for paternalism—for doing what is, all things considered, in another's best interest, notwithstanding her consent to something injurious. One might think, in other words, that consent is inoperative when it gives license to what is not in a person's own best interests, on the balance of all consequences considered. But those who sport a libertarian streak or who otherwise place significant weight on the value of autonomy will at least feel the normative force of a person's consent in circumstances in which that person wills for himself an end that is not, objectively, optimal. They will recognize in their own lives the moral absolution that consent appears to give to bar-tenders, tanning salons, amusement park ride operators, purveyors of fattening foods, fast cars, motorcycles, and stiletto heels, organizers of pick-up games of basketball, hosts of Monday night football game parties, those who give rides when walking would be better, and the list goes on. The point: we all consent to indulge in many temptations that are not, strictly speaking, in our own best interests. Were those who satisfied such temptations without (albeit stained) permission to provide them, we would all be deprived of liberties that make life worth living, even as they make it of a shorter span. Thank goodness for the moral magic of consent that allows us all to go to Hell in our own handbaskets.[10]

4.2.2.3 When consent licenses justified demonstrations of vice

Third, one can imagine instances in which not only does consent negate all deontological obligations that would otherwise prohibit an action, but the balance of first-order reasons for action either fully justifies the action or is in equipoise so as to make any choice consequentially neutral. Still, if the actor opts to do the deed to which consent has been given, he will reveal a kind of vice that will aretaically taint the deed in question. In such a situation, one might think that the proffered consent provides a stained permission to do the act, for while the act is neither deontologically prohibited nor consequentially unjustified, it is not the sort of thing that a virtuous person would do, and it is thus to be condemned on that basis.

Consider, for example, a faculty colleague who always insists on splitting lunch bills with fellow faculty members in exacting ways. He never gives or loans others money by covering any portion of their lunch bills, insisting on exact change right down to the last penny. On a given day, he has left his wallet in his car, and a colleague consents to cover his bill for him. He could readily return to his car, as he has forced his colleagues to do in the past, but instead he agrees to take the loan. He clearly does his colleague no wrong, for the taking of the money was fully consensual. And we can imagine that the consequential returns of both choices are identical. Still, we might think that his choice to take advantage of his generous colleague when he has extended no such reciprocal generosity himself is suberogatory under the circumstances, and thus, that his colleague's consent gave him a permission that is stained by his own bad character. We can again condemn him (on aretaic grounds), even though we cannot complain that he did anyone a wrong or brought about more harm than good. We can think that he is morally permitted to do what is revealing of his bad character. When he acts on the consent of his generous colleague, he stains the permission that he has been given. But consent makes all the difference between his committing a deontic wrong and his simply revealing a weakness of character. Moral magic.

4.2.2.4 When consent dissolves a dilemma but leaves a moral mark

Fourth, some scholars are convinced that there can be moral dilemmas in which people are rightly condemned no matter what they choose—circumstances in which persons are "damned if they do, and damned if they don't". Some think that circumstances of self-defense are of this sort; so that, while a person is morally permitted to take a culpable aggressor's life in order to save her own, she nevertheless does something that is forever morally tarnishing—something that goes on the negative side of her life's "moral ledger". I am not of this camp, so this is not a square in a taxonomy of logical positions that I shall occupy. But I can imagine that those who are of this persuasion could find instances in which consent would afford licenses that are of the sort imagined in the self-defense context—licenses to resolve dilemmas in ways that remain stained by the fact that, by their nature, dilemmas permit of no thoroughly right answer.

Consider, for example, the classic dilemma invented by Bernard Williams about Jim and the Indians (Williams 1973: 98–9). If Jim refuses to kill one of 20 Indians who have been lined up by gunmen in a small South American town, the gang leader will kill all 20 of them. Imagine that, as Jim wrings his hands over the prospect that his inaction might result in the death of 20 innocents, a lone Indian steps forward and consents to be the one who is killed. Those who are of the view that choices made in moral dilemmas are inevitably stained might insist that, while the Indian's consent eliminates Jim's obligation not to take his life,[11] the Indian's death remains a moral stain. His consent gives Jim a permission to sacrifice his innocent life so as to save 19 other innocent lives; but it is a stained permission that lives on to darken Jim's moral ledger.

Still, it is a permission powerful enough to relieve Jim of the charge that he has committed an unjustified killing. Even those who are not consequentialists, and who thus derive no justification for the killing from the fact that the Indian's death saved 19 others, are still likely to conclude that, under the circumstances, Jim's action did not constitute a wrong. It might have been a wrong had it reflected a crude consequential calculation, indifferent to the fact that, in actively taking a life, Jim had affirmatively authored the death of an innocent in violation of an agent-relative deontological duty not to kill innocents. But instead, it reflected respect for the autonomous choice of one who sought to save 19 others through self-sacrifice, and who could accomplish his goal only through consenting to another's otherwise wrongful shooting. Moral magic.

4.2.2.5 When consent is present but unknown

Fifth, and finally, consent could convey a stained permission in circumstances in which it is fully present, but not fully appreciated. In such a case, the stain is a function of an epistemic failure on the part of the person to whom consent has, in fact, been given. One who does a deed that is consensual, but who does not know that it is consensual, acts culpably, even as he does not act wrongly. In this fifth sort of case, then, consent removes the act's wrongfulness, but it leaves the stain of culpability.

Consider the case of someone who is incapable of visibly conveying consent, but who nevertheless wills another's actions in ways that remove their wrongfulness to her. One might think of a woman in a safe room who recognizes that one of the burglars who has broken into her new home is her son to whom she has already deeded all of her valuable possessions. As he approaches her jewelry box, she shouts pointlessly at the sound-proof glass, urging him to take all of its contents; eager for him to have now what she has already deeded over to him as his own. One might think that her consent to his taking vitiates any claim that the son, in fact, stole from his mother. But inasmuch as he thought he was stealing from her—inasmuch as he possessed the culpability of a thief, and so was *attempting to* commit theft—her permission was stained. It was not successfully conveyed, and it thus could not do the necessary psychological work to eliminate her son's culpability. He continued to operate under the false belief that he was subject to an exclusionary reason that barred the taking of his mother's property without her consent, for under the facts as he believed them to be, she had not consented to his taking of her jewelry. But she had consented; and in so doing she reduced his wrong from theft to attempted theft. Moral magic.

Many will be quick to insist that consent is not consent until it has been conveyed. They will deny that an act of will alone can work a transference of moral title—that merely intending that another do a deed is enough to make that deed consensual (Schulhofer 1995: 2181; McGregor 1994: 242; Sherwin 1996: 216–8; Wertheimer 2000: 568). I have labored elsewhere to deny that consent requires uptake of a communication on the part of the person to whom it is granted (Hurd 1996: 135–8). I have, indeed, defended the claim that consent is complete, for moral purposes, when a particular (somewhat complex) intention is formed—one that satisfies what I call "the fine-grained identity thesis" (Hurd 1996: 134). I shall not repeat myself here, because that would require that I stray from questions about the normative force of consent to questions about the nature of consent. Suffice it to say here that the fifth manner in which consent may convey a stained permission is clearly contingent upon the understanding of consent that I have elsewhere defended. If consent is deemed incomplete unless it is clearly conveyed and fully appreciated, then there is no means by which unknown consent can convey a permission, and no means by which one can construct an epistemic conception of a stained permission. But if, as I contend, one eliminates the wrongfulness *to oneself* of another's act simply by willing its commission,[12] then one can convert a completed crime into a mere attempt by an act of will alone. Moral magic.

4.3 Conclusion

I have taxonomized eight possible accounts of the normative force of consent.[13] Two of these construe consent as a source of liberty-limiting constraints upon the later actions of the person who gives consent. On these accounts, consent functions to foreclose the opportunity for later complaint about actions which may, nevertheless, remain serious wrongs. Six of the accounts I describe, however, characterize consent as a source of liberty-enhancing permissions that eliminate otherwise existing obligations on the part of those to whom consent is given. On these accounts, consent is a moral game-changer. While it may not do all the work that is required to reverse the morality of others' actions, it eliminates any claim that such actions are wrongs to the person who gives consent. As such, these liberty-enhancing accounts are true to the notion that consent is morally magical—that it can create and destroy obligations in the blink of an eye so as to constitute a normative power that allows agents to change their moral landscape, to alter others' moral legacies, and to author moral laws by will alone.

Notes

1 What seems clear is that consequentialists cannot construct accounts of consent that *necessarily* make consent a moral game-changer, for consent, by itself, cannot be thought to alter the long-term consequences of actions, and thus it cannot, by itself, guarantee that consensual actions will necessarily yield a net gain in good consequences. One can imagine, however, consequential accounts of consent that emphasize its epistemic role. It might be argued, for example, that consent reveals a person's preferences so as to permit calculations that both maximize the satisfaction of the preferences of the person who gives consent and permit preference-realizing reliance and industry on the part of persons to whom consent is extended. When preferences are clear, calculations about how to achieve net gains in preference satisfaction are more reliable, and for this reason alone, consent should be of epistemic interest to those who embrace a consequentialist theory that attends to the maximization of preferences, utility, happiness, pleasure, or any other similar subjective good.

2 It is important to be clear that my focus in this piece is on the moral force of consent. I am not here concerned with its nature (e.g., as a mental state, a performative act, or some combination of the two)—a question on which I have previously focused (Hurd 1996)—or with the pre-conditions of its morally relevant exercise (e.g., an adequate choice set and the cognitive and volitional requirements for rationality). Excellent contributions to these areas of inquiry have been made by Alexander (2014, 1996), Bergelson (2014a, 2014b, 2007, 2008, 2009), Dempsey (2013), Owens (2011, 2012), Wertheimer (2000), and Westen (2004). My interest in this piece is in unpacking what these scholars and others might mean when they commonly claim that consent is morally transformative.

3 Of course, by expanding what others can do to and with one, one can similarly expand one's own opportunity set. But this sense in which consent is liberty-enhancing is derivative rather than primary.

4 This is the language first made famous by Joseph Raz's extensive taxonomy of the sorts of reasons for action that inform practical deliberations, and further developed in the work of those who have both criticized and extended his distinctions and their application to jurisprudential questions. See Raz (1979, 1986, 1999, 2000), Green (1990), Perry (1987), Alexander (1990, 1991), and Hurd (1999).

5 My thanks to Peter Schaber for this way of putting this point.

6 Some construe John Stuart Mill's imperfect duties this way, claiming, for example, that while we have duties of charity, no given person has a right to our charity. It is also common for people to think that we have duties to dead persons, even as dead persons can have no rights; or we have duties to future generations, even as those who will comprise them cannot now have rights. And, of course, it is commonplace to suggest that we owe duties to animals and other nonhuman entities, even as such entities lack the necessary capacities required to be rights-holders.

7 Obviously consent is not a sufficient condition for there to *be* a dinner party (as Dempsey says, "this account overstates the matter considerably. . . . Turning a trespass into a dinner party requires, at least, dinner. . . ." (Dempsey 2013: 12)); it is simply a sufficient condition for a shared dinner to be moral, as opposed to immoral.

8 As Dempsey puts it, consent is not itself an explanation for *why* an action was taken (Dempsey 2013: 17–18).

9 "[C]onsent should always be at least a partial defense, because it defeats at least one aspect of harm—namely, violation of rights. A partial justification does not make a wrongful act right, it only makes it less wrongful compared to an identical but nonconsensual act" (Bergelson 2008: 732).

10 This is not to say, of course, that paternalism is never legitimate, or indeed, obligatory. But that is for another paper—indeed, one that I have already written (Hurd 2009). The point is that it is a person's consent to self-risking or self-injurious activities that puts the legitimacy of paternalism in question. One only has a problem with paternalism—one only finds it something that requires special justification—precisely because consent can make wrong actions right, and it can make wrong actions a matter of right even when they remain wrong.

11 This assumes that the right to life is alienable. Those who believe that the right to life is inalienable, and who understand this to mean that consent is ineffective in making another's taking of a life morally permissible, must reject the possibility that consent can grant a stained permission to take an innocent life.

12 Inasmuch as one cannot, strictly speaking, will another's actions, this way of putting it is elliptical for the more complicated subjective mental state that I contend is all that is needed for consent to be

morally magical. It may not, of course, be all that the law should require for purposes of recognizing the defense of consent. For a full discussion of the nature of consent and the reasons why the law might require, for evidentiary purposes, more than morality requires, see Hurd (1996).

13 As I made clear at the start, all of these are deontological in nature, for consequential accounts of the role and significance of consent can be epistemic at best.

References

Alexander, L. (1990) "Law and Exclusionary Reasons. Philosophical Topics," *Philosophy of Law* 18(1): 5–22.

Alexander, L. (1991) "The Gap," *Harvard Journal of Law & Public Policy* 14(3): 695–701.

Alexander, L. (1996) "The Moral Magic of Consent (II)," *Legal Theory* 2(3): 165–74.

Alexander, L. (2014) "The Ontology of Consent," *Analytic Philosophy* 55(1): 102–13.

Bergelson, V. (2007) "The Right to be Hurt: Testing the Boundaries of Consent," *George Washington Law Review* 75(2): 165–236.

Bergelson, V. (2008) "Autonomy, Dignity, and Consent to Harm," *Rutgers Law Review* 60(3): 723–36.

Bergelson, V. (2009) "Consent to Harm," in A. Wertheimer and F. Miller (ed.), *The Ethics of Consent: Theory and Practice*. First Edition. Oxford: Oxford University Press, 163–92.

Bergelson, V. (2014a) "The Meaning of Consent," *Ohio State Journal of Criminal Law* 12: 171–80.

Bergelson, V. (2014b) "The Defense of Consent," in M. Dubber and T. Hörnle (ed.), *The Oxford Handbook of Criminal Law*. First Edition. Oxford: Oxford University Press, 629–53.

Dempsey, M. (2013) "Victimless Conduct and the *Volenti* Maxim: How Consent Works," *Criminal Law and Philosophy* 7(1): 11–27.

Green, L. (1990) *The Authority of the State*. Oxford: Oxford University Press.

Hurd, H. (1996) "The Moral Magic of Consent (I)," *Legal Theory* 2(2): 121–46.

Hurd, H. (1999) *Moral Combat*. Cambridge: Cambridge University Press.

Hurd, H. (2009) "Paternalism on Pain of Punishment," *Criminal Justice Ethics* 28(1): 49–73.

Hurd, H. (2017) "Promises Schmomises," *Law and Philosophy* 36(3): 279–343.

McGregor, J. (1994) "Force, Consent and the Reasonable Woman," in J. Coleman and A. Buchanan (ed.), *In Harm's Way*. First Edition. Cambridge: Cambridge University Press, 231–54.

Owens, D. (2011) "The Possibility of Consent," *Ratio* 24(4): 402–21.

Owens, D. (2012) *Shaping the Normative Landscape*. Oxford: Oxford University Press.

Perry, S. (1987) "Judicial Obligation, Precedent and the Common Law," *Oxford Journal of Legal Studies* 7(2): 215–57.

Raz, J. (1979) *The Authority of Law: Essays on Law and Morality*. Oxford: Clarendon Press.

Raz, J. (1986) *The Morality of Freedom*. Oxford: Clarendon Press.

Raz, J. (1999) *Practical Reason and Norms*. Second Edition. Oxford: Oxford University Press.

Raz, J. (2000) *Engaging Reason: On the Theory of Value and Action*. Oxford: Oxford University Press.

Schulhofer, S. (1995) "The Feminist Challenge in Criminal Law," *University of Pennsylvania Law Review* 143: 2151–207.

Sherwin, E. (1996) "Infelicitous Sex," *Legal Theory* 2(3): 209–31.

Wertheimer, A. (2000) "What Is Consent? And Is It Important?" *Buffalo Criminal Law Review* 3(2): 557–83.

Westen, P. (2004) *The Logic of Consent: The Diversity and Deceptiveness of Consent as a Defense to Criminal Conduct (Law, Justice, and Power)*. Abingdon: Routledge.

Williams, B. (1973) "A Critique of Utilitarianism," in J.J.C. Smart and B. Williams (ed.), *Utilitarianism: For and Against*. First Edition. Cambridge: Cambridge University Press, 75–150.

Related topics

Ch.5 Consent and wronging a person
Ch.11 Moral obligations and consent
Ch.12 Consent and autonomy

5

CONSENT AND WRONGING A PERSON

Peter Schaber

By giving others our consent we give them permission to do things with us that without our consent would wrong us.[1] Medical treatment without consent is battery; the removal of goods without consent is theft; sexual relations without consent is sexual assault or rape. It is widely assumed that consent does change the moral property of acts if and only if it meets certain procedural requirements for valid consent: that consent was voluntary, informed, and competently given.[2] In this chapter I would like to explore two questions concerning the relationship between valid consent, permissibility, and the wronging of persons. The first is (a) the question of how consent changes the moral status of an act; and the second is (b) the question of what it is that could make consent in certain cases morally ineffective, such that it does not change the moral property of the act. Regarding the first question, a number of authors believe that it is *the interests* of the consenting person that transform an impermissible action into one that is permissible or not wrongful. I will call this theory the *interest theory* of consent. And by interests I mean things that, when they are satisfied, make our lives better. Consent changes the moral property of an act, according to interest theory, when the act being consented to is in the interest of the consenting person. It is in my interest that a surgeon operates to remove my appendix. It is in my interest to have sex with my partner. And it's in my interest to occasionally lend Jill my car. These are all examples of the acts of cooperation we routinely engage in that are mutually beneficial. It seems obvious then that it is such interests that give consent its normative power (Waldron 1993: 47; Raz 1986: 80ff; Owens 2012: 179).

However, we also consent to things that are not conducive to our interests, sometimes even to things that are detrimental to our interests. For example, a person taking part in a research experiment or lending someone their car does these actions without their being beneficial for himself. We consider this kind of consent ethically *unproblematic*, at least when it does not run significantly counter to the interests of the consenting person. We would not think my consenting to lend Jill my car over the weekend is invalid if we learned that my only reason was to do Jill a favor. And no one would demand that someone take part in an experiment only if it somehow brought them a personal benefit.

This is why many authors subscribe to an alternative to the interest theory—namely, that it is solely the will of the consenting person that makes consent something that changes an impermissible action into one that is permissible or not wrongful. In this theory it is the *autonomy* of the consenting person that plays a central role (Hurd 1996; for consent to sexual intercourse see

Archard 1998). The moral property of an act is changed when consent expresses what the consenting person wants. And this is the case regardless of its relation to that person's interests—that is, whether or not it makes the life of the consenting person better. Even when it runs counter to the interests of the consenting person, consent can make an action permissible. Consent is morally effective, according to autonomy theory, to the extent that it expresses the will of the consenting person.

Reasons can be found for both views. Consent serves our interests in many ways (Raz 1986: 85ff). Consenting to medical treatment may allow us to regain our health or it can even save our life. Consenting to someone borrowing our property encourages further acts of cooperation that are mutually beneficial. And there are many more examples of things that are beneficial for us that we would not be able to have if we could not consent to them. It seems obvious to say then that consent has its normative power because it serves our interests. On the other hand, especially when consent does not serve our interests, it seems equally obvious to say that consent is about ensuring that we are treated by others like we want to be treated by them. And this may not always be beneficial for the consenting person. But, one could argue, that is not what consent is about. Consent is about protecting a person's autonomy and not their well-being.

The autonomy theory can be understood in several different ways. One way is that someone may only do with me what I want him to do. In this view consent makes an action permissible through an expression of will. Permitting someone to do something, however, does not mean that I want them to do that particular action. I can permit someone to do something and hope that they will not do it. Some authors including Larry Alexander think that we don't need to want someone to do what we have consented to. We can even mind very much if they do what we have given our consent to. A can consent to B doing x and hope that B does not do x (Alexander 2014: 108).

It is easier to understand the different versions of the autonomy theory if we turn for a moment to the question of what we want when we give someone our consent. What we want when we do this, is what gives consent, according to these theories, its normative power. This is why the question of what we want when we consent is of such importance to understanding its normative power. This question is examined in section 5.1. In sections 5.2–5.5 the interest theory of consent is first discussed, followed by the autonomy theory. And finally section 5.6 is about the question of what it is that could make consent in certain cases morally ineffective.

5.1 What kind of moral change?

First, what kind of moral change does consent bring about? A and B are in love and want to have sex. A consents to having sex with B. A's consent makes it permissible for B to have sex with A. What would have been impermissible without consent has been made permissible. It seems thus that consent makes acts permissible that would otherwise be impermissible (Wertheimer 2000: 559). But consider the following case: A is only allowed to do x if B, C, and D consent to A's doing x. B consents to A's doing x; C and D were asked but have not yet given their consent. It is then not permissible for A to do x. C and D also have to consent to make it permissible. Thus B's consent did not make the act in question permissible. Yet B's consent does make a moral difference. If A did x she would commit a wrong but she would not wrong B. A's doing x is okay for B; this is what B's consent tells A. It might not be okay for C and D and thus be wrong, all things considered, but it is okay for B. The moral change B's consent creates consists in making it the case that B is not wronged by A's doing x. B's consent does not make the act permissible. The same applies to cases of consent where duties towards third persons are at stake. Take the adultery case: A consents to having sex with B who is married to C. A's consent makes it the case that B does not wrong A. B, however, flouts a duty he has towards C. What he does is thus impermissible but not wrongful towards A. If consent does make a moral change it makes it the case that the consented act is not wrongful to the consenter. By consenting, A releases B from the duty B has towards A. A cannot release B from the duties B has towards others.[3] The consented act is permissible if B has no duties towards others. Whether the act is permissible depends thus on background conditions A cannot control. A can only make it the case that she is not wronged by B.

One could thus argue that what the consenter does is this: By consenting she makes it the case that she is not wronged by the act she has consented to. The message thereby conveyed is: "It is fine with me if you do x". Thus, in the adultery example A makes it the case that she is not wronged by B's doing x. A needs to have the normative power to make this the case. She has the normative power when she has the power to waive the relevant right she has against B. If A does not have this power she cannot make it the case that she is not wronged by B, even if she wants to make this the case.

5.2 The interest theory

Turning to our initial question: How does consent make it the case that the consenter is not wronged anymore? First, let's consider the view that it is the interest of the consenting person that gives consent its normative power. Waldron (1993: 47) writes:

> Why does my consent make it permissible for someone to do something with me which would otherwise be impermissible? The reason lies first, in our need for control over what happens to us, as part of our general interest in controlling the course of our lives, and second, in the fact that as social beings we can help, assist, and enjoy one another in various ways.

Waldron describes two kinds of interest that account for consent being able to grant someone permission to do something. In reverse order they are: a) an interest in relationships that are beneficial to us and b) an interest in controlling what others do with us. Let us look at these two interests more closely.

About a) we could say that consent is valid if it serves an interest of the consenting person. In other words, consent is valid if I expect that it will contribute to an improvement, even if only a minor improvement, in my life. The normative power of consent results from the interests of the consenting person. When I give my consent then I am expressing that I want to permit someone to do something.[4] The normative work is being done, according to interest theory, not by this will, but, if all goes well, by the interests this will rests upon. The will to permit others to do things can coincide with the interests of the consenting person. But it is not the will but rather the interest that changes this action into one that is permissible.

According to interest theory, it is not solely the interest of the consenting person that does this normative work. Jill is allowed to use my car if I give her my consent. If I do not then she is not—regardless of whether an interest of mine is served by her borrowing it or not. Giving consent does not make it the case that the act in question is not wrongful, according to interest theory—only when the action is also in my interest.

Interest theory faces the following problem: Consent does not always lose its normative force when it is not in the interest of the consenting person. It does not lose its normative power when it is not conducive to the interests of the consenting person (Wertheimer 2011: 69). If giving Jill my consent to use my car does not benefit me whatsoever, or if it even has disadvantages, we would still think my consent is morally effective. And there are other times when it seems that it does not have to be in the interest of the consenting person in order for something to be no longer wrongful. An interest theory of consent must explain how consent has normative force in these cases. It could of course always be argued that in fact consent only makes an action permissible when it is in the interest of the consenting person. However, it would appear that this condition would excessively restrict the normative power of consent.

But the interest theory of consent is confronted with still another problem. If it is interests that do the normative work of making an action permissible, it is not clear why consent is needed at all. For example, suppose I need to undergo medical treatment and the doctor is only allowed to carry out the treatment if I give my consent. I give my consent. According to interest theory, my consent turns the medical treatment into a permissible action because it is in my interest. A proponent of the interest theory might say that because it was in my interest I gave my consent. But why is my consent needed here? What normative work is being done by the act of consent in interest theory? It must contribute something to moral transformation, otherwise it would be normatively unnecessary. The normative work would be done by interests; an action would be permissible because it was in my interest.

5.3 Control interest

Let us now turn to our interest in controlling what others do with us, an interest that, according to Waldron, is served by consent. More precisely it is the interest that others only do with me what I want them to do. When we are talking about interest here, we mean that it is good for me if I can control what others do with me. If what others do with me coincides with my will, then of course it can also be good because other interests are served. But it is good in itself, in this view, if my interest in control is being served. This is why it is also possible that I consent to something that diminishes my well-being but, because it coincides with my will, it is good for me. For example I could consent to taking part in a medical research experiment although it involves my taking medication that causes mild feelings of nausea. That is not in my interest. The fact that I want to take part in the experiment makes it good for me to do so and makes it, on the whole, better than if I did not. Those who believe that it is my interest in control that makes an action I consent to permissible would disagree with the proponent of the autonomy theory that it is the autonomous will of the consenting person that is responsible for this normative change. On the contrary, they would say that this change is due to the fact that it is good for me when others do what coincides with my will.

David Owens (Owens 2012: 166ff; see also Tadros 2016: 213ff) thinks there are a number of different reasons for a person to have an interest in controlling what happens with him: a) the fact that someone decides to undergo medical treatment is a good sign that it is also in his interest; b) in addition it is often the case that something is in the interest of a person *because* he has decided to do it: "The fact that I have chosen to Φ may actually make it the case that Φ-ing is in my interests rather than merely indicate that this is so" (Owens 2012: 167); and c) our decisions also have a social dimension. Owens (2012: 167) gives this example: "Often it is not embarrassing to be observed naked (. . .) provided one has chosen to be so observed". This is one reason why, according to Owens, it is in our interest to be able to retain control over what others can and cannot do with us.

This concept of interest might also account for a widespread intuition that consent is not able to make *every* action permissible. Consent is unable to do this—even when it serves the control interest of the consenting person—if on the whole the action is not in his interest. Some actions harm the consenting person in a way that cannot be compensated for by being in that person's interest and as a result, in interest theory, they are not transformed into permissible actions. Owens (2012: 179) writes:

> I can't make it the case that I am not wronged by a serious physical injury, for instance, simply by declaring that this is so. The significance of the injury depends on its affecting my interests (including my control interests) and though my choices might influence how it affects my interests, my declaration alone will not.

We do not have an interest in being able to change such actions into ones that are permissible. This holds for all actions that entail such severe disadvantages for the consenting person that they are not compensated for by the advantage that they serve a control interest.

This proposal faces the following two difficulties:

a) It is not clear whether it is good for us that someone can only do something with us when it coincides with our will. Is the fact that what others do with us coincides with our will something good in itself? We could say that consent does not make an action good or better. It's good for me when a doctor relieves me of my pain. But is it good simply because it coincides with my will? What makes it good is that it relieves me from my pain. And consent makes it permissible.
b) The second difficulty is that it is doubtful that when an action has been consented to it must also be in that person's interest in order for it to be changed into an action that is permissible. Conducting a medical experiment on a person, for example, can be permissible even when it is not in the interest of the consenting person. The experiment does not have to be in his interest. It only needs to coincide with what he wants.

5.4 The autonomy theory

And that is exactly what the proponent of the autonomy theory would say: In order for an action to be permissible, it has to coincide with the will of the consenting person, whether or not one of his interests is served. I want to lend my car to Jill. The fact that I want this gives her the permission she needs, regardless of whether it is in my interest or not. This is a theory held by many medical ethicists: Consent has normative force when it expresses what a person wants (Beauchamp 2010: 57; Beauchamp & Childress 2001: 78; Maclean 2009: 41ff; McLean 2010: 57). Consent should ensure that a person is treated the way she wants to be treated. In a weaker formulation we can say that consent is meant to ensure that nothing is done to a person against their will.[5] This implies that we can consent to something without wanting someone to actually do it. Sometimes by consenting we are expressing nothing more than that we do not mind if someone does something with us (Westen 2004: 31).

The main idea of this theory is that consent gives the autonomous person the ability to change a normative relationship with another person. Hurd (1996: 124) thinks that this constitutes the core of respect for autonomous persons:

> To respect persons as autonomous is to recognize them as givers and takers of rights and duties (...) when their consent to others' actions is taken to alter the morality of those actions.

Part of the autonomy of a person is, in this view, being able to change impermissible actions into permissible ones or acts that are not wrongful. Autonomy is thought of as a capacity that we can exercise and that by exercising it we can change the deontic properties of an action. We could say that the autonomy theory is related to a concept of respect for persons. When we respect the autonomous will of a person, we are respecting that person (Henning 2011: 20). My consenting that Jill borrows my car is to be respected not because or to the extent that it is good for me but because it is what *I* want. Not thinking this consent is valid would be disrespecting my person. What I want would be treated as normatively irrelevant. If we respect others, we respect what they want even if it is not beneficial for them. In this sense Darwall (2013: 113) writes: "To refuse to give weight to others' desires and cares when they have little or no reason for them is a form of disrespect for them as persons". And this is how consent, provided it is an expression of the consenting person's will, has normative power. In contrast to the interest theory of consent, it is not about the interests of the consenting person. The expressed will of the consenting person changes the deontic property of the action whether or not it is in the interest of that person.

It is important to distinguish here between the non-normative will and the normative will. Consider the following example: I consent to Jill using my car. If this means that I want her to do this, then her borrowing my car would accord with my will. However, I could also not want her to borrow my car and hope that she does not (Alexander 2014: 108). But I still give her my permission. Then her borrowing my car would accord with my normative will. In such a case I want to change the normative situation; that is, I want to change an impermissible action into one that is permissible. We could say that it is this normative will that brings about normative change, provided I have the normative power to waive the relevant right. Jill is allowed to use my car because I want her to be allowed to do that. I want, in other words, to release her from the obligation she has towards me not to use my car. This is what my consent expresses[6] and what brings about the normative change, provided I have the required normative power.

5.5 The right to release others from obligations

If I consent to Jill using my car I release her from the obligation not to use my car. However, I can only do this because I have a right to release others from the obligation not to use my car. I cannot release Jill from the obligation not to use my neighbor's car. And it's controversial whether, for example, I can release others from the obligation not to kill or seriously harm me. This raises the following question: Why, generally speaking, do we have the normative power to consent to certain actions and thus permit them? This is the question of what gives us the power to make it the case that we are not wronged by certain acts. Why are we able to do this?

And here too the interest theory and the autonomy theory give different answers. According to interest theory we have the power to release others from some duties because it's in our interest to be able to do it. If I have the power to waive the relevant right then my consent has normative force. It may be that, for the reasons discussed above, the consented act is on balance still wrong. But it ensures that someone is not violating my rights if he does what I have given him my consent to do. If I do not have such a normative power, then my consent does not have any normative force at all. And I am also unable to ensure that someone does something without violating my rights.

Why do we have the right to release others from some duties? For Owens (2012: 176ff) this right is based on a *normative interest* that we have—namely, the interest to permit others to do some things. We have, in his view, an interest in being able to ensure that others are allowed to do some things. If I permit someone to borrow my car, then this does not have to be, on balance, something that is in my interest. Nevertheless, for Owens I still have an interest in being able to release others from the duty not to use my car. It is good for me to be able to decide to do this, even when someone does something that is not in my interest. That is, it is good for me to be able to allow another person to do something to me. And provided it is good for me, I also have a right to do it. For interest theory it is the other way round: I do not have the power to waive the right not to be seriously harmed by others since it is not in my interest. If I consent to someone seriously harming me then this consent does not have, from the outset, normative force. We do not need to check whether a particular act of consent is not, on balance, in the interest of the consenting person. It is already clear from the outset that consent in cases of serious harm does not have moral consequences.

It is not clear, however, whether it is good for me to be able to make it the case not to be wronged by another person if what I am permitting him to do is not in my interest. What is not clear here is whether it is good in itself to be able to eliminate the wronging. Let us say that someone is being physically intimate with me without my consent. This is an impermissible action. And it would still be an impermissible action even if it was good for me that this person was physically intimate with me (since, for example, it would let me determine whether it was pleasurable or not). Even so, someone would not be allowed to do this without my consent. Owens (2012: 123ff) calls these kinds of action "bare wrongings". He believes that there are bare wrongings because we have normative interests; that is, we have interests in being able to make it the case that we are not wronged by others. If we did not have such interests we would only be wronging others when we violated their non-normative interests. But, as Owens argues, we can wrong others without violating their non-normative interests. In the case of "bare wrongings" we wrong them by violating their normative interests (Owens 2012: 174).

But it is not clear why we should be talking about interests here. Owens argues as follows: Even if it does not adversely affect any of a person's interests, it is wrong to be physically intimate with that person without their consent. But doing this without their consent can only be wrong if it is not good for this person, and this is only the case if an interest is adversely affected. It has to be a normative interest that is affected because non-normative interests are not affected in cases such as these. For Owens consent is about our interest in being able to determine what others are *allowed* to do with us.

If doing something with someone without their consent is still wrong when none of their interests is adversely affected, then the fact that this person did not give their consent must be not good for them. However, it is not clear whether this is correct. We could say, following the autonomy theory, that it's wrong *because* the person does not want to be treated like this. This does not necessarily mean that it is bad for her to be treated like this. It is just something she does not want. And because she does not want this, according to autonomy theory, others are not allowed to treat her like this. We have the normative power to release someone from some duties because we would like to determine how we are treated by others. We want, in other words, to be able to release others from these duties.

We might add, following Seana Shiffrin, that the ability to consent is part of a plausible concept of an autonomous life. If we did not have this ability we would not be able to have meaningful relationships with other people, and so we would not be able to lead an autonomous life: "A plausible account of autonomy (. . .) would have to include the power of consent to share at least some of the powers associated with self-sovereignty" (Shiffrin 2008: 502). We can also think of the normative power to release others from duties as being grounded in a desire to be able to shape our interactions with others in light of what is okay for us. Consent enables us to do this. This is not the same as making sure that one is treated according to one's will. Take our example: A would be very happy to have sex with B. But it is not okay for A to do so as long as B has a sexual relation with C. A says to B: "Look, I would be very happy to have sex with you; but I am terribly sorry, as long as you are still with C, it is not okay for me to have sex with you". It is not that A does not want to have sex with B. It is rather that it is not okay for A to have that kind of relation. This is the reason for A to refuse to have sex with him. It is one thing that A wants to have sex with B; it is another that it is okay for A to have sex with B. These two things do sometimes come apart. By consenting we express normative views we have about the way we want to live with others and with ourselves. The things we want do not always fit these views. It might be good for us if we get what we want. But we refuse sometimes to get what we want, not because we have another will, all things considered, but rather because we think it is not okay to get something we want.

5.6 When consent does not work

Let us now turn to the second question: What is it—if anything—that makes consent ineffective, even though it is voluntary, informed, and competently made? If I consent to an action that will cause me pain, according to interest theory, my consent will only make it the case that I am not wronged if it is in my interest. The autonomy theory says that this action can only be performed if the consenting person wants to be treated like this or wants someone to be allowed to treat him like this. However, it is also possible to have the view that even when these conditions are fulfilled this action is still morally wrong, all things considered. One can argue that this is not because consent does not have normative force. Consent can have normative force without it turning the action into one that is, on the whole, permissible. Let us return to the example of my consenting to an action that will cause me pain. One could say that my consent has brought about a normative change: My rights have not been violated, which would have been the case if I had not given my consent. But this does not necessarily mean that the action is also morally permissible. Allowing someone to inflict pain upon me cannot be, on the whole, in my interest. And so, according to interest theory, this action would be wrong, all things considered.

In the autonomy theory, too, the reasons for objecting to an action may make it morally wrong. If it is morally wrong to seriously harm other persons, then it is "wrong-making" even if the victim consents to being harmed. If the victim consents to this action, then the perpetrator may not be violating a right but he is still doing something morally wrong. If he did this action without the victim's consent, he would also be violating the victim's rights. And the action would be morally worse than if the same action had been consented to. In such cases consent has normative force but not in a way that turns an action into one that is permissible. Consent only ensures that the act does not violate the rights of the victim.

Bergelson (2010: 181) writes:

> Consent alone doesn't suffice to justify the victim's death or injury (. . .) consent, [however] should always be at least a partial defense, because it defeats at least one aspect of harm, namely, violations of rights (. . .) A partial justification doesn't make a wrongful act right; it only makes it less wrongful compared to an identical but nonconsensual act.

For the perpetrator the consent of the victim, in some cases, only serves as a partial and not a full defense. It makes it the case that the act is less wrong than the identical non-consented act. But it is still morally wrong, all things considered. Bergelson (2010: 180) believes that this is the case when the disadvantages for the consenting person clearly outweigh the advantages or when their dignity has been violated:

> In order to satisfy the second requirement of the defense of consent, the perpetrator must establish that, to the extent he set back the victim's welfare interests and, at the same time, disregarded the victim's dignity (. . .) the harmful act nevertheless produced an objectively positive outcome.

Regardless of whether or not we share this model of weighing an action's advantages against its disadvantages, we could say that an action is morally impermissible when the reasons to object to it make it wrong in itself. For example, if an action is wrong because it would seriously harm someone, then it would also be wrong even if it were consented to. By harming the consenter you would commit a wrong without wronging him. This is one way of thinking of things.

Another way of thinking about this would be to say that certain rights cannot be waived. The consenter wants to make it the case that he is not wronged but he cannot succeed in doing this. Owens (2012: 49), for instance, holds such a view: "I can't consent to enslavement (even in return for a huge donation to my favorite charity), not to torture, lobotomization, and so forth". If A cannot waive the relevant right she has against B, B commits a wrong by wronging A. But why should this be the case? One could argue that a person is unable to waive a right if doing so is not of value to her. There are different views on what the value of consent is. Consider the view according to which consent is of value to us if and only if it allows us to shape our relations and interactions in light of what is okay for us (see section 5.5). When A consents to B's doing x, A thinks that B does not wrong A if he does x and wants B to take this into account. Consent thus allows us to treat each other in ways that are okay for us. And if doing x is okay for A it is of value to A.

When A consents to B's doing x, A thinks that it is okay for her if B does x. The following, however, could be the case here: A might be wrong in thinking that it is okay for her if B does x. If this is the case A's consent has no value for her and should play no role in B's practical deliberation. B has no reason to think that it would be okay if he did x. As a matter of fact it would not be okay for A and thus not be okay for B to do x. Suppose that A consents to being regularly used by B in a way that is clearly exploiting A. A thinks it is okay if B acts accordingly. But then it is not okay because it is exploitative. Thus A might be wrong about this. And if A is wrong about this it is not okay for her to be treated by B this way and her consent is of no value to her. The same could apply to other acts such as torture and enslavement. We cannot consent to things such as torture, enslavement, or serious physical injury because there are no reasons to find it okay to be treated accordingly. Our consent to such acts has no value for us and should play no role in our practical deliberation. It would thus remain wrong to torture someone even if she consented to it. It would remain wrong as a wronging of the victim. The victim is unable to waive the relevant right if what she consents to is not okay for her.[7]

Notes

1 A number of authors believe that we are able to create obligations through consent (Hurd 1996: 121; Raz 1986: 83). This chapter is solely about permission given by means of consent.

2 See Chapter 8, Valid consent.

3 "Consent does not comprehensively justify the action as such; rather, the consenting agent is precluded from asserting that he or she has been wronged" (Beyleveld & Brownsword 2007: 61).

4 Alexander says that by consenting I want to waive a right (Alexander 2014: 107).

5 We sometimes give our consent to things we feel indifferent about.

6 Owens believes that this involves communicating the intention "of hereby making it the case that someone wouldn't wrong you by Φ-ing" (Owens 2012: 166).

7 I would like to thank Andreas Müller and Stefan Riedener for their helpful comments and discussion.

References

Alexander, L. (2014) "The Ontology of Consent," *Analytic Philosophy* 5: 102–13.
Archard, D. (1998) *Sexual Consent*. Boulder, CO: Westview Press.

Beauchamp, T. (2010) "Autonomy and Consent," in F.G. Miller and A. Wertheimer (ed.), *The Ethics of Consent*. Oxford: Oxford University Press, 55–78.
Beauchamp, T. and J. Childress (2001) *The Principles of Biomedical Ethics*. Fifth Edition. Oxford: Oxford University Press.
Bergelson, V. (2010) "Consent to Harm," in F.G. Miller and A. Wertheimer (ed.), *The Ethics of Consent*. Oxford: Oxford University Press, 163–92.
Beyleveld, D. and R. Brownsword (2007) *Consent in the Law*. Oxford and Portland: Hart Publishing.
Darwall, S. (2013) "Because I Want It," in *Morality, Authority, & Law: Essays in Second-Personal Ethics I*. Oxford: Oxford University Press, 93–113.
Henning, T. (2011) "Why Be Yourself? Kantian Respect and Frankfurtian Identification," *The Philosophical Quarterly* 61: 1–21.
Hurd, H. (1996) "The Moral Magic of Consent (I)," *Legal Theory* 2: 121–46.
Maclean, A. (2009) *Autonomy, Informed Consent, and Medical Law: A Relational Challenge*. Cambridge: Cambridge University Press.
McLean, S. (2010) *Autonomy, Consent, and the Law*. London: Routledge.
Owens, D. (2012) *Shaping the Normative Landscape*. Oxford: Oxford University Press.
Raz, J. (1986) *Morality of Freedom*. Oxford: Oxford University Press.
Shiffrin, S.V. (2008) "Promising, Intimate Relationships, and Conventionalism," *Philosophical Review* 117(4): 481–524.
Tadros, V. (2016) *Wrongs and Crimes*. Oxford: Oxford University Press.
Waldron, J. (1993) "Liberal Rights: Two Sides of the Coin," in *Liberal Rights: Collected Papers 1981–1993*. Cambridge: Cambridge University Press, 1–34.
Wertheimer, A. (2000) "What is Consent? And Is It Important?" *Buffalo Criminal Law Review* 3: 557–83.
Wertheimer, A. (2011) *Rethinking the Ethics of Clinical Research: Widening the Lens*. Oxford: Oxford University Press.
Westen, P. (2004) *The Logic of Consent*. Aldershot: Ashgate.

Related topics

Ch.4 The normative force of consent
Ch.11 Moral obligations and consent
Ch.12 Consent and autonomy
Ch.18 Consent to pain

6
THE SCOPE OF CONSENT

Neil C. Manson

6.1 The scope of consent

Consent renders permissible certain kinds of action that would otherwise be impermissible. Consent of this kind—*permissive* consent—is operative in many domains. For example, in many jurisdictions the building of new homes requires "building consent". Here consent is sought from and given by institutions. Our focus here will not be on this kind of institutional consent but upon individual consent. Whilst it is true that a "building consent" decision may be made by an individual, this is not the sense of individual consent that we are concerned with here. First, this individual only has a normative power in virtue of the role she plays: the power attaches to the role, and the institution, not the individual herself. Second, although we may refer to this kind of normative change as "consent" it is importantly different from the consent that will concern us here. Although the employee may have some discretion in her decision whether or not to give permission, the proper exercise of the normative power is constrained by the criteria for permissible building of new homes (that they have to be in certain regions, the building materials of a certain quality, and so on). The individual's role is partly an epistemic one: to ensure that the planning criteria and standards are met. It is not simply up to her whether or not to give consent. Her role is also an *executive* one: *somebody* needs to decide whether the criteria are met. The individual consent that concerns us, by way of contrast, is a radically discretionary kind of consent where it is simply up to the consentor whether or not to bring about normative change. She may consent for good reasons, for bad, on a whim, to impress her boss, to secure trust, to forge a friendship, and so on.

Individual discretionary permissive consent—from here, just *consent*—is often operative against a backdrop of individual rights. Consider the right that each of us has against bodily touching. Such a right protects the holder from the intrusive and invasive acts of others. But it may also pose a barrier to the right-holder's interests (e.g., suppose she wants medical care from another). The power to permit by consent allows us to maintain the protection of those rights whilst exercising a distinctive kind of control over others' dispositions to act. We exercise this control by changing their reasons: more specifically, consent removes a reason that another agent has for refraining from acting in certain ways.

Although consent plays this key role against a backdrop of rights, it is also operative in domains where we might not think that rights talk has any purchase. For example, one social obligation of politeness is to ask before sitting by someone in a vacant seat on a train, or on a park bench. It is not clear that the sitter has a right against being sat beside, but politeness demands that we ask before doing so. Indeed, further norms of politeness seem to place serious constraints on the exercise of the power. If the seated party refuses to permit, without good reason, we may judge that the refusal itself breaches norms of politeness.

6.2 The normative scope of the *power* to permit by consent

Consent can change the normative situation with regard to different kinds of norms: moral, social and legal, or even *ad hoc* norms introduced by agreement. In our "building" example, *legal* permission is given. Here our focus will be upon consent as something that is morally transformative, against a backdrop of rights. When consent is transformative in this way the changes it brings about are limited. Consent has a *normative scope*. We can think about the normative scope of consent in two ways. The first is in terms of the scope of the power to permit by consent. If A has a right against other parties touching her without her consent, A's power is typically restricted to creating an exception to others' directed obligations towards *A* (Wenar 2013). A has the power to permit acts of bodily touching that would breach the obligations owed *to her*. In some contexts, however, the power to permit by consent may range over rights that other parties have. Parents have the power to create exceptions to their children's rights against being touched. But here too the power to permit is restricted in its scope and concerns only obligations directed at *their own* children. The parent of child A does not have the power to permit bodily touching, or clinical treatment, for *other people's* children.

There are some challenging ethical questions to do with parental consent that are, at root, questions about the proper limits to the scope of the parents' power to permit by consent. Where parents have the power to permit their (young) children's medical treatment, those same children, at some later point, will become adults and will (normally) acquire the sole power to permit their own treatment. Should the parents' power be removed in a single step, or should there be a transitional period of power sharing where, for example, the parent has a power of limited scope (e.g., an "emergency" normative power to permit life-saving treatment in the face of an adolescent's refusal) (Manson 2015)?

The normative scope of the power to permit is bound up, more generally, with considerations of competence. This is because the exercise of the normative power in question is a discretionary one that puts a certain level of cognitive demands upon the consentor and, unlike our "building consent" example, the power must be exercised by a particular individual, not some other individual playing the same role. The individual in question must understand that she has the power to permit; she must understand what it is she is doing when she permits others to act; she must understand something about the act that consent is given *for* and the agents that consent is given *to*. If an agent is unable to adequately make decisions to permit by consent, she cannot properly exercise the discretionary power to permit by consent. A discretionary power that one cannot exercise is not a discretionary power at all.

Questions about the normative scope of the power to permit by consent will thus arise when agents have diminished or limited decision-making capacity. For example, we might coherently hold that a particular agent with dementia is competent to decide whether or not to permit her neighbour to enter her house, and create an exception to *that* right, whilst at the same time arguing that she does not have the competence to make large financial decisions or decisions about major surgery. Or, we might argue that the agent has the power to permit, or refuse, medical interventions when the stakes are low, but not when the stakes are high (where refusal would be life-threatening, say) (Wilks 1999).

We noted at the outset that the power to permit by consent allows us to set aside the protection of certain rights. Given that rights protect fundamental interests, the power to permit by consent can be a liability for the right-holder. Setting aside her rights leaves her vulnerable to intrusion, invasive acts, loss of property, and so on. Questions about the scope of the power to permit by consent direct us towards broader, deeper, normative issues to do with the balance between norms that protect us and norms—including norms that assign powers—that give us the discretion to set aside that protection. This kind of debate—often framed in terms of determining the proper balance between beneficence and respect for individual autonomy—is central to medical ethics. At root, this fundamental debate in medical ethics is one about the limits of the normative scope of the power to permit by consent, in a context where other important norms are also in play. The normative scope of the power to permit may be restricted, overridden, out-weighed, and so on, by other considerations.

6.3 The normative scope of acts of consent

The power to permit by consent is one thing; the exercise of that power is another. Suppose agent A has a right against being touched by others and a right against others' use of her property. Such rights imply obligations on others to refrain from acting in certain ways. The first point to note is that when A consents she does not set aside, or abrogate, her rights. Her rights remain in place, but a limited *exception* is made for some parties to do some things.

Second, A can create an exception to one *kind* of right, without thereby creating an exception to other rights that she has. The third point is that each kind of right applies to a range of distinct entities, objects, regions, and so on. In the case of property rights, for example, A can create an exception for the use of her car without thereby creating an exception for the use of her catapult. She can also create an exception for one person, without thereby creating an exception for others. In the case of her right of bodily integrity, the right pertains not just to the body as an undifferentiated mass; the body has distinct parts, regions or zones. One can consent to surgery on one's ear, without consenting to surgery on one's leg or eye.

An act of consent always has a more or less specific content. We can express the content of an act of consent, in ordinary English, with the permissive auxiliary "may": an act of consent is aimed at bringing it about that [some agent or set of agents] *may* [perform some kind of action F], where F *may not* be done without consent. The content of an act of consent is not the same thing as its normative scope. An act of consent may be made, even explicitly articulated, without bringing about normative change. For example, suppose A and B are joint legal owners of some item X, where the conditions of their ownership allow *either* party to transfer ownership to a third party. Suppose C asks A if she may use the item. A consents. But A did not know that B had sold the item to someone else. Here A's act of consent has a content—that D may use X, not that D may use Y, or that E use X—but the act is *normatively* inert. This is because, in that context, unbeknownst to A, she no longer held the normative power in question.

Suppose we restrict our focus to situations where A *does* have the power to permit B to do some action; even here an act of consent may lack normative force. For example, if A is *coerced* by B, with threat of death, say, into signing a "consent form" that says "B may take my prize motorbike", the *content* of the speech act is that B may take the motorbike (not that C may, or that B may perform surgery on A), but the *normative* scope of the act is the empty set: nothing is permitted by it. Though, note, we might wonder here whether we should call such an act an act of *consent*. The coerced victim feigns consent and feigned consent is no more consent than a fake diamond is a diamond. But a diamond must have a specific physical constitution (something the fake lacks). Consider a different analogy. A forged ticket might still be usefully referred to as a ticket. Indeed, a forged ticket can be viewed as having some kind of "content" even when it is normatively inert. A forged ticket for the musical *Phantom of the Opera* is not a forged ticket for *Chicago*. It has a content, but as a forgery it has no normative force: it is *void, invalid, null*.

Let us leave aside the question of whether a normatively null act of consent is properly an act of consent. Let us focus on acts of consent that are normatively transformative. What is the normative scope of such acts? Here a note of caution is needed. Suppose A consents to B's borrowing her camera. B then borrows it. B's act of taking the camera is a *unique particular* act. It takes place at a particular time, for a particular duration, involves a particular (unique) trajectory through space, and so on. In light of this, it might seem that the normative scope of A's consent is the particular action that B performs: A's consent permits *that*. But the fact that an act of consent renders permissible a particular act does not imply that the normative scope of consent is that particular act. Suppose B in fact takes the camera whilst wearing a tie with pictures of *eagles* on it. Now suppose that he had taken it wearing a tie with pictures of *beagles* on it instead. Although these differences would constitute a different token act, such differences are normatively irrelevant.

The fact that consent is directed at *types* of act feeds into a debate in medical research ethics that is often framed in terms of the normative scope of consent. Biobanks—mass research repositories of human biological samples, including genetic samples—are valuable research resources because samples and data can be endlessly re-used in an open-ended range of research projects. This creates an ethical problem because the consent for such uses is gained at the time of initial acquisition of the sample (Steinsbekk & Solberg 2011). Given that future research uses may be unknown at the time of consent, the question arises whether the subject can permit such unknown uses by her consent. If we simply consider consent, then the answer is unproblematic: of course she can. All consent is "broad" consent, and all consent involves ignorance of countless facts about the actions that are permitted by consent. If A consents to B's use of her camera, she may have no idea what pictures A will take. If A consents to B's use of her car, she may not know that at this junction she will turn left, at that, turn right, and there is no requirement at all for B to *re-contact* A every time she does something.

Because actions can be individuated indefinitely finely, or with reference to indefinitely many individuating factors, it is correct, in one sense at least, that an act of consent permits indefinitely many actions. But this does not imply that an act of consent permits *anything* or that it is somehow "open". There is nothing odd or untoward about this kind of "open-but-bounded" feature of consent; it is a general feature of communication. Suppose A makes a request to B: "Bring me five red apples". It is open as to which red apples B brings (the set of token actions that *would* fulfil the request is very large), but it is not a request for green apples, or yellow apples, or for four apples or five million apples (the set of actions is indefinitely large, but membership of the set is not "open" to all).

A biobank participant can clearly consent "broadly" to members of any of a defined set of actions—research actions—without knowing which actions will be performed. Broad consent is not "open": it does not permit the sale of her data, its use by the police, or its being made available to insurance companies. The debate, however, is not so simple. This is because medical research ethics does not work with the concept of consent alone, but, rather, with a different concept: *informed consent*. Informed consent is not simply a matter of knowing something about the actions one is consenting to, it is a distinctive doctrine that holds that there are obligations on patients and research subjects to make consent decisions in a certain way (on the basis of specific information about specific types of action), and obligations on clinicians and researchers to *facilitate* and *ensure* that decisions are made in that way by providing large amounts of specific information (Schneider 1998). Whilst there are questions about the normative scope of *informed consent* in contrast to *consent*, we cannot address those here.

A normatively efficacious act of consent renders permissible some actions but not others, for some agents, but not others. Consent to surgery on one's ear is not consent to surgery on one's foot. But such an example is one where the scope of consent seems intuitively clear. But now consider another example: B asks A "May I kiss you?" A says "Oh yes, darling, do!" If B kisses A *there and then* we will typically think that the action is permissible. But what if B (rudely) turns and runs out the room, goes off for a week's holiday, then returns and tries to kiss A. Does A's earlier act of consent permit him to do so? What if B disappears for twenty years and then, on his return, argues that he may kiss A; after all, consent *was* given. What if B goes off on a forty-minute bike ride? A quick trip round the block? What set of actions is it that A's consent permits?

What we need is a clearer articulation of what determines the normative scope of consent. Having a clear sense of what determines the normative scope of consent is not simply some abstract bit of philosophical book-keeping. A lack of clarity about the normative scope of an agent's consent may leave it unclear whether or not a consentor was wronged by another's actions.

6.4 Explaining the normative scope of acts of consent

The power to permit by consent is discretionary. It is up to us whether and how to exercise it. As such, the normative scope of an act of consent is importantly bound up with the consentor's will. When A consents to B's taking her camera, she *intends* to create an exception *for B* to do *that kind of* act. She does not intend to create an exception for other parties, or for B to do other types of act.

The normative scope of consent is thus importantly bound up with the consentor's intentions. This line of thought is further supported when we consider examples where an agent is wronged by another party acting outside the scope of her consent. Suppose B enters A's room in the dark and A has sex with B thinking that B is her partner C. Here B wrongs A—B acts without A's consent— because A did not intend to consent to sex with B, but intended to consent to sex with C. We might be tempted to generalize here: if a person does not intend to permit an action that is F, no doing of F is thereby permitted. If she does not intend to permit *B* to do F, then B is not permitted to do F.

But, as it stands, this cannot be the correct account of the normative scope of consent. For example, suppose A consents to clinician B taking blood. B takes blood with a syringe that is, in fact, made in Scotland. Insofar as A is unaware of the origins of the syringe A cannot intend that B perform the action that B in fact performs: *taking blood with a syringe made in Scotland*. If A doesn't know that an action of type G is to be performed, or is actually performed, how can she permit it? If the normative scope of consent were to be *exclusively and exhaustively* determined by what the consentor intends, *no* action would be permissible. This is because consent is directed at sets of possible actions and any action that falls within that set will be a member of countless other sets. Whenever B does some action with A's consent, there will be facts about the action that are unknown, both to A and B. Consent *always* involves an indefinitely large amount of *ignorance* with regard to the act that is actually performed (the idea of a "fully informed" consent is nonsense).

Here we need to take care to distinguish different aspects of consent. In everyday English "consent" is used as a synonym for *agreement*. Suppose B seeks A's consent for B to do X. If A does consent, we might say that A *agreed* to the proposal. We cannot agree to something in ignorance. If A does not know—or have good reason to believe—that a proposed action is F, she does not *agree* to an action that is F being performed. A did not *agree* to being touched with a Scottish syringe. But *agreeing* to something and *permitting* it are not the same thing. A can agree to cut B's grass without thereby *permitting* B to cut his grass. The problem here is that when permissive consent is offered by way of response to a proposal, we can frame it *both* in terms of agreement and permission: A *agrees* to B's proposal to do X, and *thereby* permits B's doing X. But what we *permit* by our consent need not be what we agree to. One can *permit* an action that is *in fact* F without *agreeing* to an action that is F being performed.

So what is it that the consentor needs to know, and intend, in order to permit an action? Why does she not need to know about the origins of the syringe? One simple response we might have here is that the origins of the syringe—and countless other facts about the act in question—are *irrelevant*. As we shall see, this is the right kind of response, but raises the question: *why* are facts about the origins of the syringe irrelevant? We might think something like this: *if* she would have made the same decision had she known the additional information, that additional information makes no difference to the decision made, and thus to the normative scope of consent: it is *immaterial* to her decision.

But this cannot be the whole story. We can *regret* consent with hindsight, without undermining the normative force of that consent. Suppose A is very much attracted to B and consents to casual sex with him. B, unbeknownst to A, takes A's consent to be indicative of a commitment to an ongoing relationship. B, fuelled by this false belief, pesters A. Weeks later, A wishes she had never had sex with B in the first place. Here A consented to an act *that led to her being pestered by B*. Unlike the syringe case, here A *would not* have consented to the act *had she known* all the facts about it, but her ignorance of these facts does not void her consent. The consentor's attitudes—especially her beliefs and intentions—may well determine the scope of her consent in a *psychological* sense (what she *agrees* to, or what she *intends* to permit) but what we want is an account of the *normative* scope of consent.

Part of the problem here is that any particular action will be an instance of indefinitely many types of action. Nobody can know *all* the truths about any action. Only some descriptions of an action are of *normative* relevance, most are not. The underlying issue here is one of what the consentor has in mind out of a very large set of descriptions of actions. But this issue surfaces elsewhere. When an agent breaches a norm it *may* also be appropriate to blame them, but whether or not an agent is blameworthy depends upon what she believes, knows and intends. Suppose A switches on the light in her bedroom, unaware that a terrorist has rigged the switch to detonate a huge bomb beneath a school. A's act is, unwittingly, an instance of the type *unjust killing*. But it does not follow from this that A is blameworthy for what she did. Alternatively, if A presses the light switch falsely believing that it will detonate a bomb under a school, she is blameworthy, even if, in fact, her act wrongs nobody.

Here legal theorists use the concept of *mens rea* ("a guilty mind"). Suppose B intends to perform an action of the type: *using an item made in Scotland*. There are no norms prohibiting such actions. As such, it makes no sense to ask whether B had *mens rea* with regard to the action so described. In contrast, if B intends to perform an act of the kind *puncturing another person's skin* she ought to recognise that such an action breaches norms. When B asks to take blood from A, she proposes an act of a type that *would* breach A's rights. It is *this* fact that is of importance for the question of B's blameworthiness. This is because *mens rea* and *blameworthiness* are *norm-referenced* notions.

We can draw upon the kind of norm-referencing found in *mens rea* to solve our current problem with the normative scope of consent (Hurd 1996). Permissive consent is operative against a backdrop of distinctive norms, where agents *may not* perform certain kinds of action without consent. The act of *taking blood*, by itself, may not be impermissible (suppose the blood was daubed 20,000 years ago on an ancient cave wall). However, in our example accessing the blood requires B to intrude upon A's body. The act, when performed, will also be an instance of countless other types: an instance of *doing something with an item made in Scotland; putting less than 15ml of liquid in a container; extracting liquid from an object with 19g of magnesium in its body,* and so on, *ad infinitum*. But actions of these latter types are, considered in isolation, not prohibited. An action of these latter types is only prohibited if, and insofar as, it is *also* an instance of some type of action that *is* prohibited without consent. It does not matter for B's *mens rea* that she know that the syringe is made in Scotland; similarly, it does not matter from A's point of view, in exercising her normative power, that she knows that the syringe is made in Scotland, or that it contains 15ml, or that it is 80mm long. What *does* matter is that A knows that the action in question is of a type that *would* breach A's rights—i.e., the type of action that B *would* be blameworthy for if B knowingly performed it *without* consent—and that A intends to create an exception for B to perform an instance of that type of act.

At this point it would seem that the normative scope of consent is determined by two different elements. First there is the normative background context. The background not only involves an assignment of normative powers (with limits on the scope of those powers) to various agents, it also determines *what types of action* are impermissible without consent. Second, there are the consentor's intentions. The consentor has many rights, and can create many different exceptions for many different agents. The normative scope of her act of consent is that set of prohibited actions that the agent has the power to permit, and that she intends to permit, restricted further by indexing the set of actions to a set of agents that A intends to create an exception for (in many cases this latter set will contain a unique individual agent).

Whilst this account of the normative scope of consent is both plausible and defensible, it is not quite the whole story, as it fails to properly register the distinctive way that we can and do exercise a more fine-tuned kind of control over the normative scope of consent.

6.5 Clarifying and negotiating the scope of consent

We noted at the outset that the power to permit by consent that concerns us is a radically discretionary one. But the way that we have framed things so far has been in terms of a discretion to decide *whether or not* to consent. But consent transactions are richer, and more fluid, than this. One thing that happens in consent transactions is a process of *clarification* of the scope of consent. Suppose B asks A "May I borrow your camera?" A might not know exactly how long B intends to use it: "How long do you want it for?" Here A could continue to ask B questions until a clear specification of the action is given, such that she then makes a *binary* decision to permit (rather than refuse) that type of action, so specified. Or, the clarification may work in the other direction, as it were. B may ask A "Can I just check, is it OK to take it for the whole week?"

Consent transactions may also involve *negotiation* of the scope of consent. Suppose B, in response to A's question "How long for?", says "I need it for a week". A then replies "I really need it back in five days". If B wants the camera for longer, B may then try to induce A to revise the scope of her consent: "Really? You have six cameras and mine is broken". This kind of negotiation involves one party seeking to *change* the (offered) scope of the other party's consent.

Although the scope of consent is something that can be clarified, negotiated, revised, expanded, amended, it is not always appropriate to do so. Suppose a medical researcher B needs blood from a range of subjects to use in her research into cancer. She asks A's consent to take blood for this purpose. Suppose A has a deep, violent, irrational hatred of people of religious faith X. She explicitly restricts the scope of actions that she is willing to permit: "You may take my blood, but not store it in the same building as any blood from those of faith X". This would be inappropriate, unfeasible and prejudicial. In this context, if B knows that there are many more potential donors, then a non-negotiable "consent or refuse" option can be offered to many people. The practical context means that B *need not* engage in negotiation about the scope of consent sought.

The scope of consent is revisable and negotiable. But most consent transactions proceed and succeed without very much being said. This fact raises the question of how it is that consent transactions can and do proceed with so little being said. Recall our example earlier. When A responds to B's request for a kiss with "Yes of course", how does the scope of consent get restricted to a kiss *now* (not in five years' time)? Why does A not make these restrictions explicit? Given that B risks wronging A if he gets it wrong, why does B not ask A to be more explicit by way of clarifying the scope of consent: "Do you mean *right now* or *in a few seconds*? Do you mean *just gently* or is *with unbridled passion* also in the scope of your consent?"

The short response here is that there is no more need to make things explicit in the case of consent than there is in any other form of social interaction, or any other kind of communication. Consider A's request "Five red apples". The shopkeeper does not have to ask "What? Do you want me to *throw* five red apples at you? Do you want them given to you on your deathbed? Do you want rotten apples? Pictures of apples?" All social interaction and communication takes place—and can only take place—against a backdrop of common knowledge and shared practices. Young children have to *learn* what a store is, and what to do in a store. But they also learn that they do not have to *say* very much at all: entering the store and simply *pointing* at an item may be sufficient to generate an appropriate response. Our everyday social interaction, and communication, not only involves a wide range of practices, and shared background knowledge, but there are also some very useful *pragmatic* "principles" in play. One such principle is that one ought to seek to *make known* to relevant others any *deviation* from the shared background. So, if A wants five *tiny* apples, or wants the apples to be *concealed in a bag so that he cannot see them*, he ought to *make known* these deviations from the norm.

6.6 *Making* things normatively significant and the "ontology" of consent debate

Let us return to, and amend, the "Scottish Syringe" example. Suppose A has a phobia about the use of Scottish items: she cannot bear the thought of anything Scottish touching her skin. Suppose B has no idea that A has this unusual phobia. Now consider two situations. First, A *explicitly says to B* "Look, I have this weird phobia about Scotland, you *may not* take blood if the syringe is from Scotland". Here A explicitly *restricts* the set of actions that she intends to permit. The striking thing about this kind of revision to the scope of consent is that *although there was no general prior prohibition against using a Scottish item* there is now a specific *local* prohibition on doing so. What B is doing, is, in effect *making* something normatively significant—the origins of the syringe—that would otherwise not be so. This changes the normative situation for B. If B does not know whether the syringe is Scottish, she ought to refrain from acting until she does know that it is not. If B does know that it *is* Scottish, she *may not* take the blood (though, note, B *may* seek to *negotiate* the scope of A's consent: "Look, Scottish syringes are no different from any others, and you need to get this blood taken now").

But now suppose that A does not bother to make explicit her (very unusual) restriction on the scope of consent. She has the opportunity to make her odd views known to B; she is not silenced by deference to authority, say. Although she does not *intend* that B take blood with a Scottish syringe, she *does not say so*, in a context where she readily *could* say so. The question now arises: does B *wrong* A by using a Scottish syringe?

At this point our discussion of the normative scope of consent feeds into another debate: the nature or "ontology" of consent. Some theorists hold that merely performing the appropriate kind of mental act is *sufficient* for rendering others' actions permissible (Hurd 1996; Alexander 2014). Such theorists acknowledge that public acts of behaviour, including communicative acts, play an important role in consent practices. But, they argue, the role such acts play is not a normative one. If A *mentally* sets aside her rights against B doing X, there may be good *practical* reasons for A to *communicate* that decision to B, but the *normative* work is done by what A intends to permit, not what she *says*.

An alternative account is that normatively transformative consent requires some kind of *other-directed* act (which may be verbal or non-verbal). Acts of consent, on this view, are a species of *performative* (Wertheimer 1999; den Hertogh 2011; Manson 2016). Certain kinds of performatives, like promises and commands, change the normative situation by the right kind of person, with the appropriate authority making the appropriate kind of speech act (in the right kind of conditions). Just as a promise in the mind is not yet a binding promise, or a command in the mind is not an order, so too, on this view, an act of consent in the *mind* alone does not change the normative situation.

One way of framing this debate about the "ontology" of consent is to focus on simple binary cases: B proposes to take A's blood. A says "yes, you may". The question then is: what does the *normative* change co-vary with: A's intentions alone, or something else? But our discussion of the normative scope of consent raises the question: how well does either theory deal with discretionary, perhaps unusual, revisions to the scope of consent?

On the mentalist theory, where A has in mind her unusual restriction on the scope of consent, and has the opportunity to say so but remains silent, B *wrongs* A by using the Scottish syringe but, perhaps, blamelessly so. In contrast, the performative theorist argues that, insofar as A has not *made explicit* the unusual restriction, in a situation where A *could* make the restriction explicit, B is not merely blameless, B does not wrong A. By analogy, suppose A promises B "I will help you clean your car today" but then *in her mind* thinks "but only if there is a total eclipse of the sun here today". A mentalist theory of promises would hold that A has only placed herself under a *conditional* obligation to B: she is obliged to clean the car *only if* there is an eclipse. A performative theory, by way of contrast, holds that the promise undertaken is *the promise declared*, and, given that the qualification remains undeclared, it is not part of the normative scope of the promise. Now, such an analogy is illustrative, and not at all conclusive, but the aim here is not to settle the debate about the ontology of consent, it is, rather, to highlight the fact that any account of the nature of consent has to be able to plausibly accommodate and explain, not just consent transactions of the simple "binary" proposal/response form, but also the various ways in which we negotiate, revise, amend and expand the normative scope of consent.

The underlying problem here is that the simplest way to explain why the origins of the syringe *did not matter* was to make appeal to background norms: that *type* of action is not prohibited, so A does not need to know whether or not the syringe is Scottish. But this is to solve the problem of *which* descriptions of an action are normatively relevant by making appeal to a *static* or *fixed* normative background. Yet the normative context of consent is not static, it can be shaped and transformed, and we have the power to *make* things of normative significance that would not otherwise be so. The open question here is whether this kind of positive *making* of normative significance is something that could be done in the mind alone.

6.7 Conclusion

Individual, radically discretionary, permissive consent has a normative scope. First, in the sense that the power to permit by consent is limited, especially to adjusting certain kinds of directed obligations that others have towards us. Second, *acts* of consent also have a normative scope. The normative scope of an act of consent is not the same thing as its *content*, nor is it purely a psychological matter. The normative scope of consent is determined by the consentor's intentions against a background normative framework which, in turn, fixes what it is that both consentor, and those to whom consent is given, need to have in mind for consent to be normatively transformative. The discretion involved in the power to permit by consent is not simply a discretion in deciding *whether or not* to consent, or refuse. We have discretionary control over the scope of consent. Given that consent transactions proceed with a great deal remaining implicit, we noted that there are open questions about *how* it is that we keep track of the normative scope of consent, given that it is fluid and revisable. It was suggested that here consent transactions are no different from other communicative transactions, relying upon shared background knowledge and various pragmatic principles (such as that one ought to signal deviation from common knowledge). Finally, it was noted that our ability to revise the normative scope of consent feeds into a broader debate about the ontology of consent. We did not have the space to settle this debate here.

References

Alexander, L. (2014) "The Ontology of Consent," *Analytic Philosophy* 55(1): 102–13.
den Hertogh, G. (2011) "Can Consent be Presumed?" *Journal of Applied Philosophy* 28(3): 295–307.
Hurd, H.M. (1996) "The Moral Magic of Consent (I)," *Legal Theory* 2(2): 121–46.
Manson, N.C. (2015) "Transitional Paternalism: How Shared Normative Powers Give Rise to the Asymmetry of Adolescent Consent and Refusal," *Bioethics* 29(2): 66–73.
Manson, N.C. (2016) "Permissive Consent: A Robust Reason-Changing Account," *Philosophical Studies* 173(12): 3317–34.
Schneider, C. (1998) *The Practice of Autonomy: Patients, Doctors, and Medical Decisions*. Oxford: Oxford University Press.
Steinsbekk, K. and B. Solberg (2011) "Biobanks—When is Re-Consent Necessary?" *Public Health Ethics* 4(3): 236–50.
Wenar, L. (2013) "The Nature of Claim-Rights," *Ethics* 123(2): 202–29.
Wertheimer, A. (1999) "What is Consent? And is it Important?" *Buffalo Criminal Law Review* 3: 557–83.
Wilks, I. (1999) "Asymmetrical Competence," *Bioethics* 13: 154–9.

Further reading

Relatively little has been written that focuses on the scope of consent *in general*, although discussions about whether this or that person consented to *that*, or had the power to do so, are commonplace in a wide range of discussions about consent. Hurd (1996) is an exception, and is essential reading for anyone interested in this topic (and it is Hurd's account that forms the core of the discussion in this entry). Alan Wertheimer's work on consent, both in the context of sexual consent, and in bioethics, involves a lot of careful thinking about the scope of consent, via a wealth of examples: e.g., see *Consent to Sexual Relations*, Cambridge University Press, 2003. In the context of sexual consent, Tom Dougherty's (2013) account of how *deception* undermines consent has a very useful, and focused, discussion of the scope of consent ("Sex, Lies and Consent," *Ethics* 123(4): 717–44).

Related topics

Ch.2 What is consent?
Ch.8 Valid consent
Ch.24 Informed consent

7
WHEN IS CONSENT REQUIRED?

Terrance McConnell

7.1 Introduction

In our everyday interactions with others, we often seek consent. In some cases the consent may be conveyed in a formal manner, such as a signed document or saying specific words. In other situations it may be more informal, conveyed by gestures, movements, and the like. The continuum here is broad and the possibilities are many. Similarly, consent may be denied, either explicitly or implicitly. Because of these complexities, it is sometimes difficult to determine when consent is required, when it is merely a matter of etiquette, or when it is unnecessary. This chapter will explore these issues.

The chapter will be structured as follows. I will first articulate my thesis, which is that whenever P_2 is required to get P_1's consent before acting, it is because some right of P_1's is implicated. I will then consider cases in which it is uncontroversial that consent is required and show how the thesis applies to them. After that, I will briefly consider cases in which it is uncontroversial that consent need not be obtained and explain why this is the case. I will then address what I shall call "problematic" cases; these are situations in which people commonly seek another's permission before acting, but it is not obvious that they are required to do so. Applying the thesis will enable us to determine whether and why seeking consent in the problematic cases is required. The determination that must be made in these cases is what right, if any, is implicated in the relationship between P_1 and P_2 and what the content of that right is. While it is tempting to think of many of these problematic cases as a matter of etiquette rather than morality, that is too simplistic. I shall suggest that when there is a common social practice of soliciting consent in certain types of situations, that signals that rights may be involved. I shall conclude by addressing the scope of the thesis. If P_1 does have right R, does that imply that it is *necessary* for P_2 to get P_1's consent before infringing R? And is P_1's consent *sufficient* to justify P_2's infringing R? These questions must be addressed because the control that a right gives its possessor may not be absolute.

7.2 The thesis

Let us begin by explaining some basic terms. The term "consent" can be used as a verb or a noun. The former is defined as "give permission; agree"; the latter, as "voluntary agreement;

permission".[1] Even profession-specific accounts of consent agree that this is the core meaning. A prominent legal dictionary defines "consent" as "agreement, approval, or permission as to some act or purpose, esp. given voluntarily by a competent person".[2] Consent involves a relationship between at least two people, one who gives the consent and one to whom consent is given. In some cases, the one to whom consent is given explicitly seeks permission from the other; but sometimes consent is given without such a request (see Schnüriger, this volume, Chapter 2).

I shall use the expressions *requirement*, *duty*, and *obligation* interchangeably. When I say that someone is required to do (or refrain from doing) something, or that someone has a duty/obligation to do (or refrain from doing) that thing, I mean that the person ought to do (or refrain from doing) that thing. An act can be *morally* required or *legally* required. While these two realms are related in complicated ways, the focus in this chapter is on *moral requirement*. So the question being addressed here is this: When and with respect to what is P_2 morally required to get the consent of P_1 before acting?

Consent involves giving permission, and that implies that the person giving permission has authority over the matter (see Koch, this volume, Chapter 3). The thesis of this chapter is that whenever P_2 is morally required to get P_1's consent, it is because P_1 has a right over the matter in question. Rights are normatively advantageous to their possessors. There are competing accounts of how best to understand these advantages. One view is that rights are protected interests; an alternative conception is that rights are protected choices (Sumner 1987: 45ff; Wellman 1995: 118–23). On either account, rights put restrictions on how others may treat their possessors (Sumner 1987: Chs. 1–2; McConnell 2000: 3–4). Rights are analyzed in connection with other normative ideas, especially claims, liberties, immunities, and powers. Rights involve several of these notions in various combinations, usually referred to as "rights packages". A right's content is what that right gives the right-holder a right to. The right of free speech, for example, involves immunity from legislative regulation plus certain liberties. The right to execute a will involves the power to dispose of one's property as one wants. The right to vote includes claims against one's fellow citizens that they not prevent one from voting and claims against officials of the state that they provide one with a reasonable opportunity to cast a ballot. The restrictions that claim rights put on others are in the form of obligations or duties to the possessors of the rights. So in the canonical form "P_1 has a right R against P_2", P_1 is the possessor of the right, P_2 is the bearer of the duty correlative with that right, and R is that to which P_1 has a right. Consent is a normative power that the possessor of a right has, giving her control over that to which she has a right. Consent is morally transforming; it normally changes the moral status of the act performed by the person to whom consent is given (Wellman 1995: 82).

If P_2 is morally required to secure P_1's consent because P_1 has a right over the matter in question, one might reasonably wonder why there would be problematic cases. If the thesis is correct, there should be a plausible answer to this query. In dealing with this, I shall argue that while the content of rights may be clear at their core, they are less likely to be clear at the periphery (Sumner 1987; Wellman 1995). Because of this, there are situations in which it is unclear exactly what duties P_1's rights impose on others, and so it is unclear whether others must seek P_1's consent before acting.

7.3 Easy cases

Consider clear cases where any ordinary human being should not act without the consent of another. Suppose that Helen wants to enter your house. She should seek your permission. And if she is acting properly, she will not enter without your consent, either by explicit invitation or an appropriate gesture. Your property rights in the house give you control over your abode and put restrictions on what others may do.

A physician should not take my blood pressure, examine my prostate, or remove my appendix without my consent (see Ach, this volume, Chapter 25). The forms that my consent can take in these cases are variable. If I go to my physician for a physical examination, it is likely that she will say something like "I am going to take your blood pressure now". When I extend my arm, I have given consent (or consent is implied). If I go to a urologist, he might say "I would like to examine your prostate now". My saying "Okay" and lowering my pants is taken as giving consent. But a physician should not perform surgery on me unless I sign an informed consent document that details the risks and benefits of the procedure (see Eyal, this volume, Chapter 24). These rights against the physician are based on the right of bodily integrity; this right gives people control over their own bodies and puts restrictions on what others may do to them.

These cases illustrate both why consent must be obtained and what the normative power of consent is. Don Herzog puts it clearly.

> Ordinarily, others may not enter your house or have sex with you or slice open your body in surgery unless you consent to their doing so. If they proceed without your consent, they violate your rights. Consent thus allows us selectively to admit different people to different sorts of intimacy and to repel those we're not interested in. That others need your permission in such contexts identifies you as an independent agent deserving of respect, with plans and projects of your own.
>
> *(Herzog 1989: 222)*

As the passage indicates, Herzog conceives of rights as protected choices; but the protected interests account works equally well here.

Suppose that I am organizing an academic conference. I very much want Professor Garcia to participate because she is a distinguished scholar in that area. In advertising the upcoming event, I am not permitted to list Professor Garcia as a participant without first getting her consent. The reasons are many, but the most important one appeals to Professor Garcia's rights. If she is advertised as a participant but does not attend, many will (reasonably but falsely) conclude that she backed out; her reputation will be unjustifiably sullied, thereby violating one of her rights.

Now consider cases where the consent of another is not typically sought. Suppose that I am trying to park my automobile in a public lot where few spaces are available. I see an open spot and I see another person pursuing it. If I get there first, I may park in that place. Neither I nor the other person has a (claim) right to the space, though each of us has a liberty right to pursue it.

There can be situations in which consent, though normally not required, is required because of the past actions of the agents involved. If you own your house and the land it is on, you have property rights to them. That would ordinarily give you a right to construct a fence to enclose your land. But if you and your neighbor were both concerned about the aesthetic and monetary value of your properties, you may have reached an agreement that neither of you would erect a fence on his property without the consent of the other. Your own voluntary acts put limits on your property rights. Consent is now required because your agreement created new rights for the other person and his agreement created new rights for you.

Consent need not be given for each and every act that implicates the possessor's rights. Suppose that someone is doing a repair to my house. When beginning the work, he should get my consent before entering my home. But if completing the job requires going in and out of the house multiple times, it is not necessary for him to seek my permission on each occasion. The original consent is reasonably understood to apply to all of the entrances necessary to complete the job. Though consent is required for another to enter my house, the context may be such that it is not required on each and every occasion; or, more cautiously, consent may be implied in some contexts.

7.4 Problematic cases

Now let us consider some cases where it is not obvious whether one person needs to get the consent of another before acting. Suppose that you are boarding a public bus. Before you sit down beside another patron (whom you do not know), do you need that person's consent? Notice how many possibilities there are here and how these variations influence people's conduct. If you get on the bus and there are multiple pairs of seats that are unoccupied, you will likely sit in one of those rather than sit beside a stranger. It is not obvious that it would be wrong to seek an unoccupied seat beside a stranger, but in such a situation most of us would not do so. But now suppose that all of the pairs of seats have at least one occupant. If you are going to sit, it will have to be beside some stranger. Perhaps you will look for a friendly face, or maybe you will just focus on the nearest available seat. In either case, you will likely say to the other occupant, "Is this seat taken?" or "May I sit here?" If the occupant is agreeable, you will probably take the seat. If the occupant expresses dissent, you may seek a different seat, though that decision is probably driven by prudence just as much as morality. Now consider a third possibility. When you enter the bus, all of the seats but one are occupied. You will probably take the unoccupied seat without asking for the consent of the adjacent occupant. You will probably do the same thing if all but a few of the seats are taken. These, I think, are customs followed by many. From facts alone – that certain customs exist – no normative conclusion follows directly. So seeking consent in this case may not be morally required. But, I suggest, customs often evolve for reasons, and so the practice of seeking consent may signal that something morally important is involved.

Consider a second case. You are at a social gathering. You see two people talking to each other. You are acquainted with one of the two. If she were standing alone, it would be natural for you to approach her and initiate a conversation. But may you join the conversation of these two people? If you approach them, should you solicit their consent? Notice that the context and the particulars of the situation matter here. If you are at an academic conference where the participants have many shared interests and the conversation is lively and involves five people, it is perfectly normal for you to join in; asking for the participants' consent is unnecessary and would be awkward. Similarly, if you are at a party and there is a group of four people laughing and having a spirited conversation, it is in line with social norms if you join in. But if you see two people involved in a conversation, I think that the instinct is different and for good reason. Some conversations are open and casual; others are more serious and intimate. And while they do not come labeled, the context often signals to others what kind of conversation it is. When it seems serious, I think that most of us would seek the permission of the other two as a condition of entering the conversation. If there are moral reasons for doing this, what rights are involved?

Consider now another case. You are attending an academic conference. Several of the presentations are related to a project on which you are currently working. You attend these presentations and take copious notes. A number of the points made by these authors are relevant to your project. You return home and continue to develop your own work. Part of your new work is influenced by some of the presentations that you heard at the conference.

In addition, you would like to discuss some of the specific claims made by some of the presenters. If you wish to cite a scholar's unpublished paper, do you need that person's consent? Like the other two kinds of cases, there is a practice, though somewhat ill-defined, of seeking such consent. I have received manuscripts from fellow scholars with a message at the top of the paper reading "Please do not cite without the author's permission". And I have attended a number of conferences in which all of the authors' presentations were available to attendees electronically prior to the event. In at least some of these conferences, anyone downloading the presentations was instructed not to cite any of the papers without the author's permission. Though this is anecdotal, it does suggest that something important is at stake. The reason to cite the work of others, of course, is to credit them and respect their rights to the ideas they have generated. But if there are moral reasons not to attribute ideas to them – ideas that they have expressed – what are they?

I shall focus on these three problematic cases – taking a seat next to someone on a bus, entering a conversation with two or more other people, and citing an author's unpublished paper – to illuminate the question "When is consent required?" But before turning to that, note two things about these cases. First, the practice of seeking consent described exists in at least some societies. Second, some will say that these practices are merely matters of etiquette. I do not think that we should be dismissive of such practices. In the first paragraph of Chapter XI of the *Leviathan*, Thomas Hobbes suggests that manners might be "Small Moralls" (Hobbes 1994/1668: 57). I think that there is some wisdom in this remark, and my analysis of the problematic cases will try to show this.[3]

7.5 Analysis of the problematic cases

Let us now see how the thesis applies to the more problematic cases. First, consider the case of taking a seat on the bus. It seems reasonable to hold that if a person purchases a ticket, she has a claim right to occupy some seat or other[4], and a liberty right to pursue any unoccupied seat. Notice the contrast when one has a claim right to a specific seat, such as when one boards an airplane. In that case, boarders do not seek the consent of those next to whom they are sitting, nor should they; no rights of other persons are implicated. So why is the conduct of someone boarding a public bus often different from that of boarding an airplane? I shall argue that there are rights involved, but their contents on the periphery are not always clear and vary depending on the context.

As was noted above, a person boarding a bus may encounter many different scenarios. One possibility is that there are many unoccupied spaces and there is no need to take a seat beside a stranger. Suppose that this is the situation that Maria encounters when she enters a bus. Instead of sitting alone, however, Maria takes a seat next to a stranger, John, without seeking his permission. In some cultures this would seem odd, though perhaps not wrong. But if we extend the scenario, we can see what right is involved. After Maria takes the seat, suppose that John moves to another area of the bus where he can sit alone. If Maria follows him, something is askew; she might even be accused of harassment. It seems clear that John is seeking privacy. The content of the right to privacy may not always be clear, but it at least involves the right to be let alone (Warren & Brandeis 1890). In this context, we are talking about a right to spatial privacy. A second scenario demonstrates how the content of the right to privacy varies with the context. Suppose that William boards a crowded bus and there is only one unoccupied seat remaining. It is likely that William will take that seat without seeking the consent of the person in the adjacent seat; such conduct seems normal and not morally wrong. William has a right to occupy some seat or other, and no patron has an absolute right that the seat next to him remains unoccupied. But notice a third scenario. When Helga enters the bus, multiple seats are available, but each option requires her to sit beside a stranger because each pair of seats has at least one occupant. As suggested earlier, before taking a seat, Helga is apt to ask, "May I sit here?" If the person responds in the negative, Helga will probably pursue another option. I think that many of us would behave similarly. One reason for doing so is prudential; it is just not worth it to stir up a public dispute. But there is a moral reason too; if someone values his spatial privacy that much, we will allow him to have it if it is easy to do so.

In contemporary society, the contours of this right are complex. If we live and work in a large city, often our spatial privacy is limited. In order to flourish, we need relationships with others in varying degrees of intimacy. But as the population has increased, people have less and less time to themselves; as a result, many desire some privacy. That too contributes to flourishing. The fact that we ourselves desire and value privacy explains, in part, why we may go out of our way to give others space to themselves when doing so is feasible.

A different right is at stake when people are conversing between or among themselves. It is a kind of privacy, what we might call relational or informational privacy. In the case of five people conversing at an academic conference, relational privacy does not seem to be relevant. It is likely that the topic of conversation pertains to academic matters discussed at the conference. A similar analysis applies to a group at a party. If they are laughing and jovial, it is unlikely that this is a private conversation. Seeking consent to enter such a conversation is not required because no important rights are involved. But in a situation in which two people are talking, at least one of whom is known to you, matters might be quite different. Numbers seem to matter, though they are not the only relevant factor. The participants' body language and the physical arrangement are clues that most people can read. We can often tell whether the tenor of others' conversations is serious or causal. The person whom you know might wave or gesture to you in a way that invites you to join them. But the body language of the two can also signal to you that the conversation is private. We share different information with different people; that is important to our well-being.

Informational privacy is clearly important to us when it concerns medical matters, legal issues, financial arrangements, or an evaluation of our work. Most of these conversations, however, are protected by the physical arrangement. We speak to physicians, lawyers, financial advisors, and supervisors in their offices, outside the auditory range of others. These professionals have property rights in the offices they occupy, and these rights in turn give them and their clients spatial privacy, which protects informational privacy. But we also value relational and informational privacy with friends. We sometimes converse with friends in public places about private matters. The reluctance of sensitive people to enter an apparently serious conversation between two people is a social norm. It might be regarded as mere etiquette. But a better explanation, I think, is that people acknowledge and respect that others value their relational privacy with selected others and that even though this kind of privacy lacks the formal protections that exist in relationships between professionals and clients, it can still be honored.

Privacy does not seem to be involved when deciding whether it is permissible to cite an unpublished paper without the author's consent. But rights of some sort do seem to be lurking. The focus here will be on the interests of the author, in particular her interests in her professional reputation.

Let us look at the context in which this question arises. You might want to quote from an author's unpublished paper because you are working on a related topic. If you are defending a substantive position on a topic, you will likely convey "the lay of the land", describing the competing views and identifying advocates of those positions. A "neutral" reason for citing an author's unpublished work is simply to identify and locate her work within the context of the debate. A second possibility is that you may be criticizing the position that the author defended in her paper. Criticisms can cover a wide spectrum, ranging from asserting that the author's view is absurd to saying that it is novel and raises unique challenges. A third possibility is that you are praising the author's work. You might say, for example, that the author is providing a novel but different defense of the position that you are articulating. This range of possibilities suggests that how the author's interests will be impacted depends in part on why you want to cite the paper.

Citing the author's paper for neutral reasons would seem to have the least impact on her interests. After all, you are merely identifying her as having supported a certain position at a conference. But if she no longer holds the position in question, she may prefer not to be so identified. And she might reasonably give you permission to cite her presentation but not to quote it. Most authors care about how they express their positions. They strive to be clear, articulate, original, and interesting. Most of us do not express things as well as we would like the first time around, or even the second time. So an author's interest in not having a work-in-progress quoted may be stronger than not having such a work cited. If so, that explains why seeking consent to quote is morally important. If you are criticizing the author's work, that might seem to raise the stakes because the author's interests are impacted more adversely. But that is too quick. Not all criticisms are harmful. Weak or pedantic criticisms may reflect more poorly on the critic than the author. And many would rather be criticized than ignored. If you are praising the author's work, you might be tempted to think that seeking consent is unnecessary. But that too is incorrect. In the cases of both criticizing and praising, a critical question is whether the author still affirms the view. The author's principal interest here is control over what views are attributed to her.

To clarify the right at stake, notice some contexts in which obtaining such consent is not required. If a politician gives a public speech, it may be cited, praised, or criticized without soliciting his consent. If a public figure gives a speech about one of her causes, anyone may quote it and discuss its contents. This gets at the meaning of "to publish"; that phrase ordinarily means "to declare publicly" or "to place before the public". No right is implicated in these cases because the speaker has made these ideas available to the public. The same applies to academic authors. Once they have published a piece in a book or a journal, it is in the public domain and may be cited or quoted without the author's consent.

The practice of treating works-in-progress presented at conferences differently rests on an implicit agreement among members of the community. What is common to all three cases – neutral citation, criticism, and praise – is the author's reputation. Requiring an author's consent before citing or quoting an unpublished work gives the author some control. Until a manuscript is submitted and a publisher accepts it, the author retains the rights to withhold this work from the public, disavow its content, or change the way the ideas are expressed. The practice promotes various interests, including encouraging people to try out new ideas and explore bold theses.

Property rights and the right to bodily integrity are basic and have reasonably clear cores. The rights to spatial privacy and informational privacy are often embedded in and protected by property rights and the right to bodily integrity. But in public places, the content of the rights to spatial privacy and relational privacy is less clear. Moreover, how that content is understood will vary from society to society. That is why it is not obvious that we need to ask for consent in these cases.

7.6 Scope of the thesis

P_2 is morally required to secure P_1's consent when P_1 has a right over the matter in question. In such a case, if P_2 abridges P_1's right without P_1's consent, P_2's act is *prima facie* wrong. But is consent always *necessary* to justify infringing another's right? And is the consent of the possessor *sufficient* to justify infringing the right? That is, does the possessor's consent alone cancel the correlative duty?

Let us begin with the necessity claim. If P_1's consent is necessary to justify any infringement of his right by P_2, then the duty correlative with the right in question is canceled or suspended *only when* P_1 has given consent. For many (and perhaps all) rights, the necessity claim is false. There are at least two other ways (besides consent) that the duty correlative with a right might be canceled. One way in which others may be justified in infringing an individual's right is if that person has *forfeited* that right. A person has forfeited a right when the duty correlative with that right is canceled because the possessor of the right has engaged in specified wrongdoing. Using force against another person is normally wrong, in part, because it violates her right of bodily integrity. But if she is assaulting you, you are permitted to use whatever force is necessary to repel the attack. In part, your use of force is justified because she has forfeited her right (McConnell 2000: 6–7). A second way in which others may be justified in infringing an individual's right has been *overridden* by a competing moral consideration. When a right is overridden, others are justified in acting contrary to the obligation correlative with that right. Entering another person's home without his consent infringes his property rights and is *prima facie* wrong. But if breaking into that person's home is necessary in order to save the life of a child, the obligation to save the child overrides the obligations correlative with property rights (Feinberg 1980: 230; McConnell 2000: 7).

For any right that can be forfeited, the obligation correlative with that right can be canceled by certain actions of the right's possessor. For any right that can be overridden, the obligation correlative with that right can be defeated by a stronger, competing obligation. Perhaps some rights cannot be forfeited. Perhaps some rights are absolute and cannot be overridden (Feinberg 1980: 225). These are substantive normative questions that any theory of rights must answer. But for any right that can be forfeited or can be overridden, there are situations in which others may infringe the right without the possessor's consent. In those cases, consent is not always required to suspend the correlative duty.

There is a third context in which consent is not necessary; this is when consent cannot be obtained. As noted earlier, physicians may not administer medical treatment to a person without her consent. But if someone is unconscious, severely injured, and in need of life-saving surgery, physicians are permitted – indeed, in most jurisdictions, required – to perform the surgery. A common rationale for this practice is that it honors patients' rights, either because they would have consented or it protects their vital interests (see Yaffe, this volume, Chapter 9). So again consent is not necessary to justify an act that, in other contexts, would infringe a person's right.

Let us now turn to the sufficiency claim. If P_1's consent is sufficient to justify P_2's infringement of right R, then P_1's consent by itself cancels P_2's obligation regarding R. But perhaps in some cases the possessor's consent alone does not justify infringing the right. This too is a substantive normative question about rights concerning which there is disagreement; the issue is whether all rights are alienable (Steiner 2013; Biasetti 2015). A right is alienable if the consent of the possessor alone is sufficient to justify infringing that right; the possessor's consent cancels the correlative duty. If a right is inalienable, then it is not the case that the consent of the possessor is by itself sufficient to justify infringing that right (McConnell 2000: 8–14). Consider the right to life. If that right is inalienable, then the mere fact that P_1 has given P_2 consent to kill him does not by itself cancel P_2's duty not to kill P_1 (McConnell 2000: Ch. 5).

There is at least one other situation in which P_1's consent is not sufficient to justify P_2's infringement of right R. This is when the rights of third parties would be threatened. Property rights are paradigmatically alienable, and so if P_1 gives P_2 permission to destroy some of his property, P_2 may normally do so. There are various ways that P_2 might permissibly destroy P_1's property with his consent, but setting his house on fire is not permissible if doing so threatens the property of others. If P_1 has given P_2 such consent, P_1 is not *wronged* by the act, assuming that the consent is voluntary and informed (see Dempsey, this volume, Chapter 17). But others may be wronged. P_1 himself is not permitted to set his house ablaze because of the rights of others, and so he cannot make it permissible for P_2 to do so. In this case, the interests of others are directly threatened, but in other cases it may be more nuanced. One has a right not to be hit by another person. But if two people are engaged in a sporting event such as boxing, each is permitted to strike the other; by participating in the sport, each has given the other consent to strike him. But if I am on a public street, does my consent give another permission to hit me? There may be disagreement about this, but there are good reasons not to allow consent to justify striking another in public. The state is charged with maintaining order and protecting people's rights. Allowing sports like boxing does not impede that goal because they occur in restricted spaces and there are good reasons to believe that people are participating voluntarily. But fighting on public streets is problematic because it is difficult to tell if all of the participants have given their consent and the violence is likely to spread in a way that threatens those who are not participating. So there is an argument, and I think a good one, to show that P_1's consent alone does not justify P_2 in hitting him because the setting in which such an act occurs can impact the welfare of third parties.

The sufficiency claim is controversial, then, because there is not a consensus about whether all rights are alienable and because in some cases the act to which the consent is given is independently wrong or poses a threat to others.

7.7 Conclusion

Consent can be permission-generating. When consent does have this normative force, the person giving consent has a right that may ordinarily not be infringed. But consent gives a second person permission to do what would otherwise be wrong. Some of these cases are obvious, like entering someone's house or having sexual relations with another. Other cases are not obvious. One explanation for why they are not obvious is that the scope and content of individual rights is not always clear. Context and particulars matter. That is why some cases seem initially puzzling and require further analysis. There are many situations in which we do, without thinking, ask for another's consent. When we then subject those situations to philosophical analysis, we may wonder why we seek consent. The explanation offered here is that these practices have evolved because rights are implicated, even though the content of these rights is sometimes difficult to articulate. But if we are tempted to seek consent, such an act may be a sign that rights of the other are involved. This is not always the case, however. As John Kleinig has noted, "we sometimes perpetuate rituals of consent even though no authorization is necessary" (Kleinig 2010: 8). His example is a man asking the consent of a woman's father before proposing marriage. But even this archaic practice has its roots in beliefs about rights; women were once thought to be the property of their fathers or husbands. Whether consent is necessary or sufficient to cancel the duty correlative with a given right depends on the right in question. If that right can be forfeited or overridden, consent is not necessary; if that right is inalienable, consent is not sufficient.[5]

Notes

1 *Illustrated Oxford Dictionary* (New York: Oxford University Press, 1998), p. 180.
2 Garner, B. (ed.). (2009). *Black's Law Dictionary*. Ninth Edition. St. Paul, MN: West Publishing, p. 346.

3 Gert argues that "politeness taken as a character trait involving acting so as to avoid giving offense to others even counts as a moral virtue" (Gert 1988: 171). This makes it clear that some but not all matters of etiquette have moral significance.
4 This assumes, unrealistically in many cases, that the number of tickets sold does not exceed the number of seats available.
5 Acknowledgements: I thank Andreas Müller, Peter Schaber, and Bas van der Vossen for their comments and suggestions on earlier drafts of this chapter.

References

Biasetti, P. (2015) "Infinite Regress and Hohfeld: A Comment on Hillel Steiner's 'Directed Duties and Inalienable Rights'," *Ethics* 126: 139–52.
Feinberg, J. (1980) *Rights, Justice, and the Bounds of Liberty*. Princeton, NJ: Princeton University Press.
Gert, B. (1988) *Morality: A New Justification of the Moral Rules*. New York: Oxford University Press.
Herzog, D. (1989) *Happy Slaves: A Critique of Consent Theory*. Chicago: University of Chicago Press.
Hobbes, T. (1994/1668) *Leviathan*. Indianapolis: Hackett Publishing.
Kleinig, J. (2010) "The Nature of Consent," in F. Miller and A. Wertheimer (ed.), *The Ethics of Consent: Theory and Practice*. New York: Oxford University Press.
McConnell, T. (2000) *Inalienable Rights: The Limits of Consent in Medicine and the Law*. New York: Oxford University Press.
Steiner, H. (2013) "Directed Duties and Inalienable Rights," *Ethics* 123: 230–44.
Sumner, L.W. (1987) *The Moral Foundation of Rights*. New York: Oxford University Press.
Warren, S. and L. Brandeis (1890) "The Right to Privacy," *Harvard Law Review* IV: 193–220.
Wellman, C. (1995) *Real Rights*. New York: Oxford University Press.

Related topics

Ch.2 What is consent?
Ch.3 Consent as a normative power
Ch.8 Valid consent
Ch.9 Hypothetical consent
Ch.17 The volenti maxim
Ch.24 Informed consent
Ch.25 Consent and medical treatment

8
VALID CONSENT

Emma C. Bullock

8.1 Introduction

Consent has the power to transform morally unacceptable actions into morally acceptable ones (Davis 2003: 368; Manson & O'Neill 2007: 79; Miller & Wertheimer 2010: 79; Hurd 1996: 123). This is most clearly so in the context of therapeutic treatment or sexual relationships. For instance, if Anna, a medical doctor, injects Betty with a drug then this counts as an assault unless Anna has Betty's consent. Likewise, if Chris has sexual intercourse with Daniel then this counts as rape unless Chris has Daniel's consent (Feinberg 1986: 180). Given that consent requirements protect individuals from what would otherwise be wrongful or harmful interferences – such as assaults and rapes – care must be taken to identify the conditions under which consent has its moral transformative power.

One way to determine when consent is morally transformative is by reflecting on what we take to be the moral purpose of consent. The reasons given as to why it is important to respect consent vary: whilst some argue that the presence or absence of consent is evidence that the transaction will contribute to the consenting party's wellbeing[1] (Miller & Wertheimer 2010: 82; Hanna 2011: 519), others argue that consent ought to be respected because consent requirements play a positive role in the pursuit of our autonomous lives and autonomous choices morally ought never to be overridden (Faden & Beauchamp 1986: 288; Bromwich & Millum 2015: 197). Broadly speaking, the type of constraints placed on morally transformative consent will differ depending on whether one identifies the moral purpose of consent in terms of protecting wellbeing or respecting autonomy. If the moral purpose of consent is to protect wellbeing, then the constraints on consent will likely be *substantive*[2]: we can deny that consent has its transformative power whenever acting on the consent would be detrimental to the consenting party's wellbeing. On the other hand, if the moral purpose of consent is to respect autonomy, then the constraints on consent will be *procedural*: we can deny consent its transformative power whenever it fails to meet a procedural constraint, regardless as to whether we consider the consensual transaction to be detrimental to the consenting party's wellbeing. The procedural constraint on morally transformative consent requires that the consent is autonomous, and this is usually measured in terms of whether the consent was voluntary, informed and competently made (Archard 1998: 44; Miller & Wertheimer 2010: 87). When these procedural requirements are met, an individual's consent counts as *valid*. Typically, those who identify the moral purpose of consent solely with the demand to respect autonomy will treat valid consent as both necessary and sufficient for morally transformative consent. Those who identify the moral purpose of consent with the protection and promotion of wellbeing might consider valid consent as necessary for morally transformative consent, but deny that meeting the requirements is sufficient for morally transformative consent.[3]

This chapter primarily focuses on the procedural constraints for morally transformative consent, that is, valid consent. In the following I outline the three typical requirements for valid consent. I will go on to suggest that either the strength of each of the requirements for valid consent ought to vary with context, or it will turn out that our consents turn out to be invalid more frequently than we might otherwise have thought. I end the entry with the suggestion that, even when the three conditions for valid consent are met, the validity of a consent may be insufficient for it to be morally transformative. Specifically, I argue that certain actions and behaviors might count as morally intolerable regardless as to whether the procedural criteria for valid consent are met.

8.2 Three requirements for valid consent

The three procedural requirements for valid consent are that the consent is voluntary, informed and that the consenting party is decisionally competent. A basic way to determine whether the first requirement has been met – that is, whether the consent is voluntary – is in terms of whether the consent was inappropriately influenced. Not all influences on consent undermine its voluntariness. Rational persuasion, for instance, is generally thought to be an acceptable method of procuring valid consent.[4] Thus, if a physician tries to persuade a patient to undergo a procedure by presenting reasons in favor of it, then the patient's consent to the procedure is, *ceteris paribus*, voluntary and so valid (Nelson et al. 2011: 7). Likewise, consent to purchase a car is no less voluntary should a car sales woman attempt to persuade her customer of the various virtues of a particular model.

Unlike rational persuasion, however, bypassing a person's capacity for rational deliberation through manipulative or coercive means can invalidate a consent by way of undermining its voluntariness (Nelson et al. 2011: 7; Manson & O'Neill 2007: 16–17; Hurd 1996: 139; cf. Gutmann, this volume, Chapter 19).[5] For instance, when a woman consents to sexual intercourse on threat of being stabbed with a knife her consent is properly thought of as involuntary because it is coerced (Miller & Wertheimer 2010: 86; Hurd 1996: 139). Likewise, if a physician tried to get a patient to undergo a medical procedure by using scare tactics, the patient's manipulated consent will count as involuntary. In both cases the coerced and manipulated consents are invalid, and so fail to be morally transformative: at least insofar as the consents are involuntary, the knife wielder does something morally unacceptable when he proceeds to have sexual intercourse with the consenting party, and the physician does something morally unacceptable when she carries out the medical procedure.

The second requirement for valid consent is that it is appropriately informed. Roughly speaking, a consent counts as uninformed if it was based on a mistaken belief or if the consenting party was ignorant about what was being consented to (Feinberg 1986: 152; O'Neill 2003: 4). Suppose, for instance, that a patient gives her consent for an ultrasound scan under the false impression that the machine will be used externally. Her consent no longer counts as valid when she later discovers that she will be having an internal ultrasound scan with a probe placed in her vagina. Insofar as the patient consents without relevant information, the sonographer does something morally wrong when she carries out the procedure even though the patient has consented: her consent is not valid since she agreed to the procedure while lacking relevant information and she would not have consented had she had this information (Hanna 2011: 524).

The third requirement for valid consent is that the individual offering or withholding consent is decisionally competent to do so. According to clinical psychiatry a patient has the decisional capacity to consent to medical treatment if she is able to a) understand information, b) appreciate that the information applies to herself, c) reason with that information, and d) express a choice (Grisso & Appelbaum 1998: 20). Persons who are unable to process and reason with information, or who are unable to express a choice because of a lack of cognitive capacity or mental impairment, are recognized as incompetent to consent, their consents counting as invalid (Faden & Beauchamp 1986: 10).

Decisional capacity is typically determined in terms of meeting a threshold. On a threshold measure of decisional capacity an individual is entitled to have her consent respected so long as a minimal requirement is met. The threshold criterion for decisional capacity is fairly familiar: even if a 10-year-old child is fully informed about the nature of sexual intercourse and her decision to have sex is free from coercion, her consent to sexual intercourse is invalid because she has failed to meet the threshold at which we generally suppose that she would have the decisional capacity to make such decision (Hyams 2011: 116). Anyone meeting a minimal threshold, however, will count as decisionally competent and so able to validly consent (Brock 1983: 241).

8.3 Voluntariness

As presented, there is some reason to think that these three criteria for valid consent are too strict. With regard to the voluntariness requirement, there are sometimes cases in which we might want to treat a consent as morally transformative even if coercive and manipulative tactics have been used in its procurement. Suppose, for instance, that my mother is terrified of heights but wants to overcome her phobia in order to bungee jump over the edge of the Victoria Falls, and in order to achieve this she undergoes a number of hypnotherapy sessions. A straightforward application of the voluntariness requirement would render her hypnotized consent insufficiently voluntary and so invalid. In other cases, a consenting party might rely on coercion as an aid to consent. Patients with anorexia nervosa sometimes request that coercive threats are used in order that they comply with their treatment program (Tan et al. 2003: 703). A simplistic application of the voluntariness requirement might result in classing the anorexic's consent to treatment – when it is procured with threats – as involuntary, and so invalid.

The typical response to cases like these is to develop a richer account of voluntariness. Instead of determining the voluntariness of a consent in terms of the types of influence on it, it has been suggested that voluntariness could instead be judged in terms of whether the consent is 'authentic' (Faden & Beauchamp 1986: 262–8). Specifically, rather than judging the voluntariness of a consent merely in terms of the sort of influence on it, the voluntariness of a consent should instead be measured in terms of whether the individual identifies with or resents the influences on her desires, preferences or motivations (Dworkin 1988: 24–5). My mother's hypnotically influenced consent to be put into a bungee harness and pushed over the edge of the Victoria Falls will be voluntary (and so to this extent valid) if she wishes to be influenced in this way. Likewise, the anorexic patient's consent to treatment, although brought about by threats, might count as voluntary if the patient endorses the use of coercion as an aid to accepting the treatment plan. The first constraint on valid consent is thus not only that it is voluntary, but that it is authentic. On this richer understanding of voluntariness coercive and manipulative techniques can be used, in addition to rational persuasion, to procure voluntary (and so valid) consent. Note that this is not to deny, however, that in some contexts we might think that coercion *always* undermines validity even if the resulting consent is authentic. Suppose, for instance, that Jane is attracted to Jill and would like to have sex with her, but is so nervous that whenever Jill approaches her with the opportunity she shyly refuses her consent. We might think it unacceptable for Jill to pin Jane down and initiate sex with her despite this being in line with Jane's authentic desires.

Problematically, the requirement that consent is authentic in order to be valid intuitively pulls apart from cases in which we consider consent to be morally transformative. This is because in some cases we might be inclined to think that a consent can be morally transformative even if it is both non-rationally influenced and inauthentic: i.e. the individual resents the external influence on her consent. The consent to purchase a house, for instance, can be morally transformative (and legally effective) even if the owner non-rationally influenced the buyer by baking cookies before holding an open house and even if the buyer would not have agreed to have purchased the house had she known that she had been influenced in this way. Romantic seduction or flirting with a potential sexual partner can be manipulative and non-rationally influencing but perhaps does not undermine the moral power of consent to sexual intercourse even if the consenting party resents being seduced in this way and would not have consented had she realized that she was being seduced. Likewise, we might take a Jehovah's Witness' consent to a life-saving blood transfusion as morally transformative, even when this consent is likely to be regretted and she has previously and consistently been opposed to this form of treatment.[6] Sometimes, then, it seems that inauthentic consent can be morally transformative.

If inauthentic consent can be morally transformative, then – as it stands – the requirement that valid consent is richly voluntary in this way fails to constitute a necessary condition for morally transformative consent. This is problematic for autonomy-based theories of consent, which suppose that the requirements for valid consent provide the necessary and sufficient conditions under which consent is morally transformative. At least two responses might be made to this problem. First, we could maintain that valid consent must be authentic and revise our intuitions about cases in which inauthentic consents count as morally transformative: instead, in such cases the consent in fact lacks moral transformative power. Note, however, that this would require that we revise our current consenting practices: any consent that is influenced by non-rational forces would be invalidated whenever the consenting party resented the non-rational influence on her consent.

Alternatively, we could treat the requirements for valid consent as variable, with different contexts requiring different degrees of voluntariness. However, if the criteria for voluntariness vary, then the requirements for valid consent will need to be supplemented with an account of *when* the requirements vary. This is potentially problematic for a procedurally neutral account of when consent has its moral power, since it is difficult to see how the voluntariness requirement can vary in a procedurally neutral way. Consider two cases of manipulated consents to sexual intercourse. In the former case the consenting party is deceived into believing that her partner will take her on a trip to Paris. In the latter, the consenting party is deceived into believing that her sexual partner is her husband (when in fact he is his identical twin brother). Intuitively, a manipulated consent to sexual intercourse might be voluntary enough for valid consent if the consenting party has merely been seduced with false promises of a trip to Paris, but not voluntary enough if she has been tricked into believing that the partner is her husband (we would perhaps class the latter case, but not the former, as rape).[7] It is difficult, however, to identify the relevant difference between these two cases in purely procedural terms since the type of influence in both cases is identical: the consenting party has been deceived.

One way of identifying when the voluntariness requirement varies is in terms of how harmful the transaction is or would be to individual wellbeing. We could rule a consent as not voluntary enough, for instance, when the consenting party is led to falsely believe that the sexual partner is her husband, since the transaction could be highly psychologically damaging to the consenting party and destabilize her marriage. On the other hand, we could rule a consent to sexual intercourse as meeting the voluntariness constraint even when it rests on lies about trips to Paris, since whilst such a consent might be regrettable it might not be as damaging to the consenting party's overall wellbeing. However, to appeal to the potential harmful repercussions of the consent would be to give up on procedural neutrality.

8.4 Information

The second constraint on valid consent is that the consent is informed. Intuitively, however, there might be some cases in which we want to treat an uninformed consent as morally transformative: your consent to purchase a bicycle seemingly has moral power (and is legally binding) even if the seller does not inform you of the risk of severe injury whilst cycling and you would not have bought the bicycle had you known of this risk (Chwang 2016: 273). In other cases, a consenter might wish to forgo information altogether and yet her consent retains its transformative power (Miller & Wertheimer 2010: 93). Imagine, for instance, that my acrophobic mother would rather not be informed of the (low) risk of falling to one's death from bungee jumping knowing that should she be informed of even the low risks she would 'chicken out'. Her uninformed consent to be placed in a harness and pushed over the edge remains transformative even though she would not have consented were she to have been informed of the relevant risks.

The importance of the informational component to valid consent is most strongly emphasized in medical ethics (Miller & Wertheimer 2010: 80).[8] For instance, the Declaration of Helsinki – a statement of ethical principles for medical research with human subjects developed by the World Medical Association (1964–2008) – imposes very strict criteria on the sort of information a research participant needs in order to offer valid consent, requiring that she is informed of the purpose of the research, the method(s) to be used, the likely risks (immediate and projected), the sources of funding, possible conflicts of interest, the intended benefits of the study, the subject's right to withdraw consent and any other relevant aspects of the study, in order that her consent counts as valid (Declaration of Helsinki 2008: §B24). Similar informational demands on valid consent are made in the therapeutic context (Manson & O'Neill 2007: 4).[9] Note that since it is impossible to give patients and research subjects 'full' or 'complete' information (O'Neill 2003: 5–6),[10] the informational requirement for valid consent (in the medical context) is that the patient or research participant receives an adequate amount of relevant information in order for her consent to be valid (English et al. 2004: 78), or that they have fair opportunity to access it (Bromwich & Millum 2015: 199; O'Neill 2003: 6). We might likewise think that my mother's consent to being placed in a harness and pushed over the edge of the Victoria Falls counts as valid if information about the risk is reliably available to her should she seek it.

A recent worry about the informational requirement for valid consent is that the way in which information is presented can non-rationally influence an individual's decision to consent, and so undermine the *voluntariness* constraint. Research in behavioral economics indicates that our decisions are subject to preference framing: individuals will change their preference for or against a medical procedure, for instance, depending on whether they are informed that the procedure carries a 10% chance of death or a 90% chance of survival (McNeil et al. 1982;

Thaler & Sunstein 2008). As such the way in which information is presented can non-rationally influence an individual's consent. It has been argued that these non-rational influences can be avoided if individuals are forewarned of framing effects and receive information with the intention of eliminating them (Chwang 2016: 281). However, if framing effects are unavoidable it might turn out that any consent that relies on the receipt of information is invalid, even when it is otherwise competent and informed (Hanna 2011: 529). This response would require that we radically revise our current consent practices: consents to medical procedures, for instance, which typically depends on the disclosure and receipt of medical information, would no longer count as valid.[11] Alternatively, we could once again vary the degree of voluntariness required for valid consent in accordance with the context: whilst framing effects might invalidate a consent to assisted suicide, for instance, they might not invalidate a consent to having one's pulse taken. As suggested above, the clearest way to identify when this requirement varies will be in terms of substantive considerations about the harmfulness of the transaction, thereby abandoning procedural neutrality.

8.5 Decisional capacity

In addition to thinking that the voluntariness and informational requirements for valid consent ought to vary with the circumstances, there are grounds for thinking that the degree of decisional capacity required for valid consent ought also to vary. In some contexts, decisionally competent consent does not seem to even be required for morally transformative consent. Some people, for instance, engage in drunken sex and insofar as the sex is consensual we generally take their consents to be morally transformative (Archard 1998: 45).[12] Moreover, drunken consent to sex need not be authentic: such an individual might be fully aware that when she is drunk she is sexually promiscuous and regret that she always behaves in this way and yet still we might class her consent as morally transformative. Again, two responses might be made here: we could either class all decisionally impaired consents as invalid and revise our consent practices accordingly, or alternatively we could vary the standards for decisional competence in accordance with context.

The decisional competence requirement for valid consent is typically taken to be variable. For this reason, individuals that we might usually take to be decisionally incapable are sometimes competent decision makers and so able to offer valid consent with respect to certain decisions. Both minors and the psychologically impaired have been judged as being competent to consent to or refuse treatment in certain circumstances. In Re C (1994), for instance, a paranoid schizophrenic patient was found to be competent to refuse an amputation after developing gangrene because the court found that the patient sufficiently understood the details of the proposed amputation despite having an underlying psychiatric condition (Re C 1994: 824). And whilst minors are usually treated as lacking decisional capacity to make medical decisions (Pollack & Billick 1999: 304), in the case of *Gillick v. West Norfolk and Wisbech Health Authority and Another* (1985) it was upheld that a child can sometimes be decisionally competent to consent to medical treatment if she is capable of understanding what is proposed and is able to express her wishes (Gillick v. West Norfolk and Wisbech Health Authority and Another 1985: 226).

One way of judging when decisional capacity varies is in terms of the risks posed by the decision (Buchanan & Brock 1989; Drane 1985),[13] the requirements of decisional capacity varying with the potential harms and benefits of the decision made. The level of competence required to make a decision will 'track' the riskiness of the decision so that: ". . . a person has to be more competent to make decisions that carry substantial risk than those that carry minimal risk" (Buller 2001: 102). The theory is therefore understood to be asymmetrical: consent to a low-risk life-saving procedure which requires a minimal threshold for competence would require the highest level of competence from one and the same individual if that treatment were to be refused (Buchanan & Brock 1989: 52).

Once again, if the requirement for decisional competence is to vary then we need an account of when it varies, and by how much. This is a difficult task for those who identify the moral purpose of consent with the importance of respecting individual autonomy, since (along with the requirements that the consent is voluntary and informed) the decisional competence requirement was supposed to track when consent is autonomous. It is difficult to see why we should respect consents that are less than fully autonomous, let alone when we should respect them, if the moral purpose of consent is to respect autonomy. Those that identify the moral purpose of consent in terms of protecting and promoting wellbeing, however, will be able to vary the requirement in terms of substantive considerations about whether or not the transaction is (or is likely to be) harmful.

8.6 The limits of valid consent

So far I have suggested that the three requirements for valid consent – that it is voluntary, informed and decisionally competent – must either vary with context, or our consents turn out to be invalid more often than we might have previously thought. Both options have their limitations. In the former case it is difficult to identify the contexts in which a greater or lesser degree of voluntariness, information or decisional capacity is needed for valid consent without drawing upon substantive considerations about the harmfulness or riskiness of what is being consented to. The latter response, which classes a great deal of our consents as invalid, requires that we radically revise our consent practices.

The point of determining the requirements for valid consent – on the autonomy-based approach – was to identify when consent has its morally transformative power. There is some reason to think, however, that meeting these conditions is not sufficient for morally transformative consent, even if these three conditions can be met in a procedurally neutral way. Instead we sometimes have reason to think that: "[. . .] there are contexts in which a consent transaction may not be morally transformative even when valid consent has been given" (Miller & Wertheimer 2010: 80). We might doubt, for instance, that one can effectively consent to be tortured, killed and eaten even if the consent is voluntary, competent and relevantly informed (Hyams 2011: 115). Similar doubts have been raised against the possibility of morally transformative consent to commercial surrogacy or prostitution (Yuracko 2003), or consent to surgery without medical purpose or the use of human tissues as commodities (O'Neill 2003: 5). In 'morally intolerable' cases we might thus sometimes want to treat valid consent as insufficient for morally transformative consent (Archard 1998: 54).

Those wanting to retain a procedurally neutral account of when consent is morally transformative will be reluctant to judge valid consent as insufficient for moral transformation in such situations. One way they may try to accommodate our intuitions about morally suspicious cases, whilst retaining procedural neutrality, is to argue that it is unlikely that the consent offered in any of these cases is actually valid. Instead the consent probably rests on a mistaken belief, or the consenting party is decisionally incompetent, or she has been coerced or manipulated into offering her consent. Since consent is extremely unlikely to be valid in these situations then we should always treat consent in these cases as invalid (Feinberg 1986: 79–81). This response is problematic, however, if the requirements for valid consent vary with context. First, it is not enough that the consent in these controversial cases is uninformed since on the variable approach consents can sometimes count as valid even when they are uninformed. Likewise, it is not enough that the consent in these cases is not richly voluntary or made by a decisionally incompetent person since on the variable approach consents can sometimes count as morally transformative even when they are inauthentic or impaired. One way to account for the degree to which these constraints vary is to make substantive judgments about the harmfulness of the transaction.[14] This, however, would be to abandon procedural neutrality.

Others have argued that consent in these cases can be (and perhaps often is) voluntary, informed and competent and can be valid in a procedurally neutral way, but that the validity of the consent is nonetheless insufficient for the consent to have moral transformative power. For these commentators, valid consent lacks absolute 'moral magic' if there is adequate evidence that the act will not contribute to the consenting party's wellbeing (Hanna 2011: 519). This limit on the moral power of valid consent, however, has been criticized as paternalistic, perfectionist or moralistic[15] because it denies the moral power of valid consent on the grounds that such transactions are harmful, exploitative or immoral (Hyams 2011: 116).

8.7 Summary

Consent has the power to transform morally unacceptable interactions into morally acceptable ones. As such, care must be taken to identify *when* it has this power. For some, the three procedural criteria for valid consent fulfil this role: a consent has moral power whenever the consent is voluntary, informed and decisionally competent. In this chapter I have suggested that a strict application of the requirements for valid consent will class many of our consents as invalid. We have some motivation, then, for thinking that the procedural requirements for valid consent ought to vary with context: whilst a high degree of voluntariness, information and decisional capacity might be required in some contexts, these will be needed to a lesser degree in others. The two options of either strictly applying the criteria for valid consent or varying the requirements with context have their limitations. The former position is undesirable insofar as it will require a radical revision of our consent practices. The latter option is undesirable if we want to retain a procedurally neutral account of when consent has its moral power, since it is difficult to apply the requirements for valid consent in a way that is sensitive to context without relying on judgments about the extent to which the transaction affects the consenting party's wellbeing.

I have also suggested that valid consent might be insufficient for morally transformative consent. On most wellbeing-based accounts of when consent is morally transformative, the explanation of why we judge certain consents as lacking transformative power in morally suspicious circumstances is not that these consents are invalid, but that the resulting transactions would be harmful. Note that the distinction between autonomy-based accounts and wellbeing-based accounts of when consent is morally transformative becomes blurred if it turns out that on the autonomy-based approach we must vary the procedural constraints for valid consent in accordance with substantive considerations about wellbeing. It would be interesting to consider which approach is overall preferable for identifying when consent is morally transformative, given that in the end both approaches rely on making substantive judgments about individual wellbeing.

Notes

1 In this chapter I am using the term 'wellbeing' in a very general way to mean 'the good life', 'welfare' or 'flourishing' etc.

2 It could be that only procedural constraints are needed to ensure that consent protects wellbeing on actual desire-based theories of wellbeing. With thanks to Andreas Müller for pointing this out.

3 Those that view the conditions for valid consent as neither necessary nor sufficient for morally transformative consent would grant consent morally transformative power whenever it was in the consenting party's best interests, regardless as to whether that consent was autonomous.

4 Although, for a recent argument that rational persuasion can be manipulative, see Tsai (2014).
5 Nelson et al. propose that voluntariness can be undermined via internal influences caused by mental illness or alcoholism (Nelson et al. 2011: 8). In this paper I group these sorts of influences separately in terms of the requirement for decisional capacity.
6 With thanks to Andreas Müller for suggesting the final example.
7 Although note that for Dougherty (2013) even 'run-of-the-mill' deceptions can invalidate sexual consent.
8 Although compare a similar focus on the importance of the informational component with regard to sexual consent in Dougherty (2013).
9 See for instance Department of Health (2001), International Code of Ethics for Nurses (2012), and Nursing and Midwifery Council (2008).
10 For discussions of the various standards of disclosure see Beauchamp & Childress (1989: 87–91), Grisso & Appelbaum (1998: 7–8) and Brock (1993: 47–50).
11 Note that these medical procedures might still be permissible on paternalistic grounds. The thought that our medical consent practices ought to be radically revised might therefore be quite attractive to supporters of medical paternalism. With thanks to Andreas Müller for raising this point.
12 Although their decision to get drunk in order to have sex need not itself be impaired, once such an individual is in fact drunk their decisions about whether to have sex, with whom to have sex, and the sort of sex to engage in (i.e. protected or unprotected) will be impaired on any standard account of decisional capacity.
13 Competing measures of competence include 'complexity-related' standards, see: Cale (1999), Wicclair (1991, 1999); for 'emotion-related' standards see: Charland (1998, 1999), Rudnick (2002). For a fixed-rationality standard see: Culver & Gert (1990).
14 As such, one might argue that at least in high-risk cases we can be certain that the threshold for, say, being sufficiently well informed will be quite high. Thank you to Andreas Müller for pointing this out.
15 Note that the mere fact that something counts as paternalistic is not enough to show that the practice is morally reprehensible (Bullock 2015).

References

Archard, D. (1998) *Sexual Consent*. Boulder, CO: Westview Press.

Beauchamp, T.L. and J.F. Childress (1989) *Principles of Biomedical Ethics*. Third Edition. Oxford: OUP.

Brock, D.W. (1983) "Paternalism and Promoting the Good," in R. Sartorius (ed.), *Paternalism*. Minneapolis: University of Minnesota Press, 237–60.

Brock, D.W. (1993) *Life and Death: Philosophical Essays in Biomedical Ethics*. Cambridge: CUP.

Bromwich, D. and J. Millum (2015) "Disclosure and Consent to Medical Research Participation," *Journal of Moral Philosophy* 10(4): 195–219.

Buchanan, A. and Brock, D.W. (1989) *Deciding for Others: The Ethics of Surrogate Decision Making*. Cambridge: CUP.

Buller, T. (2001) "Competence and Risk-relativity," *Bioethics* 15(2): 93–109.

Bullock, E.C. (2015) "A Normatively Neutral Definition of Paternalism," *Philosophical Quarterly* 65(258): 1–21.

Cale, G.S. (1999) "Continuing the Debate over Risk-Related Standards of Competence," *Bioethics* 13(2): 131–48.

Charland, L.C. (1998) "Is Mr. Spock Mentally Competent? Competence to Consent and Emotion," *Philosophy, Psychiatry & Psychology* 5(2): 67–81.

Charland, L.C. (1999) "Appreciation and Emotion: Theoretical Reflections on the MacArthur Treatment Competence Study," *Kennedy Institute of Ethics Journal* 8(4): 359–76.

Chwang, E. (2016) "Consent's Been Framed: When Framing Effects Invalidate Consent and How to Validate It Again," *Journal of Applied Philosophy* 33(3): 270–85.

Culver, C.M. and B. Gert (1990) "The Inadequacy of Incompetence," *The Milbank Quarterly* 68(4): 619–43.

Davis, H. (2003) *Human Rights and Civil Liberties*. Devon: Willan.

Declaration of Helsinki: Ethical Principles for Research Involving Human Subjects (1964; amended 2008). www.wma.net/en/30publications/10policies/b3/ [Accessed 27 July 2016].

Department of Health (2001) "Good Practice in Consent Implementation Guide: Consent to Examination or Treatment," Crown Copyright.

Dougherty, T. (2013) "Sex, Lies and Consent," *Ethics* 123(4): 717–44.

Drane, J.F. (1985) "The Many Faces of Competency," *The Hastings Centre Report* 15(2): 17–21.

Dworkin, G. (1988) *The Theory and Practice of Autonomy*. Cambridge: CUP.

English, V., G. Romano-Critchley, J. Sheather and A. Sommerville (2004) *Medical Ethics Today: The BMA's Handbook of Ethics and Law*. Second Edition. London: BMJ Books.

Faden, R.R. and T.L. Beauchamp (1986) *A History and Theory of Informed Consent*. Oxford: OUP.

Feinberg, J. (1986) *The Moral Limits of the Criminal Law – Vol. 3 Harm to Self.* Oxford: OUP.

Gillick v. West Norfolk and Wisbech Health Authority and Another (1985) 3All ER.

Grisso, T. and P.S. Appelbaum (1998) *Assessing Competence to Consent to Treatment: A Guide for Physicians and Other Health Professionals*. Oxford: OUP.

Hanna, J. (2011) "Consent and the Problem of Framing Effects," *Ethical Theory and Moral Practice* 14(5): 517–31.

Hurd, H. (1996) "The Moral Magic of Consent (I)," *Legal Theory* 2: 121–46.

Hyams, K. (2011) "When Consent Doesn't Work: A Rights-Based Case for Limits to Consent's Capacity to Legitimize," *Journal of Moral Philosophy* 8(1): 110–38.

International Code of Ethics for Nurses (2012) www.icn.ch/images/stories/documents/about/icncode_english.pdf [Accessed 27 July 2016].

Manson, N.C. and O. O'Neill (2007) *Rethinking Informed Consent in Bioethics*. Cambridge: CUP.

McNeil, B.J., S.G. Pauker, H.C. Sox Jr and A. Tversky (1982) "On the Elicitation of Preferences for Alternative Therapies," *New England Journal of Medicine* 306(21): 1259–62.

Miller, F.G. and A. Wertheimer (2010) "Preface to a Theory of Consent Transactions: Beyond Valid Consent," in F.G. Miller and A. Wertheimer (ed.), *The Ethics of Consent*. Oxford: OUP, 79–106.

Nelson, R.M., T. Beauchamp, V.A. Miller, W. Reynolds, R.F. Ittenbach and M.F. Luce (2011) "The Concept of Voluntary Consent," *American Journal of Bioethics* 11(8): 6–16.

Nursing and Midwifery Council (2008) *The Code*. www.nmc.org.uk/standards/code/read-the-code-online/ [Accessed 18 Oct. 2011].

O'Neill, O. (2003) "Some Limits of Informed Consent," *Journal of Medical Ethics* 29(1): 4–7.

Pollack, M.E and S.B. Billick (1999) "Competency to Consent to Treatment," *Psychiatric Quarterly* 70(4): 303–11.

Re C (Adult: Refusal of Medical Treatment) (1994) Vol. 1 All ER.

Rudnick, A. (2002) "Depression and Competence to Refuse Psychiatric Treatment," *Journal of Medical Ethics* 28(3): 151–5.

Tan, J., T. Hope and A. Stewart (2003) "Competence to Refuse Treatment in Anorexia Nervosa," *International Journal of Law and Psychiatry* 26(6): 697–707.

Thaler, R.H. and C.R. Sunstein (2008) *Nudge*. London: Yale University Press.

Tsai, G. (2014) "Rational Persuasion as Paternalism," *Philosophy and Public Affairs* 42(1): 78–112.

Wicclair, M.R. (1991) "Patient Decision-Making Capacity and Risk," *Bioethics* 5(2): 149–53.

Wicclair, M.R. (1999) "The Continuing Debate over Risk-Related Standards of Competence," *Bioethics* 13(2): 149–53.

Yuracko, K.A. (2003) *Perfectionism and Contemporary Feminist Values*. Indiana: Indiana University Press.

Further reading

S.A.M. McLean, *Autonomy, Consent and the Law* (Oxon: Routledge, 2010) investigates 'respect for autonomy' as the primary purpose of consent in the context of biomedical law. A. Wertheimer, *Consent to Sexual Relations* (Cambridge: Cambridge University Press, 2003) provides an account of some of the factors that might invalidate sexual consent. B.C. White, *Competence to Consent* (Washington DC: Georgetown University Press, 1994) provides a comprehensive overview and critique of various measurements of decisional capacity.

Related topics

Ch.5 Consent and wronging a person
Ch.12 Consent and autonomy
Ch.15 Deception and consent
Ch.18 Consent to pain
Ch.19 Voluntary consent
Ch.24 Informed consent

9
HYPOTHETICAL CONSENT

Gideon Yaffe

9.1 Introduction

In many domains of human life, consent makes an enormous moral difference. Sometimes it seems to transform the harmful into the non-harmful, or even the beneficial, as summarized in the Latin phrase *volenti non fit injuria* (roughly, "to the willing no injury is done"). Organ donation might be an example. Sometimes it transforms the impermissible into the permissible. Think of the use of another's car. In other cases, it eases a moral justificatory burden, even if the burden cannot, in the end, be met. It was not justified for the United States to engage in "enhanced" interrogations of suspected terrorists on foreign soil. But it would have been even harder to justify, and so even farther from being justified, if the countries that hosted these events did not consent to their taking place. And sometimes consent silences a moral complaint that could otherwise be legitimately raised. You cannot consent to host a party and then complain that the guests drank your wine, at least not if drinking your wine is part of what it was reasonable to expect your guests to do. And, finally, many have seen the difference between morally justified state action against citizens, on the one hand, and tyranny, on the other, as determined by consent. Only where citizens consent to be governed, that is, is the government morally justified in harming them for the sake of socially valuable ends.[1] In all of these cases, weighing all of the factors that contribute to the proper moral assessment of the conduct of one party to an interaction requires that consideration and weight be given to the consent of another.

In the paradigm case, consent is morally relevant only if actually present at the time of the conduct to be morally assessed. In the paradigm case, that is, the assertion that moral weight should be given to consent can be rebutted through showing that there was no actual consent at the relevant time. If the doctor says that he did not harm the patient because she consented to the surgery, the patient can press her claim to have been harmed by showing that she was not, contrary to his claim, actually consenting. Absence of consent, that is, very often weakens another's moral position and it does so precisely because consent, when present, strengthens it. In fact, absence of consent is of moral significance even when it is not accompanied by outright refusal. If the patient actually refused the surgery done to her, she has a strong claim. But she also has a claim if she neither consented nor refused. The absence of consent places the doctor in a weaker moral position even in that case.

It is thus quite puzzling that there are large classes of cases that we treat morally *as though* they involved actual consent, even though it is fully recognized that actual consent was absent. In many such cases, we point to the consent of some "absent" version of the person affected—consent by that person at an earlier or later time, or consent in a non-actual possible world—in order to explain why it seems that the case is morally the same as one in which consent was present.[2] When Ulysses struggles with his ropes, while listening to the song of the Sirens, he is not a kidnapping victim. The reason is that he earlier consented to his men ignoring his demands to be released, when he would later be listening to the song. When a delusional patient is restrained, kicking and screaming, and given antipsychotic medication, his autonomy might be thereby respected, rather than undermined. At least, this seems like the right description of the case if, when the medication takes effect, he looks back on the event and consents retrospectively to the drug's having been administered to him in his moments of madness.[3] And, in cases of the kind that are our concern here, when an unconscious patient arrives bleeding in the emergency room, and is treated, the patient is not a victim of battery. The reason is that, in a possible, non-actual world in which the patient is conscious, informed and capable of deciding how to direct his medical treatment, he would consent to be treated. And such is the case, also, at least arguably, when it comes to justifying the state's use of coercive power against a citizen (e.g. in exacting a tax). It is a rare citizen who consents at the time of the treatment, or before or after. (How would one even go about it? Send a letter of consent to the President?) So, if the state's behavior is justified in part by citizen consent, it is not actual consent that does the work, but, instead, citizen consent in some relevant possible world, such as, for instance, a possible world in which a citizen assesses the government's action without knowledge of whether he will be one of those harmed by it, or one of those protected by it, or both.[4] In all of these cases, we expand our gaze beyond the qualities or the behavior of the affected party at the time of the putative harm, or violation of right, and if we find consent in another part of the timeline, or in another possible world, then we evaluate the morality of the transaction as though the affected party consented.[5]

Let's reserve the term "hypothetical consent" for what we find in cases in which the affected party consents in some relevant possible world. Some such cases also involve previous or subsequent consent. Perhaps the patient has issued instructions in advance about what to do if he arrives unconscious at the hospital. Or perhaps the patient awakes and consents, retrospectively, to what was done to him. But hypothetical consent cases do not all involve previous or subsequent consent, and, more importantly, the moral position of such cases does not seem to depend on it. Rather, the fact that a particular non-actual, hypothetical version of the person consents seems, under at least some conditions, to be of such significance as to warrant a moral assessment of the conduct of the parties identical to what would have been appropriate if consent had actually been given.[6]

In one important respect, the concept of hypothetical consent is ambiguous. To say that someone consents in a *relevant* possible world is not to say which possible worlds are and are not relevant. So to say that a person hypothetically consented is to make tacit reference to a criterion of relevance. There are, of course, clear cases. A person who consents in a possible world in which he is rational, thinking clearly, and has set aside his wayward impulses and desires has hypothetically consented. The possible world in question is relevant by any measure of relevance. On the other side, the person who consents in a possible world in which he is given a dose of sodium thiopental, which purportedly causes highly compliant behavior, has not hypothetically consented. The possible world in question is not relevant. But there are many penumbral cases involving hypothetical consent given some criteria of relevance and not given other criteria. Did the hydrophobe hypothetically consent to be thrown in the pool? The possible worlds in which he consents are those in which his fear of water does not grip him. Whether such worlds are relevant will depend on what criterion of relevance we have in mind. More will be said about this issue as we move forward.

The fundamental puzzle about hypothetical consent is this: granting that actual consent makes a moral difference, why does hypothetical consent make *any* moral difference, much less the very same moral difference that actual consent makes? The answer to this question must be consistent with several striking features of hypothetical consent's moral import. In particular, it must be consistent with the facts about when hypothetical consent is, and is not, more morally important than other facts about consent.

To see this last point note, first, that hypothetical consent, when it is morally significant, typically trumps the absence of consent.

Doctor #1: We must operate immediately on the unconscious patient.
Doctor #2: But the patient has not consented to be operated on.
Doctor #1: True, but the patient would consent if he were awake and aware of his situation.

The consideration that Doctor #2 raises—namely that there is no actual consent—would, in the absence of more, be a decisive moral objection to the operation. But the fact of hypothetical consent, which Doctor #1 cites in his reply, silences this concern. We need an explanation for this that does not undermine the prima facie significance of the absence of consent. Importantly, however, hypothetical consent does not *always* trump the absence of consent. It is rape to have sex with an unconscious stranger, who has not actually consented, even if the stranger would consent were she awake and thinking clearly. Why does hypothetical consent silence the moral voice of consent's absence in the one case, but not in the other?

In addition, hypothetical consent sometimes morally trumps previous or subsequent consent and sometimes it does not. Say that the unconscious patient would consent to the treatment even taking into consideration low risks of irreparable impairments that the treatment might cause. So there is hypothetical consent. And imagine that things go wrong and, when the patient awakes, he has suffered those very impairments. Angry and in despair, he positively repudiates the earlier treatment, retrospectively refusing it. Was the earlier treatment morally equivalent to nonconsensual treatment? While it is hard to say for certain, it seems not; hypothetical consent seems to trump subsequent refusal of the treatment in that case. Since he would have agreed to the treatment, even given the risks, his repudiation of the treatment now that the risks have materialized to his detriment is not morally significant. But contrast this with a case in which there is hypothetical *refusal*. Were he awake and thinking clearly, the patient would decline the treatment, taking the risks of future irreparable impairment to be too great to take the chance. Still, he is treated and later awakes to find that, lucky for him, the risks did not materialize, he avoided suffering the impairments and benefited from the treatment. He then retrospectively consents to the treatment. Was the treatment nonconsensual? While, again, it is hard to say for certain, it seems not. In this case, that is, it seems that subsequent consent trumps hypothetical refusal. The case, that is, seems to be one of moral hazard. The doctors risked wrongdoing but they were rescued by the patient's retrospective consent to the treatment. Parallel cases involving prior consent or refusal that conflicts with hypothetical consent can also be constructed. And there too sometimes hypothetical consent trumps, sometimes it does not. A full theory of the moral import of hypothetical consent will help to elucidate the conditions in which it silences competing facts about consent and the conditions in which it is silenced by them instead.

Still, the possibility has to be considered that appeals to hypothetical consent to explain the moral position of an act are really just talk. Perhaps such appeals are disguised ways of identifying other factors that are morally significant, such as the fact that a certain act is genuinely good for the person affected by it. Perhaps there is no more substance to the assertion that the unconscious patient hypothetically consents than the assertion that the treatment is in his interests, and strongly so. If this is right, then the doctor who cites hypothetical consent in support of treating the unconscious patient can be understood only to be asserting that in this case treating is the thing to do *even though the patient does not consent.* That is, appeals to hypothetical consent are, really, just assertions to the effect that paternalistic behavior is in this instance justified. Such a view represents skepticism about the moral import of hypothetical consent.

Such skepticism has its advocates. The most prominent argument for the skeptical position is the central topic of section 9.2. Discussion of it also requires examination of the difficulty, identified above, of specifying how, exactly, to formulate the counterfactual that is to be assessed for truth in determining whether or not someone hypothetically consented. Which possible worlds are relevant? Imagine someone so subject to optimism bias as to invariably refuse medical treatment; he always thinks he will heal without aid. Is such a person incapable of hypothetical consent to medical treatment? Must we ask what he would consent to, given his optimism bias, or ought we to set the bias aside when asking the hypothetical question, asking instead what he would do if he were not biased in this way? Without confidence that there are answers to questions of this kind, we might be skeptics about hypothetical consent.

Section 9.3 proposes a theory as to why hypothetical consent is morally significant and considers the implications of the theory for the question of what facts about consent trump, and are trumped by, hypothetical consent. In short, the theory proposed is that the puzzles about hypothetical consent disappear when we pair the fact that consent matters morally because autonomy matters, on the one hand, with a defensible set of necessary conditions for autonomy, on the other. Whether what happens to one is consistent with one's autonomy, or in conflict with it instead, is a matter not just of whether one represents a treatment in a positive light at the time one suffers it, but also a matter of the attitude towards it of a variety of past, future and hypothetical people. The modal facts that are constitutive of hypothetical consent are also partly, but not wholly, constitutive of what it is for a form of treatment to be consistent with one's autonomy. To know which facts about consent trump, and are trumped by, hypothetical consent, one needs to know how the various facts in question contribute to determining what, exactly, respect for autonomy requires us to do and to refrain from doing.

9.2 Paternalistic skepticism about hypothetical consent

Modal facts are facts about what is possible or necessary; they are facts about how things *might* and *must* be. When we appeal to hypothetical consent in order to explain the moral status of an act that affected a hypothetically consenting party, we appear to be appealing to a modal property, namely the property that is present just in case the following kind of counterfactual statement is true:

If _____________, then V would consent.

In our example of the unconscious patient in need of medical treatment, the blank might be filled in in such a way as to make the following the relevant counterfactual: "If V were awake and aware of his situation, then he would consent".

While there is a live debate in metaphysics about whether modal facts are ultimately grounded in and determined by non-modal facts, facts about how things actually are, it is rare to find a metaphysician who would deny it.[7] If it is true that the apple would look orange were it bathed in yellow light, it is because of facts about the apple's actual surface structure, and facts about how yellow light actually bounces, and facts about how our sensory experiences vary with facts about the light that hits our retinae. The modal fact, that is, is determined by a non-modal *basis*: the conjunction of non-modal facts thanks to which the modal property is present and the relevant counterfactual statement is true.

The distinction between a modal fact and its basis allows us to ask an important question about hypothetical consent: if hypothetical consent is morally significant, as it appears, is this because the relevant modal fact—the fact about what the person would consent to in certain circumstances—is morally significant, or is the morally significant thing the modal fact's basis? The important moral philosopher Judith Thomson opts for the latter answer.[8] She claims that what justifies, for instance, treating the unconscious patient as though he had consented to medical treatment is not, as it might seem, a fact about a possible, non-actual version of him, but, instead, a fact about *him*, at the time of the medical treatment. The relevant fact about him, Thomson thinks, is that *it would be good for him to have the medical treatment*. The reason it is important that he would consent under certain circumstances is that in those circumstances he would see that the treatment would be good for him, and would opt for it on those grounds. The facts about what is good for him, that is, are the basis for the modal property that we identify by noting that the counterfactual is true. But it's not the modal property that is really morally significant but, rather, its basis.

If the moral situation is just as it would be were there actual consent, and if Thomson is right about the significance of hypothetical consent, then sometimes facts about what is good for a person are just as morally important as facts about what he actually consents to have done to him. But if that is so, then those who believe that hypothetical consent can place us on the same moral footing as actual consent believe that in such cases paternalism is justified. After all, paternalism is what we are engaging in when we treat someone a certain way since it is good for him to be treated that way while ignoring the fact that he does not actually consent to be treated that way. If Thomson is right, then that is what we predicate our treatment of others on when we predicate it on their hypothetical consent.

Thomson also believes that people have a lot of say in determining what is and is not good for them. She thinks that life-saving medical treatment is actually *bad for* a Christian Scientist. It is not, as some would say, that the Christian Scientist does not want what is good for her. Rather, what she wants is in part determinative of what is good for her. Similarly, what a person *actually* consents to, or refuses, is in part determinative of what is good for her. This goes some way towards making palatable the kind of paternalism that Thomson is advocating. To discover that the patient hypothetically refuses treatment is, in many cases, to discover that the treatment is not actually good for her, and so not justified to give. So many cases of egregious, refusal-ignoring behavior will be condemned by Thomson. Many such behaviors do not actually involve conduct that is good for those affected. But, still, in the end Thomson thinks that if hypothetical consent makes any kind of moral difference it is for reasons that paternalists find congenial: where we find it, we find forms of treatment that are good for the people to whom they are applied, and that is what counts in their favor, morally speaking.

To see why Thomson's position should be understood as a position skeptical of the moral importance of hypothetical consent, consider the moral importance of actual consent. The reason that actual consent and actual refusal are morally significant is that autonomy is morally significant. It is permissible to borrow your car, when you say that I can, not because it is good for you for me to borrow your car. It might be inconvenient or even downright harmful to you, and you might fully recognize that. Rather, it is permissible because your autonomous agency anointed the act. This formulation is vague and hazy, but the point should be clear. In abiding by the consent and refusal of others, we comply with our moral obligation to respect autonomy. It is because such respect is morally required of us that consent and refusal make a difference to the moral situation.

Someone who is a believer in hypothetical consent, and not a skeptic about it, needs to explain why hypothetical consent is morally significant *in the same way as actual consent*, because of something about the autonomous agency of the person who hypothetically consents. Someone who explains its relevance, instead, by talking about *what is good for* the person who hypothetically consents is a skeptic. Talk of hypothetical consent, on such a view, implicates nothing about autonomy and the need to respect it and so it is, really, just talk. We use the word "consent" when we speak of hypothetical consent, and so make it appear that we are respecting autonomy in being guided by hypothetical consent. But that's a blind. We could have said all that needs saying without using the word, or any word like it. Facts about what is good for those affected by our acts are what is really of moral significance, according to this skeptical position.

One way to reach such a view is by reflecting on the difficulty involved in specifying the difference between those hypotheticals that are and are not relevant for assessing hypothetical consent. Above it was suggested that the following hypothetical is of import in our unconscious patient case: "If the patient were awake and thinking clearly, he would consent". But, of course, if the patient were awake and thinking clearly he would not consent to any kind of medical treatment *the point of which is to help him to awaken and think clearly again*. If he were already awake and thinking clearly, such treatment would be unnecessary. This objection, however, seems to miss the point and prompts us to try to specify the hypothetical differently. Perhaps what we really want is something like this: "If the patient were awake and thinking clearly *about what should be done to him in his current state* (in which he is unconscious and not thinking clearly), then he would consent". That's better. But why? An appealing answer, congenial to Thomson's position, is that it is better because it gets closer to a hypothetical in which the consent is reflective of the agent's settled, actual judgment about what's in his interests.

Say that we imagine a world in which the patient would refuse the treatment even though it was, in fact, good for him. We could respond to that hypothetical in one of two ways: either by denying that the world is relevant to the question of what the person hypothetically consents to, or else by concluding that this is a case in which we are not warranted in proceeding with what is good for the patient. Why would we ever adopt the second option? Wouldn't we always conclude that whatever it was that led the hypothetical person astray should be imagined away when assessing hypothetical consent? If so, then it seems that the relevant hypothetical is the one in which the agent gets it right about what's good for him. All other possible worlds are to be ignored. And from there it is a short step to Thomson's position: what matters is what is good for the person, not the modal fact about what he would consent to. Why else would we limit our gaze to possible worlds in which he consents to something if and only if it is good for him?

Those who wish to avoid this skeptical line should object to the claim that the only relevant possible worlds are those in which the agent gets it right about what is good for him and consents in accordance with such judgments. Also relevant, one might think, are worlds in which the agent gets it dead wrong about what is good for him, but autonomously consents or refuses in line with his mistaken judgment. If Thomson is correct in holding that relevant to what is good for a person is what he autonomously elects for himself, then this class of worlds will be at most small. But, still, if there are any such worlds, and if the facts about consent and refusal in such worlds are morally significant, then the skeptical position is mistaken. To see the point, consider the example mentioned in the introduction: an agent who always refuses medical treatment out of excessive optimism, out of the belief that he will heal without help. When that agent arrives in the hospital unconscious, is the moral situation like that in which he consents to medical treatment, or like that in which he refuses it? If the relevant hypothetical person is the one who is just as optimistic as this person usually is, then it is a case of hypothetical refusal; if the relevant hypothetical person has removed his rose-colored glasses, then it is a case of hypothetical consent. If it is really true that the basis of the relevant modal property is the facts about what is good for the person, then it is a case of hypothetical consent (assuming that his optimism interferes, in this instance, with his ability to pursue what is good for him). But if the basis includes his excessive optimism, then it is a case of hypothetical refusal. Why acquiesce to the picture under which all that matters is what is good for the person? After all, if this person actually refused what was good for him, then the moral situation would be quite different from one of consent. Respect for the person's autonomy would require not issuing the treatment. Why should we ignore a hypothetical world that would be morally significant if actual—namely the world in which the excessively optimistic agent refuses treatment?

To summarize, we began with the question why the consent of a non-actual hypothetical person mattered to the morality of a particular treatment of him. Thomson observes, first, that it must be the basis of the modal property, rather than the modal property itself, that matters morally. She then asserts that the relevant basis is the fact about what is good for the person. This then leads her to her paternalist-friendly, skeptical position: to take hypothetical consent to be morally significant is just the same as taking the facts about what is good for a person to be morally significant, and that is just what paternalists do. If we want to resist this skeptical conclusion, we can revisit with critical scrutiny the claim that the relevant basis is the facts about what is good for the person. To accept that is to exclude as irrelevant possible worlds in which the agent autonomously consents, or refuses, in conflict with what is good for him. Does respect for autonomy require that we include those worlds in our moral calculations? The next section will provide some reasons for thinking that the answer is "yes", and so provide reasons for resisting skepticism about hypothetical consent.

9.3 Autonomy and modal facts

The first step down the skeptical road described in the last section was the claim that the modal facts cannot matter morally *in themselves*; what matters, instead, are the features of the person and his situation *thanks to which* it is true that he would consent under certain conditions. Why should we take that first step? If we could identify some reason why the modal facts—and not just any modal facts, but modal facts *about consent*—matter morally, then we would be freed from the skeptical line of thought. And, in fact, we can see why the modal facts about consent matter just by reflecting further on what it is about *actual* consent that matters morally—namely something about autonomy. Modal facts matter to autonomy. Whether what takes place is consistent with an agent's autonomy depends quite often on the happenings in non-actual possible worlds. And so it should be no surprise that hypothetical consent sometimes has precisely the same import as actual consent: both matter to autonomy and so matter morally in just the same way.

To see this, start by reflecting a bit on the relationship between autonomy and freedom. It is obvious that whether someone is free depends on various modal facts. Why is the freedom of someone in a locked room curtailed? Answer: because in possible worlds in which he tries to leave, he still stays. The actual world need not be a world in which the agent is trying to leave for the lock on the door to curtail his *actual* freedom. He is actually less free thanks in part to what does not actually takes place—namely that he is thwarted in his efforts to leave—but takes place, instead, only in a particular possible world—namely one in which he tries to leave the room. To be autonomous is to enjoy "self-rule". This is not *a theory* of autonomy; it is, instead, merely a description of what such a theory must unpack. But even this much helps us to see that there must be some close relationship between autonomy and freedom. Consider the person who has no desire whatsoever to leave the room in which he is locked, but could not leave even if he tried. Does he stay autonomously? Or, put another way: does the lock on the door interfere with his autonomy? There are conceptions of "self-rule" under which the answer is "no". After all, the man stays in the room thanks to facts about him—namely that he wants to—rather than facts about the lock on the door. But there are more expansive conceptions of self-rule under which the agent who willingly stays in a locked room is less his own ruler, as it were, than someone who willingly stays in a room that he could have left. The reason is that the idea of *being a ruler*, whether over another or over oneself, includes the idea of determining what happens in hypothetical as well as actual circumstances. That is, some forms of freedom are required for autonomy; and freedom is, in part, a modal property of those that enjoy it. The result: autonomy, too, is, in part, a modal property. It is actually possessed by people in part thanks to what is not actually, but only possibly, true of them.

In the example of the man in the locked room who stays willingly, does the moral demand to respect autonomy dictate that those who can should unlock the door? The question here is not whether all doors should, full stop, be unlocked. Of course they should not. The question is whether we are under moral pressure, perhaps overridden by other moral pressures, to unlock doors that confine those who will never, actually, walk through them. The answer is "yes". Respect for the autonomy of those who are confined demands removing their confinements, even if they would never take advantage of their new-found freedoms. The ethical life is not spent merely in busily respecting autonomy, which is why we often have no obligation to remove confinements; but, still, that is what is demanded of us by the moral demand to respect autonomy.

This, I suggest, is why hypothetical consent matters morally. It matters just in case the consent or refusal of a hypothetical version of the agent to be treated in a certain way bears on the agent's *actual* autonomy with respect to that treatment. That a hypothetical version of the unconscious patient would consent to medical treatment shows that respect for the patient's autonomy does not require refraining from the treatment. The case is just like that of the lock on the door. If the man in the room does not know of the lock, or knows of it but hasn't either consented to it or refused it, then the question of whether his autonomy is respected through removing the lock turns on whether he *would* walk through the unlocked door, not whether he *does*, nor whether he *will*.

What has been said so far provides us, immediately, with an account of which possible worlds are "relevant" to hypothetical consent and which are irrelevant. The relevant possible worlds are all and only those in which the agent retains his actual features that bear on his autonomy. We cannot justify giving medical treatment to the unconscious Christian Scientist. The reason is that a person's religious commitments, and in general his committed values, bear directly on his autonomy. They are part of what realizes his autonomy; they are part of what makes him autonomous. Since we are interested in his modal properties because we are interested in his autonomy, we are interested only in those modal properties he possesses while retaining his autonomy, and so while retaining his fundamental values, including values manifested in his settled religious views. This also explains why intuitions might vacillate about the optimistic person who refuses the treatment in the world in which his optimism is held fixed, but consents to it when his rose-colored glasses are removed. Optimism can be conceived of as a fundamental feature of the way in which the agent responds to, and recognizes value in, the world. Or it can be thought of as a distorting bias, interfering with, rather than constituting, an agent's autonomy. Depending on which conception of optimism applies in a given case, it should be classified as either involving hypothetical consent, or hypothetical refusal instead.

Recall the issue of trumping, flagged in the introduction. Sometimes previous, subsequent, or even the absence of actual, consent is morally trumped by hypothetical consent; sometimes hypothetical consent is trumped by it. What trumps what, I suggest, is determined entirely by the contributions of the relevant actual and modal properties to the agent's autonomy and the particular way in which autonomy is realized in the agent. Typically, for instance—so typically, in fact, as to make it the default position from the point of view of public policy—sexual autonomy is determined by contemporaneous actual choices favoring sexual activity. There is an open question, the answer to which would require deeper reflection on the nature of human sexuality than is possible here, as to why this is so, given that it is not true of autonomy in all domains of human life. One possibility is that this distinctive feature of sexual autonomy derives from the fact that sexual activity involves continuous and dynamic, and at least to some degree unscripted, physical contact, each moment of which must be autonomously chosen if the activity itself is to be autonomously chosen. Perhaps this fact about sexual activity makes actual consent, as opposed to hypothetical, particularly important to sexual autonomy. But, even if this is not the right direction to pursue in explaining why sexual autonomy is important, the fact remains; and that is why the absence of actual consent trumps hypothetical consent to sexual activity. It is why it is rape to have sex with an unconscious person.

By contrast, hypothetical consent to a form of government treatment typically validates and justifies that treatment even where actual consent is absent, or there is even previous or subsequent or contemporaneous refusal. The reason is that what matters to citizen autonomy is what citizens would consent to when occupying a point of view in which they set aside their parochial concerns and think about what *we* should do, *we* who live together in a state. When what is at issue is the conditions under which governmental treatment of a citizen is an expression of that citizen's autonomy, the point of view of the non-actual citizen, occupying idealized conditions, has pride of place.

And other cases of trumping also are ultimately grounded in conceptions of autonomy. The reason that subsequent refusal to a medical procedure, in light of suffering risked side-effects, does not invalidate the moral permissibility of the procedure when it was hypothetically consented to, taking into consideration the risks, is that regret is perfectly consistent with the autonomous choice of that which one does indeed regret. By contrast, part of the point of being autonomous is to attain what is good for us, and so cases of retrospective consent to risky treatments that turn out well, but were hypothetically refused, are morally in the same position as consensual treatments; they both further the fundamental end or function of autonomous agency. Retrospective acts of consent, that is, make the prior treatment consistent with autonomy, even though it was hypothetically refused.

In short, since modal properties of people often bear on their autonomy, hypothetical consent bears on autonomy. So it is not surprising that what respect for autonomy requires of us can vary, also, not just with the actual but also with modal facts. The result is that hypothetical consent and refusal are morally significant for just the same reasons that actual consent and refusal are morally significant. They matter to the moral landscape because central features of the moral terrain are autonomy and the moral requirement to respect it.

9.4 Conclusion

We began with a puzzle. How can we explain the moral import of hypothetical consent consistent with recognition of the moral import of consent's absence? As we have seen, reflection on this question can lead to the conclusion that paternalism is justified more often than we might think. But it need not lead to that conclusion, for it could be that to appreciate the contours of hypothetical consent—what it is, when it trumps, and when, instead, it is trumped by, other consent-relevant facts—requires the recognition that modal facts, including facts about what a person would consent to or refuse, matter to actual autonomy, and so to a full account of what it is to respect autonomy, in accordance with morality's demand. In the end, however, it should be acknowledged that this amounts to shifting the object of philosophical inquiry, rather than eliminating the need for further theorizing. The reason is that we are left with the puzzle of specifying the necessary and sufficient conditions of autonomy, and the precise bearing of autonomy on the moral properties of conduct that impinges, as most conduct must, on the conditions of others. In fact, this is more than a puzzle; it is a fundamental philosophical problem. In the end, it is the problem that must be solved if we are to provide a full explanation for the moral import of hypothetical consent.[9]

Notes

1 Consent-based theories of political authority and obligation have a venerable history. Perhaps the most influential is that offered in Locke ([1690] 1980).

2 This is not true of *all* such cases. A hockey player is hit in the face during a game. He did not consent previously or subsequently to being hit. Nor is there hypothetical consent: he would not have consented to being hit if he had been thinking clearly; quite the reverse. And, yet, we sometimes morally evaluate the situation as though the person consented to the treatment. I set aside these cases here, which are sometimes labeled as involving "constructive consent". I also set aside cases in which the affected party does not consent, or even refuses, but we nonetheless morally evaluate the situation as though there were consent thanks to the actual consent of some third party with authority to speak for the person affected. We often do this in assessing the morality of what we do to children with their parents' consent, or to the incompetent with the consent of their guardians or fiduciaries.

3 For discussion of temporal difference between an act that affects someone and his consent to it, see Davis (2004).

4 Of course, the tacit reference here is to John Rawls's theory of the justification of uses of state power in Rawls (1999). For a recent discussion of the relevance of hypothetical consent to political obligation, see Stark (2000).

5 Cases with the diversity of structures just described are discussed with great acuity in Westen (2004).

6 For discussion of the moral import of hypothetical consent, see Kuflik (2010).

7 Cf. McGinn (1981).

8 Thomson (1990), esp. pp. 187–92.

9 Thanks to Peter Schaber for comments on an earlier draft and to Scott Shapiro and the participants in a seminar we co-taught on consent at Yale Law School in the fall of 2014.

References

Davis, J.K. (2004) "Precedent Autonomy and Subsequent Consent," *Social Theory and Practice* 7: 267–91.
Kuflik, A. (2010) "Hypothetical Consent," in F. Miller and A. Wertheimer (ed.), *The Ethics of Consent: Theory and Practice*. Oxford: Oxford University Press, pp. 131–58.
Locke, J. ([1690] 1980) *Second Treatise of Government*. Indianapolis: Hackett Press.
McGinn, C. (1981) "Modal Reality," in R. Healy (ed.), *Reduction, Time and Reality*. Cambridge: Cambridge University Press.
Rawls, J. (1999) *Theory of Justice*. Revised Edition. Cambridge: Belknap Press.
Stark, C. (2000) "Hypothetical Consent and Justification," *Journal of Philosophy* 97(6): 313–34.
Thomson, J.J. (1990) *The Realm of Rights*. Cambridge, MA: Harvard University Press.
Westen, P. (2004) *The Logic of Consent: The Diversity and Deceptiveness of Consent as a Defense to Criminal Conduct*. New York: Ashgate Publishing.

Related topics

Ch.12 Consent and autonomy
Ch.13 Paternalism and consent
Ch.30 Consent theory of political obligation

10
GROUP CONSENT

Anna Deplazes-Zemp

10.1 Introduction

Informed consent is well known as a central element of biomedical ethics (see Ach, this volume, Chapter 25). The requirement that patients or research subjects be comprehensively informed and provide their consent to medical treatments or participation in research is a central element of good practice in medicine and biomedical research. Drawing from this influence of the informed consent paradigm, it has been suggested that, analogous to individual patients affected by a medical procedure, groups should also be asked to give consent to decisions that are relevant to them. According to this argument, certain decisions are of such relevance for the group that implementation without obtaining the group's informed consent would be unethical. Interestingly, this transfer of the informed consent paradigm from the individual to the group level happens independently in different contexts in practical as well as theoretical discussions. It is the aim of this chapter to introduce different interpretations and understandings of group consent and draw connections among them. In that sense, the question of *whether* groups can give consent will not be addressed, but I will try to show *how* the idea of consent by groups has been *interpreted* in various contexts and by different authors. I will introduce three interpretations of group consent that differ in their views on what morally justifies a requirement for group consent or their views on how a group should give consent. The first of the three interpretations, *corporate group consent*, is based on the understanding of a group as a corporate entity with moral standing and morally relevant interests. According to this interpretation, respecting such a moral status of the group requires obtaining its consent. The second interpretation, *collective group consent*, justifies the requirement for group consent with reference to the role the group has for its individual members. While these two interpretations of group consent are characterized by their understanding of a group and the right of a group to give consent, it is the consent procedure that specifies the third interpretation: *participatory group consent* understands group consent as a procedure in which the affected group can participate in shaping the decision to which it consents.

To set the background for the theoretical analysis of the different interpretations I will start with a brief introduction of three practical contexts in which the notion of 'informed group consent' has been discussed and applied. The three contexts are a) engineering and land use, b) research on groups, and c) 'Free Prior Informed Consent' (FPIC) in interactions with indigenous communities. In all of these situations, it has been emphasized that group consent must be *informed*; however, this condition will not be discussed here.[1]

10.2 Contexts of group consent

Engineering and land use: Engineering and land use seem to be the earliest contexts in which the informed consent paradigm was transferred from individuals to groups as consenting subjects. The transfer is based on an understanding of engineering as an "experiment on a societal scale" (Martin & Schinzinger 1983: 84) that affects groups comparable to the effect that biomedical research has for the individual. Accordingly, engineers should obtain informed consent by those affected by the projects (Martin & Schinzinger 1983). A recent engineering context in which the idea of informed group consent came up is climate engineering (Morrow et al. 2009). With respect to controversial land use, too, parallels were drawn between the physician's moral responsibility to obtain informed consent and the responsibility of planners involved in controversial land-use projects. One example for such projects is finding a location for hazardous waste disposal facilities. It has been argued that setting up such a facility requires obtaining informed consent from the community living in the area in question (Simmons 1987).[2]

Research on groups: The most direct shift from a demand for informed individual consent to informed group consent took place in the context of biomedical research on groups. It has been argued that the general ethical dogmas in biomedical research are too much focused on individuals and do not take account of the interests and rights of communities (Weijer 1999). The idea that informed group consent must be obtained from groups that are being studied may not only apply to the biomedical context but also to certain studies in the social sciences (Schrag 2006). However, a classical biomedical example is particularly suitable to illustrate the shift from individual to group consent. This is the example of population genetics, where both the individuals and the population are research subjects (Greely 2001). There is a clear requirement to obtain informed consent from everyone who donates a blood sample for genomic analysis. However, genetic research on populations will lead to conclusions about genetic dispositions that are characteristic of the studied community. All members of this group, not only those who participated and consented to the research in question, will be associated with these results. Therefore, it has been suggested that, in addition to individual consent, the researcher should also obtain group consent from the population that is described by the analyzed individual genomes (Greely 2001; Schrag 2006).[3]

'Free Prior Informed Consent' (FPIC) in the interaction with indigenous communities: The idea of group consent has presumably had the most practical influence in the interaction with indigenous communities, where it is known under the acronym 'FPIC'. The phrase should emphasize that genuine group consent requires that consent is given 'freely', i.e. voluntarily and without coercion; 'prior', i.e. before the activities for which consent is required are initiated; and 'informed', i.e. after all relevant information has been understood by the consenting party. The demand of indigenous groups to recognize their right to give or withhold FPIC has been traced to the mid 1980s (Colchester & Ferrari 2007). Since then FPIC procedures have been implemented in the interaction with indigenous communities, for instance in UN-REDD Programmes (UN-REDD Programme 2013),[4] forest management (van der Vlist & Richert 2012) or projects of extractive industries (Bruxton & Wilson 2013), where the FPIC standard has been incorporated into 'corporate social responsibility' policy. The notion of FPIC also entered international law.[5] The purpose of requesting FPIC in these cases is to give the communities a voice in decisions concerning their land and environment when their livelihoods and core values are at stake. This is to be accomplished by obtaining these communities' consent in a consultation and participation process.[6]

In these three practical contexts, independent commentators or the affected groups themselves suggested obtaining group consent as a step towards responsible conduct with groups. 'Informed group consent' is meant to protect the group in question against paternalistic decisions by more powerful agents who, even if their decisions may be well-intended, decide based on their own priorities rather than referring to the position of the group in question. This aim of preventing paternalism is an important similarity with the informed consent paradigm in biomedicine. In the following sections, these practical examples will be examined for the underlying theoretical understanding of group consent.

10.3 The group and its individual members in group consent

The phrase 'group consent' suggests that a group can agree or disagree with a suggestion, but how can this notion account for a group consisting of different individuals? This section discusses possible relations between the group and its individuals in group consent.

Unanimous consent: A direct integration of individual consent in the notion of group consent would require that all members of the group unanimously give their consent to the decision in question. Some authors indeed understand unanimous consent as the ideal that group consent should try to approximate (Simmons 1987; Schrag 2006). With respect to practical applications, this idea has been criticized because it would give veto power to each individual, which would forestall movement in any direction (Hansson 2006). Unanimous consent is not the way group consent should be understood because it takes individual consent as the relevant form of consent. Those authors who think unanimity amongst all involved group members is required have a form of aggregated individual consent in mind, which would be performed and justified along the same lines as cases in which individual consent of only one person has been required. Unanimous consent thus does not raise many new issues. In contrast, group consent has been introduced in this chapter as a concept that involves a *shift* from the individual to the group level, which goes along with new challenges concerning the moral legitimation of a requirement for group consent, as well as the procedure of determining whether the group consents or not. Unanimous or aggregate consent can thus be seen as a type of 'intermediate' between individual and group consent.

Implied and hypothetical consent: In practice, requiring group consent often faces the difficulty of unidentifiable or inaccessible group members.[7] One strategy to address such cases is to resort to hypothetical or implied consent. In this chapter, I distinguish between explicit, implied and hypothetical consent as follows:[8] Classical cases of explicit consent directly involve individuals in the decision procedure at hand. Implied consent, in contrast, is understood as consent inferred from the individual's actions or analogous decisions in similar situations.[9] The phrase 'hypothetical consent' is used here for assumed consent based on how rational people could be expected to decide in the situation at hand.[10] In the introduction of different interpretations of group consent, I will come back to the role of hypothetical or implied consent in certain group consent models.

Although unanimous, implied, or hypothetical consent will be mentioned in the following, the focus of this chapter lies on three interpretations of group consent: *corporate group consent*, *collective group consent* and *participatory group consent*. Amongst other things, these interpretations differ with respect to the role that individual group members play in the process, as well as in their legitimization of group consent, which is the topic of this subchapter.

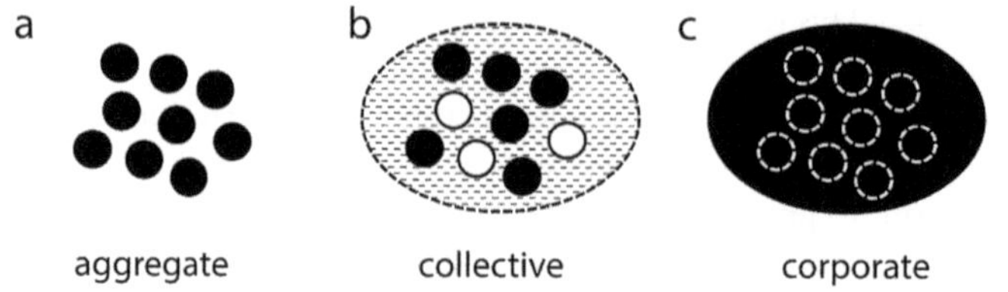

Figure 10.1 Schematic depiction of the relation between the group and its individuals in aggregate consent, collective group consent and corporate group consent. a) Aggregate consent or unanimous consent: Each individual consents individually. b) Collective group consent: The group consent is determined based on the group interests of its individuals, but they do not individually need to give consent. c) Corporate group consent: Group consent is given based on the interest of the group as an entity.

I adopt the distinction between a group as a corporate entity and a group as a collective from Peter Jones' distinction with respect to group rights (Jones 1999, 2008). His two conceptions of group rights differ in how a group holds a right. Whereas the holder of *corporate* group rights is the group as an entity, *collective* group rights are *jointly* held by the members of the group. In contrast to individual rights, collective group rights occur only in groups; it is not possible that individuals hold collective group rights separately (Jones 1999, 2008).

In the following, this distinction between corporate and collective will be adapted to the notion of group consent. A moral requirement for group consent is usually legitimized based on morally relevant interests of the group or group rights to self-determination. Therefore, Jones' distinction of group rights can be directly transferred to two different interpretations of group consent. In short, the *corporative* model justifies a requirement for group consent by referring to a particular status of the group as an entity and the rights that come along with that status. In contrast, the justification of claims for the second type of group consent –*collective* group consent – refers to the importance of group consent for the individual group members alone. According to this view, the group does not have an independent moral status or morally relevant interests, but its members identify with the group, have interests as a group, want to be considered as a group and have *collective* group rights. This notion is compatible with situations in which singular group members do not consent to a certain decision. The group as a collective is thus more than an aggregate of individuals; at the group level, there are new properties and morally relevant interests that go beyond those of the singular members. Therefore, collective group consent must not be confused with unanimous or aggregate consent as described above. Figure 10.1 illustrates the three different types of group consent.

10.4 Corporate group consent

The notion of corporate group consent is based on the understanding of a group as an entity that can act as one agent. In the legal context, this idea of a group is known from the treatment of corporations, which have certain legal duties and rights. Other examples are international interactions, where nation states are corporate agents in the global political system. Various authors generally distinguish between three conceptions of groups as corporate entities. According to the first, such groups are natural entities with moral agency and personhood. According to the second conception, corporations are artificial entities with legal but not moral personhood. According to the third, corporations are simply agglomerates of individuals and thus do not constitute a distinct entity.[11] The third position understands a group as a collective or aggregate and is thus closer to interpretations discussed in other sections of this chapter. The first position is associated with the strongest presuppositions and the strictest interpretations of a group as a natural corporate entity. Corporate group consent as discussed in this chapter is usually based on this understanding of group rights. A prominent representative of this position is Peter French. He argues that corporations have internal decision structures based on which we can attribute intentions.[12] This intentionality serves as a basis for French's attribution of agency and moral personhood to corporations (French 1979). The second position understands corporations as artificial entities with legal personhood. This view acknowledges that in law and international politics, corporations have *legal* or conventional rights ascribed to them and they perform certain acts. However, according to this view, groups are *not* natural or moral persons with moral rights.

In some of the contexts introduced at the beginning of this chapter group consent seems to be based on a corporate understanding of the group. A requirement of group consent in this sense is justified with reference to a group's moral right to self-determination as a right grounded in its moral status or interests. However, it is important to note that in the practical context a requirement for obtaining group consent is sometimes meant as a legal rather than moral requirement. These two cases must be separated from each other since arguments for the legal requirement cannot be countered by arguing that groups do not have a moral status.

An argument for the importance of group consent in the corporate sense can, for instance, be found in the context of research on groups. Authors in this field often emphasize that it is a certain population understood as a distinct entity that is the subject of research. This entity has interests that may differ from those of its individual members. Consequently, informed consent of the group as a whole must be obtained (Greely 2001). For Charles Weijer, informed group consent is required to implement an ethical principle that he calls "respect for communities" (Weijer 1999: 505). Weijer argues that this principle should protect the interests and rights of the communities in question, and he explicitly refers to the moral status of the communities that should be acknowledged (Weijer 1999). Representatives of the group could give corporate group consent in this sense. Inherent procedures of the corporation or traditional customs of the community could serve as mechanisms to select such representatives. It has been suggested that consent by representatives is a type of implied or hypothetical consent since these representatives seem to *assume* that the group members would consent (Wong 2016). However, it is the interests and rights of the group and not those of its individual members that the representative considers when giving or denying corporate consent. Therefore, corporate consent should not be understood as implied or hypothetical consent of the group members. Corporate consent by representatives authorized to represent and personify the group is how the group can give consent. Since representatives neither derive their decision from previous, more explicit group decisions nor refer to the will of a rational group agent, one could argue that corporate group consent is a type of explicit rather than implied or hypothetical consent.

Some elements of a corporate understanding of group consent can also be identified in the context of FPIC in the interaction with indigenous communities. A right of indigenous peoples to FPIC has been stated in several articles of the UN Declaration on the Rights of Indigenous Peoples (UNDRIP) (UN 2006). As indicated by its title, this declaration is phrased in the language of corporate group rights. Although in some places the rights of indigenous individuals are discussed, there is a strong focus on the group rights of indigenous people*s* (rather than indigenous people (without s)). The right to self-determination is phrased as a corporate group right.[13] This raises the question of whether indigenous groups are understood as entities with moral status or as 'artificial' entities with legal rights. The analogy that is often made between the rights of indigenous groups and nation states suggests that many authors understand indigenous groups in the second sense and their rights as legal rights. Others may indeed assign a moral status to indigenous groups; however, this is usually not explicitly expressed in the literature.

10.5 Collective group consent

Let us now have a look at the second interpretation of group consent, which understands a group as a collective rather than a corporate entity. In this view, the group is understood with respect to its role and function for the individual group members. Nevertheless, the group is still conceived as something with properties and impact beyond those of its members as individuals. As mentioned above, when I introduced Peter Jones' distinction between corporate and collective group rights, collective group rights are "rights that are held by the members of a group only as a group" (Jones 1999: 362). They are morally legitimized with reference to the moral status and the interests of the individual group members. However, only as shared interests of individual group members can these interests provide sufficient reason for a right and a corresponding duty to secure this right. This can be illustrated with the interest to attain school education in one's native language. Only the shared interest of individuals qua members of a group in education in their language may suffice to request that authorities consider such an interest.[14] This argumentation can be applied to defend a *collective* group right to self-determination based on vital human interests of the group members (Margalit & Raz 1990). When a requirement for group consent is explained with reference to a group right of self-determination, this does thus *not* necessarily depend on a *corporate* understanding of a group as an entity with moral status, as introduced in the previous section. Instead, it can also be justified based on a *collective* understanding of the group, which draws from the moral status of individual group members. This contrasts with the previously introduced understanding of the group as an aggregate of individuals that requires unanimous consent. While a requirement for collective group consent can be justified with respect to the collective interest or a group-right to self-determination of the group members, a call for unanimous consent is legitimized with the individual interests and with reference to the autonomy of the individual group members. However, that collective group consent does not include this requirement for unanimity means group consent can be given even if some members of the group do not consent. A majority vote amongst the group members could, for instance, serve the purpose. Alternative models suggest that different weight be given to different group members depending on how much they will be affected by the decision at stake. Such a weighted consent model has been suggested by Jukka Varelius, who has mainly engineering and land use examples in mind (Varelius 2008). Another model for weighted consent suggests considering the motives of individual group members to determine the (non)consenters' 'weight' in the consent procedure (Grill 2009). Besides majoritarian or weighted consent, collective group consent could also be implemented as consent by a representative. In that case, the representative would act in place of the group members and based on their interests. Such a model has, for instance, been suggested in the context of climate engineering research (Morrow et al. 2009). Due to the far-reaching implications of this type of research, it has been argued that representative governments should give consent in the name of the citizens of their states. If the representatives decide based on popular votes in their states, this would still be a form of majoritarian consent. However, a collective understanding of group consent could also be implemented by representatives who decide based on what they assume would be how the members of the group would decide. In this version, collective group consent would include certain elements of hypothetical or implied consent. This contrasts with cases in which group consent by a representative is understood as a form of corporate group consent.

10.6 Participatory group consent

The two interpretations of group consent discussed so far take consent as the final step of a decision procedure. Based on such an idea of group consent, the criticism has been made that group consent is a non-participatory decision procedure (Hansson 2006). Others, however, have argued that group consent is compatible with public participation at earlier decision steps (Varelius 2008), an interpretation which has been particularly influential in the context of FPIC. As outlined above, group consent as FPIC is embedded in a participatory approach to decision making. The idea is that if, for instance, a company aims to launch a project that directly affects an indigenous community, the company must inform the community about the project in question before taking any steps to implement it. In addition – and that is the characteristic part of this type of consent – the company must engage with the community and take up suggestions and input. The community thus participates in forming the project. Eventually, the project will only be realized if the community in question gives consent. According to this interpretation, obtaining consent requires more than just asking the affected group to accept a predetermined suggestion. Instead, respecting the rights and interests of this group implies that the group is involved in setting up the suggestion in question. With its focus on the participatory approach, FPIC is thus based on a different interpretation of what it means practically to consider the other party than the traditional paradigm of informed consent in biomedicine.[15] The World Bank, for instance, focused so much on the participatory aspect of FPIC that it abandoned the requirement for consent altogether. For the World Bank, involving members of the affected community in a consultation process is sufficient, and it thus interprets FPIC as Free Prior and Informed *Consultation* (World Bank 2005). However, other documents on FPIC point out that while consultation is an important element in the participatory FPIC procedure, it is not sufficient to characterize this process. Beyond consultation, the reference to 'consent' in FPIC implies that the community has the right to reject a project (van der Vlist & Richert 2012; Lehr et al. 2010; UN-REDD Programme 2010).

Following the distinction between corporate and collective consent outlined in the previous sections, this description of participatory consent raises the question of who is understood to be the holder of the right to this form of group consent. Is it the group (as in corporate group consent) or its individual members (as in collective group consent)? This distinction is not clearly made in the descriptions and guidelines for FPIC, and elements of both interpretations can be found. On the one hand, as mentioned before, these reports often refer to the corporate right to self-determination of indigenous groups in the UNDRIP, and, accordingly, at least in some places refer to people*s* as right holders (Bruxton & Wilson 2013; Colchester & MacKay 2004; Hill et al. 2010; van der Vlist & Richert 2012). However, the descriptions and recommendations for concrete FPIC processes generally aim to inform and engage with the individual members of the communities in question (Colchester & MacKay 2004; Hill et al. 2010; UN-REDD Programme 2010). Many authors emphasize that consent should be reached through customary processes and institutions of the group in question. According to a corporate interpretation, it would not matter how this procedure relates to the individual group members. However, contrary to this interpretation, many authors point out that the position of marginalized groups such as women or young people must be included, too, even if the customary decision processes do not include them (Lehr et al. 2010; UN-REDD Programme 2010; van der Vlist & Richert 2012). In practice, FPIC procedures usually involve different interest groups within an indigenous community and often make efforts to reach as many community members as possible. In sum, the collective understanding of a group thus seems to prevail in the practical implementation of FPIC.

10.7 Conclusion

The notion that informed group consent could be morally required has been expressed in different practical contexts as illustrated with the examples of engineering and land use, research on groups, and the FPIC model for interactions with indigenous communities. In the practice-oriented literature, the idea of a moral obligation to obtain the informed consent of the affected group is often taken for granted. Three interpretations of group consent were presented: corporate, collective and participatory. They are based on different arguments to explain why obtaining consent from the affected group can be morally required or how group consent should be obtained.

These interpretations are not necessarily mutually exclusive. As Peter Jones established in his discussion of group rights, different interpretations can be combined (Jones 1999). Defenders of moral rights to FPIC can understand such an indigenous right as a *corporate moral* right of the indigenous group but at the same time also as a *collective* right of its individuals. Depending on the focus with which FPIC is discussed, one or the other justification might be more appropriate. Both justifications can serve to support a requirement to introduce a *legal corporate* group right to FPIC in the legislation of a state. Moreover, for defenders of FPIC it is not enough to involve the group in question at the last step of accepting or rejecting a decision. Group consent is interpreted as the result of a participatory process. All three interpretations of group consent can thus play a role in the discussion of an FPIC example. Therefore, the distinction between corporative, collective and participatory group consent should not be understood as a distinction between mutually exclusive types of consent but as different interpretations that depend on the angle from which one looks at a particular instance of group consent. This is not to say, however, that *all* defenders of the view that group consent can be morally required must accept the three interpretations. Some would deny that groups have a moral status, which is what the idea of corporate group consent is based on. Unfortunately, it is often not clear on what interpretation specific requirements of group consent are based. There seem to be some tendencies towards one or the other understanding or group consent in the different practical contexts introduced at the outset. In the context of engineering and land use, there is a trend towards the *collective* understanding of group consent, whereas in connection to research on groups, a *corporate* understanding seems to prevail. Finally, the literature on FPIC is the paradigm example for a participatory understanding. However, despite these tendencies, each interpretation plays a role in different contexts.

Notes

1 For discussion of this condition see Ach (this volume, Chapter 25).

2 One important criticism of the transfer of the informed consent paradigm to the group level in this context points out that in biomedicine it is rare that the decision about a medical treatment of an individual directly harms others. In contrast, in decisions concerning land use this is the common case (Fotion 1987). Another difficulty with group consent in the context of engineering or land use is that often it cannot be known in advance who will be affected (Long 1983). Moreover, those affected usually do not form clearly identifiable groups (Hansson 2006) or are members of future generations.

3 Critics of group consent in the context of research on groups argue that a requirement for informed group consent in these studies might lead to a 'biologization of social groups' because individuals that are not members of the social groups still share genetic information with the group (for instance, Americanized children of immigrants) and others who identify with the social group may not have the related genotype (Juengst 1998). In spite of this criticism, the requirement to obtain informed consent from groups in population genetics has been implemented, for instance, by the North American Regional Committee of the Human Genome Diversity Project (Greely 2001).

4 UN REDD is a UN initiative to reduce emissions from deforestation and forest degradation (UN-REDD Programme 2013).

5 See: Convention 169 of the International Labor Organization or Convention on Biological Diversity (CBD) and its Nagoya Protocol.

6 There are different interpretations of how FPIC should be set into practice, which go along with various practical difficulties (e.g. Szablowski 2010; Mahanty & McDermott 2013). For instance, indigenous communities usually aren't homogenous groups (Brereton et al. 2011), and there are concerns that the consent procedure is structured entirely according to Western ideals, which may be in contradiction with the indigenous groups' traditional models of decision-making. Moreover, the success of the process depends to a large extent on the political and financial circumstances as well as on the conduct of the different parties involved (Szablowski 2010).

7 See notes [2] and [6].

8 The same distinction has for instance been applied by Wong (2016).

9 Some authors distinguish between different types of implied consent, such as tacit consent (assuming consent if no objections are being brought forward) and implicit consent (referring to analogous decisions in the past) (Beauchamp & Childress 2001: 65–6).

10 See Yaffe (this volume, Chapter 9) for an introduction to hypothetical consent.

11 For authors who apply this or similar distinctions between different understandings of corporate entities, see Dewey (1926), French (1979) and Phillips (1992).

12 Peter French speaks of a Corporation's Internal Decision Structure (CID), through which the intentions of the Corporation are expressed. He argues that the CID subordinates and synthesizes the intentions and acts of individual persons into a corporate decision (French 1979: 212).

13 Interestingly, an UNDP report noted that, in contrast to this corporate language of group rights in the UNDRIP, the rights of other minorities in the "*Declaration on the Rights of Persons Belonging to National or Ethnic, Religious and Linguistic Minorities (UNDM)*" are phrased as individual rights or collective group rights (UN 1992; UNDP 2010).

14 Jones adopts the collective conception of group rights from Joseph Raz (Jones 1999; Raz 1986).

15 It is interesting to note, however, that also in the interaction between patients and physicians there are initiatives known as 'shared decision making' to involve the patient in a more participatory decision procedure compared with the classical informed consent model (Charles et al. 1997).

References

Beauchamp, T.L. and J.F. Childress (2001) *Principles of Biomedical Ethics*. Fifth Edition. Oxford, New York: Oxford University Press.

Brereton, D., J. Owen and J. Kim (2011) *World Bank Extractive Industries Source Book, Good Practice Notes on Community Development Agreements*. www-wds.worldbank.org/external/default/WDSContentServer/WDSP/IB/2012/10/01/000425962_20121001122627/Rendered/PDF/712990v20WP0P100Good0Practice0Notes.pdf (accessed August 2017).

Bruxton, A. and E. Wilson (2013) *FPIC and the Extractive Industries, A Guide to Applying the Spirit of Free, Prior and Informed Consent in Industrial Projects*. http://pubs.iied.org/pdfs/16530IIED.pdf (accessed August 2017).

Charles, C., A. Gafni and T. Whelan (1997) "Shared Decision-Making in the Medical Encounter: What Does it Mean? (or it Takes at Least Two to Tango)," *Social Science & Medicine* 44: 681–92.

Colchester, M. and F. MacKay (2004) *In Search of Middle Ground, Indigenous Peoples, Collective Representation and the Right to Free, Prior and Informed Consent*. www.forestpeoples.org/sites/fpp/files/publication/2010/08/fpicipsaug04eng.pdf (accessed August 2017).

Colchester, M. and M.F. Ferrari (2007) *Making FPIC – Free, Prior and Informed Consent – Work: Challenges and Prospects for Indigenous Peoples*. www.forestpeoples.org/sites/fpp/files/publication/2010/08/fpicsynthesisjun07eng.pdf (accessed August 2017).

Dewey, J. (1926) "The Historical Background of Corporate Legal Personality," *Yale Law Journal* 35: 655–73.
Fotion, N. (1987) "Simmons and the Concept of Consent: Commentary on 'Consent and Fairness in Planning Land Use'," *Business & Professional Ethics Journal* 6: 21–4.
French, P.A. (1979) "The Corporation as a Moral Person," *American Philosophical Quarterly* 16: 207–15.
Greely, H.T. (2001) "Informed Consent and Other Ethical Issues in Human Population Genetics," *Annual Review of Genetics* 35: 785–800.
Grill, K. (2009) "Liberalism, Altruism and Group Consent," *Public Health Ethics* 2: 146–57.
Hansson, S.O. (2006) "Informed Consent Out of Context," *Journal of Business Ethics* 63: 149–54.
Hill, C., S. Lillywhite, M. Simon et al. (2010) *Guide to Free Prior and Informed Consent*. www.culturalsurvival.org/news/oxfam-guide-free-prior-and-informed-consent (accessed August 2017).
Jones, P. (1999) "Group Rights and Group Oppression," *The Journal of Political Philosophy* 7: 353–77.
Jones, P. (2008) "Group Rights," in E.N. Zalta (ed.), *The Stanford Encyclopedia of Philosophy*. Stanford: Stanford University. https://plato.stanford.edu/entries/rights-group/ (accessed August 2017).
Juengst, E.T. (1998) "Groups as Gatekeepers to Genomic Research: Conceptually Confusing, Morally Hazardous, and Practically Useless," *Kennedy Institute of Health Journal* 8: 183–200.
Lehr, A.K., G.A. Smith and F. Hoag (2010) *Implementing a Corporate Free, Prior, and Informed Consent Policy: Benefits and Challenges*. www.foleyhoag.com/publications/ebooks-and-white-papers/2010/may/implementing-a-corporate-free-prior-and-informed-consent-policy (accessed August 2017).
Long, T.A. (1983) "Informed Consent and Engineering: An Essay Review," *Business & Professional Ethics Journal* 3: 59–66.
Mahanty, S. and C.L. McDermott (2013) "How Does 'Free, Prior and Informed Consent' (FPIC) Impact Social Equity? Lessons from Mining and Forestry and Their Implications for REDD+," *Land Use Policy* 35: 406–16.
Margalit, A. and J. Raz (1990) "National Self-Determination," *The Journal of Philosophy* 87: 439–61.
Martin, M.W. and R. Schinzinger (1983) *Ethics in Engineering*. New York: McGraw-Hill.
Morrow, D.R., R.E. Kopp and M. Oppenheimer (2009) "Toward Ethical Norms and Institutions for Climate Engineering Research," *Environmental Research Letters* 4: 1–8.
Phillips, M.J. (1992) "Corporate Moral Personhood and Three Conceptions of the Corporation," *Business Ethics Quarterly* 2: 435–59.
Raz, J. (1986) *The Morality of Freedom*. Oxford: Oxford University Press.
Schrag, B. (2006) "Research with Groups: Group Rights, Group Consent, and Collaborative Research, Commentary on Protecting the Navajo People through Tribal Regulation of Research," *Science and Engineering Ethics* 12: 511–21.
Simmons, J.A. (1987) "Consent and Fairness in Planning Land Use," *Business & Professional Ethics Journal* 6: 5–20.
Szablowski, D. (2010) "Operationalizing Free, Prior, and Informed Consent in the Extractive Industry Sector? Examining the Challenges of a Negotiated Model of Justice," *Canadian Journal of Development Studies* 30: 111–30.
UN (1992) *Declaration on the Rights of Persons Belonging to National or Ethnic, Religious and Linguistic Minorities*. www.ohchr.org/EN/ProfessionalInterest/Pages/Minorities.aspx (accessed August 2017).
UN (2006) *United Nations Declaration on the Rights of Indigenous Peoples (UNDRIP)*. www.un.org/esa/socdev/unpfii/documents/DRIPS_en.pdf (accessed August 2017).
UNDP (2010) *Marginalised Minorities in Development Programming*. www.ohchr.org/Documents/Issues/Minorities/UNDPMarginalisedMinorities.pdf (accessed August 2017).
UN-REDD Programme (2010) *Manual for Interlocutors to Conduct FPIC Village Consultation Meetings*. www.unredd.net/index.php?option=com_docman&Itemid=134&view=download&alias=4245-manual-for-interlocutors-4245&category_slug=leaflets-and-brochures-2009 (accessed August 2017).
UN-REDD Programme (2013) *Guidelines on Free, Prior and Informed Consent*. www.uncclearn.org/sites/default/files/inventory/un-redd05.pdf (accessed August 2017).
van der Vlist, L. and W. Richert (2012) *FSC Guidelines for the Implementation of the Right to Free, Prior and Informed Consent (FPIC)*. https://ca.fsc.org/download.fsc-guidelines-for-fpic.177.pdf (accessed August 2017).
Varelius, J. (2008) "On the Prospects of Collective Informed Consent," *Journal of Applied Philosophy* 25: 35–44.
Weijer, C. (1999) "Protecting Communities in Research: Philosophical and Pragmatic Challenges," *Cambridge Quarterly of Healthcare Ethics* 8: 501–13.

Wong, P.-H. (2016) "Consenting to Geoengineering," *Philosophy & Technology* 29: 173–88.
World Bank (2005) *OP 4.10 – Indigenous Peoples*. https://policies.worldbank.org/sites/ppf3/PPFDocuments/090224b0822f89d5.pdf (accessed August 2017).

Further reading

Hansson, S.O. (2006) "Informed Consent Out of Context," *Journal of Business Ethics* 63: 149–54. (A critical comment on the notion of informed group consent in which the author identifies three key problems of informed group consent.)
Varelius, J. (2008) "On the Prospects of Collective Informed Consent," *Journal of Applied Philosophy* 25: 35–44. (In this article the author defends the idea of group consent against Hansson's criticism. Please note that Varelius uses the phrase "collective informed consent" for "informed group consent"; this author does not distinguish between corporate and collective consent.)

Related topics

Ch.9 Hypothetical consent
Ch.24 Informed consent
Ch.25 Consent and medical treatment

PART II

Normative ethics

11

MORAL OBLIGATIONS AND CONSENT

Andreas Müller

Whether or not a person has consented to an action often makes a crucial difference for the moral assessment of that action. An action that would wrong a person because it would breach a moral obligation owed to her is often permissible if that person gives her consent. In such cases, the consent ensures that performing the action in question no longer constitutes a wrongful breach of obligation.[1]

This chapter addresses three questions concerning the effects consent has on our moral obligations. In the first section, I discuss *whose* obligations can be affected by someone's consent. The second section addresses *which* obligations are sensitive to consent and surveys various answers from the literature. In the third section, I distinguish different accounts of *why* a person's consent sometimes ensures that an action no longer breaches an obligation.

Throughout the chapter, I am only concerned with the relevance of consent to our *moral* obligations, leaving the role of consent in the legal realm to one side. Moreover, I will assume that the consent in the cases I discuss is formally valid, i.e. that it is sufficiently informed and voluntary and that the person giving it is competent to do so.[2]

11.1 Whose obligations are affected?

11.1.1 The agent

First and foremost, consent makes a difference to the normative situation of the agent of the action that has been consented to. Touching a person intimately, drawing a blood sample from her, or slapping her in the face are wrong in the absence of her consent because each of these actions breaches an obligation that is owed to her. With her consent, however, those actions no longer constitute breaches of obligation. In that case, we can say that the person who consents to the action thereby *waives* the agent's obligation to refrain from performing it.

The obligations in the three cases just mentioned are negative obligations – obligations to refrain from performing a certain type of action. But it seems that our consent can also affect an agent's positive obligations towards us. Suppose my friend and I are on our way to the cinema to watch a movie that I have wanted to see on the big screen for a long time. Suddenly, my friend trips and injures her arm in a way that requires immediate medical care. As her friend, I have a moral obligation to accompany her to the hospital, which fortunately is right around the corner. However, if I walk with her to the hospital, I will miss the movie. Knowing that, my friend tells me: "It's really okay for me if you go to the cinema. I know how much this movie means to you, and it's no problem for me to walk to the hospital alone. You have my permission to leave now". I take it that this constitutes an act of consent on my friend's part, so that if I leave and go to see the movie, I do not wrong her by not helping her (though I might reveal that I am less than an ideal friend). This is probably not a paradigmatic case of effective consent, but it suggests that, at least in certain circumstances, the positive obligation to help someone in need can be waived by giving consent, too.

Importantly, however, the obligations on the part of the agent that can be waived in this way are *directed* obligations. Observing them is something we owe to a particular person – viz. the person who can waive it by giving her consent – and breaching them would not simply be wrong, but would be wronging that person, which usually entitles her to an apology. It is an open question whether all moral obligations are directed in this sense. Many people think that the obligation not to destroy a rare painting, for example, is a moral obligation that cannot be reduced to any obligations to its creator or to its potential viewers but that is grounded in the impersonal value of that painting. It seems clear that such undirected obligations, if indeed there are any, cannot be waived by giving consent, for whose consent would be relevant? That of any particular person, or of some group, or everyone's? If destroying the painting would also breach an obligation towards a particular person (e.g. the artist or the owner), then that person's consent does make a moral difference, because it would ensure that she is not wronged by the painting's destruction. But insofar as destroying the painting would also constitute the breach of an undirected obligation, it might nevertheless be wrong. Such wrongness without wronging, it seems, is not affected by anyone's consent.

Specifying the distinctive effect of consent on the agent's normative situation as making her action *permissible* is thus an overstatement. A person's consent makes an action permissible only if that action would otherwise be wrong solely because it would wrong that person. Hence, that an action is impermissible despite the affected person's consent does not show that her consent has been ineffective, because she might very well have succeeded in waiving an obligation towards her.

11.1.2 The consenter

Some people argue that, in addition to waiving an obligation on the part of the addressed agent, consent can also result in a new obligation for the person giving it (Archard 1998: 3; cf. Raz 1986: 82 and Hurd, this volume, Chapter 4). They have in mind cases like the following: yesterday, I consented to my colleague's using my bike. When she comes to my office today to pick it up, however, she finds out that I took the bus to work and left my bike at home. It seems that my colleague has legitimate ground to complain that I have wronged her by not bringing my bike. Is this because, by consenting to her using my bike today, I incurred an obligation to make it available to her today? Does consenting to an action impose on the consenter an obligation to facilitate or at least not to impede that action?[3]

Let us grant that, in the bike example, I wrong my colleague by not bringing my bike. In that case, I have an obligation that I would not have had without giving consent (leaving the bike at home would have been perfectly fine). Giving consent thus affects the obligations of the consenter. One might doubt that it always does so, however. In cases of consent to sex, for example, it seems questionable whether the consenter incurs an obligation to facilitate – and the addressed agent a corresponding right to such facilitation. Moreover, we can still ask whether imposing a facilitative obligation in cases like the bike example is a direct result of giving consent, in the same way as waiving the agent's obligation is, or whether the relation between the consent and the imposed duty is more indirect. What seems to explain my obligation to bring the bike in our example is that I led my colleague to believe that she could use it the next day, and perhaps to rely on that expectation by adapting her plans accordingly.

But is raising this expectation an essential aspect of my consent in that case, or does it accompany it merely as a matter of contingency? If the latter is true, it would not be the consent as such that generates the facilitative obligation. Note that I give her my consent by communicating with her, and that acts of communication often instantiate additional act types. If your boss communicates to you that there is going to be a reception with important business partners later today, she might thereby also demand that you attend. She can avoid doing so, however, by adding "But there is no need for you to come" or something along those lines. Can I similarly avoid misleading my colleague by adding "But don't count on it" to my expression of consent, without thereby rendering the consent ineffective? That is, would my amended consent still ensure that she would not wrong me by using my bike if I did bring it? If the answer is yes, then leading my colleague to expect that she will be able to use my bike is not an essential aspect of my consenting to it. And if my obligation to bring the bike is grounded in that expectation, then it is not a necessary result of my consent, either, but merely an indirect and contingent consequence of it. Thus, even though we sometimes incur a facilitative obligation when we consent to an action, this obligation might be the normative effect of something we also do when we communicate our consent on that occasion, rather than an effect of the consent as such.

11.1.3 Third parties

Consenting to an agent's action can also affect the rights and obligations of third parties. This is because some of the moral obligations that can be waived by giving consent are so weighty that we often have an obligation to prevent agents from breaching them, at least if we can do so at little or no cost for ourselves. For example, you might have an obligation to prevent someone from sexually harassing another person at a party. If, on the other hand, the intimate contact is consensual, you have no right, and certainly no obligation to get involved. Thus, if a person consents to an action that would otherwise wrong her, third parties typically lose any obligation to intervene on her behalf that they might otherwise have.

11.2 Which obligations are affected?

In the remainder of this chapter, I will focus on the effect a person's consent has on the moral obligations of the agent to whom it is given. This is arguably the most important normative effect of consent, and surely the effect most of the literature on consent is concerned with. This section addresses which obligations a person to whom they are owed can waive by giving consent. Which obligations, in other words, are *consent-sensitive*?

Most people will agree that some, but not all, moral obligations are consent-sensitive. For one thing, we already saw that undirected obligations are not. But what about directed obligations – can those always be waived by giving consent? It is tempting to argue for a negative answer by pointing to examples of wrongful actions that remain wrong even if the victim consents, such as mutilation or torture. But that seems too hasty: recall that even if a person can successfully consent to an action, that does not entail that her consent makes the action overall permissible. It only ensures that she is no longer wronged by it. If the action also breaches an obligation that is not owed to the consenter, it might be wrong even though one of the obligations it would breach has been waived by her (cf. section 11.1). Moreover, it is often controversial which obligations account for the wrongness of those actions in cases without consent. All of this makes it difficult to argue from the premise that a certain kind of action remains wrong even if the affected person consents to it, to any thesis about the consent-insensitivity of particular moral obligations.

Since my aim here is not to determine the limits of successful consent, I will not pursue this issue any further. Instead, I will focus on cases that are widely considered as paradigmatic instances of successful consent, and on the obligations that various authors have presented as consent-sensitive in order to accommodate those cases. For while the difficulties mentioned above entail that a change in the moral status of particular actions is not a necessary condition for the consent-sensitivity of a certain obligation, it is a sufficient one: if an action that is wrong because it breaches a certain obligation can be made permissible by the affected person's consent, then that obligation is consent-sensitive. Thus, if the permissibility of an action depends on someone's consent, then this shows that the underlying obligation – whichever it is – is consent-sensitive. In what follows, I will discuss three moral obligations that are perhaps most often considered to be consent-sensitive in the literature: the obligation not to harm, the obligation to respect autonomy, and the obligation not to trespass.

11.2.1 The obligation not to harm

Which obligations an author focusses on when considering the normative effects of consent often depends on the kinds of cases they have in mind as paradigmatic examples of consent. Take the case of punching someone in the face. Ordinarily, doing so wrongs that person, but it can be permissible if that person gave her consent, e.g. if the punch is part of a stage performance or a boxing match. Why is it wrong to punch someone in the face without their consent? The answer most people will give, I take it, is that it harms that person – it significantly decreases her well-being.[4] That is, they take such punches to be wrong because they breach the obligation not to harm other people. If this is true, then that obligation must somehow be consent-sensitive, because those punches can be made permissible by consent.

In her account of how consent works, Dempsey (2013) focusses on such a punching example and suggests that the obligation not to harm can be waived by giving consent. Feinberg (1988: 176–8) and Wertheimer (2003: ch. 5), too, take a person's consent to be capable of making actions permissible that would otherwise be wrong because they harm her.

Dempsey also maintains that consent can *only* be effective for actions that would otherwise be wrong because of the negative effect they have on the consenter's well-being (2013: 18–19). That is, she holds that the obligation not to harm is the only obligation that is consent-sensitive. To many, however, that thesis will appear too restrictive. In the context of medical treatment, for example, we can find many actions whose permissibility depends on the patient's consent, even though many people – and most doctors – would refuse to characterize them as harming the patient in the way a punch to the face does. Curing a patient from a serious infection by administering antibiotics increases her well-being, even if, some would argue, those antibiotics were mixed into the patient's food without informing her. One might respond that while the overall effect of such covert treatment on the patient's well-being is positive, there is still some harm involved, some aspect that, when considered on its own, detracts from the patient's well-being. But is that really why covert treatments constitute such a grave wronging of patients?

Another example that casts doubt on Dempsey's thesis is the kind of nonconsensual sex that John Gardner and Stephen Shute call "pure rape" (Gardner & Shute 2000). These are cases of rape in which the victim is "forever oblivious to the fact that she was raped", e.g. because "she was drugged or drunk to the point of unconsciousness when the rape was committed, and the rapist wore a condom" (2000: 196). In such – extremely unlikely but, according to the authors, philosophically important – cases, the victim's "life is not changed for the worse, or at all, by the rape" (ibid.), that is, the rape does not affect the victim's well-being and is thus "harmless". Nevertheless, of course, the rapist's actions constitute a grave wronging of the victim, so there must be an obligation other than the obligation not to harm that those actions breach. Gardner and Shute argue that it is that other obligation which fundamentally accounts for the wrongness of rape, even in the more common cases that involve serious physiological and psychological harms (2000: 197–8).[5] But since consent can transform rape into morally permissible sex, that obligation must be consent-sensitive, too.

11.2.2 The obligation not to violate autonomy

In much of the literature on consent, the crucial obligation that explains the normative significance of consent is not the obligation not to harm other people, but rather the obligation not to violate their autonomy.[6] The latter extends to cases that are not covered by the former: covert medical treatment might not cause any (overall) harm to the patient, but it certainly fails to respect their autonomous choices, especially if it is administered not just without, but against, the patient's will. Such covert treatment is a paradigmatic example of paternalism, i.e. of interfering with a person against her will but for her own good, and paternalistic actions are usually thought to be morally problematic because they violate a person's autonomy (cf. Dworkin 2017). The obligation not to violate autonomy is at the core of many influential discussions of the doctrine of informed consent in medical ethics (Faden & Beauchamp 1986; Beauchamp & Childress 2013: ch. 4; Dworkin 1988: ch. 7; Jonsen et al. 2010), and it has played an important role in establishing that doctrine as a binding rule of conduct for medical professionals (see also O'Shea, this volume, Chapter 23 and Ach, this volume, Chapter 25). But the focus on autonomy is not limited to medical ethics. In her seminal discussion of the "moral magic" of consent, which takes a more general perspective on the phenomenon, Heidi Hurd maintains that "consent is normatively significant precisely because it constitutes an expression of autonomy" (1996: 124).

Taking the obligation not to violate autonomy to be consent-sensitive extends the range of wrongings that can be made permissible by consent, as the case of covert medical treatment illustrates. But exactly how far it extends that range depends on how one spells out the concept of autonomy. Various authors have pointed out that this concept is notoriously ambiguous, and that the obligation not to violate autonomy has little content unless it is combined with one of the many competing theories of personal autonomy. Onora O'Neill has gone further in arguing that the importance of informed consent in medical ethics cannot be rooted in the importance of individual autonomy, because many of the decisions protected by that doctrine do not qualify as autonomous on any of the accounts on offer (O'Neill 2003: 5). Rather than ensuring respect for individual autonomy, the requirement of informed consent in medical ethics protects patients from deception and coercion (ibid.). According to O'Neill, the requirement is thus not grounded in an obligation not to violate autonomy, but in an obligation not to coerce or deceive. If she is right, it is the consent-sensitivity of this latter obligation that explains why the permissibility of medical interventions in treatment and research depends on the patient's or subject's consent.

Archard (2008), too, thinks that there are cases in which the permissibility of an action depends on a person's consent, but where performing the action without consent would not be wrong because it violates the person's autonomy. His example is that of taking a mouth swab from someone "without her agreement, yet harmlessly, painlessly, and without coercion or deception" (2008: 19). Archard argues that doing so does not amount to an assault on the person's autonomy. The value of autonomy, he suggests, lies in the value to lead one's own life, and so the obligation to respect autonomy only protects "critical" decisions that make a substantial difference to one's life, such as marrying someone, joining a political party, or becoming a vegetarian (2008: 21–2). "Trivial" decisions, by contrast, such as choosing a particular meal or selecting a phone number, do not fall within the scope of that obligation (2008: 22). Archard considers the mouth swab to be a trivial rather than a critical matter. Taking it without the person's consent, he suggests, does not "subvert the ability of its victim to lead her life as she chooses" (2008: 22). He thus concludes that "the wrong of taking the mouth swab cannot be understood by appeal to the idea of respecting personal autonomy" (2008: 22).

If the permissibility of taking the mouth swab depends on the person's consent, but taking it without consent does not breach the obligation to respect her autonomy, there must be another consent-sensitive obligation that accounts for its wrongness. Note that as Archard presents the case, it cannot be the obligation not to harm, because the mouth swab is taken without causing any pain or harm. We can imagine the patient never even being aware of it. So which obligation is breached here?

11.2.3 The obligation not to trespass

The answer Archard finds most compelling is that taking the mouth swab without the person's consent is wrong because it "is a *trespass* upon the body of that person" (2008: 27). Similarly, Judith Thomson argues that people have a general claim against bodily intrusion that can be waived by giving consent (1990: ch. 8). Like entering someone's land or foreign territory without permission, entering someone's body without consent is wrong because it crosses a certain boundary and thus constitutes "trespass" (Thomson 1990: 205).

Both Archard (2008: 27) and Thomson (1990: 209) point out that trespass need not cause any harm, so the obligation not to trespass upon someone's body extends to cases that are not covered by the obligation not to cause harm. In particular, it extends to cases like the mouth swab. Does the obligation not to trespass also explain the wrongness of Gardner and Shute's "harmless" cases of rape? Clearly, such rape involves an intrusion into the body of the victim. However, as Archard (2008: 30) acknowledges, the obligation not to trespass upon someone's body does not seem suitable to explain the *distinctive* wrong of rape, harmless or not. This is because trespass is a binary notion: you either cross the relevant boundary, or you don't. There are no degrees of severity in trespassing that depend on where or how far that boundary is crossed. If you step on my land without my permission, you are trespassing. It does not matter where you climb over the fence, or how far you walk beyond the fence. But rape does differ in severity from other intrusions into the body. It is much worse than Archard's mouth swab, for example. Hence, there seems to be something over and above the trespass, some other obligation that is breached by rape but not by trivial intrusions like the mouth swab and that explains the moral severity of rape.

Moreover, Thomson argues that we have similar claims against intrusions into our body as we have against intrusions into our land because both our body and our land are our property (1990: 225). Such a proprietarian justification of the claim against bodily intrusions has implications that many, including Archard (2008: 29), will find morally unacceptable. For one thing, it suggests that people have a right to sell or rent out their bodies or parts thereof, which would make the sale of organs, surrogacy, and prostitution seem morally unproblematic. More importantly for our context, explaining the wrongness of unconsented bodily intrusions in terms of the wrongness of unconsented use of property would classify rape as a case of unconsented and possibly violent borrowing (Archard 2008: 30), which, again, misses the distinctive wrongfulness of rape.

Yet, without the kind of unified justification Thomson's proprietarian account provides, it seems less informative to point out that bodily intrusions like the mouth swab are similar to burglary in that both involve the impermissible crossing of some boundary and can thus be called "trespassing". In other words, not much seems to be won by saying not just that the unconsented mouth swab is wrong, but that it is wrong because it constitutes a case of trespassing upon someone's body, if all we can say about the reasons for why trespassing upon someone's body is wrong is that they are different from the reasons why, e.g., trespassing upon someone's land is wrong.

*

The three obligations discussed in this section – the obligation not to harm, the obligation to respect autonomy, and the obligation not to trespass – are among the obligations that are most often considered to be consent-sensitive in the literature. Each of them deals best with a certain class of examples of effective consent, and each of them, it seems, has problems dealing with certain other examples. Our discussion thus suggests that the variety of cases in which consent can make a difference to the moral status of an action can only be accommodated by a plurality of consent-sensitive obligations. Some authors, however, espouse a more monistic view concerning this question. Dempsey does so explicitly with respect to the obligation not to harm, and many authors in medical ethics appear to view the requirement of (informed) consent exclusively as a way of ensuring respect for autonomy.

This points us to the question that will be addressed in the next section of this chapter. So far, we have approached the task of identifying consent-sensitive obligations by looking at various examples in which an action's permissibility depends on consent and identifying the underlying moral obligation. But why does consent make a difference to the moral status of certain actions at all? Why does the permissibility of some actions depend on someone's consent? An explanation of this dependency is philosophically interesting in its own right. Moreover, if that explanation is only applicable to breaches of some obligations, but not others, it also provides us with a more systematic way of identifying the moral obligations that are consent-sensitive and distinguishing them from those that are not.

11.3 Why are some obligations consent-sensitive?

A moral obligation is consent-sensitive if and only if the valid consent of the person to whom it is owed can ensure that she is not wronged by an action that would otherwise breach that obligation. Such an obligation, we have said, can be waived by giving consent. But why exactly does consent make a difference to whether or not the action breaches the obligation in those cases?

11.3.1 The removal account

Various answers to this question can be found in the literature. The first one I call the removal account. It is more often implicitly presupposed than it is explicitly endorsed. According to this account, effective consent removes the wrongmaking feature underlying the relevant obligation. The basic idea is simple: wrongness is not a brute feature of certain actions. An action that wrongs someone does so because of some other feature (or features) it has, a feature that provides a reason against performing the action. Every wrong action is wrong in virtue of such a wrongmaking feature. Which features of actions can be wrongmaking is, of course, a matter of continuing dispute in normative ethics. According to the removal account, some wrongmaking features entail the lack of a person's valid consent. In that case, giving consent ensures that the wrongmaking feature is not present. If an obligation protects us against actions with such a wrongmaking feature, it is consent-sensitive. To waive it through consent is to deliberately remove that feature.

The removal account provides a straightforward way of identifying the moral obligations that are consent-sensitive: if the wrongmaking feature that underlies an obligation entails the absence of consent, then that obligation is consent-sensitive. Consider, for example, the obligation not to violate other people's autonomy. Insofar as this obligation protects us against actions that do not conform to our autonomous will, the removal account provides a compelling explanation for why it can be waived by giving consent. For if I validly consent to an action, it does conform to my autonomous will. By doing so, I thus make it the case that the action lacks the feature in virtue of which the obligation would apply to it, just as the removal account has it.

It is less clear what the removal account entails for the consent-sensitivity of the obligation not to harm. This obligation protects us against actions that harm us, e.g. by causing us pain. Sometimes whether an action harms us seems to depend on our attitudes towards it. Usually, being bitten by someone harms me, but it arguably does not if the bite occurs as part of consensual sex (cf. Owens 2012: 180). More generally, it is often argued that our choices are a good indicator of what does and what does not diminish our well-being and thus constitutes a harm. Firstly, as many authors have pointed out, people are usually in an epistemically privileged position with respect to their interests and hence the best judges of what is good for them. Secondly, the desires or preferences that inform our choices are often considered to be at least partly constitutive of what is good for us.

However, assuming that there is such a close connection between choice and harm does not suffice to show that the obligation not to harm is consent-sensitive. This is because there are good reasons to distinguish between consenting to an action and choosing that action, or wanting it to occur (cf. Owens 2012: 165–72). Of course, the two often coincide, and in some areas, such as medical treatment, they nearly always do. Nevertheless, they should be distinguished, because they have different objects: while choosing an action or wanting it to occur are concerned with the actual performance of the action, consent is concerned with its moral status, i.e. its wrongfulness. They can also come apart, e.g. when you invite an annoying colleague to a party at your place, thereby consenting to their entering your house (they wouldn't wrong you if they did), even though you do not want them to actually come. If we draw this distinction, the considerations in the previous paragraph only show that the obligation not to harm is *choice*-sensitive. Then, advocates of the removal account could only classify that obligation as *indirectly* consent-sensitive, because its wrongmaking feature entails the absence not of consent itself, but of something that frequently coincides with it.

But even if we include the effects of the choices that coincide with our consent, the account's criterion for distinguishing obligations that are consent-sensitive from those that are not is in conflict with our everyday conception of consent. This is because in some of our paradigmatic examples of effective consent, the feature that appears to make the action wrong in the absence of consent is also present when consent has been given. But then the fact that the action no longer wrongs the person cannot be explained by the removal of the wrongmaking feature. Consider the examples of removing someone's kidney, or punching them in the face. Surely, these actions wrong the person if they are performed without her consent, and surely they wrong her because they cause her significant harm.[7] But removing a kidney constitutes a harm, not just to a victim of organ theft, but also to a voluntary donor. This harm is not always offset by any benefits the donor might draw from saving the receiver's life, especially not in cases of anonymous donations (denying this would mean denying that those donations are genuinely altruistic). The donor consents to the harm, for the sake of the recipient. But she does not thereby remove the harm. Similarly, a punch to the face is harmful even if it occurs in a consensual boxing match. Nevertheless, most of us think that the donor's consent can make the surgical removal of her kidney permissible,[8] and that the boxer is not wronged by her opponent if she consented to the fight. Thus, they waive the obligation not to harm by giving their consent, but they do not remove the wrongmaking feature (neither through their consent nor through the choices that coincide with it).

11.3.2 The exclusion account

An alternative account of why consent makes a moral difference is offered by Dempsey (2013). Dempsey holds that all wrongings that can be made permissible by consent owe their wrongness to the negative effect they have on the victim's well-being (see section 11.2). This is the feature that counts against those actions and makes them wrong. But on her account, the victim's consent does not remove that feature. Dempsey does not think that a lack of consent necessarily adds to, nor that giving consent necessarily deducts from, an action's negative effect on a person's well-being. Instead, she argues that consent provides the agent "with an exclusionary permission not to act for reasons grounded in the consenter's well-being" (Dempsey 2013: 21).[9] That is, it provides the agent with the option to exclude the action's effect on the consenter's well-being from consideration when deciding what to do. When he takes up that option and decides to deliver the punch, he does not wrong the consenter and his action does not breach any obligation towards him, even though the punch diminishes the consenter's well-being, possibly to the same extent that it would have if consent had not been given.

What allows us to present Dempsey's exclusion account as an alternative to the removal account is that Dempsey amends the notion of a wrongmaking feature introduced earlier. According to her, a feature that provides a reason against an action can only make the action wrong if the agent is not permitted to exclude it from her deliberation. The normative effect of consent, then, is that some such features may be excluded. Thus, a person's consent can explain why punching her in the face is permissible because it constitutes a defeating condition of the wrongmaking relation, not because the wrongmaking feature somehow entails its absence.

Dempsey's exclusion account does not, by itself, provide a criterion for identifying the moral obligations that are consent-sensitive. It is, in principle, applicable to any moral obligation, because the concept of an exclusionary permission does not include any limitation to a certain class of reasons. Thus, in principle, any feature that counts against an action might be kept from making the action wrong by someone's consent. Dempsey thinks that the normative effect of a person's consent is limited to the reasons that are grounded in that person's well-being, so that only the obligation not to harm turns out to be consent-sensitive. But she does not give a reason for this limitation. Perhaps she assumes that all practical reasons are grounded in well-being. But that would not yet explain why someone's consent only affects reasons that are grounded in *that person's* well-being. After all, I cannot consent to someone's punching you in the face.

One way to explain such a limitation of the power to grant exclusionary permissions appeals to the value of having that power: why can I grant permission to exclude reasons grounded in my well-being, but not reasons grounded in yours? Because it is valuable to be able to grant permissions to exclude reasons grounded in one's own well-being, but not valuable to be able to grant permissions to exclude reasons grounded in the well-being of others. Of course, fleshing out such a value-based account of the scope of our power to grant exclusionary permissions – and hence, according to Dempsey, of our power to consent – requires answering a number of additional questions: is the relevant kind of value instrumental or noninstrumental? Is it personal value ("good for") or value simpliciter? Surveying different answers to those questions goes beyond the scope of this chapter.[10] What is important here is that Dempsey's exclusion account will yield an explanation as to why some moral obligations but not others are consent-sensitive only when we add some account of the scope of our power to grant exclusionary permissions.

11.3.3 Owens' account

The removal account and the exclusion account do not exhaust the options for explaining why consent affects the moral status of an action. The explanation offered by Owens (2012: ch. 7), for example, follows neither the removal nor the exclusion account. Owens rejects a fundamental assumption that both accounts share, which is that all negative moral obligations are grounded in certain wrongmaking features that count against the actions they prohibit.[11] Instead, he postulates a class of obligations called "interested obligations" (2012: 2). These obligations do not *protect* our interests by prohibiting actions that violate them (as, e.g., the obligation not to harm does). Rather, their existence *satisfies* certain "normative interests" of ours, that is, interests in the obtaining of certain normative states of affairs (2012: 2–6). Owens' main example is the obligation that is breached by rape, including Gardner and Shute's case of harmless rape, which, on his account, is simply the obligation not to have sex with someone unless they consent to it. This obligation, Owens argues, serves "an interest in its being the case that one is wronged by the rape *unless one consents to it*", which he calls a "permissive interest" (2012: 181, his italics). Interested obligations that are grounded in such permissive interests are thus all consent-sensitive, simply in virtue of the kind of normative interest they serve. According to Owens, these are the only obligations that are consent-sensitive (2012: 164–5).

Owens' account resembles the removal account in that consenting to an action makes the moral obligation that it would otherwise breach inapplicable: it ensures that the action no longer falls under the description of actions that are prohibited by the obligation. But it does not do so by removing a wrongmaking feature, because interested obligations are not grounded in any wrongmaking features of the actions they prohibit. They do not identify anything that is bad about the actions that breach them, nor do they provide any reason against performing them (Owens 2012: 69).[12] Instead, these obligations exist because being subject to them is good for us (ibid.). For Owens, what explains why an obligation is consent-sensitive is thus not that the wrongmaking feature of the actions it prohibits entails a lack of consent (as the removal account has it), but that it serves a normative interest of ours that those actions are impermissible unless we consent to them.[13] Whether a particular class of actions is prohibited by a consent-sensitive obligation thus depends on the content of our permissive interests, that is, on whether it is good for us that the permissibility of those actions depends on our consent. Owens' account of the scope of our consent is thus similar to the value-based account we discussed above as a possible addition to Dempsey's exclusion account (though he does not understand giving consent as granting an exclusionary permission).

*

The three accounts discussed in this section offer different explanations of why consent makes a difference to whether or not an action breaches an obligation, when it does. According to the removal model, it does so because, by giving our consent, we remove the wrongmaking feature underlying the obligation. According to the exclusion model, it does so because, by giving our consent, we grant the agent the permission to exclude the wrongmaking feature from consideration when deciding whether or not to perform the action in question, which defeats the wrongmaking relation between that feature and the action. And, according to Owens' account, it does so because it is good for us that the actions in question constitute wrongings if and only if we have not consented to them.

But only the removal model comes with a criterion for distinguishing obligations that are consent-sensitive from those that are not. That criterion, however, seems to be in conflict with our everyday conception of what we can successfully consent to. The exclusion model and Owens' accounts yield such a criterion only when combined with some specific view concerning the scope of our power to grant exclusionary permissions or the content of our permissive interests, respectively. Defending such a position is what proponents of either of these accounts will have to accomplish in order to provide us with a systematic way of determining which moral obligations are consent-sensitive.[14]

Notes

1 In what follows, I will use "breach of obligation" to refer to wrongful breaches only and thus omit the qualification.

2 See Bullock (this volume, Chapter 8) for details on these conditions.

3 Consent is also sometimes thought to create an obligation for the consenter not to complain about the action. See Hurd (this volume, Chapter 4) for a discussion of this idea.

4 As I understand it here, an action *harms* a person whenever it decreases her well-being, i.e. whenever it is bad for her. This rather wide notion of harm must be distinguished from one which means that the person is wronged by the action. Whether a person is wronged by an action that harms her in the former sense – the one adopted here – is an open question. See Feinberg (1988: xxvii–xxix) for a similar distinction between two senses of "harm".

5 According to Gardner and Shute, what accounts for the distinctive wrongness of rape is the rapist's "objectification" of the victim (2000: 204).

6 See Walker (this volume, Chapter 12) for a more comprehensive discussion of the relations between consent and autonomy.

7 There might be additional wrongmaking features, but this one is surely sufficient on its own. Sometimes, an action's wrongness is overdetermined.

8 Anonymous living kidney donation is legally practiced, e.g. in the United Kingdom, cf. www.giveakidney.org

9 Dempsey adopts the notion of an exclusionary permission from Joseph Raz, who takes consent to be one main example of granting such a permission (Raz 1999: 96–7).

10 Raz (1986: 86–8) suggests a value-based explanation of the scope of our power to consent that appeals to the noninstrumental value of the human relationships and personal projects that are facilitated by our ability to consent. See also Koch (this volume, Chapter 3).

11 Though see note 12.

12 Owens need not deny that actions which breach an interested obligation have "wrongmaking features" in a weaker sense in which that term picks out those features of an action in virtue of which the obligation prohibits it. The feature of being nonconsensual sex would qualify as such a feature on his account. But, for Owens, those features do not explain why the action is wrong, they only indicate that it is. What explains their wrongness and hence "makes" them wrong in a more substantive sense is the normative interest. By contrast, the wrongmaking features that consent removes according to the removal account are wrongmaking in this more substantive sense: they (or, more specifically, the reasons they provide against the action) explain why the action is wrong, so consent removes the source of the action's wrongness, as it were. It does not do so on Owens' account.

13 Note that this normative interest is distinct from what Owens calls a "control interest", which is "an interest in having the occurrence of [certain actions] depend on our choices" (2012: 166). Whereas the former is concerned with a potential action's normative status, the latter is concerned with its actual performance.

14 I am grateful to Anna Goppel, Felix Koch, and Peter Schaber for valuable comments on a penultimate draft of this chapter.

References

Archard, D. (1998) *Sexual Consent*. Boulder: Westview.
Archard, D. (2008) "Informed Consent: Autonomy and Self-Ownership," *Journal of Applied Philosophy* 25(1): 19–34.
Beauchamp, T.L. and J.F. Childress (2013) *Principles of Biomedical Ethics*. Seventh Edition. New York: Oxford University Press.
Dempsey, M. (2013) "Victimless Conduct and the *Volenti* Maxim: How Consent Works," *Criminal Law and Philosophy* 7: 11–27.
Dworkin, G. (1988) *The Theory and Practice of Autonomy*. New York: Cambridge University Press.
Dworkin, G. (2017) "Paternalism," in E.N. Zalta (ed.), *The Stanford Encyclopedia of Philosophy* (Spring 2017 Edition). https://plato.stanford.edu/archives/spr2017/entries/paternalism.
Faden, R.R. and T.L. Beauchamp (1986) *A History and Theory of Informed Consent*. New York: Oxford University Press.
Feinberg, J. (1988) *Harmless Wrongdoing, The Moral Limits of the Criminal Law*. Vol. 4. New York: Oxford University Press.
Gardner, J. and S. Shute (2000) "The Wrongness of Rape," in J. Horder (ed.), *Oxford Essays in Jurisprudence*. Fourth Series. Oxford: Oxford University Press.
Hurd, H. (1996) "The Moral Magic of Consent (I)," *Legal Theory* 2: 121–46.
Jonsen, A.R., M. Siegler and W.J. Winslade (2010) *Clinical Ethics. A Practical Approach to Ethical Decisions in Clinical Medicine*. Seventh Edition. New York: McGraw-Hill.
O'Neill, O. (2003) "Some Limits of Informed Consent," *Journal of Medical Ethics* 29: 4–7.
Owens, D. (2012) *Shaping the Normative Landscape*. Oxford: Oxford University Press.
Raz, J. (1986) *The Morality of Freedom*. Oxford: Oxford University Press.
Raz, J. (1999) *Practical Reason and Norms*. Second Edition. Oxford: Oxford University Press.
Thomson, J.J. (1990) *The Realm of Rights*. Cambridge, MA: Harvard University Press.
Wertheimer, A. (2003) *Consent to Sexual Relations*. Cambridge: Cambridge University Press.

Related topics

Ch.3 Consent as a normative power
Ch.4 The normative force of consent
Ch.5 Consent and wronging a person
Ch.12 Consent and autonomy
Ch.17 The volenti maxim

12
CONSENT AND AUTONOMY

Tom Walker

12.1 Introduction

The relationship between consent and autonomy is complex – not least because both "consent" and "autonomy" have multiple meanings. In this chapter I will take the term "consent" to refer to a communicative act that changes the normative landscape so that an act that would have been impermissible for some reason is no longer impermissible for that reason – though this does not necessarily mean that it is permissible, all things considered (Owens 2012: 165; Feinberg 1986: 177; Raz 1986: 81; Manson 2007: 297–8). If this is what "consent" is, then there are two ways in which consent and autonomy could be linked. It could either be that consent requires an autonomous act (that is, for an act to shape the normative landscape in the required way that act must be autonomous), or that the reason it would be morally impermissible to act without a person's consent is that to do so would fail to treat that person as required by the fact that he or she is autonomous. The former takes autonomy to be a feature of acts – in particular, the act of granting permission to act in a certain way. The latter, in contrast, takes autonomy to be a feature of individuals – it is because individuals are autonomous that there are some things we ought not to do without their consent. In this chapter I aim to investigate how we should interpret "autonomy" if either of these two ways of making the link between autonomy and consent is to be plausible. In doing this I will argue for two things. First, we need to interpret "autonomy" or "autonomous" in different ways depending on how we conceptualize the relationship between autonomy and consent. Second, how these terms should be interpreted will vary depending on the context, but in many contexts they need to be interpreted in a minimal sense.

12.2 Does consent require an autonomous act?

Let us start with the claim that for an act to change the normative landscape in the way that consent does that act must be autonomous. In practice we standardly consent by agreeing to someone acting in a certain way. As such, the claim to be considered here is that only an agreement that is autonomous can make it permissible for us to act in that way. At first sight such a claim looks unproblematic. It is, at least intuitively, implausible that a non-autonomous act could alter whether it is morally permissible for one person to have sex with another, to give them medical treatment, or to carry out research on them. Furthermore, there appear to be clear cases where an act that is not autonomous would not constitute the required consent (i.e. not make the required change in the normative landscape), and where the reason it would not do so is precisely that it is not autonomous. For example, if Sue is coerced into having sex with Bill, her agreement does not make it permissible for Bill to have sex with her – and the reason is that she did not autonomously agree to him doing so.

The claim that consent requires an autonomous act is, however, ambiguous. To remove that ambiguity two things need to be made more precise. First, more needs to be said about what is required for an act to be autonomous. As is well known there are multiple different accounts of "autonomy" (Dworkin 1988: 3–6; Taylor 2005). Some of the main ones in the philosophy literature are: Kantian accounts, structural accounts (e.g. Frankfurt), and historical accounts (e.g. Dworkin) (for an overview of such accounts see Taylor 2005). An alternative that is more common in debates in bioethics states that for an act (such as a choice) to be autonomous it must be intentional, voluntary, and carried out with understanding (Beauchamp 2005). Whether a particular act is autonomous will vary depending on which of these accounts is adopted. It could be that even if autonomy in one of these senses is needed for consent, an autonomous act is not needed for consent if we adopt a different account of which acts are autonomous.

Second, more needs to be said about the wrong of acting without consent. There are many different reasons an act might be wrong if done without consent – including that it would break the law, that it would violate an individual's rights, or that it would fail to respect someone's autonomy (these are not of course mutually exclusive). A particular individual's agreement that is autonomous in some particular sense may be needed to avoid acting wrongly in one of these ways, but not needed to avoid acting wrongly in the others. For example, suppose that the law says "you must not carry out research on a competent adult unless (a) they understand what is to be done, the benefits and possible harms of acting in that way, and (b) you have their voluntary agreement to take part in the research". In that case an autonomous agreement (in Beauchamp's sense at least) would be needed for legal consent – it would be wrong to include a person as a research participant unless they have autonomously agreed to participate in that research. This is because of the way this law is written. As such, that it is required in this context does not mean that an autonomous authorization is needed for something to be consent in other contexts (e.g. to comply with the law requiring consent to sex) where the law may be different. It also will not necessarily be the case that autonomy is needed for consent where we are thinking about things other than legal consent (i.e. where the wrong of acting without consent is something other than simply that to do so would be to break the law).

These different ways in which the claim that consent requires an autonomous act can be interpreted mean that writers who appear to disagree about that claim may not in fact disagree at all. They may in their writings simply be discussing different things. Equally, even where writers do disagree about the truth of this claim on some particular way of interpreting it, there may be much about the relationship between autonomy and consent on which they agree. For example, they might agree about whether or not a patient's autonomous authorization in Beauchamp's sense is needed if a doctor is to avoid the wrong of breaking the law, but disagree about whether it is needed to avoid the wrong of failing to respect the patient's autonomy. Similarly, they might agree that an autonomous act in Frankfurt's sense of what it is for an act to be autonomous is not needed in order to avoid the wrong of failing to respect the patient's autonomy, but disagree about whether an autonomous act in Beauchamp's sense of what it is for an act to be autonomous is needed to avoid that wrong.

When assessing whether an autonomous act is necessary for consent the method we use will have to vary depending on what the wrong of acting without consent is. If the wrong would be breaking the law, for example, then to determine whether only an autonomous act (in whatever sense of "autonomous") can change the situation so that this would not be the case requires an analysis of what the law says. But where we are not concerned with legal consent a different approach will be required. In taking such an approach intuitions play an important role in two ways. First, it appears intuitively to be the case that virtually all adults are able to consent to things like sex, medical treatment, or participating in research. Second, there are many occasions in which it appears that people have consented – that is, in which they have successfully brought it about that someone else did not act wrongly where they would have been acting wrongly if no consent had been given. The account of what is required for consent needs to take account of these intuitions and this constrains the interpretation of "autonomy" in accounts of autonomy and consent (though this is not to deny that a fully worked-out account may show that our intuitions about some cases are mistaken).

These kinds of consideration mean that it is implausible that an autonomous act is needed for consent on some prominent accounts of what "autonomy" is. To begin with, such a claim will not be plausible if "autonomy" is interpreted in a Kantian sense. This is not because adults are not in most cases capable of acting autonomously in this sense; it is because there seem to be clear cases in which consent was given but where no autonomous act was performed. Suppose, for example, that Mary very strongly desires to have sex with Bill – she lusts after him. Acting purely on this desire she agrees to have sex with Bill. On Kant's account in this case Mary is acting heteronomously, rather than autonomously. But we would not want to say purely in virtue of this that she has not consented to have sex with Bill, and that (taking rape to be unconsented-to sex) he has raped her. Similar considerations would appear to rule out accounts that interpret "autonomy" in the ways proposed by writers such as Frankfurt or Dworkin. It is a feature of such accounts that an act is only autonomous if the individual in some sense endorses that act (in this case the act of giving permission), or one where they are acting on a desire they have a second-order preference that they act on. The requirement that it is only such acts that can be consent would rule out many cases that intuitively appear to be clear cases in which consent is given. Such accounts, it has been argued, are too intellectual and set the bar for what counts as autonomous too high to support the claim that consent requires an autonomous act (Manson & O'Neill 2007: 21; Beauchamp & Childress 2009: 100–1).

For reasons of this type in medical ethics and research ethics the claim that an autonomous agreement is needed for consent has typically drawn on the more minimal account of what it is for an act to be autonomous proposed by Beauchamp. According to this account three things are needed for an act or agreement to be autonomous: it must be intentional, it must be voluntary, and the actor must have sufficient understanding of what is involved (Beauchamp 2005). However, depending on how it is interpreted even this account may rule out cases in which it appears that an individual has successfully consented.

The key point here is that both voluntariness and understanding come in degrees – we can act more or less voluntarily, and with more or less understanding. As such, on this account the claim that an autonomous act is needed for consent is ambiguous. To avoid that ambiguity we would need to specify what degree of understanding and voluntariness are needed for an act to be autonomous. One option would be to specify these as referring to full understanding and complete voluntariness. However, doing this would lead to the same problems that meant it was implausible to claim that an act that is autonomous in the Kantian or Frankfurtian sense is needed for consent. Many acts that appear intuitively to be successful cases of consenting are not autonomous if this is what is meant by an autonomous act (Felson & Reiner 2011).

At the other extreme we could interpret what it is for an act to be voluntary and made with understanding in a minimal way. On all accounts of autonomy coercion undermines autonomy. As such, acting voluntarily could be interpreted as requiring only that the act was uncoerced.

That in turn plausibly leads to a requirement for a minimal level of understanding – in particular that the person agreeing understands that they have a real choice about whether or not the other person acts in the proposed way (see Manson & O'Neill 2007). This is not, however, the only thing a person would need to understand for their agreement to constitute consent (Manson 2007: 299; Walker 2012). Consent, as we have seen, makes it permissible for another person to act in a certain way. As such, in consenting a person consents to something – for example to their appendix being removed, or to anal sex – and typically does so by agreeing. Because of this the individual consenting must understand something about what is being proposed. Their agreement will not be consent to having their appendix removed unless they understand that they are agreeing to have their appendix removed. Similarly, an individual will not have consented to anal sex unless she understands that she has agreed specifically to anal sex (as opposed to some other sexual act). The information required in this way is, however, minimal – in most cases it will not include information about things like the benefits of the proposed action, any potential harmful consequences, and the method to be used – and much less than is standardly required for informed consent by institutional or regulatory codes. If we interpret the claim that an autonomous act is one that is intentional, voluntary, and done with understanding in this minimal sense, then it may well be plausible to hold that an autonomous act is needed for consent.

However, there appear to be two problems with such an account. First, it is not clear that something so minimal should appropriately be counted as autonomous. The criteria involved appear to amount to no more than those required for an act to be both an uncoerced agreement and one in which the actor understands she is making an uncoerced agreement – to say that S has autonomously agreed to T doing X would amount to saying that S has agreed to T doing X, understands that she has agreed to T doing X, has not been coerced into agreeing, and understands she has a real choice. Second, this account does not capture the idea that consent requires autonomous agreement as this idea has been developed in the literature. That account requires much more in the way of understanding for an act to count as autonomous, even if it does not require full understanding. For example, on Beauchamp and Childress's version of this account, to be sufficiently informed for one's resulting act to be autonomous one needs to understand what is being proposed where this includes: what is to be done, what the benefits of that might be, and what the potential harms or side-effects of the proposed course of action are (Beauchamp & Childress 2009: 117–24).

There is, though, a problem for any account, like that just described, that takes understanding to be required for autonomy and rejects the idea that the required level of understanding is either full understanding or the minimum understanding needed for it to be the case that a person has agreed. This is that, wherever between these two limits the line is drawn, a question will arise about why that level of understanding is needed for an act to be autonomous – rather than slightly more or less understanding. It is not clear that there is any way of drawing this line that would not be arbitrary. One way to respond to this problem would be to adopt a pragmatic approach based on why we want an account of which actions are autonomous in a certain context. If our concern is with consent then the idea would be to determine what information a person needs to understand for their agreement to change the normative situation in the way required for consent (that is, to make permissible something that would otherwise have been impermissible), and then to stipulate that that is the level of understanding needed for an agreement to be autonomous. Such an approach to determining which acts are autonomous, however, would render the claim that consent requires an autonomous act a tautology. This is because an autonomous act would be defined as one that meets the conditions required for consent, and as such the claim "consent requires an autonomous act" would be equivalent to the claim that "consent requires an act that meets the conditions required for consent".

In this section we have been considering whether consent requires an autonomous act. I have argued that it does if we interpret what it is for an act to be autonomous in a very minimal sense (though it may be doubted whether such an account is really an account of autonomy at all). Richer accounts of autonomy do not support the claim that autonomy is needed for consent because there are acts that change the normative landscape in the way that consent does which are not autonomous according to those accounts. There may be one exception to this. As was pointed out earlier, legal consent may require an autonomous act if the law is written in such a way to require this – that is, if the law states that it would be wrong to act in a certain way without the autonomous (on some sense of "autonomous") agreement of another person. Whether any actual laws have this form is an empirical question that would take us too far from our concerns here to investigate. Finally, I argued that the claim that autonomy is needed for consent could be true if what counts as an autonomous act is determined on the basis of what is needed to perform consent. However, in that case the claim is uninteresting because it is true by definition.

12.3 Is consent needed because individuals are autonomous?

The section above focuses on whether only an autonomous act can be an act that does what consent does (that is, make it permissible for someone else to act in a certain way). But this is not the only way in which consent and autonomy might be linked. Some individuals are autonomous and this places limits on what we can do to them without acting wrongly. That is, in virtue of the fact that an individual is autonomous there are things that we should not do (to them). That individual could, however, exercise their autonomy to bring it about that it would not be wrong for us to act in those ways. When they do so they are consenting – they are changing the normative situation to bring it about that something that would otherwise be morally impermissible for some reason is not impermissible for that reason. If this is right then there are some things for which we need consent if we are to avoid acting wrongly where the reason it would be wrong to act without consent stems from the fact that the other person is autonomous. Because acting in these ways without consent would involve failing to treat the individual as is called for by the fact that he or she is autonomous, in the literature the wrong here is standardly referred to as "failing to respect the individual's autonomy".

Before assessing this proposed link between consent and autonomy it is important to be clear about what exactly that link is supposed to be. It is not simply that some individuals are autonomous and it would be wrong to act in certain ways without their consent. Rather, it is that, in virtue of the fact that some individuals are autonomous, acting in certain ways (for example, doing certain things to them) without their consent would be wrong on the grounds of failing to respect their autonomy. This stronger link is needed because there are ways in which it is wrong to treat individuals who are autonomous that are wrong independently of the fact that they are autonomous. For example, where you have agreed that you will not pass information about S on without her consent, it would be wrong to do so – this gives the basis for a duty of confidentiality. But the reason it would be wrong is that you have agreed not to do so, and you should not do those things you have made a commitment not to do. This does not depend on the idea that the person to whom you made that undertaking or commitment is autonomous. That is, the reason it would be wrong is not (or at least not only) that to pass on the information would be to fail to respect S's autonomy. It would be wrong even if S were not autonomous because it would still be an act that breaks a commitment that one has voluntarily undertaken. For it to be the case that an individual's consent to your acting in some way is needed for it not to be wrong on the grounds that it would fail to respect their autonomy for you to do so, three conditions must be met: 1. to act in that way would involve a failure to respect their autonomy if done without their consent, 2. it would not involve a failure to respect their autonomy if done with their consent, and 3. it would be wrong to act in a way that fails to respect their autonomy. These three conditions can only be met by individuals who are autonomous. As such, it would be correct to say that autonomy is needed for consent, but in doing this it is important to distinguish this claim from that made above (that only an autonomous choice can be consent) if we are to avoid misunderstandings.

As with the case of autonomous actions there are a variety of different accounts of what it is for an individual to be autonomous, including: 1. the ability to decide which of her motivational states the individual will act on, 2. independence (or the absence of dependence on others), 3. independence of mind, 4. the right or authority to make decisions for oneself, 5. authenticity, 6. self-identification (that is, being a person with a harmonious and coherent self-image), 7. heroic autonomy as captured in things like Stoic *apathia* or Nietzsche's ideal of the free spirit, and 8. responsiveness to reasons (for an overview of these see Arpaly 2003: 117–48). As such, to assess the claim that S's consent is needed to avoid the wrong of acting in a way that fails to respect her autonomy, which of these accounts of what it is to be autonomous needs to be specified.

When assessing the claim that an autonomous act is needed for consent it was taken to be a desideratum that "autonomous" was interpreted in such a way that virtually all adults could act autonomously (and sometimes do act autonomously). If we do not do this, the claim that an autonomous act is needed for consent will turn out not to be plausible – given that most adults seem to be capable of giving consent. For a related reason in applied ethics the word "autonomous" in the claim that "consent is needed because individuals are autonomous" is standardly interpreted in a way that ensures most adults turn out to be autonomous. Indeed, according to Tom Beauchamp and James Childress, "Law, medicine, and, to some extent, philosophy, presume a context in which the characteristics of a competent person are also the properties possessed by an autonomous person" (Beauchamp & Childress 2009: 113). The reason for this is that nothing that one does could be a failure to respect the autonomy of an individual who is not autonomous – whatever one does it would not be the case that one was acting in a way contrary to that called for given their autonomy (since by definition they are not autonomous). As such, if it is to be the case (1) that consent is needed from all competent adults for things like medical treatment and participation in research and (2) that consent is needed to respect autonomy, then "autonomy" must be interpreted in a way such that all competent adults are autonomous. Accepting this does not rule out the possibility that it would be wrong to treat non-autonomous individuals in these ways. But if doing so is wrong, the reason could not be that to do so is wrong in virtue of the fact that the individual is autonomous (as by stipulation they are not).

This requirement means that some of the accounts of what it is to be autonomous outlined by Arpaly cannot be the correct way to interpret the claim that "consent is needed in order to respect autonomy" as it appears in these debates. For example, it rules out both accounts that take "autonomy" to refer to authenticity or independence, and accounts of heroic autonomy. This is because if we interpret "autonomy" in these ways it will turn out that many adults are not autonomous. Few of us live up to the ideals of Nietzsche or the Stoics, and few of us live authentically in the required sense. Nor, when it comes to things like health care, are we independent. Indeed it is because we are dependent on others for assistance that we seek medical treatment in the first place. Were we really independent then we would not need to do so. As such, these debates in applied ethics make use of either a capacity-based or a sovereignty-based account of autonomy (Wilson 2007). The former takes autonomy to be, as Raanan Gillon puts it, "the ability and tendency to think for oneself, to make decisions for oneself about the way one wishes to lead one's life based on that thinking, and then to act on those decisions . . ." (Gillon 2003: 310; see also Dworkin 1988). That one has this ability or capacity may not in itself be enough to impose requirements on others (or restrictions on what they do). But these will follow if it is in our interest both to be recognized as having this capacity and to be allowed to exercise it. This may well follow from the idea that this capacity is the same as that required for one to be a moral agent. Imposing something on another person who has this capacity would be a case of setting back their interest in being recognized as having that capacity (Dworkin 1988: 100–20; Raz 2001: 169–75). If this is right then it would be wrong to do things like perform surgery on an autonomous individual without his consent because to do so would be to fail to treat him in the way that someone who is autonomous (in this sense) ought to be treated (though this need not be the only reason it would be wrong to perform the surgery without his informed consent). That is, it would be a failure to recognize his interest in being the one to determine whether or not surgery is performed. On the other hand, if he voluntarily agrees to you performing the surgery it will not be a failure of this type – and hence would not be wrong on the grounds of failing to respect his autonomy. This is because in that case the act of seeking his consent to the surgery appropriately acknowledges and recognizes this interest.

According to sovereignty-based accounts, on the other hand, a person is autonomous in virtue of having a certain standing or authority either to make demands on others (Darwall 2006), or over what is done to them (including what medical treatment they receive) (Ripstein 2006; Feinberg 1986: 49–51). To use an example from Darwall – suppose you were to stand on my foot. This would be wrong because in doing so you cause me pain, but Darwall argues that is not the only way it would be wrong. It would also be wrong to stand on my foot because I have the authority to demand of you that you not stand on my foot – and I have that authority in virtue of my being autonomous. If I voluntarily agree to your standing on my foot then things are different. In that case you are not usurping or failing to recognize my authority in this matter. Hence it is not wrong for you to stand on my foot. In this way my voluntary agreement can change the situation from one that is wrong for reasons that stem from the fact that I am autonomous to one that is not wrong for those reasons.

It would appear that a range of activities – including sex, much medical treatment (such as surgery, giving injections, taking blood samples), and much research (particularly research that does something to the participant's body) – would constitute a failure to respect autonomy in one or both of these senses if done without consent. If that is right, then, in order to avoid wrongdoing, consent to things like sex, medical treatment, and research is (at least in some circumstances) needed before having sex, giving medical treatment, or carrying out research. Having said that, three questions still need to be addressed if we are to have a full account of the connection between consent and autonomy:

1. Exactly what things would be a failure to respect S's autonomy if done without S's consent? (This is a question about scope of the connection)
2. Is the claim that it would be a failure to respect S's autonomy (and hence wrong) to do X without S's consent supposed to be the claim that this is *pro tanto* wrong or the claim that it is, all things considered, wrong? (This is a question about the strength of the connection)
3. What conditions need to be met for it to be the case that S has changed the situation to one in which doing X would not be a failure to respect her autonomy? (This is a question about the nature of consent and links back to the discussion in the first part of this chapter.)

The answers to these questions will depend on which account of autonomy is adopted. This is perhaps most clearly seen in relation to the second question. Suppose that an autonomous individual does not consent to something that would prevent her from suffering pain. If we conceptualize autonomy as a capacity to make decisions for oneself and to act on them, then I argued above that this is to take it that it is sometimes wrong to act without a person's consent because to do so would be to set back their interests. However, the interest in being recognized as having this capacity is not the only interest a person has. She also has an interest in not experiencing pain. In that case we have a clash of interests and there seems to be no reason in principle to think that the former will always outweigh the latter. As such, the claim that it would be wrong to act without consent on this account appears to refer to what is at most a *pro tanto* claim – it could in some cases be overridden by other interests the individual has. In contrast, this does not look to be possible on the sovereignty-based account outlined above. To determine that it is better for this person to avoid pain than to do what she chooses is itself to usurp her authority to determine what happens to her. As such, on this type of account the wrong of acting without consent does not look as if it can be outweighed by an interest in avoiding pain (though this is not to say that the claim that it is wrong to act without consent on this interpretation is always wrong, all things considered – it may be permissible to do so to prevent harm to others, for example).

12.4 Conclusion

In this chapter I have argued that "consent" and "autonomy" are potentially related in two very different ways. On some accounts the claim is that consent requires an autonomous act on the part of the individual consenting. As we have seen, however, this is only plausible in contexts such as those involving sex, medical treatment, or research if we interpret "autonomous" in a very minimal sense. This way of interpreting the term may be too minimal and take us too far from central ideas about autonomous action for the resulting account to properly be thought of as an account of autonomous action. On the other hand it has been claimed that the reason consent is needed if we are to avoid wrongdoing is that many people are autonomous. As such, it is argued, we would fail to respect their autonomy if we were to act in certain ways without their consent. As before the plausibility of this claim depends on exactly how we interpret the idea that people are autonomous. I have argued that there are some accounts of autonomy on which it would be a failure to respect autonomy to act in certain ways without consent, but that this is not true of all ways in which we might conceptualize autonomy.

These two different ways of thinking about the relationship between consent and autonomy may in some cases be connected. That is, it may be true both that it would be wrong to act in certain ways without consent because to do so would be to fail to respect an individual's autonomy, and that an autonomous act is needed for them to have consented. But this is not necessarily the case – failing to respect autonomy is not the only way in which we can act wrongly if we act without consent. Furthermore, in this type of situation it is important to bear in mind that the word "autonomy" (or "autonomous") will have different meanings depending on whether we are referring to the wrong that would be done if we were to act without consent or to the features of the act that constitutes that consent.

References

Arpaly, N. (2003) *Unprincipled Virtue: An Inquiry into Moral Agency*. Oxford: Oxford University Press.

Beauchamp, T.L. (2005) "Who Deserves Autonomy, and Whose Autonomy Deserves Respect?," in J.S. Taylor (ed.), *Personal Autonomy: New Essays on Personal Autonomy and Its Role in Contemporary Moral Philosophy*. Cambridge: Cambridge University Press, pp. 310–29.

Beauchamp, T.L. and J.F. Childress (2009) *Principles of Biomedical Ethics*. Sixth Edition. Oxford: Oxford University Press.

Darwall, S. (2006) "The Value of Autonomy and Autonomy of the Will," *Ethics* 116: 263–84.
Dworkin, G. (1988) *The Theory and Practice of Autonomy*. Cambridge: Cambridge University Press.
Feinberg, J. (1986) *The Moral Limits of the Criminal Law: Harm to Self*. New York: Oxford University Press.
Felson, G. and P.B. Reiner (2011) "How the Neuroscience of Decision Making Informs Our Conception of Autonomy," *AJOB Neuroscience* 2(3): 3–14.
Gillon, R. (2003) "Ethics Needs Principles – Four Can Encompass the Rest – and Respect for Autonomy Should Be 'First Among Equals'," *Journal of Medical Ethics* 29: 307–12.
Manson, N. (2007) "Consent and Informed Consent," in R. Ashcroft, A. Dawson, H. Draper and J. McMillan (ed.), *Principles of Health Care Ethics*. Second Edition. Chichester: John Wiley and Sons Ltd., pp. 297–303.
Manson, N. and O. O'Neill (2007) *Rethinking Informed Consent in Bioethics*. Cambridge: Cambridge University Press.
Owens, D. (2012) *Shaping the Normative Landscape*. Oxford: Oxford University Press.
Raz, J. (1986) *The Morality of Freedom*. Oxford: Clarendon Press.
Raz, J. (2001) *Value, Respect, and Autonomy*. Cambridge: Cambridge University Press.
Ripstein, A. (2006) "Beyond the Harm Principle," *Philosophy and Public Affairs* 34(3): 215–45.
Taylor, J.S. (2005) "Introduction," in J.S. Taylor (ed.), *Autonomy: New Essays on Personal Autonomy and Its Role in Contemporary Moral Philosophy*. Cambridge: Cambridge University Press, pp. 1–29.
Walker, T. (2012) "Informed Consent and the Requirement to Ensure Understanding," *Journal of Applied Philosophy* 29(1): 50–62.
Wilson, J. (2007) "Is Respect for Autonomy Defensible?" *Journal of Medical Ethics* 33: 353–6.

Related topics

Ch.8 Valid consent
Ch.11 Moral obligations and consent
Ch.13 Paternalism and consent
Ch.24 Informed consent

13

PATERNALISM AND CONSENT

John Kleinig

13.1 Introduction

At first blush, the topic looks quite straightforward: paternalism just is unconsented-to beneficence, and that's what makes paternalism wrong (insulting, presumptuous, misguided, or counterproductive, to use some of the more common epithets). It's a good start but, as the evolving literature and further reflection make clear, it's not the end of the matter. The complaint needs to be spelled out in more detail and with greater precision, and then a diversity of challenges needs to be reviewed. Some challenges link specifically to the way in which paternalism is characterized. Some focus on the character of the consent. Others challenge the ethical conclusion. I will consider and review each of these options, while developing some conclusions about whether and, if so, under what understanding and in what circumstances paternalism may be justified.

As discussed in the present chapter, the paternalism in question is what is known as strong or hard paternalism – paternalistic impositions on those capable of taking responsibility for their actions.[1] I also take paternalism to refer primarily to a type of reason rather than as a class of act – that is, what are referred to as paternalistic acts are those in which paternalistic reasons are given a significant or determinative justificatory role rather than those for which benevolence is the sole motive. To take a well-known example, although seat belt laws probably constitute good public policy (lowered health and insurance costs) as well as protect people against the possible consequences of their risky decision making, some critical justificatory role is played by the paternalistic determination not to leave risk taking to motorists' discretion.

13.2 Paternalism

Let me start with a plausible enough definition of paternalism as a benevolently motivated imposition on another. Note that this definition does not make reference to consent (unlike the account provided in the first sentence of this essay). I will soon return to the reason for this.

The present account also makes reference to benevolence rather than beneficence, to indicate the concern with motivation rather than outcome. That may be important, because one of the frequent complaints about paternalism is that it is misguided: what the paternalist believes to be for the other person's good or welfare is not what the recipient considers to be the case.[2] To the extent that paternalistically motivated conduct and policies secure the welfare of others, whose judgment as to welfare should prevail? It was the contention of John Stuart Mill that individuals are more likely to be better judges of their welfare than others (Mill 1859: ch. 4). That, of course, is an empirically based normative claim and, even if it is fine as a generalization, it is problematic in some cases. If I take away the car keys of a friend who has been partying and put him into a taxi, even though he insists that he is sober enough to drive, I may well be in a better position than he to make a wise judgment. Sometimes one will be thanked for acting thus – though whether that could or should constitute a justification is contentious (Kasachkoff 1994; Chwang 2009).[3] When Jon Corzine refused to wear a seat belt so that he could conduct New Jersey gubernatorial business more easily with his fellow passengers, he knowingly placed his short-term convenience above his long-term welfare. Or, to complicate the matter even further, he drew questionable inferences from data about probabilities. Following the accident that almost killed him, he affirmed the wisdom of the law he had ignored (Hester 2008).

Even with these qualifications, we should probably distinguish those cases in which what is imposed on the other is something that the other can or does recognize as being for his good and what only (or only at that time) the paternalist deems to be for that other's good. When Ulysses, desiring to hear the Sirens, asked to be bound to his ship's mast and not untied even if he begged for it, he acknowledged what could harm him, and the act of his men in leaving him tied while he listened to the Sirens' song represents a form of paternalism that did not violate his own judgment of what was good for him (Homer *Odyssey* bk. 12).[4] However, should Brian prevent Alice from getting tattoos on the ground that she will later come to regret it, Brian may or may not be right about what she will later think about her tattoos. His interference, nevertheless, does not reflect Alice's judgment about what is good for her, even if, later on, she comes to share it.[5]

Paternalistic impositions may be direct – as in the case of seat belts – as well as indirect. They are indirect when the imposition is placed on someone who acts with the consent (or at the request) of the person whose welfare is thereby endangered. An indirectly paternalistic imposition might be one that requires parents to have their newborn tested for diseases[6] or that penalizes a doctor who accedes to the request to remove an otherwise healthy limb.[7] Although my focus in this chapter is mostly on the relevance of consent, it straddles the direct/indirect divide.

Let me return to the distinction between beneficent impositions and unconsented-to beneficence. An older discussion of paternalism would probably not have been concerned to differentiate them, considering them coextensive. But dissatisfaction with both traditional hard paternalism and its laissez-faire alternative, coupled with the development of behavioral economics, has led to the formulation of what has been dubbed *liberal* or *libertarian paternalism*, a strategy in which, for paternalistic reasons, certain measures are imposed, but without undermining consent. Its most prominent advocates have been Thaler & Sunstein (2008). Their widely discussed book, *Nudge*,[8] begins with a simple and plausible assumption – viz., that all our decisional transactions take place within a context, and this context has a structural impact (at least) on our decision making. Given that assumption, the question arises: where we are able to affect the decisional process, what restructurings are permissible? So far as "health, wealth, and happiness" are concerned, Thaler and Sunstein argue that decisions concerning our own health, wealth, and happiness can be enhanced by restructurings that are (also) likely to reflect our own deepest commitments concerning optimal decision making.

This chapter, however, is not the place for a discussion of what purports to be paternalism that is compatible with consent. Libertarian paternalism has garnered plenty of critical discussion (Hausman & Welch 2010; Blumenthal-Barby & Burroughs 2012; White 2013), including discussions about whether and when it challenges the traditional problematic of paternalism.

13.3 Paternalism and consent

Standard cases of paternalism involve more than the impositions to which libertarian paternalists supposedly refer. They compromise consent in some significant way, and it is because of this that they generally lack the support that "libertarian paternalism" has garnered in some circles. Consent, indeed, is usually considered to be so important to what might otherwise be seen as paternalistic transactions that highly problematic efforts are sometimes made to insinuate some reference to it into such engagements. So there are references to "prior consent", "anticipated consent", "subsequent consent", "hypothetical consent", and "tacit consent". In some, but not all, of these cases legitimate consent may be involved, but to a significant extent they draw on the moral significance of consent to legitimate what are often questionable paternalistic intrusions (Kleinig 1984: 55–67).

So I return to paternalism as it is usually conceived – viz. unconsented-to beneficence – and thus to what in liberal circles is usually opposed just because (informed or full or robust) consent is lacking. The bracketed qualification is important, because what is consented to as a result of deception may carry some of the important marks of consent, but lack others. Paternalism generally involves some compromise of consent, even if it is not coercive. So, first of all, what is it about consent that is so important and that therefore makes hard paternalism particularly problematic?

13.3.1 The moral significance of consent

Consent is often said to be morally transformative, and it is important to determine how and why this may be the case. If Alice wants Brian's bicycle she may simply take it. Alternatively, she may ask Brian, and he may consent to her having it, temporarily or permanently. In the first case, what she does constitutes theft or robbery. In the second case, the bicycle is a loan or gift. Brian's consent transforms the moral quality (and description) of what is done.

The underlying reason for this is that Brian has some special normative claim to the bicycle (in this case, ownership), and Alice's access requires Brian's dispensation (consent). Similar stories may be told about other transactions between Alice and Brian. Where one wants what the other has *as of right*,[9] then the transaction will be violative if it takes place in the absence of the other's consent.

This reflects something special about humans and their relationships.[10] At bottom, the need for consent in such transactions acknowledges that "the other" has a special claim to that which is sought, a claim ultimately rooted in a special status that we often characterize in dignitarian terms, though the status may be cast in other ways. We may resort to the language of self-authorship, of autonomy, of being the object of respect or possessor of rights. Although in some contexts it would be appropriate to explore the relations, nuances, and differences registered by these different manners of speaking, here it would take us too far afield (Kleinig & Evans 2013).

More appropriate to the present undertaking, and for the purpose of exploring its implications for the discussion of impositions, we need to consider the conditions under which a morally robust consent may be said to be given. That will help us to better understand the relations between consent and imposition and also to see more clearly what it is about consent that enables it to be morally transformative.

13.3.2 Conditions for consent

Other contributors to the present volume will have much more to say about the conditions of consent, and so I will indicate only briefly what I believe these conditions to be before suggesting how they contribute to consent's morally transformative character (see, further, Kleinig 1998, 2009, 2013). Four interconnected conditions are important – what I refer to as signification, competence, voluntariness, and intentions.

Consent is a communicative act, not simply an internal wish or desire. No matter what Anne feels, if she does not *signify* her consent to Bruce, he assaults her if he has sex with her. And that consent, once signified, may be withdrawn.[11] Signification, however, is not enough – assent is not consent. If Anne consents to Bruce's request for sex, she must be *competent* to do so, where competence is a function of various psycho-social factors. A related but distinct consideration is *voluntariness*. If Brian threatens Alice with harm if she does not lend him her bicycle, or Amelia is told that she will not be appointed to a position unless she works for below-minimum pay rates, then compliance will fall below what consent requires in terms of voluntariness. Such voluntariness will be a matter of degree, and, for consent to be valid, it will need to rise above a certain threshold.[12]

A further – and related – consideration is that consent should meet a certain *epistemic threshold*. When Alexis consents to invest her savings with Barry, the genuineness of her consent requires that she has – or has at least had adequate access to – certain information about her investment that allows us to say that her decision is responsibly taken. We have developed certain conventions about the threshold of knowledge that a person should have where monies are to be invested or medical decisions are made. A final – also related – consideration focuses on the *intentions* of the consenter. If Alice asks for Brian's bicycle and Brian consents, believing that she only wants to borrow it, he has a cause against her if she then keeps it or gives it away to someone else. Consent is usually bounded in some way, either explicitly or contextually. This is one reason why signification can be so important – lest one party to the transaction is disappointed or worse. If I consent to your use of my car, I do not *ipso facto* consent to your using it as a getaway car in a bank robbery.

True, there are some fuzzy edges here. We can debate the adequacy of a particular signification, the competence of the supposed consenter, the voluntariness of a proffered consent, whether the consent was backed by adequate knowledge, and the scope of what was consented to.

What drives such discussion is a quest to specify the conditions under which consent will be morally transformative; that is, the conditions under which, say, Alice's act of taking Brian's bicycle does not violate some special claim that Brian has to the bicycle, or Bruce's sexual intimacy with Anne does not constitute sexual assault or fraud of some kind. These consent conditions must be such as to place responsibility for Alice's taking the bicycle with Brian or Bruce's sexual intimacy with Anne. More deeply, these conditions recognize Brian and Anne as agents who have a moral entitlement to control their possessions and bodies. It is that moral entitlement that is grounded in the status they have as persons.

This is one reason why, even though Mill sometimes suggests that what is most wrong with paternalism is the fact that paternalists are less likely to make good judgments about the welfare of others than those others themselves, the deeper reason usually seen for opposing paternalism is that it violates the claims that others have by virtue of their status as persons – whether that is cashed out in terms of rights, dignity, respect, self-government, sovereignty, or autonomy.

13.4 Paternalism and the limits of consent

Given what I have so far said about the background to consent and what it achieves, it would seem reasonable to conclude that hard paternalism cannot be justified. That, certainly, is a common understanding of the matter. An old maxim – *volenti non fit injuria* (to the one who consents no wrong is done) – captures this well. Although the maxim has its origins – and, perhaps, its most common invocations – in civil liability law, it is frequently deployed in criminal contexts. And although it's a jurisprudential principle, it is commonly seen as reflecting a fundamental truth about individual sovereignty:

I am the master of my fate
I am the captain of my soul (Henley 1888 [1875]).

On this understanding, the paternalist, no matter how compassionately or benevolently motivated, violates a fundamental moral boundary. Although we may advise and perhaps even warn others about the self-harming consequences of their actions, we may not interfere.

That this is a well-supported view cannot be denied. And yet most societies have been unwilling to translate it into a robust policy. True, some have been willing to intervene only as a civil matter, but even most liberal societies have not been willing to forgo all criminal sanctions when people harm themselves or consent to be harmed. When Armin Meiwes found someone willing to participate in the realization of his cannibalistic fantasies (Bernd Brandes), the German authorities did not acquiesce in the fact that the occasion was consensual (Bergelson 2008b; Reid 2014). Initially, they took his victim's consent into account and he was convicted only of manslaughter and sentenced to 8½ years in prison. But a public outcry along with appeals by both prosecution and defense led to a new trial in which Meiwes was convicted of murder and sentenced to life imprisonment. Although some commentators think that Meiwes was unfairly treated (Wisnewski 2007) – there was no question that the killing and eating was consensual – most appeared to think that even though the act was consensual he had done something seriously wrong and that criminal charges were appropriate. Why is this so?

In some respects it does not matter too much whether the criminal law is invoked in such cases or some other kind of legal intervention is involved. Obviously, criminal charges carry a condemnatory message that may not be involved in other interventions. But in each case the intervention can count as paternalistic – preventing if not punishing someone for consenting to self-regarding harm. What, if anything, enables us to differentiate consensual cannibalism from cases in which consent offers a complete defense?

Four considerations may contribute to a differentiation:

(1) One broad philosophical strategy is to question the moral weight that the anti-paternalistic argument accords to autonomy or, put somewhat differently, the absoluteness of the individual sovereignty that argument is said to support. In other words, it might be argued that although consent is very important, and carries significant moral weight, it may not always be determinative. Something of this kind appears to have influenced the initial decision of the German court. Given that there was no statute outlawing cannibalism, and that Brandes clearly consented to what was done, Meiwes was initially convicted of manslaughter rather than murder. Brandes's consent did not carry the day, but it counted for something.

So, although we might wish to argue for a strong presumption in favor of individual autonomy – including allowing people's self-regarding decisions to stand, even though they are risky, unwise, or self-harming – it is arguably fetishistic to absolutize it. If Ambrose chooses to place himself at considerable risk for the thrill of skylarking, subway surfing, or some forms of planking, should we stop at warning him of the risks involved, or might we adopt stronger measures by either physically preventing him or penalizing him if he foolishly chooses to run them?[13] The same might be asked of consensual brawling (Syrota 1996). If two men decide to settle their differences with their fists or baseball bats or, in a past era, by duelling[14], should we let them go ahead? There may of course be some non-intrusive way of preventing some of these behaviors from occurring. But the question remains: should any and every encroachment on individual autonomy, no matter how small, except for other-regarding reasons, represent an impermissible violation? Is individual sovereignty inviolable?

It is not obvious that we should answer these questions affirmatively. The political metaphor of sovereignty is instructive: although we grant some form of Westphalian sovereignty to countries, we take seriously the question of whether it should be considered absolute. Whether we cast our question in terms of "humanitarian intervention" or "the responsibility to protect", we do not automatically presume that sovereignty excludes all outside interventions. There were strong reasons for intervention in Rwanda. True, a libertarian might argue that countries are not individuals, and that in such cases we are concerned about securing some individuals from the predations of others, but, insofar as the political metaphor is used, we should not assume that it possesses an absoluteness in the individual case that it does not have in its primary context. Some encroachments will be more invasive than others; some avoided consequences more injurious than others. This is one reason why opposition to seat belt legislation appears excessive. Too little freedom is involved, and the aggregative benefits are considerable. True, once we make exceptions, the specter of a slippery slope begins to loom. But there are slopes and slopes and, despite the doomsayers, if the slope begins to look too steep or the trade-off unreasonable, people will resist. In other words, if consent is infringed for paternalistic reasons, we need not see such infringements as all-of-a-piece. Some infringements will be more serious than others, and some paternalistic concerns will be weightier than others.

(2) An absolutist position needs, moreover, to be tempered by the data of behavioral economics to which I have already referred. Even those who have reached the stage at which they can and should take responsibility for their decisions are notoriously unreliable when it comes to decisions that impact on their welfare. Humans are wilfully careless, impulsive, and poor calculators of risk taking. Contrast the findings of behavioral economists with what Mill writes (1859: ch. 4):

> neither one person, nor any number of persons, is warranted in saying to another human creature of ripe years, that he shall not do with his life for his own benefit what he chooses to do with it. He is the person most interested in his own well-being: the interest which any other person, except in cases of strong personal attachment, can have in it, is trifling, compared with that which he himself has; the interest which society has in him individually (except as to his conduct to others) is fractional, and altogether indirect: while, with respect to his own feelings and circumstances, the most ordinary man or woman has means of knowledge immeasurably surpassing those that can be possessed by any one else. The interference of society to overrule his judgment and purposes in what only regards himself, must be grounded on general presumptions; which may be altogether wrong, and even if right, are as likely as not to be misapplied to individual cases, by persons no better acquainted with the circumstances of such cases than those are who look at them merely from without. . . . Considerations to aid his judgment, exhortations to strengthen his will, may be offered to him, even obtruded on him, by others; but he himself is the final judge. All errors which he is likely to commit against advice and warning, are far outweighed by the evil of allowing others to constrain him to what they deem his good.

Mill is making a number of empirical claims here: (1) with the possible exception of those who have "strong personal attachments", individuals are much more interested in their well-being than others, individually and collectively; (2) individuals have direct access to what will serve their well-being, whereas the knowledge that others have will only be indirect, and because of this directness, especially with regard to circumstances and feelings, an individual's knowledge (of what will serve his well-being) will "far surpass" that possessed by others; (3) even if others have better knowledge than an individual of what will serve that individual's well-being, as likely as not they will misapply that knowledge; and (4) it is likely to turn out far better for an individual's judgment and resolution if others limit themselves to advice and admonitions.

At some level, Mill's cautions are well-advised. We certainly do not want a society in which people interfere willy nilly with the self-regarding acts of others because they judge them to be acting unwisely. Although the presumptuousness of busybodies may not be the worst thing about them, there is, nevertheless, that presumptuousness. Advice and exhortation should ordinarily be the extent of our intervention into their self-regarding affairs, and often not even that. Barring the kind of situation that Mill had in mind when sanctioning interference with someone ignorantly about to cross an unsafe bridge (Mill 1859: ch. 5), as individuals we are not generally well placed to know what will or will not protect the well-being of others.

But should we allow these supposedly empirical claims to pass without qualification? Once we not only have the data from behavioral economics, but also understand some of the mechanisms involved in our poor individual decision making, might there not be an argument for some elective paternalism even when it is not (initially) consented to? I say "initially", because what we might initially resist as governmental or other intrusion, we may subsequently come to see as wise policy. We have, for example, data from compulsory seat belt wearing that lets us know, collectively, that most of us are better off individually if we wear them than if we are or had been left to decide for ourselves. We now have data about trans fats that make bans on their use in commercial cooking better for us, given the small gains from their use (Rajczi 2013). Of course, to the extent that enough of us are individually better off as the result of such interferences, we are also likely to be better off societally. That is, there will be a collective benefit if enough of us individually benefit.

Let me be clear. This is not to sanction paternalistic interferences without constraint or in the face of significant public opposition. No legislation should be too far in advance of public opinion. The time may come when cigarette smoking can be banned, but that time is not yet, and such paternalism is limited to "sin taxing" and similar measures. Also, of course, where education and admonition show good results, we should limit ourselves to education and admonition. And where we can achieve good results through minor impositions – as with nudge architecture – we should content ourselves with that. But there will almost certainly be cases in which our shortsightedness or our tendency to take risks expose us to significant harms that could be obviated by means of relatively small evidence-based interferences with our easily flawed judgment, and in these cases coercive measures that are paternalistically motivated may be justified. Clearly there will need to be some balancing or trade-off involved. We will want to know about the magnitude of the harms in question, about their reversibility, about the probability of the harms occurring, the size of the constraint on liberty, and we may of course also want to see whether similar results can be obtained at less cost. Might cars be constructed so that we need to take a breath test before we start them?

What we might reasonably argue in the case of such empirical judgments is that paternalistic interferences be reviewed on a regular basis and revised or abandoned in the event that the data fail to support them.

In several articles on legal hard paternalism, Vera Bergelson has offered two additional reasons for making exceptions to the consent exemption (Bergelson 2007, 2008a, 2008b).

(3) Where consented-to intrusions are seriously disabling, they are to be distinguished from cases in which consent is morally transformative. There is something inherently problematic

about injuring or killing a(nother) human being. True, such acts are sometimes self-defensive and justified on that account, but even in those cases the onus is on the person who injures or kills to justify the injury or killing. In such cases, harm is done, whether or not the person consents. If Arthur asks Bronwyn to shoot him, then, if Bronwyn does so, the injury caused by the shooting does not become less so because it was consented to: Arthur will be wounded or killed.

Such cases are to be distinguished from some of those we considered earlier. If Anne and Bruce become sexually intimate or if Alice uses Brian's bicycle, there is nothing inherently problematic about their acts. It is the consent or lack thereof that determines whether or not what was done was harmful, morally acceptable, or unacceptable.

The issue then will be to draw the line between acts whose morally problematic character is solely a function of their consensuality, and those whose character is inherently problematic, even if consent makes *some* difference to how we view what is done. Whether or not what is done is viewed as harmful – independent of considerations of consent – may not always be easy to determine. People who undergo extreme body modification for aesthetic or other reasons may not see themselves as harmed, even though the results sometimes appear quite bizarre (Wikipedia Editors "Body Modification"; Anon. 2015).

One consideration might be whether or not what is consented to is disabling – so that, for example, we are not merely considering aesthetics but also function, and as long as what has been consented to is not severely disruptive of functionality, then we may consider the harm ignorable. But that now raises questions about self-regarding or consented-to conduct that is disabling – for example, people with BIID, who see certain bodily parts – say, arms or legs – as grotesque protrusions of which they wish to rid themselves.

If BIID is not to be prevented, we may require a further consideration – whether on balance more good than harm is done. If the person with BIID is rendered so distraught by his arms or legs that his peace of mind is purchasable only at the cost of removing one or more limbs (there being no less invasive means available), then we might consider it regrettable but acceptable if the offending limbs are removed: what is physically disabling may be mentally liberating. An argument such as this might also be advanced in some cases in which voluntary euthanasia is sought.[15] In cases such as these, well-being is more than a matter of what we would ordinarily see as bodily integrity.

Particularly controversial as well as instructive was the British case of *R. v. Brown* (1993), which concerned a group of homosexuals who periodically indulged in various sado-masochistic practices. The videotapes they made were shared only among themselves.[16] Although injuries were sometimes sustained – injuries that would have attracted criminal penalties had they been inflicted without consent – they were not "serious or permanent". Moreover, the activities did not "get out of hand", and the consensual behavior took place in settings that excluded observation by unwilling others. After a trial judge ruled that consent could not be advanced as a defense, the men pleaded guilty inter alia to assault occasioning actual bodily harm and appealed to have the fact of their consent deemed relevant. Eventually, in a 3–2 decision, the House of Lords determined that it was not necessary to show lack of consent to hold them guilty of the offenses for which they were charged.[17]

This was a difficult case because, although injuries were sustained, they were not "serious or permanent". Additionally, in this case, the activities were conducted in private, and the tapes were not intended for public distribution. It was not "public indecency". The public interest case for intervening was therefore questionable.[18] What probably persuaded the court was the fact that the injuries were serious enough to have attracted a criminal penalty had no consent been given.

Even so, it is asserted in this case that "it is not in the public interest that people should try to cause, or should cause, each other actual bodily harm for no good reason" (Attorney-General's Reference 1981: 719). The best I can make of this is that the benefit to those involved (satisfaction of sado-masochistic desires) was not of a kind that, if ignored, served a public interest that would outweigh the harm caused by the acts in question. The question was one of whether sado-masochistic satisfactions carried enough social weight to outweigh the harms that were inflicted, even though they were not seriously disabling. For controversial reasons of its own, the court decided that they did not – even though they may have been important to the participants.

Contrast this with the case of consensual flagellation or crucifixion, where the motivation is religious. Because religious reasons are still given considerable weight in human affairs, even trumping many other societal considerations, the reasons that we would have for intruding on such inherently harmful conduct are often allowed to pass. Indeed, the religious reasons, autonomously or consensually held, are often considered to be morally transformative in this limited case: it is no longer whipping but "mortification of the flesh", an act of piety and cleansing, or of "participating in the sufferings of Christ for the world" (Camporesi 1983/1988; Glucklich 2003). To allow such "transformation" does not of course amount to approving the behavior in question. Someone may disapprove of going to prostitutes without seeing what is done as rape or assault.

Even if we accept self-harm or consented-to harm as a reason for coercive and thus paternalistic intervention, it need not follow that such interventions are punitive. In *Brown* they probably were because the harms in question were other-regarding, but if we were to intervene in a case of (attempted) suicide, we might opt for a non-punitive intervention.

(4) The second consideration advanced by Bergelson focuses on dignitarian concerns.[19] The moral power of consent is diminished when what is consented to undermines that person's dignity.

Bergelson considers situations in which we act differently to the mutilation of human bodies – on the one hand, to conducting autopsies, and on the other, to using dead bodies as crash dummies – and asks why we are inclined to different responses. For obvious reasons, it is not about the invasion of autonomy. Rather, she suggests, the former is not disrespectful of human dignity whereas the latter is. This dignitarian consideration may help to explain why we would want to outlaw consensual gladiatorial contests, despite the fact that they would be autonomously agreed to. Revulsion associated with the Meiwes/Brandes cannibalism case might also be linked with dignitarian concerns, given that the events and what led to them was a matter of record.

One deeper reason for this, though not one that Bergelson explores, is that consent in human transactions is required by human dignity. We detract from the dignitarian status of others when we treat them in ways that detract from that dignity. That is often clear in cases of rape, where unequal power and the degrading reduction of another to a sexual object are said to deny the dignity of another. But it might also be argued of certain cases in which people consent to being treated in ways that subject them to others or objectify them in certain respects. In such cases, consenting to what undermines one's dignitarian status is self-defeating if thought to express that status. In his rejection of self-enslavement, Mill argues that it is not freedom to alienate one's freedom (Mill 1859: ch. 5). Mill might have made his point less paradoxically had he said that it is not an expression of one's dignity to give up one's dignitarian status.

I do not suggest that dignitarian concerns are by themselves sufficient to justify hard paternalism. The question is whether they provide some plausible reason that, along with others, whether paternalistic or not, might provide a good enough reason for intervention. Nor do I argue that the form of intervention has to be formal (legal) or criminal. The Millian argument opposes any form of social interference with others that is motivated by considerations of their well-being (Mill 1859: ch. 1).

Dignity is a complex notion and writers have discerned several different kinds of dignity. Elsewhere I have distinguished and linked status dignity with what is sometimes termed comportment dignity – a standing that we share as human beings but that may be expected to express itself in certain ways (Kleinig & Evans 2013). Sometimes we may act in ways that are incompatible with our status dignity. Obviously, some judgment may need to be exercised as to whether a particular way of comporting oneself erodes one's status dignity to the extent that it constitutes a reason for the intervention of others (leaving the form of appropriate intervention unspecified at this stage). The practice or "sport" of dwarf-tossing is a case in point. Whereas it has sometimes been outlawed as degrading to those who are tossed, quite apart from injuries that may be caused, others, including some of those who have been tossed, have objected to the deprivation of a source of income.[20] More problematic was a German case in which mechanical "peep show" performances were outlawed on the grounds of their inherently undignifying character (Federal Administrative Tribunal 1981). Here, apparently, the "mechanical" nature of the arrangement was thought to make it more degrading than the personally engaged and interactive (albeit still somewhat objectifying) sexual performances of a strip club. In some of these cases one might suspect that what is at issue is rather more moralistic – a concern with indecency as much as indignity.

Similar dignitarian concerns manifest themselves in some arguments for voluntary euthanasia. Arguments against voluntary euthanasia sometimes see it as incompatible with a person's dignitarian status; those who favor it also appeal to dignity and the importance of "death with dignity", linking death to a concern that it not be marked by events that are seen as degrading to our persons – loss of control, humiliating situations, etc.

If, as has often been the case, we are inclined to oppose requests to be put to death or helped to die on grounds that killing someone is prima facie harmful (consideration (3) above), the argument of those who support some provision for voluntary euthanasia is that it enables a person to die in a manner that is expressive of both status and comportment dignity. In such cases, then, there is a balancing or trade-off in which a judgment about benefits and harms must be made.

Taken together, the foregoing four considerations provide, if not an unassailable argument, at least a powerful set of reasons for thinking that even robust consent – consent that expresses a willingness to take responsibility for what one does to oneself or requests or accedes to – may not always trump paternalistic interventions by others. This is not to say that robust consent or responsibility should be discounted altogether, only that in such cases it may not be sufficient to transform that which was wrong into that which is justified.

13.5 Conclusion

To the extent that we are willing to countenance libertarian paternalism as a form of paternalism, then it is possible to conceive of a range of cases in which paternalism may not be incompatible with robust consent. But there is a serious question whether the imposed benevolence that motivates libertarian paternalism is sufficient to characterize it as a form of paternalism. The more central cases – and those that, from a liberal perspective, make paternalism morally problematic – are ones in which robust consent is qualified in some significant way or is altogether absent. In these cases the lack of consent's morally transformative presence renders such paternalism deeply problematic. However, it may not be so problematic as to rule out all forms of paternalistic intervention. Despite the moral power of robust consent, there may need to be complex judgments that take into account the coherence of the interference with the person's known values, the extent of the intrusion, the magnitude of the harm to be prevented, the probability of the harm occurring, and the relationship between the paternalist and the paternalized person. Even in liberal societies consent is rarely recognized as sufficient to sanction certain types of serious harms to self. Reasons for such constraints on the moral suasiveness of consent can be found in four considerations: doubts about the inviolability of autonomy, skepticism about human rationality, the inherently problematic character of certain harms, and the weight of human dignity.

Notes

1 Two points are important here: (1) I do not want to suggest that no ethical questions are raised by "soft" paternalism. They are. Most of them, however, are also questions for hard paternalism, and it is hard paternalism that generates the most difficult ethical challenges. (2) I appreciate that my reference to "capacity for taking responsibility" does not mesh exactly with certain formal criteria, such as "being 18", or even with graduated criteria such as "14" as the age of consent for undergoing surgery, "16" for wearing a seat belt, "18" for driving a car, and "21" for consuming alcohol. As a matter of public policy we probably need proxies or bright lines; my criterion is intended to inform (often controversial) decisions about where such bright lines are most efficiently drawn.

2 A further qualification here might be that the "good or welfare" in question is to be understood as "harm minimization" rather than "welfare advancement". The latter is often included when soft paternalism is involved. Most cases of hard paternalism are construed in terms of harm prevention.

3 There is of course also the question of whether, say, friends have moral entitlements that, say, strangers or governments don't have (Richards 1989; Fox 1993).

4 We might compare this with multi-venue self-exclusion programs that authorize gambling casinos to refuse one entry for a determinate period (National Center for Responsible Gambling 2010). Some such programs also exist for problem drinkers.

5 Again, I am presuming that Alice is a responsible adult.

6 There might of course be debate about what diseases are tested for.

7 See the famous case of *R. v. Wright* (1603). This has also been an issue in BIID cases (Elliott 2000; Bayne & Levy 2005).

8 Although influential, their book can probably be criticized for ranging more widely than their paradigm cases, and hence more widely than can easily be encompassed by their conception of libertarian paternalism.

9 I use this phrase as one of a number that might be employed to indicate the normative priority that consent "surmounts".

10 If I cut the limb off a tree in the wild, I do it no wrong. I need not first seek its "consent". Consent operates within the realm of human relationships, and within the realm of human relationships of a particular kind.

11 Whether consent – given and then withdrawn – should have negative consequences will depend on the situation. Sometimes withdrawing consent may unjustifiably disadvantage someone who has relied on it. In rare cases, consent may be virtually irrevocable. See n. 4 above for an example.

12 When Joel Valdez broke into Elizabeth Wilson's apartment, put a knife to her throat, and demanded sex, Wilson said she would comply, provided that Valdez used a condom (which he did). Subsequently, a grand jury refused to indict Valdez on the ground that Wilson's request that he wear a condom indicated her consent. Given the circumstances – Wilson's fear of physical injury or HIV infection, the fact that she tried to dial 911, and her subsequent naked flight from her apartment – there is good reason, notwithstanding a Texas grand jury's decision, to believe that her compliance did not rise to a morally relevant threshold for voluntariness (da Luz & Weckerly 1993). Equally egregious, it used to be the case that unless there was evidence of physical injury, a woman could not establish that she was raped.

13 Skylarking involves clinging to the side of a moving subway train, and surfing involves lying on the top of a moving train (Wikipedia Editors, "Train Surfing"; Wikipedia Editors, "Planking (a fad)").

14 Not all see anti-duelling laws in this way (Arneson 1980).

15 Harm or benefit to whom? Such a case would require that we allow death to count as a benefit to the person in question.

16 The case was widely discussed (Bamforth 1994; Moran 1995; Bronitt & McSherry 2010, for an update on the literature).

17 Some of the participants subsequently appealed (unsuccessfully) to the European Court of Human Rights (*Laskey, Jaggard and Brown v. The United Kingdom* (1997)).

18 It is clear, though, from some of the judicial comments, that moral disapproval also figured: "perverted and depraved sexual desire", as one of the judges (Lord Lowry) put it. Whether or not that was the case, it ought not to have figured in the judicial decision.

19 I have explored some of these concerns myself in Kleinig (2017 [2010]).

20 In 1995 when the French Conseil d'État (Commune de Morsang-sur-Orge) ruled that dwarf-tossing, even when consented to, violated "ordre public" because it compromised human dignity to allow oneself to be used as a mere thing (Conseil d'État 1995). In the United States, dwarf-tossing is prohibited in a number of states – partly in response to representations by members of Little People of America.

References

Anon. (2015) "International Tattoo Festival Leaves its Mark on Venezuela," Telegraph Video (January 31). www.telegraph.co.uk/news/worldnews/southamerica/venezuela/11381515/International-tattoo-festival-leaves-its-mark-on-Venezuela.html

Arneson, R. (1980) "Mill versus Paternalism," *Ethics* 90: 470–89.

Attorney-General's Reference (No. 6 of 1980) (1981) QB 715 at 719, cited in *R. v. Brown.*

Bamforth, N. (1994) "Sado-Masochism and Consent," *Criminal Law Review* 1994: 661–5.

Bayne, T. and N. Levy (2005) "Amputees By Choice: Body Integrity Identity Disorder and the Ethics of Amputation," *Journal of Applied Philosophy* 22: 75–86.

Bergelson, V. (2007) "The Right to Be Hurt: Testing the Boundaries of Consent," *George Washington Law Review* 75: 165–236.

Bergelson, V. (2008a) "Consent to Harm," *Pace Law Review* 28: 683–711.

Bergelson, V. (2008b) "Autonomy, Dignity, and Consent to Harm," *Rutgers Law Review* 60: 723–36.

Blumenthal-Barby, J.S. and H. Burroughs (2012) "Seeking Better Health Care Outcomes: The Ethics of Using the 'Nudge'," *American Journal of Bioethics* 12: 1–10.

Bronitt, S. and B. McSherry (2010) *Principles of Criminal Law.* Third Edition. Pyrmont, NSW: Law Book Co./Thomson Reuters.

Camporesi, P. (1983; trans. 1988) *The Incorruptible Flesh: Bodily Mutation and Mortification in Religion and Folklore*, trans. T. Croft-Murray. Cambridge, UK: Cambridge University Press.

Chwang, E. (2009) "A Defense of Subsequent Consent," *Journal of Social Philosophy* 40: 117–31.

Conseil d'État (1995) www.conseil-etat.fr/ce/jurisp/index_ju_la47.shtml (October 27).

da Luz, C.M. and P.C. Weckerly (1993) "The Texas 'Condom-Rape' Case: Caution Construed as Consent," *UCLA Women's Law Journal* 3: 95–104.

Elliott, C. (2000) "A New Way to Be Mad," *Atlantic Monthly* 286(6): 72–84.

Federal Administrative Tribunal (1981) "Sittenwidrigkeit von Peep-Shows," *Bundesverwaltungsgericht* (BVerwGE) 64: 274.

Fox, E.L. (1993) "Paternalism and Friendship," *Canadian Journal of Philosophy* 23: 575–94.

Glucklich, A. (2003) *Sacred Pain: Hurting the Body for the Sake of the Soul.* New York: Oxford University Press.

Hausman, D.M. and B. Welch (2010) "Debate: To Nudge or Not to Nudge," *Journal of Political Philosophy* 18: 123–36.

Henley, W.E. (1888 [1875]) "Invictus," originally published without title in *Book of Verses*, London: D. Nutt (written 1875, published 1888), 56–7.

Hester, Jr., T. (2008) "Corzine Backs Seat Belts for All Jersey Passengers," *Courier-Post* (March 26). www.courierpostonline.com/apps/pbcs.dll/article?AID=/20080326/NEWS01/80326035

Homer (trans. 1999) *The Odyssey*, bk 12, trans. R. Fagles. New York: Penguin.

Kasachkoff, T. (1994) "Paternalism: Does Gratitude Make It Okay?," *Social Theory and Practice* 20: 1–23.

Kleinig, J. (1984) *Paternalism.* Totowa, NJ: Rowman and Allanheld.

Kleinig, J. (1998) "Consent, Problems of," in L.C. Becker and C.B. Becker (eds.) *Encyclopedia of Ethics.* Second Edition, Vol. I. Detroit, MI: Gale, 299–304.

Kleinig, J. (2009) "The Nature of Consent," in F.G. Miller and A. Wertheimer (eds.) *The Ethics of Consent: Theory and Practice.* New York: Oxford University Press, 3–24.

Kleinig, J. (2013) "Consent," in H. LaFollette (ed.) *International Encyclopedia of Ethics.* Norton, MA: Wiley-Blackwell. http://onlinelibrary.wiley.com/doi/10.1002/9781444367072.wbiee377/full.

Kleinig, J. (2017 [2010]) "Paternalism and Human Dignity," *Criminal Law and Philosophy* 11(1): 19–36. [This is an English version of "Paternalismus und Menschenwürde," in A. von Hirsch, U. Neumann, and K. Seelmann (eds.) (2010) *Paternalismus: Die Kriminalisierung von selbstschädigendem Verhalten*, trans. A. Du Bois-Pedain, Baden-Baden: Nomos Verlagsgesellschaft, 145–171.]

Kleinig, J. and N.G. Evans (2013) "Human Flourishing, Human Dignity, and Human Rights," *Law and Philosophy* 32: 539–64.

Laskey, Jaggard and Brown v. The United Kingdom (1997) 2 EHRR 39.

Mill, J.S. (1859) *On Liberty*. London: John W. Parker and Son.

Moran, L.J. (1995) "Violence and the Law: The Case of Sado-Masochism," *Social and Legal Studies* 4: 225–51.

National Center for Responsible Gambling (2010) *Evaluation: Self-Exclusion as an Intervention for Disordered Gambling*. Beverly, MA: NCRG. www.ncrg.org/sites/default/files/uploads/docs/monographs/self_exclusion_monograph_final.pdf

R. v. Brown (1993) 2 All E.R. 75; [1994] 1 AC 212.

R. v. Brown (1603) 1 Coke on Littleton 194 (127a, 127b); 1 Hale PC 412.

Rajczi, A. (2013) "Formulating and Articulating Public Health Policies: The Case of New York City," *Public Health Ethics* 6: 246–51.

Reid, Jr., C.J. (2014) "Eat What You Kill: Or, a Strange and Gothic Tale of Cannibalism by Consent," *North Carolina Journal of International Law & Commercial Regulation* 39: 423–521. www.law.unc.edu/journals/ncilj/issues/volume39/issue-2-winter-2014/eat-what-you-kill-or-a-strange-and-gothic-tale-of-cannibalism-by-consent/

Richards, N. (1989) "Paternalism toward Friends," in G. Graham and H. LaFollette (eds.) *Person to Person*. Philadelphia: Temple University Press, 235–44.

Syrota, G. (1996) "Consensual Fist Fights and Other Brawls: Are They a Crime?" *Western Australian Law Review* 26: 169–89.

Thaler, R.H. and C.R. Sunstein (2008) *Nudge: Improving Decisions about Health, Wealth, and Happiness*. New Haven: Yale University Press.

White, M.D. (2013) *The Manipulation of Choice: Ethics and Libertarian Paternalism*. New York: Palgrave Macmillan.

Wikipedia Editors, "Body Modification." https://en.wikipedia.org/wiki/Body_modification.

Wikipedia Editors, "Planking (a fad)." http://en.wikipedia.org/wiki/Planking_(fad).

Wikipedia Editors, "Train Surfing." http://en.wikipedia.org/wiki/Train_surfing.

Wisnewski, J.J. (2007) "Murder, Cannibalism, and Indirect Suicide: A Philosophical Study of a Recent Case," *Philosophy in the Contemporary World* 14: 11–21. www.hartwick.edu/Documents/PHILOS WisnewskiMurderandCannibalism.pdf.

Further reading

Among influential early contributions to the contemporary discussion, see Gerald Dworkin, "Paternalism," *The Monist* 56 (1972): 64–84; Donald VanDeVeer, *Paternalistic Intervention: The Moral Bounds on Benevolence* (Princeton, NJ: Princeton University Press, 1986), and Joel Feinberg, *Harm to Self* (New York: Oxford University Press, 1986, the paternalism volume in his magisterial four-volume work, *The Moral Limits of Criminal Law*). A useful recent collection is Christian Coons and Michael Weber (eds.), *Paternalism: Theory and Practice* (Cambridge: Cambridge University Press, 2013). Gerald Dworkin provides an excellent overview of the issues in "Paternalism," *The Stanford Encyclopedia of Philosophy* (Spring 2017 Edition), Edward N. Zalta (ed.). https://plato.stanford.edu/archives/spr2017/entries/paternalism/. For a good collection of articles on the various contexts in which consent is important, see Franklin G. Miller and Alan Wertheimer (eds.), *The Ethics of Consent: Theory and Practice* (New York: Oxford University Press, 2009).

Related topics

Ch.2 What is consent?
Ch.5 Consent and wronging a person
Ch.8 Valid consent
Ch.11 Moral obligations and consent
Ch.12 Consent and autonomy
Ch.17 The volenti maxim
Ch.18 Consent to pain

14
EXPLOITATION AND CONSENT

Matt Zwolinski

14.1 Introduction

Most of us believe that there are certain things that we should not do to or with others without their consent. For the most part, we think that it is wrong to take people's property without their consent, or to touch them in certain ways, or to enter into certain forms of relationship such as marriage or employment. We think that we should gain people's consent before interacting with them in these ways in part because we think that people have a kind of special moral status. There's something special about people that makes it wrong to use them as a mere object for the satisfaction of our desires in the way that we might a rock or a tree. Requiring that interactions be consensual is a way of recognizing that status, and thereby treating people with the respect they deserve.

Requiring consent also serves a more consequentialist goal by helping to ensure that interactions generally make *both* parties better off, by their own lights.[1] Non-consensual transactions such as theft and slavery involve a kind of social parasitism whereby one party gains only at the other's expense. Consensual interactions, in contrast, offer both parties the opportunity to say "no" to proposals that would leave them worse off than before. As a result, proposals that are able to garner the consent of both parties will tend to make both parties better off than they would have been in the absence of a transaction.

At its best, then, consensual interaction is both a token of respect and an engine of mutual benefit. Of course, not all real-world interactions live up to this ideal. Some interactions are non-consensual in the most straightforward and obvious sort of way: murder, theft, and rape being but the most glaring examples. Still other transactions *appear* to be consensual, but nevertheless seem to many to fall short of the idea of mutually respectful and beneficial interaction. Consider, for example, the interactions between the owner and employee of a sweatshop where work is done for long hours in dangerous conditions for only minimal pay. Or consider the interaction involving a price gouger who proposes to sell bottled water to a disaster victim for ten times its normal cost. Or that between a pharmaceutical company and the research subject in the developing world whose body is used to test drugs that she will never herself be able to afford. In each of these cases, both parties to the interaction *seem* to consent to the interaction taking place. Nevertheless, there is something morally troubling about them.

One way of diagnosing what troubles many of us about these exchanges is to point out that they all seem to involve a kind of exploitation. In each of these cases, and in many others like them, one party to the interaction seems to take unfair advantage of the other. That is, one party uses his or her advantage in the bargaining situation leading up to the interaction to compel the other person, who is suffering some sort of vulnerability or weakness, to make a deal that benefits the advantaged party at the vulnerable or weak party's expense. The sweatshop uses its economic advantage to compel the worker to take a job on unfavorable terms;[2] the price gouger charges a high price by virtue of the disaster victim's desperation and lack of other options;[3] and the pharmaceutical company takes advantage of its subject's hope and, perhaps, lack of information in order to secure a willing subject for its trials.

The concept of exploitation is, like many ordinary moral notions, one of which it is difficult to provide a precise philosophical analysis. There is widespread (but less than unanimous) agreement that the core of the concept consists in the notion of taking unfair advantage of another person. To call an action unfair in this sense is thus already to make a moral judgment about that action – at least a *pro tanto* one. Exploitation, or at least the sort of exploitation in which moral philosophers are interested, is by definition unfair, and hence morally wrong.[4]

Past this point of agreement, however, the proper understanding of exploitation becomes heavily contested. What makes an interaction fair rather than unfair? By what standard are the terms of an interaction to be judged so as to make this determination? Is it unfair to take advantage of another's ignorance? Is it unfair if the ignorance is culpable? And so on.

There are a number of respectable theories of exploitation, each of which provides its own plausible answers to these questions.[5] My purpose in this paper, however, is not to offer or defend a full theory of exploitation. Instead, I seek to examine merely one element of such a theory: the relationship between exploitation and consent.

That there is *some* important relationship between these two concepts is clear enough. It is clear, for instance, that some of the most egregious forms of exploitation involve, and are made possible by, non-consensual relationships in which the victim lacks the power to say "no" to the exploitative interaction. Slavery is the most obvious example of this sort, but certain forms of child exploitation serve to illustrate the phenomenon as well. It is also fairly clear that certain defects in expressed consent – such as consent given while intoxicated, or while lacking crucial information – can be taken advantage of in a way that renders the resulting interaction wrongfully exploitative.

But while there is clearly some relationship between the concepts of exploitation and consent, there are a number of important and unresolved questions regarding its exact nature. For instance, we might wonder whether *all* exploitative transactions necessarily involve a lack of valid consent on one party's part. In the sweatshop, price gouging, and pharmaceutical examples described above, it certainly *appears* that both parties have consented to the interaction. But appearances can be deceiving, especially when the question is not merely whether consent was *tokened* by both parties but rather whether both parties gave what we should regard as morally or legally *valid* consent.[6] Perhaps the consent tokened in these cases is morally invalid because of duress, lack of relevant information, or some other reason. And perhaps the invalidity of the consent is what leads us to deem the resulting interaction exploitative.

So, one question this paper will explore is whether all exploitative transactions are really non-consensual in some way. Another question is what makes non-consensual transactions exploitative. That a lack of valid consent is not a sufficient condition for exploitation seems clear enough. At the very least, exploitation involves *taking advantage* of another person, and thus non-consensual actions that are not intended to benefit the actor, such as paternalistic interference, are not exploitative, even if they are wrong in some other sort of way. Are there other conditions beyond this that are necessary to render a non-consensual interaction exploitative? And if so, what are they?

Section 14.2 of this paper will examine two sharply divergent theories which nevertheless converge on the view that exploitation necessarily involves *force*, and the absence of valid consent. I argue that this view is mistaken, and that while non-consensual exploitation might be morally *worse* than consensual exploitation, the latter is nevertheless a possibility that theorists of all stripes can and ought to recognize. Section 14.3 asks under what conditions a defect in consent will render a transaction wrongfully exploitative. In it, I look at coercion and ignorance, and argue that neither of them *by themselves* is sufficient to render a transaction wrongfully exploitative. Whether a transaction involving such a defect is exploitative will depend on a variety of factors, including the agents' knowledge of the defect, responsibility for the defect, the consequences to both parties of attempting to *avoid* taking advantage of the defect, and the context in which the interaction occurs.

14.2 Is all exploitation non-consensual?

Suppose one thinks that consent is a relatively weighty moral notion. To hold that consent is "weighty", in the sense that I mean, is to hold that whether an interaction is consensual or not has a great deal of influence on the overall moral permissibility of that interaction. Such a view might seem plausible for those who think that individual autonomy is an important moral value, and that consent is a way of expressing this value. It might also be plausible for those who think that consent is a reflection of individual preferences, and that permitting consensual exchanges is an effective tool for maximizing the satisfaction of those preferences.

Someone who thinks that consent is morally weighty in this way might be tempted to believe that wrongfully exploitative transactions are *necessarily* non-consensual. The reasoning is straightforward. If consensual transactions are morally permissible, and if exploitative transactions are morally impermissible, then consensual transactions cannot be exploitative. Just as the famous maxim *volenti non fit injuria* holds that one who consents cannot be *harmed*, so it might also be claimed that one who consents cannot be *exploited*. Whatever loss the agent suffers through the interaction, however unfair its terms may appear to a third party, so long as both parties give their valid consent, the transaction cannot be wrongfully exploitative.

Such a view of exploitation has an obvious libertarian character to it. On Robert Nozick's view, for instance, interactions are morally permissible only if they involve no violation of the individual rights of the interacting parties or any third party.[7] But because all rights on Nozick's view are property rights, and because property rights are always waivable or transferrable by consent, it follows for Nozick that voluntary, consensual interactions cannot violate the individual rights of the persons who consent. Libertarians such as Nozick will therefore not regard exploitation that occurs in the context of consensual exchange as a rights-violation, i.e. an injustice. And they will therefore regard attempts to suppress exploitation by coercive means as themselves an injustice – an initiation of force into a transaction that was itself peaceful and voluntary.[8]

What libertarians *do* count as unjustly exploitative are those interactions in which consent is lacking. When one person or group of persons uses coercion or deception in order to benefit itself at another party's expense, libertarians do not hesitate to decry the resulting interaction as exploitative and unjust.[9] Indeed, it is precisely this sort of consideration that underlies the libertarian critique of taxation. Dismissing the idea of a "social contract" as a myth, libertarians regard taxation as an involuntary transfer of resources. And because the resources taken from taxpayers are almost always used to benefit some *distinct* person or group of persons, libertarians regard taxation as a form of vicarious exploitation. The state uses its power of coercion to exploit vulnerable groups (often those groups with too little political or economic power to curry favor with the state) for the benefit of other, more politically privileged groups.[10] Transfers such as this often take the form of a mutually beneficial exchange between the group that receives the benefit and the state, which receives financial or political support from that group in exchange for using its power on its behalf. This mutually beneficial exchange comes at the expense of the taxpayer, however, who, because she lacks the power to say "no" to the exchange, is unable to avoid suffering a loss for others' benefit.[11]

The libertarian claim that taxation is morally "on a par with forced labor" should therefore not be dismissed as empty rhetoric.[12] For libertarians, taxation is exploitation, and the paradigmatic case of exploitation is slavery. In both cases, what properly belongs to one individual is taken by force or threat of force and used for benefit of another. The difference between the two is one of degree – how *much* is taken – not one of kind.[13]

In this respect, libertarians share an interesting affinity with many Marxists, including probably with Marx himself. For Marx, too, held slavery to be the paradigm case of exploitation. And like libertarians, Marx appears to have believed that *force* is an essential element of exploitation. What renders workers in a capitalist system exploited, according to Marx, is not merely the fact that the surplus value created by their labor winds up in the hands of capitalists. It is the fact that this value is taken from them by force. Not, of course, by the direct threat of violence on the part of the employer. On a surface level, the employment relation appears to be consensual and voluntary. But this surface appearance masks the deeper reality that workers are compelled to sell their labor to capitalists by virtue of the latter group's coercively enforced monopoly over the means of production.

Both many libertarians and many Marxists thus endorse what Jeffrey Reiman labeled a "force-inclusive" definition of exploitation.[14] Where they differ is not in how they define exploitation but in where they see it. Libertarians see taxation as the forced extraction of wealth from the taxpayer and therefore conclude that taxation is slavery. Marxists see wage labor as the forced extraction of surplus value from the laborer and therefore conclude that wage labor is slavery.

Whatever the merits of their particular charges against taxation and wage labor, however, both groups are mistaken in assuming that exploitation must necessarily involve force or the background threat of force. Someone who encounters a hiker lost in the desert and offers to lead her to rescue for $10,000 – or else leave her to die – does not employ force. Such a person's only threat is *inaction* – the withholding of a benefit, rather than the positive imposition of a harm. Still, most of us would think that such a person acts in a way that is grossly unfair and exploitative. If this intuition is correct, we thus have at least one example of a transaction that is wrongfully exploitative but which does not involve the use or threat of force.

To exploit someone is to take unfair advantage of their vulnerability. But that vulnerability need not be the product of force, or indeed of any injustice at all. It might simply be the product of bad luck, or even a (culpably) bad choice. One can take unfair advantage of a bad situation one had no role in creating.

Nor must exploitation involve any lack of valid consent on the victim's part. The worker who chooses to accept the sweatshop's offer of employment, for example, exercises her powers of consent in a morally transformative way. Her choice is morally transformative insofar as it makes it permissible for the managers of the sweatshop to do things (monitor her movements, issue certain authoritative commands, and so forth) that would otherwise be morally impermissible. And this is true *even if the terms of her agreement are wrongfully exploitative*. After all, the fact that the workers' choice does not authorize *everything* the managers of the sweatshop may do does not mean that it authorizes nothing at all. Even in highly constrained and less-than-fully-autonomous circumstances, an individual's choice can still express important preferences, and still be an important manifestation of (partial) autonomy.[15] To treat these choices as morally dismissible – as we would the "choice" of someone who literally acted under compulsion – would be to treat vulnerable persons with serious disrespect, and potentially to do them grave harm.[16]

In conclusion, a distinction drawn by Alan Wertheimer will be useful in illuminating the ways in which force is, and is not, relevant in assessing exploitation. Wertheimer distinguishes between the "moral weight" of exploitation – its degree of wrongness – and its "moral force" – the various moral upshots that exploitation might have for parties to the transaction or for third parties.[17] These questions are related, but importantly distinct. It is one thing to determine how bad a particular instance of exploitation is. It is quite another to determine what we should *do* about it – how we should respond to it, for instance, with legal sanctions or social pressure.

In terms of moral weight, the presence of force or coercion might indeed make exploitation *worse*. As Reiman notes, we distinguish between "robbery" and mere "theft" on roughly these grounds[18], so it is sensible that we would draw a similar distinction between sorts of exploitation. But the mere fact that forceful, non-consensual exploitation is worse than non-forceful exploitation hardly shows that the latter is not wrong at all. As noted above,[19] even a libertarian like Nozick has the logical space to admit that non-coercive exploitation is wrong in *some* sense, albeit one that falls short of a rights-violation.

What role does the presence or absence of force play in assessing the moral force of an exploitation claim? Nozick, of course, thinks that consensual exploitation is not an injustice because he adheres to a highly contestable theory according to which all rights are essentially property rights. And thus he holds that society must refrain from forcefully interfering with such exchanges. For most others, however – and even for most deontologists – what warrants societal interference will be a more context- and consequence-sensitive matter. For them, the moral force of exploitation will be at least partly dependent on the particular non-moral facts pertaining to the interaction, and the likely consequences of various sorts of interference with that action. So, for example, whether prostitution should be legally prohibited or not will not depend *solely* on the question of whether prostitution is wrongfully exploitative. It will also depend, at least in part, on whether prohibition is likely to make prostitutes better or worse off. Few of us are so adamant in our opposition to exploitation as to be willing to prohibit it even at the expense of condemning its victims to an even worse fate.

14.3 When do defects in consent render an interaction exploitative?

Ideal consent is both fully informed and voluntary. Many cases of real-world consent, however, fall short of this ideal in one or more ways. Sometimes, people try to take advantage of defects in someone else's consent for their own benefit. Under what conditions is doing so wrongfully exploitative?

14.3.1 Coercion

It might seem obvious that outright physical coercion would be sufficient to render a transaction wrongfully exploitative. And, certainly, many cases involving coercion *will* be wrongfully exploitative. If *A* threatens *B* with physical violence unless *B* does unpaid labor for *A*, then *A* has clearly exploited *B*. But what if the coercion is performed by some third party, *C*? If *C* threatens *B* with physical violence unless *B* does unpaid labor for *A*, then would it be wrongfully exploitative for *A* to take advantage of *B*'s free labor?

If *A* knows about *C*'s threat, and certainly if *A colluded* with *C* in producing it, then it seems that *A*'s action is wrongfully exploitative. If *A* knows that *B* is offering him a benefit only because *C* is wrongfully threatening *B* with violence unless he does so, then *A* would appear to be taking unfair advantage of *B* to accept the benefit. *A* is *using* the unjust coercion for his own benefit, even if he did not produce that coercion himself.

If *A* does *not* know about *C*'s threat, however, then matters become somewhat more complicated. Consider the following real-world case:

> Rebecca Burnham's husband (Victor) severely beat Rebecca until she agreed, under threat of further beating, to stand on the street in front of their house and entice motorists (such as A) to have sex with her while Victor photographed her. Although Rebecca feared physical injury from Victor, she feigned expressions of desire to the motorists.[20]

Rebecca's consent is clearly coerced in this case. But *A* neither caused nor appeared to be aware of the coercion. Nor does it seem plausible to say that *A should* have been aware of the coercion – that his ignorance was culpable. Having sex with a random person who flags you down on the street may be unusual, and risky, but it is not obviously wrong in itself. Thus, *A* appears to have acted in a way that was morally permissible, and not wrongfully exploitative, despite the fact that *B*'s consent was coerced.

Even in cases where *A knows* that *B* has been wrongfully coerced by *C*, it is not always obvious that it would be wrongfully exploitative for *A* to interact with *B* so as to benefit from this coercion. An example will help to illustrate this difficulty. Assume, for the sake of argument, that all workers have a moral right to engage in collective bargaining. And suppose that *B* is a worker in a country where workers' rights to unionize have been wrongfully suppressed by their government (*C*). In this situation, it is likely that the wages that *B* will be able to receive from her employer (*A*) will be lower than they would have been had she been able to exercise her right to engage in collective bargaining. *A* thus benefits from *C*'s wrongful coercion of *B*. But does *A* benefit *unfairly*? That is, does *A* exploit *B*?

Cases such as this are difficult to resolve. Still, two questions seem relevant to making this determination. First, what alternatives are open to *A* that do not involve taking advantage of injustice? And, second, what are the consequences to *B* (and others) of *A* taking one of these alternatives? With respect to the first question, perhaps *A* is a multinational enterprise that can hire unionized workers in a different country instead. Or perhaps it can hire non-unionized workers in the original country but pay them a wage that approximates what they would have received if they *had* been allowed to unionize. Every alternative will raise its own set of unique challenges and possibilities, but one general point can be used as a rough guide in assessing all of them: the more costly the alternatives are to *either A or B*, the less inclined we ought to be to judge *A*'s interaction with *B* to be wrongfully exploitative.

To illustrate this point, suppose that *A* is a small, family-run domestic firm whose only alternatives are to either a) hire domestic, non-unionized labor at the normal market rate, or b) relocate to a different country with more liberal labor laws. In such a situation, the burden to *A* of refraining from taking advantage of the coercion suffered by *B* seem excessively high. And this seems to at least push us in the direction of holding that either 1) *A* does not wrongfully exploit *B* in taking advantage of the coercion suffered by *B*, or 2) *A does* wrongfully exploit her, but is not morally culpable for doing so – he has a kind of moral excuse.

This may seem to let *A* off the hook too easily. Surely, some will object, we should not allow *A* to do wrong simply because it is hard for him to avoid doing so. A very successful thief doesn't get a moral license to keep stealing simply because it would be costly for him to give it up.

It is worth remembering, however, that the kind of case we are considering is one that involves a *mutually beneficial* transaction. The question is not whether *A* is morally permitted to steal from *B*, or assault her. The question is whether *A* is permitted to interact with *B* in a way that allows *A* to capture a larger share of the cooperative surplus than he would have if *B* had not been coerced. It is thus a question about the fair division of benefits between *A* and *B*.

Because the question is about the fair division of benefits between *A* and *B*, it is entirely appropriate that the burdens to *A* be taken into consideration in determining how much *A* ought to sacrifice so that *B* may gain. If what troubles us about an exploitative exchange is that *A* gains *too much* relative to *B* from an exchange, then we should try to correct the balance – but not so far that it winds up skewed in the opposite direction.

Thus, the costs and benefits of *A*'s various alternatives *to both A and B* must be taken into account in determining what is to count as a fair (non-exploitative) transaction. With respect to the costs to *B*, for instance, if *A*'s only alternative to hiring *B* at the normal market rate is to lay her off and replace her with a machine, thus putting *B* out of work altogether, then we might likewise be inclined to hold that *A* is not exploiting *B* by interacting with her on these terms. After all, it would be quite odd to say that *A* treats *B* unfairly when *A* literally does the most he can possibly do for *B*, and when him doing so leaves *B* better off than she would be under any other possible alternative.

What we can learn from this analysis is that a defect in *B*'s consent, such as the presence of coercion, is not *by itself* enough to render *A*'s interacting with *B* and benefitting from that defect wrongfully exploitative. In some cases, the costs to *A* or *B* of not transacting or transacting on different terms will be high enough to lead us to conclude that what appeared to be an unfair and hence exploitative transaction was not actually unfair after all. The presence of coercion can *contribute* to rendering a transaction unfair. But, just as clearly, it cannot be sufficient.

14.3.2 Ignorance

Much the same analysis will hold for other potential defects in consent, such as ignorance. If *B* is ignorant of some of the important facts relevant to her interaction with *A*, and *A* does not know (and is not obligated to know) of *B*'s ignorance, then *A* will generally not be guilty of wrongfully exploiting *B*, even if *A* gains as a result of *B*'s ignorance. In some cases, of course, *A* might have a *duty* to take positive steps in order to ensure that *B* knows what he is doing – a doctor might have such a duty toward a patient considering undergoing a serious medical procedure. But in many cases, including most ordinary market transactions, *A* will have no such positive duty.

And just as they were relevant with respect to coercion, the consequences of various courses of action matter with respect to ignorance, too. Specifically, if the consequences to *A* or *B* of *A not* taking advantage of *B*'s ignorance are sufficiently dire, we might hold that *A* is justified or excused in benefitting from *B*'s ignorance. To see this, consider the following example. Suppose *A* sells items at a negotiable price to many customers, some of whom are ignorant (call this class of customers "*B*") and some of whom are not. Due to their ignorance, *B* end up paying more than they otherwise would for certain goods and services, even though those goods and services are still worth more to them than what they pay (the exchange is mutually beneficial). *A* could implement measures to determine which customers are ignorant, and thus avoid taking unfair advantage of the ignorant, but the costs to him of doing so are sufficiently high that either a) they will impose a crippling economic burden on him if he absorbs them himself or b) they will cause the price of his goods to be out of reach of *B* if he passes the cost along to them. In the first case, we might hold that *A* does not benefit *unfairly* from *B* since the only way for him to avoid benefitting *too much* would be for him to benefit *too little*. In the second, we might hold that *A* does not benefit unfairly from *B* because there is no way for *A* to alter the terms of the agreement in a way that benefits *B* more.[21]

In addition to considerations of knowledge and consequences, an analysis of ignorance also highlights two other factors that play a role in determining whether a transaction involving a defect in consent is wrongfully exploitative: context and responsibility.

Unlike coercion, individuals are commonly causally and morally responsible for their own ignorance. And in at least some cases, this will matter as far as judgments of wrongful exploitation are concerned. In buying a used car, for example, the norm of *caveat emptor* is generally understood to apply, and buyers are responsible for inspecting the car or hiring a professional to do so prior to purchasing it. If a buyer does *not* conduct such an inspection, and as a result does not discover an issue with the car that would have led her to be willing to pay less than she otherwise would, the seller is not morally culpable for benefitting from the buyer's ignorance.

In some cases, of course, it *would* be morally wrong for *A* to take advantage of *B*'s ignorance, even if *B* is responsible for her own ignorance. In some cases, we have a positive duty to look out for another person's interests, one that obliges us to not take advantage of their vulnerability, even when that vulnerability is their own fault. This positive duty can arise from formal relationships such as that which exist between an attorney and her client, or a teacher and a student, or it can arise from informal relationships such as friendship or romantic partnership.

And this illustrates the second factor that is relevant to determining whether an interaction involving a defect in consent is wrongfully exploitative: context. "Context", of course, is a broad term encompassing a number of disparate factors. But this, in a way, is the point. Exploitation is built on the notion of fairness, and "fairness" is a concept that is notoriously difficult to reduce to one or even a small handful of necessary and sufficient conditions.

One part of what the term "context" is meant to capture is the social norms that govern different situations. Part of the reason why it is appropriate to push for advantage in used car transactions but not in a romantic relationship is that this is what people *expect*. Norms governing these situations are "common knowledge", and we expect that people will be able to adjust their behavior accordingly so as to exercise different degrees of caution in different contexts, as appropriate. In this respect, objective judgments of moral permissibility are at least partly a function of what people subjectively *believe* is permissible. Those beliefs, when widely shared, generate expectations about how others will act, and those expectations (sometimes) generate objective moral reasons for action that transcend the subjective beliefs from which they arose.

Of course, social norms do not arise in a vacuum. The particular social norms that govern a situation will themselves be partly a function of other morally relevant values to which they have arisen as a response. Norms dealing with what the seller of a used car does and does not have to disclose, for example, arguably advance the value of economic efficiency by placing the burden of acquiring information on the party who is able to do so at the lowest cost.[22] And the norm that permits a certain form of outright deception in poker is arguably a function of the relatively low-stakes, voluntary nature, and purpose of the game.[23]

14.4 Conclusion

In thinking about exploitation, it is easy to be misled by putting too much weight on the notion of consent. One form this error can take is to assume that, because consent is so morally weighty, all wrongfully exploitative transactions must really be non-consensual in some way. Another is to assume that, again because consent is so morally weighty, all transactions in which one party gains from a defect in the other's consent must be wrongfully exploitative.

This paper has argued that neither of these assumptions is correct. The mistake, of course, does not lie in the assumption that consent is a tremendously weighty moral notion. It is. But even the weightiest of norms cannot explain *everything* in the moral universe. The concept of exploitation, and the concept of fairness on which it is based, draw upon a wide range of moral considerations, including the considerations of welfare and responsibility that I have considered in this paper. This inherent pluralism in the concept of exploitation makes it difficult to draw any simple lessons about the relationship between exploitation and consent. The best we can do, beyond the negative lesson of what that relationship *isn't*, is to emphasize the role of context in specifying the norms and values that are relevant to considerations of exploitation, and to emphasize the importance of that context in future theorizing about the concept.[24]

Notes

1 More precisely, we might say that consent helps to ensure that transactions will advance the ends of both parties since nothing in the argument hinges on the assumption that parties' ends are always or usually self-interested.

2 This is how such interactions are frequently characterized, at any rate. As I have argued elsewhere, the reality is both empirically and normatively more complicated. See Zwolinski (2007).

3 Again, the situation is somewhat more complex than this popular description suggests. See Powell & Zwolinski (2011); Zwolinski (2008).

4 In the English language, the word "exploitation" is used in both a moralized and a non-moralized sense. In the non-moralized sense, to exploit something is simply to take advantage of it, without any connotation that the advantage-taking is morally wrong. So, for instance, a chess player might be said to exploit a weakness in her opponent's position, or a shrewd businessperson to exploit an opportunity to increase sales. If it is possible to exploit a person in this non-moralized sense (that is, if exploiting a person, rather than an object or a situation, is not always morally wrong), then one who consents might still be exploited in the non-moralized sense of the term (see Goodin 1987). But he or she will not be *wrongfully* exploited.

5 See, for an overview, Zwolinski & Wertheimer (2016). For a useful set of essays on various historical theories of exploitation, see Reeve (1987).

6 I owe the distinction between *tokened* consent and *valid* consent to Alan Wertheimer (Wertheimer 2003: 122–4, 152). To token consent is to communicate consent in some way, either verbally, through nonverbal action, or through silence or inaction. To say that consent is valid is to say that it meets whatever conditions are necessary to be morally or legally transformative – that is, to change the nature of the moral relationship between the giver and receiver of consent so that, for example, a formerly impermissible action on one party's part (e.g. kissing the other on the lips) becomes, by virtue of the consent, permissible.

7 See Nozick (1974: chapter 3). "Only if" rather than "if and only if", because Nozick's view of rights as side constraints technically leaves open the possibility that considerations other than a failure to respect individual rights might render an action morally impermissible. For instance, an action might be morally impermissible by virtue of a failure to treat one's *self* as an end. Since such a failure would not constitute a violation of rights, presumably others would not be justified in forcibly interfering with your actions in order to correct the failure. Still, it is worth noting that Nozick's view does leave open the possibility that exploitative actions involve a *kind* of moral impermissibility. We will return to this possibility later.

8 See Nozick's discussion of the libertarian side constraint against aggression in Nozick (1974: 33).

9 See, for example, Raico (1977).

10 In nineteenth-century France, libertarians such as Frederic Bastiat described this sort of process as "plunder" (Bastiat 1998). In the twentieth century, libertarians drew heavily on the discipline of public choice economics and its analysis of "rent seeking" to refine their analysis. See Stigler (1971); Tullock et al. (1988).

11 For an extended discussion, see Zwolinski (2016).

12 Nozick (1974: 169).

13 Nozick makes this point in his later discussion of "The Tale of the Slave" (Nozick 1974: 290–2). But the early libertarian Herbert Spencer made essentially the same argument, more directly applied to taxation, in his essay "The Coming Slavery" (Spencer 1981: 55–6). The success of these arguments, of course, hinges upon the assumption that there is no distinction in kind between the rights to bodily integrity and control that are violated in the case of slavery, and rights to property in external resources that are violated in taxation. Many non-libertarians will deny this assumption.

14 Reiman (1987).

15 This argument is developed in greater detail in Radcliffe Richards (1996) and Zwolinski (2007).

16 Suppose we could push a button that would prevent a sweatshop from hiring a worker who has consented to its offer of employment. Pushing the button would stop the worker from being exploited by the sweatshop. But it would do nothing to change the underlying circumstances of poverty and desperation that led her to view the sweatshop job as her best (or least bad) option.

17 Wertheimer (1996: 6).

18 Reiman (1987: 4).

19 *supra*, note 7.

20 *People v. Burnham,* 176 Cal. App. 3d 1134, 222 Cal. Rptr 630 (1985). This presentation of the case, and my discovery of it, comes from Wertheimer (2003: 149). The defendant was initially convicted of rape by a jury who found that Burnham did not genuinely consent, but that decision was overturned by the appellate court which ruled that the jury should have been instructed regarding the defendant's good faith *belief* that she had consented.

21 The situation described in this paragraph may bear a certain resemblance to the situation faced by the payday lending industry in the United States. That industry makes a large number of small, short-term, high-fee loans to individuals who for various reasons cannot obtain credit from more traditional sources. Much of the industry's profit comes from "rollovers" – cases where borrowers are unable to pay back their loan at the specified time and therefore must renew them for a new fee. And a large proportion of these rollovers come from a small group of individuals who, arguably, are poorly skilled at managing their finances and anticipating the long-term costs of repeated rollovers. Some have argued that the payday lending industry exploits these individuals and should implement measures to protect those customers who are bad at managing their financial risk. The payday lending industry typically responds that doing so would raise costs significantly and thereby make its services unaffordable for many customers – the majority of whom use them responsibly. See, for discussion, Mayer (2003, 2012).

22 See Kronman (1978).

23 See Carr (1968).

24 One of the many virtues of Alan Wertheimer's seminal text (Wertheimer 1996) on exploitation is precisely this kind of context-sensitive approach to the topic.

References

Bastiat, F. (1998) *The Law* (D. Russell, trans.). Second Edition. New York: Foundation for Economic Education.

Carr, A. (1968) "Is Business Bluffing Ethical?" *Harvard Business Review* (Jan.–Feb.) 143: 55.

Goodin, R.E. (1987) "Exploiting a Situation and Exploiting a Person," in A. Reeve (ed.), *Modern Theories of Exploitation*. London: Sage, 166–200.

Kronman, A. (1978) "Mistake, Disclosure, Information, and the Law of Contracts," *The Journal of Legal Studies* 7(1): 1–34.

Mayer, R. (2003) "Payday Loans and Exploitation," *Public Affairs Quarterly* 17(3): 197–217.

Mayer, R. (2012) "When and Why Usury Should be Prohibited," *Journal of Business Ethics* 116(3): 513–27. doi: 10.1007/s10551-012-1483-3

Nozick, R. (1974) *Anarchy, State, and Utopia*. New York: Basic Books.

Powell, B. and M. Zwolinski (2011) "The Ethical and Economic Case Against Sweatshop Labor: A Critical Assessment," *Journal of Business Ethics* 107(4): 449–72. doi: 10.1007/s10551-011-1058-8

Radcliffe Richards, J. (1996) "Nephrarious Goings On: Kidney Sales and Moral Arguments," *Journal of Medicine and Philosophy* 21: 375–416.

Raico, R. (1977) "Classical Liberal Exploitation Theory: A Comment on Professor Liggio's Paper," *Journal of Libertarian Studies* 1(3): 179–83.

Reeve, A. (1987) *Modern Theories of Exploitation*. London: Sage.
Reiman, J. (1987) "Exploitation, Force, and the Moral Assessment of Capitalism: Thoughts on Roemer and Cohen," *Philosophy and Public Affairs* 16(1): 3–41.
Spencer, H. (1981) "The Coming Slavery," in H. Spencer (ed.), *The Man Versus the State*. Indianapolis, IN: Liberty Fund, 31–70.
Stigler, G. (1971) "The Theory of Economic Regulation," *The Bell Journal of Economics and Management* 2(1): 3–21.
Tullock, G., R.D. Tollison and C.K. Rowley (1988) *The Political Economy of Rent Seeking*. Boston: Kluwer.
Wertheimer, A. (1996) *Exploitation*. Princeton: Princeton University Press.
Wertheimer, A. (2003) *Consent to Sexual Relations*. Cambridge: Cambridge University Press.
Zwolinski, M. (2007) "Sweatshops, Choice, and Exploitation," *Business Ethics Quarterly* 17(4): 689–727.
Zwolinski, M. (2008) "The Ethics of Price Gouging," *Business Ethics Quarterly* 18(3): 347–78.
Zwolinski, M. (2016) "Exploitation and Freedom," in D. Schmidtz and C. Pavel (ed.), *The Oxford Handbook of Freedom*. New York: Oxford University Press. doi: 1093/oxfordhb/9780199989423.013.23
Zwolinski, M. and A. Wertheimer (2016, 8/16/2016). Exploitation. *The Stanford Encyclopedia of Philosophy*. http://plato.stanford.edu/entries/exploitation/.

Further reading

Cohen, G.A. (1979) "The Labor Theory of Value and the Concept of Exploitation," *Philosophy and Public Affairs* 8(4): 338–60. (On the connection between Karl Marx's theory of exploitation and the labor theory of economic value.)

Steiner, H. (1984) "A Liberal Theory of Exploitation," *Ethics* 94(2): 225–41. (An account of exploitation from a libertarian perspective, on which exploitation depends on taking advantage of past rights-violations.)

Vrousalis, N. (2013) "Exploitation, Vulnerability, and Social Domination," *Philosophy and Public Affairs* 41(2): 131–57. (Attempts to revive the analytical Marxist account of exploitation, linking it to the notion of social domination.)

Wertheimer, A. (1996) *Exploitation*. Princeton: Princeton University Press. (One of the most influential contemporary accounts of exploitation as unfairness, developed and applied to a variety of topics.)

Zwolinski, M. and A. Wertheimer (2017) "Exploitation," in E.N. Zalta (ed.), *The Stanford Encyclopedia of Philosophy* (Summer Edition). https://plato.stanford.edu/archives/sum2017/entries/exploitation/. (Broad overview of historical and contemporary accounts of exploitation.)

Related topics

Ch.8 Valid consent
Ch.17 The volenti maxim
Ch.19 Voluntary consent

15
DECEPTION AND CONSENT

Tom Dougherty

15.1 Introduction

Even though April Fool's day is an inauspicious day for a wedding, you still would not expect the marriage to end with the bride suing the Cuban government for non-consensual sex. Yet that was the conclusion of Ana Margarita Martinez's marriage to Juan Pablo Roque, after he left their Florida residence, never to return (Bragg 1999). The mystery of his disappearance was resolved a few days later when he appeared on television broadcast from Havana, unveiling himself as an undercover spy sent to infiltrate the dissident community in the United States. This was surprising, and unwelcome, news to Martinez, who thought she had married a fellow dissident. Consequently, she filed a lawsuit about the deception against his employer. Since Cuba was not accustomed to defending itself in Florida's courts, it did not contest the suit, and Martinez was awarded millions of dollars in damages. Part of her case was based on her claim that the fraud meant that she did not give valid consent to sex with Roque. As her lawyer put it, "She would not have given her consent, had she known".

Martinez's case is controversial—is sex non-consensual when it results from someone disguising their career, allegiances, and motives? This question is difficult and weighty: typically, it is appropriate to censure non-consensual sex heavily in law. Consequently, sexual consent has been a focus of research into the relationship between deception and consent, and this chapter will reflect this emphasis. But the issue also arises for other types of consent. If someone impersonates a police officer, then she lacks valid consent to entering someone's home. If someone misrepresents the risks of a clinical study, then she lacks her research subjects' valid consent.

For the purposes of this chapter, let us define non-consensual behavior as behavior for which the agent needs, but lacks, the other person's valid consent. Then we can ask two key questions. First, when does deception lead to non-consensual behavior? Second, why does it do so? These questions are orthogonal to other moral evaluations of deception. Perhaps deception is *pro tanto* morally wrong, because it involves treating people as "mere means" (O'Neill 1985), and undermines valuable communication (Shiffrin 2014). Or perhaps deception can be benign or even salutary, protecting our privacy (Nagel 2006), smoothing social interactions (Calhoun 2000), or allowing mystery to build attraction (Buss 2005). These moral evaluations are separate from the relation between deception and consent. Deception that is morally objectionable in itself might not lead to non-consensual behavior, and vice versa.

This chapter focuses on "permissive consent" (see Manson, this volume, Chapter 6; Hurd, this volume, Chapter 4). Permissive consent waives a right against an interaction, releasing someone from her duty not to engage in it. So, wherever rights protect realms of our lives, permissive consent allows us to share these realms. In addition to permissive consent, the English word "consent" can refer to agreements that create obligations, such as promises. Deception can also be a problem for these agreements, but, while this topic is important, it will be passed over here.

For our purposes, let us define deception as intentionally causing someone to form a false belief. This definition includes paradigmatic lies—understood as deliberate assertions of falsehoods—as well as misleading statements and omissions. It excludes omissions that merely allow pre-existing false beliefs to persist. It also excludes concealment that does not create false beliefs. Currently, I am concealing from you my address, without deceiving you.

This chapter will discuss accounts of how and why deception leads to non-consensual behavior, introducing a distinction between "duty-first" and "awareness-first" approaches. Duty-first approaches begin by specifying key duties not to deceive a consent-giver. These approaches then hold that the consent-receiver lacks the consent-giver's valid consent because she has not carried out these duties. By contrast, awareness-first approaches start with an account of key features of an interaction of which a validly consenting person must be aware. An awareness-first theorist can then, if they like, appeal to this awareness to derive duties not to deceive. To be clear from the start, these approaches need not be exclusive, since it may be that there is more than one way that deception can lead to non-consensual behavior. Moreover, there is little reason to think they are jointly exhaustive, as it is plausible to think that there are other theoretical options waiting to be explored.[1] Still, it is hopefully a helpful distinction for orientating us to the topic of deception and consent.

15.2 Duty-first approaches

A duty-first approach begins with the thought that valid consent requires certain background conditions to be in place. For example, we might think of giving consent as a form of transaction. To ensure this is a "fair transaction", the consent-receiver may need to discharge key duties towards the consent-giver (Miller & Wertheimer 2009). These duties would plausibly include duties not to coerce the consent-giver, as well as duties to disclose information and to avoid certain types of deception. A duty-first approach then appeals to these duties in order to develop an account of when the deceiver lacks the consent-giver's valid consent to an action: when the deceiver fails to discharge one of these duties, the victim does not validly consent to the action.

This order of explanation seems to fit many people's intuitions about when a deceiver lacks valid consent, since it places importance on the aetiology of false beliefs relevant to decisions to consent (Beyleveld & Brownsword 2007: 147). If false beliefs are not caused by the consent-receiver, then the context need not be unfair. But if these beliefs result from the consent-receiver not fulfilling her duties, then the consent-receiver could lack valid consent. Placing importance on the aetiology of false beliefs is the main advantage of a duty-first approach. Its main disadvantage is that it owes us an account of the boundary between key duties not to deceive (which must be discharged for valid consent to the encounter in question) from minor duties not to deceive (which need not be discharged for valid consent to that encounter).

Determining these key duties is a complex task. The duties plausibly vary with different types of consent. For property consent, some deception seems fair game. For example, in commercial exchanges, both parties may disguise their interests and resources, in the course of arriving at a valid agreement. For example, Smith might play down her interest in leasing Jones's car, while Jones might mislead Smith about the lowest price that she would accept. Moreover, people are allowed some "puffery" when presenting the value of their property (Shiffrin 2014). This is not to say that anything goes in property exchanges. Vendors and lessors may not deceive consumers about critical features of their products. Indeed, this would frequently be fraud. Similarly, a consumer may not pay with counterfeit money. It is hard to distinguish acceptable and unacceptable deception in property exchanges, and there may be several ways of doing so. Here we encounter broader philosophical questions concerning the role for conventions in the ethics of property. Plausibly, the answers to these questions will determine much about our key duties not to deceive with respect to property consent.

What about consent to therapeutic medical treatment or participation in research? Here legal and institutional norms bear on how deception relates to consent. Professionals are obligated by institutional codes, and legally obligated by the laws of their jurisdiction. Assuming these codes and laws are adequately just, they bear on moral obligations. These codes do not just cover deception, but also duties of disclosure. These duties are linked. If a physician must disclose a risk factor, then she is required not to deceive the patient about the risk factor, and not to conceal the risk factor from the patient. Since duties of disclosure generate duties both not to deceive and not to conceal, we should take disclosure as fundamental here. Consequently, we should start theorizing how deception relates to consent to research and therapy by thinking of duties of disclosure (Manson & O'Neill 2007; see also Eyal, this volume, Chapter 24; Ach, this volume, Chapter 25; O'Neil, this volume, Chapter 26.)

For sexual consent, the issue is complicated by the fact that deception features widely in people's sexual lives (Buss 2005). The relevant philosophical debate has been framed by a distinction in Anglo-American law between "fraud in the *factum*" and "fraud in the inducement". (Feinberg 1986, following Perkins 1957: 856; Westen 2004) Fraud in the *factum* misrepresents the nature of the sexual encounter itself. The law typically conceives of this narrowly, including impersonation or disguising a sexual encounter as a medical procedure (Falk 1998). This deception would typically lead to legally non-consensual sex. All other deception is considered fraud in the inducement. A paradigm would be deception about one's romantic intentions. The thought is that if someone engages in a sexual encounter because her partner pretends to be interested in a long-term relationship, then she is not misled about the sexual encounter itself and so still validly consents to the sexual encounter. The phrase "fraud in the inducement" may suggest it covers only fraud about people's incentives. But for the *factum* / inducement distinction to be exhaustive, the inducement category must also cover deception about any "peripheral" feature of the interaction that is not fraud about one of the "core" features that constitutes fraud in the *factum*.

The *factum* / inducement distinction has received much criticism (Wertheimer 2003; Manson unpubl.). For a start, it is hard to offer a principled basis for distinguishing facts that concern the sexual encounter and facts that do not, without this distinction yielding an over-inclusive conception of fraud in the *factum*. What should we "pack into" the description of the sexual act itself (Feinberg 1986; McGregor 2005)? Should the act be described as sex with a married man? If so, then a man pretending to be single would be committing deception about the sexual act itself. In addition, it appears *ad hoc* to apply the *factum* / inducement distinction to sexual consent, given a similar distinction would bear no weight in other domains (Schulhofer 1998; Rubenfeld 2013). For example, if one person fraudulently offers inducements for engaging in a property exchange, then this fraud will typically leave the exchange legally void. These criticisms would target the *factum* / inducement distinction both as a principle for rape law, and as the basis for moral principles.

If we reject the *factum* / inducement distinction, what can we put in its place to distinguish e.g. key duties not to impersonate people (which must be fulfilled for valid consent to the encounter in question) from minor duties not to lie about one's income (which need not)?

One option appeals to people's expectations about the likelihood of different harms. Perhaps an impersonator lacks their victim's valid consent because impersonation is so unexpected. Meanwhile, people lie so often about their income that detecting such a lie would not lead to a deep sense of harm. This option could yield either normative principles for framing the criminal law (McGregor 2005: 181–9), or moral principles. Indeed, it seems independently plausible to emphasize expectations if we think that morally valid consent consists in communication. What a speech-act communicates depends on conversational participants' shared assumptions (Stalnaker 2014). These assumptions will typically depend on the social and legal context.

Another option distinguishes types of information which someone is required or permitted to share with sexual partners. For example, someone might be required to disclose STIs, but not whether they were a victim of a sex crime. In addition, it could be that we are required to disclose some information on request, but we need not provide it of our own accord. This gives us an account of our duties of disclosure. We could use this account to say that a deceiver lacks their victim's valid consent to sex if and only if the deception involves failing to discharge a duty of disclosure (Lazenby & Gabriel 2017). Thus, we would derive norms governing deception from norms of disclosure, in the way that we do for medical and research consent.

A more radical option holds that we have duties not to deceive others about *any* feature that is materially relevant to their decisions to consent (Dougherty 2013).[2] We might worry that alternative views implicitly rely on a notion of sex that is moralized insofar as certain features of a sexual encounter are deemed more objectively important than other features, independently of what the participants consider important (Dougherty 2013). Moreover, we may think that a "fair transaction" account suggests a radical position on deception and consent (Miller & Wertheimer 2009). Deception that is materially relevant to someone's decision-making is a paradigm of manipulating someone or treating her "merely as a means" (O'Neill 1985; Pallikkathayil 2010). Consequently, material deception would typically bring about an unfair context for consent. This option is radical because it implies that deception about one's income will lead to non-consensual sex when income is material to someone's decision to consent to sex. Consequently, we would need to either revise down our estimate of the moral and legal importance of consent (Rubenfeld 2013), or revise up our estimate of how morally wrong deceiving someone into sex is (Dougherty 2013) and how stringently the law should penalize it (Larson 1993; Herring 2005).

15.3 Awareness-first approaches

Awareness-first approaches start with an account of the awareness that someone must have of an interaction, in order to validly consent to it. Proponents of these approaches can then, if they like, use this account to derive our duties of disclosure and our duties not to deceive.

Consequently, a principal benefit of an awareness-first approach is potentially that it provides us with a framework to determine the nature of these duties. To complete this task, we would need to consider other interests, such as consent-receivers' interests in privacy or in avoiding various costs of disclosure. But once we have factored in these interests, we have an underlying rationale for the existence and shape of these duties: their goal is to provide consent-givers with the awareness necessary for valid consent.

The principal cost of an awareness-first approach is that it does not place any intrinsic importance on the aetiology of false beliefs or ignorance when determining whether these lead to non-consensual behavior. If a consent-giver's false belief by itself is enough for an absence of valid consent, then it would not matter, with respect to the validity of the consent, whether this false belief has arisen by an innocent mistake, by non-disclosure, or by deception. This will strike many as counterintuitive. An awareness-first theorist could sweeten this pill by allowing that other moral phenomena are sensitive to this aetiology. For example, the consent-receiver's *blameworthiness* for non-consensual behavior could depend on whether she knew of the false belief, and in turn this knowledge may depend on the belief's aetiology. Similarly, this knowledge may influence how morally problematic the interaction is in other respects; for example, the knowledge may influence the extent to which someone is being manipulated, and manipulation may be wrong independently of considerations of consent.

How do we determine what awareness is necessary for valid consent? To answer this, we might start with the thought that the validity of consent depends on the voluntariness of the consent. In paradigmatic voluntary agency, an action is imputable to an agent because the action is caused and rationalized by the agent's conative and cognitive states. Coercion weakens the causal links between her conative states and the action—the agent does not otherwise want to perform the action except to avoid the coercer's threats. Consequently, to the extent that someone's action is coerced, the action did not flow from her own voluntary agency. According to one view, for consent to be morally valid, it must meet a threshold for voluntariness; so, coercion could invalidate consent by making it insufficiently voluntary.[3]

We might think that, similarly, deception can invalidate consent by making it insufficiently voluntary (McGregor 2005: 181). Just as coercion weakens the connection between the agent's conative states and her action, false beliefs and ignorance could weaken the connections between her cognitive states and the action. If the agent is unaware of features of her action, then she does not intend these features. So if we were to describe what the agent does intentionally, we would not mention these features. In the case of consent, we might say that only to the extent that the agent is aware of an action's features does she voluntarily consent to *this action*. In this way, we might hold that, the more an agent is misled about an action, the less willingly she engages with it, and she is wronged to the extent that her will is not implicated in the act (Archard 1998: 50).

Along these lines, we might classify features of an act according to how undesirable the consent-giver finds these features. If a feature of an action only puts her off the action in a limited range of circumstances, that feature would be a reasonably weak deal-breaker. But if the feature put her off the action in nearly all circumstances, then it would be a fairly strong deal-breaker. Consequently, we could determine the voluntariness of a decision to consent to an action according to the strength of any deal-breakers that are being concealed (Manson 2017).

Alternatively, for the purposes of determining the validity of consent, we could distinguish gradations of voluntariness in terms of the means by which the deception is achieved, e.g. whether it involves promises, threats, harms, or non-benefits (Feinberg 1986). This approach leaves us with the further question of how exactly a lack of awareness makes one's consent involuntary. This seems as substantive as a prior question of how a lack of awareness could lead to an absence of valid consent. So it is unclear how much progress has been made with this approach.

Instead of appealing to voluntariness, we could focus on the *content* of someone's consent. For example, we might claim that, for some types of consent, someone validly consents to an encounter only if they intend to consent to that encounter. This claim follows straightforwardly if consent consists in a mental attitude (Hurd 1996; Alexander 1996, 2014; see Schnüriger, this volume, Chapter 2). But it could also follow if we think that such an intention is necessary (although not sufficient) for some types of consent to be valid. Sexual consent might be a plausible example. If an intention to consent to an encounter is necessary for validly consenting to the encounter, then we should consider the content of such an intention. This will determine whether the actual encounter that took place is one such that the consent-giver intended to consent to that encounter (rather than an entirely different, merely hypothetical, encounter) (Dougherty 2013; Manson unpubl.).

Let us start with the fact that an intention is a propositional attitude. Suppose Jane intends that John cuts her hair. The content of Jane's intention is the proposition that John cuts Jane's hair. In attributing this intention to Jane, we need not suppose that this is the only relevant intention of Jane's. For example, we should also attribute to Jane an intention whose content is the proposition that the man in front of her cuts her hair. In this way, our attributions of intentions are similar to our attributions of other mental states, such as belief. When the haircut begins, Jane will not only believe that John is cutting her hair; she will also believe that the man in front of her is doing so.

At this juncture, we must say more about the nature of these propositions that constitute the content of these mental states. Consider a case of impersonation. Suppose Brian impersonates Robert Redford. As Brian is standing before Alice, she intends to have sex with him, thinking he is Robert Redford. It becomes tricky to characterize Alice's attitudes because there is a man in front of her, and she takes herself to be consenting to that man; but this man is Brian and Alice does not take herself to be consenting to sex with Brian. We could say that the contents of Alice's intentions are "mental descriptions" (Hurd 1996). For example, Alice is consenting to sex with someone under the mental description of "Robert Redford". Since this description picks out a man distinct from Brian, we can point to a key intention of Alice's that does not include Brian in its content. Consequently, we can point to this mismatch between the event in the world, and the content of Alice's intentions, in order to explain why she did not validly consent to the event (Hurd 1996).

Although we theorists would be forced to use language to characterize these mental descriptions, we should not assume that the mental descriptions themselves are linguistic entities. In other words, we need not think that mental descriptions are either natural language sentences that are consciously brought before the consent-giver's mind, or sentences in a language of thought. Indeed, there is no reason to think that a natural language like English is sufficiently expressively rich that we can always adequately articulate the relevant mental description using this language (McDowell 1984).

The idea that Brian does not fall within the content of Alice's intention has sometimes been put in terms of a distinction in the philosophy of language between *de dicto* and *de re* attributions of attitudes. Heidi Hurd takes this approach in a passage that has been so influential that it is worth quoting in full:

> Suppose that Alice slept with a man she thought was Robert Redford. He was not. Did she consent to sleep with him? The answer turns on whether her intention was *de re* or *de dicto*. If she intended to sleep with "that man"—whatever his name, profession or personal characteristics—then her intention was *de re*. Insofar as she slept with "that man", she did what she intended to do, and hence, she consented to his actions.
>
> If, on the other hand, she intended to sleep with "the Sundance Kid of movie fame", then her intention was *de dicto*. Insofar as the man with whom she slept was not the famous Robert Redford, she did not intend, and hence, did not consent, to engage in sexual intercourse with him.
>
> Most intentions are *de dicto*, not *de re*. That is, most intentions are held under discrete descriptions.
>
> *(Hurd 1996: 127; see also Liberto 2017)*

Hurd is right to focus our attention on the exact content of Alice's consent. Using square brackets to indicate the "mental description" under which Alice conceptualizes her intention, we can see that there is an important difference between these two intentions:

(1) Alice intends that [she has sex with that man, whoever he is]
(2) Alice intends that [she has sex with the Sundance Kid of movie fame]

However, we should not follow Hurd in characterizing (1) as a *de re* intention, and (2) as a *de dicto* intention. Instead, if we use the *de re / de dicto* terminology in the standard way that it is used in the philosophy of mind and language, then both (1) and (2) are *de dicto* intention ascriptions. This is because both characterize the "mental description" of Alice's intention in terms of concepts that Alice herself must possess (Burge 1977). By contrast, *de re* ascriptions of attitudes merely indicate relations of acquaintance. Consequently, these ascriptions can be made when someone is acquainted with the subject matter of her attitude (Lewis 1979). We can make such an ascription in the case of Alice, since she is acquainted with someone—Brian:

(3) Of Brian, Alice intends that she has sex with him

Unlike (1) and (2), there are no square brackets in (3), since the *de re* intention ascription does not characterize the "mental description" under which Alice intends sex. Consequently, *de re* ascriptions need not employ terms that express concepts employed by the subject herself. For example, (3) does not imply that Alice is thinking of Brian under the mental description "Brian". Indeed, (3) can be true even if Brian has falsely said his name is "Robert". The point that is crucial for our purposes is that, simply because Alice is directly acquainted with Brian as her sexual partner, (3) will be true. Consequently, (3) will be true regardless of whether (1) is true or (2) is true. But if (2) and (3) are both true, then Alice does not validly consent to sex. As a result, (3) is insufficient for Alice to validly consent to sex with Robert. In other words, a *de re* intention is insufficient for valid consent. This point generalizes widely: because (conscious) sex involves acquaintance, *de re* sexual intentions are ubiquitous, and so will always be present when deception leads to non-consensual sex.

Again, it is important to bear in mind that a consent-giver will typically have multiple intentions. For example, Alice will no doubt also have this intention:

(4) Alice intends that [she has sex with the man standing in front of her]

Indeed, we need to attribute to Alice a *de dicto* intention that employs an indexical concept like "in front of her", in order to explain e.g. her physical interactions with this man (Lewis 1979). Moreover, it is a *de dicto* attitude ascription like (4) that grounds the *de re* attitude ascription of (3). In other words, it is true that, of Brian, Alice intends to have sex with him because Alice intends that [she has sex with the man standing in front of her]. As we have already noted, this attribution of the intention in (4) does not exclude attributions of more specific intentions like (1) and (2). Clearly, Alice will have intention (4) if she has intention (1). But she will also have intention (4) if she has intention (2). (Compare the analogues of predictive belief attributions to (1), (2) and (4): clearly, Alice has the unspecific belief that she will have sex with the man standing in front of her.) So, if we assume that Alice does not give valid consent if Brian has impersonated Robert Redford and (2) is true, then we should conclude that (4) is insufficient for Alice's giving valid consent. To put that point in the language of "mental descriptions", it is not enough for Alice to validly consent to sex with Brian that Alice consents under *some* description to sex with Brian.

Assuming Alice does not validly consent to Brian, how should we explain this? It is natural to look for mental descriptions, such that if someone gives sexual consent under one of these descriptions, and the description is not true of her sexual partner, then she does not validly consent to the sex. This is a difficult and substantive issue. One promising approach is to consider the question of which rights we have in the first place. One answer is that we only have coarse-grained rights not to have sex with someone (which we can waive for any reason at all), but lack fine-grained rights not to have sex with someone-with-a-headache (Liberto 2017). On this view, if Jones intends to consent to sex with Smith under the description "Smith", then this intention could constitute valid consent, even if Smith has a headache and Jones does not intend to consent to sex with Smith under the description "Smith with a headache".

Alternatively, we could adopt a radical view that focuses on the features of the sexual encounter that are material to someone's decision to consent to sex. Let us define a "deal-breaker" as any feature of an encounter, such that the consent-giver is opposed to consenting to the encounter, given that it has this feature.[4] Now a consent-giver does not intend to consent to any encounter that has a deal-breaker. So if such an intention is necessary for valid consent to this encounter, then the following result holds: if an encounter only occurs because the consent-giver was deceived about a deal-breaker, then she does not validly consent to that encounter (Dougherty 2013). This result will strike many people as counterintuitive, since it entails that even deception about someone's income could lead to non-consensual sex, if a certain income was a deal-breaker for the consent-giver. The result may be more palatable if we allow that some forms of non-consensual sex are only minor wrongs, e.g. when the sex imposes only minor harms on the consent-giver (Boonin unpubl.).

In our discussion, we have been looking at the content of a consent-giver's intentions. But, in closing, we should note that there is another option: we could look at the content of their expressions of consent, and consider when and how deception might result in this content failing to include the interaction that actually takes place. This option will seem particularly appealing if we think that communication is necessary for valid consent (Dougherty 2013). But it is an option that has received little attention to date, and so for now must remain an avenue for future research.

15.4 Conclusion

This chapter has discussed different accounts of the relation between deception and consent, organized around a novel distinction between duty-first and awareness-first approaches. While analytically distinct, these approaches need not be competitors, as there may be more than one way that deception relates to consent. The approaches have different advantages and disadvantages. Duty-first approaches start with an independent account of key duties not to deceive, and then use this account to say that, when these duties are not met, the deceiver lacks her victim's valid consent to the action in question. These approaches have the advantage of making the aetiology of false beliefs intrinsically morally relevant—they claim that there is no valid consent only when the false beliefs are caused by the consent-receiver failing in her duties. But a disadvantage of duty-first approaches is that they now owe us an account of what these key duties are. This disadvantage is not faced by awareness-first approaches. These approaches begin by specifying an independent account of the awareness necessary for valid consent. This opens up the possibility of appealing to this account in outlining the rationale for our duties not to deceive. But the approaches come with the cost of failing to make the aetiology of false beliefs intrinsically relevant to whether consent is valid.

Duty-first and awareness-first approaches both need to choose which features of an encounter are such that deception about these features will lead to an absence of valid consent to this encounter. They are choosing between similar options. For example, they could focus narrowly on some special features, or broadly include any features that the consent-giver considered materially relevant to her consent. But while both duty-first and awareness-first approaches share these options in common, their motivations for choosing between these options may differ. On duty-first approaches, we would fundamentally be concerned with identifying the duties that one must fulfil in order to create an e.g. adequately fair context for a consent transaction. This would frame our choice as one to be guided by concerns of fairness. On an awareness-first approach, we would fundamentally be concerned with identifying true beliefs that one must have either for consent to be voluntary, or for the consent's content to include the actual encounter. In this way, the distinction between duty-first and awareness-first approaches is not only useful for characterizing the internal justificatory structure of a view of consent. It also helps make clear how different approaches should go about determining which types of deception lead to non-consensual behavior.

Notes

1 One option, which may turn out to be an alternative to both approaches, is the idea that deception leads to an absence of valid consent for an encounter when the deception has a sufficiently adverse effect on the meaning and value of the encounter (Tadros 2016).
2 For criticism of this option, see Manson (2017), Jubb (2017), Lazenby & Gabriel (2017), and Liberto (2017).
3 For (to my mind, decisive) criticism of this view of why coercion debilitates consent, see Liberto (unpubl.). See also Tadros (2016).
4 As a flawed rule of thumb, we might employ counterfactuals: for most deal-breakers it will be the case that, were the consent-giver aware of the feature, then she would not have decided to consent. But this counterfactual test is only good as a rough and ready heuristic and faces counterexamples—see (Chadha 2016; Tadros 2016). To canonically state what a deal-breaker is, we should not consider counterfactual mental states, but instead focus on the actual content of the consent-giver's actual mental states (Dougherty 2013).

References

Alexander, L. (1996) "The Moral Magic of Consent (II)," *Legal Theory* 2: 165–74.
Alexander, L. (2014) "The Ontology of Consent," *Analytic Philosophy* 55: 102–13.
Archard, D. (1998) *Sexual Consent*. Oxford: Westview.
Beyleveld, D. and R. Brownsword (2007) *Consent in the Law*. Oxford: Hart Publishing.
Boonin, D. (unpublished manuscript) "Sex, Lies and Harm: Dougherty on Deceptive Seduction".
Bragg, R. (1999) "Ex-Wife is Suing Cuba over a Spy's Deception," *New York Times*, August 15, accessed on February 1, 2013. www.nytimes.com/1999/08/15/us/ex-wife-is-suing-cuba-over-a-spy-s-deception.html.
Burge, T. (1977) "Belief *De Re*," *The Journal of Philosophy* 74: 338–62.
Buss, S. (2005) "Valuing Autonomy and Respecting People: Manipulation, Seduction and the Basis of Moral Complaints," *Ethics* 115: 195–235.
Calhoun, C. (2000) "The Virtue of Civility," *Philosophy & Public Affairs* 29: 251–75.
Chadha, K. (2016) *Sexual Consent: Sketching a Liberal Account*. Thesis submitted in partial fulfilment of the requirements for the degree of BPhil in Philosophy, University of Oxford.
Dougherty, T. (2013) "Sex, Lies and Consent," *Ethics* 123: 717–44.
Falk, P. (1998) "Rape by Fraud and Rape by Coercion," *Brooklyn Law Review* 64: 39–149.
Feinberg, J. (1986) "Victims' Excuses: The Case of Fraudulently Procured Consent," *Ethics* 96: 330–45.
Herring, J. (2005) "Mistaken Sex," *Criminal Law Review*: 511–24.
Hurd, H. (1996) "The Moral Magic of Consent (I)," *Legal Theory* 2: 121–46.

Jubb, R. (2017) "Consent and Deception," *Journal of Ethics and Social Philosophy* 12: 223–9.
Larson, J. (1993) "Women Understand So Little, They Call My Good Nature 'Deceit': A Feminist Rethinking of Seduction," *Columbia Law Review* 93: 374–472.
Lazenby, H. and I. Gabriel (2017) "Permissible Secrets," *The Philosophical Quarterly*. Advance online publication, https://doi.org/10.1093/pq/pqx044.
Lewis, D. (1979) "Attitudes *De Dicto* and *De Se*," *The Philosophical Review* 88: 513–43.
Liberto, H. (2017) "Intentions and Sexual Consent," *Philosophical Explorations*. Special Issue, "The Normative Significance of Intentions," 20: 127–41.
Liberto, H. (unpublished manuscript) "Moral Debilitation".
Manson, N. (2017) "How Not to Think about the Ethics of Deceiving into Sex," *Ethics* 127: 415–29.
Manson, N. (unpublished manuscript) "Why Deception Does Not Undermine Consent".
Manson, N. and O. O'Neill (2007) *Rethinking Informed Consent*. Cambridge: Cambridge University Press.
McDowell, J. (1984) "*De Re* Senses," *Philosophical Quarterly* 34: 283–94.
McGregor, J. (2005) *Is it Rape? On Acquaintance Rape and Taking Women's Consent Seriously*. Aldershot: Ashgate.
Miller, F. and A. Wertheimer (2009) "Preface to a Theory of Consent Transactions: Beyond Valid Consent," in F. Miller and A. Wertheimer (ed.), *The Ethics of Consent*. Oxford: Oxford University Press.
Nagel, T. (2006) "Concealment and Exposure," *Philosophy & Public Affairs* 27: 3–30.
O'Neill, O. (1985) "Between Consenting Adults," *Philosophy & Public Affairs* 14: 252–77.
Pallikkathayil, J. (2010) "Deriving Morality from Politics: Rethinking the Formula of Humanity," *Ethics* 121: 116–47.
Perkins, R. (1957) *Perkins on Criminal Law*. First Edition. New York: Foundation.
Rubenfeld, J. (2013) "The Riddle of Rape-by-Deception and the Myth of Sexual Autonomy," *Yale Law Review* 122: 1372–443.
Schulhofer, S. (1998) *Unwanted Sex*. Cambridge, MA: Harvard University Press.
Shiffrin, S. (2014) *Speech Matters: On Lying, Morality and Law*. Princeton, NJ: Princeton University Press.
Stalnaker, R. (2014) *Context*. Oxford: Oxford University Press.
Tadros, V. (2016) *Wrongs and Crimes*. Oxford: Oxford University Press.
Wertheimer, A. (2003) *Consent to Sexual Relations*. Cambridge: Cambridge University Press.
Westen, P. (2004) *The Logic of Consent*. Aldershot: Ashgate.

Related topics

Ch.4 The normative force of consent
Ch.6 The scope of consent
Ch.8 Valid consent
Ch.16 Sexual consent
Ch.24 Informed consent
Ch.25 Consent and medical treatment
Ch.26 Consent in clinical research

16
SEXUAL CONSENT

David Archard

16.1 Introduction

The crime of rape is defined by most jurisdictions as unconsented sex. More particularly, the sex in question is normally defined as penetrative sex, and the *mens rea* will be defined in terms of the intentional, reckless or negligent disregard of or indifference of the putative rapist for the non-consent of the victim. Given that rape is also standardly regarded as one of the most serious of crimes – second only in severity of punishment to murder – it should be obvious why it is important to understand the nature of consent to sex (henceforward "sexual consent").

The legal definition of rape is closely related to but distinct from the view that sex without consent is morally wrong. That view is one half of what might be termed the liberal moral orthodoxy of sex that can be formally set out as:

Sex is morally permissible if and only if it is consensual.

In illustration of the distinction between the legal definition of rape and the liberal moral orthodoxy we should note that not all forms of impermissible sex need be criminalised. Thus, some forms of unconsented physical contact might be morally wrong but judged not so serious as to constitute criminal behaviour, even if they were subject to non-criminal sanctions (such as workplace penalties). Consider forms of sexual harassment that include unwanted physical closeness.

Moreover, not all forms of criminalised sex amount to rape. Inasmuch as the unconsented sex of rape is penetrative it is open to any jurisdiction to classify as lesser crimes – perhaps crimes of sexual assault – those forms of unconsented sex that are non-penetrative (for instance, sexual molestation, attempted penetration).

The liberal moral orthodoxy comprises two claims:

Non-consensual sex is impermissible; and
Consensual sex is permissible.

Few will deny the first claim. At most one might imagine somewhat far-fetched scenarios in which a token of non-consensual sex is *pro tanto* but not, all things considered, wrong: A rapes B under credible threat from C of some egregious harms to many others; A's rape of an unwilling B ensures the procreation of future humans and thus the survival of the species.

However, the second claim *is* controversial. I assume that there are no third-party harms. The claim, fully spelled out, is thus that, "Consensual sex is permissible only if it does not harm others not engaged in the sex in question". Some might think adultery between willing adults is nevertheless wrong insofar as it injures the spouse(s). Even with that qualification the second claim will be denied by those who are normally characterised as conservative sexual moralists. These will probably be, but need not be, those who endorse religious beliefs. The denial of the claim is, however, not dependent on the truth of any religion. For the conservative view will standardly appeal to the idea that only those sexual acts that are procreative in kind or in intent are morally allowed. In turn such a view may appeal to the idea of the proper nature or end (*telos*) of sexual activity.

A distinct conservative view is that consensual sex is only permissible if it is the expression of romantic love. Or it is permissible only if it is the expression of the right kinds of intentional attitude towards the other (Scruton 1986).

We should note that a defender of the liberal moral orthodoxy may – and indeed should – distinguish between permissibility and goodness (Primoratz 1999). Thus it can be argued that every instance of consensual sex is permissible, but that not all forms of consensual sex are of the same moral value. A liberal might regard some forms of consensual behaviour as worthless or base (for instance, promiscuous sex with strangers).

I do not intend here to evaluate the respective merits of these two views – the liberal moral orthodoxy and the conservative. Nor will I spend any time on the question of what counts as sexual. This latter metaphysical question is interesting but should not deflect us from attending to the principal question: what is the nature of sexual consent? However, it is important to acknowledge one point. Consent operates in a number of domains. Of interest to normative philosophers there are three principal ones: sex, biomedicine and the legitimate exercise of political power. In all three domains consent has what we will see is the same morally transformative power, rendering licit what would otherwise be illicit. Nevertheless, we should allow for two possibilities: first, consent can function as it does, can be morally transformative, in different ways in each domain; second, the legitimating function of consent can have a greater or lesser moral significance in each domain.

This second possibility is closely linked to the idea that sexual morality may be *sui generis* – that is, that what makes sexual behaviour morally right or wrong can only be properly understood through an appreciation of what is distinctive and different about *sexual* behaviour.

16.2 The moral magic of consent

Following Hurd (1996) it is standard to characterise the morally transformative power of consent as "magic". The thought appealed to by the use of this term is that – quite remarkably – by a single word or minor physical movement (such as a nod of one's head) a moral agent can transform what would otherwise be illicit into licit behaviour. I can give permission to another to do to me what in the absence of my consent would be wrong. Indeed, as suggested above, by giving my *sexual* consent I can change what would be *very* wrong – rape – into what is allowed. This fact about consent makes it all the more important to be clear when and how it is given.

However, it is worth noting a certain oddity in the description of what is going on in the case of sexual consent. Consider the parallel domain of medical consent. A doctor who gains my agreement to take blood then does to me what would be wrong if done without that consent (it would be an assault). He sticks a needle in my arm and extracts blood. Yet he does something *to* me whether he does it with or without my consent. Whilst it sounds right to say that sex without consent is something that is done to me, it sounds curious to describe consensual sex as sex in which two parties do things to one another. It sounds better – and the sex would surely be better – if it was rather a case of two persons having sex together. It is not so much a case of John doing things to Mary just as Mary does things to John but rather one of John having sex *with* Mary (and conversely Mary having sex *with* John). Consider – to emphasise the point – whether it makes much sense to describe the blood test as the doctor and her patient "having a blood taking together".

This oddity reveals something about the nature of sex – namely that it is a joint enterprise (and nothing in the foregoing should be taken as limiting the numbers engaged in that enterprise to two). It also hopefully shows up the fact that there is a real and radical difference between consensual sex and non-consented sex, something that will be returned to in a later section on the wrong of rape.

We should also distinguish consent from what Singer (1974: 47–52) has characterised as "quasi-consent" and which is closely related to the legal doctrine of *estoppel*. This is behaviour by somebody that gives rise to a reasonable expectation in others that she will do or allow something, such that the others can legitimately complain if their expectations are disappointed. The person does not consent but it is *as if* she did, and, arguably, it is as good as if she did. Someone might be liable for payment if she ordered a meal and led the restaurant to expect that she would pay. She could not complain that she did not agree to pay; she did enough for it to be true that she might as well have agreed.

However, in the case of sex, the idea of quasi-consent is troubling. It seems that it would be wrong to have sex with a woman who did not consent to the sex but who did what the other took as giving rise to an expectation that sex would be forthcoming. One should only have sex with someone who consents; one should not have sex with someone who causes you to believe that she will not complain if you do have sex with her. One may not be blameworthy for reasonably believing that the other does consent; one is arguably to blame for having sex only because you think the other did what is as morally good as consent.

16.3 Intention and performance

A first question to ask about sexual consent is what it is. This could be termed the "ontology of consent". Two main answers have been given to the question: one is that it is a state of mind, an intention to have sex or willing that sex; the other is that sexual consent is a behaviour or act, a performance of some kind. A third allows for a hybrid mixture of both and is defended by Wertheimer (2003). We might call the first the *attitudinal* account – defended by Hurd (1996) – and the second the *performative* – defended by McGregor (2005). The attitudinal account considers that someone has an attitude towards the sex, whereas the performative account considers that someone does something.

We can allow that on the performative account someone consents to sex by intentionally or deliberately doing something. One cannot accidentally consent to sex. We should also be clear that, on an attitudinal account, the willing of sex (perhaps better willing that sex) is distinct from a mental disposition to favour sex, what one could term taking up a "pro-attitude" to sex. Consider, thus, a dutiful wife who finds sex with her husband distasteful, such that she would rather not have sex with him. Or consider that, on some particular occasion, she is not well disposed to have sex with him. Nevertheless, she freely agrees to sex. Indeed, we might say that she agrees to sex with him even whilst she does not find the sex agreeable, or even that she does not agree *with* the sex *to* which she agrees. She might consistently – if unhappily – combine an attitude of willing that sex with a negative attitude towards the sex in question. One can will that someone may do X without willing that they actually do X, nor wanting them to do X, nor, again, being unhappy if they fail to do X.

The attitudinal account will allow for cases in which a performance that would otherwise be indicative of agreement is not accompanied by the appropriate attitude. Consider someone who intentionally says "I do" at a marriage ceremony whilst not willing that she be married. She does not wish to be married to the groom; nor does she want to allow others to marry her to the groom. The use of "intentionally" is important in order to distinguish such a case from one in which the utterance of "I do" is accidental or results from a linguistic misunderstanding, or is coerced (the "shotgun wedding"). She, for instance, utters the words knowing what they mean, but does so mischievously or playfully and insincerely. The insincerity of the utterance means that, in Austin's celebrated terminology, it is "infelicitous"; it thereby fails to do what those words normally do (Austin 1962).

Now a defender of the performative view will hold that her behaviour – the utterance of the words "I do" – *is* consent, whilst a defender of the attitudinal view will hold that consent is absent. In her heart she does not will that she be married, whether or not this is wanting to marry. A third "hybrid" view is then possible: that consent involves *both* a willing that something be the case and the outward behavioural communication ("objective expression") of that willing to the other (Westen 2004). The woman only consents if she utters the marriage vows as an outward expression of her inward will to be married.

However, it is surely hard to hold onto the idea of someone not willing what they deliberately and freely express in their actions. It is also important not to confuse the ontological question of whether someone does or does not consent by what they do or will from the normative question – to which we will turn – of whether the other is blameworthy for believing that there is consent, and behaving appropriately in the light of that belief.

The striking – if very unfortunate – test case for a choice between the attitudinal and performative accounts is the person whose extreme physical disability means that she can give no sign whatsoever of her agreement to sex (not even by an eye blink). Hurd (1996: 137) takes it on her preferred attitudinal account that such a person can consent whilst Wertheimer (2003: 152), who believes she cannot, views the case as evidently favouring the performative account. The point at issue is not whether the severely disabled person can enjoy sex; nor whether she is denied the opportunity to enjoy sex if denied the power of consenting to it. The point is whether someone who cannot do *anything* in the world can sensibly be thought of as someone who can change her moral relations to others – such as waive her rights over their possible actions – in that world. That would indeed be 'magical'.

One might invoke the analogy of promising and emphasise that the whole point of morally transforming one's relations to another is to secure the right kinds of beliefs – as to what may or will be done – on their part (Dougherty 2015). This change in beliefs can surely only be done by successful communication.

16.4 A note on terminology

Mary says "yes" to sex with John. Does she consent to that sex? Many who write on this topic will say that her consent is "real" or "genuine" or "valid" only if her affirmative utterance is informed and voluntary. Thus she may consent if forced to say "yes" but not "really" or "validly" consent. Such language can be confusing. Better, it would seem, to say that one either consents or does not consent to sex. If Mary is forced to say "yes" to sex with John she does not consent to that sex. It is not that she does consent but somehow not "really". At best it would be better to distinguish between *assent*, and its signs, and consent proper.

16.5 Actual consent to sex

The question of what consent consists in (the ontology of consent) is to be distinguished from the question of how someone might on any particular occasion actually consent. On the attitudinal account a simple willing that sex takes place will suffice. By contrast, defenders of the performative view owe an account of what kinds of behaviour are enough to communicate sexual consent. In more formal terms the question is what can count as *tokens* of consenting. One very stringent view is what might be termed the affirmative verbal standard, according to which sexual consent is given if and only if one utters, sincerely and voluntarily, words such as "I agree to sex", "Yes" or "OK". Such a standard has been defended philosophically (Pineau 1989) and can also be found in enforceable sexual offenses policies, especially those in operation on a number of American university campuses.

Some will criticise such a standard on the grounds that it seeks to impose an overly rigorous understanding of what might count as consensual on a sphere of human activity marked by passion, spontaneity and unpredictability. It will be replied that the costs of getting it wrong about the sexual consent of the other are too great to permit the running of risks that can easily be avoided by seeking, and securing, explicit confirmation of consent. Nevertheless, it will be said that the standard applies best to first-time sexual encounters with erstwhile strangers where understandings of what is sought and allowed need to be negotiated. Conversely, then, the affirmative verbal standard of consent seems inappropriate in longstanding sexual relationships whose parties have come to understand, and value, what the other wants and will tolerate, and where outward signs of agreement are otiose.

A different challenge to the affirmative verbal standard comes from those who appeal to the existence and use of conventions whereby certain kinds of behaviour may reasonably be taken to signal sexual consent. Their use may, further, be defended by citing evidence of those – especially, it is said, women – who are putatively unhappy with having to make explicit and verbal their agreement to sex (Husak & Thomas 1992). The response to the use of such conventions is that there need not, and evidence suggests there is not, agreement between the genders as to what these rules are or license. Furthermore, the risk of using them is unwarranted where it is possible to secure explicit confirmation of agreement to have sex (Archard 1997).

16.6 Reasonable beliefs as to sexual consent

The question of what consent is and the separate one of what should count as a giving of consent in any particular circumstance are in turn distinct from that of what it is reasonable for anyone to believe is sexual consent. The answer to this question is of direct relevance to the ascription of culpability for having sex in the absence of consent. It is thus the means of establishing the *mens rea* of rape. How the law understands the fault of the rapist was given dramatic focus by the notorious decision of the English Law Lords in the case of *DPP v. Morgan* [1975]. The Lords there determined that an honest belief by a man that a woman with whom he had sex was consenting did constitute a valid defence to the charge of rape, irrespective of whether that belief was based on reasonable grounds.

The judgment attracted considerable jurisprudential criticism (Pickard 1980; Thornton 1982). Some claim that it is impossible, or virtually impossible (Telling 1983: 138), for a man to make a mistake as to the woman's sexual consent on the grounds that it is in the nature of sex as an intimate activity that one's dispositions are evidently and immediately disclosed to the other. Indeed, Duff thinks that "there is no logical space for either doubt or mistake about the consent of either party" (Duff 1981: 58). Yet such a claim is open to the challenge of cases, both imagined and real, in which such mistakes do indeed seem all too possible. Moreover, if no such mistake is even conceivable, then rape is not wrong but rather unimaginable. In *Morgan* the defendants discounted the very evident and distressing protests of Mrs Morgan. Yet a woman might have good reason not to resist or show dissent in circumstances where a man might understandably not know those reasons and form, reasonably, a belief in her consent. To insist that any false belief in consent is culpable would mean seeing rape as a strict liability offense.

What is needed is an account of when and why a man's mistaken belief as to the woman's consent to sex is unreasonable. If the affirmative verbal standard is endorsed then a failure to secure a positive response and consequent reliance on other putative signs of consent will be conclusive evidence of an unreasonable belief in consent. Yet, in those circumstances where a demand for that standard seems implausibly stringent, a belief as to consent might reasonably be based on non-verbal behaviour. Nevertheless, a man is culpable if he discounts the evidence of circumstances in which sincere and voluntary consent is highly unlikely to be given (a woman's behaviour notwithstanding). The English *Sexual Offences Act* (2003) lists those "evidential presumptions" that should be sufficient if known by a defendant to take his belief in any consent as unreasonable. These include the use of or threat of violence, as well as the administration to the victim of a "stupefying" substance. Moreover, it would be clearly wrong of a man to discount the testimony of a woman as to her non-consent, whatever he might take other evidence to show (Archard 1999). In *Morgan* the defendants unreasonably relied on the testimony of Captain Morgan as to how they should interpret the protests of his wife.

16.7 Defeating conditions of sexual consent

Any comprehensive account of consent must provide a description of who can give and withhold consent, and of those circumstances in which consent is vitiated. These are fairly standard descriptions across all instances of consent. Only those human beings possessed of certain capacities can consent. Children are thus excluded, as are those suffering from some permanent serious mental incapacity. The conditions that defeat consent are a lack of voluntariness and ignorance.

In respect of children and sexual consent we should note two possible normative principles. One is that below a certain age a child cannot give consent. Thus sex with a minor below that age is non-consensual and morally impermissible. This is so even if the minor voluntarily assents to sex. The crime of "statutory rape" captures this wrong. A second "protective" principle allows that at some age minors can consent. Nevertheless, it might be thought appropriate to protect such minors from entering into sexual relations with others (Scottish Law Commission 2007: Part 4). This could be to guard against their exploitation, or because it is thought that sex below a certain age, even if consensual, is intrinsically wrong.

Sexual consent is absent if someone has sex non-voluntarily or in ignorance of some important, salient fact concerning the sex. A classic definition of rape is that it is sex obtained by "force, fear or fraud". "Force" is understood as meaning the physical overpowering of a person; "fear" as submission before the credible threat of significant physical harm. (We will turn to "fraud" in due course.) Such a definition is restrictive and narrow in that it excludes forms of coercion that are non-physical but nevertheless such as to leave the victim with no reasonable choice but to comply. Consider a man who threatens to expose a woman's secret such that she would lose her job and suffer severe reputational damage.

The definition also reflected a particular patriarchal view of women as only prepared to undergo sex with someone other than their husband if overpowered or on pain of death or serious injury. On such a view a woman is expected to "resist to the utmost" the unwelcome sexual advances of another. Indeed, only credible evidence of such resistance – in the injuries suffered by a woman – might be sufficient to secure the conviction of the rapist.

In respect of fraud there is a distinction to be considered later. However, we may note that if a woman is misled as to some salient material fact about the sex to which she assents then her consent is, *prima facie*, vitiated and she is raped.

However, on this initial characterisation of the defeating conditions of sexual consent there is an apparent puzzle. This is that the view of rape as non-consensual sex is in tension with its characterisation as seriously morally wrongful if it is allowed that sexual consent is vitiated by some forms of coercion and of deception. Consider, as oft-cited examples, the insistent but subtle pressure of a man saying, "Have sex with me or I will end the relationship"; and the lie of the skilled seducer, "I am actually a secret agent for the government/earn a huge salary for a leading financial institution". Such men who thereby obtain sex do not – common sense would insist – do anything *seriously* wrongful.

One response to this puzzle would be to give up the definition of rape as non-consensual sex. This is unwelcome inasmuch as that definition represents a major advance on earlier definitions that were seriously prejudicial to women's interests. Another response is to retain the definition of rape but allow that not all instances of rape are seriously morally wrongful. I will consider the wrongfulness of non-consensual sex in the next section.

We can acknowledge that a man may behave in a morally disreputable manner by pressurising the other to have sex with him, or by misrepresenting himself to her so that she agrees to sex. However, the important question is not whether he behaves badly but whether his bad behaviour vitiates her consent.

A proper response to the puzzle can acknowledge that deception and non-forceful or non-physical coercion come in degrees. However, the crucial point is whether these exceed a threshold such that the other's consent to sex is vitiated. Thus, one might identify as coercive pressure, following Wertheimer (1987), a wrongful worsening of the other's situation to a point where there is no reasonable choice but compliance (Conly 2004). Similarly, one might define the deception or lie that vitiates sexual consent as a "deal breaker" – namely a lie about some feature of the sexual encounter such that the other would not be willing to have sex if she knew it had that feature (Dougherty 2013). In both cases (deception and pressure) a "but for" counterfactual account is used: had Smith not used pressure or lied as he did then Jones would not have agreed to sex with Smith.

On this kind of account there will then be standard problems of aggregation and context. Imagine that Jones is only just unwilling to have sex with Smith, but that the pressure or withheld fact tips her into agreement. It is true that "but for" this pressure or lie she would not have consented. However, arguably, each, in making the difference between consent and non-consent, did not, in themselves, make *that much* difference.

This kind of case could be contrasted with one in which the pressure or lie is very significant. It makes the difference between consent and non-consent by being sufficient for Jones to have sex with Smith. Yet it does so *whatever* the circumstances and *however* weighty the considerations that might have, in the absence of the pressure or lie, otherwise disposed Jones not to have sex with Smith. Must then the pressure or lie that vitiates consent be causally sufficient to secure agreement irrespective of all other factors in the decision-making circumstances?

There is a further difficulty that attends the use of deception to vitiate sexual consent. Traditionally, Anglo-American law has distinguished in this context between "fraud in the *factum*" and "fraud in the inducement". Essentially, the former concerns fraud as to the nature of the act, whereas the latter concerns fraud as to the purported consequences of the act. An example of the former would be a doctor falsely telling a naïve female patient that he is conducting a medical examination when he is in fact penetrating her vagina with his penis. An example of the latter would be a doctor duplicitously telling a patient that she can only be cured of some medical condition by having sex with him (see Falk 1998 for a comprehensive survey of cases of rape by fraud).

Anglo-American law has been disposed to view fraud in the *factum* but not in the inducement as constituting rape. One explanation for this is the presumption that the inducements to sex that significantly reduce voluntariness would nevertheless suggest that the sex thereby induced is not especially harmful to the "victim" (Feinberg 1986). After all, in the cited case the woman is willing to have sex with the doctor even if she does so on a false promise of what it will deliver. By contrast, in the "fraud in the *factum*" case the woman is *not* willing to have sex with the doctor. However, the distinction between the types of fraud is not perspicuous. After all, any material deception as to what follows from the sex can be construed as a false characterisation of the act. The woman, in the suggested example, consents only to "curative sex" and not to sex *simpliciter*.

The background worry about fraud in the inducement is the sense that the skilled seducer who falsely represents what will follow on the morrow of sex is not properly represented as a rapist. He is at worst a cad. However, saying this may underestimate the background context of unequal gender relations within which a male seducer operates (Anderson 2006). The response may also miss the threshold point. What is critical is whether the pressure applied is such that but for the lie told about the sex there would not have been agreement to it. This still allows that there may be a range of deceptions, falling short of those that vitiate consent, that render the resultant sexual acts morally wrongful (Larson 1993).

16.8 Wrong of rape

The previous section identified a puzzle about viewing some forms of non-consensual sex as seriously wrongful. One response to the puzzle would be to distinguish between kinds of sex and to deny that all forms of non-consensual sex amount to rape. One might maintain that rape is only a sub-set of seriously wrongful non-consensual sexual acts, those that involve penetration, for instance.

The other response to the puzzle denies that all instances of rape, even when understood as non-consensual penetrative sex, are seriously wrongful. One way to do this is to argue that "Rape is *typically* or *likely* seriously morally wrongful". It is so inasmuch as it is *experienced* as harmful (Wertheimer 2003). All instances of non-consensual sex are of a kind that makes it likely that they will be experienced as (especially) harmful. The problem for such an account is the "hurt-less" rape, one in which a woman does not know that she has been raped and thus does not experience the rape as distressing. She may not know at the time or subsequent to the event (Shute & Gardiner 2000).

One surely wants to insist that a wrong is done to a woman who does not know that she has been raped. Further, that the wrong in question is independent of her experience of it. There is then a question of what that wrong is. An answer to that question must explain what it is that makes rape *seriously* wrongful. To specify the wrong as a disregard for the other's consent may capture the "moral injury" (Hampton 1999) or "dignitary harm" (Westen 2004: 149) of rape. However, someone who would have sex with the other even if the other did not consent does such injury even if the other does consent. He does so for he is indifferent to her as a source of agreement.

Something else is involved in the wrong of rape. This is the violation of sexual integrity. How exactly that is captured requires attention to two important points (Archard 2007). First, a violation of sexual integrity is radically distinct from a violation of bodily integrity. Successfully expressing that distinction means attending to the significance of our nature as sexed beings. This in turn is not the same as the significance or value we may, as individuals, attach to sex. Second, non-consensual sex is not sex from which consent has somehow been subtracted. This would suggest that even non-consensual sex has some value for the person or some residual capacity for pleasurableness. However, non-consensual sex is of an entirely different order to consensual sex.

Acknowledgement of these two points provides the means to respond to those who think that the rape of some – such as a prostitute or promiscuous person – does less injury inasmuch as they are generally more willing than others to have sex. It should also rebut the presumption that a willingness of Smith to have sex with Jones in the past does not lessen the injury done her when Jones compels Smith to have sex against her will on some particular occasion.

16.9 Limits of consent

A liberal, despite initial sympathies with the moral orthodoxy outlined at the outset, might be moved to think that the principle expressed by the second claim – consensual sex that injures no third parties is permissible – is false inasmuch as some kinds of consensual sex are impermissible. Two kinds of consensual sex in particular trouble the liberal: prostitution and adult incest. The worry raised by the controversial English judgment of *R v Brown* [1993] was that extreme sado-masochistic activity between consenting adults is not exempt from criminalisation insofar as the harms consented to in that kind of case are egregious. However, if this is a legitimate worry it is not exclusively one about *sexual* conduct; the judgment would, in principle, extend to any consensual practice that caused or risked very serious harms.

The concerns about prostitution can be variously expressed. If it is that prostitutes do not really agree to the sale of sex (in virtue, for instance, of "economic coercion") then the liberal moral orthodoxy is unchallenged. The same would be true if the concerns were about third-party harms – such as to those injured by their partners' use of prostitutes, or to women in general, or to the public good.

The other principal concern is that prostitution is exploitative, in which case it can be argued that any complete normative theory of sexual conduct should be modified as follows: Consensual and non-exploitative sex that injures no third parties is permissible. A distinct concern is that prostitution is injurious to prostitutes, and that, although freely chosen, it should be regulated so as to prevent those harms (De Marneffe 2009). In such a case, the respect for autonomy that underlies granting consent its normative power is seriously qualified by a concession to paternalism.

The other problem case is incest. Instances of consensual sex between adult siblings can be envisaged that run no significant risks of third-party harms (such as those of transmitting genetic abnormalities). Yet it may still be said that there is something very wrong with incest. Such a judgment will be left with little recourse other than to the idea of a fundamental taboo against such a form of sexual activity (Neu 1976). If that is the case then moral theorising arguably gives way to the brute fact of ingrained human responses that do not admit of any possible rational justification.

16.10 Conclusion

If consent works its moral magic in the domain of sexual activity, does it do so in the very same way as it works elsewhere? This is not so much a question of how consent to sex is given as opposed to consent to other things – although that clearly matters. Rather it is a question of whether sexual consent can be morally transformative to the same degree as consent is elsewhere. If not, the issue is whether that says something about the *sui generis* nature of sexual morality, or whether sex is such as to raise interesting questions about the proper limits of consensuality.

References

Anderson, S. (2006) "Sex Under Pressure: Jerks, Boorish Behaviour, and Gender Hierarchy," *Res Publica* 11: 349–69.

Archard, D. (1997) "'A Nod's as Good as a Wink': Consent, Convention, and Reasonable Belief," *Legal Theory* 3(3): 273–90.

Archard, D. (1999) "The *Mens Rea* of Rape: Reasonableness and Culpable Mistakes," in K. Burgess-Jackson (ed.), *A Most Detestable Crime: New Philosophical Essays on Rape*. New York: Oxford University Press: 213–29.

Archard, D. (2007) "The Wrong of Rape," *Philosophical Quarterly* 57: 374–93.

Austin, J.L. (1962) *How to Do Things with Words*. Oxford: Oxford University Press.

Conly, S. (2004) "Seduction, Rape and Coercion," *Ethics* 115 (October): 96–121.

De Marneffe, P. (2009) *Liberalism and Prostitution*. New York: Oxford University Press.

Dougherty, T. (2013) "Sex, Lies and Consent," *Ethics* 123 (July): 717–44.

Dougherty, T. (2015) "Yes Means Yes: Consent as Communication," *Philosophy & Public Affairs* 43(3): 1–30.

DPP v Morgan [1975] UKHL 3.

Duff, R.A. (1981) "Recklessness and Rape," *The Liverpool Law Review* 3: 49–64.

Falk, P.J. (1998) "Rape by Fraud and Rape by Coercion," *Brooklyn Law Review* 64(1): 39–180.

Feinberg, J. (1986) "Victims' Excuses: The Case of Fraudulently Procured Consent," *Ethics* 96 (January): 330–45.

Hampton, J. (1999) "Defining Wrong and Defining Rape," in K. Burgess-Jackson (ed.), *A Most Detestable Crime: New Philosophical Essays on Rape*. New York: Oxford University Press, 118–56.

Hurd, H. (1996) "The Moral Magic of Consent (I)," *Legal Theory* 2(2): 121–46.

Husak, D. and G.C. Thomas (1992) "Date Rape, Social Convention, and Reasonable Mistakes," *Law and Philosophy* 11: 95–126.

Larson, J.E. (1993) "'Women Understand So Little, They Call My Good Nature Deceit': A Feminist Rethinking of Seduction," *Columbia Law Review* 93(2): 374–472.

McGregor, J. (2005) *Is It Rape? On Acquaintance Rape and Taking Women's Consent Seriously*. Aldershot: Ashgate.

Neu, J. (1976) "What is Wrong with Incest?" *Inquiry* 19: 27–39.

Pickard, T. (1980) "Culpable Mistakes and Rape: Relating *Mens Rea* to the Crime," *University of Toronto Law Review* 30: 5–98.

Pineau, L. (1989) "Date Rape: A Feminist Analysis," *Law and Philosophy* 8: 217–43.

Primoratz, I. (1999) *Ethics and Sex*. London: Routledge.

R v Brown [1993] UKHL 19, [1994] 1 AC 212.

Scottish Law Commission (2007) *Report on Rape and Other Sexual Offences*. Edinburgh: Stationery Office. www.legislation.gov.uk/ukpga/2003/42/contents

Scruton, R. (1986) *Sexual Desire: A Philosophical Investigation*. London: Weidenfeld and Nicolson.

Sexual Offences Act (2003) London: HMSO. www.legislation.gov.uk/ukpga/2003/42/contents

Shute, S. and J. Gardiner (2000) "The Wrongness of Rape," in J. Horder (ed.), *Oxford Essays in Jurisprudence*, 4th series. Oxford: Oxford University Press, 193–217.

Singer, P. (1974) *Democracy and Disobedience*. London: Oxford University Press.

Telling, D. (1983) "Rape – Consent and Belief," *Journal of Criminal Law* 47: 129–39.

Thornton, T.M. (1982) "Rape and *Mens Rea*," *Canadian Journal of Philosophy* 8: 119–46.

Wertheimer, A. (1987) *Coercion*. Princeton, NJ: Princeton University Press.

Wertheimer, A. (2003) *Consent to Sexual Relations*. Cambridge: Cambridge University Press.

Westen, P. (2004) *The Logic of Consent, The Diversity and Deceptiveness of Consent as a Defence to Criminal Conduct*. Aldershot: Ashgate.

Further reading

Alan Soble and Nicholas Power (eds.), *The Philosophy of Sex: Contemporary Readings*, 5th edition (Lanham, MD: Rowman and Littlefield, 2008) is a comprehensive collection of the most important writings on the philosophy of sex. Alan Soble (ed.) *Sex from Plato to Paglia: A Philosophical Encyclopedia* (Westport, CT: Greenwood Press, 2006) is an impressively wide-ranging collection of commissioned entries on philosophical sexuality.

David Archard, *Sexual Consent* (Boulder, CO: Westview, 1998) provides a critical overview of what consent means in a sexual context and an evaluation of particular instances of sexual consensuality. Catherine MacKinnon, *Toward a Feminist Theory of the State* (Cambridge, MA: Harvard University Press, 1989), Andrea Dworkin, *Intercourse* (New York: Free Press, 1987), and Carole Pateman, *The Sexual Contract* (Stanford, CA: Stanford University Press, 1988) all offer important, and interestingly different, feminist critiques of the very possibility under patriarchy of mutual consent to sex by equals. Stephen J. Schulhofer, *Unwanted Sex: The Culture of Intimidation and the Failure of the Law* (Cambridge, MA: Harvard University Press, 1998) gives an excellent and provocative account of how American law has failed to safeguard consensual sexual relationships.

Related topics

Ch.2 What is consent?
Ch.4 The normative force of consent
Ch.5 Consent and wronging a person
Ch.15 Deception and consent
Ch.21 Rape as non-consensual sex

PART III

Legal theory

17
THE VOLENTI MAXIM

Michelle Madden Dempsey

17.1 The volenti maxim: a brief introduction

In its simplest terms, the volenti maxim means what it says: "to one who consents, no wrong is done". As Heidi Hurd memorably puts it, consent has a kind of "moral magic" that can turn "a battery into a handshake; a sexual assault into a kiss . . . a theft into a gift", etc. (cf. Hurd, this volume, Chapter 4; Hurd 1996). Primarily, the volenti maxim functions as a tag-along to its more famous cousin, the harm principle. As articulated by John Stuart Mill, the harm principle provides as follows: "[T]he only purpose for which power can be rightfully exercised over any member of a civilized community, against his will, is to prevent harm to others" (Mill 2002 [1859]: 8).

As a supplement to the harm principle, the volenti maxim helps us identify when a case involves "harm to others" in the sense of a "*wrongful* harm to others". Identifying which harms count as *wrongful* harms matters because the harm principle is not designed to prevent all harms whatsoever. Rather, the universally accepted interpretation of the harm principle limits its concern to *wrongful* harms. (Thus, properly stated, the harm principle should read, ". . . [T]he only purpose for which power can be rightfully exercised over any member of a civilized community, against his will, is to prevent *wrongful* harm to others".) The volenti maxim steps in to inform us that *consensual* harms are *not wrongful* harms. As Joel Feinberg explains:

> One class of harms . . . must certainly be excluded from those that are properly called wrongs, namely those to which the victim has consented . . . The harm principle will not justify prohibition of consensual activities . . .; its aim is to prevent only those harms that are wrongs.
>
> *(Feinberg 1984: 35–6)*

Modern philosophers have attributed the origins of the volenti maxim to Aristotle, but the attribution is shaky at best (Feinberg 1984: 255, n. 12; Westen 2004: 115). While it is true that something like the basic gist of the volenti maxim might be read into the *Nicomachean Ethics* – where Aristotle claims that "no one is voluntarily treated unjustly; for no one wishes to be unjustly treated" (Aristotle 1999: 86) – two points are worth noting. First, at least on W.D. Ross's translation, Aristotle uses a term closer to "wishes" – not "consents". As such, Aristotle's actual claim may be closer to something like: "to one who *wishes* to be treated in a certain way, no wrong is done in treating him that way". Now, of course, *consenting* to something is not nearly the same as *wishing* that it would happen – just ask anyone consenting to painful medical procedures, while wishing for a pain-free return to full health. Given this gap between *consenting* to certain treatment and *wishing* to be treated in that way, there is space to wonder if the volenti maxim can plausibly claim Aristotelian lineage.

Second, at this point in the *Ethics* (book 5, ch. 9), Aristotle's claim is mere stipulation. The closest he comes to fleshing out an argument in defense of the claim comes in book 5, chapter 11, where he takes up the question of "whether a man can treat himself unjustly or not". The argument runs roughly as follows: (1) one who voluntarily harms another acts unjustly against (wrongs) the person who was harmed; (2) one who voluntarily harms himself also acts unjustly – but *not* against the person who was harmed (that is, he does not act unjustly against *himself*); (3) rather, one who voluntarily harms himself acts unjustly against the state (community); (4) thus, the state may punish one who voluntarily harms himself. On this reading, Aristotle seems to reject the volenti maxim, at least as applied to criminal law, where the state (rather than the harmed party) prosecutes the legal action (and thus claims the role of the "wronged party").[1]

As a legal doctrine, the volenti maxim's origins can be traced back to sixth-century Roman Law, with its modern formulation ("volenti non fit injuria") taking form by the end of the thirteenth century (Ingman 1981: 1–2). As the maxim developed and was recognized in English law, it became closely associated with (and some would argue, confused with) legal doctrines such as assumption of risk and contributory fault (Ingman 1981: 5–6; Hurd 2005). Over time, however, interpretations of the maxim began to require a more robust showing that the plaintiff/complainant voluntarily consented to the alleged harm, rather than merely requiring proof that s/he knowingly assumed a risk of such harm.[2]

In modern legal doctrine, the impact of the volenti maxim is most clearly on view in the private law of tort – where it bars causes of actions in which plaintiffs allege that they have suffered a legal wrong, despite having genuinely consented to the conduct in question. In this limited context, the maxim undoubtedly has *legal* magic. For, as a matter of tort law, anyway, consent does indeed turn (the tort of) battery into a non-tortious touching; (the tort of) trespass into a non-tortious entry onto another's property; and (the tort of) conversion into a non-tortious use of another's property, etc. None of this is controversial.

Things become more contentious, however, when the volenti maxim is extended into the *criminal* law. For, as Aristotle observed, even if an individual is not *directly* wronged by an act to which s/he consented – the act done to him/her might nonetheless constitute a wrong to the broader community. This possibility is particularly salient in cases where the act makes a causal contribution to creating, promoting, or sustaining social forms that harm community members who do *not* genuinely consent – or whose consent is compromised by a lack of social power to transform or dismantle these harmful social forms. Consider two examples: (1) the commercial sex industry (2) the junk food/sugary drinks industry.[3] First, while some percentage of people in the commercial sex industry may genuinely consent to trade sex for money, no doubt others do not consent. Per the volenti maxim, let us assume that those who genuinely consent are not wronged, and so (in those cases) buying sex does not wrong those people directly. And yet, if buying sex makes a causal contribution to expanding the commercial sex trade generally (by normalizing the purchase of sex), and the expanded market demand is met by increasing the non-consenting supply (that is, if the expanded demand is met by increasing the number of sex trafficking victims), then the act of buying sex (even with a consenting-seller) nonetheless constitutes a wrong to victims of sex trafficking.

Second, while some people with plenty of healthier options choose to eat fattening foods, many people living in "food deserts" lack an adequate range of healthy options. Per the volenti maxim, let us assume those who have better options genuinely consent to the harm they experience through eating a diet of fatty foods and sugary drinks, and thus are not wronged by those who sell such food/drinks. Now, if we think only of the wrongs done to those who have an adequate range of healthy options, we might be tempted to view the situation as Hurd describes:

> [W]e all consent to indulge in many temptations that are not, strictly speaking, in our own best interests. Were those who satisfied such temptations [here, purveyors of fatty foods/sugary drinks] without . . . permission to provide them, we would all be deprived of liberties that make life worth living, even as they make it of a shorter span. Thank goodness for the moral magic of consent that allows us all to go to Hell in our own handbaskets.
>
> *(Hurd, this volume, Chapter 4)*

Yet, if we think about those who eat such foods out of a lack of healthier options, and a lack of social power to transform or dismantle the harmful social forms that create, sustain, and promote "food deserts", then the broader community harms come into view. We can then see it is not simply a matter of each one of us individually choosing to "go to Hell in our own handbasket". Rather, it is a matter of the contributions that each of us make – as sellers, buyers, voters, etc. – that wrongfully harm others in our community. Of course, questions of whether and when such causal contributions to wronging others should be prohibited under force of law requires us to answer many other questions. My point here is simply that a straightforward, simplistic application of the volenti maxim hardly resolves the issue.

17.2 The who, what, and why of the volenti maxim

For now, let us assume that the volenti maxim is true – that is, "to one who consents, no wrong is done". In order to unpack the meaning of the maxim and better understand the debates it inspires, it will be helpful to frame our initial investigation in terms of three "W" questions – the who, what, and why of the volenti maxim.

17.2.1 Who?

First, *whose* normative position is impacted by the volenti maxim? Before we attempt to answer this question, consider four categories of people whose role may prove relevant to our considerations. (Not all the people in these categories will have their normative position impacted by the volenti maxim, but for the sake of getting all relevant actors in view, it is worth setting out these four categories at this point in our discussion):

The person who consents ("A");
The person to whom consent is given ("B");
Non-consenting others who are harmed indirectly by what B does to A ("C");
Those who seek to prohibit the kind of conduct B does to A, on grounds that it indirectly harms people in category "C" (the non-consenting others) ("D").[4]

Imagine that Ben slaps Amy. Absent Amy's consent, Ben's conduct would wrong Amy.[5] Yet, let us imagine that Amy consents to being slapped by Ben while playing the game "Red Hands", pursuant to the "free slap" rule, after Amy pulls her hands away too quickly. Also, let us assume that Amy's consent is fully competent, voluntary, and knowing, such that it bears whatever normative force consent might bear under ideal circumstances.[6] If this is all true, whose normative position is impacted by operation of the volenti maxim?

At a basic level, the volenti maxim surely impacts Amy's and Ben's normative positions. Without her consent, Amy is a victim and Ben her assailant. With Amy's consent, Amy is not a victim, and Ben is not her assailant. Below, we will examine what this change of normative position means in terms of how it impacts Amy's and Ben's rational horizons.[7] For now, however, imagine that Amy and Ben's game catches on, such that other people (Carla, Candace, and Charlie) are slapped while playing Red Hands. In some sense, Carla, Candace, and Charlie consent to being slapped, just like Amy, since they have agreed to play the game. Yet imagine that Carla's consent is not fully competent (e.g., due to youth or disability), Candace's consent is not fully voluntary (e.g., she has been pressured into playing the game), and Charlie's consent is not fully knowing (e.g., he doesn't understand the consequences of pulling his hands away too quickly). Since Carla, Candace, and Charlie are not fully consenting to being slapped (at least, not in the fully competent, voluntary, and knowing sense in which Amy consented), it seems that Amy's consent has no impact on their normative position. That is, the fact that Amy fully consented to being slapped by Ben does nothing to change the fact that Carla, Candace, and Charlie are (to some degree, at least) wronged by being slapped, since they are being slapped without giving full consent. Moreover, imagine that Amy and Ben's slapping game inspires a variant of non-consensual slapping, such that Clark is slapped while walking down the street, minding his own business. Surely, the fact that Amy consented to being slapped by Ben does nothing to impact Clark's normative position: he is a victim, and his slapper is an assailant.

What about the fourth category of people outlined above: those who seek to prohibit the kind of conduct B does to A – that is, those who seek to prohibit the game of Red Hands? Imagine that Daniel, Dana, Donald, and Declan seek to prohibit the game. Their motivations vary: Daniel is an advocate for people like Carla (the disabled and others who lack full competence to consent to the game); Dana is an advocate for people like Candace (those who are vulnerable to being coerced into playing the game); Donald is an advocate for people like Charlie (those who lack the knowledge of the "free slap" rules); and Declan is an advocate concerned with public safety and the rise of non-consensual slapping inspired by Red Hands. (Let us refer to them collectively as the anti-Red Hands advocates.) Does the volenti maxim impact the normative position of these advocates? At first glance, one might be tempted to conclude the answer is no. After all, the advocates are seeking to prohibit the game because of the harm it does to those whose consent is either defective or absent (as in the cases of Carla, Candace, Charlie, and Clark). Since the volenti maxim only applies in cases of genuine, full consent (as in the case of Amy and Ben), it does not seem relevant to the normative position of those such as the anti-Red Hands advocates, who merely seek to protect the non-consenting. And yet the fact that Amy has genuinely consented to being slapped while playing the game does seem to impact the advocates' normative positions to some degree, at least if the anti-Red Hands advocates are seeking to abolish the game completely. For, if they are successful in prohibiting the game altogether, they will have not merely prevented harms to those whose consent is defective or absent – they will have effectively prevented consenting partners from partaking in the game as well.[8] Thus, it seems that the volenti maxim does impact the advocates' normative position, to some degree, since it means that Daniel, Dana, Donald, and Declan are not merely well-intentioned advocates seeking to protect those whose consent is defective or absent – they are also (to some extent, at least) busybodies seeking to prevent perfectly competent, voluntary, knowing participants from playing an amusing, albeit occasionally painful, game.

17.2.2 What?

Second, *what* normative force does the maxim have for the three categories of people whose normative positions are impacted by the maxim (A, B, and D)?[9] That is, how does the volenti maxim alter the rational horizons of folks like Amy, Ben, and the anti-Red Hands advocates? Let's begin with Amy. If she had not consented to being slapped by Ben, she would have reason to complain, to call Ben to account for his behavior, to condemn Ben's conduct, etc. Indeed, it might be thought that Amy would have a *duty* to do some or all of these things (Marshall 2004; Dempsey 2009: 185–210). Moreover, Amy would have a right to expect that her community would both support her efforts to hold Ben accountable directly to her, and take it upon itself to condemn and punish him, etc. (Marshall & Duff 1998; Dempsey 2009: 185–92).

Given her consent, however, Amy's rational horizons are dramatically different. By operation of the volenti maxim, no wrong was done to her by Ben. As such, she has no reason to complain about being slapped by him, no reason to call him to account, nor to condemn his behavior. Indeed, it may be thought that Amy's consent (per the volenti maxim) does not merely cancel reasons she might otherwise have had to complain, but that it grounds a duty on her part *not* to complain about being slapped by Ben (cf. Hurd, this volume, Chapter 4).[10] Moreover, she no longer has any right to expect her community to do anything to see that Ben is condemned or punished for slapping her – and, indeed, she may be obligated not to seek such community action.

What normative force does the volenti maxim have for Ben? Absent Amy's consent, Ben would have a duty to apologize for slapping her, a duty to make amends for any injury caused by the slap, and would have forfeited his right not to be punished for his wrongful conduct (Wellman 2012).[11] All of this would be the case because slapping Amy without her consent would be wrong all-things-considered.[12] Yet *all-things-considered wrongs* are not the only kinds of wrongs. Rather, there are also *pro tanto wrongs* (Kagan 1989: 17). *Pro tanto* wrongs can be justified, in which case they are not wrong all-things considered (Gardner 1996), and thus do not trigger the kinds of duties and forfeiture of rights noted above.[13] Yet, even when fully justified, *pro tanto* wrongs can leave a "rational remainder" that continues to ground reasons for action, belief, or emotions in the future (Gardner 2011: 35; Dempsey 2016).[14] So the question becomes: which kind of wrong is referenced by the volenti maxim in the claim, "to one who consents, no *wrong* is done"? Does it mean that Ben's conduct is not wrong *pro tanto*, or does it mean that his conduct is simply not wrong *all-things-considered*?

Consider the first option: if the volenti maxim means, "to one who consents, no wrong is done, even *pro tanto*", this means that the normative force of consent completely negates any kind of wrongdoing on Ben's part whatsoever. According to this reading, the volenti maxim dramatically transforms Ben's rational horizons, by making it the case that Ben has not wronged Amy *at all*. Rather, Amy's consent "literally reverses the morality of [Ben's] deed" (Hurd, this volume, Chapter 4).

However, if the volenti maxim means, "to one who consents, no wrong is done *all-things-considered*", then things are somewhat different. On this reading of the maxim, Ben's *pro tanto* wrong (slapping Amy) is *justified* by her consent and thus is not wrong all-things-considered. In that case, Amy's consent transforms Ben's practical reasons in at least three important ways. First, Ben would have no duty to apologize for slapping Amy. Second, he would have no duty to make amends for any injury caused by the slap. And, third, he would retain his right not to be punished for slapping Amy. Importantly, however, Ben might still have first-order reasons for actions, beliefs, or emotions in virtue of the fact that slapping Amy was *pro tanto* wrong (albeit, a *pro tanto* wrong that was justified in virtue of Amy's consent).

Imagine that the day after an especially raucous game of Red Hands, Amy develops bruises on her hands.[15] When Ben sees the bruises, he would have no *duty* to apologize, make amends, or submit to punishment for slapping Amy – but surely he would have some *reason* to inquire as to how Amy is feeling and perhaps extend some sign of regret that Amy is suffering. Of course, it might be the case that *anyone* would have such reasons upon seeing Amy's bruised hands. Simply as a matter of politeness, anyone may have reason to say something along the lines of, "Ouch, your hands look sore. I'm sorry you're in pain. How are you feeling?", etc. My point here, however, is that Ben has reasons to say these things not merely out of politeness, but rather out of the "rational remainder" (Gardner 2011: 35) that continues to bear normative force on Ben's rational horizons simply in virtue of the fact that *he* was the one who caused the bruises by slapping Amy.[16]

Interestingly, the force of Ben's first-order reasons to ask Amy how she is feeling, to express sympathy, and perhaps to extend some sign of regret for her suffering may vary according to how Amy feels about having been slapped, now that she has developed bruises. Imagine two responses Amy might have to Ben's inquiry upon seeing her bruises. First, she might respond playfully, "I'm fine, thanks. Just wait till I heal up and it's game-on for round two of Red Hands! Next time, I'm gonna smack you down!" In this scenario, Ben has acted on the first-order reasons he had to show appropriate concern for having caused Amy's bruises, and Amy has playfully rebuffed his concern. Now consider an alternate scenario, in which Amy responds as follows: "Thanks for asking. My hands really do hurt a lot. I kind of wish we hadn't played for so long. I think I'm done with Red Hands for a while". In this scenario, Amy's regret might very well strengthen the first-order reasons Ben has to express concern for her suffering or even to make amends for having caused the bruises. For example, there might now be reason for Ben to offer to carry Amy's book bag, to alleviate the pain in her hands – or simply to say, "Gee, I'm sorry".

Of course, Amy's subsequent regret would *not negate* her previous consent. Thus, it would remain the case that Ben is under *no duty* to apologize or to make amends for any injury caused by the slap, nor could he be properly subject to punishment for slapping Amy. So, in those respects, the "moral magic" (Hurd 1996) of Amy's consent would continue to bear its normative force on Ben's rational horizons, despite Amy's subsequent regret. Moreover, the normative force of Amy's consent on her *own* rational horizons would remain as well. As such, she would still have no reason to complain about being slapped by Ben, no reason to call Ben to account, no reason to condemn his behavior.[17]

What normative force does the volenti maxim have for the fourth category of people outlined above: anti-Red Hands advocates (Daniel, Dana, Donald, and Declan) who seek to prohibit the game of Red Hands in the interest of those whose consent is either defective or absent? The risk identified above was that the volenti maxim might impact the advocates' normative position by making the advocates into "busybodies seeking to prevent perfectly competent, voluntary, knowing participants from playing an amusing, albeit occasionally painful, game". If this is so, then what does that mean for the rational horizons of these advocates? Primarily, it means that they will have reason to pursue their advocacy in a way that preserves space for consensual Red Hands game players, to the extent possible.

Put differently, the impact of Amy's consent is that it creates an *auxiliary* reason for the advocates (Raz 1990: 34), which helps identify the kinds of policies the advocates should use to achieve their goal. Specifically, the kinds of policies they pursue should not only eliminate non-consensual slapping, but should also (to the extent possible) preserve opportunities for people like Amy and Ben to engage in consensual Red Hands game playing.[18] The strength of this auxiliary reason will vary to some extent based on how many people in the relevant community engage in consensual Red Hands games, and how many (or how often) others are harmed through playing Red Hands without fully consenting to do so.[19] For example, if a large number of people consensually play Red Hands, the volenti maxim (more precisely, the harm principle as moderated by the volenti maxim) will mean that the advocates should pursue strategies that allow such games to continue, while still reducing the amount of non-consensual slapping.[20] However, where few people engage in genuinely consensual Red Hands games (that is, where the vast majority of such games involve either no consent or defective consent), then the strength of the auxiliary reason to preserve a space for Red Hands games will be correspondingly diminished. Of course, if it is easy enough to preserve a space for folks like Amy and Ben to continue playing Red Hands consensually then the advocates should remain attentive to the possibility of doing so and integrate that concern into their overall advocacy strategy. Yet, if it is not feasible to achieve both goals (that is, to eliminate/reduce non-consensual slapping, and to preserve space for consensual game playing), then the advocates may be justified in pursuing a strategy of total prohibition, even at the cost of preventing Amy and Ben from playing.

17.2.3 Why?

Finally, *why* does the volenti maxim bear the normative force that it does? The answer to this question requires attention to the normative context in which is it posed. In a *legal* context, if we ask why the volenti maxim bears normative force, the answer is relatively straightforward, at least for a legal positivist (Hart 2012; Raz 1979; Gardner 2001). According to legal positivism, legal norms bear *legally* normative force because they are *valid* legal norms of a legal system – and legal norms are valid based on social facts about their sources. The legal validity of the volenti maxim is based on the social fact that judges, in deciding cases, interpreting laws, and creating legal doctrines, have endorsed, adopted, relied upon, or otherwise engaged with the volenti maxim as a valid legal norm. Importantly, however, the fact that the volenti maxim bears *legally* normative force does not mean that it bears *morally* normative force – which is to say, legal validity does not establish moral validity (Green 2009). As such, there may be instances in which the application of the volenti maxim as a *legal* norm is morally sound (as when it turns "a battery into a handshake; a sexual assault into a kiss . . . a theft into a gift", etc. (Hurd, this volume, Chapter 4)), and instances in which it is morally suspect (as in cases where the maxim was used to systematically deprive employees of the right to pursue tort actions against negligent employers (Ingman 1981: 8–16)).

In a *moral* context, if we ask why the volenti maxim bears the normative force that it does, the answer is rather less straightforward. Consider two perspectives from which we might ask the question. The first, which I will refer to as a perspective of *political morality*, is one in which we are particularly concerned with practices such as holding one another to account, imposing blame (or praise), punishment (or reward). That is, the perspective of political morality is concerned with the appropriateness of our public *responses* to others' actions and their (perceived) moral status, whereas pure moral evaluation (discussed below) is solely concerned with the moral status of an action itself. What matters most from the perspective of political morality is not simply the moral quality of Ben's conduct when he slapped Amy – but whether Amy, or anyone else, would be justified in calling him to account, condemning him, punishing him, etc.

The second perspective, which I will refer to as a perspective of *pure moral evaluation*, is one in which "all individuals are responsible for all their voluntary behavior . . . [and] must answer, at the very least, to their own consciences for what they have done" (Feinberg 1988: 214). From this perspective, we are decidedly *not* concerned with practices such as holding one another to account, imposing blame (or praise), punishment (or reward). Rather, this perspective focuses simply on "moral judgment [. . .] on some ideal record . . . [where] it will be forever to [one's] credit of blame . . . that he acted wrongly or rightly, badly or well" (ibid.).

From the perspective of political morality, it is easy enough to see why the volenti maxim bears normative force. In the normal course of human interactions, basic notions of fairness require that we not hold others accountable, blame them, or (worse yet) punish them for things they did to another person, if the other person genuinely consented to what was done.[21] If the volenti maxim did not bear its normative force from this perspective, we would never be able to shake hands, hug, kiss, or have sex, without opening ourselves up to an accusation of battery, sexual assault, or rape. Moreover, we would never be able to give a gift to a friend, or invite colleagues to dinner, without being regarded as victims of theft and trespass. Quite simply, from the perspective of political morality, the volenti maxim bears the normative force that it does because, otherwise, living in a society with normal, everyday, valuable, community-promoting activities would be impossible.

From the perspective of pure moral evaluation, however, it is not entirely clear why the volenti maxim bears normative force. The most common explanations are grounded in a deontological morality, according to which a person's consent amounts to an exercise of his right to autonomy (Feinberg 1986: 59–61; Westen 2004: 127–8; Hurd, this volume, Chapter 4; Hurd 1996). As such, it is ultimately the right to autonomy that explains why consent possesses its "moral magic". Indeed, the volenti maxim continues to bear its full moral force on this account, even if those who consent choose unwisely – consenting to being treated in ways that harm their happiness, health, and even their lives. As Feinberg put it, "autonomy is even more important than personal well-being" (Feinberg 1986: 59). Just so long as the consent constitutes an exercise of one's right to autonomy, the moral force of the volenti maxim remains. For, according to this account, a person's right to consent to being treated by others in particular ways (even in ways that are ultimately detrimental to the consenting person's well-being) is paramount.

A more moderate view links the exercise of autonomy (and, thus, the "moral magic" of consent) to the promotion of human well-being, instrumentally. According to this view, the power to transform the moral quality of another person's act through our consent is valuable primarily because it is an instrument by which we open up a vast range of valuable opportunities that promote our well-being, and ultimately contribute both to individual human flourishing and the common good of all humanity. Without the morally transformative power of consent, every massage would be a battery, all sex rape, every guest a trespasser, and every gift a theft. Since massages, sex, guests, and gifts all make valuable contributions to human well-being, flourishing, and the common good – the instrumental role consent plays in making these valuable experiences possible grounds the normative force of the volenti maxim.

A more radical view denies that consent has any "moral magic" at all, at least when viewed from the perspective of pure moral evaluation, and thus denies the moral validity of the volenti maxim. This radical view claims instead that, at best, consent provides a useful epistemic guide for judging what will promote another's well-being. The basic idea is this: most often, individuals will be in the best position to know what will promote their own well-being, and so, most often, they will only consent to things that do so. As it happens, of course, folks are sometimes deeply mistaken about what will promote their own well-being (as when dieters take pills advertised as "healthy weight loss supplements", only to suffer serious illness or death). Moreover, folks often find themselves consenting to things that they know are contrary to their well-being (e.g., overeating, failing to exercise, etc.). Ignorance of consequences and weakness of will result in many cases where people simply are not in the best position to know what will promote their well-being, or they will, nonetheless, knowingly consent to things that are detrimental to their well-being. According to the radical view, consent does not magically turn wrongs into rights in such cases. Rather, at best, an individual's consent is regarded as a helpful guide that will often (but not always) provide knowledge regarding what might promote that person's well-being.[22] So, on this radical view, the answer to the question, "Why does the volenti maxim bear the normative force that it does?" goes something like this: "Oh, from the perspective of pure morality, it doesn't actually bear any normative force whatsoever – but it can often be a helpful guide to knowing how to treat other people".

17.3 Conclusion

This chapter has provided an introductory overview of the volenti maxim ("to one who consents, no wrong is done"). Primarily, the chapter examined questions regarding *whose* normative position might be impacted by the force of the maxim, *what* kind of normative force the volenti maxim might have, and *why* the volenti maxim bears such normative force. Throughout, the chapter has pushed back (gently) against a broad reading of the maxim, by challenging the maxim's application to the criminal law, arguing that those who receive consent might nonetheless have reason to apologize or make amends for the harm they have caused, and suggesting that (at least from the perspective of pure moral evaluation) consent might very well lack any normative force whatsoever.

Notes

1 The maxim has clearer philosophical pedigree in the writing of J.S. Mill: "that is not unjust which is done with the consent of the person who is supposed to be hurt by it" (Mill 1871: 84), and was most fully developed in Feinberg (1984, 1988).

2 Some appellate cases continue to link the volenti maxim with legal assumption of risk. *Austin v. Kroger Texas, L.P.*, 465 S.W.3d 193, 208 (Tex. 2015), citing *Robert E. McKee, Gen. Contractor v. Patterson*, 153 Tex. 517, 519, 271 S.W.2d 391, 393. See also Bergelson (2005).

3 The first example draws on Dempsey (2010). The second is borrowed from Hurd (this volume, Chapter 4).

4 The discussion below might be thought to imply that C and D are mutually exclusive categories, but this thought should be avoided. Indeed, it is likely that there will be overlap between people in categories C and D.

5 The discussion that follows imagines Amy and Ben in a consensual game of Red Hands (https://en.wikipedia.org/wiki/Red_hands), but it is easy enough to see the analogy to other consensual harmings in more contentious circumstances, such as sadomasochism, prostitution, euthanasia, etc. See endnotes 8 and 18, below.

6 Further assume in what follows that Ben is aware of Amy's consent such that he would not have slapped her without her consent. That is, assume that Ben is "consent-sensitive" (Dempsey 2013: 25–6).

7 By "rational horizons", I mean to refer to reasons for action, belief, and emotion that apply to human beings, and the nature and force of such reasons (e.g., first-order, exclusionary, mandatory, categorical, etc.) (Raz 1990, 2000). For our purposes, there will be little need to get into many of these distinctions, so, below, I will sometimes collapse all of these considerations under the label "practical reasons".

8 We can draw out the analogy to sadomasochism, prostitution, and euthanasia. Advocates seeking to protect those who do not fully consent (or consent at all) to these practices often seek to abolish the practices completely, rather than opting for a regulatory scheme that might protect potential victims while allowing the consensual practices to continue. The rationale behind promoting abolition rather than regulation depends on empirical assumptions regarding what would happen if consensual practices were allowed to continue. For example, if prostitution is legalized and regulated, will sex trafficking increase? At least some empirical research suggests the answer is yes (Cho et al. 2013), and, as such, some advocates promote abolition over regulation (Dempsey 2010). Of course, in determining the best policy to adopt (abolition, regulation, etc.), the number of people in categories A and C matter,

comparatively. If many more people in category C will be victimized for the sake of only a relative few in category A, that fact speaks in favor of abolition. Yet, if there are many people in category A and only a few in category C, that fact speaks in favor of legalization, regulation, etc. That said, we should be careful not to suppose that the reasons to allow category A and B people to participate in the consensual activities are equally as weighty/strong as the reasons to protect people in category C – for the mere fact that conduct is consensual does not mean that it is valuable. That is, consent does not ground a reason in favor of an action. On an account I've outlined elsewhere, consent merely presents people in category B with an exclusionary permission (Dempsey 2013). (When it comes to playing Red Hands, I'm assuming that consensual playing has some value. See endnote 19, below.)

9 Recall, the volenti maxim does not impact the normative position of those such as Carla, Candace, Charlie, or Clark.

10 In legal doctrine, the normative force of the volenti maxim sometimes functions as a form of estoppel and is closely associated with notions of assumed risk and contributory fault. See discussion on p. 188. For explanation of why consent-as-estoppel is not the most satisfying account of the volenti maxim as a matter of political or moral philosophy, see Hurd, this volume, Chapter 4).

11 I'm assuming Ben would have no excuse for slapping Amy – e.g., he was not under duress, he did not reasonably but mistakenly believe that Amy consented, etc. (Gardner 1998).

12 I'm assuming that there are no exceptional circumstances that would otherwise justify the slap, such as self-defense.

13 By *pro tanto* wrong, I mean that there are non-trivial *pro tanto* reasons against the act, such that doing the act calls for justification. See Kagan (1989: 17n): "A pro tanto reason has genuine weight, but nonetheless may be outweighed by other considerations. Thus, calling a reason a pro tanto reason is to be distinguished from calling it a prima facie reason, which I take to involve an epistemological qualification: a prima facie reason appears to be a reason, but may actually not be a reason at all".

14 In previous work, I referred to this rational remainder as a "moral residue of regret" (Dempsey & Herring 2007: 488–91).

15 Assume that bruising is to be expected and that Amy fully consented to the probability of bruising, so this is not a case where the injuries exceeded the scope of Amy's consent.

16 To be clear, the reasons that speak against Ben slapping Amy are not canceled/eliminated by Amy's consent – they are merely permissibly excluded (Dempsey 2013). Excluded reasons can still function as a "rational remainder" on Ben's rational horizons, grounding reasons for Ben to apologize, etc. – even if the slap was done with Amy's full consent.

17 A fortiori, Amy would also not have any right to have Ben held accountable or punished by her community, despite her subsequent regret.

18 To draw out the analogy to sadomasochism, prostitution, and euthanasia, the claim here is that advocates opposing these practices have auxiliary reasons to preserve opportunities for people to engage in these activities. This point, however, does not resolve the debate regarding abolitionism versus regulation, etc. One may still advocate for abolitionism if the conditions are such that regulation, legalization, etc. will have the results discussed at endnote 8. My point here is simply that, even in advocating for abolition, these auxiliary reasons mean that advocates should remain alive to the possibility that changed conditions could, in the future, mean that consensual practices should be permitted.

19 It will also vary according to whether the consensual Red Hands games involve bare consent, or a genuine wish to play, experiences of genuine value contributing to human flourishing, etc.

20 Such strategies might include what Feinberg calls "soft paternalism", in which temporary interventions are used to ensure that someone's apparent consent "does not stem from ignorance, coercion, derangement, drugs, or other voluntariness-vitiating factors" (1986: 12–6).

21 I include "in the normal course of things" to bracket the unusual cases where the volenti maxim is often thought to lack normative force to transform the moral quality of one's conduct. See, for example, the case of the German cannibal, Armin Meiwes, whose victim consented to being killed and eaten (Reid 2014).

22 Mill appears to endorse this radical thesis: "[One's] voluntary choice is evidence that what he chooses is desirable, or at least endurable, to him, and his good is on the whole best provided for by allowing him to take his own means of pursuing it" (Mill 2002 [1859]: 87). That said, Mill did defend the genuine moral force of the volenti maxim, albeit because (he assumed) the disvalue of interfering in another's choices would always outweigh the disvalue of bad choices s/he might make. "All errors he is likely to commit, against advice and warning, are far outweighed by the evil of allowing others to constrain him" (Mill 2002 [1859]: 65).

References

Aristotle (1999) *Nicomachean Ethics*, trans. W.D. Ross. Kitchener: Batoche Books.
Bergelson, V. (2005) "Victims and Perpetrators: An Argument for Comparative Liability in Criminal Law," *Buffalo Criminal Law Review* 8: 385–487.
Cho, S.Y., A. Dreher and E. Neumayer (2013) "Does Legalized Prostitution Increase Human Trafficking?" *World Development* 41: 67–82.
Dempsey, M.M. (2009) *Prosecuting Domestic Violence: A Philosophical Analysis*. Oxford: Oxford University Press.
Dempsey, M.M. (2010) "Sex Trafficking and Criminalization: In Defense of Feminist Abolitionism," *University of Pennsylvania Law Review* 158: 1729–78.
Dempsey, M.M. (2013) "Victimless Conduct and the *Volenti* Maxim: How Consent Works," *Criminal Law and Philosophy* 7: 11–28.
Dempsey, M.M. (2016) "Against Liability: A Reasons-Based Account of Self-Defense," in C. Coons and M. Weber (ed.), *The Ethics of Self-Defense*. New York: Oxford University Press.
Dempsey, M.M. and J. Herring (2007) "Why Sexual Penetration Calls for Justification," *Oxford Journal of Legal Studies* 27: 467–91.
Feinberg, J. (1984) *Harm to Others: The Moral Limits of the Criminal Law*. Oxford: Oxford University Press.
Feinberg, J. (1986) *Harm to Self: The Moral Limits of the Criminal Law*. Oxford: Oxford University Press.
Feinberg, J. (1988) *Harmless Wrongdoing: The Moral Limits of the Criminal Law*. Oxford: Oxford University Press.
Gardner, J. (1996) "Justifications and Reasons," in A.P. Simester and A.T.H. Smith (ed.), *Harm and Culpability*. Oxford: Clarendon Press.
Gardner, J. (1998) "The Gist of Excuses," *Buffalo Criminal Law Review* 1: 575–98.
Gardner, J. (2001) "Legal Positivism: 5½ Myths," *American Journal of Jurisprudence* 46: 199–227.
Gardner, J. (2011) "What is Tort Law for? Part 1: The Place of Corrective Justice," *Law and Philosophy* 30: 1–50.
Green, L. (2009) "Legal Positivism," *The Stanford Encyclopedia of Philosophy*. https://plato.stanford.edu/archives/fall2009/entries/legal-positivism/.
Hart, H.L.A. (2012) *The Concept of Law* (with introduction by Leslie Green). Oxford: Oxford University Press.
Hurd, H.M. (1996) "The Moral Magic of Consent (I)," *Legal Theory* 2: 121–46.
Hurd, H.M. (2005) "Blaming the Victim: A Response to the Proposal That Criminal Law Recognize A General Defense of Contributory Responsibility," *Buffalo Criminal Law Review* 8: 503–22.
Ingman, T. (1981) "A History of the Defence of Volenti Non Fit Injuria," *Juridicial Review* 26: 1–29.
Kagan, S. (1989) *The Limits of Morality*. Oxford: Clarendon Press.
Marshall, S.E. (2004) "Victims of Crime: Their Station and its Duties," *Critical Review of International Social and Political Philosophy* 7: 104–17.
Marshall, S.E. and R.A. Duff (1998) "Criminalization and Sharing Wrongs," *Canadian Journal of Law & Jurisprudence* 11: 7–22.
Mill, J.S. (1871) *Utilitarianism*. London: Longmans, Green, Reader, and Dyer.
Mill, J.S. (2002 [1859]) *On Liberty*. Mineola, NY: Dover Publications.
Raz, J. (1979) *The Authority of Law*. Oxford: Oxford University Press.
Raz, J. (1990) *Practical Reason and Norms*. Second Edition. London: Hutchinson and Sons.
Raz, J. (2000) *Engaging Reason: On the Theory of Value and Action*. Oxford: Oxford University Press.
Reid, C. (2014) "Eat What You Kill: Or, A Strange and Gothic Tale of Cannibalism by Consent," *North Carolina Journal of International Law and Commercial Regulation* 39: 423–521.
Wellman, C. (2012) "The Rights Forfeiture Theory of Punishment," *Ethics* 122: 371–93.
Westen, P. (2004) *The Logic of Consent: The Diversity and Deceptiveness of Consent as a Defense to Criminal Conduct*. Burlington, VT: Ashgate Press.

Further reading

Dempsey, M.M. (2013) "Victimless Conduct and the *Volenti* Maxim: How Consent Works," *Criminal Law and Philosophy* 7: 11–28. (Explaining the normative force of consent in terms of exclusionary permissions.)
Feinberg, J. (1984) *Harm to Others: The Moral Limits of the Criminal Law*. Oxford: Oxford University Press. (The classic work arguing that the maxim should serve as a limiting constraint in criminalization.)

Ingman, T. (1981) "A History of the Defence of Volenti Non Fit Injuria," *Juridicial Review* 26: 1–29. (Providing a detailed history of the development of the maxim in legal doctrine from Roman Law through late-1970s English caselaw.)

Westen, P. (2004) *The Logic of Consent: The Diversity and Deceptiveness of Consent as a Defense to Criminal Conduct*. Burlington, VT: Ashgate Press. (Providing comprehensive overview of the consent in U.S. criminal law.)

Related topics

Ch.4 The normative force of consent
Ch.5 Consent and wronging a person
Ch.12 Consent and autonomy
Ch.18 Consent to pain

18
CONSENT TO PAIN

Vera Bergelson

Should people have the power to consent to the infliction of pain? Does society have valid reasons to prohibit rational adults from willingly submitting to a painful experience? And if the answer is yes, do those reasons justify criminal punishment of a person who has inflicted pain on the willing victim?

Most of us hate pain even when it is transitory and does not indicate serious problems with our health or well-being. We hate pain because it is experientially unpleasant; it intervenes with our plans and diminishes our opportunities; and at times it is demeaning. In most circumstances, pain has a negative value: we spend time and money; avoid tasty foods and other enjoyable things; agree to various inconveniences in life – all to avoid pain. Moreover, many of us believe that pain is also intrinsically bad and worth avoiding for its own sake.[1]

Then why might a person consent to pain? There is a whole range of reasons. Pain may be an inevitable side-effect of a desired result (a cosmetic procedure may be painful but effective). Pain may be an instrument of obtaining a benefit (consenting to beating for money; participating in a slapstick comedy). Finally, pain may carry its own value (masochistic sexual pleasure; religious mortification).

Consent is a waiver of rights. By giving consent, a person releases others from certain obligations they used to have with respect to that person and gives them the privilege, power, or immunity to do what they could not legitimately do before (Hohfeld 1923). In some cases, consent operates to prevent the commission of a crime: consensual intercourse is not rape; consensual taking of property of another is not theft; and consensual entering of someone's home is not trespass (Hurd 2005: 503–4). And yet there are many examples of the conduct that remains wrongful or illegal despite its consensual nature. Consensual homicide, riot, bribery, and bigamy are among those (*Model Penal Code* § 2.11 cmt. 1).

The Model Penal Code ("MPC") explains this incongruity: "consent is given defensive effect by the law when it is logically relevant either to negative a prescribed element of the offense or to preclude the occurrence of the harm or evil that the law defining the offense seeks to prevent" (ibid.). Accordingly, consent precludes conviction of theft because the objective of the theft law is to protect the property rights against unauthorized infringement. Consent negatives the unauthorized character of the infringement and precludes the harm and evil of theft. But consent is powerless to preclude the harm or evil of homicide, riot, bribery or bigamy where the objectives of the law go beyond the interests that may be asserted by an identifiable victim.[2] So, where does consent to pain stand in this dichotomy? Is it a private matter, in which case consent should shield from the moral condemnation and criminal punishment the person who inflicts pain on the willing victim, or does the harm or evil of pain infliction go beyond the private interests of the participants?

Historically, consent has been functioning differently in cases that involve bodily harm and cases that do not. For the past few centuries, the law has been reluctant to give legal power to one's consent to bodily harm. Today too, under the U.S. law, consent provides a defense to a charge of assault only in three sets of circumstances: (i) when the injury is not serious; (ii) when the injury results from a lawful athletic activity; and (iii) when the bodily harm was inflicted in the course of a recognized medical treatment.[3]

Based on this rule, one would think that consent to pain, unaccompanied by life-threatening, permanent or long-lasting injuries, should be valid even outside of the sports and medical contexts.[4] The reality, however, is much more ambiguous. It is less than clear whether infliction of pain alone is – or should be – targeted by criminal law. Many penal codes list physical pain as a variety of "bodily harm" but then many do not.[5] The MPC includes pain in the definition of "bodily injury" but not "serious bodily injury" (*Model Penal Code* §§210.0(2), (3)).[6] These definitions, however, are located in the Special Part (section on homicide); thus, there is an uncertainty as to whether they apply to the overall consent provision located in the General Part (*Model Penal Code*, §2.11). If they are judged to apply to the consent provision, and if "serious bodily *injury*" of the Special Part is interpreted to mean the same as "serious bodily *harm*" of the General Part, then, under the MPC, one should be able to consent to the infliction of pain that does not present significant health risks (ibid. at §210.0(3)).

If those provisions are judged not to apply, however, a person inflicting consensual pain on another may be found guilty of assault or battery.[7] The MPC assault section explicitly adopts the definitions given in the homicide section, including those of "bodily injury" and "serious bodily injury" (*Model Penal Code* §211.0). The assault section reads: "A person is guilty of assault if he . . . attempts to cause or purposely, knowingly or recklessly causes bodily injury to another; or . . . negligently causes bodily injury to another with a deadly weapon" (ibid. at §211.1(1)). In addition, a person is guilty of aggravated assault if he "attempts to cause or purposely or knowingly causes bodily injury to another with a deadly weapon" (ibid. at §211.1(2)). Thus, a person who causes another *any* physical pain is *prima facie* guilty of assault or aggravated assault (depending on the means he used). Whether or not he will be able to exonerate himself by using the defense of consent would depend on whether or not the court considers the inflicted pain to be "serious bodily harm" (under the MPC, outside of the sports and medical exceptions, consent is a defense to assault only if the bodily harm is not serious) (ibid. at §2.11(2)(b)). And courts tend to answer the question differently depending on whether they approve or disapprove of the activity that has caused the pain.[8]

In *State v. Guinn*, for example, the court rejected the defendant's defense of consent and the defendant was convicted of assault for inflicting "serious physical injury" in the course of a sexual encounter (Wash. App. LEXIS 502). There was no evidence that the victim "ever required any medical attention or suffered any wounds of any sort" (ibid. at *34). Yet the appellate court sustained the assault conviction, reasoning that the sadomasochistic paraphernalia the defendant used must have caused serious physical pain (candle wax was "hot and it stung" and nipple clamps were "tight and cutting"), and "serious physical pain" satisfied the requirement of "serious physical injury" (ibid.).

When the law is ambiguously written and inconsistently applied, one way to make sense of it is to look at the *rationales* permeating judicial decisions.[9] These rationales are intended to justify the state's interference with the right of an individual to make personal choices. Quoting Paul Roberts,

> [T]he advocate of any particular criminal prohibition needs to supply a good reason, not just for generalized state interference in the lives of individuals, but for that special form of state regulation represented by criminal sanctions: that is, hard treatment (with serious implications for personal autonomy) administered through procedures specially designed to communicate the sting of blame or "censure".
>
> *(Roberts 2001: 217)*

Of course, state invalidation of an individual's consent presents a problem only so far as consent is voluntary – that is, freely given and informed.[10] Consent obtained by duress or fraud regarding the nature of the perpetrator's act is void *ab initio*.[11] Certain groups of people (e.g. children, mentally ill, seriously intoxicated) in most instances are deemed incapable of granting valid consent.[12] Thus, if there is a problem with the voluntariness of consent or the decision-making power of the consenter, the court must declare the consent null and void. Such decision enforces rather than impedes personal autonomy.[13] In contrast, state annulment of private arrangements – including those involving physical harm or pain – made by fully responsible agents encroaches upon the personal autonomy, which, at least in the liberal tradition, is believed to be essential for a free society.[14]

There is no developed legal doctrine dealing specifically with pain alone. There is, however, a significant body of law involving consent to physical harm. Since in many legislative and judicial documents pain is considered to be a subcategory of physical harm, it may be instructive to consider whether the arguments for denying legal weight to one's consent to physical harm would justify denying one's consent to the infliction of pain.

Traditional reasons for invalidating consent to physical harm have included at least three sets of theories: harm to self; harm to others; and general public policy. The first theory presumes that the apparent consent was not truly rational or voluntary and, therefore, is invalid. The second maintains that, unless the consensual injurious act is prohibited, society will suffer significant harm. Finally, the third one seeks to protect the values beyond the direct harm to either the interests of the participating parties or society, such as the respect to the law and social order, public morality, and dignity.

18.1 Harm to self

There may be reasons to dismiss one's consent if the consent has been given either not rationally or not voluntarily. In *People v. Samuels*, for example, the court has questioned the victim's capacity for *rational* decision-making (58 Cal. Rptr. at 504–5). Samuels was convicted of aggravated assault for whipping an apparently willing victim in the course of production of a pornographic movie (ibid. at 503–4). The case was complicated by the fact that the victim could not be found to confirm his consent (ibid. at 506). The court dismissed the very possibility of such consent, however, saying: "It is a matter of common knowledge that a normal person in full possession of his mental faculties does not freely consent to the use, upon himself, of force likely to produce great bodily injury" (ibid. at 513–14). The *Samuels* court's argument is a perfect example of circular reasoning: a person who consents to X is insane because one has to be insane to consent to X. After the victim's insanity is thus established, the conviction follows automatically because consent of an insane person is invalid.

Concerns over the *voluntariness* of consent to bodily harm have been expressed in *R v. Brown*, a case involving the activities of a group of gay men engaged in consensual sadomasochistic sex. Lord Templeman, in his opinion, has characterized consent of the masochists in the group as "dubious or worthless", suggesting that these individuals were younger than the men on the sadist side and psychologically vulnerable (*R v. Brown* [1994] 1 AC 212).

Those concerns should not be dismissed lightly. People can be manipulated into consenting to something they do not subjectively wish or something that objectively goes against their best interests. Psychological, emotional or financial pressure may lead a vulnerable individual to undergo a painful experience that is consensual only in a very superficial way. H.L.A. Hart cautioned:

> Choices may be made or consent given without adequate reflection or appreciation of the consequences; or in pursuit of merely transitory desires; or in various predicaments when the judgment is likely to be clouded; or under inner psychological compulsion; or under pressure by others of a kind too subtle to be susceptible of proof in a law court.
>
> *(Hart 1963: 33)*

Few would disagree that people can make "bad" decisions (no matter how we define this term) and that their choices are seldom, if ever, free from various influences. Moreover, as Robin West persuasively argued in her critique of Richard Posner's rationalistic vision of the world, people are often driven by self-destructive forces, desires of failure or humiliation, and the ultimate yearning for authority (West 1985: 384). In many instances, people's consent is socially predetermined, and choices people make may not reflect their true preferences.[15]

It is thus utterly possible that a person may later regret consenting to a painful experience, and that the person may be psychologically or emotionally harmed by it. Yet it is dubious that this person's harm would reach the level at which the state may be justified in interfering in people's personal choices. After all, practically any consensual activity – from attending a friend's poetry reading to the first-date lovemaking – carries a risk of a later regret and psychological or emotional harm. Unrequited love would easily carry this risk but we would hardly want the state to regulate people's affections.

18.2 Harm to others

Among the harms an individual can inflict upon society by consenting to a physical injury, the following two have most often been cited: (a) public violence may disturb peace; and (b) the injured person may become a public charge. Let's explore how those concerns apply to consent to pain.

Breach of the peace. The traditional reasoning behind prohibiting consent to bodily harm has been that, when assaults are committed publicly or in the presence of others, they tend to incite riotous and disorderly or offensive behavior (*State v. White*, 28 A. 968). Duels and prize fights have been held to threaten peace; therefore, an agreement to fight has been held invalid (*Bissell v. Starzinger*, 83 N.W. 1065; *Bundrick v. State*, 54 S.E. 683).

To the extent this rationale is applied to violent public outbreaks, it may be pertinent. However, it makes little sense when used in connection with private consensual actions, such as sadomasochistic sex. The counsel for the appellants in *Brown* has persuasively, if unsuccessfully, argued to the court that:

> The activities had all taken place in private, and in all save one occasion the incidents took place on private property, that is, in a private house or garden, or on occasion in the privacy of a hotel room. Participation in the acts complained of was carefully restricted and controlled and was limited to persons with declared like-minded sado-masochistic proclivities who wished to participate. The acts were not witnessed

by the public at large. There was no desire on the part of the participants that they should be so witnessed. There was no danger or likelihood that they would ever be so witnessed.

(*R v. Brown [1994] 1 AC 212)*

Even when the consensual infliction of pain is public, it does not have to jeopardize peace. If that were the case, public screening of slapstick comedies in movie theaters should have been banned long ago. Finally, in the current era of a well-established police force and numerous statutory offenses directed at specific instances of public disorder, the "breach of peace" rationale for overriding people's autonomy is outdated and unpersuasive (*A-G's Reference* 1981: 719).

Public charge. A more general argument in favor of the state's right to strike individuals' consensual actions is based on the risk that those individuals would become a "public charge" (*State v. Bass,* 120 S.E.2d at 49–50). Courts have held that the state has an interest in preventing citizens who are capable of being productive members of society from disabling themselves if they or their dependents would be forced to rely either on the gifts of others or on the state itself for support (Note 1976: 165). Critics of this rationale maintain that a society that respects its members may not use this logic as a basis for its social policies. Those arguments are particularly powerful when applied to consensual actions that do not involve the risk of serious, permanent or irreversible injuries. It is highly unlikely that a member of a sadomasochistic club of the type that existed in *Brown* would become a public charge as a result of experiencing pain. The counsel for the *Brown* appellants raised this point, saying: "No serious or permanent injury had been sustained by any of the appellants as a result of the activities complained of" (*R v. Brown* [1994] 1 AC 212). The court, however, dismissed the argument, opining that the inflicted injuries cannot be described as merely "transient or trifling" (ibid.).

18.3 Public policy

The requirement that the consensual conduct should not violate public policy has been cited by courts and legislatures alike to deny the defendants the defense of consent. For example, the German Criminal Code provides: "Whoever commits bodily injury with the consent of the injured person only acts unlawfully if the act is, despite the consent, contrary to good morals" (Strafgesetzbuch 2013: §228). The specific rationales invoked in this regard include: disrespect for law and social order; immorality; and violation of dignity.

Disrespect for law and social order. The rationale of respect for law and social order is typically used to explain why one set of rules is "good for all" and why the state may not permit individuals to contract around the law. As one court said, "To allow an otherwise criminal act to go unpunished because of the victim's consent would not only threaten the security of our society but also might tend to detract from the force of the moral principles underlying the criminal law" (*State v. Brown,* 364 A.2d at 30–31).

When applied to the consensual infliction of pain, this rationale does not appear particularly persuasive. True, causing pain to another is defined as assault or battery under some penal codes, including the MPC (*Model Penal Code* §211.0–1). Thus, an argument could be made that, by negotiating consent to pain, the parties "contract around the law".[16] Yet it is hard to see why the negotiations that involve private, consensual, and virtually harmless conduct should concern the state or affect the law and order. And in many circumstances the state is not concerned.

In *State v. Beck*, for example, the defendant, a store owner, caught a thief and gave him a choice: be whipped or go to jail (1 Hill 363). The thief chose the former. In fact, he begged the defendant to administer the punishment, which the defendant reluctantly did. The defendant was convicted of assault and battery but the conviction was reversed, the court saying that, while under some circumstances a license to beat another would be void, this would only happen if the person administering the beating entertained hostile dispositions toward the other, and in this case the defendant had no evil disposition toward the victim but acted only at the victim's own earnest request and to save him from what the victim considered a greater evil.

In its consultation paper, *Consent in the Criminal Law*, the U.K. Law Commission sympathetically describes a woman who belongs to the liberal edge of the Roman Catholic Church and "takes her religion seriously" (Law Commission 1995: Part X).

> For many years she has occasionally found self-mortification the appropriate penance, if she has behaved in a way that falls gravely short of what a committed Christian faith involves . . . Now that she is married, her husband helps her. He inflicts an adequate level of pain to ensure that the punishment is full and effective.
>
> *(ibid.)*

People may approve or disapprove of the way this couple practices religion. However, under the current law, both in theory and in practice, the "religious" husband is not guilty of any offense.

Similarly, the state is not concerned when people consent to pain in the context of cosmetic procedures, tattooing, body-piercing and such. For example, in *R v. Wilson*, a man was convicted of assaulting his wife when, at her request, he branded his initials on her buttocks with a hot knife ([1997] 1 AC 212).[17] The appellate court reversed the conviction, saying that what the defendant did was rather akin to tattooing and, therefore, legitimate. If respect for law and social order is not jeopardized in those circumstances, why would it be in other instances of consensual infliction of pain? It appears that respect for law and social order would suffer much more if citizens perceive the rules applied in particular cases as unfair or unnecessarily intrusive.[18]

Immorality. Courts have used the immorality argument primarily to ban perceived sexual transgressions, such as sodomy, fornication, bigamy, adultery, incest, sadomasochism, and prostitution. In *State v. Collier*, for example, the court refused to recognize one's ability to consent to sadomasochistic beating, thus opining: "It is obvious to this court that the legislature did not intend [to legitimize] an activity which has been repeatedly disapproved by other jurisdictions and considered to be in conflict with the general moral principles of our society" (*State v. Collier,* 372 N.W.2d at 307). Similarly, in *R v. Brown*, Lord Templeman wrote: "Society is entitled and bound to protect itself against a cult of violence. Pleasure derived from the infliction of pain is an evil thing. Cruelty is uncivilised" (*R v. Brown* [1994] 1 AC 212).

In contrast with the sadomasochistic activities, religious beatings have been traditionally regarded as morally appropriate and lawful (Law Commission 1995: Part 10.1). In an 1847 Scottish case, the court said: "In some cases, a beating may be consented to as in the case of a father confessor ordering flagellation; but this is not violence or assault, because there is consent" (ibid., quoting *William Fraser* 1847: 302). The practice still exists in a number of nations with a strong Roman Catholic tradition. Opus Dei, a conservative Catholic movement, encourages "corporal mortification", which can include flagellation done by another person (Ruppe 2001). "Such acts are said to help bolster self-discipline and recall the suffering of Christ" (ibid.).

In the United States, religious flagellation is practiced mainly in southwestern states (Law Commission 1995: Part 10.4). Although courts have said that the law "may prohibit religiously impelled physical attacks", research has revealed no legal cases, which suggests that religious flagellation has not been subject to criminal prosecution (*U.S. v. Meyers,* 906 F.Supp 1494, 1496

(D. Wyo.1995)).[19] Moreover, some states have statutes regulating ritual torture. The Illinois Criminal Code, for instance, provides that

> A person commits the offense of ritual mutilation, when he or she . . . tortures another person as part of a ceremony, rite, initiation, observance, performance or practice, *and the victim did not consent, or under such circumstances that the defendant knew or should have known that the victim was unable to render effective consent.*
>
> *(720 Ill. Comp. Stat. Ann. 5/12-32(a) (West 2005))*

The italicized language implies that if the religious torture is done *with* the otherwise valid consent of the victim, such activity should be lawful.

At the same time, if the primary motive for the infliction of pain is not religious but sexual, the defendant is likely to be convicted of assault or battery.[20] Compare the "religious" husband in the story above with someone who causes pain for the sexual pleasure of his partner. In both instances the perpetrator may perform the exact same acts, with the consent of his partner, and for the purpose of satisfying the partner's emotional need. Yet, if that emotional need has a sexual undertone, the perpetrator is likely to be convicted of a crime. This is a typical example of morals legislation intended to punish the perpetrator for causing a "wrong" kind of satisfaction. But should the state regulate morality by the means of criminal law?

Historically, there has been little doubt that protecting morality, even within the private relationships of adult citizens, is a legitimate state interest. The legitimacy of this interest, however, became the subject of considerable public debate starting the middle of the twentieth century (Wolfenden Report 1957). In a famous exchange between Lord Patrick Devlin and H.L.A. Hart that followed the publication of the Wolfenden Report, Hart, who supported the decriminalization of homosexual sex and prostitution, wrote: "We have ample evidence for believing that people will not abandon morality, will not think any better of murder, cruelty, and dishonesty, merely because some private sexual practice which they find abominate is not punished by the law" (Hart 1959: 162).

In the years that followed, many countries confronted their laws regulating morals. In the United States, the Supreme Court held in *Lawrence v. Texas* that the majority may not "use the power of the State to enforce [their] views on the whole society through operation of the criminal law" (*Lawrence v. Texas*, 539 U.S. at 571). The Court invalidated anti-sodomy laws and overturned its conflicting earlier decision, holding: "*Bowers* was not correct when it was decided, and it is not correct today" (ibid. at 578). The court admitted that for centuries homosexual conduct was condemned as immoral, and for many people it is still completely unacceptable (ibid at 571). Yet these considerations were held not to be sufficient for criminal prosecution (ibid. at 570).[21] Criticizing the Court's changed views, Justice Scalia wrote in his dissenting opinion:

> The Texas statute undeniably seeks to further the belief of its citizens that certain forms of sexual behavior are "immoral and unacceptable" – the same interest furthered by criminal laws against fornication, bigamy, adultery, adult incest, bestiality, and obscenity. *Bowers* held that this *was* a legitimate state interest. The Court today reaches the opposite conclusion . . . This effectively decrees the end of all morals legislation.
>
> *(ibid. at 599)*

Indeed, the *Lawrence* opinion seems to prohibit any legislation adopted on purely moral grounds. Some of the laws listed by Justice Scalia (e.g. against fornication, adultery, and, to a much lesser extent, adult incest) had been repealed even prior to *Lawrence*.[22] The *Lawrence* decision added strength to the argument that "immorality" alone is insufficient to rationalize prosecution for private intimate conduct by consenting adults (ibid. at 582). The opinion was cited, for example, to strike down the laws criminalizing "fornication" by unmarried partners.[23] Yet, in other contexts featured in Justice Scalia's parade of horrors, *Lawrence* has not had much impact.[24] In *State v. Van*, the Supreme Court of Nebraska held *Lawrence* inapplicable to sadomasochistic activities, explaining that, in that decision, the U.S. Supreme Court "did not extend constitutional protection to *any* conduct which occurs in the context of a consensual sexual relationship" but only to such that does not involve injury to a person or abuse of an institution protected by law (*State v. Van*, 688 N.W.2d at 615). The issue has not yet been reviewed by the U.S. Supreme Court. It is thus unclear whether criminal law may reach consensual infliction of pain. A better policy, it would seem, is keeping the state out of the grown-ups' consensual, private sexual affairs. But it remains to be seen how the law in this area develops.

Violation of dignity. This argument is more academic than legislative or judicial. In the view of its proponents, certain harmful actions violate their victims' dignity regardless of the consent of the latter. Such actions may include: slavery; gladiatorial matches; and the barroom practice known as "dwarf tossing". Meir Dan-Cohen, for example, argues that the reason society must outlaw slavery, even in the hypothetical case of voluntary "happy slaves",[25] is because slavery represents a "paradigm of injustice", which by its very terms denies people's equal moral worth and thus treats them with disrespect (Dan-Cohen 2000: 770).[26] Similarly, R.A. Duff finds voluntary gladiatorial contests unacceptable because of the "dehumanization or degradation perpetrated by the gladiators on each other, and by the spectators on the gladiators and on themselves" (Duff 2001: 39).

Proponents of the dignity rationale maintain that the law should not allow people consenting to the actions that violate their dignity because dignity is so essential to people's humanity that, in the case of a conflict between autonomy (the power to consent) and dignity (the recognition of the other person's humanity and equal moral worth), the former ought to yield (Wright 1995: 1399; Dan-Cohen 2000: 777–8; Dubber 2004: 568). Opponents usually cite the vagueness of the concept of "dignity" and express concern that the rationale would bring back all criminal bans based on the "immorality" rationale (Glensy 2011: 111–20).

This debate may be relevant to the question of whether consensual infliction of pain should be legally recognized. Consider this: the public's fascination with watching pain is certainly not a new phenomenon. In recent years, this fascination has become particularly widespread and particularly public. Here are some examples of the scenes featured in popular British reality TV shows, *Balls of Steel* and *Dirty Sanchez*:

- The "perpetrator" pressing onions into the opened eyes of the "victim";
- The "perpetrator" hitting the buttocks of the "victim" with a cane or foil;
- The "perpetrator" hitting the "victim" on the head with a toilet seat, breaking the toilet seat in the process.

(von Pahlen 2011)

In another popular TV series produced in the United States, *JackAss,* the performers deliberately inflict pain on each other and on themselves for entertainment. A scholar interested in this cultural phenomenon and its legal status writes: "The vast success of this television show speaks for itself. There is a real demand for real pain . . . and for *Schadenfreude*" (ibid.).

To many of us, this kind of entertainment is quite repugnant and violative of the participants' dignity. The participants do not treat each other with much respect. Moreover, just like in Duff's gladiators' example, this entertainment is objectionable because of the dehumanization or degradation perpetrated by the participants on each other, and by the TV viewers on the participants and on themselves (Duff 2001: 39). And yet the question remains: may the state criminally punish the people involved in the production of such shows by invalidating the participants' consent to pain? I suggest that it may not, mainly for the reasons of political morality: a liberal state that bases its legitimacy on the "consent of the governed" may not deny its citizens the right of consent in private matters. Additionally, not punishing someone's conduct does not mean approving of it; instead, that can mean the lack of standing to judge or condemn it (ibid. at 37). The state has many tools to influence public opinion besides its most intrusive and suppressive power to punish. In the current age of over-criminalization, expanding the reach of criminal law, particularly with respect to consensual conduct, is the last thing we need. These considerations of course are even more applicable to sadomasochistic encounters – not only do they not violate the participants' dignity but they are also neither public nor commercial.

All in all, there is no clear answer to the question of whether the law recognizes consent to the infliction of pain. Sometimes it does (TV "pain" shows; religious mortification) and sometimes it does not (sadomasochistic activities). This divide is frustrating. Whatever the answer be – and I suggest that the answer should be the recognition of consent to pain in all circumstances – it would be desirable to have a consistent approach. So far, we do not have it.

Notes

1 See e.g. Nagel (1986: 158–60). Avoidance of pain has not only agent-relative value (i.e. each of us has a reason to avoid his own pain) but also agent-neutral value (i.e. anyone has a reason to stop anyone's pain).

2 For the sake of the argument, I do not discuss here the question of whether consensual homicide is a private or public matter. I have addressed that question earlier in Bergelson (2007).

3 In other common law jurisdictions, the specific legal provisions may differ from the MPC but, conceptually, they treat consent to bodily harm in a similar fashion. For a review of sadomasochistic assault convictions in Scotland, England, and Wales see Cowan (2010).

4 See *R v. Donovan* [1934] KB 498 at 509 ("'Bodily harm' has its ordinary meaning and includes any hurt or injury calculated to interfere with the health or comfort of the prosecutor. Such hurt or injury need not be permanent, *but must, no doubt, be more than merely transient and trifling*").

5 For examples of penal codes that list physical pain as a variety of "bodily harm" see: WASH. REV. CODE. § 9A.04.110(4)(a) (2004) ("'Bodily injury', 'physical injury', or 'bodily harm' means physical pain or injury, illness, or an impairment of physical condition"); ALA. CODE § 13A-11-260 (2013) (defining "physical harm" as "[a]ny physical harm that . . . causes pain or suffering of any gravity or duration"); Mo. Rev. Stat. § 556.061(2011) ("physical injury" means physical pain, illness, or any impairment of physical condition). Penal codes that do not provide definitions of "bodily harm" include: CAL. PENAL CODE § 243 (Deering 2015) ("'Injury' means any physical injury which requires professional medical treatment"); ARIZ. REV. STAT. ANN. § 13-105 (2015) ("'Physical' injury means the impairment of physical condition").

6 *Model Penal Code,* § 210.0(2) ("'bodily injury'" means "physical pain, illness or any impairment of physical condition"); § 210.0(3) ("'serious bodily injury' means bodily injury which creates substantial risk of death or which causes serious, permanent disfigurement, or protracted loss or impairment of the function of any bodily member or organ").

7 *Jaske v. State*, 539 N.E.2d 14 (Ind. 1989) (observing that lack of consent is not included among statutory elements of battery and, since the state code expressly recognizes victim's cooperation as a mitigating circumstance in sentencing, it is clear that the legislature did not intend for a victim's consent to operate as bar to conviction).

8 *Model Penal Code,* § 2.11 cmt 2, n 8 (acknowledging that the "iniquity of the conduct involved" tends to affect judicial assessment of the seriousness of the harm).

9 *R v. Brown* [1994] 1 AC 212 (HL) (Templeman LJ) ("The question whether the defence of consent should be extended to the consequences of sado-masochistic encounters can only be decided by consideration of policy and public interest").

10 Alexander (1996: 166–7), observes that, to be able to give valid consent, one must be of a certain age, lack serious mental disease, irrationality, or intoxication, and have a certain minimum degree of self-control.

11 Shipley (2005: 666), observes that "consent obtained by fraud, or from one without capacity to consent, will not be a defense to a charge of criminal assault and battery".

12 Feinberg (1989: 316) – "[i]f he is so impaired or undeveloped cognitively that he doesn't really know what he is doing, or so impaired or undeveloped volitionally that he cannot help what he is doing, then no matter what expression of assent he may appear to give, it will lack the effect of genuine consent".

13 *People v. Kevorkian*, 527 N.W.2d 714, 750–1 (Mich. 1994) (Levin, J., concurring in part and dissenting in part) ("[w]here an otherwise healthy person is depressed or mentally disturbed, the personal liberty interest is weak, and the state has a strong interest in protecting the person's interests in life").

14 Mill (1993: 518). Mill wrote:

> Whenever . . . there is a definite damage, or a definite risk of damage, either to an individual or to the public, the case is taken out of the province of liberty, and placed in that of morality or law. But with regard to the merely contingent, or, as it may be called, constructive injury which a person causes to society, by conduct which neither violates any specific duty to the public, nor occasions perceptible hurt to any assignable individual except himself; the inconvenience is one which society can afford to bear, for the sake of the greater good of human freedom.
>
> *(Ibid.: 524)*

15 Gibson (1977: 214–16), discussing how people's choices are determined by their socialization); West (1987: 96–7), arguing that women often consent and redefine relationships as consensual in order not to be violated).

16 *R v. Donovan* [1934] KB 498 (CA) 509 (Swift J) ("if an act is unlawful in the sense of being in itself a criminal act, it is plain that it cannot be rendered lawful because the person to whose detriment it is done consents to it").

17 *R v. Wilson* [1997] 1 AC 212 (HL) (explaining that the defendant assisted his wife in "what she regarded as the acquisition of a desirable piece of personal adornment, perhaps in this day and age no less understandable than the piercing of nostrils or even tongues for the purposes of inserting decorative jewellery").

18 See Robinson and Darley (1997) for a discussion of the negative effect of the laws that go against people's perception of justice on their general respect for the law.

19 See also *Ogletree v. State*, 440 S.E.2d 732, 733 (Ga. Ct. App. 1994) (opining that, even had the victim consented, the severe beating ordered by a pastor would still constitute battery).

20 *People v. Samuels*, 58 Cal Rptr. 439, 446-447 (Cal. Dist. Ct. App. 1967) (ruling that "consent of the victim is not generally a defense to assault or battery, except in a situation involving ordinary physical contact or blows incident to sports such as football, boxing or wrestling").

21 *Lawrence v. Texas*, 539 US at 570 ("Our obligation is to define the liberty of all, not to mandate our own moral code") (quoting *Planned Parenthood v. Casey*, 505 U.S. 833, 850 (1992).

22 See e.g. N.J. Stat. Ann. § 2A:114-2 (1951) (repealed 1979) (criminalizing incest); Vt. Stat. Ann. tit. 13, §§ 201, 202 (1947) (repealed 1981) (criminalizing adultery); R.I. Gen. Laws. §§ 11-6-3, 11-6-4 (1956) (repealed 1989) (criminalizing fornication and incest).

23 *Martin v. Ziherl*, 607 S.E.2d at 369 (holding that a statute prohibiting sexual contact between unmarried persons is unconstitutional under *Lawrence*).

24 See *Beard v. State*, No. M2004-02227-CCA-R3-PC, 2005 Tenn Crim App LEXIS 568, at *6 (Tenn. Crim. App. June 7, 2005) ("[I]ncestuous relationships are not protected by our state constitution and the *Lawrence* decision in no way alters our holding . . ."); *Bronson v. Swensen*, 394 F. Supp. 2d 1329, 1334 (D. Utah 2005) ("[T]his court cannot hold that *Lawrence* can be read to require the State of Utah to give formal recognition to a public relationship of a polygamous marriage") (judgment vacated and appellants' claims dismissed for lack of subject matter jurisdiction by *Bronson v. Swensen* 500 F.3d 1099 (10th Cir. 2007).

25 See Herzog (1989).

26 Dan-Cohen defines dignity as "an expressive value demanding that people's behaviour, physical and verbal, convey a certain attitude to other people – namely, an attitude of respect" (ibid.).

References

720 Ill. Comp. Stat. Ann. 5/12-32(a) (2005).
A-G's Reference (No 6 of 1980) (1981) QB 715.
Ala. Code § 13A-11-260 (2013).
Alexander, L. (1996) "The Moral Magic of Consent (II)," *Legal Theory* 2(2): 165–74.
Ariz. Rev. Stat. Ann. § 13-105 (2015).
Beard v. State, No. M2004-02227-CCA-R3-PC, 2005 Tenn Crim App LEXIS 568 (Tenn. Crim. App. June 7, 2005).
Bergelson, V. (2007) "The Right to Be Hurt. Testing the Boundaries of Consent," *George Washington Law Review* 75(2): 165–236.
Bissell v. Starzinger, 83 N.W. 1065 (Iowa 1900).
Bronson v. Swensen, 394 F. Supp. 2d 1329 (D. Utah 2005).
Bronson v. Swensen, 500 F.3d 1099 (10th Cir. 2007).
Bundrick v. State, 54 S.E. 683 (Ga. 1906).
Cal. Penal Code § 243 (Deering 2015).
Cowan, S. (2010) "The Pain of Pleasure: Consent and the Criminalisation of Sado Masochistic 'Assaults'," in James Chalmers, Fiona Leverick and Lindsay Farmer (eds.), *Essays in Criminal Law in Honour of Sir Gerald Gordon.* Edinburgh: Edinburgh University Press, 126–40.
Dan-Cohen, M. (2000) "Basic Values and the Victim's State of Mind," *California Law Review* 88(3): 759–78.
Dubber, M. (2004) "Toward a Constitutional Law of Crime and Punishment," *Hastings Law Journal* 55(3): 509–72.
Duff, R.A. (2001) "Harms and Wrongs," *Buffalo Criminal Law Review* 5(1): 13–46.
Feinberg, J. (1989) *The Moral Limits of Criminal Law: Harm to Self.* Oxford: Oxford University Press.
Gibson, M. (1977) "Rationality," *Philosophy and Public Affairs* 6(3): 193–225.
Glensy, R. (2011) "The Right to Dignity," *Columbia Human Rights Law Review* 43(1): 65–142.
Hart, H.L.A. (1959) "Immorality and Treason," *The Listener* 62(July 30): 162–3.
Hart, H.L.A. (1963) *Law, Liberty, and Morality.* Stanford: Stanford University Press.
Herzog, D. (1989) *Happy Slaves: A Critique of Consent Theory.* Chicago: University of Chicago Press.
Hohfeld, W. (1923) *Fundamental Legal Conceptions as Applied in Judicial Reasoning: And Other Legal Essays.* New Haven: Yale University Press.
Hurd, H. (2005) "Blaming the Victim: A Response to the Proposal that Criminal Law Recognize a General Defense of Contributory Responsibility," *Buffalo Criminal Law Review* 8(2): 503–22.
Jaske v. State, 539 N.E.2d 14 (Ind. 1989).
Law Commission (1995) *Consent in the Criminal Law.* The Law Commission Consultation Paper No 139.
Lawrence v. Texas, 539 US 558 (2003).
Martin v. Ziherl, 607 S.E.2d 367 (Va. 2005).
Mill, J.S. (1993) *On Liberty.* Oxford: Oxford University Press.
Model Penal Code § 2.11
Model Penal Code § 211.0
Model Penal Code § 211.1
Nagel, T. (1986) *The View from Nowhere.* Oxford: Oxford University Press.
N.J. Stat. Ann. § 2A:114-2 (1951) (repealed 1979).
Note (1976) "Consent in Criminal Law: Violence in Sports," *Michigan Law Review* 75(1): 148–79.
Ogletree v. State, 440 S.E.2d 732 (Ga. Ct. App. 1994).
People v. Kevorkian, 527 N.W.2d 714 (Mich. 1994).
People v. Samuels, 58 Cal Rptr. 439 (Cal. Dist. Ct. App. 1967).
Planned Parenthood v. Casey, 505 U.S. 833 (1992).
R.I. Gen. Laws. §§ 11-6-3, 11-6-4 (1956) (repealed 1989).
Roberts, P. (2001) "Philosophy, Feinberg, Codification, and Consent: A Progress Report on English Experiences of Criminal Law Reform," *Buffalo Criminal Law Review* 5(1): 173–254.
Robinson, P. and J. Darley (1997) "The Utility of Desert," *Northwestern University Law Review* 91(2): 453–99.
Ruppe, D. (2001) "Opus Dei on the Rise: Conservative Catholic Group Grows Quietly," *Great Dreams,* viewed 21 February 2016. www.greatdreams.com/sacred/Opus_Dei.htm
R v. Brown [1994] 1 AC 212 (HL) (Templeman LJ).
R v. Donovan [1934] KB 498 (CA) 509 (Swift J).

R v. Wilson [1997] 1 AC 212 (HL).
Shipley, W. (2005) "Annotation: Consent as Defense to Charge of Criminal Assault and Battery," ALR 3d 58, pp. 666.
State v. Bass, 120 S.E.2d 580 (N.C. 1961).
State v. Beck, 1 Hill 363 (Ct of App. of S.C. 1833).
State v. Brown, 364 A.2d 27 (N.J. Super. Ct. Law Div. 1976).
State v. Collier, 372 N.W.2d 303 (Iowa Ct App 1985).
State v. Guinn, No. 23886-1-II Wash. App. LEXIS 502 (Wash. Ct. App. Mar. 30, 2001).
State v. Van, 688 N.W.2d 600 (Neb. 2004).
State v. White, 28 A. 968 (R.I. 1894).
Strafgesetzbuch (2013) Penal Code (StGB) § 228, viewed 1 September 2017. www.gesetze-im-internet.de/englisch_stgb/
U.S. v. Meyers, 906 F. Supp. 1494 (D. Wyo.1995).
von Pahlen, K.J. (2011) "Painful TV," *Entertainment and Sports Law Journal* 9(1): 14–23.
VT. STAT. ANN. tit. 13, §§ 201, 202 (1947) (repealed 1981).
WASH. REV. CODE. § 9A.04.110(4)(a) (2004).
West, R. (1985) "Authority, Autonomy, and Choice: The Role of Consent in the Moral and Political Visions of Franz Kafka and Richard Posner," *Harvard Law Review* 99(2): 384–428.
West, R. (1987) "The Difference in Women's Hedonic Lives: A Phenomenological Critique of Feminist Legal Theory," *Wisconsin Women's Law Journal* 3: 81–146.
William Fraser [1847] Ark 280, 302.
Wolfenden Report (1957) "Report of the Departmental Committee on Homosexual Offences and Prostitution." Committee on Homosexual Offences and Prostitution. London: Her Majesty's Stationery Office.
Wright, R. (1995) "Consenting Adults: The Problem of Enhancing Human Dignity Non-Coercively," *Boston University Law Review* 75(5): 1397–440.

Further reading

Ashford, C., A. Reed and N. Wake (2016) *Legal Perspectives on State Power.* Cambridge, UK: Cambridge Scholars Publishing. (A volume of interdisciplinary works addressing the balance of state power and individual autonomy.)
Westen, P. (2004) *The Logic of Consent: The Diversity and Deceptiveness of Consent as a Defense to Criminal Conduct.* Burlington, VT: Ashgate Publishing. (A fundamental book on consent that analyzes the varied nature of consent arguments in criminal law.)
Hurd, H. (1996) "The Moral Magic of Consent (I)," *Legal Theory* 2(2): 121–46.
Alexander, L. (1996) "The Moral Magic of Consent (II)," *Legal Theory* 2(2): 165–74. (These two influential articles, initially intended as one but later published separately due to some differences between Hurd and Alexander, present a fascinating debate about fundamental issues of capacity, autonomy, and consent.)
Hanna, C. (2001) "Sex Is Not a Sport: Consent and Violence in Criminal Law," *Boston College Law Review* 42(2): 239–91. (The article criticizes the liberal treatment of sadomasochism as a matter of sexual autonomy and argues that recognizing consent in that context may lead to glorification of sexual violence.)

Related topics

Ch.4 The normative force of consent
Ch.5 Consent and wronging a person
Ch.12 Consent and autonomy
Ch.17 The volenti maxim
Ch.19 Voluntary consent

19
VOLUNTARY CONSENT

Thomas Gutmann

19.1 Introduction

It is generally thought that valid consent (cf. Bullock, this volume, Chapter 8), which is morally and/or legally transformative, must be suitably competent, informed and voluntary. A lack of voluntariness renders a person's consent invalid.

(1) "Voluntariness" describes a basic feature of actions for which we can attribute responsibility to the actor. There are different dimensions of how an agent's responsibility (in a broad sense) might be negated because she has acted involuntarily. Consequently, there are discrete types of normative claims that give rise to the question of whether there has been coercion; the truth conditions that sustain an affirmative answer for one type of claim may be quite different from those that constitute "coercion" for purposes of the other (Berman 2002). In the realm of *consent*, it is not whether the agent can be excused for his action or whether his action can be justified that is of interest to us, but rather whether the agent's consent loses its validity and its transformative effects within the respective moral or legal relationship because we cannot hold it to sufficiently reflect the agent's *own* will, preferences and values. In short, in order to be an instance of a valid exercise of a normative power to bring about a change in the nexus of rights and duties within a relationship (cf. Hart 1982; Raz 1999: 97 ff.), a token of consent needs to be voluntary.

(2) The term "voluntariness" can be used in a broad as well as in a narrow way. If we distinguish voluntariness, information and competence as different criteria for valid consent (cf. Wertheimer 2003: 7), coercion is the only defect in consent in the dimension of its voluntariness. In a broader notion, lack of voluntariness could also consist in cognitive defects (lack of information or understanding, including error and deception; see Feinberg 1986: 151; Wertheimer 1987: 4 and 224, 1996: 26) since a person's choices made without access to the relevant information cannot reflect her values or judgements. Arguably, lack of competence (failure to attain a certain threshold of cognitive and volitional capabilities necessary for giving valid consent) can also be qualified as lack of voluntariness for the same reason. In this broader view, error, misrepresentation and fraud, on the one hand, and immaturity, mental handicaps or intoxication, on the other, are examples which may invalidate consent because these also qualify it as *involuntary*. In this chapter, we pursue the narrow conception of voluntariness focusing on coercion only and make the case for a specific normative conception of voluntariness and coercion that does

not refer to the preanalytic image of "coercion" as mere psychological pressure or the difficulty of one's choices (see 2.2–2.5). The question of whether a token of consent is voluntary cannot be resolved solely by reference to non-moral facts.

(3) Moreover, this chapter focuses on "horizontal" coercion between persons, setting aside the general relationship of voluntary consent and coercion with regard to the legitimate authority of the state, which has been discussed in political philosophy at least since Hobbes, and also the question of whether even justified, freedom-enhancing legal systems backed by democratic states are necessarily coercive structures because "right and authorization to use coercion [. . .] mean one and the same thing", as put by Kant (1996 [1797]: 26).

(4) "Consensual minimalism" (Wertheimer 2003: 130) refers to the idea that B's valid consent is necessary and sufficient to render it permissible for A to proceed (while in some legal systems consent is thought to be necessary, but not sufficient to render certain acts permissible, as in the English doctrine of consent to bodily harm, for example). In any case, B's valid consent can only make A's action permissible with regard to B's rights and interests. Consensual actions may still be regarded as wrong or even impermissible if they generate negative externalities to third persons or to collective goods (Wertheimer 2003: 131). In this sense, the concept of valid consent can capture a lot (albeit not all) of what is morally and/or legally *impermissible*, but not much more. When A acts upon B's valid consent, B is not wronged, i.e. her rights are respected. This does not necessarily imply that the act B has consented to fosters her long-term interests or that this act makes A, B or both of them more virtuous persons or that the world will be better or a more just place.

19.2 Consent and coercion

19.2.1 Voluntariness and coercion

At least for legal purposes, consent must include a performative component, i.e. some token of consent, a verbal or non-verbal act of authorization (Feinberg 1986: 173). Coerced tokens of consent are invalid. The question is when we have reasons to apply this principle. What exactly are the truth conditions for coercion claims?

Coercion as the antonym of voluntariness is clear in regard to acts of pure force (*vis absoluta*), i.e. direct use of force or constraint applied to the body without the involvement of any willed cooperation or acquiescence on the victim's part. However, the notion of "involuntariness" not only comprises non-voluntary (non-volitional) movements (as in cases of *vis absoluta* and reflex actions or spasms) or non-voluntary acts (where the will is impaired or overborne by inner conditions such as compulsive behaviour, phobia or psychosis), but also cases of constrained volition where, in a specific sense, the agent's choice is *against* her will (*vis compulsiva*, coercion via the will).

Since Aristotle's ambivalent and eventually undecided analysis of whether "the things that are done from fear of greater evils" (*vis compulsiva*) are done voluntarily or involuntarily (Aristotle 1908: 1110a, b), there has been a discussion of the so-called *coactus volui*-paradoxon (cf. Gutmann 2001: 34–66), which results from the fact that the coerced person can still act deliberately under coercion in the form of *vis compulsiva*. Even in a "your money or your life" situation, B, the victim of an armed robbery by A, has a choice and can act upon a preference for realization of one of the two possible consequents. Nevertheless, she is not acting voluntarily when she hands over her money or consents to the robber taking it. Therefore, Frankfurt's suggestion that coercion which bars the ascription of moral responsibility and invalidates consent must affect the victim's ability to choose by triggering desires and motives that are beyond her control (Frankfurt 1973: 77) does not seem convincing. Rather, under *vis compulsiva*, B can still choose, but A's coercive threats imperil B's autonomy by making B's choice responsive to A's reasons or will, and not to her own (Wertheimer 2003: 126).

19.2.2 Coercive proposals and baseline approaches

Coercive proposals are the main form in which we face coercion that compromises the voluntariness and validity of consent. According to Alan Wertheimer's two-pronged definition, which (as a philosophical abstraction derived from an analysis of legal institutions (see Wertheimer 1987: part 1)) still sets the current standard in the theory of coercion, A coerces B "when (i) A proposes to make B worse off relative to the appropriate baseline if she does not acquiesce and (iia) it is reasonable for B to succumb to A's proposal rather than suffer the consequences [. . .]".[1]

Let us take a look at (i) first (we return to (iia) in 2.8). Both threats and offers are bi-conditional proposals with the same basic structure: A claims that (A will bring about consequences X if and only if B does Y). Threats and offers have the common elements that each can make some actions more or less attractive for the addressee. In both cases, the motivational effect on the recipient is induced by the fact that she prefers the realization of one of the two possible consequents (X/Y or non-X/non-Y, respectively). With regard to (i), the central idea is that (successful) threats coerce while offers don't; relative to the appropriate baseline, (credible) threats worsen the coercee's situation prior to the proposal, while offers do not. When the armed robber A demands B's money or B's life, B goes from being able to have both to being unable to have both. *This* option has essentially become foreclosed. With an offer, regardless of how attractive it is, the case is different: whether the employer A offers B a job for $ 1 (minimum wage laws aside), $ 10 or $ 500 per hour, B receives an additional option while retaining the option to decline and stay in her status quo ante (transaction costs, i.e. the costs and burdens of choosing and processing information not taken into account).

From Nozick's seminal article onwards (Nozick 1969), there has been intense discussion on how this "baseline relative to which B may not be worse off" if she rejects A's proposal must be defined in order to distinguish coercive proposals (conditional threats) from non-coercive proposals (conditional offers). Nozick's definition of this baseline as the "normal or natural or expected course of events" (Nozick 1969: 447) is deliberately ambivalent in regard to whether it refers to normative (moral or legal) or non-normative (empirical) criteria. At closer look, we see four main possibilities: (1) A may propose to make B worse off than B's status quo; (2) A may propose to make B worse off than what B can "statistically" expect in the normal course of events; (3) A may propose to make B worse off relative to what B subjectively experiences or prefers as her baseline (Nozick 1969: 460; Gorr 1986: 398; see also Rhodes 2002); (4) A may propose to make B worse off relative to where B has a right to be vis-à-vis A. The latter may be called a normative (or moralized) baseline (Wertheimer 2003: 165).

These baselines will often converge. In many hard cases, however, they do not, so a theory of coercion has to reach a decision in respect of this. The current state of debate (cf. Anderson 2015; Miller & Wertheimer 2010) seems to assess possibility (4) as clearly superior to the others. In possibility (1), it is unclear how B's status quo is to be defined. If taken at face value as the *factual* status quo, option (1) would yield the counterintuitive result that a seller makes a coercive threat when she merely raises the price of her commodity (Frankfurt 1973: 70; Zimmerman 1981: 126). Neither can mere factual or statistical expectations as in possibility (2) carry the normative weight of attributing responsibility and deciding about the validity of tokens of consent. A husband who beats his wife once a week and proposes to spare her the next time if she consents to Y (cf. also Nozick's (1969: 450–1) slave case) does not threaten to make her worse off than her status quo or than what she can *factually* expect in the normal course of events; this, however, does not seem to provide a reason for considering her consent voluntary and valid. Option (3) does not seem very promising either. Athough Nozick (1969: 462) has a point in saying that, while a formally rational person would normally be willing to go from the status quo ante, i.e. the pre-offer stage, to the offer stage, she would not be willing to go from the pre-threat stage to the threat stage, this does not do the trick because (a) recipients like the abused wife in our example, who are already in an overall coercive situation in the pre-proposal stage, will nonetheless be disposed to go from the pre-proposal stage to the proposal stage. Vice versa, (b) most recipients would just as little want to go from the status quo ante to the offer stage in cases where the transaction partner makes a worse (utility-reducing) offer for further transactions, e.g. by legitimately raising the fees for his future services. When landlord A has the right to raise the rent for B's flat every three years (or terminate the contract), B's acceptance of the landlord's proposal to prolong the contract with the increased rent for another three years cannot be held as involuntary and therefore invalid just because B would have preferred to stay in the pre-offer stage (and continue to pay a lower rent). So, with possibility (3), the distinction between coercive threats and legitimate hard bargaining gets lost. A fully preference-based baseline account cannot avoid seeing coercion in many situations where not only our pre-theoretic views (Anderson 2015: sub 2.3), but also our normative principles and practices would deny it. At least for the attribution of *legal* responsibility and answering the question of whether a token of consent is valid and transformative, we need an objective criterion which is not at the discretionary power or in the subjective experience of the consenting person alone, as is the case in (3). For this reason, Nozick's suggestion (1969: 451) for using the baseline preferred by the recipient of the proposal when the "predictive" (3) and the "moral" (4) baselines diverge is not convincing.[2]

This leaves us with possibility (4) as the most plausible one: A's proposal is coercive if A indicates that she will make the recipient B worse off than B ought to be if A's demand is denied. This approach implies that a coercion claim is never a value-free or empirical claim. Although coercion has descriptive features (see Nozick 1969: 441; Raz 1986: 148; Gutmann 2001: 66–91), the truth of a coercion claim requires normative (moral or legal) judgements at its core.[3]

19.2.3 Coercion and rights

The normative (moral or legal) judgements at the core of a coercion claim are, however, of a special sort: *A's proposal is coercive – and hence nullifies the transformative power of consent on grounds of coercion – if and only if A proposes to violate B's rights (or fails to fulfil a rights-based obligation to B) should B reject A's proposal.*

Starting with Pufendorf (1672: III ch. 6, § X), the central insight of coercion theory is that any attempt to explicate the notion of coercion as a criterion for the moral and legal validity of the coercee's consent in abstraction from the rights and obligations of the parties involved must fail (Ryan (1980: 492) calls this the "State of Nature Fallacy"). The appropriate baseline for telling threats apart from offers is the recipient's (moral or legal) *rights* (Wertheimer 1987: 217), simply because there is no other form in the realm of morals (and law) than the concept of rights that could better serve to define the mutual legitimate expectations of the persons involved. This approach seems especially promising for legal analysis, given the structural significance of individual rights for our legal systems and the fact that the concept of subjective rights "is probably the most important achievement of the evolution of law in modern times" (Luhmann 2004: 76 and 269). However, A may propose to violate B's moral rights without proposing to violate B's legal rights (or vice versa), so we have to distinguish between proposals that are "morally coercive" and those that are "legally coercive", thus making A's consent morally invalid, legally invalid, or both. Vice versa, B's consent is voluntary (in the moral and/or legal sense) in all the cases when she succumbs to a proposal that A has the (moral and/or legal) right to make (Wertheimer 1987: 301). So, in the final analysis, the matter to be assessed "is not the situation of the person consenting, but the behavior of the person obtaining the consent" (Radcliffe-Richards 2010: 295).

19.2.4 The normative core of the concept of voluntariness

For this reason, voluntariness is a normative concept which does not concern itself exclusively with the consenter's situation (beliefs, options, capacities). Above all, it cannot be adequately explained in descriptive psychological terms. In order to invalidate B's consent, it is necessary, but not sufficient, for B to feel "under pressure" to consent or to find the alternative to acquiescence to be grim, distasteful or painful (which, by and large, is the preanalytic image of "coercion") (Wertheimer 2003: 151; Murphy 1981: 84–5). This is true with the exception of cases where severe psychological pressure affects the addressee's ability to choose at all, i.e. her competence. Even voluntary decisions between Scylla and Charybdis are possible. If B is diagnosed with cancer and has to choose between an early death and painful chemotherapy to avoid death, she can voluntarily exercise the second option and give valid consent to the therapy proposed by her oncologist A (Wertheimer 2003: 173). Hard choices are not incompatible with valid consent (Murphy 1981: 83–5). Therefore, the fact that a person reasonably believes that she has "no choice" or "no reasonable alternative" but to opt for consenting is not sufficient for the conclusion that her consent is not valid, as long as "having no choice" or "having no reasonable alternative" means that it would not be rational for the agent to forgo a bad option for an even worse one. Offers that one cannot reasonably refuse in this sense are still offers because the "dictates of reason" do not coerce. Neither do moral norms, virtues or role models the agent identifies with: a father who decides to donate part of his liver for his critically ill child because it seems evident to him that this is what a person like him who strives to be a good father does to save the child in the absence of other options, acts perfectly voluntarily. So even "volitional necessities" in Frankfurt's sense (Frankfurt 2006: 44), i.e. values and principles with which we identify wholeheartedly, ends that we cannot but accept and whose rejection is unthinkable for us, are perfectly compatible with acting and consenting voluntarily. On the other hand, the thesis that voluntariness cannot be adequately understood in descriptive psychological terms also explains why a positive attitude towards the chosen option is not an essential component of voluntary consent. We do not have to desire what we choose (e.g. chemotherapy) in order to choose it voluntarily. And finally, coercion cannot be defined by a psychological criterion which only recurs to the degree of pressure experienced by the addressee of a proposal while neglecting the difference between threats and offers (as Joel Feinberg does (1986: 199 et seq.) by calculating the "differential coercive pressure" or "total coercive burden" of the proposals; cf. also Held (1972: 55)). Offers are never coercive, even if they seem to be without eligible alternatives or are so seductive that they create motivational force or "pressure" quantitatively similar to that associated with coercive threats, and will, with a high degree of probability, induce the consent of the addressee. In view of the foregoing, it becomes equally clear that voluntariness as a normative notion is a *binary* concept; a token of consent is either voluntary or it is not. Voluntariness does not come "in degrees" (for a different approach see Walker, this volume, Chapter 12).

Voluntariness as a normative concept without reference to psychological pressure or the intricacy of one's choices (cf. Murphy 1981: 83–5 and 44; Scanlon 2001: 114) is not only a conceptual argument, but also one about a core normative function of self-determination and the value of choice. If hard choices were not voluntary ones, people could not give valid consent in situations where entitlement to choose for oneself matters most. The need for morally transformative consent arises especially in critical life decisions that can have a dramatic life-altering impact, in situations in which we face hard (or incommensurate) choices or find ourselves under serious constraints or in dire straits. Self-determination is sometimes reduced to choosing between the worst and the second worst possibility or to consenting to transactions that will move one from a very unfortunate situation to an only slightly better one. It is highly questionable whether any principle of respect for persons and their autonomous choices (or whether the goals of enhancing their autonomy or their welfare) would be compatible with denying persons the transformative power of their consent under such circumstances. And, finally, if we were not entitled to decide for ourselves in such situations, then who would decide for us?

19.2.5 Coercive offers?

Although quite a number of authors claim that conditional offers, too, can be coercive[4], a plausible concept of coercive offers has not yet been put forward (Gutmann 2001: 149–200). Many of the examples given can be analyzed as coercion *simpliciter*, e.g. Zimmermann's examples (1981: 133) in which A makes an offer to B while actively preventing B from obtaining a situation for herself that would be better than the situation A proposes (thus violating B's rights). Most authors who think that offers can also be used coercively, however, describe instances of exploitation (cf. Frankfurt 1973: 71–2; Lyons 1975: 33; Benditt 1979; McGregor 1988–9). This is also the case with Feinberg's paradigmatic example of the lecherous millionaire A who makes the proposal to B that he will pay for the expensive surgery that is the only possibility for saving her child's life, provided that she become his mistress for a period. Feinberg (1986: 229 and 233), recurring to a psychological account of involuntariness, argues somewhat paradoxically that, despite not being responsible for the situation B finds herself in and having no duty to help her, A makes a freedom-enhancing but nevertheless coercive offer. The moral problem of such an offer, however, does not lie in the fact that it undermines voluntary consent (see 2.7).

Inducements per se, including economic inducements, cannot be a general problem for morally transformative consent (provided that they do not, in themselves, severely distort the addressee's capability for judgement), as long as our notion of personal autonomy fosters the idea that being an autonomous agent includes, among other things, the ability to pursue one's subjectively defined ends rationally (cf. Radcliffe-Richards 2010: 289). There are bad or even toxic offers – seductive offers (inducing a person to make a choice that does not advance her long-term interests, all things considered, cf. Wertheimer 2003: 126), exploitative (see below, 2.7), harassing, corrupting or even humiliating offers. They may be criticizable for being seductive, exploitative, harassing, corrupting or humiliating. But, as long as they are offers (i.e. as long as they do not threaten to violate a right of the recipient), they add to the range of options available to B when measured against her normative baseline and do not propose to make B worse off relative to this baseline if she does not acquiesce. All a (competent) recipient has to do is to reject such an offer without losing anything she is entitled to. Even when such offers exert high motivational force and will very probably lead to the action of B desired by A, they are not coercive and thus cannot invalidate B's consent on account of lack of *voluntariness*.

19.2.6 Voluntariness and injustice

In a just world, people would have better options to choose from and face less hard choices. And if "the ideal of personal autonomy", which means that people should be the authors of their own lives, "requires not merely the presence of options, but of acceptable ones" (Raz 1986: 205), people would also lead more autonomous lives. So the ideal of autonomy requires social justice. For the time being, however, we do live in societies with unequal and unjust basic structures (Rawls 1971: 3). We therefore need a theory of voluntariness and coercion that can be applied to the non-ideal circumstances in which we find ourselves. For this reason, a justifiable concept of voluntary (and hence, valid) consent will "hold that, from A's (and B's) perspective, B's circumstances – even if unjust – may properly define the background against which their transactions occur and from which we must evaluate their moral [and legal] status" (Wertheimer 2003: 177, 1996: 270). There is a distinction to be made between the problems in our objective circumstances in which choices are made and the problems in the quality of the choice that we are making, given the background conditions. Social inequality or inequality of bargaining power (see McGregor 1988–89: 25) per se do not invalidate consent although we often agree to transactions we would reject under more just or equal background conditions. When unjust background conditions which cannot be changed here and now are the problem, an offer that allows its addressee to improve on those background conditions is always at least one option more for her and very often the best option available.

Again, this is not only a conceptual argument, but also one about a core normative function of consent and personal autonomy and about the social inclusiveness of our institutions. It seems important to respect a person's capacity to make decisions under the circumstances in which she finds herself (Wertheimer 2003: 128). If being in a weaker position than one's partner in a transaction were to imply that one could no longer give morally transformative consent or enter a contract (which are both instances of exercising a normative power to bring about a change in the nexus of rights and duties within a relationship; cf. Bix, this volume, Chapter 20), this would mean adding incapacitation to inequality. We would have to create procedures for proxy consent within a system of general tutelage for the majority of people, amounting to their extensive exclusion from the institutions of our autonomy-orientated society.

19.2.7 Voluntariness and exploitation

Although voluntary consent presupposes neither equality nor equal bargaining power between the parties, nor fair background conditions for their transaction, there is one complex normative concept whose consequences for the validity of consent merit further exploration. This is exploitation (in its strictly analytic, not in its Marxian meaning), i.e. a situation where a person takes unfair advantage of someone else's vulnerabilities or desperation to strike a deal (cf. Wertheimer 1996; Zwolinski & Wertheimer 2016). A transaction may be *substantively* unfair in reference to the outcome of the transaction ("excessive benefit") or *procedurally* unfair, implying that there is some sort of defect in the process by which the outcome has come about (in this sense, coercion can be seen as a subform of exploitation, albeit with special structural features).

The crucial point, however, is that exploitation is generally compatible with voluntary action (on both sides) and hence with voluntary consent because, in its paradigmatic cases ("consensual exploitation", see Wertheimer (1996: 14)), it involves offers by which the exploiter proposes to make her victim better off if the victim does as the exploiter proposes (Zwolinski & Wertheimer 2016: sub 2.2; Zwolinski, this volume, Chapter 14). Therefore, exploitative proposals do not coerce, and the exploitee can give valid and "fully voluntary consent to the exploitative behaviour".[5]

Moreover, exploitation is a tricky and even somewhat paradoxical (Ferguson 2016) concept, with a moral force less clear than coercion since it can be mutually beneficial. It may even be harmful for vulnerable individuals to be protected from being exploited because this often means that they are deprived of one (or even the only) possibility for improving their situation by engaging in a mutually beneficial (albeit unfair) transaction, while preventing exploitative transactions by itself does nothing to alleviate this vulnerability or to change the unfair background conditions (cf. Radcliffe-Richards 2010: 295). Finally, it is far from clear which forms of exploitation should count as a kind of wrong that can justify state intervention (Wertheimer 1996: 29 ff.).

Using another person's vulnerability for one's own benefit is, in general, unfair and wrong (and it may well be appropriate for the exploitee A to issue complaints against the exploiter B, even though A has consented). This constitutes good reasons for the law to set limits to such practices. The motive for this, however, is *not* that voluntary and valid consent is not possible under exploitative conditions. Therefore, rational legal systems have to develop different institutions to translate into doctrine the structurally different concepts and foci of coercion, on the one hand, and exploitation, on the other. Within different national legal systems, coercion, on the one hand, and exploitation, on the other, are currently being addressed in a rather non-systematic way by a plethora of theoretically blurry concepts, for example by different legal notions of "coercion" or "duress" and by certain aspects of "undue influence" and "unconscionability" (or "good morals", in German law)(cf. Bigwood 2004; Gutmann 2007; Bix, this volume, Chapter 20). One main task of a legal theory of consent aiming at doctrine is the reconstruction of these legal notions along the lines of the different analytical structures of the two concepts of coercion and exploitation. However, *The Draft Common Frame of Reference for a European Private Law* (Von Bar & Clive 2009: vol. I, Art. II–7:206 and 207) (with regard to contracts) clearly distinguishes between threats

> Art. II.–7:206: Coercion or threats: (1) A party may avoid a contract when the other party has induced the conclusion of the contract by coercion or by the threat of an imminent and serious harm which it is wrongful to inflict, or wrongful to use as a means to obtain the conclusion of the contract. (2) A threat is not regarded as inducing the contract if in the circumstances the threatened party had a reasonable alternative.

and exploitation, requiring a combination of procedural and substantive unfairness:

> Art. II.–7:207: Unfair exploitation: A party may avoid a contract if, at the time of the conclusion of the contract: (a) the party was dependent on or had a relationship of trust with the other party, was in economic distress or had urgent needs, was improvident, ignorant, inexperienced or lacking in bargaining skill; and (b) the other party knew or could reasonably be expected to have known this and, given the circumstances and purpose of the contract, exploited the first party's situation by taking an excessive benefit or grossly unfair advantage.

Nevertheless, a new approach in consent theory may jeopardize this distinction. Miller & Wertheimer (2010) try to answer the central question of whether a consent transaction between A and B is morally transformative and, in particular, whether a consent transaction renders it permissible for A to proceed – however, not with the prevailing theory of valid consent, which they call "the lock-and-key/autonomous authorization model (LK/AA) of consent transactions" and which, according to the authors, fails to do justice to the bilateral nature of consent transactions. Instead, they have developed a "fair transaction model" of consent transactions that claims that A is only morally permitted to proceed on the basis of a consent transaction "if A has treated B fairly" (Miller & Wertheimer 2010: 81) and responds in a reasonable manner to B's token or expression of consent (or what A reasonably believes is B's token or expression of consent). As the requirement of "treating a person fairly" also specifies refrainment from all instances of consensual exploitation (Miller & Wertheimer 2010: 103–4), consent given in coercive circumstances and consent given under exploitative circumstances are both instances of non-transformative (and hence invalid) consent. This result is, however, derived by neglecting the structural normative differences between coercion and exploitation, thus disregarding the interests of all persons who voluntarily prefer an unfair, but valid, transaction to no transaction at all. In any case, the "fair transaction model" of consent transactions is not a theory about distinguishing between voluntary and involuntary consent.

19.2.8 Coercion and resilience

Not all threats coerce, as threats may be wrongful, but too trivial to provide a good reason to acquiesce. Therefore, the question is when the person giving consent is *entitled* to yield to the coercer's proposal and thus be released from the normal moral and legal consequences of her consent (Wertheimer 1987: 267). So, given A's proposal is a threat, a second criterion for coercion is that it must be "reasonable for B to succumb to A's proposal rather than suffer the consequences" (see above, 2.3). We would not hold B's consent to a sexual act with A involuntary just because A threatened to destroy B's favourite coffee mug otherwise. This resilience criterion not only excludes trivial threats where we expect the addressee to stand his ground, but also generally addresses the question of whether there was another reasonable (or tolerable) alternative for the coercee. Sometimes (e.g. when our partner threatens not to perform our contract) the legal system does provide us with such an alternative (e.g. to sue for breach of contract). This "choice prong" of the two-pronged theory of coercion is generally applied in a contextualized way by the law, especially when it comes to duress or necessity as a criminal defence (cf. Christie 1999; for American law on criminal responsibility, confessions, plea bargaining, blackmail, contracts and consent to searches and medical procedures in general, see Wertheimer (1987: part 1)). At the same time, the two-pronged theory of coercion serves as a general principle in the law of contracts (cf. 2.7; Bix, this volume, Chapter 20), cf. Art. II–7:206 of the *Draft Common Frame of Reference for a European Private Law* ("A threat is not regarded as inducing the contract if in the circumstances the threatened party had a reasonable alternative"). In general, this "choice prong" criterion also reflects voluntariness as a normative concept with regard to what we rightfully expect of the recipient of a potentially coercive proposal. While there are few legal examples where the reasonable-alternative test is applied in cases of one party consenting to medical procedures, the question of what degree of resilience shall be expected from the victim plays a contested role in the definition of different offences against sexual autonomy (Hörnle, this volume, Chapter 21).

Notes

1 For the whole definition, see Wertheimer (2003: 165, 1987: 172). For non-baseline approaches to coercion, cf. Anderson (2015: sub 2.5); for a different attempt that tracks the specific form of power associated with "coercion" within a non-moralized, coercer-focused approach to coercion, cf. Anderson (2010).

2 For other descriptive (non-evaluative) analyses of coercion that face difficulties in explaining the legal or ethical significance in coercion thus conceived, see e.g. Gorr (1986) and Rhodes (2002).

3 Gunderson (1979), Ryan (1980), Raz (1986: 148), Wertheimer (1987: 7 et seq.), Berman (2002).

4 Cf. Held (1972), Lyons (1975), Benditt (1979), Zimmerman (1981), McGregor (1988–9), Feinberg (1986: 229).

5 Feinberg (1990: 176), cf. Wertheimer (1996: 248 ff.), Jansen & Wall (2013), Radcliffe-Richards (2010).

References

Anderson, S. (2010) "The Enforcement Approach to Coercion," *Journal of Ethics and Social Philosophy* 5: 1–31.

Anderson, S. (2015) "Coercion," in E.N. Zalta (ed.), *The Stanford Encyclopedia of Philosophy* (Summer 2015 Edition). http://plato.stanford.edu/archives/sum2015/entries/coercion/.

Aristotle (1908) *Nicomachean Ethics*, transl. W.D. Ross. Oxford: Clarendon Press.

Benditt, T. (1979) "Threats and Offers," *Personalist* 58: 382–4.

Berman, M. (2002) "The Normative Functions of Coercion Claims," *Legal Theory* 8: 45–89.

Bigwood, R. (2004) *Exploitative Contracts.* Oxford: Oxford University Press.

Christie, G. (1999) "The Defense of Necessity Considered from the Legal and Moral Points of View," *Duke Law Journal* 48: 975–1042.

Feinberg, J. (1986) *Harm to Self. The Moral Limits of the Criminal Law.* Vol. III. New York: Oxford University Press.

Feinberg, J. (1990) *Harmless Wrongdoing. The Moral Limits of the Criminal Law.* Vol. IV. New York: Oxford University Press.

Ferguson, B. (2016) "The Paradox of Exploitation," *Erkenntnis* 81: 951–72.

Frankfurt, H.G. (1973) "Coercion and Moral Responsibility," in T. Honderich (ed.), *Essays on Freedom of Action.* London and Boston: Routledge & Kegan Paul, 65–86.

Frankfurt, H.G. (2006) "Getting it Right," in *Taking Ourselves Seriously and Getting it Right.* Stanford: Stanford University Press, 27–52.

Gorr, M. (1986) "Toward a Theory of Coercion," *Canadian Journal of Philosophy* 16: 383–406.

Gunderson, M. (1979) "Threats and Coercion," *Canadian Journal of Philosophy* 9: 247–59.

Gutmann, T. (2001) *Freiwilligkeit als Rechtsbegriff.* München: C.H. Beck.

Gutmann, T. (2007) "Zwang und Ausbeutung beim Vertragsschluss," in R. Schulze (ed.), *New Features in Contract Law.* Munich: Sellier. European Law Publishers, 49–66.

Hart, H.L.A. (1982) "Legal Powers," in *Essays on Bentham. Studies in Jurisprudence and Political Theory,* Oxford: Oxford University Press, 194–219.

Held, V. (1972) "Coercion and Coercive Offers," in J.R. Pennock and J.W. Chapman (ed.), *Coercion* (Nomos XIV). Chicago/New York: Aldine Atherton, 49–62.

Jansen, L. and S. Wall (2013) "Rethinking Exploitation: A Process-Centered Account," *Kennedy Institute of Ethics Journal* 23(4): 381–410.

Kant, I. (1996 [1797]) *The Metaphysics of Morals*, transl. M. Gregor. Cambridge: Cambridge.

Luhmann, N. (2004) *Law as a Social System*, transl. K.A. Ziegert Oxford: Oxford University Press.

Lyons, D. (1975) "Welcome Threats and Coercive Offers," *Philosophy* 50: 425–36.

McGregor, J. (1988–9) "Bargaining Advantages and Coercion in the Market," *Philosophy Research Archives* 14: 23–50.

Miller, F.G. and A. Wertheimer (2010) "Preface to a Theory of Consent Transactions: Beyond Valid Consent," in F.G. Miller and A. Wertheimer (ed.), *The Ethics of Consent. Theory and Practice.* Oxford/New York: Oxford University Press, 79–106.

Murphy, J.G. (1981) "Consent, Coercion, and Hard Choices," *Virginia Law Review* 67: 79–95.

Nozick, R. (1969) "Coercion," in S. Morgenbesser, P. Suppes and M. White (ed.), *Philosophy, Science, and Method: Essays in Honor of Ernest Nagel.* New York: St. Martin's Press, 440–72.

Pufendorf, S. von (1672) *De jure naturae et gentium libri octo.* Lund.

Radcliffe-Richards, J. (2010) "Consent With Inducements: The Case of Body Parts and Services," in F.G. Miller and A. Wertheimer (ed.), *The Ethics of Consent. Theory and Practice.* Oxford/New York: Oxford University Press, 281–304.

Rawls, J. (1971) *A Theory of Justice.* Cambridge, MA: The Belknap Press of Harvard University Press.

Raz, J. (1986) *The Morality of Freedom.* Oxford: Oxford University Press.

Raz, J. (1999) *Practical Reasons and Norms.* Oxford: Oxford University Press.

Rhodes, M. (2002). *Coercion: A Nonevaluative Approach.* Amsterdam: Rodopi.

Ryan, Ch. (1980) "The Normative Concept of Coercion," *Mind* 89: 481–98.

Scanlon, T.M. (2001) "Promises and Contracts," in P. Benson (ed.), *The Theory of Contract Law.* Cambridge: Cambridge University Press, 86–117.

Von Bar, C. and E. Clive (eds.) (2009) *Principles, Definitions and Model Rules of European Private Law. Draft Common Frame of Reference (DCFR).* Full Edition, Vol. I. Munich: Sellier.

Wertheimer, A. (1987) *Coercion.* Princeton: Princeton University Press.

Wertheimer, A. (1996) *Exploitation*. Princeton: Princeton University Press.
Wertheimer, A. (2003) *Consent to Sexual Relations*. Cambridge: Cambridge University Press.
Zimmerman, D. (1981) "Coercive Wage Offers," *Philosophy and Public Affairs* 10: 121–45.
Zwolinski, M. and Wertheimer, A. (2016) "Exploitation," in E.N. Zalta (ed.), *The Stanford Encyclopedia of Philosophy* (Fall 2016 Edition). http://plato.stanford.edu/archives/fall2016/entries/exploitation/.

Related topics

Ch.8 Valid consent
Ch.12 Consent and autonomy
Ch.14 Exploitation and consent
Ch.20 Consent and contracts
Ch.21 Rape as non-consensual sex
Ch.24 Informed consent

20
CONSENT AND CONTRACTS[1]

Brian H. Bix

20.1 Introduction

Consent – in one form or another[2] – is at the core of the modern understanding of contract law. In Anglo-American law,[3] commentators suggest that what is distinctive about contract law is "freedom of contract" – that is, the notion that legally enforceable obligations are those, and only those, that individuals freely choose to impose upon themselves. In contrast, in other areas of law, *e.g.*, criminal law and tort law, the duties apply regardless of the individuals' choices or preferences (cf. Symposium 2004). In Continental Europe, commentators espoused a "will theory" of contract (*e.g.*, Gordley 1991: 161–229) that is comparable to "freedom of contract": grounding contractual obligations on the convergence of the acts of will of the contracting parties.[4]

This chapter will show how the nature of consent involved in contractual transactions is distinctively different from the consent involved in other sorts of events and transactions. While consent in other contexts (*e.g.*, medical care and sexual relations, even invitations of strangers into one's home) can be said to be primarily about the removal of an obligation, making an act that would otherwise be a wrong not a wrong (Owens 2012: 164), consent in contract law is primarily about the creation of new obligations (and their correlative rights). With contracts, we *consent to* the imposition of certain duties upon ourselves, but these duties are connected to (exchanged for) legal rights to some good or performance from the other contracting party. Additionally, as will be discussed, modern contracting practice frequently involves transactions where defects in knowledge or lack of reasonable alternatives raise concerns about the (level of) consent of one or both parties.

The chapter will also observe the way that issues of consent are in tension with another important aspect of contracts and contracting: that contracts – and their predictable enforceability – are central to modern commercial life (Oman 2016). Firms need to make investments and plans in reliance on the enforceability of their transactions, and the reliable enforceability of contracts is required for many types of business financing (*e.g.*, where accounts receivable are used as collateral). However, as a requirement of the other party's consent (or, if needed, that party's "full consent" or "informed consent") at the time of a transaction may be both hard to discern at the time of a transaction and difficult for courts to determine after the fact, consent requirements could lead to unpredictability in enforcement. This tension between concerns about consent and the need for certainty in enforcement is also reflected in theoretical discussions of contract law: *e.g.*, in the way that justification for contract law based on any of the related concepts of promise, consent, will, or autonomy, will usually be supplemented by justifications based on some version of the related consequentialist concepts of utility and welfare, showing how and why some contracts are and should be enforced even when consent is absent or defective.[5]

The chapter begins by offering some general reflections on the nature of consent. It then considers the connection between consent and various doctrinal defenses to the enforcement of contracts. A subsequent section describes the way in which modern contracting practice generally falls far short of consent in its fullest sense. Finally, the chapter will reflect on the practical effects "defective" consent may have for the enforcement of agreements,[6] as well as the moral implications of defective consent for individual obligations to keep contracts.

20.2 The nature of consent

Commentators tend to view consent either as a certain state of mind (*e.g.*, Hurd 1996: 124–5) or as an act of will. As modern contract law focuses on the objective manifestations of assent, the difference for our purposes is likely not important. Consent (or its absence) will be found based on what contracting parties do and say,[7] even if their actual mental states indicate a different conclusion.[8]

Consent in its fullest form is often thought to entail knowledge by the actor of all material circumstances, alternatives, and consequences (thus, the reference to "*informed* consent", especially in the medical context). It is "full *and free* consent" when the action or decision is not coerced and when there are reasonable alternatives (see generally Schnüriger, this volume, Chapter 2). As will be discussed below, contemporary contracts frequently involve a level of consent far below its fullest form. However, *legal* consent is usually a binary: there either *was* sufficient consent (to the contract, the medical treatment, the sexual contact, the presence of the stranger on one's property, etc.) or *there was not;* the level of knowledge, available and reasonable alternatives, and lack of coercion was either collectively sufficient or it was not.[9] That noted, the legal regulation of contract law has ways of responding to the complexity of consent – most commonly, by adding in some cases other (usually procedural) requirements. For example, for some transactions there is a waiting period during which time the party consenting is allowed to withdraw its consent (cancel the transaction), or there is a requirement that certain provisions be presented in a more salient way (*e.g.*, larger or bolder font) or be separately signed or initialed (cf. Eisenberg 1995). Additionally, certain defects in consent play a role in decisions regarding certain (equitable) remedies.[10]

The significance of consent is that it is a normative power, changing the normative status of the person consenting and others with whom the consenting party is interacting (see Hurd, this volume, Chapter 4). In particular, consent makes actions permitted that would otherwise be forbidden – *e.g.*, with sexual relations, medical treatment, allowing a stranger to enter one's property, etc. As already noted, with contracts, consent is part of a transaction that creates both duties and rights for the consenting party.[11]

There are other distinct differences in the nature and role of consent in contract law,[12] compared with its role in other areas, such as medical treatment and sexual relations (cf. Ach, this volume, Chapter 25; Archard, this volume, Chapter 16). At first glance, the difference may appear to be related to the ability to change one's mind: that one is allowed to change one's mind with consent to medical care or consent to sexual relations in a way that one cannot (without liability) change one's mind in contract law. Generally, one can tell a treating physician that one no longer consents to the current treatment, and the physician would be under a legal obligation to stop that treatment. Similarly, once one tells a sexual partner that one no longer consents to sexual contact, that partner must stop the contact or be subject to criminal and tort liability. One can consent now for tomorrow's surgery, but what one cannot do is consent in such a way that it prevents one from tomorrow, just before the surgery, validly withdrawing that consent. By contrast, once one has consented to (agrees to) a contract that is otherwise legally valid, one is not legally authorized to simply change one's mind. If one does change one's mind, and does not perform as required under the contract, one will have breached the contract and be subject to damages for that breach. If one contracts to have the surgery, one may withdraw one's consent before the surgery, preventing its occurrence, but one will likely still be legally liable as a matter of contract law.

It is probably more precise to think of the difference between the kinds of consent, not in terms of a right to change one's mind, but instead either in terms of the subject of the consent or in terms of the period of time over which the consent is effective. As already discussed, consent in connection with medical treatment, sexual contact, and another person's presence on one's property is the removal of another person's duty – making an action that would have been wrongful no longer wrongful. That consent is understood as operating at the time the consent is expressed, and until it is withdrawn. By contrast, one's consent to a contract is consent to an imposition of a duty on oneself. Once given, it cannot be validly withdrawn (without the permission of the other contracting party).

Commentators often note that a promise, agreement, or act of consent only counts as such if the party intended to do that action.[13] For something to be a valid promise, one must *intend* to promise, and similarly with consent and agreement. At the same time, many legal systems (including the American legal system) will enforce contracts without any requirement that one prove that the other party intended to agree or intended to contract (though clear language in a written agreement indicating that the parties intend *not to be legally bound* will usually be followed).[14] The "objective standard" of modern contract law involves enforcing contracts where one party *reasonably believes* that the other party intended to agree (consent), even where that belief was false.[15]

What is the connection between consent and contractual obligation? Do we have an obligation to keep our contracts, to act according to the undertakings we have made? This is a deceptively difficult and surprisingly controversial question. Even if one confines oneself to the seemingly simple and tautological assertion that one has a *legal* obligation to act according to one's duties under a *legally valid* contract, commentators differ on *what that entails*. A view that is associated with Justice Oliver Wendell Holmes,[16] and which is a fundamental assumption of most economic models of contract remedies (*e.g.*, Craswell 1988), is that a legal obligation generally[17] means only that one must *either* act as promised under the contract or one must *pay damages,* nothing more.[18]

Many other commentators resist this idea, asserting that one has a (presumptive) legal – and moral – duty to perform as one has agreed to do in one's contracts. Assuming that there is some kind of (prima facie) moral obligation to perform as one's contract prescribes, what is the ground of that obligation? And here, again, there is a surprising amount of uncertainty and controversy. As already indicated, commentators disagree on whether contractual obligations are ultimately grounded on promise, consent, will, utility, welfare, or some combination of these. And even if one were to equate the moral obligation to keep contracts with the moral obligation to keep promises,[19] theorists going back at least to David Hume (Hume 1978: Book III, Part 2, ch. 5, 469–70) have disagreed over whether *that* obligation is some sort of foundational duty, or whether it, in turn, is grounded on ("mere") social convention or social practices (*e.g.*, Scanlon 1990).[20]

Consent tends to play a role, albeit a somewhat changing role, as one moves among the different understandings of the grounding of contractual and promissory obligation. Consent (in a sufficiently full/valid form) can be seen as a necessary expression of will for will theories and autonomy theories, an invocation of the convention of promising for a promissory theory, as well as a good indication of what will maximize wealth or utility for consequentialist theories. We will return later to the question of what different theories might prescribe for situations when consent is far less than "full" or "optimal".

20.3 Consent and doctrinal defenses to enforcement

American contract law contains defenses to the enforcement of agreements based on certain types of failures of consent (most other contract law systems have comparable defenses). These defenses include duress, undue influence, misrepresentation, mistake, and unconscionability.[21] These are all doctrines that courts apply only in highly exceptional circumstances, for courts do not want to undermine the general reliability and predictability of enforcement.[22] It is likely that some degree of coercion, over-persuasion, misrepresentation, and mistake occur in a significant percentage of transactions that are enforced, even when they do not appear at the level necessary to persuade a court to refuse enforcement of the underlying contracts.

Duress is a doctrine that applies when one party only entered an agreement because of an unacceptable type or level of coercion by the other party. Under current US contract law principles,[23] the party claiming duress must show that his or her consent was induced by a wrongful act by the other party, and that the party claiming duress had no reasonable alternative to assenting to the agreement.[24] Undue influence occurs when one party uses coercive forms of persuasion to induce assent to an agreement by a party left vulnerable by his or her condition or circumstances.[25] Defenses based on this doctrine are rarely successful (it seems to have somewhat greater success in challenges to wills than in attempts to rescind contracts, but even with wills its success is infrequent). A party can, in extreme circumstances, void an otherwise valid contract on the basis of mutual mistake, if that party can show that, at the time of contracting, both parties were mistaken about some matter central to their agreement.[26] Here, the claim is that the parties did not effectively consent, because both were ignorant of facts important to the transaction.

There are two different understandings of unconscionability, or, perhaps, two different roles that doctrine plays, each with a different connection with consent. Under the first understanding (see Epstein 1975), the doctrine should be applied in circumstances where, perhaps because of one-sided terms, the court suspects that the agreement is the product of misrepresentation, duress, or mistake (or some combination of those), but the party challenging enforcement is unable to prove in court all the elements needed for the defense. Under this view, unconscionability is a doctrine to be applied where there are serious concerns about the (level of) consent of one of the parties. Under the second understanding of unconscionability, the doctrine is available to negate the enforceability of agreements that are so contrary to justice, dignity, or basic respect that the agreements are not to be enforced (if challenged), regardless of the challenging party's level of consent at the time of contracting. This understanding of unconscionability is a small example of a point to be discussed later: that consent is by no means the only moral consideration in the decision whether to enforce an agreement, and the factor of consent (or its absence) may be overridden by other considerations (cf. Shiffrin 2000).

20.4 Problems of consent in contemporary contracting practice

While courts and commentators still regularly refer to "freedom of contract", the fact is that in the vast majority of contracts that most people enter, the consent of one or both parties to the terms of the agreement falls far short of consent in its fullest form.[27] In particular, the concern is with transactions that occur on long standardized forms,[28] especially when those terms are presented online (usually with the contracting party being required to register assent through a "click", though sometimes the terms are simply presented without any requirement that the contracting party express assent) or when the terms are presented at a later point, often in the packaging of the item being shipped to the contracting party.[29]

There are a number of problems. First, consumers are sometimes unaware that they have even entered a contract.[30] This is particularly the case where the terms are provided on an internet site without any requirement that the consumers check a box to indicate their assent to the terms, or where (additional) terms are placed in the box in which goods have been provided to the consumer. Second, even parties aware that there are terms rarely read the terms, and, third, if they do read the terms, they rarely fully understand their significance (many of the provisions in standard forms are difficult even for trained lawyers to understand on first reading). Fourth, even when consumers and employees know of and fully understand one-sided terms, they are likely to discount the significance of those provisions, for reasons summarized by behavioral law and economics scholars (*e.g.*, Korobkin 2003; Bar-Gill 2013).[31] Fifth, parties often lack reasonable alternatives to taking on the unwanted obligations and limitations on their rights under those contractual obligations. The lack of alternatives is constituted by some combination of reasonable necessity (*e.g.*, it is very hard to function well in our society without credit cards, a cell phone, or internet access) and lack of variety (all providers have nearly identical terms – *e.g.*, regarding mandatory arbitration, class action waivers, limitations of liability, etc.).

Both Karl Llewellyn and Randy Barnett have argued that contracting parties should be held to have consented to the negotiated terms, or those most salient to the parties, and to have given a general or "blanket" consent to all generally reasonable terms hidden in the form provisions they have not read (or have not understood) (Llewellyn 1960: 370; Barnett 2002: 638). For some, this will stretch the idea of "consent" further than it should be stretched; others may be concerned about likely wide disagreements regarding what constitutes a "generally reasonable term".

There are some categories of cases that exemplify consent problems in modern contracting practice or that raise distinctive versions of such problems: post-employment restrictive covenants, premarital agreements, and provisions covering mandatory arbitration and other procedural terms.[32] These will be discussed, briefly, in turn.

Many employment agreements include provisions that purport to limit the rights of employees after the end of the employment. "Non-competition clauses" are common also in partnership agreements and in the sale of businesses. Such terms can be reasonable, justifiably protecting party interests based on training, sharing of customers and patients, and business good will.[33] At the same time, employers often overreach, imposing limitations that are broader in scope and geography, and longer in duration, than would be justifiable. The main issue of consent here is one of cognitive biases and bounded rationality[34]: that people are not good at focusing rationally on events far into the future, or thinking clearly about the possibility that employment that begins with hope and good feeling could end badly.

Premarital agreements are contracts entered on the eve of marriage that purport to waive or modify the rights of one or both parties upon divorce, or upon the death of the other spouse. These agreements are structurally similar to the post-employment covenants just discussed, in that parties who have never been divorced or widowed may not focus with sufficient care on provisions that will take effect far into the future and only if negative events occur that they are too hopeful to believe will occur. (It is common for such agreements to be entered between one party who has gone through a divorce and a partner who has not; in such cases, the parties' levels of cognizance of the possibility and consequences of divorce would obviously be very different.)

Most consumer contracts today (as well as many employment contracts and franchise agreements) contain provisions requiring disputes to be sent to arbitration (usually with an express waiver of any right to class actions within arbitration).[35] Also, many contracts contain choice-of-law provisions and terms selecting the choice of forum (the location where litigation or arbitration must take place), often creating a legal context much more favorable to one party than the other. This is not the time or place to discuss at any length the controversies about arbitration and other forms of "alternative dispute resolution". Only a few comments are offered to note some of the issues. While some commentators have shown that at its best arbitration can be (relative to conventional litigation) affordable, fast, and generally fair (*e.g.*, Drahozal & Zyontz 2010), at its least attractive it can be a form of dispute resolution that sharply deters consumer challenges (due to cost and inconvenience) and shows strong apparent bias against any consumer complaints that are actually brought (*e.g.*, Sternlight 2005; Resnik 2015; see generally Consumer Financial Protection Bureau 2015).

The question about consent to procedural provisions would be mostly one of knowledge: in those cases where arbitration is expensive, inconvenient, and possibly biased, such facts are rarely known to the consumer prior to assenting to the form with the mandatory (pre-dispute) arbitration provision. There are also questions of reasonable alternatives, in that consumers looking to obtain credit cards, cell phones, and many other services and goods will be hard pressed to find providers whose contracts do *not* contain mandatory arbitration provisions.

20.5 What follows? – practical and moral considerations

As mentioned earlier, the predictable enforceability of (the vast majority of) agreements is an important part of commercial life. Even at the level of simple agreements between individuals, there are moral reasons for enforcing even agreements where one of the parties may not have fully consented to the terms.[36] For example, one reason for imposing an "objective" rather than a "subjective" standard to determine questions of contract formation (and, to a lesser extent, issues of contract interpretation[37]) is that contracting parties reasonably rely on people's words and actions having their conventional meaning, rather than some subjective and idiosyncratic meaning (Fried 2015: 58–63, 86–91).[38] Individuals make plans and expend money in reliance on the enforceability of their agreements and on those agreements being interpreted in line with the usual understandings of the language used. In general, the predictable enforceability of agreements allows contracting parties – whether individuals or businesses – to make investments that will maximize the value of performance, and also to be able to use existing agreements as collateral, which in turn can help to prevent cash flow difficulties for ongoing business ventures.

At the same time, the problems of consent discussed in Section 20.3 raise serious worries, especially concerning less sophisticated parties, such as (many) consumers and employees, and for electronic or standard-form contracts generally. If parties are merely acquiescing to terms out of ignorance or because they have no real choice, the moral and policy reasons for enforcing agreements seem to be undermined. (*e.g.*, Radin 2013) The actual response of courts and legislatures has varied significantly, with a major difference to be found in the comparison of the US and the EU.

The American approach to defective consent in connection with standard forms and electronic contracting is to create a strong presumption for enforcement, with a variety of doctrines to avoid enforcement (only) in the most extreme cases, but with issues of general fairness left to market forces to police (Bebchuk & Posner 2006; Ben-Shahar 2010). Through a combination of trust in the market and distrust in regulation, the result in the US is that most terms are enforceable. Scholarly commentary (especially from law and economics scholars, but not exclusively so) tends to show how attempts to protect contracting parties are futile (because they can be contracted around),[39] counter-productive (because they harm the groups they mean to protect), and/or inefficient (creating costs for one or both parties while creating little benefit) (*e.g.*, Posner 2014: 95–158; Shavell 2004: 289–385). Apologists for enforcing standard forms, boilerplate, contracts of adhesion, etc., argue that competition among vendors will lead to efficient terms, and that, even if few parties read and understand terms, vendors will need to produce fair terms for the few (educated or activist) parties who do (Bebchuk & Posner 2006; Ben-Shahar 2010; Oman 2016: 133–59). Not all American scholars apologize for standard forms and the like, or defend their enforcement. There have been many prominent scholarly arguments for non-enforcement or regulation (*e.g.*, Slawson 1971; Rakoff 1983; Radin 2013), but there is little indication that these efforts have deflected courts or legislatures from maintaining a strong presumption in favor of enforcement without significant regulation.

There are two (connected) major differences between the EU approach and the American approach. First, in the EU, transactions involving consumers fall under a different set of rules than business-to-business transactions, rules that tend to be far more protective and intrusive. (There is consumer protection legislation, at both the state and federal level, in the United States, but its effects are far less than those of their EU counterparts (*e.g.*, Macaulay 1989).) The second difference is in the way consumer transactions are regulated in the EU: through the classification of certain terms as either mandatory, prohibited, or presumptively unenforceable (Amato 2013). Of course, while legislature-imposed or court-imposed contractual terms (and prohibited terms) may avoid certain one-sided terms in agreements,[40] they obviously do not solve the problem of party consent: they simply offer terms imposed by government in place of terms imposed by powerful contracting parties (Craswell 1989).

One possible moral "take-away" from the problem of defective consent in modern contracting practice is that government should do more to protect vulnerable parties and regulate the fairness of agreements. Whether this can be effectively done at all (a large question we cannot resolve here), it is clear that in the US, at least, suggestions by some commentators and reformers that problems with consent should lead to significant regulation of the contracting process have not been followed by American courts and legislatures (with occasional exceptions). And in the current political and judicial context,[41] it does not seem likely, in the short and medium term, that this will change.

From the perspective of individual contracting parties, even if it may be a mistake to equate contracts with promises (Pratt 2008; cf. Shiffrin 2007, 2012), they are analogous for the purpose of many issues of morality and practical reasoning. For example, while we have a presumptive moral obligation to keep our promises, that moral obligation can be overridden either by other moral obligations (*e.g.*, we should break our promise to meet a friend for lunch when a sick child needs us) or by the nature of the promise made (we do not have a moral obligation to keep a promise to commit a murder or to defraud a client).[42] Similarly, our moral obligation to keep a contract may be weakened or overridden either by other moral obligations or by problems with the contract itself (Bagchi 2014: 203), including problems of consent.[43]

20.6 Conclusion

Contract law, like other forms of private law (*e.g.*, property law and tort law), involves state enforcement in the service of private interests. The government offers state resources for enforcement because it believes that society will benefit over the long term. For contract law, the judgment is that it is generally beneficial to enforce agreements (allowing individuals to make legally enforceable commitments), though certain categories of agreements come to be excluded (*e.g.*, agreements that involve illegal activity or other activity strongly contrary to public policy, or agreements that were entered through fraud or coercion), on the view that refusal of enforcement in those cases will do more good than would enforcement (Cohen 1933).

There is an obvious and significant role for consent in determining which agreements are or should be enforced, though we should be careful not to overstate it. Party consent makes it more likely that a transaction will increase party autonomy and maximize social welfare. The more weakened or defective the consent, the less likely it is that enforcing agreements will serve those purposes. However, enforcement of contracts might still bring more benefits than costs (particularly in commercial contexts), even where consent is far from optimal (cf. Oman 2016: 133–59).

Notes

1 Frederick W. Thomas Professor of Law and Philosophy, University of Minnesota. A previous version of this chapter was presented at University of California-Irvine. I am grateful for the comments and suggestions of those present at the U.C.-Irvine talk, as well as those from Lisa Bernstein, William A. Edmundson, Michael S. Green, Claire A. Hill, Andreas Müller, Peter Schaber, and Kenneth W. Simons.

2 The term "consent" is not as common in the discourses within and about contract law as it is in discourses relating to (*e.g.*) medical decision-making and sexual relations (though one prominent commentator labeled his theory of contract law as a "Consent Theory" (Barnett 1986)). However, as will be explained, issues of choice or lack of choice come up in many topics connected with contract law, even if the term "consent" is not used.

3 This chapter focuses primarily on the doctrines and principles of American law, with hope that the observations will apply more generally to the contract law of other legal systems.

4 In this approach, "will" comes from the Augustinian and Kantian traditions and denotes something far richer than just a voluntary/uncoerced action.

5 I have argued elsewhere (Bix 2012: 147–62) that theories of contract law should be pluralistic, but that topic takes us too far afield to be investigated here.

6 In this chapter "agreement" and "contract" will be used interchangeably (where "agreement" is used more broadly to include non-enforceable arrangements, that will be clear from the context).

7 Some commentators suggest that uncommunicated consent might be sufficient in a tort case (*e.g.*, Simons 2014: 336–46). It would be unlikely, at best, for consent that was not manifested in some way to be relevant to the interpretation or enforcement of a contract.

8 Legal standards sometimes refer to "implied consent", indicating that there has been some action – or, sometimes, some failure to act – which in some way expresses a choice. (I do not mean to conflate "choice" and "consent". As David Owens points out, there are circumstances "in which a normatively significant choice is made but no power of consent is exercised" (Owens 2014: 86).)

9 "Fullness" of consent (and, thus, "defects" of consent) refer to the actual state of mind or will, though contract law, again, will ultimately focus on objective manifestations.

10 Defects of consent may also be considered when determining what kind of remedy to offer. Cf. *Restatement (Second) of Contracts* § 90 (remedy for relied-upon promise only "if injustice can be avoided only by enforcement of the promise"), § 364 (unfairness as a factor to consider in determining whether to order specific performance).

11 The analogy here is to promises, where one's action creates duties in oneself (and may create rights in another party).

12 And here, the role of consent in marriage is similar to its role in contract law, perhaps not surprisingly, as it is common to think of marriage as a kind of contract (even more in traditions of Islam and Judaism than in most Western civil legal systems).

13 See, *e.g.*, Anscombe (1957, 1963).

14 On the treatment of intention to contract in US (and English) contract law, see Klass (2009).

15 Fried (2015: 61) refers to the objective standard in formation and interpretation as "the inevitability of using noncontractual principles to resolve failures of agreement . . . ".

16 Holmes (1897: 462): "The duty to keep a contract at common law means a prediction that you must pay damages if you do not keep it – and nothing else".

17 Other than in the highly exceptional case where a court would be willing to order "specific performance" – an order that a party perform its obligations under the contract.

18 This would make most contracts the equivalent of a "pay or play" agreement.

19 On this issue, compare Fried (2015) with Pratt (2014).

20 Compare Raz (2014) and Owens (2014), where the theorists disagreed about whether the obligation to keep promises is grounded on the promisor's interest in being able to shape her life or on the promisee's interest in normative assurance (Raz); or primarily grounded on the promisee's authority interest (Owens). See also Pratt (2014).

21 A fuller discussion of the role of consent in various contract law doctrines appears in Bix (2010: 256–66).

22 Where these doctrines apply, the agreement can be voided at the option of the aggrieved party. That party, however, also has the option to enforce the agreement despite the wrongdoing.

23 See, *e.g.*, *Restatement (Second) of Contracts* § 175 (American Law Institute 1981).

24 *Restatement (Second) of Contracts* § 175, Comment b. Reasonable alternatives might include obtaining the good or service from another supplier, or (in the case of a threatened breach of contract) bringing a lawsuit. Many courts also require the party claiming duress to show that the other party's wrongful act either caused the lack of reasonable alternatives or was a knowing exploitation of that lack.

25 *Restatement (Second) of Contracts* § 177.

26 On the traditional test for mutual mistake, the party claiming the defense would also have to show that the mistake went to the "essence" of the subject of contracting, and not just to its "value". The foundational case involved a cow that the contracting parties had thought to be barren at the time of contracting, but which was in fact with calf. *Sherwood v. Walker*, 33 N.W. 919 (Mich. 1887).

Under the modern *Restatement* test, there is no talk of "essence" versus "value," but the party must show (along with the centrality of the mistake) that the agreement did not expressly or implicitly place the risk of error on the party now claiming the defense. *Restatement (Second) of Contracts*, §§ 152, 154. In a rare case, with the proper equities, even a unilateral mistake by one party might be grounds for rescission. *Id.*, §§ 153, 154.

27 While the consent issues mentioned are most severe in standard forms and electronic contracting, it is important to remember that many of the same issues are present, in some form, in almost all contracts (Boardman 2014; cf. Drobac 2015).

28 There is a substantial literature on standard forms and their implication for contract law and contract theory. E.g., Ben-Shahar (2007), Barnett (2002), Hillman & Rachlinski (2002), Kessler (1943), Kim (2013), Korobkin (2003), Lemley (2006), Marotta-Wurgler (2007), Radin (2013), Rakoff (1983), Slawson (1971), and Wilkinson-Ryan (2014).

29 See, e.g., *Hill v. Gateway 2000,* Inc., 105 F.3d 1147 (7th Cir. 1997) (enforcing terms sent with a purchased computer); *ProCD v. Zeidenberg,* 86 F.3d 1447 (7th Cir, 1996) (enforcing terms inserted in packaging); *Nguyen v. Barnes & Noble, Inc.*, 763 F.3d 1171 (9th Cir. 2014) (refusing enforcement of "browsewrap" – terms present on a website, but consumer is not required to "click" assent to them – where the site did not call attention to the terms); *Register.com, Inc. v. Verio, Inc.*, 356 F.3d 393 (2nd Cir. 2004) (enforcing browsewrap where defendant was aware of terms); see generally Hillman & Rachlinski (2002), Kim (2013).

30 This refers to exceptional browsewrap cases where parties are downloading free software or games or the like, and may not even be aware that the download was subject to legal terms. For most conventional contracts, consumers obviously know they have entered a contract.

While this chapter focuses on problems from the perspective of vulnerable individuals – consumers and employees – often businesses, especially smaller businesses who are not repeat players in the market in question, may be comparably vulnerable (e.g., Lemley 2006; Hesselink 2010).

31 For an argument that the terms in electronic contracting forms are not significantly more one-sided than other standard forms, that the terms are not read, and that advanced disclosure would make little difference, see Marotta-Wurgler (2007, 2009, 2011), Bakos et al. (2014), Ben-Shahar & Schneider (2014).

32 A longer list and more extended discussion appears in Eisenberg (1995).

33 Unusual among US states, California refuses to enforce non-competition clauses. *Cal. Bus. & Prof. Code* § 16600.

34 On cognitive biases and bounded rationality, see, e.g., Kahneman (2011), Thaler (2015). As a related point, it is sometimes a matter of "rational ignorance" not to spend too much time learning or negotiating over provisions whose likelihood of application is truly small; however, post-termination restrictive covenants do not fall into that category.

35 There are indications that mandatory arbitration provisions are significantly less common in business-to-business agreements (Eisenberg et al. 2008).

36 Radin (2013: 96–7), responding to my earlier works (Bix 2010, 2012), accuses me of being unduly complacent about the problems of consent in consumer contracting, and unduly pessimistic about the possibility of comprehensive reform. I disagree, but leave it to readers to come to their own judgment on these matters.
37 Some states recognize a doctrine of "reasonable expectations", under which consumers facing standard forms (most states limit this doctrine to insurance contracts) will be held only to their reasonable understanding of an agreement, even when the clear language of the form has a different meaning. See *Restatement (Second) of Contracts* § 211 (3), Schwarcz (2007: 1426–35). This doctrine, in the rare case where it is applied, gives priority to the consumer's subjective understanding and consent over the objective meaning of the legal text to which the parties assented (through their signatures).
38 It is also the case that a subjective standard for contract formation or interpretation would create a motivation/temptation for parties to claim (falsely) that their words and actions were intended to mean something other than the usual and conventional meaning.
39 There is often a sort of back-and-forth game. If a protective provision is only a default, the more powerful party will often insist on its waiver. If a state law makes a provision unwaivable, the more powerful party may try to circumvent it by a choice-of-law provision that invokes the law of another state. If the state forbids enforcement of choice-of-law provisions in consumer and employee contracts, the response may be a mandatory arbitration provision with high fees and a class-action waiver. If state legislation, regulation, and court decisions somehow blunt all of these business responses, companies will complain about the infringement of freedom of contract, and how the mandatory terms are increasing costs and decreasing options for consumers.
40 Critics would claim that mandating and restricting terms may lead to certain harms, like higher costs and reduced choices, but this is not the time to evaluate the costs and benefits of such regulation.
41 A context that includes the fact that many state court judges are elected or subject to elective recall, meaning that it will be unlikely that courts in those states will consistently or persistently support views that business interests strongly oppose.
42 It is important to remember, though, that whether I should keep my contracts (or my promises) is inevitably distinct from the moral (and political) question of whether the state should enforce that same contract (or promise) (e.g., Webb 2014: 148–9).
43 Leo Katz has shown how the force the law (or morality) gives to consent often turns on the grounds for the agent's preference, leading to seeming paradoxical outcomes where claims are allowed for some reasons and objects but not in other, seemingly analogous cases (Katz 2006).

References

Amato, C. (2013) "The Europeanisation of Contract Law and the Role of Comparative Law: The Case of the Directive on Consumer Rights," in J. Devenney and M. Kenny (ed.), *The Transformation of European Private Law: Harmonisation, Consolidation, Codification or Chaos?* Cambridge: Cambridge University Press, 45–62.
American Law Institute (1981) *Restatement of the Law (Second) of Contracts*. Washington, DC: American Law Institute.
Anscombe, G.E.M. (1957) *Intention*. Cambridge, MA: Harvard University Press.
Anscombe, G.E.M. (1963) "The Two Kinds of Error in Action," *Journal of Philosophy* 63: 393–401.
Bagchi, A. (2014) "Distributive Justice and Contract," in G. Klass, G. Letsas and P. Saprai (ed.), *Philosophical Foundations of Contract Law*. Oxford: Oxford University Press, 193–211.
Bakos, Y., F. Marotta-Wurgler, and D.R. Trossen (2014) "Does Anyone Read the Fine Print? Consumer Attention to Standard-Form Contracts," *Journal of Legal Studies* 43: 1–35.
Bar-Gill, O. (2013) *Seduction by Contract: Law, Economics, and Psychology in Consumer Markets*. Oxford: Oxford University Press.
Barnett, R.E. (1986) "A Consent Theory of Contract," *Columbia Law Review* 86: 269–321.
Barnett, R.E. (2002) "Consenting to Form Contracts," *Fordham Law Review* 71: 627–45.
Bebchuk, L.A. and R.A. Posner (2006) "One-Sided Contracts in Competitive Consumer Markets," *Michigan Law Review* 104: 827–35.
Ben-Shahar, O. (ed.) (2007) *Boilerplate: The Foundation of Market Contracts*. Cambridge: Cambridge University Press.
Ben-Shahar, O. (2010) "One-Way Contracts: Consumer Protection without Law," *European Review of Contract Law* 6: 221–49.

Ben-Shahar, O. and C.E. Schneider (2014) *More Than You Wanted to Know: The Failure of Mandated Disclosure*. Princeton: Princeton University Press.

Bix, B.H. (2010) "Contracts," in F.G. Miller and A. Wertheimer (ed.), *The Ethics of Consent*. Oxford: Oxford University Press, 251–79.

Bix, B.H. (2012) *Contract Law: Rules, Theory, and Context*. Cambridge: Cambridge University Press.

Boardman, M.E. (2014) "Consent and Sensibility," *Harvard Law Review* 127: 1967–90.

Cohen, M.R. (1933) "The Basis of Contract," *Harvard Law Review* 46: 553–92.

Consumer Financial Protection Bureau (2015) *Arbitration Study: Report to Congress*. http://files.consumerfinance.gov/f/201503_cfpb_arbitration-study-report-to-congress-2015.pdf.

Craswell, R. (1988) "Contract Remedies, Renegotiation, and the Theory of Efficient Breach," *Southern California Law Review* 61: 629–70.

Craswell, R. (1989) "Contract Law, Default Rules, and the Philosophy of Promising," *Michigan Law Review* 88: 489–529.

Drahozal, C.R. and S. Zyontz (2010) "An Empirical Study of AAA Consumer Arbitrations," *Ohio State Journal on Dispute Resolutions* 25: 843–930.

Drobac, J.A. (2015) "The Myth of 'Legal' Consent in a Consumer Culture," in A. Pawar (ed.), *Facets of Consumerism in a Global Economy*. India: Twenty First Century Publications. http://papers.ssrn.com/sol3/papers.cfm?abstract_id=2647488.

Eisenberg, M.A. (1995) "The Limits of Cognition and the Limits of Contract," *Stanford Law Review* 47: 211–59.

Eisenberg, T., G.P. Miller and E. Sherwin (2008) "Mandatory Arbitration for Customers but Not for Peers," *Judicature* 92(3): 118–23.

Epstein, R.A. (1975) "Unconscionability: A Critical Reappraisal," *Journal of Law and Economics* 18: 293–315.

Fried, C. (2015) *Contract as Promise: A Theory of Contractual Obligation*. Second Edition. Oxford: Oxford University Press.

Gordley, J. (1991) *The Philosophical Origins of Modern Contract Doctrine*. Oxford: Clarendon Press.

Hesselink, M.W. (2010) "Towards a Sharp Distinction Between B2B and B2C? On Consumer, Commercial and General Contract Law after the Consumer Rights Directive," *European Review of Private Law* 18: 57–102.

Hillman, R.A. and J.J. Rachlinski (2002) "Standard Form Contracting in the Electronic Age," *NYU Law Review* 77: 429–95.

Holmes, O.W. (1897) "The Path of the Law," *Harvard Law Review* 10: 457–78.

Hume, D. (1978) "A Treatise of Human Nature," in P.H. Nidditch (ed.), Second Edition. Oxford: Clarendon Press.

Hurd, H.M. (1996) "The Moral Magic of Consent (I)," *Legal Theory* 2: 121–46.

Kahneman, D. (2011) *Thinking, Fast and Slow*. New York: Farrar, Straus and Giroux.

Katz, L. (2006) "Choice, Consent, and Cycling: The Hidden Limitations of Consent," *Michigan Law Review* 104: 627–70.

Kessler, F. (1943) "Contracts of Adhesion – Some Thoughts about Freedom of Contract," *Columbia Law Review* 43: 629–42.

Kim, N.S. (2013) *Wrap Contracts: Foundations and Ramifications*. Oxford: Oxford University Press.

Klass, G. (2009) "Intent to Contract," *Virginia Law Review* 95: 1437–503.

Korobkin, R. (2003) "Bounded Rationality, Standard Form Contracts, and Unconscionability," *University of Chicago Law Review* 70: 1203–95.

Lemley, M.A. (2006) "Terms of Use," *Minnesota Law Review* 91: 459–83.

Llewellyn, K.N. (1960) *The Common Law Tradition: Deciding Appeals*. Boston: Little & Brown.

Macaulay, S. (1989) "Bambi Meets Godzilla: Reflections on Contracts Scholarship and Teaching vs. State Unfair and Deceptive Trade Practices and Consumer Protection Statutes," *Houston Law Review* 26: 575–601.

Marotta-Wurgler, F. (2007) "What's in a Standard Form Contract? An Empirical Analysis of Software License Agreements," *Journal of Empirical Legal Studies* 4: 677–713.

Marotta-Wurgler, F. (2009) "Are 'Pay Now, Terms Later' Contracts Worse for Buyers? Evidence from Software License Agreements," *Journal of Legal Studies* 38(2): 309–43.

Marotta-Wurgler, F. (2011) "Will Increased Disclosure Help? Evaluating the Recommendations of the ALI's 'Principles of the Law of Software Contracts'," *University of Chicago Law Review* 78: 165–86.

Oman, N.B. (2016) *The Dignity of Commerce*. Chicago: University of Chicago.

Owens, D. (2012) *Shaping the Normative Landscape*. Oxford: Oxford University Press.

Owens, D. (2014) "Does a Promise Transfer a Right?" in G. Klass, G. Letsas and P. Saprai (ed.), *Philosophical Foundations of Contract Law*. Oxford: Oxford University Press, 78–95.

Posner, R.A. (2014) *Economic Analysis of Law*. Ninth Edition. New York: Wolters Kluwer.
Pratt, M. (2008) "Contract: Not Promise," *Florida State University Law Review* 35: 801–16.
Pratt, M. (2014) "Some Features of Promises and Their Obligations," *Southern Journal of Philosophy* 52: 382–402.
Radin, M.J. (2013) *Boilerplate: The Fine Print, Vanishing Rights, and the Rule of Law*. Princeton: Princeton University Press.
Rakoff, T.D. (1983) "Contracts of Adhesion: An Essay in Reconstruction," *Harvard Law Review* 96: 1173–274.
Raz, J. (2014) "Is There a Reason to Keep a Promise?" in G. Klass, G. Letsas and P. Saprai (ed.), *Philosophical Foundations of Contract Law*. Oxford: Oxford University Press, 58–77.
Resnik, J. (2015) "Diffusing Disputes: The Public in the Private of Arbitration, the Private in Courts, and the Erasure of Rights," *Yale Law Journal* 124: 2808–943.
Scanlon, T. (1990) "Promises and Practices," *Philosophy and Public Affairs* 19: 199–226.
Schwarcz, D. (2007) "A Products Liability Theory for the Judicial Regulation of Insurance Policies," *William and Mary Law Review* 48: 1389–463.
Shavell, S. (2004) *Foundations of Economic Analysis of Law*. Cambridge, MA: Harvard University Press.
Shiffrin, S.V. (2000) "Paternalism, Unconscionability Doctrine, and Accommodation," *Philosophy and Public Affairs* 29: 205–50.
Shiffrin, S.V. (2007) "The Divergence of Contract and Promise," *Harvard Law Review* 120: 708–53.
Shiffrin, S.V. (2012) "Is a Contract a Promise?" in A. Marmor (ed.), *The Routledge Companion to Philosophy of Law*, 241–57.
Simons, K.W. (2014) "Consent and Assumption of Risk in Tort and Criminal Law," in M. Dyson (ed.), *Unraveling Tort and Crime*. Cambridge: Cambridge University Press, 330–55.
Slawson, W.D. (1971) "Standard Form Contracts and Democratic Control of Lawmaking Power," *Harvard Law Review* 84: 529–66.
Sternlight, J.R. (2005) "Creeping Mandatory Arbitration: Is it Just?" *Stanford Law Review* 57: 1631–75.
Symposium (2004) "Freedom *from* Contract," *Wisconsin Law Review* 2004: 261–836.
Thaler, R.H. (2015) *Misbehaving: The Making of Behavioral Economics*. New York: W.W. Norton and Company.
Webb, C. (2014) "Contract as Fact and as Reason," in G. Klass, G. Letsas and P. Saprai (ed.), *Philosophical Foundations of Contract Law*. Oxford: Oxford University Press, 135–50.
Wilkinson-Ryan, T. (2014) "A Psychological Account of Consent to Fine Print," *Iowa Law Review* 99: 1745–84.

Cases

Hill v. Gateway 2000, Inc., 105 F.3d 1147 (7th Cir. 1997)
Nguyen v. Barnes & Noble, Inc., 763 F.3d 1171 (9th Cir. 2014)
ProCD v. Zeidenberg, 86 F.3d 1447 (7th Cir. 1996)
Register.com, Inc. v. Verio, Inc., 356 F.3d 393 (2nd Cir. 2004)
Sherwood v. Walker, 33 N.W. 919 (Mich. 1887)

Statutes

Cal. Bus. & Prof. Code § 16600

Restatements

Restatement (Second) of Contracts §§ 90, 152, 153, 154, 175, 177, 211, 364

Further reading

R.E. Barnett, in "A Consent Theory of Contract," *Columbia Law Review* 86 (1986): 269–321, and "Contract is Not Promise; Contract is Consent," *Suffolk University Law Review* 45 (2012): 647–65, argues for the centrality of consent to modern contract law. F.G. Miller & A. Wertheimer, *The Ethics of Consent: Theory and Practice*

(Oxford: Oxford University Press, 2010), is a volume parallel to the present one, offering valuable perspectives on the role of consent in moral theory and practical ethics. N.B. Oman, *The Dignity of Commerce* (Chicago: University of Chicago Press, 2016), offers a market-centered theory of contract law, which de-emphasizes the importance of consent; this is clearest in chapter 7, on "Boilerplate".

Related topics

Ch.2 What is consent?
Ch.4 The normative force of consent
Ch.16 Sexual consent
Ch.18 Consent to pain
Ch.25 Consent and medical treatment

21
RAPE AS NON-CONSENSUAL SEX

Tatjana Hörnle

21.1 The importance of consent for the assessment of sexual acts

For centuries, the line between rightful and wrongful sexual conduct was not drawn by examining consent. Moral and legal assessments depended on marital status and the nature of the sexual act ("normal intercourse" versus "acts against nature", often with references to religious laws) (West 2005; Gaca 2003). Sexual activities were considered wrongful if they disregarded fathers' and husbands' rights to control the chastity of females (Dripps 1992: 1781–3; Rubenfeld 2013: 1388–92). The description of rape as a violent appropriation of women belonging to others can be traced back to Medieval laws,[1] that is to epochs when most persons would have found the idea of sexual autonomy (particularly for women) bizarre. It is a rather new idea that consent suffices to make a sexual encounter rightful and that lack of consent constitutes wrongdoing (see for a history of sexual offenses Farmer 2016: 264–96).

In contemporary liberal societies, agreement is growing that the crucial criterion for assessing the moral and legal permissibility of sexual conduct should be consent. The expressions "moral magic" (Hurd 1996) and "transformative power" (Kleinig 2010: 4–5) capture this idea. There is some debate whether consent is a sufficient condition to make conduct immune against moral criticism and criminal prosecution. Even with consent on both sides, it is conceivable that one agent or both might still deserve blame, for example in instances of prostitution (Gardner & Shute 2000: 208; Plaxton 2016: 4) or if reciprocity or equality is lacking (see the discussion in Wertheimer 2003: 135–40). However, a sophisticated analysis should distinguish between the question of whether conduct is morally praiseworthy or recommendable on the one hand and moral and legal interferences with what others are doing on the other hand. One can argue that a sexual interaction is morally defective but nevertheless declare it permissible (Wertheimer 2003: 142–3).

The flip side of consent's transformative power is blame if consent is lacking. On this point, there is less debate: consent is a necessary condition for permissible sexual conduct and it is wrong to involve a non-consenting person in a sexual act, particularly if the act involves penetration. However, it needs to be explained *why* sex without consent is wrongdoing. Liberal criminal law theory bases prohibitions on the concept of harm. In the tradition of John Stuart Mill (Mill 1859), it is considered a good reason to prohibit conduct if it harms other persons, but, in the absence of harm, liberty should not be curtailed. From this starting point, it can be a puzzling question why sexual assaults are serious offenses. Such acts can cause tangible harm such as bodily injuries. In cases involving penetrations, victims typically experience serious psychological suffering, which might be related to the way evolution has shaped patterns of human sexuality (Wertheimer 2003: 89–118). One could, however, argue that some non-consensual sexual acts, for instance, groping genitals or breasts, are rather trivial incidences. The same might be true for intercourse under certain conditions. Describing what they call a "pure case of rape", John Gardner and Stephen Shute refer to a woman who never learns that she was subjected to sexual intercourse while she had lost consciousness (Gardner & Shute 2000: 196–9). Without injuries, pregnancy or diseases, it is difficult to establish harm.[2] However, unconsented sexual touching is considered wrong in both a moral and legal sense and intercourse with an unconscious person means serious wrongdoing. The essence of the wrong done is the violation of sexual autonomy rights (McGregor 1994: 234; Schulhofer 1998: 102; Archard 2007; Spena 2010: 501; Dempsey 2016: 520–1).

21.2 Sexual autonomy

Autonomy in sexual matters comprises two types of autonomy and freedom (Dripps 1992: 1785–6; Green 2015: 207): thick autonomy involving positive freedom – that is, to have a sexual life according to one's own desires and needs – and thin autonomy/negative freedom. Negative freedom means not to be subjected to others' sexual acts. Positive freedom can only be supported indirectly with moral and legal norms, by not narrowing down options through prohibitions. Whether persons will be able to lead the sexual life they want depends on other factors as well – for instance, on the attractiveness of their body and personality as well as their luck in meeting others. Thin autonomy or negative freedom, on the other hand, can be protected in a more direct way by norms that prohibit unwanted interferences[3] and grant a right against interference, viz. the right not to be touched in a sexual way. The use of the phrase "moral magic of consent" in legal theory has been criticized because explanations seem preferable to magic (Dempsey 2013: 12–15). However, there is a rather simple explanation of what consent does: it is a waiver of the right against interference (McGregor 1994: 242).

Why are these rights against interference important? The starting point for an explanation is the dominant role of autonomy in contemporary thinking. Autonomy as a (or even *the*) central value figures in moral philosophy, political and constitutional theory, and law. Some popular authors question the value of autonomy as positive freedom: making choices is characterized as a tiresome task with a negative impact on the quality of life (Ehrenberg 1998; Han 2010). But skepticism does not extend to sexual autonomy. Freedom of choice and protection against unwanted sexual acts continue to be taken very seriously (McGregor 1994: 235; Archard 2007: 390–3; Dougherty 2013: 724).

The importance of negative sexual autonomy stems from the fact that sexuality involves the body (Archard 1998: 20–1; Schulhofer 1998: 111): to exercise autonomy over what happens to one's body is considered particularly important. One possible explanation for this fact points to the sexual value of the body as a commodity (Dripps 1992: 1785–92). This description captures *one* dimension of sexual autonomy, but the focus on the body as a means for exchange is too narrow. The increased meaning of the body and autonomous choices concerning its treatment are a wider phenomenon. In medical ethics and law, the notion of patients' autonomy has displaced the paternalistic view of doctors being in a better position to judge patients' interests.[4] The emphasis on personal choices concerning the body can be explained by pointing to its identification value (to be contrasted with use value; for the distinction see Gardner & Shute 2000: 201). Use value has lost its significance in consumer worlds with an abundance of replaceable goods. At the same time, the identification value of non-replaceable goods, and specifically one's own body, has grown.

It is not only the interference with another person's body, but its sexual nature, that carries the assessment "serious wrongdoing". To fully grasp the wrongdoing of rape and other non-consensual sexual acts, another aspect needs to be emphasized: disregard of a person's sexual autonomy is also disregard for this person's human dignity. References to human dignity require some thoughts about what constitutes a violation of human dignity. Some authors point to the Kantian verdict against "using the other merely as a means" and sexual instrumentalization (Gardner & Shute 2000: 204; Plaxton 2016). This, however, does not fully explain why unwanted sexual contact entails a meaning that other ways of using a person's body do not (Statman 2012: 108 f.). A full picture must include the notion of severe humiliation. Humiliation is not the same as feeling humiliated: rather, the social and symbolic significance from an observer's perspective matters. Performing a sexual act using a non-consenting person's body or forcing a person to act in a sexual way means to humiliate this person in a substantial way (therefore rape is used as an instrument of subjugation in war; see Allen 1996).

The high significance of sexual autonomy is also connected to women's rights, which might be a reason why, until recently, the rape of male victims (see Mezey & King 2000) has not been much discussed. With the surge of feminist literature (Brownmiller 1975; Henderson 1992; Estrich 1986), the topic of rape gained prominence. Historically and in many societies until today, there was and is no consensus that women are entitled to decide when, with whom, and how to have sex (Munro 2014: 747–8). Women's right to sexual autonomy (both as a thick and a thin concept, as positive and negative freedom) needs to be affirmed and defended against gender-biased views.

21.3 Coercion-based vs. consent-based: the diversity of criminal laws

Many legal definitions of sexual assault and rape still require coercion, typically by force or threats; see for instance Art. 222-22, 23 French Penal Code, Art. 189, 190 Swiss Criminal Code. Under the coercion-based model, offenders must resort to violence or threats of violence to subjugate victims (see for a defense of this approach Rubenfeld 2013). The law of rape traditionally was constructed to determine whether a woman who had sex outside of marriage ought to be punished for fornication or adultery (Wertheimer 2003: 14). In the 20th century, offense descriptions were modernized: for example, offenders and victims were described in gender-neutral ways and marital rape was included. However, the coercion-based model persists, despite growing awareness that coercion and lack of consent are two different elements of wrongdoing (Dripps 1992; McGregor 1994; Schulhofer 1998: 101; Archard 2007; Tuerkheimer 2015). Coercion means increased wrongdoing, but should not be considered a necessary condition. Lack of coercion does not indicate that sexual acts are consensual. It can be superfluous to apply force or threats if a surprised, overwhelmed, or slow person does not resist physically, but victims' physical passiveness can be and often is combined with verbal protests or other circumstances that demonstrate lack of consent.

Recent reforms of criminal law show a trend towards the consent-based model. European legal bodies such as the Council of Europe promote a consent-based approach.[5] In Germany, after controversial public debates, the parliament changed the law on sexual offenses in 2016: since then coercion is no longer a necessary condition for sexual assaults and lack of consent has become the central notion (Hörnle 2017; see for the legal situation until 2016 Hörnle 2000). In Anglo-American legal systems, some statutes describe sexual offenses as sexual acts without consent; see for instance the English Sexual Offences Act 2003 (see Sect. 1–4), the criminal laws of a few US states (Tuerkheimer 2015: 15; Anderson 2016a: 1951–3) and the Canadian Criminal Code (Sect. 165). The rape provisions in the American Model Penal Code 1962 (see for a critical assessment Estrich 1986: 1134–47; Schulhofer 1998: 20–5) are under revision (Tuerkheimer 2015: 15).

21.4 The concept of consent

Considerations about how a consent-based criminal law should look must begin with conceptual issues. The first question is whether consent refers to a mental state or a performative act.[6] Should the fact that the other person wanted or was content with sex be considered consent in a legal sense? Or does she have to express approval or refusal? From the perspective of moral philosophy, it has been argued that the "moral magic" is done by the mental state, not by its expression (Hurd 1996: 137; Alexander 2014). However, the mental state approach deserves criticism, particularly for legal purposes. It is neither easy to define the required mental state (wanting? accepting?) nor to re-construct it retrospectively. The subjective experience of wanting or not wanting something is often fuzzy and multilayered. Legal judgments should refrain as far as possible from relying on mental states. They should trace interactions and communications (Archard 1998: 4; Wertheimer 2003: 144–52; Dougherty 2015; Healey 2015). Furthermore, if the crucial element is a mental state, this can lead to unfair outcomes for both sides involved. Consider a person who is accused based on the other's testimony not to have wanted sex. Criminal proceedings are troublesome even if the case is finally dismissed after the accused points out that he had no idea of this "true will". In *mens rea*-based systems, the "consent as mental state" approach works to the disadvantage of victims, too. It invites dishonest statements of the kind: "She did not say anything, but I believed that her mental state was in favor of sex". False claims are somewhat easier to debunk if offenders need to invent communicative elements rather than simply refer to their beliefs about victims' mental states.

If one defines consent as an act of communication, the next question arises – namely: what kind of communication is required? Two options are discussed: an affirmative consent model ("only yes means yes") (McGregor 1994: 245–6; Schulhofer 1998: 283) and a veto model ("no means no"). The first claims that affirmation must be expressed. According to the narrower veto approach, blame is in order if the actor has ignored an expression of refusal (Estrich 1986: 1182–3; Dripps 1992: 1807). Under both models, communication can take different forms: words, gestures, active participation in the sexual activities (tokens of consent; see Wertheimer 2003: 152). The difference between the two approaches becomes relevant if a person remains silent, passive, and submissive before and during the sexual encounter. Proponents of an affirmative consent model will point to lack of expressed consent, while, according to a veto-based model, silence is not per se sufficient to label the other person's conduct as wrongful.

In the United States, colleges and universities have adopted the affirmative consent model for campus rules of conduct (see Tuerkheimer 2015; Baker 2016; Anderson 2016a). Lack of compliance is not a criminal offense but can be sanctioned. Criticism can be raised on procedural grounds (for instance, regarding the neutrality and competence of the examining bodies, rules of procedure, displacement of criminal investigations). Also, it is not evident that colleges and universities are entitled to regulate conduct that is not directly related to academic issues but concerns adults in the most personal and intimate aspects of their lives. Questions of procedure and standing-to-judge in university settings cannot be examined here. The pertinent question for our analysis is: what duties do persons have towards each other in sexual encounters?

One source of objections against the affirmative consent approach is uncertainties concerning the content of rules. When and how often must consent be expressed? What constitutes "a sexual act"? Consent is required at the beginning, once the threshold into sexuality has been crossed but it will not be sufficient to express general willingness "to have sex now". Because this can mean rather different acts, it will be necessary to repeat consent once the next stage is reached, which leads to a threshold problem. The more demanding rules are, the more one has to expect confusion about what must be done. A "no means no" model makes compliance easier because the rule is simple: listen to a veto expressed by the other person and stop.

The main dispute concerns the fair balance of duties. Proponents of affirmative consent argue that it amounts to a simple duty, too: if in doubt, just ask. This presupposes, however, another more demanding duty: the duty to monitor the other's reactions and to evaluate facial expressions and body language. Such a duty can be justified as a moral duty if the background is an ongoing relationship of love and mutual care. But it would be unrealistic and too moralistic to assume that sex is or should be restricted to relationships of love. At this point, one could contend that paying attention to the other's reactions is trivial and a matter of minimal considerateness. However, the duty is not as undemanding as it might appear (see Tuerkheimer 2015: 13). The quality of sex can be defined by pointing to mental states such as passion, euphoria, and obliviousness. This is a gender-neutral argument: it is not about dominant males, but about closing one's eyes and retreating into the realm of physical pleasure. The requirement to stay fine-tuned to the other person's reactions all the time can interfere with the quality of the sensual experience.

Duties to monitor and ask should be weighed against an obligation of the sexual partner: the obligation to express oneself clearly if consent is lacking. This does not involve physical resistance – such an obligation could not be justified because this would require more difficult and risky activities (risky because physical resistance might trigger violence from the other side). Nor does one have to repeat a veto if it is evident that the other person is well aware of the situation but does not care. However, if the situation is genuinely ambiguous, saying "no" is not an unreasonable or unduly challenging demand.

In the end, the choice between an affirmative consent model and a veto model depends on the purpose that rules of conduct serve. If the context is education and the perspective forward-looking, it makes sense to set standards high – they will be diluted in real life. Good advice for adolescents could be: treat the other *as if* this were a relationship with duties of care and consideration (it might develop this way), but, sometimes, you are also entitled to relax and close your eyes. However, the burden of justification is heavier if the perspective is retrospective and the consequences are blame and sanctions. Reactions of blame are appropriate if a "no" has been ignored. If the other person remained silent and passive, moral blame is also deserved under certain conditions, for instance, if there were strong indicators that the "partner" was suffering (if, for example, someone remains silent and does not move a limb, resembling a corpse rather than a living human being). Situations of genuine ambiguity are, however, different. They involve mixed signals (partly encouraging, partly discouraging). If the context is not easy to decipher, the obligation of the unwilling participant to express his true will is the overriding duty.

In the realm of moral judgments, not everyone will agree with this conclusion. But if one turns to legal consequences, additional arguments can be raised against an affirmative consent model. Moral and legal assessments are not identical. This point is neglected by legal theorists (see for instance Plaxton 2016) who adopt moral philosophers' ideas without discussing the differences between virtue ethics and moral duties on the one hand and legal rules and sanctions on the other hand (Wertheimer 2003: 5–7). Criminal law theory should include moral evaluations but should not stop there. Criminal punishment for a sexual offense and further consequences such as being registered as a "sex offender" (Anderson 2016a: 1956) have the potential to destroy the convicted person's life. Therefore, the criminal law requires more restrictive rules. Borderline cases that create dispute about the weight of moral duties should be excluded from criminalization.

Criminal norms should be formulated in ways that make duties as plain and as easy to follow as possible. In some legal systems, constitutional provisions demand that the law defines the scope of prohibitions[7] (which means: legislatures must specify what is prohibited). If such a clause is not part of a national constitution, its rationale can be invoked as a matter of political philosophy: citizens should find as much guidance as possible in the law. For this reason, the simple norm of conduct derived from a veto model is preferable to the more demanding duties under an affirmative consent approach.

21.5 Consent-based criminal law reform

Overhauling traditional coercion-based criminal laws in favor of a consent-based approach means introducing new offense descriptions. Unfortunately, a thoughtful, systematic reform of sexual offenses is rather demanding. Legislators should be aware of the above-mentioned controversies regarding the concept of consent and they should reach an agreement about the meaning of consent. In a second step, these considerations need to be converted into prohibitions. A general commitment to consent-based law can find rather different expressions in the texts of criminal laws.

A straightforward approach uses elements in offense descriptions that directly mirror consent as a concept, such as the element "without consent" or a similar wording; see, for instance, Sect. 1-4 Sexual Offences Act UK 2003 ("does not consent"). Drafting prohibitions in this way could make sense if the underlying assumption was either "consent is a mental state" or "expression of affirmative consent is necessary". But even if this is the conceptual premise, the word "consent" as an element of offense descriptions has drawbacks. Because the concept of consent is complicated and ambiguous, this legislative choice has the effect of leaving the definition of wrongdoing mainly to the courts (Tadros 2006: 520–3). It is preferable to introduce differentiated offenses (Tadros 2006), particularly if the conceptual starting point is a veto model. The reform of sexual offenses in Germany takes such a differentiated approach (see § 177 German Criminal Code, since 2016). First, the core situation must be captured – that is, cases in which the victim has expressed "no" in words or behavior. Possible offense descriptions could be "against the expressed will" or "against the recognizable will" (see for the latter § 177 I German Criminal Code). Second, prohibitions should cover scenarios in which a "no" was not expressed because this was plainly impossible – for instance, if the victim was unconscious (in a coma, fainted, narcotized, sleeping) or if the assault was fast and surprising. Regarding impossibility cases, narrow exemption clauses for married partners or other couples should be considered (for instance, if one touches the other during sleep; Plaxton 2016: 11–12). Generally, the status of marriage or co-habitation cannot substitute consent. However, a waiver of rights may be assumed under certain conditions – for instance if the sexual act is of a minor nature and if it does not express hostility.

Finally, legislators have to draft criminal prohibitions that capture situations in which victims express approval. One needs to distinguish between consent in a normative sense – that is, valid consent, and consent in a factual sense (Green 2015: 212). For the latter, I will use the word "approval". From a normative, moral, and legal perspective, saying yes or giving other signs of approval does not necessarily mean that this constitutes valid consent. It is an important task for criminal law theory to examine conditions such as lack of competence or situational pressures that render factual approval irrelevant.

The starting point should be a non-perfectionist account of decision-making. References to autonomy need to acknowledge human imperfection (Arpaly 2004: 180). A strong ideal of truly autonomous choices would be demanding. Decision-makers would need to know all relevant facts, be competent to assess them and to make a well-balanced decision, and be capable of asserting themselves against others. In real life, human beings hardly ever conform to this ideal. Awareness of facts tends to be fragmentary and assessments distorted, and many persons are vulnerable even to minor pressures by others and situations. In his defense of the traditional coercion-based model of rape, Rubenfeld argues that sexual autonomy cannot be protected completely and therefore cannot be the legal interest protected (Rubenfeld 2013: 408). However, rather than presupposing ambitious notions of autonomy and consent, for the criminal law it must suffice that consent is valid enough (Archard 1998: 82–3). The notion of citizenship implies a duty to take responsibility for one's choices. Being entitled to follow one's own preferences (positive autonomy) can entail, as its flipside, forfeiture of complaints about regrettable decisions.

The challenge is to define where to draw the red line for legal assessments – that is, how to describe those severe deficiencies that render approval irrelevant. Heidi Hurd argues in favor of a symmetrical relation: circumstances that will not exculpate offenders should not make victims' consent invalid, either (Hurd 1996: 141–2). However, the assumption of symmetry can be challenged: conditions required for waiving a right can be somewhat more demanding than what is necessary to understand criminal norms. Both an affirmative consent model and a veto model must deal with these problems. If "without consent" is the central element of an offense description, statutes or courts have to develop criteria for valid consent. On the basis of a veto model, criminal statutes must include offenses that describe such circumstances, in addition to "expressed no" and "impossibility to declare one's will" scenarios. Three sets of circumstances should be taken into account: errors and deceptions,[8] young age, or severe cognitive or mental deficits and coercive circumstances.

21.6 Circumstances that render approval irrelevant

Some criminal laws penalize sexual acts if the offender obtained approval by deception about the nature of the act or his identity (see for instance Sect. 76 Sexual Offences Act UK 2003; for US law Green 2015: 200–1). This is, however, not the approach in all legal systems. For instance, German law does not mention deception as an element in sexual offenses.[9] From a moral perspective, one can argue that it is wrong to deceive the other person about facts of central importance to her (Dougherty 2013). However, moral standards should not be simply transferred to legal evaluations (Wertheimer 2003: 213–14). With regard to the intrusiveness of criminal punishment, a gray zone of morally reprehensible but not punishable conduct is acceptable. German criminal law doctrine distinguishes between deceptions that concern the core wrong of the specific offense and deceptions concerning motives, such as deceptions about feelings, marriage, or financial or social standing. Only the first category invalidates consent (Roxin 2006: 581–2). In a similar vein, English legal terminology refers to "fraud in the factum" and "fraud in the inducement" (Archard 1998: 46–50; Green 2015: 198). The essentials one needs to know are that one is going to have sex, what kind of sex, and with whom. Sexual meaning is obscured if the offender feigned a non-sexual touching (typically claiming to perform "healing treatment"). Deception about the degree of physical intrusiveness includes lies about the use of a condom. If a person is deceived about these essentials or about the identity of the other person, expression of approval does not amount to valid consent (Schulhofer 1998: 284; Green 2015: 225–34). This kind of conduct could be criminalized.

Young age can be another relevant factor. If minors say "no" or are subjected to surprise attacks, punishment need not be justified differently from cases involving adult victims. The interesting cases are those when minors express approval. The notion of citizens' autonomy and a liberal assumption of competence refer to adults. Regarding minors, the law should take a closer look at real vulnerability. For children, obstacles to autonomous decisions are: lack of communicative skills or lack of understanding of what sex means, lack of awareness of self as clearly distinguishable from others, and inability to maintain and assert volitions against others' instructions and incentives. Within legal proceedings, it would be impossible to establish an individual child's competence at a certain point in time retrospectively. Legal systems therefore avoid individualized judgments and establish strict age limits, creating offenses that in English terminology are called "statutory rape" (Green 2015: 238–51). These age limits should reflect empirically sound judgments about when children are typically competent enough to give valid consent (Wertheimer 2003: 222). It will hardly be possible to prove that this must be twelve, thirteen or fourteen years – there is some leeway (see for US law Robinson & Williams 2018: Chap. 20). Because maturity is achieved gradually, prohibitions should distinguish between children and juveniles. European legal instruments unfortunately ascribe the status of "child" to all persons under eighteen.[10] However, a seventeen-year-old cannot be compared to a child of seven. Juveniles should be granted the positive freedom to explore sexuality in teenage encounters. At the same time, it needs to be taken into account that they are not yet adults. Juveniles are vulnerable to more or less subtle pressures by older persons, particularly within hierarchical social roles, for example, in encounters with teachers. Criminal laws therefore should define two age thresholds (Archard 1998: 128–9). Up to a certain age, sexual contact ought to be absolutely prohibited. Beyond that age, juveniles need only protection against "partners" who exploit superiority in age and social status.[11]

Competence also becomes an issue if intellectually disabled persons approve of sexual contact. Severe mental handicaps make valid consent impossible (Feinberg 1989: 316; Archard 1998: 44; Bergelson 2008: 701). However, it needs to be reconsidered whether in the presence of factual approval lack of competence must without any exception lead to criminal punishment for the other person. This imposes an absolute ban on sexual activities for adults with severe mental disabilities who would like to experience sexual pleasure. This is a restriction that is detrimental to adults' quality of life, and an example that reminds us that it is impossible to maximize negative and positive autonomy at the same time (Wertheimer 2003: 3). Two solutions should be considered. Criminal laws could avoid references to severe mental handicaps, but this would allow persons without benign attitudes towards the handicapped person to exploit lack of judgment or lack of assertiveness. The second, preferable, solution attempts a compromise by drafting provisions with clauses such as "exploitation" (Hörnle 2017).

Criminal decisions often have to deal with the impact of intoxication on the validity of consent. The easy cases are those when the offender sedates or intoxicates an unknowing victim. They should be discussed under the heading of "coercion". However, if large quantities of alcohol (or other drugs) were voluntarily consumed, the question arises whether a drunken person's expression of approval constitutes valid consent. With regard to a high degree of intoxication that does amount to a severe temporary mental handicap, the considerations are similar to those regarding permanent mental retardation. A general prohibition would neglect the fact that people often desire and enjoy sexual contact under the influence of alcohol and other disinhibiting substances (Wertheimer 2003: 257). Offense descriptions should include an exploitation clause. In defining what constitutes exploitation, a set of circumstances should be taken into account: prior sexual relations and the degree of attachment between the persons involved as well as elements of the interaction (such as hostility or signs of affection).

Another group of circumstances that can render expression of approval irrelevant can be summarized as coercion. The classical offense descriptions relying on coercion by violence or threat of violence should not be eliminated from criminal laws. They should no longer be treated as a necessary condition for punishment (see for a different view Anderson 2016b), but still figure in definitions of invalid consent and as an aggravating factor. For violent assaults, labeling and sentencing should reflect that coercion is a particularly serious version of a sexual offense. Threats must not necessarily be threats of violence. Similar considerations apply when offenders threaten victims with other illegal acts that would lead to a serious detriment. Small-scale blackmail commonly used by people (for example: "I will not spend the weekend with your parents") does not seriously impact the other's autonomy. Threats with serious and illegal harm, however, such as to fail someone arbitrarily in an exam, render consent invalid.

In ordinary language, references to coercion are often used in a wider sense, not limited to a threat of violence or other illegal acts but referring to any kind of an individuals' perception "to be under pressure" by circumstances (see for such cases Archard 1998: 54–65; Schulhofer 1998: 137–67; Wertheimer 2003: 166–92). Economic and social vulnerabilities can create considerable psychological pressure, and, from a moral point of view, it can be blameworthy if others exploit this to obtain sexual benefits. In legal contexts, however, moral perfectionism should be avoided (Archard 1998: 136). Within the normative framework of autonomy and responsibility, the default line is that persons have to stand by their decisions. It is part of sexual autonomy in a thick sense to use sexuality independent of erotic or emotional interests as a means to (perhaps) improve sad living conditions (Hurd 1996: 145). From the perspective of virtue ethics, such choices might not be recommendable. However, for legal purposes the distinction between offers and threats is important. The state should only punish the other person involved if she has created the unfortunate situation through illegal acts or if her proposal to improve circumstances amounts to a threat with illegal acts or ignoring a legal obligation to help (Wertheimer 2003: 163–92).

21.7 Abuse of office

Under certain conditions, criminal prohibitions may restrict sexual contact for reasons that are independent of sexual autonomy. Abuse of office and abuse of profession can be an issue if, for example, police officers, public prosecutors, prison wardens, or persons working in hospitals have sexual contact with defendants, inmates, or patients. Criminal law norms addressing such situations can be explained in a dual way: either as a matter of deficient consent, for instance, if the office or profession confers charismatic powers (Schneebaum 2015), or as an abuse of office or abuse of a profession. The latter refers to collective interests regarding the functioning of institutions and public trust in these institutions. It weakens respect and cooperation if professionals favor inmates for personal reasons. Also, practices of favoritism, like other cases of corruption, weaken the public's trust that institutions are run in a fair and efficient way.

21.8 Offenders' subjective fault

Defendants in sexual offense cases frequently argue that they did not know the relevant facts, such as lack of consent or the age of the other person. Legal systems come to different outcomes for such cases. Systems with a strong emphasis on intention require proof of knowledge for all objective elements in the statutory descriptions. For instance, according to German law on sexual offenses, the irrefutable claim to have wrongly believed in the other's consent or to have erred about another relevant fact will result in acquittal[12] – even if the error was plainly stupid and any other person in the same situation would have seen the obvious. Criminal law systems of that type make it rather easy to escape conviction.

Other legal systems rely on strict liability with regard to the consent of the other person or her age. Strict liability means that the offender will be convicted even if a most careful person in the same situation would not have suspected that the other person did not consent or was under age. The Sexual Offences Act UK 2003 does not require that the offender knew or could have known that the victim was under thirteen.[13] Some US states leave leeway for courts to take similar approaches regarding consent (Dempsey 2016: 518–9). Strict liability is a radical departure from general principles that presuppose some form of fault. Such legal constructions deserve criticism because they overshoot their aim: if legislatures want to block off feeble "well, I did not see that" excuses, they should introduce negligence offenses rather than strict liability crimes (Hurd 1996: 136).

Regarding erroneous assumptions of consent, a strong tradition in American case law (Husak & Thomas 1992: 99; Dempsey 2016: 518–9) and the English Sexual Offences Act 2003 rely on a reasonable person standard.[14] If the defendant's belief in consent was reasonable, he will not be found guilty of sexual assault or rape. If the false belief was, however, unreasonable, he will be convicted of sexual assault and rape like an offender who positively knew that the victim did not consent. This approach deserves criticism, too (Husak & Thomas 1992: 97; Tadros 2006: 534), because it equates insufficient attention with positive knowledge about lack of consent. Not paying sufficient attention to the question of consent is wrong (Archard 1998: 144–5) – but it is a different wrong from intentional disregard of the other person. Intentional crimes should be labeled and sanctioned differently from behaving unreasonably by not paying sufficient attention.

Solutions are possible on a middle ground between the two extremes of foregoing punishment despite gross carelessness on the one hand (such as in German law) and punitive instruments in form of the reasonable person standard and strict liability in English and American law on the other hand. A separate offense could be introduced that covers gross negligence concerning consent, with lower sanctions than intentional disregard for signs of disapproval. A rare example of this approach can be found in Norwegian law.[15]

Notes

1 See the definition in the Constitutio Criminalis Carolina from 1532; for an essence of traditional English common law Blackstone's Commentaries On the Laws of England, 210.

2 In traditional societies, there would be additional issues such as loss of virginity and marriage prospects. Forcible intercourse with a disreputable woman was not considered rape in Medieval laws; see for instance Constitutio Criminalis Carolina (Nr. 119 "Straff der Nottzucht").

3 Rubenfeld (2013: 1417–23) argues convincingly that a thick conception of sexual autonomy cannot be supported with the means of the criminal law. But he downplays the importance of negative freedom. Even if a person perceives her life as dismal, this does not mean that negative freedom becomes unimportant: if one *also* had to endure sexual assaults, life would be *even more dismal.*

4 See O'Shea (this volume, Chapter 23).

5 See Art. 36 I Istanbul-Convention (Council of Europe Convention on preventing and combating violence against women and domestic violence), entry into force: August 1, 2014.

6 See also Schnüriger (this volume, Chapter 2).

7 See Art. 103 II Grundgesetz, the German Constitution: "An act may be punished only if it was defined by a law as a criminal offense before the act was committed".

8 See also Dougherty (this volume, Chapter 15).

9 The 19th-century prohibition concerning errors about the marital nature of intercourse was abolished in 1969.

10 See Art. 2 (a) Directive 2011/92/EU, Combating the Sexual Abuse and Sexual Exploitation of Children and Child Pornography.

11 See §§174, 176, 182 German Criminal Code. Some of these norms protect minors until the age of sixteen, others until the age of eighteen.
12 This was also the approach in English law before the Sexual Offences Act UK 2003; see the infamous Morgan case (Alexander 1995).
13 Sect. 5-8 Sexual Offences Act 2003.
14 Sect. 1-4 Sexual Offences Act 2003.
15 Sect. 192 Criminal Code Norway. In Sweden, a reform commission proposed a similar solution in 2016; see Ett starkare skydd för den sexuella integriteten, Statens Offentliga Utredningar, SOU 2016:60, at 55 (summary, in English).

References

Alexander, D. (1995) "Twenty Years of Morgan: A Criticism of the Subjectivist View of *Mens Rea* and Rape in Great Britain," *Pace International Law Review* 7: 207–46.
Alexander, L. (2014) "The Ontology of Consent," *Analytic Philosophy* 55: 102–13.
Allen, B. (1996) *Rape Warfare: Hidden Genocide in Bosnia-Herzegovina and Croatia.* Minneapolis: University of Minnesota Press.
Anderson, M. (2016a) "Campus Sexual Assault Adjudication and Resistance to Reform," *Yale Law Journal* 125: 1940–2005.
Anderson, S. A. (2016b) "Conceptualizing Rape as Coerced Sex," *Ethics* 127: 50–87.
Archard, D. (1998) *Sexual Consent.* Boulder: Westview.
Archard, D. (2007) "The Wrong of Rape," *The Philosophical Quarterly* 57: 374–93.
Arpaly, N. (2004) "Which Autonomy?" in J. K. Campbell, M. O'Rourke and D. Shier (ed.), *Freedom and Determinism.* Cambridge: MIT, 173–88.
Baker, K. (2016) "Campus Sexual Misconduct as Sexual Harassment: A Defense of the DOE," *Kansas Law Review* 64: 861–90.
Bergelson, V. (2008) "Consent to Harm," *Pace Law Review* 28: 683–711.
Brownmiller, S. (1975) *Against Our Will: Men, Women and Rape.* New York: Simon and Schuster.
Dempsey, M. (2013) "Victimless Conduct and the *Volenti* Maxim: How Consent Works," *Criminal Law and Philosophy* 7: 11–27.
Dempsey, M. (2016) "Smith and Hogan at Villanova: Reflections on Anglo-American Criminal Law, the Definition of Rape, and What America Still Needs to Learn from England," *Villanova Law Review* 61: 509–23.
Dougherty, T. (2013) "Sex, Lies, and Consent," *Ethics* 123: 717–44.
Dougherty, T. (2015) "Yes Means Yes: Consent as Communication," *Philosophy & Public Affairs* 43: 224–53.
Dripps, D. (1992) "Beyond Rape: An Essay on the Difference between the Presence of Force and the Absence of Consent," *Columbia Law Review* 92: 1780–809.
Ehrenberg, A. (1998) *La fatigue d'être soi.* Paris: Odile Jacob.
Estrich, S. (1986) "Rape," *Yale Law Journal* 95: 1087–184.
Farmer, L. (2016) *Making the Modern Criminal Law.* Oxford: Oxford University Press.
Feinberg, J. (1989) *The Moral Limits of the Criminal Law, Vol. 3: Harm to Self.* Oxford: Oxford University Press.
Gaca, K. (2003) *The Making of Fornication: Eros, Ethics, and Political Reform in Greek Philosophy and Early Christianity.* Berkeley and Los Angeles: University of California Press.
Gardner, J. and Shute, S. (2000) "The Wrongness of Rape," in J. Horder (ed.), *Oxford Essays in Jurisprudence.* 4th series. Oxford: Oxford University Press, 193–217.
Green, S. (2015) "Lies, Rape, and Statutory Rape," in A. Sarat (ed.), *Law and Lies: Deception and Truth-Telling in the American Legal System.* Cambridge: Cambridge University Press.
Han, B.-C. (2010) *Müdigkeitsgesellschaft (Fatigue Society).* Berlin: Matthes und Seitz.
Healey, R. (2015) "The Ontology of Consent: A Reply to Alexander," *Analytic Philosophy* 56: 354–63.
Henderson, L. (1992) "Rape and Responsibility," *Law and Philosophy* 11: 127–78.
Hörnle, T. (2000) "Penal Law and Sexuality: Recent Reforms in German Criminal Law," *Buffalo Criminal Law Review* 3: 639–85.
Hörnle, T. (2017) "The New German Law on Sexual Offenses," *German Law Journal* 18: 1309–29.
Hurd, H. (1996) "The Moral Magic of Consent (I)," *Legal Theory* 9: 121–46.
Husak, D. and G. Thomas (1992) "Date Rape, Social Convention, and Reasonable Mistakes," *Law and Philosophy* 11: 95–126.

Kleinig, J. (2010) "The Nature of Consent," in F. Miller and A. Wertheimer (ed.), *The Ethics of Consent. Theory and Praxis*. Oxford: Oxford University Press.

McGregor, J. (1994) "Force, Consent, and the Reasonable Woman," in J. Coleman and A. Buchanan (ed.), *In Harm's Ways: Essays in Honor of Joel Feinberg*. Cambridge: Cambridge University Press.

Mezey, G. and M. King (2000) *Male Victims of Sexual Assault*. Oxford: Oxford University Press.

Mill, J. S. (1859) *On Liberty*, London: John Parker and Son.

Munro, V. (2014) "Sexual Autonomy," in M. Dubber and T. Hörnle (ed.), *The Oxford Handbook of Criminal Law*. Oxford: Oxford University Press.

Plaxton, M. (2016) "Nussbaum on Sexual Instrumentalization," *Criminal Law and Philosophy* 10: 1–16.

Robinson, P. and T. Williams (2018) *Mapping the American Criminal Law. An Exploration of the Diversity Among the States*, forthcoming.

Roxin, C. (2006) *Strafrecht Allgemeiner Teil Vol. 1*. Fourth Edition. Munich: C.H. Beck.

Rubenfeld, J. (2013) "The Riddle of Rape-By-Deception and the Myth of Sexual Autonomy," *Yale Law Journal* 122: 1372–443.

Schneebaum, G. (2015) "What is Wrong with Sex in Authority Relations?" *The Journal of Criminal Law and Criminology* 105: 345–85.

Schulhofer, S. (1998) *Unwanted Sex: The Culture of Intimidation and the Failure of Law*. Cambridge, MA: Harvard University Press.

Spena, A. (2010) "Harmless Rapes? A False Problem for the Harm Principle," *Diritto & Questione Publiche* 10: 497–524.

Statman, D. (2012) "Gardner on the Wrongness of Rape," *Jerusalem Review of Legal Studies* 4: 105–9.

Tadros, V. (2006) "Rape Without Consent," *Oxford Journal of Legal Studies* 26: 515–43.

Tuerkheimer, D. (2015) "Rape On and Off Campus," *Emory Law Journal* 65: 1–45.

Wertheimer, A. (2003) *Consent to Sexual Relations*. Cambridge: Cambridge University Press.

West, D. (2005) *Reason & Sexuality in Western Thought*. Cambridge: Polity Press.

Related topics

Ch.2 What is consent?
Ch.12 Consent and autonomy
Ch.15 Deception and consent
Ch.16 Sexual consent

22
CONSENT AND PRIVACY

Bart Custers, Francien Dechesne, Wolter Pieters, Bart Schermer, and Simone van der Hof

22.1 Introduction

Consent to personal data-processing practices has become quite a mundane activity in the digital world. When downloading apps to our smartphones, we – almost automatically – consent to the privacy policies associated with the particular services they provide. Also, when subscribing to social networking services, consenting to their privacy policies is inescapable. Another particularly visible practice is to ask internet users to accept cookies (i.e., small pieces of data stored on people's computers to "remember" their actions and preferences).

The (consent to) disclosure of personal data and the subsequent use of such data is the domain of privacy and data protection. This chapter explores the discussion on the role of consent in privacy and personal data protection. It is shown how legal, ethical, economic and technological studies point to similar core issues related to the limitations of communication and decision making, inhibiting the effectiveness of consent for privacy protection. In section 22.2 the relation between privacy and consent is examined. In section 22.3 ethical and legal requirements for (informed) consent in relation to privacy and personal data protection are discussed. Special attention is given to the issues concerning children's consent. Next, the limits of consent in privacy and personal data protection are discussed from a technological perspective (section 22.4) and from the perspectives of legal, social and (behavioral) economics (section 22.5). In section 22.6 potential solutions to the issues regarding privacy and consent are offered and analyzed. In section 22.7 conclusions are provided.

22.2 Privacy, data protection and consent

In relation to privacy and personal data, informed consent is often described in terms of informational self-determination (Westin 1967), stating that each person should have a right to determine for himself when, how and to what extent information about him or her is communicated to others. Consent requests fulfil a practical purpose, as they allow individuals to express their preferences. In a sense, a consent transaction also functions as a warning that there may be consequences of a particular choice, consequences that may be beneficial for the individual, but also consequences that may be non-beneficial or potentially harmful.

In the context of information technology, sharing and disclosing personal data by organizations typically requires consent of the person whose personal data are involved. However, when not all conditions for informed consent are met, the consent may be ethically and/or legally flawed (see section 22.3), and even when all such conditions are met, the consent may not always be effective (see sections 22.4 and 22.5). For instance, informed consent to the use of personal data can only be given if the context of such data use is clear – a concept referred to as *contextual integrity* (Nissenbaum 2010). In other words, the consent is only valid against a fixed and clear (knowable) setting of roles, activities, norms and values for the use of the data.

Before addressing these ethical issues of (the limits of) consent in privacy and personal data protection, a short note on the concepts of privacy and personal data protection may be useful. Privacy has many connotations and perceptions of privacy can be different depending on individual preferences and historical, cultural or social contexts. One such conception of privacy is control over personal data or informational self-determination. On such a conception, personal data protection can be subsumed under the broader notion of privacy. However, privacy and data protection are sometimes also perceived as different legal tools to regulate our private (information) spheres. Privacy as an opacity tool (i.e., protection of the private life) has a prohibitive nature and aims at the protection of individual liberty and autonomy against state interference. Contrastingly, personal data protection schemes (i.e., fair processing of personal data) are of a regulatory rather than a prohibitive nature and focus on "channeling, regulating and controlling legitimate powers" (Gutwirth & De Hert 2008).

Privacy is often contrasted with security and law enforcement. This is particularly the case when interests of national security (such as counterterrorism) lead to requests for access to personal data, such as private communications. In such situations consent to collect and process personal data may not be required, if specific laws (e.g., criminal law, anti-terrorism legislation) overrule privacy and data protection legislation. It is argued that, in order to protect security in society, it is sometimes justified to override consent. The privacy versus security distinction only applies to actors from the public sector. The government has a duty to protect citizens (security) and may, in this context, sometimes violate individual rights (such as privacy) and override consent. Private actors typically are not authorized to violate such rights and may depend on consent as a basis for processing personal data.

22.3 Requirements for consent

22.3.1 Criteria for valid consent

In the context of privacy and data protection, it is usually assumed that consent is only valid when it is informed consent. An essential aspect of informed consent is that the person who is asked for consent should be properly informed of what exactly he or she is consenting to and is to some extent (made) aware of the consequences such consent may have. In the context of information technology, consent decisions concern the sharing and disclosure of personal data. From an ethical and legal perspective, several crucial criteria can be identified in the context of automated information processing.

Criteria for informed *consent* may include criteria regarding the person who consents (is the person an adult, capable and competent to consent?) and criteria on how to give consent (for instance, is the consent written or oral, is the consent partial or full, is the conviction behind the consent reasonably strong and is the consent an independent decision?) (Custers et al. 2013).

Criteria for *informed* consent can include criteria regarding the extent to which persons are enabled to consider the consent decision well, such as what information should be provided and how this information should be provided (Custers et al. 2013). It is generally held that the information that should be provided includes at least contextual information about which data

Table 22.1 Overview of the criteria for consent

Criteria regarding the *decision to consent*	Criteria regarding the *person who consents*	Is the person who consents an adult? If not, is there parental consent? Is the person who consents capable of consenting? If not, is there a legal representative to consent? Is the person who consents competent to consent? If not, is there a legal representative to consent?
	Criteria on *how to give consent*	Is the consent written? Is the consent partial or full? In case of partial consent, does the consent cover the purpose? Is the conviction behind the consent decision reasonably strong? Is the consent an independent decision? Is the consent up to date?
Criteria enabling the *well-consideredness of the decision to consent*	Criteria regarding *what information should be provided*	Is it clear which data are collected? Are the purposes clear? Is it clear which security measures are taken? Is it clear who is processing the data and who is accountable? Is it clear which rights can be exercised? Is it clear how these rights can be exercised?
	Criteria regarding *how information should be provided*	Is the information provided specific and sufficiently detailed? Is the information provided understandable? Is the information provided reliable and accurate? Is the information provided accessible?

are collected, used and shared and for which purposes the data are used. Furthermore, information on which security measures are taken, information about who is processing the data and who is accountable as well as information on user rights and how they can be exercised are potentially relevant for the consent decision. Moreover, it is generally held that the information provided should be specific, sufficiently detailed, understandable, reliable, accurate and accessible. Apart from situations in which it is obvious that some of these criteria are not met (such as absent policies, or policies in a completely different language), it is not clear for many of these criteria when they are sufficiently met. An overview of these criteria for valid informed consent is shown in Table 22.1. This overview includes the legal criteria for the validity of individual consent, which will be discussed in more detail in the next subsection.

22.3.2 Consent in data protection legislation

Through official guidelines and legislation, many of the criteria mentioned in Table 22.1 are included in the legal frameworks for personal data protection in many countries, including the US and the EU. Therefore, these criteria are not only ethical criteria but also legal criteria that a consent decision must meet in order not to be flawed. In the US, the criteria can be found in the Fair Information Practice Principles (FIPPs) of the Federal Trade Commission. Although these principles are only recommendations, they form the basis of specific legislation, including the Fair Credit Reporting Act, the Right to Financial Privacy Act, the Electronic Communications Privacy Act and the Video Privacy Protection Act.

In the EU, the legal framework for informational privacy and personal data protection is established by the Data Protection Directive,[1] which will be replaced by the General Data Protection Regulation (GDPR) as of 25 May 2018.[2] Both these laws contain most of the criteria mentioned in Table 22.1.

In European data protection legislation, consent plays a vital role, because it is one of the most important reasons legitimizing personal data processing. The Data Protection Directive and its successor, the GDPR, stipulate that personal data may be processed based on the unambiguous consent of the person to whom the data relate.[3] Consent under EU data protection legislation must be freely given, specific and informed in order to be valid. Furthermore, EU data protection legislation sets requirements for the form in which consent is given: consent must be unambiguous and, in certain cases, explicit.

For consent to qualify as "unambiguous" there must be no uncertainty about the intent of the person to whom the data relate. This intent can be expressed in the form of an action carried out by the person who must give the consent (e.g., ticking a checkbox), but also through a more general action carried out by the individual (e.g., walking through a door with a sign above it saying "if you enter you consent to having your picture taken"). Inferring consent from *in*action can never count as an unambiguous consent. However, inferring consent from an action that is not specifically or solely aimed at consent is possible, given that it is unambiguous. The burden of proof for the unambiguity of the consent rests upon the organization responsible. In the GDPR, the requirements for consent are strengthened by requiring that consent is expressed "either by a statement or a clear affirmative action". This will likely leave less room for the inference of consent.

For special categories of data that are more sensitive (e.g., health data), the higher standard of *explicit* consent needs to be met in order to legitimize data processing. For explicit consent, individuals need to be asked to agree or disagree with a particular use or disclosure of their personal information and they need to respond actively to the question.[4]

22.3.3 Children's consent

Both the US Children's Online Privacy Protection Act (hereafter: COPPA) and the GDPR hold special provisions on children's consent that take into account the level of maturity of children in determining whether they are capable of consenting to the processing of their personal information. Their level of maturity is mostly derived from their cognitive abilities to sufficiently understand their (legal) position and, hence, to give consent to certain actions. In the landmark case of Gillick, the UK House of Lords formulated the capacity to consent as: *a sufficient understanding and intelligence to be capable of making up his own mind on the matter requiring decision* as well as the capability *of understanding what is proposed, and of expressing his or her own wishes*.

When it comes to the provision of online commercial services, such as social media, video websites and games, both COPPA[5] and the GDPR[6] aim to provide children with special protection from (re)use of their personal data for marketing and other commercial purposes. Basically, children's capability to consent can be challenged in three ways. First, children might not be capable of understanding the *nature* of personal data processing. What personal data are used? How are they being used and by whom? Second, children might not be capable of understanding the *consequences* of personal data practices. Third, children might not be capable of understanding their *legal position* and of effectively using their privacy and data protection rights.

In privacy and data protection law in the US and the EU, the required level of maturity is reflected in the ages set for children's consent. From a certain age, children are considered to be capable of consenting on their own to the use of their personal information. However, this age can vary depending on the particular legal system. Under COPPA, the age is set at 13 years, whereas the GDPR provides that children are capable of consenting at the age of 16. However, the GDPR also leaves room for EU member states to set lower ages as long as they are not below 13. Below the age of consent, children require the consent of their parents to use online commercial services, even if such services are for free. Both COPPA and the GDPR require that parental consent is *verifiable.*

Verifiable parental consent entails that "reasonable efforts" must be taken by the responsible organization to make sure that it actually is the parent who is consenting. What verifiability of consent means more precisely and how it can be ensured is a matter for further scrutiny and not easily determined (Van der Hof 2014).

The provisions on children's consent are problematic in a number of ways (Van der Hof 2016). Remarkably enough, parental consent requirements might lead to tensions between parents and children in terms of privacy. Social media are, for instance, not only a venue for teens to socialize with their peers but also provide private spaces unbeknownst to parents (boyd 2008, 2014). Additionally, these requirements potentially encourage intrusive parental surveillance (Van der Hof 2014). Moreover, given the limits to consent discussed in the next sections, it might be questioned whether the provision indeed protects the use of children's personal data as envisioned by COPPA and the GDPR.

22.4 Limits of consent: the technological view

When one or more criteria for consent mentioned in Table 22.1 are not met, the individual consent is likely to be invalid, for example, in the case where a person is not properly informed.[7] However, even if the individual consent is valid, a consent mechanism may still be inadequate in the context in which it is used. Since informed consent is a mechanism that is used to ensure that people make well-considered decisions, the consent mechanism may also be *ineffective* and not very meaningful when people do not take notice of the information offered (e.g., because it is too much information or hard to understand). This section discusses limits of effective consent mechanisms from a technological perspective and the next section discusses the limits of consent from legal, social and (behavioral) economics perspectives.

From a technological perspective, a first issue is that information on the use of personal data may be difficult to provide. As data-processing tools in the context of Big Data, including data mining and profiling tools, continue to evolve, it can be extremely difficult to predict future data-processing technologies and the future potential of personal data. Developments in information and communication technology allow data, including personal data, to be aggregated, archived and analyzed ("mined") across domains on an increasingly vast scale and for longer periods of time. For example, if a person consents to the sharing of electricity consumption data with a network provider for network management and billing purposes, such consent does not cover selling the data to marketing firms.

Big Data developments (exponentially more data, more real-time data and more diverse datasets) provide opportunities for data coupling across domains such that unexpected relations and patterns may be discovered in the data. The increasing reuse of data in new ways and contexts may not be transparent or understandable for everyone and potentially undermines the possibility to make well-considered consent decisions. On top of that, Big Data allows so-called Privacy Merchants to combine apparently innocuous facts not privileged by law into highly sensitive personally identifiable information. Etzioni (2012) suggests calling such processes "privacy violating triangulation". In this respect, the combination of data across domains and across time means the use of the data is re-contextualized ("context creep"), in some cases beyond the scope of the original consent. Changing or even discarding the context under which the data were consensually collected, and the impossibility to be truly informed about the consequences of granting data use, means the informed consent loses its validity.

A second issue is that withholding consent (i.e., refusing to disclose personal data) does not necessarily guarantee better privacy protection. The use of Big Data increasingly enables the prediction of characteristics of people who withheld consent on the basis of the information available from people who did consent. When large numbers of people consent to the use of their personal data, it is possible to predict missing values of other people (Custers 2012). This may be pretty accurate: Kosinski et al. (2013) show how a range of highly sensitive personal characteristics, including sexual orientation, ethnicity, religious and political views, personality traits, intelligence, happiness, use of addictive substances and parental separation can be predicted very accurately on the basis of what a person has "liked" on Facebook. Such predictions limit the effectiveness of withholding consent. Obviously, predicting missing values is also possible for people who provided partial consent or for people who (whether on purpose or not) provided false information. Nevertheless, when data are inaccurate or incomplete, for instance because they are outdated, such predictions may become less accurate, resulting in wrong conclusions about people.

A third issue is that consent has a temporal aspect that may become increasingly important given the rapid technological developments. For instance, consent is usually asked for when registering for social media or websites, but rarely renewed afterwards. As a result, consenting once often implies consent "forever" (i.e., until it is actively withdrawn), even though the consent may rapidly get outdated (i.e., no longer match the initial preferences of a user), for instance, because the user has changed her mind, the technology and design of the service or website have changed, the terms and conditions or policies have changed or because the data-processing practices have changed significantly. Custers (2016) has suggested starting a debate on expiry dates for consent.

Given this temporal aspect, a fourth issue concerns the difficulties of withdrawing consent. Here it is important to focus on the debate on the right to be forgotten. This right enables people to have personal data about themselves deleted after it has become public. Amongst others, the right is relevant in situations in which an individual withdraws consent (or objects to the processing of his or her personal data). The right is of particular importance as it allows individuals to start again with a clean (online) slate. Reasons for consent withdrawal can be manifold, including changes in privacy policies, augmented concerns about the use of personal data, contextual changes (e.g., implementation of privacy-intrusive technologies or practices). The discontinuation of a particular service or transaction (e.g., by closing and deleting a social media account or exercising the right of withdrawal from an online consumer contract) could entail consent withdrawal. After consent withdrawal, the personal data initially collected may no longer be pertinent to the contractual relationship, once completely finished, and, hence, new obligations arise, one of which might be to erase such personal data. In that respect, the right to be forgotten is often more adequately referred to as "the right to erasure". For instance, the GDPR indeed requires subsequent erasure of data upon consent withdrawal, unless other lawful grounds for processing personal data of the individual remain. However, in practice this obligation might not always be easy to comply with or may potentially even be ineffective, given that the internet architecture largely undermines the ability to control data flows as a result of its open, end-to-end character. Unless personal data have been contained within a system strictly controlled by the service provider, it might be hard or even impossible to meet this requirement.

22.5 Limits of consent: the legal, social and (behavioral) economics view

Besides the technological perspective, the effectiveness of informed consent mechanisms as a means to establish informational self-determination in the context of personal data processing can also be challenged from a legal, social and economic point of view (Pollach 2007; Acquisti 2009; Böhme & Köpsell 2010; Adjerid et al. 2013; Solove 2013).

The first issue is that models for informed consent based on informational self-determination fail to offer adequate protection to people, as such models have too many hurdles (Solove 2013). *First*, people do not read privacy policies. Each time consent is asked for, the information provided is often very extensive. It may take a lot of time to read privacy policies and to make a decision based on this information. McDonald & Cranor (2010) have estimated that if people actually read all the privacy policies presented to them, it would take them 244 hours annually. This may explain findings of empirical studies indicating that people simply consent whenever confronted with a consent request (Custers et al. 2013). Such consent mechanisms are likely to be ineffective and their value may be disputed. *Second*, if people do read privacy policies, they may not understand them, as the information provided may be too difficult. In many situations, the text is highly legalistic in nature or contains technical details beyond the comprehension of the average user. *Third*, if people read and understand the policies, they often lack sufficient background knowledge to make an informed decision. While an abbreviated, plain-language policy would be quick and easy to read, it is the hidden details that carry significance (Toubiana & Nissenbaum 2011). Related to this issue is the asymmetry in power distribution. Those who collect and process the data have technological expertise that the average user usually lacks (Acquisti & Grossklags 2005; LaRose & Rifon 2007). *Fourth*, if people read privacy policies, understand them and can make an informed decision, they are not always offered the choice that reflects their preferences.

A second issue is related to this: people seem to become increasingly disengaged in the consent processes, such that the consent decision fails to have the intended moral effect of giving agency to individuals as autonomous decision makers (Hurd 1996; Kleinig 2010). Using the internet, there are (too) many requests for consent (Schermer et al. 2014). Most of the time, users blindly accept consent boxes when they resemble other dialog boxes (Böhme & Köpsell 2010). Browsing and surfing would take a lot of time if internet users were to actually consider every consent request. Moreover, it feels as if they have no choice when encountering consent decisions, since these are framed as take-it-or-leave-it offers: refusing consent means that access to a website or internet service is plainly denied or severely hampered. People are concerned about their privacy, but at the same time they routinely disclose personal information out of convenience or a lack of understanding of the consequences, or for discounts and other incentives (Dutton & Blank 2013; Regan 2002). People may consider this a trade-off in which they "pay" with their personal data, but it may also be the case that they feel they do not have a real choice. There is an important difference between accepting terms and conditions and agreeing with their contents: the former may yield legally valid consent, but the latter regards the actual effectiveness and meaningfulness of the consent mechanism.

A third issue is information asymmetry. A decision to consent to data processing may depend on the level of protection of personal data. However, how to communicate this information adequately is unclear, which makes it difficult for online service providers to compete on the quality of privacy protection,[8] or, more generally, information security (Anderson 2001). From an economic point of view, this creates a "market of lemons", in which high-quality goods are outcompeted by low-quality goods, as the difference cannot be perceived by buyers. A high level of privacy protection cannot be distinguished from low(er) levels of protection, making it difficult for users to decide whether to give consent to a particular scheme based on their security preferences, the consequence being that they may simply consent to anything.

A fourth issue with consent is framing. For instance, social network services usually collect user data for a variety of purposes and provide users with extensive access to each other's profiles. The privacy settings can allow users to distinguish between different (groups of) contacts that have access to (particular parts of) their personal profile. This is referred to as audience segregation (Van den Berg & Leenes 2010; Van den Berg & Van der Hof 2012). In such a situation, privacy is framed as an issue of inter-user access. However, framing privacy as inter-user access potentially takes attention away from data-processing practices by service providers. Hence, the questions asked in a consent request may be used to frame or mediate the interpretation of the problem and may become part of a strategic game (Adjerid et al. 2013; Johnson et al. 2002; Pieters 2010).

A fifth issue is that there are limits to the idea that privacy and consent are always about data that persons themselves control (or ought to be able to control). Developments in social media and Big Data already make that assumption problematic, as many data are being generated without the individual being aware (for instance, cell phones generating location data or smart watches collecting biometrics) and control cannot be expected given the volume of the data (for instance, when datasets are too large for human intuition to overview). What is more, data collected and used may be(come) anonymous or aggregated data, and both are not necessarily *personal* data. In that case, consent may not be required or may be difficult to obtain as it is not clear whom to address; yet such anonymous or aggregated data can be used to generate (sensitive) profiles that can have an impact on individual people nonetheless. An example is the (alleged) relation between crime and ethnicity. In establishing or verifying such a relation, using anonymous or aggregated data can circumvent consent decisions. However, such correlations can have a serious impact on individuals and society, as it may result in stigmatization, discrimination and social polarization.

Under the GDPR, individuals will have a right to object to profiling for direct marketing purposes. It remains to be seen to what extent such a right can be effectively implemented in practical processes and how it pertains to the concept of consent. Moreover, there may be data that a person does not want to control or does not want to know of (e.g., life expectancies). In such cases, consent may be required for providing particular information to a subject, for example, in the case where genetic data point to a high likelihood of contracting a serious disease (Tavani 2004; Van den Hoven et al. 2014). Subjects may choose *not to know* such data and forcing it upon them without consent could be problematic (Chadwick et al. 1997).

22.6 Potential ways forward

A possible solution for addressing some of the limits of consent lies in simplifying the consent process. This can be done in several ways. First, the representation of the information in the consent process can be simplified. Rather than presenting a long text to the user, the information can be condensed in privacy icons, colors, etc. (e.g., Holtz et al. 2011). The obvious question is whether such simplified representations contain enough information to be able to speak of informed consent. The subtleties of different privacy policies, risk profiles, etc. could be lost in the process of simplification. In this approach, the user would still have to consent separately for each service, but the individual indications of consent may take less time, assuming that the meaning of the simplified representations is clear to the user or becomes clear after getting used to the system.

A different approach entails reducing the number of acts of consent. If users can specify once which policies and risks they find acceptable or unacceptable, it may be possible to reuse this information when being asked for consent for different services. Typically, the choices would be formally represented in a privacy profile for the user. Similarly, each service would provide a formalized privacy policy. By matching the user policy against the service policy, acceptability of the conditions to the user could be derived (e.g., Broenink et al. 2010). If there is a match, consent could be given automatically or a positive advice could be given to the user. If the policies do not match, the system could indicate where the policies differ. In this case, the reduction of complexity lies not in the simplification of the policy representation, but in the reduction of the number of acts of consent. The user may still need to confirm, but the policy matching is done automatically.

Another solution that may improve the current situation is to move from take-it-or-leave-it consent to empowering users to choose a balance between functionality and privacy. For example, rather than giving a travel advice app access to all requested data including location (app permissions), a user may choose to keep the location private at the cost of not being able to use the current location in the app. This requires a different interface and consent mechanism for app permissions (and probably more effort on the part of the developers, in order to be able to work under different access conditions).

Anonymization of data has long been regarded as an important solution to protect privacy, and as such is often included in consent forms. However, research demonstrates that the digital traces that people leave behind, for example, by using credit cards or streaming video, can nowadays be effectively used for de-anonymizing (meta)data (e.g., Narayanan & Shmatikov 2008).

Another important concept in the solutions discourse is privacy-by-design (see e.g., Cavoukian 2010; Langheinrich 2001; Schaar 2010). The central idea is that, when designing information systems, architectural choices can be made that are beneficial to privacy protection. In particular, distributed rather than centralized storage of data can be an important choice, because decentralized storage makes it more difficult to process large volumes of data. Less fundamentally tied to the system architecture, default settings also form a crucial factor in the actual distribution of privacy-sensitive data. The idea is that the way in which choices are presented influences the resulting choice behavior. Default settings provide a so-called choice architecture (Thaler & Sunstein 2003) that encourages (nudges) people to stick with the default, and to change the settings only if they consider it worth the effort. Therefore, privacy-friendly defaults can contribute significantly to the protection of personal data. In the privacy context, this often involves opt-in (giving explicit consent, with non-consent being the default) in contrast to opt-out (explicitly withdrawing consent, with consent being the default) (Johnson et al. 2002). Following the consent criteria we outlined, opt-in would then be preferred, as it involves explicit consent, whereas opt-out assumes implicit consent. At the same time, if users cannot get what they want done without opting in too often, they may simply click without reading the information. An example is the EU legislation on web browser cookies, requiring explicit permission for storing (tracking) cookies, used among other things for personalized advertisements (Bond 2012). Apart from design criteria, it is also important to consider procedures in which citizens can report violations of the consent requirement in data processing. This solution concept focuses on monitoring and feedback, which have been put forward as requirements for responsible experimentation with new technologies in society (Pieters et al. 2014). User education is crucial to make such solutions work in practice.

22.7 Conclusions

Consent is a fundamental concept in privacy and personal data protection. In this context, consent is often characterized in terms of informational self-determination. From a legal perspective, there are several criteria to determine the validity of individual consent. However, even when individual consent is valid, the consent mechanisms may be ineffective (or not meaningful) when they do not meet several additional criteria. An assessment of these criteria shows that it may be extremely difficult to meet all these criteria in the context of digital technologies, as there are many hurdles. For instance, people do not read privacy policies, may not understand them, lack background knowledge or are offered choices that do not reflect their preferences. Things get more complicated when children's consent is required. Furthermore, it may be extremely difficult to predict the future potential of personal data, data may be processed and used for data mining and profiling that yields unpredictable results and withholding consent may not prevent undisclosed data being predicted anyway. Finally, on the internet people are confronted with so many consent requests that they increasingly become disengaged in the consent process. When consent mechanisms are not effective or meaningful, their value may be disputed.

Several solutions have been offered to address these issues. The consent process can be simplified, the number of consent requests can be reduced, more privacy settings can be offered and privacy-preserving measures can be built into the architecture of information technology. Anonymization can be a useful tool, but may not always guarantee privacy. Note, however, that all these solutions only address one or several of the issues of consent. Hence, a combination of measures is recommended in order to ensure that consent decisions actually make people pause for a moment and make them think actively about the consequences of consent.

Notes

1 Directive 95/46/EG of the European Parliament and the Council on the protection of individuals with regard to the processing of personal data and on the free movement of such data. OJ EU, L281/31, 23.11.1995.
2 Regulation (EU) 2016/679 of the European Parliament and of the Council of 27 April 2016 on the protection of natural persons with regard to the processing of personal data and on the free movement of such data, and repealing Directive 95/46/EC (General Data Protection Regulation), OJ EU, L119/1, 4.5.2016.
3 Apart from consent, the GDPR also offers other legal grounds for the processing of personal data. For instance, when the processing is necessary for the performance of a contract to which the data subject is party or in order to take steps at the request of the data subject prior to entering into a contract, for compliance with a legal obligation to which the controller is subject, for the performance of a task carried out in the public interest or in the exercise of official authority vested in the controller.
4 Article 29 Data Protection Working Party, Opinion 15/2011 on the definition of consent, 01197/11/EN WP187.
5 See Electronic Privacy Information Center, Children's Online Privacy Protection Act (COPPA), available at: https://epic.org/privacy/kids/ (last accessed: 11 May 2016).
6 See recital 38 of the GDPR.
7 Note that, in this respect, validity of consent depends on the jurisdiction and the specific situation or context.
8 The quality of privacy protection may be improved by, for instance, transparency, clear purpose specifications, not outsourcing data processing, limiting third-country data transfers, not selling data to data brokers, etc.

References

Acquisti, A. (2009) "Nudging Privacy: The Behavioral Economics of Personal Information," *Security & Privacy Economics* 7(6): 72–5.

Acquisti, A. and J. Grossklags (2005) "Privacy and Rationality in Decision Making," *IEEE Security and Privacy* 3(1): 26–33.

Adjerid, I., A. Acquisti, L. Brandimarte and G. Loewenstein (2013) "Sleights of Privacy: Framing, Disclosures, and the Limits of Transparency," *Proceedings of the Ninth Symposium on Usable Privacy and Security*. Newcastle, 24–6 July. New York: ACM.

Anderson, R. (2001) "Why Information Security Is Hard – an Economic Perspective," *Proceedings of the 17th Annual Computer Security Applications Conference (ACSAC)*. IEEE.

Böhme, R. and S. Köpsell (2010) "Trained to Accept? A Field Experiment on Consent Dialogs," *Proceedings of the SIGCHI Conference on Human Factors in Computing Systems*, pp. 2403–6.

Bond, R. (2012) "EU E-Privacy Directive and Consent to Cookies," *The Business Lawyer* 68: 215–24.

boyd, d. (2008). *Taken Out of Context: American Teen Sociality in Networked Publics. Managing*. https://doi.org/10.1056/NEJMcps0801308.

boyd, d. (2014). *It's Complicated: The Social Lives of Networked Teens*. New Haven, CT: Yale University Press.

Broenink, G., J.-H. Hoepman, C. van't Hof, P. van Kranenburg, D. Smits and T. Wisman (2010) "The Privacy Coach: Supporting Customer Privacy in the Internet of Things," in *Pervasive 2010 Conference Workshop on What Can the Internet of Things Do for the Citizen*. pp. 72–81. *arXiv preprint arXiv:1001.4459*. Helsinki, May 17.

Cavoukian, A. (2010) "Privacy by Design: The Definitive Workshop. A Foreword by Ann Cavoukian," *Identity in the Information Society* 3(2): 247–51.

Chadwick, R., M. Levitt and D. Shickle (1997) *The Right to Know and the Right Not to Know*. Aldershot: Ashgate Publishing.

Custers, B. (2012) "Predicting Data that People Refuse to Disclose; How Data Mining Predictions Challenge Informational Self-Determination," *Privacy Observatory Magazine*, Issue 3. www.privacyobservatory.org/

Custers, B. (2016) "Click Here to Consent Forever: Expiry Dates for Informed Consent," *Big Data and Society*, January–June 2016: 1–6. doi: 10.1177/2053951715624935.

Custers, B., S. Van der Hof, B. Schermer, S. Appleby-Arnold and N. Brockdorff (2013) "Informed Consent in Social Media Use. The Gap between User Expectations and EU Personal Data Protection Law," *SCRIPTed, Journal of Law, Technology and Society* 10(4): 435–57.

Dutton, W.H. and G. Blank (2013) *Cultures of the Internet: The Internet in Britain*. Oxford Internet Survey 2013. http://oxis.oii.ox.ac.uk/reports.

Etzioni, A. (2012) "The Privacy Merchants: What is to Be Done?" (March 1, 2012). *University of Pennsylvania Journal of Constitutional Law* 14(4): 929–51.

Gutwirth, S. and P. De Hert (2008) "Regulating Profiling in a Democratic Constitutional State," in M. Hildebrandt and S. Gutwirth (ed.), *Profiling the European Citizen*. Heidelberg: Springer, pp. 271–302.

Holtz, L., H. Zwingelberg and M. Hansen (2011) "Privacy Policy Icons," in J. Camenisch, S. Fischer-Hübner and K. Rannenberg (ed.), *Privacy and Identity Management for Life*. Heidelberg: Springer, pp. 279–85.

Hurd, H.M. (1996) "The Moral Magic of Consent (I)," *Legal Theory* 2: 121–46.

Johnson, E.J., S. Bellman and G.L. Lohse (2002) "Defaults, Framing and Privacy: Why Opting in-Opting Out," *Marketing Letters* 13(1): 5–15.

Kleinig, J. (2010) "The Nature of Consent," in F. Miller and A. Wertheimer (ed.), *The Ethics of Consent: Theory and Practice*. New York: Oxford University Press, pp. 3–25.

Kosinski, M., D. Stillwell and T. Graepel (2013) *Private Traits and Attributes Are Predictable from Digital Records of Human Behavior*. PNAS. www.pnas.org/cgi/doi/10.1073/pnas.1218772110.

Langheinrich, M. (2001) "Privacy by Design – Principles of Privacy-Aware Ubiquitous Systems," in G.D. Abowd, B. Brumitt and S. Shafer (ed.), *Ubicomp 2001: Ubiquitous Computing*. Heidelberg: Springer, pp. 273–91.

LaRose, R. and N. Rifon (2007) "Promoting i-Safety: Effects of Privacy Seals on Risk Assessment and Online Privacy Behaviour," *Journal of Consumer Affairs* 41(1): 127–49.

McDonald, A.M. and L.F. Cranor (2010) "The Cost of Reading Privacy Policies," *I/S Journal for Law and Policy for the Information Society* 4(3): 543–68. www.aleecia.com/authors-drafts/readingPolicyCost-AV.pdf

Narayanan, A. and V. Shmatikov (2008) "Robust De-anonymization of Large Sparse Datasets (How to Break Anonymity of the Netflix Prize Dataset)," in *Proceedings of 29th IEEE Symposium on Security and Privacy*. Oakland: IEEE Computer Society. May 2008, pp. 111–25.

Nissenbaum, H. (2010) *Privacy in Context – Technology, Policy and the Integrity of Social Life*. Stanford: Stanford University Press.

Pieters, W. (2010) "Reve {a, i} ling the Risks: A Phenomenology of Information Security," *Techné: Research in Philosophy and Technology* 14(3): 194–206.

Pieters, W., D. Hadžiosmanović and F. Dechesne (2014) "Cyber Security as Social Experiment," in *Proceedings of the 2014 workshop on New Security Paradigms Workshop*, ACM, pp. 15–24.
Pollach, I. (2007) "What's Wrong with Online Privacy Policies?" *Communications of the ACM* 50(9): 103–8.
Regan, P.M. (2002) "Privacy and Commercial Use of Personal Data: Policy Developments in the US," Paper Presented at the Rathenau Institute Privacy Conference. January 17, Amsterdam.
Schaar, P. (2010) "Privacy by Design," *Identity in the Information Society* 3(2): 267–74.
Schermer, B.W., B.H.M. Custers and S. Van der Hof (2014) "The Crisis of Consent: How Stronger Legal Protection May Lead to Weaker Consent in Data Protection," *Ethics & Information Technology* 16(2): 171–82.
Solove, D.J. (2013) "Privacy Self-Management and the Consent Dilemma," *Harvard Law Review* 126: 1880–903.
Tavani, H.T. (2004) "Genomic Research and Data-Mining Technology: Implications for Personal Privacy and Informed Consent," *Ethics and Information Technology* 6(1): 15–28.
Thaler, R.H. and C.R. Sunstein (2003) "Libertarian Paternalism," *American Economic Review* 93(2): 175–9.
Toubiana, V. and H. Nissenbaum (2011) "An Analysis of Google Logs Retention Policies," *Journal of Privacy and Confidentiality* 3(1): Article 2, 3–26.
Van den Berg, B. and R. Leenes (2010) "Audience Segregation in Social Network Sites," in *Proceedings for SocialCom2010/PASSAT2010 (Second IEEE International Conference on Social Computing/Second IEEE International Conference on Privacy, Security, Risk and Trust)*. Minneapolis (Minnesota, USA): IEEE: 1111–17.
Van den Berg, B. and S. Van der Hof (2012) "What Happens to My Data? A Novel Approach to Informing Users of Data Processing Practices," *First Monday* 17(7). http://firstmonday.org/ojs/index.php/fm/article/view/4010.
Van den Hoven, J., M. Blaauw, W. Pieters and M. Warnier (2014) "Privacy and Information Technology," in E.N. Zalta (ed.), *The Stanford Encyclopedia of Philosophy* (Winter 2014 Edition). http://plato.stanford.edu/archives/win2014/entries/it-privacy/.
Van der Hof, S. (2014) "No Child's Play: Online Data Protection for Children," in S. van der Hof, B. van den Berg and B. Schermer (ed.), *Minding Minors Wandering the Web: Regulating Online Child Safety*. The Hague: TCM Asser Press/Springer Press, pp. 127–41.
Van der Hof, S. (2016) "I Agree . . . or Do I? — A Rights-based Analysis of the Law on Children's Consent in the Digital World," *Wisconsin International Law Journal* 34(2): 409–45.
Westin, A. (1967) *Privacy and Freedom*. London: Bodley Head.

Related topics

Ch.8 Valid consent
Ch.24 Informed consent

PART IV

Medical ethics

23
HISTORICAL PERSPECTIVES IN MEDICAL ETHICS

Tom O'Shea

23.1 Introduction

The ethics of consent is conspicuous by its absence from much of the history of medicine. What we would now recognize as the practice of soliciting informed consent from competent patients has only seldom been taken to be a necessary condition of administering treatment or conducting medical research. Similarly, the surviving writings on medical ethics and doctoral etiquette rarely address the participation of patients in decision-making, and on this matter often confront us with a "stark silence" (Katz 2002: 3). These omissions are also reflected in the historiography: for instance, among its sixty-three chapters, there are no entries dedicated to consent in the monumental *Cambridge World History of Medical Ethics* (Baker & McCullough 2009).

Nevertheless, we can find various attempts to inform and secure the cooperation of patients in the history of medical treatment – even if they are rarely driven by concern for individual autonomy. Furthermore, it is possible to survey the development of the social and intellectual infrastructure that underpins modern medical consent, despite its progenitors not conceiving of themselves as contributors to any such project. This chapter charts this history in broad brush-strokes as it appears in medical thought and practice in ancient Greece, medieval Europe and the Middle East, and the history of Western law and medical ethics from the early modern period onwards. It concludes with some brief comments about possible future directions for ethical approaches to medical consent and competence that would depart from the models that arose in the twentieth century.

23.2 Medicine in ancient Greece

Plato's discussions of law inadvertently reveal some salient features of the relationship between doctors and patients in fourth-century Athens. In *The Laws*, he contrasts two approaches to medicine in order to illustrate by analogy the advantages of legislation that not only coerces but persuades. Doctors who are slaves administer to slaves; they give orders "like a tyrant" and "never talk to their patients individually" (Plato 2000: IV.720), whereas the freeman doctor attends to fellow freemen, "enters into discourse with the patient and with his friends", and "will not prescribe for him until he has first convinced him" (ibid.).

Some commentators claim that Plato thereby recognizes a requirement for consent from freemen that reveals an understanding of "the relation of consent to autonomy of the person as the expression of his right to self determination and free will" (Dalla-Vorgia et al. 2001: 60). However, we ought to be cautious here. Plato says that the freeman doctor who talks to his patients is "at once getting information from the sick man, and also instructing him as far as he is able", which suggests a diagnostic and therapeutic function for dialogue rather than a primarily ethical one (IV.720). Furthermore, when Plato tells us that a freeman doctor will convince their patient before prescribing for him, this is to first bring "the patient more and more under his persuasive influences and set him on the road to health" (ibid.). Indeed, the purpose of the medical analogy is to show that persuasion can serve as a tool to help legislators secure a prosperous *polis*, without implying that the legitimacy of this legislation depends upon the consent of the citizenry. Similarly, there is no indication that the patient who is the target of persuasion is granted a veto in the event that the doctor fails to win them around. Thus, there is a lack of textual evidence for the claim that Plato or his contemporaries recognized consent as a specifically ethical demand in medicine.

Plato earlier employs a medical analogy in *The Statesman* to discuss persuasion and force, which more definitively shows that he would have been no supporter of what we would understand as an ethical requirement for medical consent. He asks us to imagine that "a physician who has right knowledge of his profession does not persuade, but forces, his patient, whether man, woman, or child, to do the better thing" (Plato 1925: 296). Plato says that, irrespective of whether the physician acts lawfully, "the patient so forced might rightly say anything else rather than that he had been treated in a baneful or unscientific way by the physicians who used force upon him" (ibid.). This expresses a strongly paternalistic understanding of the doctor–patient relationship, which Plato evidently expects his audience of educated Greek men to share.

The Hippocratic Corpus echoes the medical paternalism that we find in Plato. Beneficence and non-malfeasance are said to be the guiding values of the physician, whereas there is no explicit discussion of consent (Faden & Beauchamp 1986: 61–2). While this does not prove that consent was not usually sought from patients, it does suggest that consent was not regarded as an important ethical prerequisite for medical treatment. Given comprehensive Hippocratic prohibitions on certain medical interventions, the lack of discussion of consent then also appears to indicate that neither was the consent of a competent patient to treatment by a skilled doctor considered sufficient to render those interventions ethically sound. For example, there are no exceptions identified to the commitments outlined in the Hippocratic Oath to refuse to provide pessaries for abortion or lethal drugs to those wanting to end their own lives (von Staden 2009: 354). Therefore, *a fortiori*, the consent of the patients cannot be sufficient to render these acts permissible.

Contemporary understandings of medical consent normally require that voluntary assent has been given in a context where a competent patient has been informed about any diagnosis, the proposed treatment, and available alternatives. In other words, valid consent must be informed consent. Yet the Hippocratic texts endorse measures that actively impede the disclosure of information that would enable an informed consent to be given or refused. For example, they recommend "concealing most things from the patient, while you are attending to him" (1923: 297).

Despite its later prominence, Hippocratic medicine was only one amongst several approaches, with only a limited influence in Greek antiquity. Other understandings of the duties of doctors were less grounded in beneficence and more capacious in accommodating certain choices made by patients. For example, some doctors were willing to help people commit suicide despite Hippocratic injunctions against this (Faden & Beauchamp 1986: 62). Even those heavily indebted to Hippocratic teachings can be found stressing competing ideals. The towering Graeco-Roman physician Galen makes much of the importance of the physician's truthfulness. He forbids major lies to the patient, and demands that doctors are completely honest with the patient's carers, yet he does concede that omitting truths and telling minor untruths can be justified if the patient benefits (von Staden 2009: 357). Nevertheless, despite this marginally more sanguine attitude towards truthfulness in how the patient is informed, it is still the case that consenting does not seem to have acted as a gatekeeper for the legitimacy of medical treatment in ancient Greece, nor is there an evident and sustained ethical concern with enabling or respecting such consent.

23.3 Medicine in medieval Europe and the Middle East

While there is no single radical development in the ethics of medical consent in medieval Europe, we can begin to identify more clearly some emerging functions of the solicitation of consent that extend beyond the pragmatic benefits of doctors knowing they have willing patients. One of the most important is the use of consent in defensive medicine. This can be seen in a nascent but recurring consent ritual devised by doctors in order to protect themselves from being unfairly blamed for the fate of their patients. The ritual is first recorded in the late sixth century, when Byzantine physicians were reluctant to operate on the gravely ill Emperor Justin II lest they be held responsible for his death. Despite his promise that they would not be punished, they reportedly asked that the Emperor personally hand them the scalpel as an explicit sign of his willingness to undergo surgery (Dalla-Vorgia et al. 2001: 60). The public expression of consent through this scalpel-handing ritual serves an exculpatory purpose. It mirrors in more ceremonial fashion the practice recorded from the fourteenth century onwards of obtaining explicit documentation releasing surgeons from claims for blood money upon the death of their patients (Ajlouni 1995; Leclercq et al. 2010). The need for public exculpation remains in modern law, where consent has been described as a "flak jacket" for liability (*Re W (A Minor) (Consent to Medical Treatment) [1993] 1 FLR 1*). Consent manifested through the handing of the scalpel likewise acts as a kind of chainmail that protects the consent-seeker rather than simply the consent-giver.

The scalpel-handing ritual is recorded numerous times in the following centuries, and not merely for powerful patients (Dalla-Vorgia et al. 2001: 60). Significantly, it is sufficiently widespread as to attract criticism from the seventh-century author of the *Miracles of St Artemios* for allowing surgeons to disavow responsibility for their mistakes. Nevertheless, its functions are relatively narrow, and it does not demonstrate that operating on someone without their consent was seen as wrong. Instead, the ritual of handing the scalpel implicitly invokes the principle *volenti non fit injuria*: that no injury is done to a willing person. It remains silent about the injuries done to the unwilling.

Medical paternalism was still alive and well in medieval Europe. For instance, in the late thirteenth century, the French surgeon Henri de Mondeville tells us that patients "should obey their surgeons implicitly in everything appertaining to their cure" (Mondeville 1977: 15). Furthermore, he has no reservations about recommending that doctors lie about the prospects for a patient's recovery when this would serve to promote their health. Again, if there are significant informational requirements for an ethically robust consent, then this advice actively undermines the ideal of voluntary and informed consent as we would presently understand it. Furthermore, while Mondeville does caution against coerced treatment, the reasons for this are not primarily ethical. Instead, they arise from concerns about reputational damage as well as the effectiveness of such treatments, which were naturally very risky or impractical in surgery undertaken without reliable general anesthetic.

We find similar attitudes towards noncompliant patients in the Middle East during this period. For Ibn Jumay, the twelfth-century Arabic physician, there is a compelling therapeutic reason to ensure that the patient cooperates with the doctor, since the recalcitrant patient is given to imprudent behavior that can impede a cure (Weisser 2009: 368). The concern once more is the danger for the patient of disobeying the doctor rather than establishing that there are cases in which patients might legitimately refuse treatment or disregard medical advice. While doctors were expected to conform to the expectations of patients regarding their attire and demeanor, some considered themselves duty-bound to bring about the most salubrious behavior in those patients. For instance, al-Ruhāwī stresses the importance of educating patients, attendants, and visitors, so that they do not act in ways that disrupt the work of the physician (Weisser 2009: 398–9). The emphasis on cooperation throughout this medical literature is ultimately asymmetrical: its focus is securing obedience to the doctor rather than the doctor accommodating themselves to the will of the patient. What rudimentary consent there is in evidence therefore never seems to escape the limits of a pervasive medical paternalism.

23.4 Conceptual and social foundations of modern medical consent

Why is consent now so integral to medical ethics when for millennia it was marginal at best? Its emergence as an ethical ideal rather than simply a pragmatic benefit was not foreordained. Instead, the ethical entrenchment of medical consent was dependent upon significant developments in how individuality, authority, and freedom came to be understood within much modern social life. This slow accretion of conceptual and institutional innovations from outside of medicine provided the cognitive and social infrastructure that has helped make the ethical demand for medical consent not only intelligible to us but also compelling.

Civil law has provided much of the architecture for the concept of individual consent. In particular, Roman law of contract crafted a sophisticated set of tools for enabling consensual agreements to be made legally enforceable (Johnston 2009: 39–41). This was an important step in beginning to normalize the idea that consensual transactions can create and alter rights and obligations (Johnston 2009: 41). Papal reform of marital law in the High Middle Ages provides a further legal foundation, with the free consent of bride and bridegroom becoming a necessary and sufficient condition for marriage when there were no clear impediments like consanguinity or bigamy (d'Avray 2005: 130). Importantly, to be authoritative, this consent had to be freely given, with the Church threatening to withdraw sacraments from those impeding or compelling the consent of another (Noonan 1973: 434). Thus, the notion that voluntary consent was required for the legitimacy of certain social relationships was established long before it was embraced within medical ethics.

The increased prominence of consent within social institutions such as marriage reflected broader social and cultural changes in Europe in the twelfth and late eleventh centuries, which some scholars have called "the discovery of the individual" (Morris 1972; cf. Melve 2006). This is manifested politically in a shift towards greater numbers of individuals being taken to possess the status of citizens rather than mere subjects. Likewise, the individual becomes a renewed focus in religious life, with "a new concern with self-discovery and psychological self-examination, an increased sensitivity to the boundary between self and other, and an optimism about the capacity of the individual for achievement" (Bynum 1982: 83). Both developments strengthen a conception of individuals as a primary locus of moral concern, which subsequently underpins an increased respect for their consent and dissent.

Deepening individualism is also a hallmark of early modern European thought and society. The social contractarian tradition associated with Hobbes, Locke, and Rousseau grounded legitimate political authority and obligation in the consent of the people – albeit consent that was typically historical, implicit, or hypothetical, rather than explicitly avowed and revocable by each individual (see Riley 1973). Furthermore, we find uneven but significant advances in religious toleration in early modern life, which gradually moves away from the sixteenth-century principle of *cuius regio, eius religio* – that whoever rules a region determines the religion – towards a more ecumenical ideal of respect for individual conscience in matters of religious confession. Similar ideas find a more expansive ethical expression in the late eighteenth century with what Charles Taylor calls "the modern ideal of authenticity": the belief that we should be true to our own inner voice – not merely because it issues accurate guidance on how to act, but because fidelity to our own particular sentiments and convictions is independently necessary for human self-fulfillment and self-realization (Taylor 1992: 31; Trilling 1972). As John Stuart Mill put it in his hugely influential nineteenth-century treatise *On Liberty*: "the free development of individuality is one of the leading essentials of well-being" (Mill 1999: III.2). Indeed, Mill's conclusion that nothing other than preventing harm to others can ordinarily justify non-consensual interference with someone's self-regarding actions continues to animate contemporary liberal ideology.

23.5 Consent in seventeenth- to nineteenth-century medicine

The trend of increasing respect for individual liberty in the history of modern culture did not uniformly suffuse all aspects of medical practice for all people in all places. Some early modern legal regulation of medical practitioners sounds strikingly contemporary in its demands for the consent of individuals. For example, the 1665 Duke of York's Law in the British colonies made the use of experimental medical techniques on competent patients conditional upon their active consent. It forbade those engaged in healthcare

> to set forth or exercise any act contrary to the known approved rule of art upon or towards the body of any [. . .] without the [. . .] consent of the patient or patients if they be *mentis compotes*, much less contrary to such consent.
>
> *(Walsh quoted in Baker 2013: 233–4)*

Another significant episode in early modern experimental medicine illustrates professional conventions concerning the ethics of consent – namely, the 1767 English legal case of *Slater v. Baker & Stapleton* (95 Eng. 860, 2 Wils. KB 359). Slater sought treatment for a broken leg from the surgeon Baker and apothecary Stapleton, who reset his femoral fracture in an experimental device – a heavy steel contraption replete with teeth – without his consent and without giving him sufficient prior warning. Since it was customary amongst physicians to obtain consent before resetting fractures in these circumstances, the judge ruled that in failing to do so Baker and Stapleton were remiss in their professional conduct. While his reasoning foregrounds the importance of patients being forewarned of medical procedures so that they may "take courage", rather than emphasizing an independent right to self-determination, it is significant that the courts recognized some legal duties to respect treatment decisions in research contexts (cf. Faden & Beauchamp 1986: 116–7).

English law of the nineteenth century was explicit about the need to both inform experimental patients and obtain their consent. For instance, we are told by J.W. Willcox's treatise on medical law in 1830 that:

> When an experiment of this kind is performed with the consent of the party subjected to it, after he has been informed that it is an experiment, the practitioner is answerable

> neither in damages to the individual, nor on a criminal proceeding; [. . .] But if the practitioner performs his experiment without giving such information to, and obtaining the consent of, his patient, he is liable to compensate in damages any injury which may arise from his adopting a new method of treatment.
>
> *(Willcox quoted in Howard-Jones 1982: 1430)*

While it may be tempting to conclude that we have a clear articulation of the doctrine of informed consent here, it is important to distinguish the responsibilities to both tell the patient of the experiment and elicit their consent from the responsibility to ensure that the patient sufficiently understands and appreciates the implications of their treatment decision, such that their consenting itself qualifies as informed (Howard-Jones 1982: 1430). It is furthermore worth noting that, in all three examples we have considered, the juridico-ethical function of consent is not to authorize ordinary medical treatments which would otherwise wrongfully trespass upon the body. Instead, consent indemnifies practitioners when they depart from the uncontroversial background norms of medical treatment by administering an as-yet untested technique. Therefore, no comprehensive requirement for medical consent is implied.

In non-experimental medicine, the sick also sometimes enjoyed considerable *de facto* latitude in their treatment as a result of their economic or social relationship to medical practitioners. Medicine that was practiced at the domestic bedside – before the dominance of the clinic – strengthened the hand of patients, their friends, and families to shape treatment (Lindemann 2009: 397). An educated seventeenth- or eighteenth-century patient would likely proffer their own thoughts on their diagnosis and its remedies rather than merely passively acquiescing to those of their medical practitioner. For example, we find Samuel Johnson recounting that he bullied and bounced his apothecary into changing the production of a salve to a formulation he believed would be superior (Porter & Porter 1989: 78). Furthermore, wealthy individuals could and did summon several doctors – enabling them to follow the prescriptions that they deemed most congenial or salubrious. For instance, Andrew Fletcher writes to John Locke to say that his sister-in-law luckily decided to follow Locke's medical advice in preference to that of two other physicians who were sent for (Porter & Porter 1989: 80). However, the sick poor were often at the mercy of infirmaries, where they might fall prey to the scientific pretensions of young doctors keen to make a name for themselves, who could all too readily deem patients incurable in their haste to commence experimenting upon them (McCullough 2009: 404–5).

In early modern mental health, non-consensual detention and treatment was typically taken to present even fewer social, legal, or ethical difficulties. Domestic care and confinement was commonplace, as it had been for millennia, and many others with psychosocial disabilities found themselves in prison or the workhouse (Porter 2002: ch. 5). Consider later developments in nineteenth-century England, where the public financing of institutions precipitated a steady increase in patient admissions and the widespread use of mechanical restraints (Fennell 1996). The 1840s saw the growth of a non-restraint movement, and the Lunacy Commission was mandated to conduct inspections requiring each use of restraint to be recorded and a rationale for it given. In reaction to the decline in restraint resulting from this regulation, medication without consent then became the so-called "sheet anchor" for subduing disruptive patients (Fennell 1996: 41). Arguably, this presented little to no advance, since the extensive use of powerful sedatives – such as opium, ether, and bromide – could be equally debilitating, shackling the mind and not merely the body.

Dissatisfaction with the side-effects and addictive properties of sedatives towards the end of the nineteenth century in England allowed the pendulum to swing back to physical management of behavior, such as the "wet packing" of mental health patients in sheets (Fennell 1996: 47).

Concerns about abuse of these techniques arose from the knotty relationship between their punitive, custodial, and therapeutic employment – leading them to be removed from the discretion of orderlies and mandating medical supervision for their use. However, now that these techniques were understood as medical treatments founded upon the authority of psychiatric expertise, this legitimized them in the eyes of wider society. Thus, non-consensual treatments of highly dubious value were still commonplace in late-nineteenth-century mental health care.

23.6 Consent in twentieth-century medicine

Cardozo J makes a landmark judgment in 1914 which articulates the requirement that the decisions of competent patients who withhold consent for treatment should be respected:

> Every adult person of sound mind has a right to determine what shall be done with his own body; and a surgeon who performs an operation without his patient's consent commits an assault, for which he is liable in damages.
>
> *(Schloendorff v. Society of New York Hospital [1914] 105 NE 92.)*

This championing of individual consent has resonances with Mill's defense of self-sovereignty: "Over himself, over his own body and mind, the individual is sovereign. [. . .] Each is the proper guardian of his own health, whether bodily, or mental and spiritual" (Mill 1999: I.9 and I.13). Despite the important implications for consent that arise from such a right to determine what happens to one's own body, this does not itself impose substantial informational obligations on others. It is only in later U.S. bioethical and legal thought that we begin to find much more stringent requirements concerning the extent to which valid consent must be highly informed.

The ethics of systematic medical research further drove the development of medical consent in the twentieth century. While the Department of Health under the Weimar Republic issued strict *Richtlinien* in 1931 mandating consent in medical research (Sass 1983), the German state soon oversaw medical experimentation of extreme cruelty and brutality in the concentration camps, including deliberatively infecting wounds with gangrene and tetanus, attempting to conjoin twins by sewing, and conducting hypothermia experiments in tanks of ice water (Berenbaum 1993: 194–5; Bogod 2004: 1155). At the subsequent Nuremburg war crimes tribunals, those indicted sought to defend themselves by arguing, unsuccessfully, that genuinely voluntary consent was not obtained by other physicians in their medical research. The tribunal's judges subsequently drew up the 1947 Nuremberg Code, which outlined in a non-legally binding form the fundamental principles that were to govern human subject research – foremost among these being a requirement for consent that was voluntary, competent, informed, and comprehending. Despite the Code often being taken to mark a turning point in medical research ethics, its immediate influence was limited, with Katz astutely describing how it was received among medical practitioners: "It was a good code for barbarians but an unnecessary code for ordinary physicians" (Katz 1992: 228).

The Declaration of Helsinki relaxed the Nuremberg principles and allowed greater scope for medical research by requiring consent only "if at all possible, consistent with patient psychology" (World Medical Association 1964: II.1). Yet even these looser standards were periodically transgressed. Most prominently, the Tuskegee syphilis study withheld information and life-saving treatment from hundreds of infected black men, who were falsely led to believe participation was beneficial for their health. The study was only finally shut down when its existence was widely publicized in 1972 – after over a hundred people had died of syphilis-related complications (Reverby 2009). The combination of public outrage about Tuskegee with earlier influential work by Beecher (1966) recounting problematic post-war human subject research has contributed to the U.S. spearheading extensive efforts to validate consent to medical research.

The first explicit formulations of requirements for "informed consent" in medicine more widely are also concentrated in the U.S., where this term initially appears in *Salgo v Leland Stanford Jr University Board of Trustees et al.* ([1957] 154 Cal App2d 560). We find two ethical imperatives for the physician in this judgment that can stand in tension: the duty to ensure that consent is "intelligent" by disclosing relevant information, and the duty to "place the welfare of his patient above all else" by exercising discretion in how far beyond minimum disclosure requirements to go if it will cause apprehension or psychological distress. This discretion has become circumscribed by a shift in the justificatory grounds for disclosure in juridico-ethical reasoning, where U.S. courts are said to have

> explicitly repudiated the traditional beneficence-based rationale for disclosure in stating that the duty to disclose does not arise from "medical custom and practice" (as it would be if it were done as part of the doctor's role to promote the patient's welfare), but instead arises from "the patient's prerogative to decide".
>
> *(Kim 2010: 8)*

The increased emphasis upon disclosure by medical practitioners was subsequently accompanied by a focus upon the nature of the competency to employ this information in deciding to grant or withhold consent. The much-vaunted right to refuse medical treatment therefore has not been extended to the many patients deemed to lack the requisite functional abilities. For example, these are often taken to include the ability to understand relevant information, as well as to appreciate and reason with it, or otherwise use or weigh the information in decision-making (Kim 2010: 12–14).

The implicit rationale for such functional accounts of competency can be understood in one of two ways. Firstly, the absence of decision-making competence might *justify overriding* a person's right to autonomy. So understood, incompetence provides a warrant for giving less weight to patients' autonomy than their health or wider best interests. Secondly, the absence of decision-making competence might be thought to *preclude* autonomy itself. Making decisions for someone would not override or breach their autonomy rights, since achieving such autonomy depends on capacities which they already lack. So understood, deciding on behalf of those without decision-making capacity does not deprive them of autonomy for the sake of some more important good, since a meaningful autonomy was never available to them in the first place.

Detention and involuntary treatment for mental health conditions in common law jurisdictions is often governed by criteria other than someone's capacity to make competent decisions. The formalization of grounds for compulsory admission begun in the late nineteenth century has focused upon risk to self or others. For instance, English law in the twentieth century settled on the necessary and sufficient grounds that the patient has a mental disorder of a nature or degree that means treatment in hospital is both appropriate and necessary for the health or safety of the patient, or for the protection of other people (*The Mental Health Act 1983*: §3.2). The ethical justifications for these criteria are a mixture of paternalism and respect for the liberty of others. While detention and involuntary treatment on the grounds of the health or safety of the patient might seem to depart from Mill's defense of self-sovereignty, his qualification that "this doctrine is meant to apply only to human beings in the maturity of their faculties" rather than "those still in a state to require being taken care of by others" (1999: I.10) can appear to render them consistent. Whatever the implication of Mill's own position, there remains concern about the extent of paternalistic intervention in both formal and informal mental health care, as well as restricting liberty on the grounds of assessments of risk to others rather than harms actually committed.

23.7 The future of medical consent

We have encountered the model of respect for informed and competent consent for physical treatment and the prohibition on involuntary mental health detention and treatment for those not a danger to themselves or others. Its rise is historically intelligible without being historically inevitable – nor is it necessarily an end-point for ethico-juridical thinking about consent in medicine. We can conclude by considering two challenges to the competency model of informed consent recounted here.

The first challenge comes from critics who believe that consent requirements became overly entrenched in bioethics and medical law in the second half of the twentieth century (Foster 2009). One sceptical explanation for the prominence of consent requirements holds that an excessive reliance on the value of autonomy in medical ethics has stemmed from the fact that "only autonomy is easily codified into a set of rules and regulations pertaining to day-to-day clinical health care" (Wolpe 1998: 47). Furthermore, some question whether appeals to autonomy have been genuinely patient-driven, with empirical research appearing to suggest that patients often simply want a relationship of personal concern wherein they are kept informed, without a "mandatory autonomism" that forces them to decide for themselves even if they would rather voluntarily defer to others (Schneider 1998: xii). Others doubt consent is meaningfully solicited in modern medicine and suspect that the consent-seeking practices codified in the twentieth century predominantly function as a way of "producing assent" for actions that medical workers have already decided upon (Anspach 1993: 24). From these perspectives, the late twentieth century has seen an unnecessary and unpopular increase in bureaucratized consent requirements, which represents a wrong turn in medical ethics.

The second challenge is to the requirement for decision-making capacity as a condition of respect for medical consent or other decisions. Critics claim that such approaches deny equal recognition before the law to people with disabilities – who will be disproportionately affected by competency requirements. These critics take inspiration from Article 12 of the recent *UN Convention on the Rights of Persons with Disabilities*, which mandates "that persons with disabilities enjoy legal capacity on an equal basis with others in all aspects of life" (2007: §12.2). They propose that we dispense with demanding tests of decision-making abilities. All they require for attributing legal capacity, and therefore grounding respect for a person's consent, is that some meaningful human agency can be identified – i.e. that a person "act in a way that at least one other person who has personal knowledge of an individual can reasonably ascribe to one's actions, personal will and/or intentions, memory, coherence through time, and communicative abilities to that effect" (Bach & Kerzner 2010: 66). This would constitute a radical break with the individualistic competence-based model of medical consent that has been fundamental to medical ethics in the twentieth century – where it remains to be seen whether such a transition is a necessary step in advancing equality or would leave those with illnesses and impairments even more vulnerable.

References

Ajlouni, K.M. (1995) "History of Informed Medical Consent," *Lancet* 346: 980.

Anspach, R. (1993) *Deciding Who Lives: Fateful Choices in the Intensive-Care Nursery*. Berkeley, CA: University of California Press.

Bach, M. and L. Kerzner (2010) *A New Paradigm for Protecting Autonomy and the Right to Legal Capacity*. Toronto: The Law Commission of Ontario.

Baker, R. (2013) *Before Bioethics: A History of American Medical Ethics from the Colonial Period to the Bioethics Revolution*. Oxford: Oxford University Press.

Baker, R.B. and L.B. McCullough (ed.) (2009) *The Cambridge World History of Medical Ethics*, vols. 1–2. Cambridge: Cambridge University Press.

Beecher, H. (1966) "Ethics and Clinical Research," *New England Medical Journal* 274: 1354–60.

Berenbaum, M. (1993) *The World Must Know: The History of the Holocaust as Told in the United States Holocaust Memorial Museum*. Boston: Little, Brown & Co.

Bogod, D. (2004) "The Nazi Hypothermia Experiments: Forbidden Data?" *Anaesthesia* 59(12): 1155–9.

Bynum, C.W. (1982) *Jesus as Mother: Studies in the Spirituality of the High Middle Ages*. Berkeley: University of California Press.

Dalla-Vorgia, P., J. Lascaratos, P. Skiadas and T. Garanis-Papadatos (2001) "Is Consent in Medicine a Concept Only of Modern Times?" *Journal of Medical Ethics* 27(1): 59–61.

d'Avray, D. (2005) *Medieval Marriage: Symbolism and Society*. Oxford: Oxford University Press.

Faden, R. and T. Beauchamp (1986) *A History and Theory of Informed Consent*. Oxford: Oxford University Press.

Fennell, P. (1996) *Treatment Without Consent: Law, Psychiatry and the Treatment of Mentally Disordered People Since 1845*. London: Routledge.

Foster, C. (2009) *Choosing Life, Choosing Death: The Tyranny of Autonomy in Medical Ethics*. Oxford: Hart.

Hippocrates (1923) "Decorum," in W.H.S. Jones (trans.), *Hippocrates*, vol. 2. Cambridge, MA: Harvard University Press.

Howard-Jones, Norman. 1982. "Human Experimentation in Historical and Ethical Perspectives," *Social Science Medicine* 16(15): 1429–48.

Johnston, D. (2009) "A History of Consent in Western Thought," in F. Miller and A. Wertheimer (ed.), *The Ethics of Consent: Theory and Practice*. Oxford: Oxford University Press.

Katz, J. (1992) "The Consent Principle of the Nuremberg Code: Its Significance Then and Now," in G.J. Annas and M.A. Grodin (ed.), *The Nazi Doctors and the Nuremberg Code: Human Rights in Human Experimentation*. Oxford: Oxford University Press, pp. 227–39.

Katz, J. (2002) *The Silent World of Doctor and Patient*. Baltimore: Johns Hopkins University Press.

Kim, S.Y.H. (2010) *Evaluation of Capacity to Consent to Treatment and Research*. Oxford: Oxford University Press.

Leclercq, W.K.G., B.J. Keulers, M.R.M. Scheltinga, P.H.M. Spauwen, and G.J. van der Wilt (2010) "A Review of Surgical Informed Consent: Past, Present, and Future. A Quest to Help Patients Make Better Decisions," *World Journal of Surgery* 34(7): 1406–15.

Lindemann, M. (2009) "The Discourse of Practitioners in Eighteenth-Century France and Germany," in R.B. Baker and L.B. McCullough (ed.), *The Cambridge World History of Medical Ethics*, vols. 1–2. Cambridge: Cambridge University Press.

McCullough, L.B. (2009) "The Discourse of Practitioners in Eighteenth-Century Britain," in R.B. Baker and L.B. McCullough (ed.), *The Cambridge World History of Medical Ethics*, vols. 1–2. Cambridge: Cambridge University Press.

Melve, L. (2006) "The Revolt of the Medievalists. Directions in Recent Research on the Twelfth-Century Renaissance," *Journal of Medieval History* 32(3): 231–52.

Mill, J.S. (1999) in E. Alexander (ed.), *On Liberty*. Ontario: Broadview Press.

Mondeville, H. (1977) "On the Morals and Etiquette of Surgeons," as entitled and reprinted in S.J. Reiser, A.J. Dyck and W.J. Curran (ed.), *Ethics in Medicine: Historical Perspectives and Contemporary Concerns*. Cambridge, MA: MIT Press.

Morris, C. (1972) *The Discovery of the Individual 1050–1200*. Toronto: University of Toronto Press.

Noonan, J. (1973) "Power to Choose," *Viator* 4: 419–34.

Plato (1925) *Statesman*, trans. R.G. Bury. New York: Heinemann.

Plato (2000) *Laws*, trans. B. Jowett. New York: Prometheus Books.

Porter, R. (2002) *Madness: A Brief History*. Oxford: Oxford University Press.

Porter, D. and R. Porter (1989) *Patient's Progress: Doctors and Doctoring in Eighteenth-Century England*. Stanford: Stanford University Press.

Reverby, S. (2009) *Examining Tuskegee: The Infamous Syphilis Study and its Legacy*. Chapel Hill: University of North Carolina Press.

Re W (A Minor) (Consent to Medical Treatment) [1993] 1 FLR 1.

Riley, P. (1973) "How Coherent is the Social Contract Tradition?" *Journal of the History of Ideas* 34(4): 543–62.
Salgo v Leland Stanford Jr University Board of Trustees et al. [1957] 154 Cal App2d 560.
Sass, H.M. (1983) "Reichsrundschreiben 1931: Pre-Nuremberg German Regulations Concerning New Therapy and Human Experimentation," *The Journal of Medicine and Philosophy* 8(2): 99–111.
Schneider, C. (1998) *The Practice of Autonomy: Patients, Doctors, and Medical Decisions*. Oxford: Oxford University Press.
Slater v Baker & Stapleton [1767] 95 Eng. 860, 2 Wils. KB 359.
Taylor, C. (1992) "The Politics of Recognition," in A. Gutmann (ed.), *Multiculturalism: Examining the Politics of Recognition*. Princeton: Princeton University Press, pp. 25–73.
The Mental Health Act 1983. London: The Stationery Office.
Trilling, L. (1972) *Sincerity and Authenticity*. Cambridge, MA: Harvard University Press.
UN General Assembly (2007) *Convention on the Rights of Persons with Disabilities*.
von Staden, H. (2009) "The Discourses of Practitioners in Ancient Europe," in R.B. Baker and L.B. McCullough (ed.), *The Cambridge World History of Medical Ethics*, vols. 1–2. Cambridge: Cambridge University Press.
Weisser, U. (2009) "The Discourses of Practitioners in the Ninth- to Fourteenth-Century Middle East," in R.B. Baker and L.B. McCullough (ed.), *The Cambridge World History of Medical Ethics*, vols. 1–2. Cambridge: Cambridge University Press.
Wolpe, P.R. (1998) "The Triumph of Autonomy in American Bioethics," in R. DeVries and J. Subedi (ed.), *Bioethics and Society: Constructing the Ethical Enterprise*. Upper Saddle River, NJ: Prentice Hall.
World Medical Association. (1964; amended 2008) *Declaration of Helsinki: Ethical Principles for Research Involving Human Subjects*. www.wma.net/en/30publications/10policies/b3/.

Further reading

On the history of informed consent, see Faden, R. and T. Beauchamp (1986) *A History and Theory of Informed Consent*, Oxford: Oxford University Press. For an excellent short history of consent more generally, see Johnston, D. (2009) "A History of Consent in Western Thought," in F. Miller and A. Wertheimer (eds.) *The Ethics of Consent: Theory and Practice*, Oxford: Oxford University Press. A lucid overview of the dominant framework for understanding modern medical consent can be found in Kim, S.Y.H. (2010) *Evaluation of Capacity to Consent to Treatment and Research*, Oxford: Oxford University Press. For a strident critique of the rise of consent in medical ethics and law, see Foster, C. (2009) *Choosing Life, Choosing Death: The Tyranny of Autonomy in Medical Ethics*, Oxford: Hart.

Related topics

Ch.8 Valid consent
Ch.24 Informed consent
Ch.25 Consent and medical treatment

24
INFORMED CONSENT

Nir Eyal

24.1 The requirement, and the need to identify its grounds

Medicine has a more demanding approach to consent than most areas of practice.[1] Medical interventions in our bodies, and use of personal medical information, are conventionally thought to require not only our consent but our informed, voluntary, capacitated, and current consent—for short, informed consent.

As I understand the standard requirement of informed consent, it states, roughly, that when a sufficiently capacitated adult does not give sufficiently informed and voluntary consent to an intervention in her body or her private sphere, then, at least when the intervention is experimental or nontrivial, and absent severe jeopardy for third parties, the intervention is impermissible—even when it seeks to assist her, physicians recommend it, third parties would benefit from it, and the patient herself had repeatedly consented to it before expressing a change of mind (Eyal 2011).

Contemporary medical culture and central human rights documents support something like this requirement. In the US, federal funding for research usually requires institutional review of informed consent procedures (HHS 2009), and the constitutional right to privacy binds government to honor patients' refusal of care. Absence of informed consent can be used to establish negligence (and hence malpractice and torts), or battery and assault.

Informed consent matters in medicine, and not only for providers' legal cover and customer relations. It seems to matter morally, as intuitions on a real-life case may illustrate. Ongoing early-phase trials to identify a strategy for cure or sustained remission of HIV have great social value (Kuritzkes 2017), but many of them put fairly healthy study participants at great medical risk, with little hope of any medical improvement (Eyal 2017a). Ethicists are debating how much such studies can be justified (Eyal 2017b). Intuitively, the higher the quality of participants' consent to trial risks, the easier these trials are to justify. That a person volunteers to put her life and limb at risk in full understanding and voluntariness, say, for a cause that she sees as noble or because she hopes to gain from its pursuit in nonmedical and potentially idiosyncratic ways of which physicians might be oblivious helps somewhat to justify placing her at that risk, and it rarely undermines such a justification (Eyal 2017b). Perhaps attesting to that intuition, bioethicists have demanded especially high-quality informed consent in these trials (Henderson 2015), and study participants reportedly find it offensive that, notwithstanding their highly informed consent, regulators hesitate to permit patients to join these risky studies (Evans 2017).

Nevertheless, many philosophical questions remain about the standard requirement of informed consent. Some surround what precisely is meant by "informed", "voluntary", "capacitated", "consent", and other key terms in the definition (Eyal 2011). Take "informed". For most bioethicists, what enables autonomous authorization is the patient's comprehension, not the clinician's disclosure—so "informed" designates primarily *comprehending* (Beauchamp & Childress 2008; Manson & O'Neill 2007; Candilis & Lidz 2010). For such bioethicists, this is precisely why, when the patient is known to be a medical specialist who fully comprehends the intervention on offer even without disclosure, disclosure is unnecessary (Faden & Beauchamp 1986; Beauchamp 2010).

But there are also reasons to hold that comprehension is unnecessary, or insufficient, for meeting the "informed" part of the consent requirement. Concerning lack of necessity, some count consent as informed whenever investigators have provided full opportunity for autonomous authorization, and good disclosure can provide such opportunity even absent full comprehension, e.g. when the information is easy to comprehend and candidate participants' failure to comprehend it is their own fault alone (Sreenivasan 2003). A related position is that full information that is easy to comprehend is already *fair* toward candidate participants, so nothing additional is owed them by way of informing (Miller & Wertheimer 2010).

Nor is it clear that comprehension suffices for properly "informed" consent. Disclosure may turn out to matter independently. Disclosure may turn out to matter independently. Documented disclosure can facilitate accountability even when misunderstood, e.g. by making later complaints easier to file. And even when a person lacks full consent rights, such that full informed consent including monitoring for comprehension is unnecessary, disclosure may still show courtesy and remain valuable (Faden et al. 2013; Dickert et al. 2017).

Questions remain even regarding aspects of informed consent and its "informed" component, on which the bioethics literature is in general agreement. According to the literature, what the patient should be informed about is those aspects of the medical intervention with the greatest impact on her—primarily the risks and benefits of the relevant intervention and of any alternatives to it (see e.g. Beauchamp & Childress 2008). Couldn't bioethicists instead demand that she be informed regarding where such information could be easily gotten? Wouldn't that, along with information on where to file complaints and a rigorous review process, be enough to put her in charge and protect her against abuse?

To settle these and other questions about the scope, force, and detail of the requirement of informed consent, it seems inevitable to ask after its philosophical grounds. The nature of these grounds might tell for or against different answers to such questions. As we shall see, in different circumstances, the potential functions of informed consent are variably applicable and variably strong, and they dictate different specifications for the requirement.

At the same time, strong intuitions about the subjects of the requirement make some grounds more plausible than others. Plausible grounds must allow a combination of what we shall call *variability* and *continuity* in the requirement. First, they must allow some *variability* of force and detail because informed consent is intuitively more important in some areas than in others: in experiments, more than in clinical care; in risky or in transformative care, more than in benign care; in care that involves touching or moving body parts, especially intimate or internal ones, or peering into highly personal parts or information, more than care involving no perceived trespass.

The requirement's grounding must also allow for some *continuity* (or *constancy*, or *homogeneity*) as well, because the intuition is that the informed consent requirement does not become wholly inapplicable, or even very weak, with just any potentially relevant yet superficial change of circumstance. For example, despite a possible account according to which informed consent is necessary solely because patients who notice its violation may sue providers, the fact that a patient is fully anaesthetized such that some violations of her legal consent rights would pass unnoticed is usually *not* enough to remove informed consent requirements. We need an account of the grounds of informed consent that accounts both for this variability and this continuity. Both can function as partial constraints on acceptable accounts.

Let us assess then some potential philosophical grounds for informed consent in light of the constraints of variability and homogeneity. Which grounding best accommodates these constraints: protection, autonomy, trust, self-ownership, several grounds that I shall dub second-order, or a combination? A discussion will then suggest that, partly because a second-order account of the grounds for the informed consent requirement seems unavoidable for meeting these constraints, the status of the requirement is more elusive than it is usually taken to be.

24.2 Protection

John Stuart Mill opposed paternalistic coercion and manipulation for a person's own good, alleging partly that people know best and care the most about their personal good so paternalism is likelier to harm them than to benefit them (Mill 2003). Suspicion of exceedingly harmful research played a historic role in institutionalizing the requirement of informed consent. Is informed consent justified, then, to protect patients and study participants from harm?

The frequent need for such protections is surely part of what appeals about informed consent, but it cannot be everything. First, we stick by informed consent even when protections are not so necessary. Other regulations imposed following these historical abuses already protect study participants—too much per many bioethicists, patients, and scientists—and participants often lack the information or skills to protect themselves further effectively (their veto rights lose them opportunities to improve their medical prospects), yet everyone agrees that we should retain the requirement, at least in part. Intuitively, no matter how many additional protections are added in e.g. risky trials (e.g. how many additional layers of institutional review by fellow patients implementing a conservative risk–benefit ratio requirement), individual informed consent would remain important. Indeed, greater emphasis on participant decision making would have sometimes reduced protection. In risky HIV cure-related trials, it is currently patients who clamor to participate (and not only when that would rationally promote their nonmedical aims: Dubé et al. 2017), and clinicians, researchers, regulators, and institutional review boards who are trying to protect them from participation.

Likewise, in clinical care, practitioners already have incentives to succeed in helping patients, such as courting the good opinion of their peers (a key to many practitioners' career promotion). Most patients cannot reliably assess the quality of their medical services (Arrow 1963). Yet something by way of informed consent seems valuable, even when it enables patients to forego substantial opportunities for medically helpful interventions.

Consent requirements forbidding forced intrusions into patients' and study participants' bodies and intimate spheres are surely not just protections against harmful medical intrusions and against damaging revelations of personal details. They protect them against any forced medical intrusion, any violation of privacy, and any forced sexual advances. Their point seems broader than mere medical protection.

Similarly, forced single-kidney redistribution, from patients with two kidneys to those with none (Fabre 2008), is everywhere opposed as a gross violation of informed consent. But in health terms, the risk from a safely performed single kidney extraction is surprisingly low, and does not depend on whether the extraction is forced or a part of a voluntary kidney donation, which all agree is legitimate, so the ground cannot be solely protection of strict medical interests (Eyal 2009).

24.3 Autonomy

These gaps in the account from the need for protection undermine what we called homogeneity. Sometimes, any added protections from informed consent seem nil, yet informed consent remains necessary. Such gaps are usually cited so as to motivate a more fundamental account, in terms of personal autonomy. The freedom to choose on our own concerning central matters, to be the authors of our own lives, to be sovereigns over our bodies and fates, strikes many as a more solid ground for the requirement of informed consent (Faden & Beauchamp 1986; Beauchamp & Childress 2008).

A complete autonomy-based justification for the informed consent requirement would explain both why personal autonomy, under a plausible precisification, matters, at least in the health arena, and how honoring the informed consent requirement engages with this value correctly (Eyal 2011).

Critics of the account from autonomy complain that it is impossibly vague (Dworkin 1988; O'Neill 2003). Is autonomy the same thing as having many (valuable) options among which to choose? Relative paucity of desires that one wishes one lacked? Relatively strong personal power to form, pursue, and if necessary revise personal plans? Respect for one's "privacy rights" over one's body? Or is it something else still? Though frustrating, the slipperiness of bioethics writing on autonomy is no proof that all possible precisifications would founder as accounts of informed consent.

Other critiques of grounding informed consent in autonomy may cut deeper. First, when there are gaps in an entire medical community's medical knowledge, such that honest attempts at full disclosure remain false and misleading (Millum & Bromwich 2013), patients' capacity to make an intelligent decision in light of their personal values and commitments is arguably as suboptimal as when an abusive researcher deliberately lies to a candidate participant. Yet in the former case consent usually counts as fully "informed", or at least there is no legal or ethical transgression, whereas the latter is a clear violation of informed consent. Therefore, the requirement seems to rely on something other than or in addition to autonomous authorization.

Personal autonomy is often thought to refer to a certain form of governance over one's *actions*, more than e.g. over one's option set in general (Buss 2012). Paradigm violators of autonomy arise in brainwashing, addiction, and other factors standing between the person and her acts (Buss 2012). Ironically, the informed consent doctrine is most stringent in the area of medical research, which rarely implicates the consenter's *actions* at all. Study participants are often subjected to interventions in their bodies, with no special need for them to act in this or in that way. While, in some medical studies, participants' actions are the object of study (e.g. in studies of what improves medical adherence), the requirement of informed consent holds in full force in other studies (including many of the HIV cure-related studies mentioned), where what researchers are checking is a physiological process, not participants' actions. In that respect, and in others (Eyal 2011), the autonomy account fails the test of homogeneity.

It may also fail the test of variability. Done safely and without the victim's antecedent or posterior awareness, the nonconsensual harvest of a single kidney need not transform the victim's character, person, or life-plans, any more than a safe and secret nonconsensual skin biopsy. On central specifications of autonomy, the transgression of autonomy can be similar either way, and low. Intuitively, however, forced kidney extraction is a far worse transgression of informed consent (Eyal 2009)—a variability that appeal to the autonomous life might be unable to explain. Admittedly, forced kidney extraction would violate many people's strong desires to keep both their kidneys and not to lose any by force. In that sense, it would transgress their autonomous will. But failure to procure kidneys for transplantation would violate the potential kidney recipients' equally strong desires. That the former desires prevail seems to rest on a requirement for informed consent before kidney extraction. Therefore, such a requirement cannot itself rest on the comparable strength of desires. Likewise, in many areas of medicine, recently obtained advance directives are broadly assumed to respect autonomy enough for informed consent purposes. Intuitively, however, to impose participation in a risky HIV cure trial on a protesting patient because she had earlier autonomously consented to participate in it (and then had a change of mind) would transgress her consent rights. If, based on our culture around advance directives, such a patient has autonomously authorized the study, then respect for autonomous authorization fails to capture a certain variability in the standard informed consent requirement.

24.4 Trust

Several authors defend informed consent as a matter of preserving social trust in doctors and in the medical enterprise (Bok 1992, 1999; Tännsjö 1999; Jackson 2001; Kass et al. 1996; O'Neill 2002; Mastroianni 2008). In ideal form, this account may argue:

1 Social trust, especially trust in caretakers and medical institutions, is necessary so that, for example, people seek medical advice, comply with it, and participate in medical research.
2 Therefore, it is usually wrong to jeopardize that trust.
3 Coercion, deception, manipulation, and other violations of the standard informed consent requirement seriously jeopardize that trust.
4 Thus, the standard informed consent requirement is justified.

This account carries much appeal (Eyal 2014), but it also falls short of our continuity criterion. Violations of the standard informed consent requirement continue to be wrong even when clearly no one will discover them and so the public's trust is not at risk. Trust is not always a good thing, when doctors are unworthy of trust. There are other problems, too. For one thing, the trust of patients and research subjects would have been far less important if doctors could force citizens to undergo checkups and potential forced treatment or experiments—in violation of informed consent. Our moral repugnance at this prospect and our consequent reliance on patients and research participants to trust physicians and approach them voluntarily presuppose at least some parts of the requirement of informed consent, and cannot fully ground it (Eyal 2014).[2]

24.5 The mere means formula

Immanuel Kant's mere means formula enjoins us to use persons always as ends in themselves and never as mere means, e.g. to others' ends (Kant 2012 [1785]). This formula has often been presented as the reason why one should not force or manipulate people to serve as study participants. To do so, in violation of informed consent, is thought to treat them as mere means, or as "guinea pigs" (Jonas 1969; Donagan 1977; National Commission for the Protection of Human Subjects of Biomedical and Behavioral Research 1998).

But most contemporary interpretations of Kant understand him not as saying that, for justified intervention, actual (informed) consent is necessary, but as saying instead that, for justified intervention, the possibility of rational consent is necessary. A proposal can remain rational to consent to even when the person fails to consent to it (Wertheimer 2014).

The mere means formula's relevance to clinical care is especially questionable. Unlike experiments, clinical care is tasked to promote the patient's own interests, often including her interests in retaining her full moral powers and what Kant would call "humanity". Can a person really be used as a mere means and in contempt of her dignity when what is pursued are her own ends and continuous dignified "humanity", simply because she did not consent to this pursuit? Such challenges question the mere means formula's ability to meet the test of homogeneity.

24.6 Self-ownership

In some settings, we strongly condemn invasion into the private sphere. Often we do so even when the expected impact on the victim's health, welfare, and ability to exercise moral powers is small. We would find it difficult to approve of forced kidney redistribution even if the (already small) health risks and impact on capabilities and personal character were nil. Many would explain this by arguing that we own our bodies and internal parts and should retain the power to decide on their fates. For someone else to poke inside us and help herself to parts remains a breach, even if it is medically safe and we are oblivious to it. This rationale may better explain why we must normally grant our permission, even for medical intervention that is safe, low-impact, and clearly beneficial, and requires no choice or action on our parts. Trespass into a truly private sphere can be forbidden even when it involves only touching, and even if the owner would be either extremely foolish or extremely selfish to reject it (Archard 2008: 27f; Thomson 1990: ch. 8; Nozick 1986). Self-ownership may initially seem to provide an especially straightforward account of our privacy rights over intimate details about ourselves. Perfectly voluntary disclosure of intimate details is normally no transgression at all. What counts as a transgression of privacy is forced exposure (Fried 1968). And this may suggest self-ownership over that information—which informed consent ensures.

However, the self-ownership account cannot alone explain why interventions that are relatively risky usually require stronger justification than ones that are not. For instance, while any forced research may be wrong, forced *and* invasive (risky, transformative of body or character, taking place deep inside the body) research is arguably far worse than forced benign research. And the quality of informed consent required for invasive research is much higher. Nor does the self-ownership account explain wherefore the moral difference between consent standards in research and in clinical care, respectively. Either type of intrusion trespasses what intuition views as a privately owned sphere, to the same degree. In these ways, a purely self ownership account fails to capture the variability in the requirement of informed consent.[3]

Even as a single component of a larger account of informed consent that leaves it to other components to explain why some transgressions of informed consent are worse than others, self-ownership may fail. First, some transgressions of informed consent involve simply no transgression of self-ownership, just of deciding with full information or voluntariness. A risky study knowingly performed with consent but without adequate comprehension of risks is a case in point. Second, some have argued that self-ownership, far from grounding consent requirements, simply means that consent is required, and hence cannot substantiate these requirements (Cohen 1995).

24.7 Wertheimer's second-order account

So far, it seems fair to say that the purported justifications of the standard informed consent requirement work only in some cases. All or most admit of gaps. This is a serious problem. While the standard informed consent requirement might not always obtain, some gaps take place in areas where intuitively, and legally, the requirement does obtain. So what we called continuity is being frustrated. Where might the more consistent nature of the requirement of informed consent come from, then?

Alan Wertheimer argued that, while it would often be legitimate and potentially justifiable to coerce people to participate in research as a matter of first-order moral principles such as refrain from harm, respect for autonomy, and the mere means formula, there are good reasons to adopt a more general prohibition on coercive participation as a matter of what he called "second-order morality". By that he meant that "Given that the use of coercion would only rarely be justified, and given the choice between an unreliable mechanism for determining when coercion should be used and the adoption of a rule that prohibits its use, it might be preferable to draw a bright line around interventional biomedical research and simply bar the use of coercion" (Wertheimer 2014). While he did not state this explicitly, Wertheimer seems to have worried about this unreliability simply because of the medical risks and burdens that it may create (Eyal 2015). Using our terms, he might have said that, combined with first-order accounts, a particular second-order account that is focused on refrain from harm assures homogeneity.

Fair doubts arise about this second-order account. As mentioned already, sometimes ample protections are already in place, making any medical risk from consent violations small in a certain category of intervention research, yet, intuitively, we should preserve informed consent. That suggests additional grounds beyond refrain from harm, as either a first-order or second-order moral principle (Eyal 2015). Likewise, the requirement of informed consent can last, fairly immutable, across experimental interventions concerning which we have very different levels of advance knowledge. For example, we know much less in advance about the likely effects of an intervention on the first participant of a trial than on the last participant needed in order to reach statistical power in that trial. Yet the requirement of informed consent is equally applicable. The requirement therefore seems justified not (only) by our lack of full advance knowledge but by additional factors (Eyal 2015).

24.8 A dignitary-harm reduction second-order account

I wish to emphasize another type of second-order account (Eyal 2015). Incorrect as it may be (Eyal 2008), the perception that extreme coercion or manipulation in either clinical or experimental contexts necessarily disrespects autonomous dignified persons is both prevalent and persistent. We typically perceive e.g. highly intrusive coercive care and experiments as evincing utter disrespect toward the patient or the study participant, no matter what the doctor explains to convince us or them otherwise, potentially generating what one may call "dignitary" harms and risks—roughly, harms and risks whose causes or central components must be specified in terms like "dignity", "respect", "esteem", "stigma", and the like. For the patient or study participant, a painful sense of humiliation and potential damage to her subjective self-respect, mood, and willingness to pursue plans; for determinate populations chronically coerced or manipulated in care or in research in ways broadly perceived as disrespectful, a potential long-term negative effect on the respect and concern of third parties and a resulting potential for neglect, stigma, exclusion or discrimination; and, for a society where doctors impose intervention on all, potential decline in the beneficial culture of respect for autonomy. In brief, coercive or manipulative actions that jeopardize, touch, penetrate or alter our bodies without informed consent carry high risk of dignitary harm. No matter how much an individual investigator or clinician tries to convince other people that imposing such interventions can be perfectly respectful toward autonomous beings, it seems safe to predict that, in the foreseeable future, most people will continue to perceive such imposed interventions in the body as disrespectful, leading to dignitary harms. Interventions that are risky, experimental, or trespass into the body and highly personal information, especially if they e.g. concern solid parts like kidneys, not only soft or liquid ones like hair and plasma, are typically perceived as especially disrespectful absent informed consent (especially if the person actually refused them). That makes them (especially) prone to causing severe dignitary harm. Instituting a requirement of informed consent across interventional research and care (and not only in cases where first-order moral reasoning or Wertheimer's consideration justify it), with special strength in areas of severe dignitary risk, can help mitigate that dignitary harm.

In conjunction with the first grounds we reviewed above and Wertheimer's second-order factors, a second-order approach to dignitary-harm reduction may provide a much fuller account of the standard requirement of informed consent specifically. In order to reduce the potential dignitary harm of forced intervention in the body, many moral theories will tell investigators and clinicians to preserve and foster their natural tendencies to believe (falsely) that invasive (e.g. risky or inside the body) medical intervention on an autonomous adult, by always (grossly) violating her autonomy, is always (grossly) disrespectful of her. Once an investigator or clinician cultivates these inclinations, she will be inclined to follow the standard requirement of informed consent, out of respect for the ethos of autonomy and dignity that typically underlies that requirement, even on occasions that the balance of first-order factors is known to permit coercion, manipulation, and other transgressions of the standard requirement. She would do so out of genuine belief in the requirement, and condemn others who transgress it. Why should she preserve and cultivate this belief? Because, inaccurate as the belief may be, it would preempt behaviors that are widely perceived as disrespectful, thus preempting offence, humiliation, encouragement of stigma, and so forth.

It may seem as though cultivating such beliefs is unnecessary in order to minimize the dignitary harm that one causes. Isn't stopping oneself from actively violating informed consent enough? A clinician might explain, "I actually believe that there is nothing truly disrespectful about coercive intervention, which, after all, would benefit you medically and arguably protect your long-term wellbeing and autonomy on this occasion. But patients usually perceive coercive intervention as disrespectful. Therefore, to protect you from incorrectly feeling offended, I will not impose care" (Eyal 2015). But to say so would usually offend patients and study participants in its own right. It appears either condescending or neglectful, and could *exacerbate* dignitary harm.

What about hiding one's real motivation, then? A clinician might lie to patients about why she avoids coercive care, falsely citing their autonomy and dignity. But to say so while believing otherwise runs a big dignitary risk. Involuntary facial gestures, for instance, might betray the clinician's deceitful scheme, and most patients would feel doubly offended. Over the course of the many years in which such a deceitful scheme were enacted, clinicians would usually cause a lot of serious offense.

The simplest way to reduce dignitary harm over one's career is to cultivate or preserve a belief in common-sense narratives about autonomy, dignity, and the mere means formula. Inaccurate as these narratives may have been shown to be, they come naturally to most of us, and are trusted and expected by most. They would help reduce the dignitary harm we cause. To insist to reject such beliefs and instead deliberate, either openly or secretly, as a cold calculator about the pros and cons of violating informed consent in particular cases (and given different patients' very different levels of personal sensitivity) would exacerbate overall dignitary harm. It could offend and humiliate on many everyday occasions. A certain type of second-order moral consideration therefore tells doctors to maintain and cultivate belief in the requirement of informed consent and in its alleged foundation in autonomy and dignity.

If coercion and extreme manipulation did not *typically* cause more harm than good in medical and nonmedical first-order terms then admittedly this concern about dignitary harm would rarely suffice to justify cultivating that deep belief in informed consent. After all, dignitary harm is merely one type of evil, and the requirement of informed consent comes at a substantial moral cost. However, some of the first-order considerations above already make coercive medical interventions *typically* wrong. What dignitary harm does is to explain why common sense tells us to oppose coercion in many more cases, and rather homogenously. Once we cultivate the deep beliefs about autonomy, dignity, etc. that are *necessary* for curbing dignitary harm, these deep beliefs prompt us to follow a fairly homogenous requirement of informed consent somewhat regardless of the circumstances on particular occasions. It tells us to do so out of lasting deep beliefs and not only out of cold and opportunistic concern for minimizing medical harm if and when that factor is relevant.

This account is "second-order" in factoring in beliefs *about* first-order factors and *about* their relative importance. It involves norms *about* which first-order norms to cultivate belief in, follow, and respect. Part of what makes it second-order is these "meta" beliefs and norms. Unlike Wertheimer's account, which is essentially about uncertainty, this account accepts variability stemming from ontological differences, such as whether coercive interventions take place deep inside the body (Eyal 2009). Admittedly, this account depends on factual generalizations, such as about the tendency of low self-esteem or of stigma to harm people, the tendency of core violations of informed consent to be perceived as disrespectful, and the tendency of conduct widely perceived as disrespectful to undermine self-esteem and exacerbate stigma. But these empirical generalizations seem plausible.

24.9 Implications: the status of the requirement

Let us summarize the inquiry thus far. "First-order" accounts of the grounds for the standard informed consent requirement contain some truth. Nonetheless, they fail tests of variability and continuity. Alan Wertheimer proposed a fruitful alternative account of the requirement, in the context of informed consent to interventional research. I rooted for a further layer of justification, which is "second-order" in a different way than his, and that focuses on reduction of dignitary harm. It is the combination of these many first-order and second-order accounts of informed consent that comes closest to saving the standard requirement from remaining groundless.

What does all that imply for the status of the informed consent requirement? First, when informed consent is necessary, what kind of requirement does it constitute? Here, several questions are worth mentioning, so that others may explore them.

If indeed the requirement of informed consent requires some second-order grounding, can it contribute a first-order objective duty? Or must the requirement be about which decision rules to use given uncertainty and other reasons not to aim deliberately at meeting any objective informed consent duties? Is it, in other words, like the requirement "Do not drop stones from the roof of the skyscraper!" when its only justification is that you can never be quite sure that no people will pass by when the stone reaches the ground and that, if they are hit, then a first-order duty would be violated? If the informed consent requirement is only for certain decision procedures, some would argue further that it does not specify what would be wrong to do, but only who is blameworthy, or perhaps who should have earlier cultivated stronger inclination to honor these procedures.

It may seem as though the second-order rationale that focuses on dignitary-harm reduction is directly about moral rightness (not mere blameworthiness or rightness of earlier choices on what inclinations to cultivate). Kantian norms of respect for dignity pertain directly to moral rightness. However, note that the proposed account is ultimately nested not in dignity and autonomy but in reducing dignitary harm, a construct that can be central to consequentialist, "Sidgwickian" moralities just as easily. For Sidgwickian consequentialists, we should often engineer ourselves to follow, even internalize, moral rules that are wrong in a first-order sense. The justification of doing so is the rightness of following, trusting, and hence internalizing these rules, even if their content is incorrect (Sidgwick 1981; Hare 1981, 1984).

Another question about status is whether the informed consent requirement correlates to a natural right, to a legal right, or to something in the middle. Many bioethicists and human rights lawyers assume that informed consent is a natural right that generates a correlative moral requirement and, downstream, legal and institutional ramifications. But future research could explore whether some justifications for informed consent do not better support other statuses.

Consider a second-order variant on the account from trust. It points out that there is something particularly unappealing about associating one's body and intimate person with things that one perceives as highly unethical and offensive to oneself. Because the public expects informed consent (correctly or not), when the public perceives its absence, it is put off by what it perceives as immoral treatment, and may lose trust and stay away from clinics. In this vein, historical abuses by study investigators including violations of informed consent that were more widely perceived (in this case, correctly) as violating research ethics may have harmed trust in investigators and clinicians among US minorities, with woeful consequences for medical adherence (Corbie-Smith et al. 2002; Alsan & Wanamaker 2016). To protect against this risk, we—quite appropriately—institutionalize and internalize informed consent practices that are more sweeping than morality objectively requires. On this account, legal rights and institutional protections of informed consent are morally appropriate, but they do not assume a correlative natural right.

It is entirely possible that, even with all of these potential grounds combined, the standard requirement simply cannot be defended in full. Indeed, in US law, informed consent is not always necessary. Informed consent requirements for research admit of various waivers (HHS 2009), recently expanded (Department of Homeland Security et al. 2017; FDA 2017). And informed consent might be unnecessary even for many interventions in our bodies and health that are substantial and invasive. Consider three examples of (nonsuperficial!) factors that may make informed consent unnecessary. First, when the health of the public is at real risk, nonmedical exemptions from vaccination arguably do not amount to personal rights, notwithstanding the invasive nature of reaching into the body and imposing some risk through vaccination (Emhoff et al. 2016). It may be politically savvy to provide such exemptions, but not because of a right of ignorant vaccine skeptics to place others at risk. It may be preferable to force vaccination through external threats not physical compulsion, but it remains permissible to force vaccination somehow, in seeming violation of informed consent "requirements". Second, the need to obtain drug prescriptions in order to take certain medications may also violate the standard requirement as charted above, for actively intervening in how the patient interacts with other consenting adults to shape her body and health (Flanigan 2012), yet it is surely permissible (Eyal 2012). Third, informed consent can easily give way when the intervention is part of sovereign government policies in certain areas where government is perfectly authorized to govern, even absent individual consent. In particular, some bioethicists have argued plausibly that, when experimental interventions take place at the level of health systems, e.g. a clinic network or an entire town or nation, the express prospective consent of all individuals involved is often unnecessary (Faden et al. 2013). As an illustration, in 2016, the US Food and Drug Administration sought to test the release of previously tested genetically modified mosquitoes, to fight Zika and other infections on the island of Key Haven, Florida, where these infections were endemic. Opponents placed "no consent" signs on their front lawns, presumably to argue that for this experimental activity, which could affect any island resident, informed consent is necessary. But individual informed consent was eventually deemed unnecessary. A referendum was held and opponents lost (Langston 2016). Arguably, this was no transgression of basic human rights. Trials of alterations to entire health systems need not require individual informed consent (Faden et al. 2013), whether or not something else by way of consent (such as a referendum, or collective deliberation: Barker & Polcrack 2001) remained necssary.[4]

24.10 Conclusion

According to common-sense morality, the requirement of informed consent that prevails in medical settings is more demanding than many consent requirements outside of medicine. Whether or not the informed consent requirement can be justified, and which concrete form of it is most justified, depends on its grounds. I reviewed some of the main controversies regarding the potential grounds of the informed consent requirement, applying new criteria that I called "variability" and "homogeneity" to that critical review, and argued that a dignitary-harm based "second-order" ground plays a central part in a full justification. This, however, makes the status of the requirement more complex and tenuous than usually assumed. Future research should therefore identify what can and what cannot be saved in the standard requirement of informed consent e.g. from worries about groundlessness, even on a combination of the most plausible grounds for that requirement.

Notes

1 Thanks to Joe Mazor and Lisa Holtzman for useful comments. Work on this chapter was funded by NIAID AI114617-01A1 and Wellcome 208766/Z/17/Z.
2 Another trust account is backward-looking. It grounds consent rights in doctors' duties to remain faithful fiduciaries to their patients. For exposition and critical discussion, see Eyal (2014).
3 For additional responses to the self-ownership account, see Archard (2008), Eyal (2011).
4 Some other questions prompted by the informed consent requirement's complex combination of first- and second-order grounds pertain to the requirement's detailed content. For instance, under what circumstances does informed consent permit substituting express, specific, prospective consent with retrospective permissions, advance directives, defeasible default rules, nonspecific consent, and proxy consent by a surrogate?

References

Alsan, M. and M. Wanamaker (2016) "Tuskegee and the Health of Black Men," *NBER Working Paper, no. 22323.*

Archard, D. (2008) "Informed Consent: Autonomy and Self-Ownership," *Journal of Applied Philosophy* 25: 19–34.

Arrow, K.J. (1963) "Uncertainty and the Welfare Economics of Medical Care," *The American Economic Review* LIII: 941–73.

Barker, J.H. and L. Polcrack (2001) "Respect for Persons, Informed Consent and the Assessment of Infectious Disease Risks in Xenotransplantation," *Medicine, Health Care and Philosophy* 4: 53–70.

Beauchamp, T.L. (2010) "Autonomy and Consent," in F.G. Miller and A. Wertheimer (ed.), *The Ethics of Consent.* New York: Oxford University Press, 55–78.

Beauchamp, T.L. and J.F. Childress (2008) *Principles of Biomedical Ethics.* Oxford: Oxford University Press.

Bok, S. (1992) "Informed Consent in Tests of Patient Reliability," *JAMA* 267: 1118–19.

Bok, S. (1999) *Lying: Moral Choice in Public and Private Life.* New York: Vintage.

Buss, S. (2012) "Autonomous Action: Self-Determination in the Passive Mode," *Ethics* 122: 647–91.

Candilis, P.J. and C.W. Lidz (2010) "Advances in Informed Consent Research," in F.G. Miller and A. Wertheimer (ed.), *The Ethics of Consent: Theory and Practice*. New York: Oxford University Press, 329–46.

Cohen, G.A. (1995) *Self-Ownership, Freedom, and Equality*. Cambridge: Cambridge University Press.

Corbie-Smith, G., S.B. Thomas and D.M. St George (2002) "Distrust, Race, and Research," *Archives of Internal Medicine* 162: 2458–63.

Department of Homeland Security, Department of Agriculture, et al. (2017) "Final Rule: Federal Policy for the Protection of Human Subjects," *Federal Register* 82: 7149–274.

Dickert, N., N. Eyal, S.F. Goldkind, et al. (2017) "Re-Framing Consent for Clinical Research: A Function-Based Approach," *American Journal of Bioethics* 17: 3–11.

Donagan, A. (1977) "Informed Consent in Therapy and Experimentation," *Journal of Medicine and Philosophy* 2: 307–29.

Dubé, K., D. Evans, L. Sylla, J. Taylor, B.J. Weiner, A. Skinner, H. Thirumurthy, J.D. Tucker, S. Rennie and S.B. Greene (2017) "Willingness to Participate and Take Risks in HIV Cure Research: Survey Results from 400 People Living with HIV in the US," *Journal of Virus Eradication* 3: 40–50 e21.

Dworkin, G. (1988) *The Theory and Practice of Autonomy*. Cambridge: Cambridge University Press.

Emhoff, I.A., E. Fugate and N. Eyal (2016) "Is There a Moral Right to Nonmedical Vaccine Exemption?" *American Journal of Law and Medicine* 42: 598–620.

Evans, D. (2017) "An Activist's Argument That Participant Values Should Guide Risk Equations in HIV Cure Research," *Journal of Medical Ethics* 43: 100–3.

Eyal, N. (2008) Utilitarianism and Coercion. *Notizie di Politeia* 90: 108–23.

Eyal, N. (2009) "'Is the Body Special?'" Review Article of Cécile Fabre, *Whose Body Is it Anyway? Utilitas* 21: 233–45.

Eyal, N. (2011) "Informed Consent," in E.N. Zalta (ed.), *Stanford Encyclopedia of Philosophy*. Fall 2011 ed.

Eyal, N. (2012) "Reconciling Informed Consent with Prescription Drug Requirements," *Journal of Medical Ethics* 38: 589–91.

Eyal, N. (2014) "Using Informed Consent to Save Trust," *Journal of Medical Ethics* 40: 437–44.

Eyal, N. (2015) "Informed Consent to Participation in Interventional Studies: Second-Order in a Different Sense," *Journal of Law and the Biosciences* 2: 1–6.

Eyal, N. (2017a) "The Benefit/Risk Ratio Challenge in Clinical Research, and the Case of HIV Cure: an Introduction," *Journal of Medical Ethics* 43: 65–6.

Eyal, N. (2017b) "How to Keep High-Risk Studies Ethical: Classifying Candidate Solutions," *Journal of Medical Ethics* 43: 74–7.

Fabre, C. (2008) *Whose Body Is it Anyway? Justice and the Integrity of the Person*. Oxford: Oxford University Press.

Faden, R.R. and T.L. Beauchamp (1986) *A History and Theory of Informed Consent*. New York: Oxford University Press.

Faden, R.R., N.E. Kass, S.N. Goodman, P. Pronovost, S. Tunis and T.L. Beauchamp (2013) "An Ethics Framework for a Learning Health Care System: A Departure from Traditional Research Ethics and Clinical Ethics," *Hastings Center Report* 43: 16–27.

FDA (2017) *IRB Waiver or Alteration of Informed Consent for Clinical Investigations Involving No More than Minimal Risk to Human Subjects*. Maryland: FDA.

Flanigan, J. (2012) "Three Arguments Against Prescription Requirements," *Journal of Medical Ethics* 38: 579–86.

Fried, C. (1968) "Privacy," *Yale Law Journal* 77: 475–93.

Hare, R.M. (1981) *Moral Thinking*. Oxford: Oxford University Press.

Hare, R.M. (1984) "Rights, Utility and Universalization: Reply to J.L. Mackey," in R.G. Frey (ed.), *Utility and Rights*. Minneapolis: University of Minnesota Press, 106–20.

Henderson, G.E. (2015) "The Ethics of HIV 'Cure' Research: What Can We Learn from Consent Forms?" *AIDS Research Human Retroviruses* 31: 56–63.

HHS (2009) 45 CFR 46 (Human subjects research). USA.

Jackson, J. (2001) *Truth, Trust and Medicine*. London and New York: Routledge.

Jonas, H. (1969) "Philosophical Reflections on Experimenting with Human Subjects," *Daedalus* 98: 219–47.

Kant, I. (2012 [1785]) *Groundwork of the Metaphysics of Morals*. Cambridge: Cambridge University Press.

Kass, N.E., J. Sugarman, R. Faden and M. Schoch-Spana (1996) "Trust, The Fragile Foundation of Contemporary Biomedical Research," *The Hastings Center Report* 26: 25–9.

Kuritzkes, D.R. (2017) "Why Cure, Why Now?" *Journal of Medical Ethics* 43: 67–70.
Langston, E. (2016) "Voters in This Florida County Just Approved GM Mosquitoes to Fight Zika," *Mother Jones*, November 9.
Manson, N.C. and O. O'Neill (2007) *Rethinking Informed Consent in Bioethics*. Cambridge: Cambridge University Press.
Mastroianni, A.C. (2008) "Sustaining Public Trust: Falling Short in the Protection of Human Research Participants," *Hastings Center Report* 38: 8–9.
Mill, J.S. (2003) "On Liberty," in M. Warnock (ed.), *Utilitarianism and On Liberty*. Second Edition. Walden, MA: Wiley-Blackwell, 88–180.
Millum, J.R. and D. Bromwich (2013) "Disclosure and Consent to Medical Research Participation," *Journal of Moral Philosophy* 10: 195–219.
National Commission (1998) *The Belmont Report* [Online]. www.fda.gov/oc/ohrt/IRBS/belmont.html
Nozick, R. (1986) *Anarchy, State, and Utopia*. Oxford: Oxford University Press.
O'Neill, O. (2002) *Autonomy and Trust in Bioethics*. Cambridge: Cambridge University Press.
O'Neill, O. (2003) "Autonomy: The Emperor's New Clothes," *Aristotelian Society Supplementary Volume* 77: 1–21.
Sidgwick, H. (1981) *The Methods of Ethics*. London: Macmillan, 1907; repr. Indianapolis, Hackett.
Sreenivasan, G. (2003) "Does Informed Consent to Research Require Comprehension?" *Lancet* 362: 2016–18.
Tännsjö, T. (1999) *Coercive Care*. London: Routledge.
Thomson, J.J. (1990) *The Realm of Rights*. Cambridge, MA: Harvard University Press.
Wertheimer, A. (2014) "(Why) Should We Require Consent to Participation in Research?" *Journal of Law and the Biosciences* 1: 137–82.

Further reading

Dworkin, G. (1988) *The Theory and Practice of Autonomy*. Cambridge: Cambridge University Press. (A classical exploration of consent in bioethics.)
Manson, N.C. and O. O'Neill (2007) *Rethinking Informed Consent in Bioethics*. Cambridge: Cambridge University Press. (A somewhat revisionary approach to informed consent.)
Miller, F.G. and A. Wertheimer (ed.) (2010) *The Ethics of Consent*. New York: Oxford University Press. (An excellent recent edited volume.)

Related topics

Ch.8 Valid consent
Ch.12 Consent and autonomy
Ch.25 Consent and medical treatment
Ch.26 Consent in clinical research

25
CONSENT AND MEDICAL TREATMENT

Johann S. Ach

25.1 Introduction

The doctrine of informed consent has been anchored in countless legal and institutional rules since the 1970s, and has since been one of the most widely discussed subjects in biomedical ethics and medical law. It is generally accepted that medical research involving (competent) human subjects is permissible only on the condition that the research subjects have freely consented to participate (cf. O'Neil, this volume, Chapter 26). The same holds true for medical treatment, dealt with in the following: there is hardly any dissent that medical interventions such as diagnostic or therapeutic measures require the informed consent of (competent) patients. If consent is not available, the intervention usually is considered morally and legally inadmissible. This is the case even in situations where the intervention is comparatively harmless and not very risky, and the physician does it for respectable motives and in the best interest of the patient. The consent of a patient may not normally be waived even if omitting the intervention is, to the best knowledge of the attending physician, to a considerable extent detrimental to the patient's health and well-being or might even lead to his death. Following the doctrine of informed consent, in other words, is regarded as mandatory – although adherence to the doctrine may be cumbersome and time-consuming on the part of the physician and may cause considerable harm on the part of the patient.

From the physician's point of view, the requirement of informed consent appears as the *obligation* to properly educate patients on a planned intervention and to obtain their consent to the action; from the perspective of the patient, on the other hand, the informed consent appears as the *right* to medical information and as a right to decide for herself upon the admission and type of medical treatment (Berg et al. 2001: 14).

In what follows I will first give a short outline of what I take to be the conventional understanding of the doctrine of informed consent and its core elements. Subsequently, I will focus on the disclosure element of the doctrine. I will show that both scope and content of the physician's obligation to disclose information about a proposed medical treatment to the patient depend upon the kind of justification that is given for the informed consent rule as a whole. In the concluding part, I will outline an argument that is meant to justify the conventional understanding of the disclosure obligation in medical contexts.

25.2 The doctrine of informed consent

25.2.1 Background

The emergence of the doctrine of informed consent has its roots in legal and philosophical, rather than medical, debate and can only be understood adequately against the background of medical and social developments in the second half of the 20th century (cf. Jonsen 1998; O'Shea, this volume, Chapter 23).

Medicine and the health system underwent significant changes in the second half of the 20th century, and this had profound effects on medical ethics as well: on the one hand, as a result of new technological possibilities for interventions (artificial respiration, organ transplantation, gene diagnostics), the problems that could be treated medically increased massively in both their number and their complexity, which raised new ethical questions and put a great deal of pressure on traditional values. On the other hand, the character of the health system changed fundamentally in the direction of specialization, fragmentation and, as a consequence, anonymization (Pellegrino 1993; Rothman 1991).

Moreover, reports on human experiments carried out in the United States until far into the 1970s (in particular, the *Tuskegee Syphilis Study*), where basic principles of research ethics had been blatantly violated and the rules laid down in the *Nuremberg Code* had been more or less completely ignored, had clearly shown that professional self-control in medicine had failed. As a result, medical research as well as clinical medicine increasingly attracted public attention and were pushed into the arena of public discourse.

Finally, the then-changing cultural climate of the United States played an important role in the emergence of modern medical ethics in the late 1960s and early 1970s – and thus also for the doctrine of the informed consent. Among other things, the American civil rights movement not only put the idea of democratic political participation on the agenda, it also led to an increase in public awareness of the discrimination against minorities.

Against this background, numerous authors consider the doctrine of informed consent to be one of the central characteristics of modern medical ethics.

25.2.2 Core elements

The doctrine of informed consent establishes that (ethically and legally) admissible medical interventions require both disclosure of information to the patient and the patient's consent to a proposed treatment. According to the usual ethical and legal understanding, the following core elements belong to the doctrine of the informed consent:

Decision-making competence: In order to be able to give an informed consent to a proposed medical treatment a patient has to have decisional capacity in regard to the decision at hand. Decision-making competence is frequently spelled out as a set of different abilities, such as the abilities to understand and process information, to relate situations and the consequences of actions to one's own convictions, desires and values, and the ability to communicate decisions and realize them effectively (cf. Buchanan & Brock 1990; Charland 2011; Grisso & Appelbaum 1998). Accordingly, a physician's assessment of competence assumes a *gate-keeping function*: the result of this assessment determines whether an informed consent must be obtained from a patient prior to starting the treatment.

This is usually consistent with the practice of *presumption of competency*, according to which the physician normally assumes the patient's capacity to consent, and questions it only in cases where the patient either belongs to a group whose competence is often questionable, or if there is reason for doubt in a different respect (Buchanan & Brock 1990: 21).

It is controversial whether the adequate standard for assessing a patient's decision-making competence is a fixed or a variable one. According to the *fixed threshold conception of competence*, decision-making competence depends solely on whether the patient possesses certain competencies such as those mentioned above. According to this view, the specific content of the decision in question is irrelevant for the physician's determination of the patient's decision-making competence. This, however, does not rule out the possibility that particularly risky or complex decision-making situations might call for special diligence of the physician in the assessment of competences (see also Feinberg 1986: 113ff). According to the *variable-standard conception of competence*, decision-making competence is a *relational property*: "The greater the risk relative to other alternatives – where risk is a function of the severity of the expected harm and the probability of its occurrence – the greater the level of communication, understanding, and reasoning skills required for competence to make that decision"(Buchanan & Brock 1990: 55).

Disclosure: The doctrine of informed consent requires the physician to provide the patient with sufficient information on the scope and importance of a proposed intervention. This means that the patient is at least informed about the diagnosis for which an intervention is being proposed, about the proposed action and the significant opportunities and risks associated therewith, and about the likely consequences of abstaining from the intervention and possible alternative courses of action (and the significant opportunities and risks associated with them). The information communicated during the disclosure must, as a rule, be specific; a general disclosure, which is not aimed at the concrete intervention, is, for the most part, not regarded as sufficient for the doctrine of informed consent.

Understanding: The claim that a patient approves to a proposed measure usually presupposes that she has grasped the information communicated during the disclosure and comprehends what has to be decided upon. The doctrine of informed consent obliges the physician to ensure that this is the case. In addition to the facts relevant to the content of the decision, the patient must, among other things, also understand that her act of consenting authorizes the physician to carry out the proposed intervention (Faden & Beauchamp 1986: 300ff.). In this context, Faden and Beauchamp have made it clear that an adequate understanding on the part of the patient often cannot be achieved by merely informing the patient, but only in a joint conversation (Faden & Beauchamp 1986: 314).[1]

Voluntariness: The doctrine of informed consent requires the physician to make sure that the patient arrives at her decision voluntarily – that is, sufficiently free from controlling influences by others (cf. Gutmann, this volume, Chapter 19).

Consent: Finally, the informed consent doctrine requires the physician to obtain the (usually) explicit consent of the patient to a proposed intervention. By consenting the patient gives the physician permission to carry out a proposed action. According to the usual understanding, only the act of consent turns the (otherwise prohibited) intervention into a (morally and legally) permitted action. This act of consent usually has to be adequately expressed and documented, for example, in written form.

25.2.3 Exceptions to informed consent

The literature discusses a number of situations in which exceptions to informed consent should be morally and legally justifiable or appropriate (Berg et al. 2001: 75ff.; Meisel 1979; Wear 1998: 20ff.).

Many agree that a patient's education and consent can be dispensed with in emergencies where there is a significant risk to the health or life of a patient if the intervention is not carried out directly (*emergency exception*). In the opinion of some, a waiver of disclosure (and thus a departure from the informed consent rule) is also permissible if the patient expressly renounces the information owed to her (*waiver exception*). Others argue that disclosure can be dispensed with if it can be assumed that the information to be communicated is generally known (*common knowledge exception*). The most controversially discussed exception to the informed consent rule even allows a deviation from the rule if disclosure would seriously harm the patient according to the physician's opinion (*therapeutic privilege exception*).

25.3 Justificatory approaches and the disclosure requirement

As early as 1979, Robert M. Veatch distinguished and discussed three different justifications for the informed consent rule, with a view to research contexts (Veatch 1979). These approaches still play a prominent role in the present discussion on informed consent. Veatch called them the *Patient Benefit Theory of Informed Consent*, the *Social Benefit Theory of Informed Consent*, and the *Self-Determination Theory of Informed Consent*.[2] In what follows I will briefly discuss these theories in turn. In the course of this discussion I will show that, and how, the scope and the content of the obligation to disclose information about a proposed medical treatment to the patient depend upon the kind of justification given for the informed consent rule.

25.3.1 The patient benefit theory of informed consent

According to the medical ethos, preventing harm to patients and fostering their well-being is the foremost task of physicians. The focus here is on the question of what the physician should or should not do to the (health-related) benefit of the patient, what attitudes a physician should exhibit towards patients, and what virtues should be guiding her. This is also expressed in the so-called *Hippocratic Oath*, at the center of which lies the obligation of the *primum nil nocere*, which is decisive for the medical ethos up to the present day.

Even if the requirements set out in the doctrine of informed consent are not part of the Hippocratic tradition, a number of authors nevertheless believe it is possible to justify the doctrine with reference to the benefit of patients. Robert Veatch, for example, writes: "Indeed, if we recognize that judgment about what is beneficial to a particular patient will vary from patient to patient depending upon the particular norms and values of that patient, a strong case can be made that informing patients of treatment alternatives so that they can participate in or even control the decision-making process will increase the likelihood that patient-benefits will be maximized"(Veatch 1979: 26–8).[3]

There are several reasons for thinking that informed consent is a suitable instrument for preventing harm to patients or for promoting their benefit or their well-being (see the considerations in Wear 1998: 66ff.). In particular, two arguments are relevant here: first, there is what we might call the interest and authority argument, which is already found in Mill. Each of us, as Mill claims, has a special interest in his happiness and well-being. Compared with this the interest that others take in us is, under normal circumstances, rather low. Moreover, as Mill adds, individuals are in a privileged epistemic position: they usually know best what is good for them. At the very least, it is not clear why others, including physicians, should *in principle* be in a better position to determine what is in one's best interest.

Second, numerous empirical studies as well as clinical experience have shown that the active participation of patients in the therapeutic process not only has a beneficial effect on the physician–patient relationship and communication, but can also promote therapeutic success. The communication between the physician and the patient taking place during the informed consent procedure has multiple beneficial effects: it enables patients to better cope with their situation, it can lead to a reduction in anxiety and a reduction in pain perception, and ultimately also results in patients being more likely to accept a proposed medical intervention. In a nutshell: the doctrine of informed consent promotes trust, understanding, and acceptance on the part of patients, which is indispensable for their compliance and thus also for the success of the therapy.

Nevertheless, the *Patient Benefit Theory of Informed Consent* is inadequate. This becomes visible in situations where a physician believes compliance with the informed consent rule to be detrimental to the welfare of a patient. This may be the case, for example, if the physician believes that the explanation of her health state or the prospects for her possible treatment might unsettle the patient or unnecessarily frighten her, or hold her back from consenting to a proposed medical treatment. In cases like this the *therapeutic privilege exception*, even framed narrowly, opens the floodgates for all kinds of paternalistically motivated interventions. In fact, the *therapeutic privilege exception* would cease really being an exception.

The *Patient Benefit Theory of Informed Consent* can, therefore, make it plausible why in many, perhaps even most, clinical situations, there is an obligation of disclosure on the part of the physician. Understood as a rule which should ensure or promote the benefit of patients, however, it can neither ground nor justify a (largely) exceptionless obligation to disclosure, nor a patient's right to be informed adequately.

25.3.2 Social benefit theory of informed consent

The *Social Benefit Theory of Informed Consent* justifies the informed consent rule with reference to its social benefit. This benefit can, for example, consist in ensuring or even promoting patients' trust, which is necessary for a functioning health care system. This trust would be violated where patients are being treated under the influence of manipulation, coercion or fraud in a way that they do not want. The informed consent rule thus can be justified as a *safeguard* against these and similar behaviors and situations (Eyal 2012).

The argument of social utility, as well as the argument of patient benefit, is essentially a consequentialist argument. Torbjörn Tännsjö introduced a decidedly utilitarian version of the argument:[4] "My argument is based on hedonistic utilitarianism. [. . .] The thrust of the argument is as follows: In many cases, we should allow people to refuse treatment for the simple reason that they presumably know best what is in their interest. [. . .] But even in cases where they are mistaken, it is crucial that they are treated in the manner they want. Otherwise they will not seek medical advice when they need it, and they must have fear that they will be treated in a manner they dislike, should they end up in certain situations. This means that their right to informed consent should be granted, even at some cost in the individual case (where they are not taken best care of). This is so because if they – we – could not in this way trust the medical system, the price would be even higher"(Tännsjö 2014: 445). Hence, according to Tännsjö, there are good utilitarian reasons for adherence to the informed consent rule insofar as general acceptance of the rule promotes social benefit: "My hypothesis is that, if the principle is honored, we will have a *better* system of health care and social services than if the principle is flouted" (Tännsjö 1999: 20).

It has been objected that utilitarian arguments for the informed consent rule (as well as consequentialist arguments in general) are inadequate due to their dependence on empirical assumptions and thus cannot provide a free-standing justification (for example Levine 2003: 1281). In fact, Tännsjö's argument in favor of the informed consent rule only succeeds if it can be shown or at least made plausible that complying with the rule actually holds the benefits expected of it and that there are no instruments better suited for reaching the goal than the – demanding and time-consuming – adherence to the rule.

More serious is the objection that the argument from social benefit proves inadequate because it has counter-intuitive consequences. According to Eyal it is intuitively problematic "to sacrifice a currently needy person for the sake of future benefits to others. But that is what an argument from trust-promotion alone tells us to do" (Eyal 2012: 7). Eyal's example, which is intended to make the objection plausible, is a patient who is urgently dependent on a certain medical treatment but rejects it for ill-considered reasons. Physicians who follow the argument from social benefit will nevertheless respect these wishes of the patient and thus refrain from a medical treatment which they consider to be in the best interests of the patient – in order to maintain the trust of future patients in the health system and thus to safeguard the well-being of future patients. What is intuitively problematic with the argument for *social benefit*, hence, is not so much that the patient in Eyal's example is being treated according to her (ill-considered) wishes instead of treating her according to her best interest. The problem rather seems to be that the failure to perform the treatment is not based on anti-paternalistic reasons, but solely serves to promote the general benefit. Even if the argument from social benefit, as Tännsjö thinks, is based on the current practice of the informed consent rule, this would somehow be due to the wrong reasons: i.e. for reasons which have nothing to do with either the duty of the attending physician towards an individual patient, or with some right of an individual patient to make a well-informed decision about her treatment.

Whether the argument from social benefit is suitable to justify the doctrine of the informed consent, however, is questionable anyway. This is because the argument, at least in the form that Tännsjö gives it, cannot explain why physicians should be obliged to adequately inform patients about a planned medical treatment. If the function of the informed consent rule is essentially to protect patients from manipulation, coercion or fraud, then the physician's obligation to disclose information seems to be initially limited to not exerting controlling influence on patients. In any case, the *safeguard* function of the informed consent rule seems to be met sufficiently well if the physician does not lead the patient to a certain decision which she would otherwise not have made, or to accepting a certain treatment which she would otherwise not have chosen. Omitted, erroneous, or negligent information by the physician may therefore be disadvantageous to the patient, by depriving her of the benefit which would otherwise have accrued to her from an appropriate explanation. But it does not constitute an inadmissible *interference* in the patient's decision.[5]

Thus, if the *Social Benefit Theory of Informed Consent* is to provide an adequate justification for the informed consent rule, a further argument would be necessary, which goes beyond the safeguard argument, and which makes it plausible that, and why, medical disclosure is a suitable tool for the promotion of the welfare of patients and a better health care system. Moreover, it would also be necessary to show that and why both duties – on the one hand, the duty to promote the well-being of the patient through adequate disclosure and, on the other hand, the duty to respect her decisions irrespective of the reasons for which the decision was taken – are compatible with one another.

25.3.3 Self-determination theory of informed consent

A third theory of justification for the informed consent rule focuses on respect for the self-determination of patients. Already in the *Belmont Report*, the doctrine of informed consent had been anchored in the principle of respect for the autonomy of patients (Beauchamp and Faden 2003: 1276). At least since the mid 1970s, the principle of respect for the autonomous decisions of patients has become the "primary justification [. . .] for requirements of informed consent" (Beauchamp & Childress 2013: 121). In this perspective, the informed consent rule can be understood as essentially a "practical application of respect for the patient's autonomy" (Jonsen et al. 2010: 51).

Ruth Faden and Tom L. Beauchamp have systematically worked out the proposal to found informed consent on the principle of respect for the autonomy of patients in their influential book *A History and Theory of Informed Consent* (1986). There, Faden and Beauchamp analyze informed consent as "autonomous authorization", i.e. as the action of a decision-competent patient who authorizes the physician to perform a certain medical intervention. According to Faden and Beauchamp, an informed consent occurs when "a patient or subject with (1) substantial understanding and (2) in substantial absence of control by others (3) intentionally (4) authorizes a professional" (Faden & Beauchamp 1986: 278). Informed consent is, from this perspective, a particular type of autonomous action: it differs from other autonomous actions which must also satisfy conditions (1) to (3) by the authorization condition (4).

Consequently, the disclosure to which a physician is obliged under the usual understanding of the doctrine of informed consent is neither a sufficient nor a necessary condition for informed consent according to Faden and Beauchamp: "There is nothing about the nature of an informed consent per se that requires disclosure as a necessary condition, and certainly nothing that would *orient* its *meaning* around disclosure" (Faden & Beauchamp 1986: 276). On the one hand, disclosure by the physician, even if carried out *lege artis*, cannot guarantee that a patient's consent constitutes an autonomous authorization; on the other hand, a physician's refrainment from disclosure does not rule out the possibility of autonomous authorization on the part of a patient.

This is not to say that disclosure would be waivable in every case. However, if one follows this line of reasoning, the question of whether or not disclosure is necessary at all, and what kind and amount of information has to be disclosed, is determined by the patient's ability to make an autonomous decision and thus by the "specific informational needs of the individual patient" (Faden & Beauchamp 1986: 306). The sole function of disclosure consists in putting the patient in a position to make a self-determined decision. Thus, in the strict sense of the term, "medical disclosure" is disclosure that enables self-determination. This requires that the patient understands the decision-problem sufficiently well and has the information which is material for her decision.

In the literature, three different standards of disclosure are discussed (Beauchamp & Childress 2013: 125ff; Berg et al. 2001: 46ff; Faden & Beauchamp 1986: 30ff): according to the *professional practice standard*, the kind and amount of information to be disclosed is determined by the expertise and the practices of the professional community. The *reasonable person standard*, on the other hand, is oriented on what information a (hypothetical) reasonable person would consider relevant in regard to a decision. Finally, the *subjective standard* demands disclosure of information which the person concerned, i.e. the patient, regards as relevant for her decision.

Faden and Beauchamp hold that a subjective standard of disclosure is preferable to its alternatives. From the perspective of the principle of autonomy, it is decisive that the individual patient retains normative authority regarding a medical treatment. For this, it is essential that the patient's consent to a proposed medical treatment be an informed decision made in a situation of sufficient absence of external controlling influences. Against this background, Faden and Beauchamp argue that the material aspects of an action are those aspects which the patient herself considers to be material in light of her convictions, desires and evaluations. The mere fact that the patient considers these aspects material for her decision is what *makes* them material (Faden & Beauchamp 1986: 304). Those aspects of the action a patient views as material for her decision thus need not in any way be causally or "objectively" relevant. "Subjective, personal assessment rather than causal outcome is the appropriate criterion of materiality" (Faden & Beauchamp 1986: 304).

If disclosure is understood as disclosure for self-determination, the physician has to provide the information that the patient considers material for her decision in light of her convictions, desires and evaluations. Disclosure so understood can, but obviously does not have to, provide the kind of information that is usually required by the doctrine of informed consent. To give an example: usually a physician following the doctrine of informed consent must inform her patient about possible alternatives to the proposed therapeutic intervention. This would, however, not be necessary for disclosure for self-determination if the patient was not in the least interested in those alternatives. On the other hand, information regarding a surgeon's sexual orientation could be necessary for disclosure for self-determination in case this information was material for a (homophobic) patient. However, no obligation of such disclosure can be found in the doctrine of informed consent as it is usually understood.

Can the obligation of disclosure as formulated in the doctrine of informed consent nevertheless be justified by recourse to the principle of autonomy? In their *Principles of Biomedical Ethics* Beauchamp and Childress explicitly emphasize that the principle of respect for autonomy not only justifies a physician's negative obligation to abstain from subjecting the patient's decision to controlling constraints, but also the positive obligation to foster the patient's autonomous decision-making (Beauchamp & Childress 2013: 107). This is of some importance as a failure to disclose information as well as (unintentionally) incorrect or negligent disclosure would be fully compatible with the physician's (negative) obligation to *non-interference* (for more details, cf. Taylor 2009: 130ff). It is only the physician's *positive* obligation to foster autonomous decision-making of patients that obliges the physician to offer disclosure and – when the offer is accepted – to inform patients with due diligence.

However, it is often difficult and sometimes impossible for the physician to determine what aspects of a medical treatment are material for the individual patient. As suggested by Faden and Beauchamp, a disclosure *conversation* can be helpful in such cases. In this sense, the obligation of disclosure often does not only require the physician to (one-directionally) provide the patient with information on facts and circumstances. Rather, it requires the physician to create a communicative situation in which the patient can figure out her desires, convictions and values. Part of this can include the physician giving the patient certain information at the patient's request and encouraging the patient to ask questions. Whether or not the patient would like to take advantage of this of course remains the patient's own decision. The obligation of disclosure thus essentially comes down to an *offer* for disclosure and conversation.

According to the theory of *self-determination* a sufficiently well-informed patient may autonomously consent to a medical intervention although she has not been adequately informed according to the standards of the doctrine of informed consent. For the same reason dissent between physician and patient on what is material in regard to a certain decision does not exclude autonomous authorization on the part of the patient. At times, however, according to Faden and Beauchamp, this discrepancy can even go so far as to call into question whether physician and patient are really talking about the same matter: "Sometimes the set of propositions a person views as material to his or her decision to authorize R is not sufficiently comprehensive to ensure that the 'R' the person intends to authorize is, by an *objective* account, the *same* R the person being authorized believes he or she has been given permission to implement"(Faden & Beauchamp 1986: 309). In order to avoid such a discrepancy of perspectives, Faden and Beauchamp suggest the necessity for an "*extra subjective component* to the knowledge base" (Faden & Beauchamp 1986: 309). In order to achieve some kind of common understanding in such situations, it might be necessary, Faden and Beauchamp argue, for patient X not only to be sufficiently well aware of the aspects she considers material for making the decision, but also to understand sufficiently well what physician Y considers material in regard to the decision. "Specifically, X should understand (1) what an informed professional in Y's position would judge to be of value for most patients or subjects in deciding whether to authorize R, (2) what a professional in Y's position judges that most patients or subjects view as material for authorizing R and (3) what it means for X's consent to R to be an authorization"(Faden & Beauchamp 1986: 309). In cases where the respective views of physician and patient diverge significantly, it is this *extra subjective component* that enables what Faden and Beauchamp call "substantial understanding" (Faden & Beauchamp 1986: 309).

Now, whether or not a (at least rudimentary) shared understanding of what is at stake really is a necessary precondition for an informed consent might depend upon the logic of consent (cf. Manson, this volume, Chapter 6). But it does not contribute to the patient's consent being an *autonomous* authorization. If it is true that the mere fact that the patient considers certain aspects of a decision material is what actually makes these facts and aspects material for the decision, why then should it be necessary for the patient's autonomous decision that she and the physician reach some consent or mutual understanding in regard to what is material in the decision at hand? Consequently, Faden and Beauchamp are cautious here, stating that "effective communication or shared decision making" is not a *necessary* condition for the informed consent of a patient, but "frequently the most available and critical means to the end of understanding by the patient" (Faden & Beauchamp 1986: 314).

Thus, neither an obligation of the physician to support the patient and foster her decision-making capacities nor the idea of shared decision-making can really change something about the character of the disclosure required within the framework of the *theory of self-determination*. Disclosure is oriented solely on the kind and amount of information the patient requires for being able to make an autonomous decision. In other words, such disclosure is oriented solely on the "specific informational needs" of the patient. Thus, it also seems apparent that the *theory of self-determination* cannot be the sole normative basis for the doctrine of informed consent.

25.4 Informed consent and the instrumental value of autonomy

The survey of various theories for the justification of the doctrine of informed consent reveals that none of these theories can serve as the sole normative basis for the obligation to disclosure included in the doctrine of informed consent as it is conventionally understood. Thus, they cannot serve as the sole normative basis for the doctrine itself, either. The *Patient Benefit Theory* may justify a disclosure obligation on the part of the physician, but this obligation ends at the very moment the physician believes that disclosing information does the patient more harm than good. Neither a (largely) exceptionless obligation of disclosure nor a patient's right to be informed can be derived from the *Patient Benefit Theory*. The *Social Benefit Theory*, which essentially understands informed consent as a *safeguard*, obligates the physician only to restrain from exercising controlling influences on patients. The *Self-Determination Theory* finally can only justify disclosure in the sense of disclosure for self-determination.

There are three basic options left if one nevertheless wants to stick to the conventional understanding of the disclosure obligation as it has been presented above. The first of these options is essentially pragmatic. Faden and Beauchamp distinguish between two meanings of informed consent. Specifically, they distinguish informed consent (*sense*1) as the autonomous authorization of a patient from informed consent (*sense*2) as the (legally) effective authorization: "'Informed consent' in this second sense does not refer to *autonomous* authorization, but to a legally or institutionally *effective* (sometimes misleadingly called *valid*) authorization from a patient or subject. Such an authorization is 'effective' because it has been obtained through procedures that satisfy the rules and requirements defining a specific institutional practice in health care or in research"(Faden & Beauchamp 1986: 280). Informed Consent (*sense*1) should, as Faden and Beauchamp argue, be the *benchmark* for the formulation of the formal requirements for informed consent (*sense*2). Since, however, there is no strictly logical connection between the criteria of the informed consent (*sense*1) and (*sense*2), the design of informed consent (*sense*2) leaves room for further, essentially pragmatically motivated, considerations and requirements.[6] This, as critics argue, not only opens up the possibility that irrelevant points are unduly weighty when formulating the corresponding criteria; the distinction between the two meanings of informed consent also nourishes the suspicion that informed consent (*sense*2) is a *legal fiction* "since it presupposes – that is, claims to reflect – genuine task specific autonomy, however baselessly" (Epstein 2006).

According to a second option, the justification models discussed above can be supplemented by further normative considerations. In the first place, one will particularly think of an approach combining welfare-based considerations on the one hand and autonomy-based arguments on the other. Other aspects that could play a role here are prevention of abusive conduct, trust, self-ownership, non-domination or personal integrity (Eyal 2011). The advantage of such a hybrid approach, which is based on different normative principles or points of view, is that existing intuitions can be reconstructed in a particularly accurate way. However, such explanatory models are, of course, problematic whenever the principles or points of view point in divergent directions. And this seems to be exactly the case in view of the obligation of disclosure within the doctrine of informed consent, as can be seen in the controversy about the *therapeutic privilege exception*. While there may well be grounds for exceptions to the informed consent rule from the perspective of a non-harm or welfare argument, the *therapeutic privilege exception* can hardly be justified, if at all, from the perspective of the principle of autonomy.

A third option, which provides not only a pragmatic explanation of the informed consent rule, but also a monistic justification, and can thus avoid the disadvantages of the two previous options, is at least to be indicated at the end: the obligation of disclosure for self-determination as discussed in the last section, as well as the obligation of disclosure as formulated in the doctrine of informed consent, can both be justified by the claim that autonomy is of instrumental value, and that "the value that autonomy is instrumental in securing is that of enabling persons to act to attempt to satisfy their own desires and secure their own goals" (Taylor 2009: 141).

To respect a patient's autonomy is to recognize that the patient has the normative authority to accept or reject a medical intervention. This requires the physician to respect the desires of the patient, which form the background against which the patient decides what aspects of a decision are material to her. In doing so, the physician has to assist the patient in reflecting on and clarifying her desires. This is, as emphasized above, the function of disclosure for self-determination. Given that health care providers have a duty to secure or enhance the instrumental value of the autonomy of patients, the physician must also inform the patient about the diagnosis, the significance and the scope of a proposed intervention, as well as possible alternatives. That is, the physician is obliged to confront the patient with the relevant medical information available from the professional point of view and by doing this to confront her with *points to consider*. This should and can help the patient to avoid mistakes in her decision-making process, such as overlooking options for action, not reasonably considering the consequences of an action, not adequately taking into account future desires, etc. Disclosure as required by the doctrine of informed consent is therefore ultimately morally imperative, for one thing, because the patient otherwise lacks the possibility of recognizing that certain alternative options and possibilities for treatment which she did not consider might fulfill her desires better than the action she currently prefers. And it is morally imperative because without disclosure a patient could lack the chance to revise her desires in the light of new information. Therefore, disclosure by the physician helps enable the patient to come to a reflected decision, and it therefore also helps to ensure that the desires of the patient, whatever they may be, are met as far as possible.

The doctrine of informed consent can thus be justified in a way which avoids substantial deviation from the conventional understanding of the obligation of disclosure and thus preserves one of the core elements of the doctrine: it follows from the principle of respect for the autonomy of patients that medical treatment of competent patients requires the patient's *informed consent after medical disclosure*. This obliges the doctor not only to provide the patient with the information the patient herself considers material, but also to confront her with information on the facts and aspects which the physician considers to be material from a professional point of view.

Notes

1 The special importance of the communicative aspect of informed consent has been emphasized many times. However, a lot of commentators lament that the communicative aspect is often neglected in practice in favor of a ritualized legalistic use of informed consent – with disastrous consequences for the individual patient as well as for the health care system as a whole (Manson and O'Neill 2007).
2 The "partnership" justification model of informed consent primarily based on considerations by Jonas (1969) and Paul Ramsey (1970) is not discussed on its own here. See, however, for this proposal, for example Levine (2003).
3 Veatch himself, however, considers the argument for autonomy discussed later on to be more convincing.
4 The trust argument can also be spelled out in a non-utilitarian manner. See, for example, Manson and O`Neill (2007) and O'Neill (2002).
5 For discussion regarding the extent to which an omitted, faulty or negligent disclosure is suitable for undermining the autonomous decision of a patient, see Taylor (2009: 130ff).
6 Miller and Franklin contest that informed consent (*sense*1) should be the *benchmark* for informed consent (*sense*2) and instead suggest a *fair transaction model of informed consent* (Miller and Wertheimer 2011).

References

Beauchamp, T.L. and J.F. Childress (2013) *Principles of Biomedical Ethics*. Seventh Edition. Oxford: Oxford University Press.

Beauchamp, T.L. and R.R. Faden (2003) "Informed Consent," *Encyclopedia of Bioethics*. Third Edition. New York: Macmillan, 1271–7.

Berg, J.W., P.S. Appelbaum, C.W. Lidz and L.S. Parker (2001) *Informed Consent. Legal Theory and Clinical Practice*. Second Edition. Oxford: Oxford University Press.

Buchanan, A.E. and D.W. Brock (1990) *Deciding for Others. The Ethics of Surrogate Decision Making*. Cambridge: Cambridge University Press.

Charland, L.C. (2011) "Decision-Making Capacity," *Stanford Encyclopedia of Philosophy*. http://plato.stanford.edu/entries/decision-making-capacity/ (Accessed 26.07.2017).

Epstein, M. (2006) "Why Effective Consent Presupposes Autonomous Authorization: A Counter-Orthodox Argument," *Journal of Medical Ethics* 32: 342–5.

Eyal, N. (2011) "Informed Consent," *Stanford Encyclopedia of Philosophy*. http://plato.stanford.edu/entries/informed-consent/ (Accessed 26.07.2017).

Eyal, N. (2012) "Using Informed Consent to Save Trust," *Journal of Medical Ethics* 40: 437–44.

Faden, R.R. and T.L. Beauchamp (1986) *A History and Theory of Informed Consent*. Oxford: Oxford University Press.

Feinberg, J. (1986) *Harm to Self*. Oxford: Oxford University Press.

Grisso, T. and P.S. Appelbaum (1998) *Assessing Competence to Consent to Treatment: A Guide for Physicians and other Health Professionals*. Oxford: Oxford University Press.

Jonas, H. (1969) "Philosophical Reflections on Experimenting with Human Subjects," *Daedalus* 98: 219–47.

Jonsen, A.R. (1998) *The Birth of Bioethics*. Oxford: Oxford University Press.

Jonsen, A.R., M. Siegler and W.J. Winslade (2010) *Clinical Ethics. A Practical Approach to Ethical Decisions in Clinical Medicine*. Seventh Edition. New York: McGraw-Hill.

Levine, R.J. (2003) "Informed Consent: Meaning and Elements," in *Encyclopedia of Bioethics*. Third Edition. New York: Macmillan, 1277–90.
Manson, N.C. and O. O'Neill (2007) *Rethinking Informed Consent in Bioethics*. Cambridge: Cambridge University Press.
Meisel, A. (1979) "The 'Exceptions' to Informed Consent Doctrine: Striking a Balance Between Competing Values in Medical Decision-making," *Wisconsin Law Review* 79: 413–88.
Miller, F.G. and A. Wertheimer (2011) "The Fair Transaction Model of Informed Consent: An Alternative to Autonomous Authorization," *Kennedy Institute of Ethics Journal* 21: 201–18.
O'Neill, O. (2002) *Autonomy and Trust in Bioethics*. Cambridge: Cambridge University Press.
Pellegrino, E.D. (1993) "The Metamorphosis of Medical Ethics. A 30-Year-Retrospective," *Journal of the American Medical Association* 269: 1158–62.
Ramsey, P. (1970) *The Patient as Partner: Explorations in Medical Ethics*. New Haven: Yale University Press.
Rothman, D.J. (1991) *Strangers at the Bedside*. New York: Basic Books.
Tännsjö, T. (1999) *Coercive Care. The Ethics of Choice in Health and Medicine*. London: Routledge.
Tännsjö, T. (2014) "Utilitarianism and Informed Consent," *Journal of Medical Ethics* 40: 445.
Taylor, J.S. (2009) *Practical Autonomy and Bioethics*. London: Routledge.
Veatch, R. (1979) "Three Theories of Informed Consent: Philosophical Foundations and Policy Implications," in The National Commission for the Protection of Human Subjects of Biomedical and Behavioral Research (ed.), *The Belmont Report. Ethical Principals and Guidelines for the Protection of Human Subjects Research. Appendix*. Vol. 2. Washington, 26-1–26-6.
Wear, S. (1998) *Informed Consent. Patient Autonomy and Clinician Beneficence within Health Care*. Second Edition. Washington: Georgetown University Press.

Further reading

Forgó, N. (2018) *Informed Consent in Europe: Legal, Ethical and Clinical Perspectives*. Baden-Baden: Nomos.
Mazur, G.O.P. (2013) *Informed Consent, Proxy Consent, and Catholic Bioethics: For the Good of the Subject*. Dordrecht: Springer.
Maclean, A. (2009) *Autonomy, Informed Consent and Medical Law: A Relational Challenge*. Cambridge: Cambridge University Press.

Related topics

Ch.8 Valid consent
Ch.23 Historical perspectives in medical ethics
Ch.24 Informed consent
Ch.26 Consent in clinical research

26
CONSENT IN CLINICAL RESEARCH

Collin O'Neil

26.1 Introduction

The defining goal of clinical research is to generate knowledge that can be used to enhance the therapeutic capacities and decision-making of clinicians and policymakers. Achieving this goal often requires experimenting on or collecting information about human subjects[1] in ways that would, without consent, infringe their rights. Guidelines for human subjects research, such as the Nuremberg Code, the Declaration of Helsinki, the Belmont Report, and the Common Rule Regulations exist because of notorious studies that, among other things, failed to obtain voluntary and informed consent from human subjects. The Nazi doctors forced prisoners into harmful experiments (Claims Conference 2007). The Tuskegee Syphilis Study tricked subjects into accepting a painful non-therapeutic lumbar puncture under the guise of "special free treatment" (Brandt 1978). Had the investigators in these experiments sought voluntary and informed consent, subjects would have refused and avoided serious harm. But protection from unwanted harm is not the only function of consent. In another much-discussed study, patients at the Jewish Chronic Disease Hospital were injected with live cancer cells for a purely scientific purpose, without being told that the injection was not for their benefit and that it contained live cancer cells (Arras 2008). The researchers argued that, since the injection posed no serious risk, the patients did not need to be informed about the contents or purpose of the injection to protect themselves from harm. Nevertheless, by injecting the patients without their informed consent, the researchers had clearly infringed on the patients' rights to decide what is done to their bodies.

The lessons of these early scandals have been learned. The norm of obtaining voluntary and informed consent is now deeply entrenched in clinical research. Yet the topic of consent in clinical research remains a focus of discussion. There are two principal areas of continuing controversy. One centers on the question of when consent to low-risk research is necessary and when it is not. It can be very costly or even infeasible to seek consent for certain types of studies, such as research on biological samples and emergency research. If consent is unnecessary in such studies this would be a boon to science, but there is disagreement about the conditions under which low-risk research may go forward without consent.

Another source of controversy derives from a worry that, even when consent is sought from subjects, the consent they provide is often defective. Consent should be adequately informed and voluntary. But empirical research has shown that subjects frequently have deficits in their understanding of the studies they are participating in, especially those aspects that set research apart from the patient-centered settings they are accustomed to (Mandava et al. 2012). Furthermore, researchers routinely offer money to healthy individuals and sometimes even to patients as an incentive to enroll in their studies. Many ethicists and institutional review board (IRB) members are concerned that these payments and other incentives such as free health care may be compromising the voluntariness of the consent that researchers obtain.

This article begins with an overview of several types of clinical research that have sparked debates about the necessity of consent, followed by a brief discussion of the considerations relevant to resolving those debates. The focus will then turn to the question of what conditions must be satisfied for consent to be effective. This is the issue of the "validity conditions" for consent to research. The earliest and still most influential account of these conditions is non-moralized, in the sense that the validity conditions make no essential reference to whether the researcher soliciting consent from a subject has obtained it in a way that wrongs the subject or not. Recently new approaches that moralize some of these conditions have been put forward. As we'll see, the non-moralized and moralized approaches to consent in research yield very different implications for how we should evaluate the use of payment and other incentives to increase enrollment and how troubled we should be by the data indicating that subjects often misunderstand various aspects of study design.

26.2 When is consent to research necessary?

Consent communicates an intention to make it the case that someone else would not wrong you by treating you in a certain way (Owens 2012: 165). That is, it purports to waive a right. When consent is "valid", it successfully waives that right. When a researcher proposes to treat a subject in a way that would infringe a right without consent, then obviously consent is necessary to avoid infringing that right. But if the researcher plans to involve the subject only in ways that would not wrong the subject without their consent, there are no rights that need to be waived. Since seeking consent can impede the progress of research, it is important to get clear on exactly what ways of involving a subject in research would infringe on their rights without their consent.

There are some types of clinical research that are routinely conducted without obtaining consent. Epidemiological research on medical records, for example, dispenses with consent. So long as confidentiality is protected, this practice is fairly uncontroversial (Miller 2010). This may be in part because this research does not include interventions on human subjects. But storing patients' tissues or blood for research purposes (after they have been removed, with consent, for therapeutic reasons) does not intervene on the bodies of subjects themselves either, nor does any of the research that is subsequently conducted on those tissues. Yet many believe that storing those samples for research purposes requires consent, and some even argue that subjects must be re-consented for every study that is subsequently done on those samples, even though this would discourage valuable research (for discussion, see Grady 2015).

There is also clinical research that does intervene on the bodies of human subjects and yet proceeds without consent from the subject or even a surrogate. Emergency research randomizes subjects with acute and life-threatening illnesses between experimental and standard emergency care. This is sometimes done without their consent (and without the consent of a proxy) not only when consent would be impossible to obtain in time, but also when prospective consent would be possible but would greatly reduce the enrollment rate or lead to imbalanced enrollment (Karlawish 2008). Randomized controlled trials comparing two approved and widely used treatments typically do seek consent to research from the subjects, but recently some ethicists have argued that consent to the particular treatment they receive suffices and that consent to research is unnecessary (Faden et al. 2014).

At least three considerations are relevant to settling the question of whether consent to research must be obtained in a given study. The first is whether there are any rights that the research would infringe without consent. Do subjects have any rights against the use of their biological samples for research purposes, assuming there are already safeguards in place to protect them from embarrassing or harmful disclosures? If they do have privacy or perhaps property rights in relation to those samples, then the mere fact that the risks are very low would not be enough on its own to justify dispensing with consent. But if they do not, or if there are ways to work around those rights (e.g., by anonymizing the samples), there would be no need for consent. Regarding comparative effectiveness trials, do subjects have a right not to be experimented upon that is distinct from their right not to be treated without consent? If they do then consent to research may be necessary (O'Neil 2014), but if not then consent to the particular treatment they receive would suffice.

When the research would infringe a right without consent, the second factor to consider is the strength of the right and the opportunity costs of seeking consent. Rights may sometimes be justifiably infringed. If the pertinent rights are weak, the fact that obtaining consent would slow important scientific progress could be enough to override them (Miller 2010). But whether this fact is indeed enough to override them may also depend on a third factor, namely, whether the justification treats subjects' hypothetical consent as a constraint. Some justifications for dispensing with consent procedures do not presuppose that anyone would refuse if asked. The reason for dispensing with consent is only that the process of seeking consent would require so much time and resources that the research would no longer be worthwhile.[2] But other justifications do presuppose that there would be high or imbalanced rates of refusal. Both kinds of justifications cite impediments to scientific progress, but they differ in their relation to hypothetical consent. The former justification is consistent with recognizing hypothetical consent as a constraint on human subjects research. The legitimacy of the latter justification is highly questionable because it flouts that constraint. Not only does it anticipate that subjects would *not* consent if asked, that is the very basis of the justification.

26.3 When is consent to research valid?

Once we are convinced that a study involves a subject in a way that would, without the subject's or a surrogate's consent, infringe a right, a new question arises. Under what conditions is consent effective in making it the case that the subject is not wronged by that involvement? Here it is important to distinguish between failures that are due to limits on the power of consent and failures that are due to defective consent. It may be the case that consent, no matter its quality, is incapable of cancelling duties to subjects not to expose them to serious risks of harm for a trivial reason (Tadros 2016: 265–80), to transact with them on terms that distribute the benefits fairly (Wertheimer 2011: 191–254), and to provide them with certain forms of ancillary care (Richardson 2012: 133–43).[3] In what follows I set aside issues about the limits on the power of consent and ask only, when a right is waivable by consent, under what conditions is consent effective in waiving the right? This is the question of the "validity conditions" for consent to research.

26.4 Competent consent

One condition that must be met for an act of consent, on its own, to waive a right against an intervention is that the consenter be competent with respect to the decision: that is, possess sufficient decision-making capacity to make the decision. Decision-making capacity is the capacity to make a decision that best reflects one's values. This capacity calls on both cognitive abilities to form a judgment about what one ought to do in light of the facts, and volitional abilities to form, maintain, and execute an intention that reflects that judgment. Young children are regarded as incompetent to waive their rights against involvement in research. Adults who suffer from advanced dementia may have cognitive impairments that render them incompetent to consent to research, and adults suffering from severe depression or addiction may have volitional impairments that render them incompetent to consent to certain kinds of research. Findings of incompetence are relative to the decision being made. Arguably an adult who has sufficient capacity to make a decision about treatment may not have sufficient capacity to make a similarly complex decision about research, if they are incapable of appreciating the relevant differences between clinical care and research (Rosenstein & Miller 2008).

What is the upshot of a determination of incompetence? Although the Nuremberg Code appears to rule out experimenting on anyone who is incompetent to consent to research, current guidelines and regulations permit some experimentation on incompetent subjects, so long as consent is obtained from a surrogate. Also, although incompetent subjects cannot by themselves effectively waive their rights against experimentation, they retain, at least when they are considered sufficiently capable of exercising it, veto power. (The bar for this capacity is lower than for competence.) The surrogate's consent is usually treated as waiving the subject's rights only so long as the subject also "assents".

The reliance on surrogate consent is a feature of both clinical practice and research. But there is one very striking difference. In clinical practice, apart from exceptional cases such as kidney donations, it is never justifiable to impose net risks on a patient for the benefit of others. But research that imposes risks without an expectation of greater benefit for the subject is conducted not only on subjects capable of consenting to it, but also on incompetent subjects when their surrogate consents. Patients who were previously competent may have expressed a wish when they were competent to make such a sacrifice after they lose competence. Involving them in such a study seems unobjectionable since it accords with their earlier competent wishes, so long as they do not now dissent. But this kind of justification cannot be extended to young children who have never been competent. Permitting children to be exposed to minor research risks for the benefit of other children is relatively uncontroversial in practice. But at the level of justification, it remains puzzling how parental consent could not only waive parental rights against researchers experimenting on their child, but also the child's own right against being exposed to risks for the benefit of others (Ramsey 1976; Wendler 2010).

26.5 Voluntary consent

Even when a subject is competent to consent to a research intervention, their consent will be invalid if it is involuntary. Mrs. M, a survivor of experiments that took place at Auschwitz, reports that she agreed to be experimented on by Dr. Mengele only because "As soon as I stood up I was whipped with a leather whip which broke my flesh, then I was told the whipping was a sample of what I would receive if I did not follow instructions and orders" (Claims Conference 2007). Obviously Mrs. M's consent to Mengele's injecting her with drugs and other chemicals did not make it the case she was not wronged by it.

Beyond this uncontroversial sort of case, however, much is in dispute. Some ethicists see involuntariness exemplified in the cases below[4]; others do not.

(1) very poor or homeless subjects that consent to research in order to receive a substantial payment;
(2) subjects that are uninsured or under-insured and that consent to research in order to receive health care;
(3) prisoners that consent to research to obtain spending money or better conditions or sentence reductions;
(4) subjects that consent to research because an authority figure in their lives wishes it;
(5) drug addicts that consent to research that involves giving addicts their drug of choice.

One disagreement about voluntariness is just terminological, although if it is not sorted out it can lead to confusion. Everyone agrees that consent may be rendered invalid because of the way the external situation in which the subject chooses is altered, as in Mrs. M's case. Everyone also agrees that consent can be rendered invalid because of the way the subject's ability to recognize or respond to his or her external situation is impaired, as in cases involving the use of deception or temptation. Some authors (Beauchamp 2010; Nelson et al. 2011) prefer a broad conception of "voluntariness" that covers both types of invalidating conditions, whereas others (Appelbaum et al. 2009; Wertheimer 2012) reserve the label for conditions that invalidate because of the way they alter the subject's external situation (see also Gutmann, this volume, Chapter 19). In what follows I will adopt the narrower use of "voluntariness" that confines it to the external situation and discuss the other type of invalidating condition under the label "impairment". Since ethicists that regard the drug addict example (5) above as displaying involuntariness presumably have impairment in mind, we can dismiss it at the outset.

26.6 The autonomous authorization approach to voluntariness

With this terminological dispute out of the way, we can focus on the substantive disagreement, which concerns the facts about a subject's external situation that could render their consent involuntary. According to the standard approach in research ethics, the autonomous authorization (AA) approach, a subject's consent is involuntary when it is "substantially controlled" by changes someone else has made to their external situation (Faden et al. 1986; Beauchamp 2010; Nelson et al. 2011). Put another way, whether consent is involuntary depends on the *degree of pressure* to consent that is brought to bear on their decision by the exercise of someone else's control over their situation. I'll describe the AA approach to involuntariness first, and then introduce a recent competing view. These two views deliver different verdicts about the consent in cases (1)–(4) above.

In Mrs. M's case, the pressure to consent derived from the removal of an option she would have preferred, namely, the option of not participating in research and avoiding a whipping. Following the Belmont Report, advocates of the AA approach tend to label pressure that results from removing more attractive options, as in Mrs. M's case, as potentially "coercive" and pressure that results just from creating more attractive options, like the option of participating in research and making money, receiving access to health care, or other benefits, as potentially "undue inducement". (However, some ethicists (Macklin 1989) and many IRB members (Largent et al. 2012) call pressure from both sources "coercive".) But the AA approach to voluntariness is, ultimately, indifferent to whether the pressure to consent derives from the removal of a more preferable option or just from the creation of a preferable option. At the end of the day, voluntariness is a matter of whether the pressure, no matter its source, is excessive.

When is pressure excessive? According to some adherents of the AA approach, including many IRB members (Largent et al. 2012), an offer of payment or other benefits exerts excessive pressure whenever it induces a subject to participate in research. This is a puzzling view, since normally the fact that someone accepts risks to make money is not taken to impugn the voluntariness of their acceptance. What lies behind it, presumably, is Hans Jonas's influential idea that participation in clinical research ought to be intrinsically motivated. Jonas (1969) regards subjects as having been "conscripted" into a study unless they consent to it for the same reason the researcher conducts it, namely, because they identify with the goals of the research. Jonas's view has had a major influence on the way IRBs think about payment for research participation. But it is far from clear why we should treat extrinsically motivated consent to research as involuntary when we treat extrinsically motivated consent to other risky jobs as voluntary.

A less demanding version of the AA approach claims that an incentive is excessive when it leaves the subject with no *reasonable* alternative but to consent. Notice however that a subject might have no reasonable alternative to participation, not because their status quo is so bad, but only because the benefits of participation are so good. Consider a subject who is financially secure and consents to a risky study in order to receive a payment that vastly exceeds the amount necessary to compensate for the risks. Recall that we are assuming that the subject's consent in these cases is clear-headed. That is, the incentive is not distorting the subject's ability to recognize or respond to their situation, e.g., by blinding the subject to the risks or tempting the subject to accept them against their better judgment. So long as that assumption is kept firmly in mind, it is hard to believe that offering someone who is financially secure substantially more than their reservation price would invalidate their consent.

The AA approach can avoid this problem by treating pressure as excessive only when the subject's alternatives are *unacceptable*. Financially secure subjects who consent to a risky study offering an extremely generous payment may have no reasonable alternative but to consent, but their status quo is acceptable. A homeless person in need of money or an uninsured person in need of health care, on the other hand, may consent to a study offering payment or health care only because their alternatives are unacceptable. Their consent would still be involuntary, according to this version of the AA approach.

Is this plausible, keeping in mind the assumption that the incentive is not distorting their practical reasoning? A desperate subject may feel forced to consent to a study offering payment or health care by the lack of acceptable alternatives. But a cancer patient also accepts the risks of chemotherapy only because the alternative, certain death, is unacceptable. Surely the cancer patient's consent to chemotherapy is not rendered involuntary by the absence of acceptable alternatives? Granted, there is a difference between the risks of chemotherapy and the risks of research: whereas the benefits of chemotherapy are not detachable from its risks, a researcher could offer money or health care without requiring research participation. But if the researcher does not owe the subject the money or health care without any strings attached, why would conditioning these benefits on research participation render the subject's consent invalid, any more than conditioning the provision of chemotherapy on receipt of payment would render the patient's consent invalid?

26.7 The moralized approach to voluntariness

According to the competing approach to voluntariness, what is invalidating about the circumstances of Mrs. M's consent is not that she had no acceptable alternative to consenting, but that the reason she had no acceptable alternative is because the researcher had *wrongfully* removed an option that she would have preferred, namely, the option of refusing participation and not suffering a whipping. Mrs. M has a right against being whipped that is not conditional on her choice about participating in research. Such an account of voluntariness is *moralized* (Wertheimer 2012). Consent to research is involuntary, according to this kind of approach, when and only when it is caused by the wrongful removal of or refusal to create an option that the subject would have preferred. Creating an option for a subject can never render their consent involuntary, since adding an option cannot wrong the subject, although their consent to that new option will be involuntary if it is a product of the wrongful removal or refusal to create an option they would have preferred.

Mrs. M illustrates how consent can be rendered involuntary by wrongfully removing an option from the subject. Consent is also rendered involuntary when it is prompted by a wrongful failure to create or sustain an option the consenter would have preferred. It is wrong for a physician to abandon a patient. Suppose that a physician decides to motivate her patient to enroll in a study she is conducting by threatening to stop treating him if he refuses. If the patient consents to the study only because of the physician's threat to discontinue an option that he is owed, namely, the option of continuing the physician–patient relationship without participating in the study, then the patient's consent to the study is involuntary.

Whereas the AA approach implies that consent to research that responds to payment is involuntary when the payment is too high or when the subject's need for money is too severe, the moralized approach never implies that an offer of money renders consent involuntary. The payment may help to make it the case that the subject has no reasonable alternative or no acceptable alternative but to consent, but this does not make the consent involuntary. However, the subject's consent to a study that offers payment would be involuntary if it was caused by a wrongful denial of a preferable option. Suppose that a researcher promises a subject that they will receive $100 for each stage of a four-stage study that they complete. The subject completes the first two stages, and then decides to withdraw. If, in order to incentivize the subject to complete all four stages, the researcher goes back on the promise and decides that the subject will be given $400 only if he completes the two remaining stages and nothing if he drops out now, then the subject's consent to the remaining stages of the study would count as involuntary. It is not the attractiveness of the $400 for completing the remaining stages that makes it involuntary, however. Rather, it is the fact that the subject is consenting to the remaining stages only because the subject was wrongfully denied his preferred option – namely, stopping after two stages and receiving $200 as promised.[5]

When it comes to the incentive of health care, again, the moralized view will deny that it is ever the offer of health care in itself that renders consent involuntary, since the offer just creates an option and the creation of an option cannot wrong the subject. However, the moralized view does imply that if the subject's consent to research is a product of the researcher's wrongful failure to offer a health care option that the subject would have preferred, then it will be involuntary. A public hospital may owe treatment to patients without strings attached. If it makes participation in a randomized controlled trial a condition on delivery of treatment, the subjects' consent would be involuntary if it is prompted by the hospital's wrongful refusal to offer treatment without research participation. But institutions such as the NIH or private hospitals that do not owe potential subjects treatment outside the context of research can make participation in a trial a condition on delivery of treatment without rendering subjects' consent to the research involuntary (Fried 2016: 43–7). And even public hospitals do not owe patients access to *experimental* therapies. Suppose that experimental therapy is offered to a patient but only on the condition that they enroll in the clinical trial that is evaluating it. If the therapy offers the subject their last best hope for survival, there would be tremendous pressure on the subject to consent. The subject may much prefer the option of receiving the therapy outside the trial, especially if the trial is placebo-controlled. But insofar as the subject is not owed that therapy outside the context of a trial, the subject's consent to the study is not based on the wrongful denial of an option they would have preferred (cf. Schuklenk & Lowry 2009).

It should now be clear how the moralized approach would handle the case of prison research. If the institution incentivized prisoners to consent to research by threatening to otherwise extend their sentence or remove privileges they had earned, then the prisoner's consent would be involuntary, so long as it was caused by the denial of these options. But if instead the institution offered a reduction in the prisoner's sentence or privileges they were not already entitled to, then the prisoner's consent to the study would be voluntary, since it is not prompted by a removal or denial of an option the prisoner is entitled to.

But suppose the details of the prison research are as follows. The researcher comes in from the outside and seeks volunteers. The researcher has no problem enrolling subjects, but it turns out this is because prison staff (acting on their own and not at the direction of the research team) are threatening to make life worse for prisoners who refuse to sign up. Is their consent still voluntary? A similar concern might lie behind the case of the subject who consents to research under the influence of an authority figure, such as a husband or a tribal leader. This raises an issue about the significance of third-party coercion. On the moralized approach as I've described it, consent to research is involuntary only when it is the product of the *researcher's* wronging of the subject (Miller & Wertheimer 2010). (Note that researchers may sometimes have duties to relieve third-party pressure on subjects, and if the subject consents to the study only because the researcher fails to discharge such a duty, the consent would be involuntary.)[6] The AA approach would not differentiate these cases, since the degree of pressure applied is the same. But there are other versions of a moralized approach that do claim that at least illegitimate third-party coercion can render a subject's consent to the researcher's intervention involuntary even in the absence of any wronging by the researcher (Millum 2014).

26.8 Informed (unimpaired) consent

At the beginning of the previous section I distinguished between consent that is invalid because it is involuntary and consent that is invalid because it is impaired. Certain ways of controlling the external situation in which the subject chooses can render consent involuntary. Impaired consent occurs when the subject's ability to recognize and respond to their external situation is distorted. There are a variety of ways in which a researcher could, intentionally or negligently, interfere with a subject's practical reasoning about whether to participate in a study. Although attaching rewards to participation, like payment or health care, cannot as such render consent involuntary, it may interfere with the exercise of subjects' cognitive capacities by blinding them to the risks of the study or their volitional capacities by tempting them into consenting against their better judgment (Wertheimer 2011: 150).[7] Similarly, the fact that an addict's drug of choice is administered in the study, though not intended as an inducement, could interfere with the exercise of the addict's volitional capacities. (See Walker (2008) for a strategy to obtain consent from addicts that circumvents this problem.) Even making use of the fact that subjects have a hard time saying no to doctors – the so-called "white-coat effect" – could impair the subject's practical reasoning by injecting an irrelevant consideration into their deliberations (Mandava & Millum 2013).

Attention to the varieties of impairments and the question of when they invalidate consent is an important research program in research ethics (Mandava & Millum 2013; see Faden et al. (1986) for an early treatment). In this section, however, I will focus on the question that has received the bulk of the attention in the literature on consent – namely, the question of when consent is adequately informed (See also Eyal, this volume, Chapter 24). The autonomous authorization (AA) approach embodies the standard answer to this question. But as in the case of voluntariness, the AA approach has come under criticism and competing approaches have been proposed. I will describe these approaches, and draw out their implications concerning the question of whether so-called "therapeutic misconceptions" and other misconceptions invalidate consent.

There is broad agreement that clinical researchers are under duties to disclose extensive information about the study to potential subjects, e.g., about the purpose of the study, what will be done to the subjects, the risks and benefits of the interventions, and appropriate alternatives to participation. In many other contexts in which consent is sought, such as commerce, jobs, sex, and gambling, there is at most a duty not to deceive, or when there are duties to disclose information, they are very modest (Miller & Wertheimer 2010). In clinical care, however, we traditionally regard clinicians as under a duty to make an extensive disclosure to patients, since it is so hard for patients to learn the relevant facts on their own and relatively easy for the clinicians, who should already know these facts, to disclose them. The same asymmetry applies to researchers and subjects. Indeed, since the primary aim of clinical research is not to benefit the subject but to advance knowledge, researchers are usually regarded as having even more extensive duties of disclosure than clinicians. Since clinicians can be presumed to be acting solely in the patients' best interests, patients arguably have less need for information from their clinicians than potential subjects do from researchers (Chwang 2010).

There is a question about the exact content of the extensive duty of disclosure, e.g., whether it is governed by the professional practice standard, reasonable person standard, or a standard more tailored to each individual subject (Brock 2008). I will assume, for simplicity, that the content of the duty of disclosure is to disclose to the subject all of the facts about the study interventions that the researcher knows or ought to know would be material to the subject's decision. These facts should also be disclosed in a manner that makes them accessible to the subject. Describing the injection in Jewish Chronic Disease Hospital as containing "live neoplastic cells" would not satisfy the duty of disclosure. But the duty of disclosure is only a duty to *try* to inform the subject, i.e., to give the subject a fair opportunity to become adequately informed. It is not a duty to succeed. Thus it is possible for a researcher to fully comply with their duty of disclosure while the subject remains ignorant of or mistaken about material facts. This raises the question of whether consent based on ignorance or mistake could be valid, so long as it is not attributable to a failure to fully discharge the duty of disclosure.

26.9 The autonomous authorization approach to informed consent

Although there is broad agreement about the duty of disclosure, important disagreements emerge when we consider different views about the *relation* between compliance with the duty of disclosure and the conditions under which ignorance or mistaken beliefs undermine the validity of consent. According to the standard view of informed consent, the autonomous authorization (AA) view, consent is valid only when all of the information about an intervention that is material to the subject's decision to consent is actually understood by the subject (Faden et al. 1986; Beauchamp 2010).[8] If it were the case that disclosures invariably brought about the corresponding understanding in subjects, then the question of whether this understanding is truly necessary for valid consent would be of merely academic interest. But it turns out that, even after scrupulous disclosures, subjects frequently misunderstand material facts about study interventions and procedures.

One particularly recalcitrant type of misunderstanding is known as the "therapeutic misconception" (Appelbaum & Lidz 2008). The defining goal of clinical research is to generate clinically useful information, not to benefit the subjects of that research. In order to achieve this goal, clinical research frequently involves departures from the individualized care one would expect in a clinical setting. Even when this different purpose and the differences between the design of the study and clinical care are disclosed, subjects frequently continue to expect individualized care in the research setting. For example, they may continue to believe that their treatment will not be selected by a random process, that they would never be given a placebo, that any burdensome or risky intervention must be intended for their direct benefit, and so on. These departures from clinical care will often be material to the subject's decision to consent, at least when the alternative to receiving the therapy in the context of the study is receiving it in clinical practice. Yet these misunderstandings are highly resistant to disclosure.

The AA approach takes the fact that subjects are under a therapeutic misconception as having a straightforward implication for the validity of their consent. Insofar as the subjects are ignorant of or misinformed about material aspects of the study, their consent is invalid, no matter how careful the disclosure was. Given the data about the prevalence of therapeutic misconceptions (Mandava et al. 2012), this in turn implies the rather alarming conclusion that researchers have for years been engaged in the wholesale violation of their subjects' rights. Possibly this conclusion is so implausible as to be reason enough to reject the theory that implies it. But even if not, there is still a powerful reason to rethink the AA theory. Notice that if researchers enhance the disclosures in light of this data, as they should given that the goal of these disclosures is to bring about understanding, there are no measures they could take that would *guarantee* that subjects are adequately informed. Surely at some point the responsibility for the mistake must belong to the subject, not the researcher. Yet the AA approach does not make any room for this moral possibility.

26.10 The minimal understanding approach

Three alternative approaches to the question of when ignorance or mistake on the part of the subject invalidates their consent have recently emerged. Each approach accepts that researchers have an extensive duty of disclosure and that at least a "minimal" understanding of a research intervention is necessary to validly consent to it. Unlike the AA approach, none of these alternatives imply that ignorance or mistake about any material fact undermines the validity of the subject's consent. But they differ as to the conditions under which ignorance or mistake does render a subject's consent invalid.

One kind of approach takes the minimal understanding of an intervention as not only necessary for validity, but also sufficient. A failure to discharge the full duty of disclosure would still wrong the subject, but it would not have the effect of rendering the subject's consent invalid unless as a consequence the subject lacked a minimal understanding of the intervention. What counts as minimal understanding? On the most fully developed version of this approach (Walker 2012; see Sreenivasan 2003 for an earlier version), consenting to a researcher's doing X requires at a minimum that the subject understand all the descriptions of X under which doing X would, without consent, infringe a right of the subject's. The fact that X would involve bodily contact or invasion is a morally relevant description. So is the fact that it imposes a risk of harm, although only if the level of risk is such that the subject would, independently of the bodily contact, have a right against being exposed to it.

This "minimal understanding" approach is very liberal about ignorance and mistakes concerning research. It seems likely that, on this account, many of the common misunderstandings subjects have about research would not compromise the validity of their consent. But it is in danger of being too liberal about misunderstandings. Suppose that a researcher is seeking a subject's consent to a placebo-controlled randomized trial, which gives her only a 50% chance of receiving the treatment she needs and that also involves painful non-therapeutic biopsies. In fact, the treatment she needs is readily available outside the trial and if she knew this she would never consent to the trial. The researcher purposefully withholds this crucial information from her. Surely the subject is wronged by the biopsies. But on the minimalist approach, she appears to possess the minimal understanding needed to validly consent to the biopsies. The fact that the treatment she needs is available outside the trial is not a description of the biopsy at all, much less a description of it under which it would wrong her without her consent.

26.11 The partially moralized approach

The next two approaches do not regard a minimal understanding of the intervention as sufficient for valid consent (Bromwich & Millum 2013; Miller & Wertheimer 2010). Unlike the AA approach, however, these theories do not imply that ignorance of *any* material fact about the intervention invalidates consent. Ignorance of a material fact renders the subject's consent invalid only if the ignorance is attributable to the researcher's failure to discharge the duty of disclosure. Regarding the case above, both views would regard the subject's ignorance of the availability of treatment outside the trial as invalidating, because this ignorance is due to the researcher's withholding that information in violation of their duty of disclosure. But if the researcher had disclosed this information in a manner that satisfied this duty and the subject still failed to grasp it, the subject's consent would not necessarily be invalidated.

Moralized theories of validity can be compellingly motivated by the following pair of cases (Bromwich & Millum 2013: 7–8). In the first case, a researcher is aware that the drug she is testing has side-effects A and B and discloses both side-effects to the subjects. It is later discovered that the drug also has side-effect C, although no one in the expert community, including the researcher, knew it at the time. Although the subjects are consenting to the drug in ignorance of the material fact that it has side-effect C, their consent seems valid. In the next case, the same researcher, after learning that the drug has side-effect C, initiates another study. She discloses side-effects A and B to the subjects, but withholds what she now knows about side-effect C from them. These new subjects are consenting to the drug in ignorance of the material information about C, just like the previous subjects, but their consent seems clearly invalid. Yet both groups of subjects have the same understanding of the same intervention in both cases.

A plausible explanation for the difference in validity is that the subjects' ignorance of C in the first case is not attributable to the researcher's failure to discharge their duty of disclosure, whereas the subjects' ignorance in the second case is. On Bromwich's and Millum's view, however, it turns out that only a subclass of the violations of the duty of disclosure can invalidate consent. Returning to the first case, suppose that side-effect C was well known in the expert community and that the researcher should have known about it, but failed to keep up with the literature. When she fails to disclose C to the subjects, she is in violation of the duty of disclosure, since this is not merely a duty to disclose what one does know, but what one should know. But they claim that when the failure to discharge the duty is due to ignorance, no matter how negligent, it cannot invalidate consent because it cannot count as an exercise of illegitimate *control* over the subject's practical deliberations (Bromwich & Millum 2013: 13).

This account, like the minimal understanding account just discussed, is in danger of being too liberal. Consider a Phase I oncology trial, in which the researcher sincerely tells a cancer patient that the drug has a small but real prospect of arresting the progress of his cancer. In fact, however, patients are to be given only a subtherapeutic dose of the drug in this trial, something the researcher does not know but certainly should have known. In this case, the researcher is not merely failing to disclose something important to the patient, but is *misinforming* the patient about something that would have changed the patient's mind about consenting. Yet, on this approach, this failure to discharge the duty of disclosure would still not invalidate the patient's consent to the trial, because the researcher does not know that she is misinforming the patient, and is therefore not exercising illegitimate control over the subject's decision-making.

26.12 The fully moralized approach

If the consent in the oncology case seems invalid, this is a reason to prefer a fully moralized account of validity, like that on offer in Miller & Wertheimer (2010) and Owens (2007). On such an account, *any* failure to discharge the duties of disclosure that results in ignorance of a material fact about the intervention would invalidate consent. This account would imply that the consent in the oncology case is invalid. Although the researcher did not know she was failing to discharge her duties of disclosure, she was. And since the subject's mistaken belief was due to this failure, the subject's consent, which was based on that mistaken belief, is invalid. The fully moralized account seems to be able to capture all the cases where, intuitively, consent is invalid, yet without implying, as the AA approach does, that each and every material misunderstanding invalidates consent.[9]

Notes

1 I use the term "subject" rather than "participant" because the topic of consent is the topic of what is needed to turn a mere subject into a participant.

2 Studies that use deception for certain methodological reasons can also be consistent with respect for subjects' hypothetical consent (O'Neil 2013).

3 The claim that subjects cannot release researchers from certain duties directed *towards them* is stronger than the uncontroversial claim that consenting to X does not always make X permissible, all things considered. E.g., subjects' consent to involvement in a study lacking social value does not release publicly funded researchers from their duty to the taxpayers not to waste resources.

4 These examples are drawn from Appelbaum et al. (2009). These authors are skeptical that (1)–(5) display involuntariness, but see their article for citations of the literature that views (1)–(5) as examples of involuntariness.

5 Suppose that, rather than offering $400 for finishing the study, the research ups the offer to $10,000, but still denies the subject the promised option of receiving $200 after completing two stages. If the subject would prefer to continue the study and receive $10,000 rather than stop now and receive the $200 he is owed, then the consent is not involuntary. Although the subject is wrongfully denied the option of receiving $200 now, the subject's consent to continue on with the study is not *caused* by the denial of that option. I.e., the subject would have consented to continue the study even if the option owed the subject had been available.

6 I owe this observation to Yulia Gamper.

7 Interestingly, there is evidence that the higher the payment, the more attentive subjects become to the risks of the study (Cryder et al. 2010).

8 They do recognize some exceptions, such as "open withholding" (Faden et al. 1986: 312–3).

9 I am grateful to Marcello DiBello, Andreas Muller, and Peter Schaber for helpful written comments, and to the participants in my Research Ethics seminar at the Center for Bioethics, NYU, Summer 2017, for valuable discussion.

References

Appelbaum, P.S. and C.W. Lidz (2008) "The Therapeutic Misconception," in E. Emanuel, C. Grady, R. Crouch, R. Lie, F. Miller and D. Wendler (ed.), *The Oxford Textbook of Clinical Research Ethics*. New York: Oxford University Press, pp. 633–44.

Appelbaum, P.S., C.W. Lidz and R. Klitzman (2009) "Voluntariness of Consent to Research: A Conceptual Model," *Hastings Center Report* 39(1): 30–9.

Arras, J.D. (2008) "The Jewish Chronic Disease Hospital Case," in E. Emanuel, C. Grady, R. Crouch, R. Lie, F. Miller and D. Wendler (ed.), *The Oxford Textbook of Clinical Research Ethics*. New York: Oxford University Press, pp. 73–9.

Beauchamp, T.L. (2010) "Autonomy and Consent," in F. Miller and A. Wertheimer (ed.), *The Ethics of Consent: Theory and Practice*. Oxford, New York: Oxford University Press, pp. 55–78.

Brandt, A.M. (1978) "Racism and Research: The Case of the Tuskegee Syphilis Study," *The Hastings Center Report* 8(6): 21–9.

Brock, D. (2008) "Philosophical Justifications of Informed Consent in Research," in E. Emanuel, C. Grady, R. Crouch, R. Lie, F. Miller and D. Wendler (ed.), *The Oxford Textbook of Clinical Research Ethics*. New York: Oxford University Press, pp. 606–12.

Bromwich, D. and J. Millum (2013) "Disclosure and Consent to Medical Research Participation," *Journal of Moral Philosophy* 10(4): 195–219.

Chwang, E. (2010) "A Puzzle about Consent in Research and Practice," *Journal of Applied Philosophy* 27(3): 258–72.

Claims Conference (2007) "Personal Statements from Victims of Nazi Medical Experiments," Conference on Jewish Material Claims Against Germany, Inc. Last Modified January 1, 2007. Accessed October 16, 2016. www.claimscon.org/about/history/closed-programs/medical-experiments/personal-statements-from-victims/

Cryder, C., A.J. London, K.G. Volpp and G. Loewenstein (2010) "Informative Inducement: Study Payment as a Signal of Risk," *Social Science & Medicine* 70: 455–64.

Faden, R.R., T.L. Beauchamp and N.E. Kass (2014) "Informed Consent, Comparative Effectiveness, and Learning Health Care," *New England Journal of Medicine* 370(8): 766–8.

Faden, R.R., T.L. Beauchamp and N.M.P. King (1986) *A History and Theory of Informed Consent*. Oxford, New York: Oxford University Press.

Fried, C. (2016) "Medical Experimentation: Personal Integrity and Social Policy," F. Miller and A. Wertheimer (ed.). New York: Oxford University Press.

Grady, C. (2015) "Enduring and Emerging Challenges of Informed Consent," *New England Journal of Medicine* 372(9): 855–62.

Jonas, H. (1969) "Philosophical Reflections on Experimenting with Human Subjects," *Daedalus* 98: 219–47.

Karlawish, J.H.T. (2008) "Emergency Research," in E. Emanuel, C. Grady, R. Crouch, R. Lie, F. Miller and D. Wendler (ed.), *The Oxford Textbook of Clinical Research Ethics*. New York: Oxford University Press, pp. 280–9.

Largent, E.A., C. Grady, F.G. Miller and A. Wertheimer (2012) "Money, Coercion, and Undue Inducement: Attitudes about Payments to Research Participants," *IRB* 34(1): 1–8.

Macklin, R. (1989) "The Paradoxical Case of Payment as Benefit to Research Subjects," *IRB* 11: 1–3.

Mandava, A. and J. Millum (2013) "Manipulation in the Enrollment of Research Participants," *Hastings Center Report* 43(2): 38–47.

Mandava, A., C. Pace, B. Campbell, E. Emanuel and C. Grady (2012) "The Quality of Informed Consent: Mapping the Landscape. A Review of Empirical Data from Developing and Developed Countries," *Journal of Medical Ethics* 38(6): 356–65.

Miller, F.G. (2010) "Consent to Clinical Research," in F. Miller and A. Wertheimer (ed.), *The Ethics of Consent: Theory and Practice*. Oxford, New York: Oxford University Press, pp. 375–404.

Miller, F.G. and A. Wertheimer (2010) "Preface to a Theory of Consent Transactions: Beyond Valid Consent," in F. Miller and A. Wertheimer (ed.), *The Ethics of Consent: Theory and Practice*. Oxford, New York: Oxford University Press, pp. 79–106.

Millum, J. (2014) "Consent Under Pressure: The Puzzle of Third Party Coercion," *Ethical Theory and Moral Practice* 17(1): 113–27.

Nelson, R.M., T. Beauchamp, V.A. Miller, W. Reynolds, R.F. Ittenbach and M.F. Luce (2011) "The Concept of Voluntary Consent," *American Journal of Bioethics* 11(8): 6–16.

O'Neil, C.C. (2013) "Methodological and Inducement Manipulation," *American Journal of Bioethics* 13(11): 55–7.

O'Neil, C.C. (2014) "Consent and Rights in Comparative Effectiveness Trials," *AMA Journal of Ethics* 16(4): 289–94.

Owens, D. (2007) "Duress, Deception, and the Validity of a Promise," *Mind* 116(462): 293–315.

Owens, D. (2012) *Shaping the Normative Landscape*. Oxford: Oxford University Press.

Ramsey, P. (1976) "The Enforcement of Morals: Nontherapeutic Research on Children," *The Hastings Center Report* 6: 21–30.

Richardson, H. (2012) *Moral Entanglements: The Ancillary-Care Obligations of Medical Researcher*. Oxford: Oxford University Press.
Rosenstein, D.L. and F.G. Miller (2008) "Research Involving Those at Risk for Impaired Decision-Making Capacity," in E. Emanuel, C. Grady, R. Crouch, R. Lie, F. Miller and D. Wendler (ed.), *The Oxford Textbook of Clinical Research Ethics*. New York: Oxford University Press, pp. 437–45.
Schuklenk, U. and C. Lowry (2009) "Terminal Illness and Access to Phase 1 Experimental Agents, Surgeries and Devices: Reviewing the Ethical Arguments," *British Medical Bulletin* 89: 7–22.
Sreenivasan, G. (2003) "Does Informed Consent to Research Require Comprehension?" *Lancet* 362: 2016–18.
Tadros, V. (2016) *Wrongs and Crimes*. Oxford: Oxford University Press.
Walker, T. (2008) "Giving Addicts Their Drug of Choice: The Problem of Consent," *Bioethics* 22(6): 314–20.
Walker, T. (2012) "Informed Consent and the Requirement to Ensure Understanding," *Journal of Applied Philosophy* 29(1): 50–62.
Wendler, D.S. (2010) *The Ethics of Pediatric Research*. Oxford: Oxford University Press.
Wertheimer, A. (2011) *Rethinking the Ethics of Clinical Research*. Oxford: Oxford University Press.
Wertheimer, A. (2012) "Voluntary Consent: Why a Value-Neutral Concept Won't Work," *Journal of Medicine and Philosophy* 37(3): 226–54.

Related topics

Ch.7 When is consent required?
Ch.8 Valid consent
Ch.12 Consent and autonomy
Ch.19 Voluntary consent
Ch.24 Informed consent
Ch.25 Consent and medical treatment

27
CONSENT AND ORGAN DONATION

Ben Saunders

Organ donation requires surgical procedures to remove organs from the donor and to transplant them into the recipient. Thus, it is generally assumed that consent is needed from both parties.[1] The main issue of contention around transplantation concerns consent for posthumous organ donation. Where organs are taken from a deceased person, they are no longer able to consent. Common solutions are for the individual to give their consent beforehand, for instance by registering as a potential donor, or for surviving relatives to be asked for consent. More will be said about these issues, but first it is worth briefly considering one issue that receives less attention – namely the need for consent from the recipients of transplants.

27.1 Consent of recipients

The literature on organ transplantation is overwhelmingly focused on donor consent. Less attention is paid to the consent of those who receive organs. This may be because it is taken as obvious that most people will consent to receive a transplant if the alternative is bad enough, for instance death or a lifetime on dialysis machines. However, receiving a transplant requires invasive surgery and has life-changing consequences which are not entirely beneficial, for instance the need for immunosuppressive drugs to prevent their bodies from rejecting the transplant organ (Clatworthy et al. 2012: 40–7). Potential recipients must be informed of the dangers of organ donation; otherwise, their consent will not be informed. This raises wider issues about what information patients need for their consent to be informed (O'Neill 2003).

Some people may wish to refuse a transplant even when their life depends on it. Some might feel uneasy at the thought of having other people's organs inserted into their body, while others might have religiously motivated objections to transplantation. It is important that patients are, where possible, given the opportunity to give or refuse consent before being placed on waiting lists, and the necessary information to make this decision. There are cases where this is not possible, for instance where the patient is a minor or unconscious, but, if possible, the patient's consent should be secured. This means that patients should also be able to refuse particular transplants, which may result in them passing over a potential "high-risk" organ in the hope that a better one will become available. This can make it more difficult to use some organs, except when potential recipients are desperate.

One possible reason for the relative lack of focus on recipient consent is that, in most countries, demand for transplant organs usually far outstrips supply (Sheehy et al. 2003; Rieu 2010; Giubilini 2015). It is difficult to estimate the size of this disparity, first because it is hard to predict supply (not everyone who registers as a potential donor actually becomes one) and second because it is unclear exactly how many potential recipients could benefit from a transplant since not everyone who might benefit from a transplant is included on waiting lists when their chances of actually receiving an organ are low (Rieu 2010: 534). Were the supply of donor organs unlimited, and the cost of transplant procedures reduced, far more people could potentially benefit from receiving a transplant. Nonetheless, whatever the exact numbers, it is clear from the existence of waiting lists that there are more people wanting to receive transplants than there are organs available for transplant. Thus, while any given individual might refuse a transplant, there are almost certainly willing recipients for any available organ. Hence, while it is important that potential recipients are given the opportunity to refuse a transplant if they wish, lack of consent on the part of recipients is not normally an obstacle to transplantation. Even if some people refuse a transplant, it can generally be assumed that those on the waiting list have given their informed consent.

While these considerations explain why the focus is usually on donors, rather than recipients, this does not mean that recipient consent is entirely straightforward. It is possible to question whether the consent given by recipients is truly voluntary. Ordinarily, valid consent requires not only that one have the capacity to give consent and the information necessary to decide, but also that one's choice be voluntary. However, if someone chooses X only because they have no acceptable alternative, this is normally thought to make their choice non-voluntary (Olsaretti 1998). It seems likely that most people only consent to transplants because they will otherwise die or suffer other serious repercussions, such as a lifetime relying on dialysis machines. It might be objected that, since they have no satisfactory alternatives but to accept an organ, transplant recipients are not really free to choose. Thus, there may be concern that the consequences of refusing a transplant are such as to undermine the voluntariness of their consent. However, while it is presumably true that most organ recipients would not receive a transplant unless it were necessary, this should not be seen as invalidating their consent. Were that the case, then it would follow that no one can validly consent to life-saving surgery. The "voluntariness" condition here should be understood as excluding outside interference from other agents, but the medical conditions that require transplants should not be seen as undermining the voluntariness of consent (Nelson et al. 2011).

27.2 Consent of donors

The case of organ recipients is relatively straightforward. No one should receive an organ transplant against their will and there may be some who, for whatever reason, refuse a transplant, even at the cost of their lives. However, it can generally be assumed that there are others on transplant waiting lists who do give their consent to a transplant. Moreover, recipients can usually be asked for their consent in the hospital, whereas this is often not possible for donors (at least, posthumous ones). Thus, it is unsurprising that *donor* consent has been the main issue of contention. The main issues arise in the case of posthumous donors, but it makes sense to begin by considering the simpler cases.

27.2.1 Living donors

There are certain organs that people can live without, such as their second kidney or a section of the liver (Clatworthy et al. 2012: 16–19). Consequently, it is possible for living people to donate an organ to someone in need. This typically occurs between friends or family, for instance one sibling donating a kidney to another, though sometimes if the willing donor is not a compatible match with their desired recipient it is possible for them to participate in an exchange with another donor–recipient pair, or even as part of a long chain of exchanges (Rees et al. 2009). There are also sometimes cases, often referred to as "altruistic donation", where an individual volunteers to donate to a stranger (Rees et al. 2009: 1096). Such non-directed living donation is not legal in all jurisdictions (Evans 1989) and, even where it is, stringent checks are often required to ensure that the donor appreciates the risks involved, is not being paid, etc.

Since the removal of an organ involves invasive surgery and attendant risks, not only of the surgery but of being without the organ, the donor's consent is needed. Assuming that the donor is a competent adult, and fully informed of the risks, this is not normally problematic. Nonetheless, there are cases where the validity of their consent may be questioned. When someone donates to a family member, they may be under considerable pressure from other relatives to do so, which may mean that their consent is not truly voluntary (Valapour 2008). Note that the point here is not simply that they agree to donate, though, in some sense, they would rather not. Rather, the worry is that other family members may, wittingly or otherwise, place potential donors under such emotional pressure that they have, or feel that they have, little choice but to donate (Lennerling et al. 2003). Even without family pressure, it can be very difficult for an individual to refuse donation, knowing that a friend or family member may die as a consequence. The potential loss of a loved one itself is not normally taken to undermine voluntariness, since it is not controlling influence by another agent, but family pressure to donate can cross that line, rendering apparent consent invalid because non-voluntary.

There are a range of other factors that might undermine donor consent. In particular, there is controversy regarding incentive payments. Some countries allow for non-financial incentives; for instance in Israel registered donors get priority if they need a transplant (Quigley et al. 2012). Australia has recently gone further, in allowing living donors to be paid compensation (Giubilini 2015). Most states, however, formally prohibit market exchange of organs.[2] This is so despite a number of calls for allowing the buying and selling of organs (Radcliffe Richards et al. 1998; Barnett et al. 2002; Taylor 2005). Such bans can be seen as forbidding acts of capitalist exchange between consenting adults (cf. Nozick 1974: 163). If there is a general presumption in favor of respecting the wishes of the individual, then such prohibitions on organ sales need to be justified.

One possible justification for prohibiting the buying and selling of organs would be that the poor may be forced to sell their organs, due to the lack of acceptable alternatives (Hughes 2009). That is, there may be concern that most people would not freely consent to the sale of their organs and so the apparent consent in any financial transaction is likely to be defective. Of course, there are already many other dangerous or otherwise unpleasant things that people are prepared to do for money, if desperate enough, and, it is sometimes added, the lot of the poor is hardly improved by barring them from entering into a transaction that they deem to be in their interests (Zwolinski 2007). However, one worry could be that, even if some people are genuinely willing to sell their organs, allowing them to do so would have negative consequences for others; for instance, if organ sales are permitted, money lenders might require people to stake their kidneys or other organs as collateral for loans (Greasley 2014: 54).

Whatever the reasons for prohibiting organ sales, since most jurisdictions do, at least formally, prohibit such sales, it seems that most assume either that financial inducements can vitiate consent or that even valid consent to donate can be overruled. The latter possibility serves as a useful reminder that, while consent may be necessary for donation, it is not sufficient. Just because someone is willing to donate an organ, whether for money or not, they have no right to be a donor (this point will be relevant when considering family objections, below).

27.2.2 Posthumous consent

The case of living donors is relatively straightforward, but some organs can only be taken from deceased donors. Since the donor is no longer able to give their consent, it is unclear whose consent is needed or how it should be given.

One possible position is to deny the need for consent. Though, on some accounts, people's interests persist after their deaths, making it possible for them to suffer posthumous harms (e.g. Pitcher 1984; Wilkinson 2002), it is debatable whether they continue to have rights (Kramer 2001; Winter 2010). If I have no rights over my body after I die, then no one can wrong me by taking my organs, regardless of my views or preferences. Thus, it might be argued that consent is unnecessary for posthumous organ donation (Delaney & Hershenov 2009). However, even if the deceased no longer has rights over his or her body, it may be that surviving relatives do, so their consent might be needed. Indeed, it is possible that consent is needed from the next of kin even where it has already been given by the deceased, since both parties may have independent moral standing. Let us first consider how consent may be secured from the deceased, before turning to the next of kin.

Since individuals cannot consent to donation after they die, it is common to allow them to specify their wishes before they die. The mechanisms through which this is done vary between countries. Some countries use an "opt-in" system, sometimes referred to as "informed consent" (e.g. Bilgel 2012) or "explicit consent" (e.g. Thaler & Sunstein 2008: 176).[3] In such a system, an individual's organs are not used unless consent is actively granted. Often this consent comes from the individual, who may give consent by signing up to a donor register and/or carrying a donor card. Sometimes consent may come from the next of kin, who authorize donation even where the individual's own wishes are not known (Rieu 2010: 534). In either case, however, consent must actively be given by some authorized party. Without such consent, organs are not to be removed.

Other countries use an "opt-out" model, according to which an individual's organs are considered available for transplant unless some objection is registered to this. Again, this objection might come from either the individual or the next of kin, and a distinction is sometimes drawn between a "hard" opt-out, in which the family is not consulted, and a "soft" opt-out, which grants surviving relatives a veto (e.g. Rieu 2010: 534–5). The role of the family will be discussed later; for present purposes, the important feature of opt-out systems is that the default is donation. Such systems are sometimes termed "presumed consent" (e.g. Gill 2004: 37; Neades 2009). While some have argued that this presumption is justified, given that most people do consent to organ donation (Gill 2004), the identification of an opt-out system with presumed consent is unfortunate (den Hartogh 2012: 196). To refer to such systems as "presuming consent" suggests, first, that consent is needed for donation and, second, that surgeons proceed on the basis of a mere presumption that this consent is or would be given. If we accept that consent is needed, then it seems morally dubious to proceed on a mere presumption, without actual consent. Presumed consent seems a flimsy basis for organ retrieval, if consent is needed. Indeed, it has been argued that if consent can simply be presumed, then this would justify doctors simply taking organs, which has been associated with public scandals (English & Sommerville 2003).

However, an opt-out system can be interpreted and defended in other ways. It might be thought, for instance, that consent is not needed for posthumous donation, since the deceased no longer has rights over his or her body (Winter 2010), or any rights that they do have are overridden by the needs of those waiting for transplants (den Hartogh 2012: 196). This position would be compatible with the mandatory conscription of organs, but individuals might be given the opportunity to opt out even if they do not, strictly, have any right to veto what happens to their organs after they die. Alternatively, one might think that there is no presumption against removing organs from a cadaveric body, and thus no need for consent from the individual, but that individuals *do* still have the right to veto the use of their organs, even after their death. That is, posthumous donation may merely require an absence of refusal, rather than consent (Douglas & Douglas 2009). In these case, an opt-out system would not presume consent, since consent would not be needed to begin with.

The idea that consent from the individual is unnecessary may strike some as even more controversial than the idea of presuming consent and hence of little use in justifying an opt-out system of donation. However, it has also been argued that opt-out systems do secure some form of consent, rather than a mere presumption of consent. In particular, it has been suggested that, when one knows that an opt-out system is in place, inaction can be construed as tacit or implied consent (den Hartogh 2011; Saunders 2012). Consent is not always given through explicit acts; sometimes consent is tacitly given or implied by people's actions. If people can easily register any objection to donation, we can take their not doing so as showing their consent. This may be the logic underlying the recent adoption of an opt-out system in Wales, where those who do not register an objection are "deemed" (rather than "presumed") to have given their consent (Douglas & Cronin 2015; Shaw 2017). Nonetheless, this argument is not without its critics (Mackay 2015). One problem is that this tacit consent will only be informed and voluntary if people are aware that their inaction will be taken as consent and it is easy and relatively costless for them to opt out.

Another possible justification for an opt-out system rests on the notion of normative consent, originally developed by Estlund (2008: 117–35). According to this proposal, an individual's lack of consent can sometimes be considered null and void where they have an obligation to give their consent. Estlund suggests that this is attractive for two reasons. First, it is generally recognized that consent may be null and void in certain circumstances, such as when given under duress, so there is a pleasing symmetry to this proposal. Second, it ensures that people cannot escape obligations simply by wrongly refusing their consent. The notion of normative consent itself is controversial, both as a justification for authority (Edmundson 2011; Koltonski 2013; Huseby 2014) and when related to organ donation (Potts et al. 2010; Manson 2013). Nonetheless, it has been suggested that, if it is accepted, it could justify opt-out donation systems (Saunders 2010). Plausibly, most people have a duty to donate their posthumous organs, where possible for them to do so; hence most people have a duty to consent to donation. If some people withhold consent, their failure to do so is void, because wrongful, and they can be treated as donors anyway. Nonetheless, explicit refusals of consent (opt-outs) carry more force than mere non-consent and may still be respected.

Each of these justifications for an opt-out donation system is controversial, but the mere availability of such justifications suffices to show that an opt-out system should not be conflated with presumed consent. There is no reason for advocates of an opt-out system to *presume* that people do or would consent to donation, since the system might be justified in other ways. It might still be objected that these alternatives are not sufficient to license donation. For instance, tacit consent may not be informed consent if people are not aware of what is involved in organ donation.

The key difference between an opt-in and an opt-out system is the default that will be applied in the absence of any active choice. In an opt-in system, the default is no donation, whereas in an opt-out system the default is donation. Since the findings of behavioral science suggest that many people stick with defaults, the expected outcome is that an opt-out system will increase the number of donors (Thaler & Sunstein 2008: 175–82). Nonetheless, this has not always been the case in practice. Brazil introduced an opt-out system in 1997, but switched back to an opt-in system as many people opted out (Csillag 1998). It is possible that more people were actively opting out than had previously failed to opt in. That is, some of those who were willing to donate when they had to opt in to do so were no longer willing to do so under an opt-out system. One possible explanation is that people objected to what they saw as a presumption of consent or, perhaps, a presumption that their active consent was not needed. The success of any procurement strategy depends on public acceptance and support.

Either an opt-in or an opt-out system risks treating people in ways contrary to their wishes if those wishes are not recorded, or if the record is incorrect or vague (Shaw 2017). Another approach seeks to avoid reliance on any default, by requiring all individuals to make an explicit choice, either giving or refusing consent. Such systems are generally known as "mandated choice" regimes (Thaler & Sunstein 2008: 180), since individuals have to choose. In practice, however, it is difficult – and perhaps morally objectionable (Taylor 2005: 12) – to force people to make this choice (Gill 2004: 53). Some regimes allow individuals to select a "don't know" or "undecided" option, which means that they do not really have to choose after all. In the first six months of a mandated choice system in Virginia, USA around 24% of respondents chose the undecided option, perhaps because they wished to leave the decision to their next of kin (Klassen & Klassen 1996: 72).

It is often proposed that the individual's choice will be binding, thus avoiding the need to consult next of kin (Spital 1996: 66). However, there is no logical inconsistency in requiring the individual to make a choice and holding that the next of kin have a right to veto that choice. Since the term "mandated choice" refers only to the requirement that one choose, it seems sensible to call this a mandated choice system. It would, however, be useful to distinguish between those systems that allow next of kin a say and those that do not. Perhaps the most appropriate terms are "hard mandated choice" and "soft mandated choice", following the terminology used when discussing opt-out systems.

While hard mandated choice is preferable, if the only aim is to respect individual autonomy, a soft system may be preferred, if the next of kin's wishes must also be respected. However, if the main purpose is to protect individual autonomy, or avoid burdening the family, this does not require mandated choice. These ends could be achieved simply by excluding the family and applying the appropriate default where an individual has not expressed any contrary wish (den Hartogh 2012: 203–4). This would not guarantee that an individual's organs were treated in accordance with her wishes, if she failed to record those wishes, but it would mean that every individual had the opportunity to determine what would happen to her organs, without fear that her directives may be overridden.

It has also been suggested that medical professionals should be allowed, or even required, to encourage consent to donation. Chouhan & Draper (2003: 161) propose this in what they call "modified mandated choice", though the issue arises in any donation system, whether or not choice is required. It may be objected that, if medical professionals seek to influence patients' decisions, most likely in favor of donation, this threatens to undermine consent. But informing and persuading should be distinguished from undue influence, such as coercion or manipulation. Medical professionals may have a duty to correct biases and misinformation, and perhaps even to offer advice when asked (Shaw & Elger 2013). It is understandable that medical professionals may wish to avoid the appearance of undue influence but, by maintaining neutrality rather than offering advice, they may be failing to give patients necessary information (Shaw & Elger 2013: 1689). Hence, it is unclear whether neutrality is required or appropriate.

Another possibility, which may be incorporated in a mandated choice regime or implemented without it, would be to allow individuals to nominate someone to decide on their behalf (Spital 1996: 68). This would enable individuals who are undecided about organ donation to delegate the decision to someone of their choosing. It would also mean that those who want to defer to the wishes of their next of kin, for instance to avoid causing them greater distress, are able to do so. There are more general questions over the appropriate role of next of kin in decisions over organ donation. Currently, many jurisdictions allow the next of kin to make decisions, even when these override the recorded wishes of the deceased individual. This practice is controversial.

27.2.3 The role of the family

While the wishes of the deceased are generally taken into consideration, if known, surviving relatives or other next of kin are also often consulted before organ retrieval takes place. The next of kin may have their own legal standing to give or refuse consent, or they may be asked only for information about the wishes of the deceased.[4] Even where the next of kin may have no legal right to be consulted at all, healthcare professionals may not proceed with procurement when the next of kin object (Neades 2009: 274). Introducing the next of kin creates an additional point at which consent may be given or refused.

In practice, since many people do not leave explicit record of their wishes, or the wishes recorded are vague (Shaw 2017), the next of kin are often left to decide. In the UK, only around 20% of donations come from individuals on the donor register, with around 80% authorized by the next of kin (Rieu 2010: 534, 537). However, even where the donor's wishes are known, one US study found that next of kin veto donation in over 50% of cases where they are approached (Siminoff et al. 1995: 15). The reasons behind such refusals are doubtless complicated and a proper understanding of them is important for those seeking to increase donation rates within systems that, formally or informally, allow such vetoes (Sque et al. 2006). My concern here, however, is not with *why* families might veto donation, but with *whether* they should be allowed to. For simplicity, I will assume that the next of kin are of one mind, though in practice there are often disagreements.

The impact of the next of kin on the donation process depends on the system in question. In what might be called a "pure" opt-in system, the only option available is to give consent to donation (otherwise, without consent, no donation takes place).[5] If consent can be given by either the individual or by the next of kin, but is only needed from one, then the chances of donation are increased. In such a system, if the individual has already given consent, then the next of kin are irrelevant: their consent would be redundant and their lack of consent is ineffective. The next of kin are only consulted where the individual has not already given consent, so the possibility that they will give consent can only lead to consent being given where it was not given before. Conversely, in a system where the only option is to block donation (a "pure" opt-out system), the next of kin could only reduce donation, by expressing an objection where there was no objection from the individual.

Most donation procurement schemes are more complicated than these pure or ideal types. It might be, for example, that the individual has the opportunity to opt in, thereby giving consent to donation, but this can be overridden if the next of kin object. This is a mixed or hybrid system, where the individual has the right to opt in but the next of kin can exercise an opt-out. However, we could have an opt-in system in which consent is needed from *both* the individual *and* their next of kin, rather than from only one party. If consent is needed from both parties, then this creates an additional barrier to donation; requiring consent from the next of kin, as well as the individual, can only reduce donation compared with a system where only one consent is needed.

In cases like this, the next of kin's wishes may effectively override those of the individual, for instance blocking donation that he or she had consented to in life. Whether the next of kin should be able to override the individual's expressed wishes is controversial. Some think that it should be up to the individual to decide what happens to his or her body, after death as in life, and that there is no good reason to allow surviving relatives to veto this decision, whatever it is. At least where consent from next of kin is not legally required, it has been argued that medical professionals who allow the next of kin to override an individual's consent to donation are neglecting their duties (Kluge 1997; Shaw 2012). However, there is certainly no logical inconsistency in holding that consent (or absence of dissent) is needed from both the individual and the next of kin, creating a "double veto" (Wilkinson 2005).

Consulting the next of kin is most attractive when the individual has not left any explicit record of his or her wishes. As noted above, in an opt-in system, permitting the family to give their consent increases the likelihood of consent. However, it is unclear what justifies this. One possible justification for consulting the next of kin is that it is what the individual may have wanted. But, while this may be the case, it is not necessarily so. To presume that this is the case, in the absence of any expressed wishes of the deceased, seems no more reliable than to presume that the individual was willing to donate their organs. Thus, it seems that anyone who objects to "presumed consent", on the grounds that it does not adequately respect individual autonomy, ought to be equally critical of what might be called "presumed delegation" (den Hartogh 2012: 197). Alternatively, it might be supposed that the next of kin are most likely to know what the deceased wanted. However, if the deceased was undecided, then asking the next of kin to identify what he or she wanted is asking the impossible (den Hartogh 2012: 198).

A more promising justification for consulting the next of kin is that they have moral standing, in their own right, to decide what should be done, perhaps even overriding the wishes of the deceased individual. Even if we accept that the deceased individual has an interest in what happens to his or her posthumous body, living relatives may have at least as much at stake. The next of kin are already suffering emotional distress and, for many, the proper disposition of their relative's body is an important part of the grieving process (May et al. 2000: 325). Particularly where the deceased is a child, the parents may feel a sense of ownership over the body and a duty to care for their child's remains (Brazier 2003: 31). Taking the body away for organ procurement may prevent relatives from saying a last goodbye (Klassen & Klassen 1996: 72). Further, the surviving relatives have to live with whatever decision is reached. Thus, it might be that the next of kin have a right to be included in decision making, and perhaps even to override the deceased individual's wishes, for instance if the individual wants to donate but it would cause significant distress to relatives.

Conversely, it has been argued that it may be wrong to consult the next of kin, at least where the individual's wishes are known (Kluge 1997; Shaw 2012) and perhaps even where they are not (den Hartogh 2012). The family are already likely to be suffering great emotional distress and burdening them with this decision may simply add to that. Even if disposed to donate, they may not wish to be troubled with the details necessary to inform their decision (Knowles 2001). Further, given their emotional state, the next of kin may make a decision that they later regret. Some studies suggest that many of those who veto donation in the heat of the moment later regret this (English & Sommerville 2003: 150). This, again, raises questions about whether medical professionals should encourage consent to donation (Shaw & Elger 2014). Alternatively, a record of the individual's wishes might be used as a persuasive tool, without the need for medical practitioners to intervene (Shaw 2014).

Persuasion is only necessary, of course, if next of kin are given the opportunity to authorize or veto donation in the first place. Some donors suggest that part of their reason for signing up to a donor register is to spare their family from having to make this decision, but if the family are asked to give consent anyway this purpose is defeated (May et al. 2000: 329). Consulting the family on this matter is inconsistent with ordinary practice in other areas, since the family are not allowed to override an individual's will, even if they dislike it. Many donors incorrectly believe that their expressed wishes are binding, and many think they should be, even if the family object.

27.3 Conclusion

Organ transplantation is an invasive procedure, for both donor and recipient. It is generally accepted that some form of consent is needed but, as we have seen, there is much disagreement about who should give consent and how.[6]

Notes

1 Some prefer to speak of *authorization*, rather than consent, to mark distinctions between the practice of permitting organ procurement and the regular practice of informed consent (Brazier 2003: 30). This term is used in Scottish law (Shaw 2016).
2 A notable exception is Iran, where living, unrelated kidney donors receive compensation from the Charity Foundation of Special Diseases (Larijani et al. 2004; Bagheri 2006). Other states tolerate organ sales in practice, even though it is formally illegal (Greasley 2014: 53).
3 "Informed consent" is something of a misnomer, since even those who opt in may not satisfy the normal conditions for informed consent (Rieu 2010: 537; Shaw 2017).
4 Tottoczko (2003: 1196) suggests that consent from next of kin is a form of "presumed consent". This seems to assume that the consent we are concerned with must be that of the deceased individual, rather than the next of kin per se.
5 What I mean by "pure" here differs from den Hartogh (2012: 195), as his use of the term precludes decision by relatives.
6 I thank Andreas Müller, Peter Schaber, and David Shaw for helpful comments on earlier drafts.

References

Bagheri, A. (2006) "Compensated Kidney Donation: An Ethical Review of the Iranian Model," *Kennedy Institute of Ethics Journal* 16(3): 269–82.
Barnett, A.H., R.D. Blair and D.L. Kaserman (2002) "A Market for Organs," in A. Tabarrok (ed.), *Entrepreneurial Economics: Bright Ideas from the Dismal Science*. New York: Oxford University Press, pp. 89–105.
Bilgel, F. (2012) "The Impact of Presumed Consent Laws and Institutions on Deceased Organ Donation," *European Journal of Health Economics* 13: 29–38.
Brazier, M. (2003) "Organ Retention and Return: Problems of Consent," *Journal of Medical Ethics* 29: 30–3.
Chouhan, P. and H. Draper (2003) "Modified Mandated Choice for Organ Procurement," *Journal of Medical Ethics* 29: 157–62.
Clatworthy, M., C. Watson, M. Allison and J. Dark (2012) *Transplantation and a Glance*. Oxford: Wiley-Blackwell.
Csillag, C. (1998) "Brazil Abolishes 'Presumed Consent' in Organ Donation," *Lancet* 352: 1367.
Delaney, J. and D.B. Hershenov (2009) "Why Consent May Not Be Needed for Organ Procurement," *American Journal of Bioethics* 9(8): 3–10.
den Hartogh, G. (2011) "Tacitly Consenting to Donate One's Organs," *Journal of Medical Ethics* 37(6): 344–7.
den Hartogh, G. (2012) "The Role of the Relatives in Opt-in Systems of Postmortal Organ Procurement," *Medical Health Care and Philosophy* 15: 195–205.
Douglas, J.F. and A.J. Cronin (2015) "The Human Transplantation (Wales) Act 2013: An Act of Encouragement, Not Enforcement," *The Modern Law Review* 78(2): 324–48.

Douglas, T.M. and N.M. Douglas (2009) "Absence of Significant Dissent Should be Sufficient for Deceased Donor Organ Procurement in New Zealand," *Australian and New Zealand Journal of Public Health* 33(5): 449–54.

Edmundson, W.A. (2011) "Consent and Its Cousins," *Ethics* 121(2): 335–53.

English, V. and A. Sommerville (2003) "Presumed Consent for Transplantation: A Dead Issue after Alder Hey?" *Journal of Medical Ethics* 29(3): 147–52.

Estlund, D. (2008) *Democratic Authority: A Philosophical Framework*. Princeton: Princeton University Press.

Evans, M. (1989) "Organ Donations Should Not be Restricted to Relatives," *Journal of Medical Ethics* 15(1): 17–20.

Gill, M.B. (2004) "Presumed Consent, Autonomy, and Organ Donation," *Journal of Medicine and Philosophy* 29(1): 37–59.

Giubilini, A. (2015) "Why and How to Compensate Living Organ Donors: Ethical Implications of the New Australian Scheme," *Bioethics* 29(4): 283–90.

Greasley, K. (2014) "A Legal Market in Organs: The Problem of Exploitation," *Journal of Medical Ethics* 40: 51–6.

Hughes, P.M. (2009) "Constraint, Consent, and Well-Being in Human Kidney Sales," *Journal of Medicine and Philosophy* 34(6): 606–31.

Huseby, R. (2014) "Normative Consent and the Scope of Democratic Authority," *Politics* 34(4): 334–44.

Klassen, A.C. and D.K. Klassen (1996) "Who Are the Donors in Organ Donation? The Family's Perspective in Mandated Choice," *Annals of Internal Medicine* 125(1): 70–3.

Kluge, E. (1997) "Decisions About Organ Donation Should Rest With Potential Donors, Not Next of Kin," *Canadian Medical Association Journal* 157(2): 160–1.

Knowles, D. (2001) "Parents' Consent to the Post-mortem Removal and Retention of Organs," *Journal of Applied Philosophy* 18(3): 215–27.

Koltonski, D. (2013) "Normative Consent and Authority," *Journal of Moral Philosophy* 10(3): 255–75.

Kramer, M.H. (2001) "Do Animals and Dead People Have Legal Rights?" *The Canadian Journal of Law & Jurisprudence* 14(1): 29–54.

Larijani, B., F. Zahedi and E. Taheri (2004) "Ethical and Legal Aspects of Organ Transplantation in Iran," *Transplantation Proceedings* 36(5): 1241–4.

Lennerling, A., A. Forsberg and G. Nyberg (2003) "Becoming a Living Kidney Donor," *Transplantation* 76(8): 1243–7.

Mackay, D. (2015) "Opt-out and Consent," *Journal of Medical Ethics* 41(10): 832–5.

Manson, N.C. (2013) "Normative Consent Is Not Consent," *Cambridge Quarterly of Healthcare Ethics* 22: 33–44.

May, T., M.P. Aulisio and M.A. DeVita (2000) "Patients, Families and Organ Donation: Who Should Decide?" *Milbank Quarterly* 78(2): 323–36.

Neades, B.L. (2009) "Presumed Consent to Organ Donation in Three European Countries," *Nursing Ethics* 16(3): 267–82.

Nelson, R.M., T. Beauchamp, V.A. Miller, W. Reynolds, R.F. Ittenbach and M.F. Luce (2011) "The Concept of Voluntary Consent," *American Journal of Bioethics* 11(8): 6–16.

Nozick, R. (1974) *Anarchy, State and Utopia*. Oxford: Basil Blackwell.

O'Neill, O. (2003) "Some Limits of Informed Consent," *Journal of Medical Ethics* 29(1): 4–7.

Olsaretti, S. (1998) "Freedom, Force and Choice: Against the Rights-Based Definition of Voluntariness," *Journal of Political Philosophy* 6(1): 53–78.

Pitcher, G. (1984) "The Misfortunes of the Dead," *American Philosophical Quarterly* 21(2): 183–8.

Potts, M., J.L. Verheijde, M.Y. Rady and D.W. Evans (2010) "Normative Consent and Presumed Consent for Donation: A Critique," *Journal of Medical Ethics* 36(8): 498–9.

Quigley, M., L. Wright and V. Ravitsky (2012) "Organ Donation and Priority Points in Israel: An Ethical Analysis," *Transplantation* 93(10): 970–3.

Radcliffe Richards, J., A.S. Daar, R.D. Guttmann, R. Hoffenberg, I. Kennedy, M. Lock, R.A. Sells and N. Tilney (1998) "The Case for Allowing Kidney Sales," *The Lancet* 351(9120): 1950–2.

Rees, M.A., J.E. Kopke, R.P. Pelletier, D.L. Segev, M.E. Rutter, A.J. Fabrega, J. Roger, O.G. Pankewycz, J. Hiller, A.E. Roth, T. Sandholm, M.U. Ünver and R.A. Montgomery (2009) "A Nonsimultaneous, Extended, Altruistic-Donor Chain," *New England Journal of Medicine* 360(11): 1096–101.

Rieu, R. (2010) "The Potential Impact of an Opt-out System for Organ Donation in the UK," *Journal of Medical Ethics* 36: 534–8.

Saunders, B. (2010) "Normative Consent and Opt-Out Organ Donation," *Journal of Medical Ethics* 36: 84–7.
Saunders, B. (2012) "Opt-out Organ Donation without Presumptions," *Journal of Medical Ethics* 38: 69–72.
Shaw, D. (2012) "We Should Not Let Families Stop Organ Donation From Their Dead Relatives," *British Medical Journal* 345: e5275.
Shaw, D. (2014) "Personalized Organ Donation Directives: Saving Lives with PODDs," *Critical Care* 18: 141.
Shaw, D. (2017) "The Consequences of Vagueness in Consent to Organ Donation," *Bioethics* 31(6): 424–31. doi: 10.1111/bioe.12335.
Shaw, D. and B. Elger (2013) "Evidence-Based Persuasion: An Ethical Imperative," *JAMA: Journal of the American Medical Association* 309(16): 1689–90.
Shaw, D. and B. Elger (2014) "Persuading Bereaved Families to Permit Organ Donation," *Intensive Care Medicine* 40: 96–8.
Sheehy, E., S.L. Conrad, L.E. Brigham, R. Luskin, P. Weber, M. Eakin, L. Schkade and L. Hunsicker (2003) "Estimating the Number of Potential Organ Donors in the United States," *New England Journal of Medicine* 349(7): 667–74.
Siminoff, L.A., R.M. Arnold, A.L. Caplan, B.A. Virnig and D.L. Seltzer (1995) "Public Policy Governing Organ and Tissue Procurement in the United States," *Annals of Internal Medicine* 123: 10–17.
Spital, A. (1996) "Mandated Choice for Organ Donation: Time to Give It a Try," *Annals of Internal Medicine* 125: 66–9.
Sque, M., S. Payne and J. Macleod Clark (2006) "Gift of Life or Sacrifice?: Key Discourses for Understanding of Organ Donors' Decision-Making by Families," *Mortality* 11(2): 117–32.
Taylor, J.S. (2005) *Stakes and Kidneys: Why Markets in Human Body Parts are Morally Imperative*. Aldershot: Ashgate.
Thaler, R.H. and C.R. Sunstein (2008) *Nudge: Improving Decisions About Health, Wealth and Happiness*. New Haven: Yale University Press.
Tottoczko, T. (2003) "Presumed Consent: What Does It Mean?" *Transplantation Proceedings* 35: 1195–7.
Valapour, M. (2008) "The Live Organ Donor's Consent: Is It Informed and Voluntary?" *Transplantation Reviews* 22(3): 196–9.
Wilkinson, T.M. (2002) "Last Rights: The Ethics of Research on the Dead," *Journal of Applied Philosophy* 19(1): 31–41.
Wilkinson, T.M. (2005) "Individual and Family Consent to Organ and Tissue Donation: Is the Current Position Coherent?" *Journal of Medical Ethics* 31(10): 587–90.
Winter, S. (2010) "Against Posthumous Rights," *Journal of Applied Philosophy* 27(2): 186–99.
Zwolinski, M. (2007) "Sweatshops, Choice and Exploitation," *Business Ethics Quarterly* 17(4): 689–727.

Further reading

Excellent book-length discussions of organ donation and transplantation can be found in J. Radcliffe Richards *The Ethics of Transplants: Why Careless Thought Costs Lives* (Oxford: Oxford University Press, 2012) and T.M. Wilkinson *Ethics and the Acquisition of Organs* (Oxford: Oxford University Press, 2011). Though focused on blood donation rather than organs, R. Titmuss *The Gift Relationship: From Human Blood to Social Policy* (London: Allen & Unwin, 1970) continues to be a key reference in debates over altruistic donation and payment. Markets in kidneys and other organs are discussed in D. Satz *Why Some Things Should Not Be for Sale: The Moral Limits of Markets* (Oxford: Oxford University Press, 2010), chapter nine, and S. Wilkinson *Bodies for Sale: Ethics and Exploitation in the Human Body Trade* (London: Routledge, 2003), especially chapter five (on consent) and chapter seven (on organs). D. Sperling *Posthumous Interests: Legal and Ethical Perspectives* (Cambridge: Cambridge University Press, 2008) addresses the rights of the dead, including over bodily disposal (chapter four).

Related topics

Ch.8 Valid consent
Ch.19 Voluntary consent
Ch.28 Consent for others

28
CONSENT FOR OTHERS

Anthony Wrigley

28.1 Introduction

Providing consent for those unable to do so for themselves has received comparatively little attention in the bioethics literature.[1] Despite this, there is pressing need to make decisions for others. An aging population with an increasing incidence of dementia and other cognitive impairments, medical science's ability to keep people alive for longer, the ever-advancing range of treatment options available, concerns as to how we should treat those with a mental disorder that compromises their autonomy, and changing social attitudes towards determining our future care have all contributed to this need. All cases raise similar sorts of questions: who should make these decisions, what sort of decisions about consenting should be made, when should we seek consent from others, and how should decision-makers go about making such decisions?[2]

Underpinning this is a question as to the basis of providing consent for others. It is widely held that autonomous (adult) individuals have a right to self-determination and are free to make any decision they like about their treatment.[3] Yet, in preparation for when they may lose their autonomy, many individuals seek means to maintain control over their lives, rather than accept the instigation of a blanket paternalistic approach.[4] This has given rise to conceptions of extended autonomy, whereby a currently autonomous individual seeks to make provision to determine important decisions about them for when they are no longer able to do so for themselves.

Whether or not autonomy can actually be so extended is a matter of philosophical debate, with questions ranging from the nature of personhood, to limits on the scope of autonomy, and what might constitute decision-making authority by a third party.[5] Although there are practical and legal dimensions that also surround consenting for others, arising from the pressing demand for decisions needing to be made about individuals and pressures on the state to safeguard the welfare of the vulnerable, these philosophical questions play an important role in clarifying key conceptual issues and establishing the moral basis for such consent.

28.1.1 Precedent autonomy and extended decision-making

The central normative foundation for consenting for others is often based on the "extension view" of precedent autonomy.[6] Drawing on conceptions of personal autonomy, precedent autonomy is the right of an autonomous individual to make decisions for a time in the future when they are no longer autonomous, such as through loss of competence due to cognitive decline. This right is derived from a simple extension of our current autonomy to cover future times. The moral authority of decisions based on our precedent autonomy is thereby considered no different to that of our usual, contemporaneously made autonomous decisions. What rights and authority this imparts on someone else to consent on behalf of another will therefore depend upon what conception of autonomy we are relying on. If autonomy, seen as something akin to a "right to make decisions for and about yourself", allows us virtually unlimited authority to make decisions about our own lives, then this right requires respect for decisions about our future selves. On this view, autonomy grants us an important degree of self-governance or sovereignty over ourselves; hence our decisions can equally cover all future aspects of the self.

The philosophical literature is, however, replete with varying accounts as to what autonomy is, and only some can serve as a basis for an account of precedent autonomy.[7] Accordingly, although the extension view just outlined is generally seen as the "orthodox" position, slightly different explanations have also been offered, depending upon the conception of autonomy being used as a basis for the account of precedent autonomy. These other explanations of precedent autonomy include allowing people to develop integrity of character whilst currently autonomous and allowing people to pursue "whole of life" wishes that allow them to live and shape their lives by values they hold as most important.[8] Regardless as to which interpretation is held, a failure to respect past decisions would be seen as a violation of autonomy.

The importance of respect for precedent autonomy is also explained through another distinction, introduced by Dworkin (1993), between "experiential" and "critical" interests. Experiential interests are the sort of thing we have in the present moment; they are felt or thought and so are often described as "welfare interests". Critical interests, on the other hand, are those concerning the values one holds, such as living in accordance with a view of what it is to have a dignified life. The desire to avoid the perceived indignity of living with dementia, for example, can be satisfied even if the individual is no longer able to understand what this critical interest is in their current state. The distinction highlights a tension that exists between making decisions in accord with the previous wishes of an individual who is no longer autonomous and making decisions that respond to welfare concerns affecting their immediate circumstances. Critical interests are what an individual is often seeking to protect when they make provision for consent to be made on their behalf, so that the course of action they indicated as being of most value to them can be adhered to, even should it not appear to be in their most immediate best interest. Precedent autonomy is therefore seen to protect an individual's critical interests by allowing them the scope to live their entire life in the way they wished it to be lived rather than have paternalistic decisions made about them.

28.1.2 Determining who to consent for

Knowing when we need to provide consent for others is a question of whether an individual is an autonomous agent. In practice, this has primarily (although not exclusively) been about determining whether a person is sufficiently competent to consent.[9] Although competence is a necessary feature of autonomy, it is important to proceed with some caution when considering this. How we understand competence does not always capture all the aspects one might consider important in a relevant determination of autonomy, which may include, for example, emotional maturity, aspects of authenticity, or ability to communicate.[10] The picture is further confused because there is no universally accepted account of what competence is, although it is generally considered to involve a number of capacities or abilities. Whether this is characterised in terms of meeting some absolute minimum threshold of intellectual capacity, as relative to individual decisions, or some other means, is not a settled matter.[11]

There are a wide range of people for whom decisions need to be made because they are not autonomous. Broad groupings include: (i) previously autonomous adults who have made provisions for their wishes and views to be known concerning future decisions; (ii) previously autonomous adults who have not made such provisions; (iii) adults who have never been autonomous; (iv) adults with fluctuating capacity, such as those with a mental illness or addiction; and (v) children. Some of these may involve clear-cut cases where there is no possibility of consent, or even communication, taking place, such as when dealing with comatose patients or very young children. There are, however, large numbers of cases where it is much more difficult to determine whether or not consent is required on behalf of another. Many of these involve people with a gradation of abilities to communicate and consent that can make the determination much more challenging as to whether or not, at any particular point in time and for any particular type of decision, consent on their behalf is required. This includes those in various stages of cognitive decline as well as children in various stages of cognitive and emotional development, where the boundaries between being and not being autonomous are unclear.

28.2 Approaches to consenting for others

Where it is considered that an individual is unable to provide consent for themselves, different approaches can be taken to determine decisions about their treatment. There are two major approaches that seek to allow an individual to exercise their precedent autonomy and make provision for future decisions: (i) appointing a surrogate or "proxy" decision-maker or (ii) creating an advance directive. In other cases where provision has not or could not be made, a range of alternative decision-making options arise.

28.2.1 Proxy decision-maker

A proxy decision-maker is an individual who is appointed to assume decision-making power for another person. In some cases, the proxy will have been appointed whilst the individual they will be consenting for was still an autonomous agent. Alternatively, it may be the identification of an individual (such as a family member, friend, or trusted associate) to indicate any known wishes they may have about medical interventions, although such cases are more about an attempt to discover the wishes of an individual rather than a strict extension of their precedent autonomy and, as such, are not the focus of discussion here. Where there is no legal authority attached to the proxy, their views are only advisory even if a proponent of precedent autonomy considers them to have moral authority, and it is up to those charged with making the treatment decisions to determine what weight to give the proxy's judgements in practice. Whether there are or should be limitations as to the nature and scope of the sorts of decisions a proxy can make forms a significant part of the philosophical debates surrounding their use.

The authority of a proxy to make decisions for another person can be seen in terms of legal provision, practical requirements for someone to fill the role of decision-maker (such as determining immediate medical attention), and moral authority. Moral authority is a difficult concept to delineate but a simple account of it can be given as a normative relation between persons, such that the decision of a person is sufficient to give us a moral obligation to assent to, obey or respect that decision.[12] The (still autonomous) appointing individual is relying on precedent autonomy to establish that the proxy has their authority to make decisions on their behalf. The proxy's decision-making thereby becomes a direct extension of the subsequently incapacitated individual's contemporaneous autonomous decision-making in virtue of this appointment.

28.2.2 Advance directives

An advance directive, also known as an advance statement or living will, allows an autonomous person to record their values, wishes, and preferences for decisions regarding their treatment for when they are no longer autonomous agents. A legally binding advance directive is a written document containing instructions that outline the sorts of treatment options that may be carried out, continued, or refused, and under what circumstances. The moral basis for adhering to the instructions contained in an advance directive are much the same as those for respecting the decisions of a proxy – an individual is extending their autonomous decision-making to allow them to consent at a future time when they are no longer autonomous.

Although it is supposed to be a direct record of the wishes of an individual, a written document containing these can cause problems. This is largely due to the need for someone to understand and interpret the content of the document so that it can be applied in practice. Therefore, they need to be sufficiently clear to help provide a determinate answer as to what is being consented to. If the content is too specific then the directive will apply only in very limited circumstances or may not sufficiently resemble circumstances that actually arise. If too general, advance directives can be difficult to interpret or apply. However, it is widely held that a clear, properly constructed advance directive provides the most accurate account of a person's wishes that it is possible to reasonably obtain.

Concerns over the validity of an advance directive might arise in cases where it was thought that a person's views had changed from those contained in the directive. The static nature of advance directives is one of the reasons for the growing use of proxy decision-makers, either as an alternative to or used in tandem with an advance directive. Proxies are seen to provide a more dynamic response to changes in situation and circumstance that may not have been foreseen at the time an advance directive was created.

28.2.3 Other approaches to decision-making for others

Not all approaches to decision-making for individuals lacking autonomy will be explicitly authorised by the individual they concern. The basis for determining such a role is usually found in social and legal precedents in virtue of a role or relationship that people or groups have towards an individual who is unable to consent. This includes a reliance on family members, medical teams, or direct decisions from the courts. However, it is questionable whether any of these methods constitute genuine consent as opposed to presenting us with various legal or practical solutions to having to make decisions about someone.

Historically, a great deal of weight was placed on the views of family members when it came to making medical decisions for an incompetent individual as they were the default, presumptive decision-maker. Often, close family members are taken to be the most knowledgeable about the incompetent individual's values and preferences, as well as having a vested interest in promoting the welfare and good of that individual. There are also well-established social norms that treat families as important units of personal relationships which make decisions about their members on a regular basis. Of course, this will not hold true of all families or family members and it may be stronger in certain relationships (such as parent–child) than others. Moreover, decisions in terms of views about best interests or preferences would not necessarily be seen as consent but only an indication of a preferred course of action. So, although seen as an important source – and often the most practical means – of establishing a patient's wishes, they are not a source of consent for another but only of advice about them.

Allowing medical treatment decisions to be made by physicians or medical teams has certain practical advantages for the immediacy of decisions and the utilisation of specialist knowledge as to the nature and implications of various treatment options. However, most decisions require not only an understanding of the medical effects but also an appreciation of the effects of the treatment upon any known values and interests the patient might have previously expressed. It is also unlikely that a medical team would make a judgement about medical options that go beyond day-to-day treatment, such as the decision to withdraw life-sustaining medication, without further ratification due to the significant moral dimensions that attach to that sort of decision. This also acts as a form of safeguard that any such decisions are in the patient's interests.

A court is, in many ways, the ultimate arbiter of decision-making for an incompetent person simply because they are the final mechanism of determining who has the legal authority to consent for another person. What sorts of decisions a court is willing or able to make will depend upon individual cases as well as the constraints imposed by statute. Where a patient is deemed incompetent due to a diagnosable mental illness, for example, even a court may be limited in what medical treatments it can authorise consent for.

Although legal authority to determine who can consent for another – and for what purpose – is in the hands of the courts, there is also a normative underpinning to much of their decision-making that lends court judgments moral authority to determine such cases. This includes a highly precautionary approach to maintaining bodily integrity, with court judgments often being guided by the view that only the least invasive and most vital treatment options should be considered. That an intervention is considered to be in the best interests of the patient is therefore not sufficient reason to authorise it by itself; it must also conform to preserving bodily integrity as much as is reasonably possible. For example, the forced sterilisation of an incompetent individual may be deemed in their best interests but would unlikely be countenanced unless there was some pressing need for it to maintain that individual's health due to the extremely invasive nature of the procedure. Furthermore, cases with a strong moral as well as medical dimension, such as cessation of life-sustaining treatments, are often seen as falling within the province of the justice system because they provide the best route to obtaining an open and impartial judgement as to the acceptability of such an action whilst also providing an important safeguard to both the patient and the medical institution.

28.3 Different standards of consent for others

Aside from questions of who can consent for another, there are standards that guide the way in which a proxy makes their decision. The two most commonly recognised guidance principles are substituted judgement and best interests. There is also scope in certain cases to account for the assent or dissent of the individual for whom consent is being given, which can be important influences as to how decisions should be made.

28.3.1 Substituted judgement and best-interests standards of consent

The substituted judgement standard requires the proxy to use their special knowledge of the incapacitated individual's preferences to make decisions that the individual would have made, were they still able. The best-interests standard allows the proxy to make an assessment of the various interests a patient may have and determines what they think will be best overall to promote those interests. Opinion is divided as to which principle should be followed, depending upon how one balances the relative merits of one against the other.[13]

With substituted judgements, as an attempt is made to replicate the actual decision-making process of the incapacitated person, it is often considered the closest we can get to determining what their wishes would have been, were they still competent. Accordingly, it is often described as the "gold-standard" of surrogate decision-making. Whether such forms of judgement are possible or coherent will be discussed in section 28.4.

With best-interests judgements, although the proxy may use their knowledge of the patient's preferences and values, their judgement is not supposed to be a direct reflection of the patient's wishes. Instead, the basis for the decision is what the proxy would consider best for the patient in a particular set of circumstances. This means it does not require the proxy to get inside the complex psychology of another person (except insofar as this is necessary to determine what may be in the best interests of that person, such as an understanding of their relevant desires, views, etc.) and can allow decisions to take into account the nuances of the particular circumstances the patient is in without having to strictly adhere to a set of values or principles a patient may have possessed.

28.3.2 Assent and dissent

Assent or dissent is a form of agreement or disagreement that assumes a lower standard of information assimilation, voluntariness, and decision-making to that of consent. However, they are concepts that are not well defined in the literature and their use can lead to some confusion.[14] They are used with those individuals who are not fully autonomous and so cannot give valid consent but who can still grasp something of the nature of the decision to be made and thereby communicate their preferences. Although not fully autonomous, individuals may have a limited or developing autonomy that can be respected through seeking their assent or dissent. Assent is not simply a modest version of consent but something to allow an individual involvement with a situation over which he or she has no direct authority to determine by being able to consent. The satisfaction of these preferences is also likely to form an important element of a best-interests assessment by indicating experiential states of that individual, giving further reason to seek and respect them where these preferences do not conflict with other central interests. Conflict may occur in situations where an individual's assent or dissent appears to be at odds with their overall best interests; for example, when a young child refuses an injection that is part of their treatment. In such circumstances, it may be appropriate to override their dissent in pursuit of their overall best interests. The challenge for the appointed decision-maker is to determine the extent to which the person's interests will be advanced by respecting their assent or dissent.

This raises an important issue where assent and dissent may be at odds with an advance directive or the judgements of a proxy. This is the tension that lies between experiential interests and critical interests raised in section 28.1. The case of an individual whose experiential interests are in conflict with their previously acknowledged wishes is one that tests exactly how much weight we are willing to give to someone's precedent autonomy. Just such a concern is presented in Dworkin's (1993) famous example of the Alzheimer sufferer Margo, which has become something of a paradigm case in the literature. Dworkin's example is used to support his argument that respecting precedent autonomy is part of a broader "integrity" view of autonomy: that the general value of autonomy is to be distinguished from the particular consequences for a particular person that arise as a result of autonomous decisions. Therefore, although there may be a conflict between the precedent autonomy of a demented person, such as Margo, and their contemporary experiential interests, respecting their precedent autonomy is consistent with their critical interests. As these critical interests were present when fully autonomous,

Dworkin argues that to resist or reject them when the individual is no longer autonomous would be to fail to respect their autonomy in the same way that it would were they still competent. This is not to say Dworkin fails to recognise the tension that may arise as a result of this concerning an individual's care, only that he considers critical interests should be judged as they were at the time they were made and treated with the same respect as all forward-looking autonomous decisions. However, as I shall go on to discuss in the next section, there are other arguments that may lend weight to an opposing view.

28.4 Philosophical issues with consenting for others

A variety of philosophical problems surrounding consenting for others exist, including concerns over how we can represent the views of another person, how we determine the validity of a proxy's judgements, disagreement over the best course of action, the lack of continuity of interests over time, and moral authority. I here focus on three of the most prominent issues: questions of identity, epistemic concerns, and the nature of transferring or "bequeathing" decision-making authority to another person.

28.4.1 Personal identity objections

Personal identity is one of the more widely discussed concerns about the moral authority of advance directives, although it may also apply to the appointment of a proxy. Metaphysical accounts of personal identity are combined with ethical reflections about autonomy and authority to raise questions as to whether an individual is the same person, or whether they become a different person (or even lose personhood altogether), after a substantial loss of competence. The pertinent question for consent becomes whether the wishes of a patient who might be considered a previous, different person before the loss of competence should have any authority over the current individual. The thought being that, as one's autonomous decision-making only has moral authority over oneself, then a necessary condition for the moral authority of an advance directive or appointment of a proxy would be that the person who issued it is identical with the one to whom it applies.

Quite what constitutes personal identity can be a matter of lengthy philosophical debate.[15] The concept of personal identity relevant to this discussion is primarily one about persistence: how do we determine whether or not we are referring to the same or different person between two points in time? It is not to be confused with other uses of "personal identity", which are used to describe what we think are our most important properties with which we identify ourselves (that "make you the person that you are"). Moreover, talk of persons being those things that have the "highest moral status" does not mean that anything which is not a person has no moral status; rather, it means persons are the sort of thing that we associate as having properties from which this status is derived.[16]

There are two major accounts of personal identity, the Psychological view and the biological or "Animalist" view.[17] The Psychological account is derived from early discussion by Locke (1690), who characterised our personal identity in terms of psychological continuity and reflective self-consciousness. Locke was concerned with a range of complex psychological attributes but perhaps the one that is most salient is continuity of consciousness, or memory, of one's psychological processes and experiences.[18] Accordingly, a person at time t_1 and a person at a later time t_2 are the same person if and only if there is a sufficient level of psychological continuity between them. This approach is often seen as attractive because it allows a strong connection to our moral concerns and our intuitions about what is most important: that we identify more closely with our minds than our bodies.[19]

The alternative view of personal identity takes a biological criterion as primary. This is the "Animalist" theory supported by Olsen (1997), Snowdon (1990), Wiggins (2001), and DeGrazia (1999). What is crucial to personal identity on this view is that we can lay claim to being a certain natural kind of animal of the species *Homo sapiens*. Our identity conditions are now those of this particular animal, and are decided in terms of biological properties rather than any account of our psychological continuity. Accordingly, a person at time t_1 and a person at a later time t_2 are the same person if and only if there is a continuity of vital biological functions (often associated with some basic functionality of the brain).

Which account we follow impacts on how we might view the moral authority of advance directives and the appointment of proxies. With the Psychological account, the substantial loss of psychological continuity – a process that typically renders the individual incompetent and brings the advance directive or proxy into use – also determines that we are no longer dealing with the same person as the one who originally made the directive or appointed the proxy. Where the psychological disruption is severe and permanent, the claim would be that we were no longer dealing with a person at all. This is referred to by DeGrazia (1999) as "The Somebody Else Problem". The problem is that the preferences of an autonomous individual do not extend over that of another individual. Hence the wishes conveyed by a person prior to their becoming incompetent lose any moral authority to determine decisions for the individual who remains after the loss of competence just at the very point they are meant to come into use. Either a new person succeeds the old one, so the previous person has no moral authority to determine treatment options over this new person, or there is no person left, in which case there is an end to moral authority altogether – it stops at the point where the necessary conditions to hold it cease. Although in practice many considerations of an individual over their future body are taken to have legal or moral authority, such as concerning organ donation or one's will, these must ultimately have a different basis to that of extension of autonomous wishes.[20]

Animalist accounts, by contrast, would hold that such a loss of psychological continuity would not result in a loss of personhood and hence would not be subject to the same identity concerns about moral authority as the psychological account. The same person continues to survive just so long as their animal functions continue to surround their most fundamental biological processes, such as metabolism, capacity to breathe, and circulation. However, even if one were to take an Animalist approach, concerns over authority may linger for other reasons, such as those in the next two sections.

28.4.2 Epistemic concerns: knowledge of the future and representation of another's thoughts

Challenges to the coherence of relying on precedent autonomy, creating advance directives, or making substituted judgements are all raised by appeal to our concerns about our epistemic states. The first of these, initially raised by Buchanan (1988), are variations of concerns about lack of information on our future conditions, attitudes, treatment options, and suchlike, and our ability to gather such information. The most basic is a worry about information provision. This is largely based on an analogy with the demands of valid consent: that a person needs to be adequately informed before consent can be given. The simplified argument can be laid out in a series of steps:

(1) Patient decision-making is only ethically valid if it is adequately informed.
(2) A patient can never be adequately informed about all the possible future medical conditions they might suffer from, or all the possible treatments that may become available.

(3) Therefore, it follows from (1–2) that treatment decisions based on precedent autonomy may not be informed (if, for example, new treatment options become available after the person has become incapacitated).
(4) Therefore, it follows from (1), (2), and (3) that decisions based on precedent autonomy may not be ethically valid.

This argument, however, has only a limited application, as it won't include very specific advance directives that cover treatment areas of which the patient was well-informed when they made the directive and for which the information still holds. At the very least, however, it does provide good reason as to why advance directives should be regularly updated to avoid concerns surrounding the levels of relevant information informing those decisions.

The other significant epistemological challenge concerns our ability to represent the thoughts of another. The issue is partly practical and partly an ongoing debate in Epistemology and the Philosophy of Mind that is relevant to how well a proxy can make a substituted judgement. On a practical level, the few studies available seem to indicate that we are not particularly good at making accurate substituted judgements for other people, even in the case of close relatives.[21] Although this may be simply reflective of the lack of discussion about personal values and the lack of experience at making such judgements, there is a more substantial concern that, given our best theories of representation and simulation of another person's decision-making process, it is virtually impossible to do this accurately in a substituted judgement setting.[22]

The difficulty faced by a proxy in capturing there being some "fact of the matter" as to what decisions a person would have made, were they able, impacts on the way we might understand proxy authority. It seems unlikely that the moral authority of a proxy can be established on the basis of their having epistemic privilege over others that allows them to capture the decisions that would have been made.[23] Although this does not rule out their being endowed or bequeathed the authority to simply make their own decisions on behalf of someone else, it does make the perceived "gold standard" of the substituted judgement standard of proxy decision-making appear a less plausible standard for proxy consent to aim for.

28.4.3 Challenges to the moral authority of proxies

If the moral authority to make decisions on behalf of another is viewed as an extension of our own contemporaneous autonomous decision-making authority, then whether it is ever possible to transfer or "bequeath" moral authority to another person lies at the very heart of considering what grounds we might have for respecting the decision of the proxy, rather than the decisions of some other person or group of people. The response that it is simply because they are the ones designated to do so does not provide us with a convincing philosophical explanation.

This problem has been addressed in detail by Wrigley (2015), in which a two-horned dilemma is posed. On the one horn, if proxy decisions lack the moral authority of a contemporaneous autonomous decision, their use is undermined because we would lack the moral obligation to respect a proxy's decisions as if they were the decisions of the still-autonomous individual. The other horn of the dilemma arises in response to a particular concern about the transfer or "bequeathing" of decision-making authority. If proxy decisions do have moral authority akin to contemporaneous autonomous decisions, this creates the possibility for the repeated application of the extension of authority process, allowing a proxy to potentially appoint their own proxy to make decisions for both themselves and the person they were acting as proxy for. This results in decisions being made by decision-makers to whom the authority had not been initially extended. Reflecting upon this dilemma tells us something about the foundations of proxy decision-making, the extent to which it offers us control over future treatment decisions, and whether this can really be said to be an extension of the original appointing individual's autonomy. The implication is that, either way, we should view proxy decision-making as offering much less scope over how we wish future decisions to be made on our behalf than may currently be anticipated.

This is not to say that justifications for respecting the decisions of a proxy are not available to us on moral grounds other than as a bequeathed extension of our own autonomy, such as making appeal to the status of the proxy themselves as being in some way trustworthy or worthy of respect, or the way in which guardians or other decision-makers are appointed for children or people who have never been competent, often with a default to the "next of kin".[24] Moreover, there are plenty of cases where we grant limited decision-making authority to others to act as our agents whilst we are ourselves still competent, autonomous agents. However, the reason for addressing the transfer of authority in the way suggested by Wrigley (2015) is that it is a direct challenge to the "extension view" of our precedent autonomy. What ultimately gives someone else the authority to consent on behalf of another may have a very different foundation than it being simply an extension of an individual's autonomous wish that they do this.

28.5 Conclusion

Although we might lack an entirely compelling account of the moral authority underpinning some of the approaches to obtaining consent, practical imperatives force us to seek some means of making decisions for others. Although legal and practical approaches provide us with sanctioned decision-makers, whether their decisions constitute consent is unlikely to be established unless we are able to provide a convincing account of how the moral authority to consent for others is established.

Notes

1 One major exception to this is the comprehensive and compelling work by Buchanan & Brock (1990), which has grounded much of the subsequent debate in this area since its publication and remains one of the foremost works on the topic.
2 Although recognising the wide range of areas this may apply to, such as financial, lifestyle, and relationship choices, the focus here is on medical treatment decisions. It will also be on consenting for adults rather than for children.
3 There are well-recognised limitations to this, such as enforced quarantine to limit communicable diseases, requests within what is legally permissible, and that there is no right to simply receive any treatment that is demanded.
4 Mill (1859) famously advocated a paternalistic approach to those lacking autonomy.
5 Concerning the former, see Buchanan (1988); Buchanan & Brock (1990), and Wrigley (2007a). Concerning the latter, see Davis (2004, 2009), Dworkin (1988), and Wrigley (2015).
6 The "extension view" is a term famously used by Davis (2009: 349–74), although the underlying principle goes back earlier and is advocated by, e.g. Buchanan & Brock (1990). The term "precedent autonomy" is itself usually attributed to Dworkin (1993).
7 This makes it almost impossible to talk of autonomy without specifying what one takes "autonomy" to be in any given context. A significant distinction is often drawn between Kant's conception of autonomy as the foundation of morality and Mill's conception of autonomy as independently and intrinsically valuable. Here, it is a form of what Dworkin (1988) called "personal autonomy" (also called "individual autonomy"), more akin to Mill's conception, that is in play. However, there are multiple variations on what that might be; for example, Feinberg (1989) identified four central meanings of "autonomy" used in moral and political philosophy alone.
8 As developed in Dworkin (1993).

9 There is sometimes a distinction drawn between "competence" and "capacity". Little of any substance hangs on such a distinction for our purposes and they may be used interchangeably in this context.
10 Other major concerns may include adequate information provision or the liberty or voluntariness of the decision. These elements can often be addressed by changing the circumstances surrounding the consent. However, there may be rare cases where lack of voluntariness may require consent to be provided by another person. For example, lack of voluntariness that arises from problems such as a mental disorder which impedes free decision-making. Alternatively, a person may find themselves in such a restricted situation that one may plausibly maintain that they do not meet the requirement for voluntariness demanded by valid consent, for example, people detained in concentration camps or even prisons.
11 For a discussion of competence see Buchanan & Brock (1990) chapter 1.
12 This is broadly the account given in Anscombe (1981).
13 For example, Buchanan & Brock (1990) tend to favour substituted judgements whereas Harris (2003) has argued for a best-interests approach. Different jurisdictions can also require a certain approach be taken by proxies for their decisions to be considered as legally appropriate.
14 See Sibley et al. (2012).
15 See Noonan (1989).
16 This follows Locke's use of the term in his (1690) *Essay*, where he takes "person" to be a "forensic" (i.e. legal and moral) term. I have, however, refrained from defining "person" in terms of the properties with which we attribute the making of moral decisions and being morally responsible for their actions, as this might be seen to beg the question against certain accounts of personhood.
17 Other accounts include, for example, narrative accounts of personal identity often traced back to MacIntyre (1984). See also the discussion in DeGrazia (2005). Parfit (1984) has even argued that questions of identity may not be what matters at all.
18 This approach has been refined numerous times to involve greater degrees of continuity and connectedness, for example, by Mackie (1976) and Parfit (1984).
19 Various thought experiments involving losing our bodies but having our minds preserved and the subsequent favouring of preferring to consider that our existence continues to follow our minds tend to support this view. More challenging cases involve "split brain" considerations. See Parfit (1984).
20 See Wrigley (2007a).
21 See, for example, Seckler et al. (1991), Suhl et al. (1994), and Sulmasy et al. (1998).
22 As advanced by Wrigley (2007b). These concerns utilise the theories of mental representation given in Davies & Stone (1995a, 1995b).
23 This debate has been pursued in much further detail concerning the validity of substituted judgements as based on "counterfactual wishes" models in terms of "what the other person would have decided had they been able to do so for themselves". See Wierenga (1983), Barnbaum (1999), and Wrigley (2011).
24 See e.g. Aiken & LaFollette (1980).

References

Aiken, W. and H. LaFollette (ed.) (1980) *Whose Child? Children's Rights, Parental Authority and State Power*. Totowa, NJ: Rowman & Littlefield.

Anscombe, G.E.M. (1981) *Ethics, Religion and Politics*. Oxford: Basil Blackwell.

Barnbaum, D. (1999) "Interpreting Surrogate Consent Using Counterfactuals," *Journal of Applied Philosophy* 16: 167–72.

Buchanan, A. (1988) "Advance Directives and the Personal Identity Problem," *Philosophy and Public Affairs* 17(4): 277–302.

Buchanan, A.E. and D.W. Brock (1990) *Deciding for Others: The Ethics of Surrogate Decision Making*. Cambridge: Cambridge University Press.

Davies, M. and T. Stone (ed.) (1995a) *Folk Psychology: The Theory of Mind Debate*. Oxford: Blackwell.

Davies, M. and T. Stone (ed.) (1995b) *Mental Simulation: Evaluations and Applications*. Oxford: Blackwell.

Davis, J.K. (2004) "Precedent Autonomy and Subsequent Consent," *Ethical Theory and Moral Practice* 7: 267–91.

Davis, J.K. (2009) "Precedent Autonomy, Advance Directives, and End-of-Life Care," in B. Steinbock (ed.), *The Oxford Handbook of Bioethics*. New York: Oxford University Press, pp. 349–74.

DeGrazia, D. (1999) "Advance Directives, Dementia and 'the Someone Else Problem'," *Bioethics* 13: 373–91.
DeGrazia, D. (2005) *Human Identity and Bioethics*. Cambridge: Cambridge University Press.
Dworkin, G. (1988) *The Theory and Practice of Autonomy*. Cambridge: Cambridge University Press.
Dworkin, R. (1993) "Life Past Reason," in R. Dworkin (ed.), *Life's Dominion*. New York: Vintage Books, pp. 218–41.
Feinberg, J. (1989) "Autonomy," in J.P. Christman (ed.), *The Inner Citadel: Essays on Individual Autonomy*. New York: Oxford University Press, pp. 27–53.
Harris, J. (2003) "Consent and End of Life Decisions," *Journal of Medical Ethics* 29: 10–15.
Locke, J. (1690) *Essay Concerning Human Understanding*, reprinted 1975, ed. P.H. Nidditch. Oxford: Oxford University Press.
MacIntyre, A. (1984) *After Virtue: A Study in Moral Theory*. Notre Dame: University of Notre Dame Press.
Mackie, J. (1976) *Problems from Locke*. Oxford: Oxford University Press.
Mill, J.S. (1859) *On Liberty*. London: Penguin Classics, repr. 1985.
Noonan, H. (1989) *Personal Identity*. London: Routledge.
Olsen, E. (1997) *The Human Animal*. Oxford: Oxford University Press.
Parfit, D. (1984) *Reasons and Persons*. Oxford: Oxford University Press.
Seckler, A.B., D.E. Meier, M. Mulvihill and B.E. Cammer Paris (1991) "Substituted Judgement: How Accurate are Proxy Predictions?" *Annals of Internal Medicine* 115: 92–8.
Sibley, A., M. Sheehan and A.J. Pollard (2012) "Assent is Not Consent," *Journal of Medical Ethics* 38(1): 3.
Snowdon, P.F. (1990) "Persons, Animals and Ourselves," in C. Gill (ed.), *The Person and the Human Mind*. Oxford: Clarendon Press.
Suhl, J., P. Simons, T. Reedy and T. Garrick (1994) "Myth of Substituted Judgement: Surrogate Decision Making Regarding Life Support is Unreliable," *Archives of Internal Medicine* 154: 90–6.
Sulmasy, D.P., P.B. Terry, C.S. Weisman, D.J. Miller, R.Y. Stallings, M.A. Vettese, et al. (1998) "The Accuracy of Substituted Judgements in Patients with Terminal Diagnoses," *Annals of Internal Medicine* 128: 621–9.
Wierenga, E. (1983) "Proxy Consent and Counterfactual Wishes," *The Journal of Medicine and Philosophy* 8: 405–16, at p. 406.
Wiggins, D. (2001) *Sameness and Substance*. Second Edition. Cambridge, MA: Harvard University Press.
Wrigley, A. (2007a) "Personal Identity, Autonomy and Advance Statements," *Journal of Applied Philosophy* 24(4): 381–96.
Wrigley, A. (2007b) "Proxy Consent: Moral Authority Misconceived," *Journal of Medical Ethics* 33(9): 527–31.
Wrigley, A. (2011) "The Problem of Counterfactuals in Substituted Judgement Decision-Making," *Journal of Applied Philosophy* 28(2): 169–87.
Wrigley, A. (2015) "Moral Authority and Proxy Decision-Making," *Ethical Theory and Moral Practice* 18: 631–47.

Further reading

Feinberg, J. (1986) *Harm to Others: The Moral Limits of the Criminal Law*. Oxford: Oxford University Press.
Newson, A.J. (2007) "Personhood and Moral Status," in R.E. Ashcroft, A. Dawson and H. Draper (ed.), *Principles of Health Care Ethics*. Chichester: John Wiley & Sons, pp. 277–83.
O'Neill, O. (2002) *Autonomy and Trust in Bioethics*. Cambridge: Cambridge University Press.

Related topics

Ch.8 Valid consent
Ch.12 Consent and autonomy

PART V

Political philosophy

29

HISTORICAL PERSPECTIVES IN POLITICAL PHILOSOPHY

Alex Tuckness

Consent is now one of the most powerful concepts in political and moral philosophy. For many people on many topics, "Was it consensual?" is the decisive question in forming a moral evaluation of an action. In politics, the U.S. Declaration of Independence's claim that "Governments are instituted among Men, deriving their just powers from the consent of the governed" has gone from revolutionary to commonplace. It has not always been so. Although there are important precursors in earlier stages of history, in the West the increasing importance of consent is a feature of the modern period, which began in the 17th century. This chapter will look at the concept of consent in political philosophy over the last 400 years with the aim of improving our understanding of contemporary debates about consent. The paper will do so by looking at consent as a five-dimensional concept and comparing different ways of understanding consent in four of the most influential philosophers of the modern period: Thomas Hobbes (1588–1679), John Locke (1632–1704), David Hume (1711–1776), and John Stuart Mill (1806–1873). These four British philosophers have been very influential in shaping the conception of consent that is currently dominant in the English-speaking world. Space will only permit a discussion of the broad outlines of their theories – for more nuances and qualifications consult the suggestions for further reading.

The claim that consent is a five-dimensional concept means that when confronted with a political claim about consent it is helpful to differentiate five different questions:

1. What is the *domain* of consent? (Whose consent is required?)
2. What is the *range* of consent? (For what sorts of situations is consent relevant?)
3. What are the *characteristics* of a legitimate act of consent? (Under what circumstances is a putative act of consent invalid?)
4. What is the *source* of consent's normative force? (Why does an act of giving or withholding consent change what is morally acceptable or legitimate?)
5. What is the *effect* of consent? (A different moral evaluation? Different legal rights? The legitimacy of government?)

Often in contemporary debates we focus on only a subset of these questions, thinking that the answers to the other questions are uncontroversial. Our historical study will help us see ways in which all of these questions are controversial and make us more aware of what people are actually doing today when they make consent arguments. For each thinker, we will examine the conception of consent along the first four dimensions. For the fifth dimension, we will use the following terminology and indicate the relevant type as appropriate. If the presence or absence of consent changes our moral evaluations of particular actions, we will call it "moral consent". If it changes legal rights, duties, permissions, or immunities we will call it "legal consent". If it affects the legitimacy of government we will call it "political consent". Since this chapter focuses on political philosophy, the focus will be on legal and political consent. In the conclusion to this chapter I will show how all five dimensions of consent have been contested in the quest for equal rights for women.

29.1 Hobbes

The first question, about the *domain* of consent, is perhaps the one most frequently overlooked but is actually one of the most important. In our eagerness to argue about the characteristics of valid consent and the range of cases where consent is needed we ignore the fact that there is a prior question: who has a status such that their consent is needed? Different societies have answered this question in different ways, but all restrict it in some ways. The legal consent of an adult is normally required for medical treatment, but for children the consent of a parent or guardian is sufficient. Likewise, adults who have been declared mentally incompetent may not enter into legally binding contracts. Debates about consent are in part debates about the relative status of different groups within a society. While the above examples are by no means exhaustive, it is fair to say that, historically, a much larger percentage of the population was excluded from "consent needed" status. Social class, race, and gender have frequently been used to declare that the consent of some people, but not others, is required in otherwise similar circumstances. This is what we mean by the domain of consent.

It is against this background that we can appreciate one of the most radical aspects of the philosophy of Thomas Hobbes. Hobbes argued in his most famous work, *Leviathan* (published in 1651), that all rational people (and even children who lacked the full use of reason) were ultimately obligated to obey the government because they had consented to do so (Hobbes 1996: 120–1). Previous theories had typically viewed political obligation as natural or a divinely imposed duty.

Hobbes began by describing people in a state of nature where there was no government and life was characterized as a war of all against all. In such a state, there were no moral duties, no enforceable social hierarchies. In such a state all people, male or female, rich or poor, were free to act as they thought best to try to preserve themselves. A telling example of Hobbes's radical approach is family obligations. Hobbes claims that husbands have legal power over their wives only if the sovereign so decrees and that the power of husbands is grounded in the consent of their wives. Similarly, even children are obliged to obey their parents because they have consented to do so, either implicitly or explicitly (Hobbes 1996: 139–40). Hobbes's radical answer to the domain question meant that women and children were capable of giving consent and that their actual consent explained their obligations.

Hobbes's egalitarian answer to the domain question was interestingly paired with a very authoritarian approach to the *range* of consent. Hobbes claimed that the range of legal consent is whatever the sovereign declares it to be (Hobbes 1996: 124–5). We give political consent to obey the sovereign in order to escape the state of war that exists under conditions of anarchy. Since limiting the power of the sovereign would invite a return to civil war, the sovereign decides the limits of liberty including the sorts of actions that are determined by legal consent. Should commercial exchanges take place if both buyer and seller consent? Only if the sovereign says they should. Is the legal consent of a parent needed for a teenager to get an abortion? Only if the sovereign says that it is. For Hobbes, there is nothing in the fabric of the universe that dictates specific answers to these questions. The sovereign is to make decisions about how big the range of consent should be with a view to promoting peace and stability.

Hobbes's explanation of the *characteristics* of consent is very permissive, meaning that there are few circumstances which render an act of consent invalid. He thinks that consent merely requires an intelligible sign (explicit or tacit) from both parties that they consent, and consent leads to an obligation if there is a sovereign to enforce the contract (Hobbes 1996: 94–5). That means that a contract entered into under duress is still a binding contract for Hobbes unless the sovereign has prohibited such contracts. Hobbes thinks that submitting to someone who could have killed us counts as consent. In practice, Hobbes thinks this explains much of the obligations of children to parents and subjects to sovereigns. The characteristics of legal consent would depend on the rules set by the sovereign, but there is no reason that fear-induced consent cannot legitimate particular actions or consent to the legitimacy of the sovereign.

Why would Hobbes think that a subject who agrees to obey the sovereign when threatened with death if she refuses is morally bound by such an act of consent? Hobbes's answer is that otherwise there would be no escape from the state of nature. We fear death there and consent to political authority to escape death. If fear of death invalidates political consent, there is no way out of the state of nature. We enter into many contracts because we fear some negative consequence – I take a job I don't like because I fear defaulting on my mortgage. If we really allowed people to avoid the obligations of contracts because their motive in signing was to avoid a harmful outcome, it would actually undermine many of our practices.

Although there is some disagreement, a common interpretation is that Hobbes thought the *source* of consent's normative force was self-interest. In fact, there is disagreement about whether "normative" is even the right word for it. Hobbes thought the keeping of covenants was the only way out of the state of nature and that therefore it is in our interest to perform them (Hobbes 1996: 100–1). If self-interest is our only motive for respecting consent, some question whether this counts as an authentically moral reason. Thus Hobbes included women and children in the domain of consent, gave the sovereign free reign over the range of consent, and took a permissive view of the characteristics of valid consent – even including consent that is given under duress, as that is just another way for self-interest to motivate consent.

29.2 Locke

John Locke continued in Hobbes's path by using the state of nature and a social contract as the basis for his political philosophy, but developed these ideas in a very different direction. His version of the argument much more closely resembles contemporary understandings of consent. Like Hobbes, Locke makes political consent the basis for political obligation for all citizens and thus reaffirms the egalitarian starting point of Hobbes regarding the *domain* of consent. It is noteworthy that Locke's account of marriage in the state of nature renders it roughly a contract between equals (Locke: 2.81).[1] The two parties are free to specify whether the union is permanent or for a period of time and presumably many other "Conditions" so long as these do not thwart the purpose of marriage, which is to care for any resulting children. The woman has as much freedom to agree to the marriage, or not, as the man. Locke does fall short of marriage equality since he argues that once in marriage one person's will must prevail and that it is "natural" that this be the man's (Locke: 2.82). Nonetheless, viewing the woman as having standing to decide whether or not to marry by giving her legal consent is significant. Locke is also explicit that those lacking full use of their rational faculties (children for example) are not subjects whose consent is needed (Locke: 2.60).

One interesting question is whether, for purposes of political legitimacy, Locke thought the domain of political consent extended to all economic classes. Locke argues that people consent to create a political community in order to protect their property (Locke: 2.123). He also argues that God gave property "to the use of the industrious and rational" who acquire property through their labor (Locke: 2.34). What then is the status of people who don't own property? One answer is that they are not full members of the political community. Minimum property requirements for voting were used in Locke's day to restrict the domain of political consent. Another interpretation of Locke points out that Locke used the term "property" broadly as including not just money, land, and possessions but also life and liberty (Locke: 2.123). In that sense, all people have property to protect.

Locke's *range* of consent differs from Hobbes in that there are universal moral principles (the laws of nature) that Locke thinks constrain what one can consent to. Whereas in Hobbes the laws of nature are in our self-interest, Locke thinks that there are moral principles that can be known by reason in the state of nature that set limits on the pursuit of our self-interest. Locke identifies that fundamental law of nature as "as much as may be, all the members of the society are to be preserved" (Locke: 2.159). From this Locke derives rights to the protection of life, liberty, and property (Locke: 2.6). A contract where people consent to do something contrary to natural law would be void. For example, Locke indicates that individuals do not have the right to commit suicide since doing so is contrary to the fundamental law of nature (Locke: 2.6). Locke would thus reject the claim that moral consent to physician-assisted suicide would make such an act permissible. Once political society is formed, consent may be further constrained by positive laws. The legislative power can stipulate rules for marriage, contracts, and so forth so long as these rules do not violate natural law and promote the public good (Locke: 2.135). For example, Locke assumes that there can be some regulation of inheritance and bequest to ensure that surviving children are not left indigent (Locke: 1.88–9, 2.72).

Locke also has a more demanding test than Hobbes regarding the *characteristics* of consent. Here and elsewhere it will be helpful to draw a comparison between promises and consent. They are different in that the former normally means that the promisor incurs a new obligation, while consent normally involves giving someone else permission to act in some way or other. They are similar in that both change our normative situation by an act of the will and both are often thought suspect if not the result of an informed, voluntary choice. They also often rely on similar sources of justification related to the value of respecting considered choices and commitments. For this reason we will sometimes use discussions of the characteristics of a valid promise to shed light on what some of the thinkers thought were the conditions of valid consent. Likewise, the reasons promises are binding often shed light on the reasons they thought consent was binding.

Locke denied that "men are bound by promises, which unlawful force extorts from them" (Locke: 2.176, 186). Force used contrary to natural law or the legitimate laws of the government makes subsequent "consent" void. Locke also thought that political consent that is merely "tacit" was sufficient to give someone an obligation to obey the laws of the government although not sufficient to make someone a full member of political society. For example, inheriting property or traveling on the highway counts as tacit political consent (Locke: 2.119). In both cases a person is choosing to enjoy the benefits of living under the protection of the government and is therefore obliged to obey (assuming that government has not lost its legitimacy by violating the trust placed in it).

Turning lastly to the *source* of consent's normative force, Locke leaned heavily on a theory of natural law. The keeping of contracts and agreements is extremely beneficial for helping preserve mankind and thus the keeping of contracts can be justified as a derivation from the fundamental law of nature. If one asks about the moral force of the fundamental law of nature, Locke's answer was theological: human beings belong to God and are ultimately God's property (Locke: 2.6). Locke thinks we can reasonably infer that God intends for his property to be preserved.

29.3 Hume

David Hume's (1711–1776) views on the *domain* of consent were fairly conventional for 18th-century England. He wrote in his essay *Idea for a Perfect Commonwealth* in favor of "allowing none to vote in the county elections who possess not a property of 200 pounds value" (Hume IPC: 231).[2] One of his reasons was the high value he placed on stability of possessions and property. Those who already have substantial wealth have the greatest incentive to maintain that stability.

Hume's views on the *range* of consent, by contrast, sought to overthrow the dominance of the social contract tradition typified by Hobbes and Locke. Both of them thought that we should obey government *because* we have consented to do so. Hume's *Of the Original Contract* (1748) challenged the claim that acts of political consent, whether tacit or express, were the real explanation for political obligation. He acknowledged that in one sense the political consent theorists had a point. No one is strong enough to govern without the voluntary cooperation of the governed (Hume OC: 187). What Hume denied was that the reason the voluntarily cooperating subjects would give for why they were voluntarily cooperating was that they had consented to do so.

In *Of the Original Contract,* Hume advanced several reasons for doubting both the existence of and relevance of some act of political consent by previous generations that explains our political obligations. Hume pointed out that in practice most political regimes gained their current territories by war, not consent, and that their subjects nonetheless tend to regard them as legitimate. Most people never stop to think about why they regard the law as legitimate, which is strange if an act of political consent is what grounds the obligation to obey the law. In many countries, proclaiming that government exists by the consent of the governed would be considered treason. Why are people bound by the political consent of their ancestors who allegedly consented to the government under which they now live? Can we plausibly say that holding an election means that people thereby consent to the rule of the government?

Hume continues his argument by dismissing the claim that tacit political consent solves the problem. Tacit consent is where consent is implied by some action (for example choosing to continue living in one's country of birth after becoming an adult). On the contrary, "such an implied consent can only have place where a man imagines that the matter depends on his choice" (Hume OC: 193). While it is possible to communicate consent nonverbally, one must still be conscious that one is consenting and most people don't think the legitimacy of the government depends on what they do or do not consent to. Nor does mere residence in a community count. "Can we seriously say, that a poor peasant or artisan has a free choice to leave his country, when he knows no foreign language or manners, and lives from day to day, by the small wages which he acquires?" (Hume OC: 193).

Hume's rejection of political consent as an explanation for the legitimacy of government does not mean he thought there was no appropriate range within which moral or legal consent carried normative force. Hume assumed that both law and social convention would create significant spaces (such as market transactions) where the mutual consent of parties determined what could and could not be done (Hume T: 3.2.4). Similarly, promises are an extremely valuable way of coordinating human activity and promises require the consent of the appropriate parties. The range of consent is therefore set by the gradual development of conventional norms about the spheres in which allowing consent to play a substantial moral role is beneficial (Hume T: 3.2.5). Thus Hume would reject both the doctrinaire libertarian claim that consent more or less always trumps competing consideration and the alternative view that consent is unimportant.

In the process of explaining his reasons for why the range of consent did not extend to legitimating governments Hume also set out a number of important claims about the *characteristics* of consent. Hume accepted Locke's claim that threats mean that a person did not have a real opportunity to make a choice when agreeing to a contract but went further. Hume makes it clear that consent requires a conscious decision where one is aware of what it is one is consenting to and where one thinks that moral, legal, or political consequences follow from whether one gives or withholds consent. Thus if I am to legally consent to a medical procedure I must have enough information to know that I am doing so, and be aware that I have communicated somehow (even by just the nod of my head) that I do consent. The legitimacy of the doctor commencing treatment depends in large part on whether I have in fact consented. Hume also expands the range of factors that plausibly mean a person had no choice. Hume thinks that not only violent threats take away choice but also poverty and lack of resources (as in the case of the peasants who have no plausible way of emigrating to a foreign country and thus do not register consent merely by continuing to reside in their current location). He also thinks that an unacceptably hard choice (needing to leave one's extended family and move to another country where one knows neither language nor customs) also fails as an example of genuine consent.

Lastly, Hume gave a clear and influential answer to the question of the source of consent's normative power. He wrote:

> We are bound to obey our sovereign, it is said; because we have given a tacit promise to that purpose. But why are we bound to observe our promise? It must here be asserted, that the commerce and intercourse of mankind, which are of such mighty advantage, can have no security where men pay no regard to their engagements. In like manner, may it be said, that men could not live at all in society, at least in a civilized society, without laws and magistrates and judges, to prevent the encroachments of the strong upon the weak, of the violent upon the just and equitable. The obligation to allegiance being of like force and authority with the obligation to fidelity, we gain nothing by resolving the one into the other. The general interests or necessities of society are sufficient to establish both.
>
> *(Hume OC: 196–7)*

There is nothing magical about uttering the mere words "I promise" or "I agree". To merely invoke promising as an explanation for why consent is binding leads to the question of what grounds the obligation to fulfill promises. A simpler explanation is that we recognize governments as legitimate because they are useful and promises as binding for the same reason (promising is a useful practice).

Hume is not arguing that moral or legal consent are irrelevant; he is only arguing that consent is not the ultimate justification. The reason I have an obligation to fulfill a specific promise is that I consented to make the promise. Our acts of consent shape the set of moral obligations we have. Instead, Hume is making two related points. First, the practice of promising derives its justification from the fact that the practice of promising is useful. Second, unlike typical instances of consent in everyday life, there is no evidence that citizens have given the necessary consent to legitimate government and so it makes much more sense to simply note that governments and law are socially beneficial practices and that people obey their governments because they value the benefits that government provides.

29.4 Mill

John Stuart Mill (1806–1873) was one of the foremost utilitarian philosophers. Utilitarians advanced the claim that right actions are those that maximize human well-being (often measured in terms of pleasure and pain). Since utilitarianism claims to be the answer to more or less all moral questions, it also claims to provide answers for all of the questions we have raised about consent. According to utilitarians, we should extend the *domain* of legal consent in whatever manner maximizes utility. The *range* of consent is set by asking when leaving matters to the mutual consent of the agreeing parties will maximize utility. We specify the *characteristics* of legal consent based on what legal framework maximizes utility (making the conditions too strict might fail to recognize genuine acts of consent while making them too lax might recognize consent where none has been given). The *source* of consent's binding power (as with Hume) is the utility that the practice produces. The above considerations apply whether we are talking about moral, legal, or political consent. What makes Mill of special interest is that the particular way he went about answering these questions from a utilitarian perspective has been very influential.

Mill was a proponent of representative government. One of his main arguments in his book *Considerations on Representative Government* is that democratic government gives people an opportunity to actively develop their higher intellectual faculties, while absolutism leads to passivity. Representative government allows for democratic participation in large societies. He proposed institutions that would allow people to select representatives who shared their positions.

It is against this background that we can consider his views on the *domain* of consent. Mill sought to further enlarge the domain, though not as much as some might have wished. In *Considerations on Representative Government* Mill makes a series of observations about the sorts of populations "suitable" or "fit" for representative government. Mill assumed that there is a threshold of education, commitment to democracy and the rule of law, and commitment to the public good that must be present before democracy is desirable. In doing so, Mill attempted to justify British colonial holdings, which were run in an authoritarian rather than democratic manner, by arguing that it is right to impose "despotic" government on "savage" people until such time as the savages have progressed to the point where they are ready for self-government (CRG: 47).[3] Those who rule a savage people must do so with the goal of improving their condition and helping them progress to that point.

It is against the background of Mill's support for imperialism that we can assess his views about the expansion of the franchise within Britain. After all, in the same way that there can be differences of competence between people groups, there can also be differences between individuals. Mill writes that:

> it is a personal injustice to withhold from anyone, unless for the prevention of greater evils, the ordinary privilege of having his voice reckoned in the disposal of affairs in which he has the same interest as other people. If he is compelled to pay, if he may be compelled to fight, if he be required to implicitly obey, he should be legally entitled to be told what for; *to have his consent asked,* and his opinion counted at its worth, *though not at more than its worth.*
>
> *(CRG: 173, emphasis added)*

Notice several things about this passage. First, Mill is following Locke and others in stretching the term "consent" to cover things like voting. In cases like this, voting "no" may still lead to a change in your legal status if more people vote "yes". This is not a case where withholding individual legal consent necessarily maintains the status quo. Second, the question of who gets to vote on matters of general interest is equivalent to "whose consent is asked?" While voting no on a law or against a candidate does not insure that you can veto that law or candidate (others may out vote you), you have at least been asked if you consent. Third, whether a person's consent is asked is an important marker of a person's status within a community, and the failure to ask for consent from someone may be an injustice against that person. Mill, therefore, sees questions about the domain of consent as raising important questions of justice. Fourth, Mill stops short of insisting that everyone's opinion counts the same: "his opinion counted at its worth, though not more than its worth".

Practically speaking, the implications were these: Mill advocated an expansion of the suffrage both economically and with respect to gender but stopped short of advocating for universal suffrage. He thought that only those who pay taxes should have the right to elect the legislators who set the rate of taxes (CRG: 176), meaning that the poorest in society were excluded from the domain of consent in this sense, although they might still have been recognized as having standing to enter into binding contracts. Beggars and those living off the dole would be excluded from full citizenship for several years until they demonstrated an ability to support themselves and contribute to the treasury. While narrower than the suffrage rules of contemporary democracies, this was not an unusual position to hold in Mill's day.

What was more unusual was the way he sought to expand, rather than contract, the domain of consent. He argued that wage laborers should be able to vote, though their votes might be weighted less than those of their more educated fellow citizens. Mill was trying to balance two considerations: making sure that hard-working laborers are not insulted by being told their consent is unnecessary and making sure that the wisest have the most influence on policies. "Every one has a right to feel insulted by being made a nobody, and stamped as of no account at all. No one but a fool, and only a fool of a particular description, feels offended by the acknowledgement that there are others whose opinion, and even whose wish, is entitled to greater amount of consideration than his"(CRG: 181). Technically it is education and intelligence, not property, that qualifies a person for extra votes, although Mill acknowledges correlations among these possible qualifications. Certain people would be given extra votes by virtue of being certified in a learned profession or graduating from a prestigious university, but others might receive extra votes simply by demonstrating their knowledge on an exam (CRG: 185). Mill also argued that for the same reason women ought to be able to vote and enter into legal contracts on the same basis as men (see CRG: 190–5 and *The Subjugation of Women* printed in OL). Women should be allowed to pursue education and professional careers and be asked whether they consent to representatives or policies in the same way men are asked.

In the same way that Mill expanded the boundaries of the domain of consent, he also expanded the boundaries of the *range* of consent. In his classic book, *On Liberty*, Mill argued that governments should normally intervene in a person's life only to protect others from harm (OL: 13) and that mutually consensual actions do not normally count as harms (OL: 15). For this reason, Mill argues that many areas of life where government prohibitions limit individual freedom should instead be areas where individuals may undertake risks if they give legal consent to do so. Mill argues against the prohibition of alcohol and against prohibiting drunkenness (where no harm is caused to others), Sabbatarian legislation, sumptuary laws, prohibitions on the sale of poisons, religious persecution, and for the legalization of polygamy. Although he hedges on complete legalization, he shows clear sympathy for legalizing prostitution and gambling (OL: chapters 4–5). Mill is thus carving out a large space within which the decisive consideration from the standpoint of the law is whether the individuals participating give legal consent, not whether society as a whole approves.

Mill also placed some restrictions on the *range* of consent. Like Hume, Mill affirms that the range of consent does not extend to a contract legitimating government (OL: 75). Rather, political obligations are best explained by the benefits people receive from participating in a political society. Respect for the law is a principle which, if acted upon by all, improves the overall happiness of society. Like Hume, he is skeptical of political consent in its more demanding forms. Second, Mill noted that consent should be restricted when a person consents to something that will foreclose particularly important decisions in the future. People may not consent to a marriage with no possibility of divorce because people cannot meaningfully know before marriage the sorts of experiences they may have in marriage and what their future self will want (PPE: 5.11.10). Mill similarly rejects the idea that a person could consent to sell himself into slavery (OL: 102–3).

Mill was also very clear about the *characteristics* of valid consent. Society has only indirect interest in actions that affect only the person performing them or others "with their free, voluntary, and undeceived consent and participation" (OL: 15). Hobbes had argued two centuries beforehand that "nothing done to a man, by his own Consent, can be injury" (Hobbes: 104). Mill, however took what for Hobbes had been a justification for restricting individual liberty (you cannot be injured by the sovereign because you consented to his rule, albeit perhaps at knife point) and turned it into an argument for restricting state power to further individual liberty. Mill argues that we can normally assume that mature adults are the best judges of what is in their interest and that therefore activities which they consent to participate in freely, voluntarily, and with accurate information do not count as harms the government should legally prohibit, though of course things might still go badly for a person. The gambler who gambles freely, voluntarily, and with full information is not harmed, in Mill's sense, even if he loses a substantial sum of money.

Mill also acknowledged that economic conditions might cause individual acts of consent to not reflect the desires of those who enter into them. In *Principles of Political Economy* (5.11.12) Mill notes that workers might prefer to limit their hours but are unable to do that unless they can coordinate their demands with those of other workers. The legal consent of persons working in sweatshops is, for this reason, suspect. Legal remedies (perhaps maximum-hour laws or collective bargaining) are needed to make it possible for workers to consent to their preferred arrangements.

Like Hume, Mill answers the final question about the *source* of consent's normative force by pointing to the usefulness of a practice where consent determines many areas of life. Mill explicitly embraces utilitarianism, claiming that it provides the ultimate explanation for why some courses of action are right and others are wrong. Some interpret Mill as a rule-utilitarian, meaning that he does not apply the principle of utility to particular decisions, but instead uses the principle of utility to derive rules which then guide moral decision making. Even if Mill is not a rule-utilitarian, it is nonetheless true that he sees the practice whereby individuals can, by their consent, shape the moral and legal rights and duties that apply to them as essential for human happiness.

One interesting complication to this story is that Mill places such a high emphasis on the value of autonomous individuality as the path to the highest happiness that the line between utilitarianism and virtue theory begins to blur. In earlier versions of utilitarianism, utilitarians prided themselves on not taking sides on the question of what makes for a good human life but instead tried to maximize the happiness and minimize the pain of other people as those people experienced it. Mill, on the other hand, can be read as arguing that autonomous individuality is the best sort of life and that, therefore, laws and customs should encourage the development of these qualities. This interpretation points to an alternative justification for the power of moral and legal consent which finds it valuable in the role it plays in fostering autonomy, independent of its contribution to happiness.

29.5 Conclusion: the five-dimensional model as one way to understand feminist claims related to consent

The five-dimensional model provides a lens through which we can look at more contemporary debates about consent. For example, first-wave feminism was largely about expanding the *domain* of *legal* consent: the consent of a woman should be required in any instance where the consent of a man is required. This was John Stuart Mill's main point in *The Subjugation of Women*. Insofar as voting is construed as an act of *political* consent, moves to expand the franchise change this aspect of the domain.

Later debates have noted specific situations and dilemmas that women face that men do not face, which require an expansion of the *range* of consent. For example, questions about whether the permissibility of abortion should be determined by the legal consent of the pregnant woman may raise issues that transcend the normal principles of requiring patient consent to medical procedures. One point of Judith Jarvis Thomson's famous article *A Defense of Abortion* (1971) defending abortion was to show that the law has placed a heavier burden on women to preserve the lives of others than it has placed on men in other instances. There are a range of issues related to reproductive freedom that may require different considerations for men and women since pregnancy affects them differently. For example, U.S. marriage laws at one point declared that a woman, when legally consenting to marriage, thereby gave legal consent to her husband to have sex with her at his will as long as they were married. Laws to repeal this have argued both that the marriage contract should not be assumed to imply such consent and that such consent, even if explicitly given at the time of marriage, is not binding thereafter.

A third set of debates involves the characteristics of valid consent. If a husband and wife agree that the wife will work part-time instead of full-time in order to handle increased domestic duties after they have children, is the normative force of the *moral* consent compromised if the background culture tends to discriminate against women in salary and puts greater social pressure on them to stay home and do unpaid housework? In other words, what counts as freely given or voluntary consent is contested and its voluntariness may be undermined not only by threats or severe economic hardships but perhaps also by some forms of socialization.

Lastly, feminist authors have suggested a range of different sources for normative force of consent. One strain of argument we see historically is an argument based on equality. Such arguments hold that the reason differential treatment of men and women is bad is that the current range or domain of consent leads to equals being treated unequally. Thus one answer to the question of why the disenfranchisement of women is wrong is that it fails to respect the value of equality. A second normative foundation is utility. Here the argument is that some or all peoples' lives would go better if consent were accepted as a regulative ideal. For example, one might argue that allowing women (rather than their fathers) to decide whether to marry and whom they will marry leads to happier people and happier marriages. One might argue that allowing women to enter professions without legal hindrances by mutual consent of employer and employee leads to better, more satisfied workers and consumers. Third, the normative force of consent can stem from a commitment to liberty as intrinsically valuable, not just as a means to promoting utility. Proposals to better protect women from sexual assault can be justified not just by the fact that sexual assaults decrease utility but also because nonconsensual sex fails to respect the autonomy of women.

Contemporary debates about consent often bracket some of the dimensions of consent while foregrounding others. One simply takes for granted the domain of consent and asks questions about the range, or one simply assumes a particular ground for consent and then asks, in light of it, what should count as an act of consent. While it is perfectly legitimate to focus on a specific aspect of the problem of consent, ideally one should be aware of the other dimensions. Historical analysis of consent allows us to be more aware of the variety of possible options along each of these dimensions.

Notes

1 References to Locke (1988) are by Treatise and Section number rather than page number.
2 References to Hume are either an abbreviation for the title of the essay and page number if it is taken from *Political Essays* (1994) or *T* followed by the Book, Chapter, and Section if taken from Hume's *Treatise* (1978).
3 For Mill, OL refers to *On Liberty* (1989), and CRG refers to *Considerations on Representative Government* (1991). Relevant selections from *Principles of Political Economy* are found in Mill's *Collected Works, vol. 3* (1965). Full citation information is in the references.

References

Hobbes, T. (1996) *Leviathan*. Cambridge: Cambridge University Press.
Hume, D. (1978) "A Treatise of Human Nature," 2nd edn. Oxford: Clarendon Press.
Hume, D. (1994) *Political Essays*. Cambridge: Cambridge University Press.
Locke, J. (1988) *Two Treatises of Government*. Cambridge: Cambridge University Press.
Mill, J.S. (1965) *Collected Works of John Stuart Mill*. Toronto: University of Toronto Press.
Mill, J.S. (1989) *On Liberty; with the Subjection of Women and Chapters on Socialism*. Cambridge: Cambridge University Press.
Mill, J.S. (1991) *Considerations on Representative Government*. Buffalo, NY: Prometheus Press.
Thomson, J.J. (1971) "A Defense of Abortion," *Philosophy and Public Affairs* 1(1): 47–66.

Further reading

Archard, D. (1990) "Free Not to be Free: The Case of the Slavery Contract in J.S. Mill's *On Liberty*," *The Philosophical Quarterly* 40(161): 453–65. (A discussion of Mill on the range of consent.)
Boucher, D. and P.J. Kelly (ed.) (1994) *The Social Contract from Hobbes to Rawls*. London: Routledge. (A collection of essays on the development of the social contract idea in the modern period.)
Buckle, S. and D. Castiglione (1991) "Hume's Critique of the Contract Theory," *History of Political Thought* 12(3): 457–80. (A helpful source on Hume and consent.)
Johnson, D. (2010) "A History of Consent in Western Thought," in F.G. Miller and A. Wertheimer (ed.), *The Ethics of Consent*. Oxford: Oxford University Press. (An account of the history of consent that goes back to ancient times.)
Simmons, A. John (1993) *On the Edge of Anarchy: Locke, Consent, and the Limits of Society*. Princeton: Princeton University Press. (Explicates Locke's consent argument and reframes it in contemporary terms.)

Related topics

Ch.30 Consent theory of political obligation

30

CONSENT THEORY OF POLITICAL OBLIGATION

George Klosko

In both the history of political theory and popular consciousness, the idea that political obligations rest on consent has played a dominant role. It is a common feature of popular discourse and important public documents. For instance, according to the *Declaration of Independence*, governments derive "their just powers from the consent of the governed". The idea that people must consent to their obligations to government is supported by the great weight liberal political theory places on values of liberty and autonomy. As Harry Beran puts this, rights to self-determination should extend to political self-determination. People should be under political authority only if they put themselves under it (Beran 1987).

In his essay "Of the Original Contract", David Hume notes the great appeal of consent as a basis for political obligations: "Where it has place", he writes, "it is surely the best and most sacred of any". But Hume also notes that "it has very seldom had place in any degree" (Hume [1748] 1985: 474). In this essay, I support Hume's assessment. I argue that consent is a powerful basis for political obligations, but only on a theoretical level. It suffers from the significant defect of inapplicability to actual political conditions. Attempts to make it apply have been unsuccessful, either failing to account for the obligations of most citizens or distorting what is ordinarily meant by consent in attempting to do so.

By political obligation, theorists generally mean a moral requirement to obey the law of one's country. Traditionally, this has been viewed as a requirement to obey the law *because it is the law*, which is generally taken to mean that political obligations are "content-independent". In other words, reasons to obey stem from the authority of the legislator as opposed to the content of particular laws (see Hart 1958, 1982). This view has a long provenance, dating back at least to the time of Thomas Hobbes. According to Hobbes: "Command is where a man saith, *Doe this* or *Doe not this*, without expecting other reason than the Will of him that sayes it" (*Leviathan*, Chap. 25; [1651] 1991: 176). Since moral requirements to obey laws follow from the means through which they are made rather than their content, legislators are able to establish obligations to obey all the laws that they make. A great strength of consent theory is its comprehensiveness, its ability to account for all political obligations.

In interpreting political obligations based on consent, it is helpful to use as a model promises, which are a clearly recognized means through which obligations are assumed.[1] To the extent that consent follows this model, it too is intuitively clear, a basis that "[n]obody doubts", according to John Locke (Locke [1690] 1988: Sec. 119). In general, a promise is made by invoking appropriate conventions in a given society, generally by uttering some formula along the lines of "I promise that . . .", or "I swear that . . .", although a range of conventions may be employed, as long as the promisor communicates her intention of making a promise. However, considerable complexity is encountered in regard to conditions that must be satisfied for a promise to be successfully completed. Three conditions are generally noted. The promisor must not be forced to make the promise. She must do so freely, and so must have reasonable alternatives to making it. Second, she must be aware of what the promise entails. This includes such matters as exactly how the promise is made, to whom it is made, and to what it commits the promisor. Third, the promisor must be competent to make it. Generally, this includes age requirements, while similar restrictions hold in regard to various psychological conditions, including mental illness and intoxication. If any of these conditions is not satisfied, a given promise will not create a binding obligation. Accordingly, these conditions may be described as "defeating conditions", as failure to satisfy one or more of them will generally prevent a binding promise from being completed (Beran 1987: 5–9). Although various additional conditions could be noted, in general, if Adam makes some promise to Beth, we may presume that the promise is valid, unless it can be shown that one or more of the defeating conditions is present. As we will see, analogous defeating conditions play a significant role in the consent theory of political obligation.

30.1 John Locke's consent theory

John Locke's *Second Treatise of Government* is the locus classicus for consent theory and one of the most familiar accounts of political obligation in the liberal tradition. A brief look at Locke's view provides an overview of both strengths and weaknesses of the position. According to Locke, people are by nature free. They originally exist in a state of nature, which is a situation without government, and so without moral requirements to obey. Because people are naturally free, nothing can remove them from this condition but their own consent (Locke [1690] 1988: Sec. 95). People in this condition are subject to the law of nature. But because there is no authority to enforce this law, Locke subscribes to the "strange Doctrine" (Sec. 13) that all men have the right to enforce it for themselves. While the state of nature is relatively peaceful, self-enforcement leads to conflict, and so people are willing to surrender this power and establish government, which they do by consenting to join together in political society and agreeing "to be concluded by the majority" (Locke [1690] 1988: Sec. 96).

The advantages of Locke's theory are apparent. In addition to its intuitive clarity, consent provides a clear basis for content-independence. In leaving the state of nature and consenting to be concluded by the majority, Adam undertakes an obligation to do whatever the majority decides – though not without limits, on which more directly. As noted above, this feature grounds political obligations that are comprehensive. Moreover, consent theory has the great advantage of accounting for what Leslie Green calls "the self-image of the state". As Green says, the state conceives of itself as a "duty imposer". By issuing directives, it is able to change people's normative status, to impose duties and other requirements on them, the content of which it, rather than they, determines (Green 1988: 86). As Green also argues, other theories of political obligation encounter difficulties accounting for this feature of political obligations, which is presumably a strong reason for the continuing attraction of consent theory.

An additional advantage is that consent to government accounts for the fact that government's authority is limited. Historically, the doctrine of consent arose in connection with limitations placed upon royal authorities that originated in their need to secure the agreement of other grandees to their plans or projects (see Klosko 2011). In a simple case, a king would summon nobles who would be asked to agree to a plan to raise taxes or undertake some war. Their consent would strengthen his position, although, in order to secure it, he would also have to make concessions. Similarly, according to consent theory, when people surrender their power to government, this is done on certain conditions. They enter into a contractual relationship with government – "the social contract" – agreeing to obey it as long as it performs the specific functions for which it was established. If it fails to fulfill these or oversteps the bounds of its original commission, it loses its legitimacy and can be resisted or overthrown. Thus consent theory is especially useful in justifying revolutions, as in Locke's *Second Treatise* and the *Declaration of Independence*.

30.2 Tacit consent and its requirements

At first sight, Locke's doctrine of consent provides strong protection for individual liberty. Political obligations require personal consent. One is not bound by the consent of one's father, or by the terms of an original contract made at the foundation of society. Each individual must agree himself (Locke [1690] 1988: Secs. 116–8). However, although "express consent" establishes clear political bonds, Locke recognizes that few people consent in this way. And so he turns to what he calls "tacit consent", other actions that people perform that are capable of binding them:

> And to this I say that every Man, that hath any Possession, or Enjoyment of any part of the Dominions of any Government, doth thereby give his tacit Consent, and is as far forth obliged to Obedience to the Laws of that Government, during such Enjoyment, as any one under it; whether this his Possession be of Land, to him and his Heirs for ever, or a Lodging only for a Week; or whether it be barely traveling freely on the Highway; and in Effect, it reaches as far as the very being of any one within the Territories of that Government.
>
> *(Locke [1690] 1988: Sec. 119)*

The actions Locke lists would account for the political obligations of all or virtually all inhabitants of the relevant territory. Frequently in modern societies, the only people who may be viewed as consenting expressly are naturalized citizens, who voluntarily move from country A to country B, and, in doing so, voluntarily assume obligations to B. For all intents and purposes, then, the consent theory of political obligation is a theory of tacit consent. However, careful examination of exactly what constitutes tacit consent reveals that, like express consent, it has difficulties accounting for the obligations of more than a fraction of society.

As A. John Simmons has argued in one of the most celebrated criticisms of tacit consent, in its essential characteristics, it is equivalent to express consent. It differs from express consent not because it is not communicated but in the manner through which it is communicated, that is, it is communicated through inaction rather than action (Simmons 1979: 80–2). For instance, imagine that I tell my class that I am going to reschedule an examination unless anyone objects, and I give them adequate opportunity to speak up. If no one raises an objection, then I may take it that they have agreed, although no one has explicitly said so. Consideration of such examples indicates the role of defeating conditions. In this case, competence may be assumed. More importantly, for the students' tacit consent to bind, they must not be forced to give it. They must consent voluntarily. In addition, as Simmons says, the means of expressing lack of consent should not be unduly difficult to perform (Simmons 1979: 81). Thus, if I tell my students that, rather than expressing themselves verbally, the means through which they should object is by doing standing backflips, their failure to perform this action would ordinarily not be viewed as constituting consent. For tacit consent, the awareness requirements are especially significant. One must not only not be forced to consent, one must be aware that tacit consent is called for and how one goes about giving it and not giving it. One must be aware of the period of time – if there is one – during which one may or may not consent. One must also be aware of what one would be committing oneself to, and the fact that this commitment would not exist unless one consented. In regard to obligations to obey the law, then, one must recognize that if one did not consent tacitly, one would not have moral requirements to obey.

The defeating conditions cause severe difficulties for acts that have been claimed to constitute tacit consent. Consider staying in one's country, which is widely viewed as the most plausible basis – as in Locke's theory. Most people are probably aware that, if they remain in a given country, they will be required to obey its laws, while this requirement will no longer obtain if they leave. Along similar lines, most people probably recognize that they undertake similar requirements when they voluntarily enter another country. For instance, a tourist entering Canada is probably aware that, if she drives, she must abide by Canadian traffic laws and may be required to pay fines if she does not. But do these considerations support the view that staying in one's country and not emigrating to another constitutes consent to obey its laws? In order for this conclusion to hold, failure to leave must not fall foul of the defeating conditions. However, how many people actually believe that continued residence constitutes consent? Unlike naturalized citizens, most people are simply born into their societies and live there largely because they have always lived there. They probably recognize that, if they leave country A for country B, they will no longer have requirements to obey the laws of A. But it seems unlikely that they recognize that tacit consent is called for, or that there is a definite period of time in which to consent or not to. Severe problems follow from the voluntariness requirement. Hanging over this form of tacit consent is the criticism of Hume, who rejects the claim in question, because the means of expressing lack of consent are not ordinarily available:

> Can we seriously say that a poor peasant or artizan has a free choice to leave his country, when he knows no foreign language or manners, and lives from day to day, by the small wages which he acquires? We may as well assert, that a man, by remaining in a vessel, freely consents to the dominion of the master, though he was carried on board while asleep, and must leap into the ocean, and perish, the moment he leaves her.
>
> *(Hume [1748] 1985: 475)*

Certainly, continued residence does not constitute tacit consent, if one is actively prevented from leaving, e.g., if borders are closed and guarded, as in the former East Germany. But as Hume says, even if borders are open, for many people it may not be possible to leave, while others would find the costs of leaving prohibitively high. If Adam is to leave country A, another country must be willing to take him. Even then, financial costs of moving could be prohibitively high, while he must be able to function adequately in B. For instance, he must know the language, be able to find a job, etc. Even if all these conditions are satisfied, it still may be extremely difficult to leave. As Simmons argues, much of what is precious in life cannot be taken with one: family, friends, a particular culture (1979: 99). Therefore, choice of either leaving or consenting tacitly could well be viewed as coercive.

Given the problems with continued residence, theorists have identified other actions that might serve. An attractive possibility is voting. If Beth votes in an election, one could argue that she has agreed to be governed by the winners, and so to obey the law (Plamenatz 1968: 168–71; Singer 1974). This argument is supported by an analogy with games. If she starts to play chess with another person, she is ordinarily viewed as agreeing to abide by its rules. But this analogy takes us only so far. First of all, in the US, many citizens do not vote. The vote in the 2016 presidential election was around 60%, which is actually high for the US (United States Elections Project, n.d.). But does this mean that the 40% of citizens who did not vote do not have political obligations? In order to make the argument bind most or all citizens, we must move from the act of voting to possessing the right to vote as constituting tacit consent. In regard to voting, knowledge requirements are especially damaging. It is unlikely that many people vote with the idea that, by doing so, they are agreeing to obey the laws of their countries, and that, if they did not vote, they would not have obligations to do so. In addition, does voting in one election bind one for the rest of one's life, or must one vote continually? Moreover, how many people would vote – and continue to vote – if they realized that, by not voting, they would free themselves from moral requirements to obey the law, including, e.g., requirements to pay their taxes? It seems clear that these and perhaps other knowledge conditions as well prevent voting from constituting tacit consent to obey the law. Although it may seem that someone who votes is among other things expressing support for her political system, this is not enough for voting to ground political obligations. To use a distinction of Simmons', we may say that voting is "consent implying" (Simmons 1979: 88–91). By this Simmons means that voting is the kind of act one would ordinarily perform only if one had consented to obey the law. But in spite of this, in itself voting does not constitute consent.

Consider other possible actions, e.g., saying the Pledge of Allegiance or taking the appropriate oath upon joining the armed forces. If we carefully assess these actions against the necessary conditions, we will likely conclude that they too come up short. While most people may be presumed to say the Pledge of Allegiance voluntarily, do they do so in the belief that saying it constitutes an agreement to obey the laws of their society? Once again and more importantly, do they believe that, if they did not say it, they would not be bound to obey? Although the oath one takes upon entering the armed forces does appear to generate moral requirements in regard to its contents, it ordinarily binds only as long as one is serving. When one leaves the armed forces, such oaths ordinarily expire.

An additional distinction of Simmons' is helpful in understanding the significance of these actions. It is likely that, when people talk about "consenting" to their government, they frequently use the term in a loose sense. Rather than accepting a moral requirement to obey the law, they have in mind an "attitudinal" sense of consent, which amounts to little more than an attitude of approval. When Claudia says that she consents to her government, what she frequently means is that she approves of it, she views it as legitimate (Simmons 1979: 93–4). Perhaps she would give it her consent, if she had an opportunity to do so – on which, more below. But this does not mean that she has actually undertaken moral commitments to obey its laws through acts of tacit consent.

30.3 Acceptance of benefits

An additional possible basis for tacit consent is that citizens consent in this manner by accepting benefits from government. An attractive quality of this position is that it connects political obligations with central functions that government performs. According to basic themes in liberal political theory, we need government to provide important services, e.g., law and order, national defense, and other necessary benefits. And so, when we make use of these benefits, we consent to obey the laws through which they are produced.

Careful examination of Locke's doctrine of consent provides evidence that he subscribed to this position, although perhaps not entirely consciously. In the passage quoted above, Locke speaks of tacit consent as given by "every man, that hath any possessions, or *enjoyment*, of any part of the dominions of any government" (Locke [1690] 1988: Sec. 119; italics supplied). In a later section, he speaks of a foreigner living in another territory "and enjoying the privileges and protection of it" as bound to obey its laws (Sec. 122). Locke is not entirely clear on what he means, but these remarks could help to fill in his view on residence as the basis for consent. One reason residing in a country could establish obligations to obey its laws is because of the benefits society or government provides. There is a certain plausibility to this position; because one receives these benefits, it seems reasonable that one should give something in return. This is especially plausible in regard to benefits that depend on the behavior of large numbers of people. For instance, law and order requires that most people obey the law. National defense requires that large numbers of people serve in the military, pay taxes to support defense industries, etc. Thus, if one benefits from the cooperative efforts of one's fellow citizens, it makes sense to hold that one too should cooperate in a similar manner (see Hart 1955). However, regardless of how plausible we view this position, it has little to do with consent. One could perhaps claim that, because Adam receives benefits from government, he has consented to obey it and should obey the law. This claim makes a certain sense in regard to benefits that Adam accepts, e.g., when he makes use of public parks or clean water. But does he do so in the belief that accepting these benefits commits him to obeying the law? More importantly, the main benefits provided by government are public goods, which Adam does not voluntarily accept. Law and order, national defense, and other similar benefits of government may be described as non-excludable. They cannot be provided to certain members of the community without being made generally available, provided to everyone else in the relevant territory who cannot help receiving them. Consent, including tacit consent, above all requires intentional actions, which, if the relevant benefits are simply provided, Adam does not perform. Once again, if we assess this position against the defeating conditions, we will see that the awareness conditions are damaging. It is unlikely that, in enjoying the benefits of law and order, Adam believes himself to be consenting to obey the laws. It seems more likely that few if any citizens make these connections.

Further examination of the connections between receipt of benefits and political obligations would take us beyond consent theory. While receipt of benefits from government can plausibly be interpreted as giving rise to political obligations, the latter can be accounted for without invoking consent. Rather, the relevant moral principles turn on reciprocity, a requirement to make appropriate return for benefits one receives. Proponents of these positions typically argue that government benefits generate the relevant moral requirements, either from gratitude or from a principle of fair play, that one should not profit from the labors of other people without performing similar labor oneself. The literature is replete with developed versions of these notions (see Walker 1988; Klosko 1992). But, once again, these theories leave consent and tacit consent behind.

30.4 Hypothetical consent[2]

In response to the difficulties of tacit consent, theorists have extended what they mean by consent. One possibility is that the consent in question need not actually be performed.

Instead, if conditions in one's country are such that one *would* consent to obey the laws if given the opportunity to do so, then this hypothetical consent could ground moral requirements to obey the law. Historically, a position along these lines can be traced back to Immanuel Kant, who contends that government's power is limited by the requirement that the legislator should "frame his laws in such a way that they could have been produced by the united will of a whole nation" (Kant [1793] 1970: 79). In a celebrated article, Jeremy Waldron argues that a conception of hypothetical consent underlies fundamental commitments of liberal political theory. Waldron views the liberal mindset as rejecting "tradition, mystery, awe and superstition as the basis of order" (1987: 134). Because of its determination to subject authority to requirements of reason, liberalism requires that laws be *transparent*. Society's fundamental principles should be capable of being understood by all individuals who are subject to them (Waldron 1987: 146). However, as bases for political obligation, these conceptions of hypothetical consent are immediately subject to criticism. To use the words of Ronald Dworkin: "A hypothetical contract is not simply a pale form of an actual contract; it is no contract at all" (Dworkin 1977: 151). The fact that the laws are such that we would consent to them does not entail that we actually have consented. Rather than grounding obligations to obey the law, hypothetical consent is a useful device for assessing the moral quality of the laws, whether they should be viewed as legitimate, or the kind of laws it would be acceptable to obey, but again, not as the actual basis for requirements to obey. Hypothetical consent performs a useful service in drawing attention away from voluntary actions performed or supposedly performed by citizens in order to assume political obligations to aspects of the political system that would justify consenting to it. But because it itself is not able to establish moral requirements to obey the law, if it is to ground these, it must be supplemented by additional moral principles.

30.5 Normative consent[3]

A notable recent development in consent theory is David Estlund's theory of "normative consent", which is related to hypothetical consent (Estlund 2008: Chap. 7). Estlund recognizes the difficulties with express and tacit consent noted above. Normative consent proceeds from the fact that, under certain circumstances, it would be wrong to consent to a given authority – e.g., if the authority is unjust or immoral. Invoking a kind of symmetry, Estlund argues that there are circumstances in which it would be wrong *not to* consent. In these circumstances, one attains obligations equivalent to those one would have if one had consented. As an example, consider a plane crash. A flight attendant is best positioned to get the passengers out safely if they coordinate their activities in accordance with her directions (2008: 124–5). Estlund claims that, under these circumstances, it would be wrong for people not to consent to obey her, and so they have obligations to obey her that are equivalent to those they would have if they had consented to do so. According to Estlund, normative consent, unlike hypothetical consent, is an actual contract theory. The reason the passengers should listen to the flight attendant is not that they would consent to do so if they had the opportunity, but because of actual obligations rooted in normative consent. However, there is an obvious weakness in this position. If there are moral reasons of sufficient weight to make it wrong not to consent to some authority, it is not clear why consent is necessary. Why are not the reasons themselves sufficient to establish the obligation? (Sreenivasan 2009) In regard to the flight attendant example, it seems that duties to help others in distress, not to cause harm, and similar moral principles provide plausible explanations for why the passengers should listen to her. Like the benefit arguments discussed above, normative consent does not require a role for consent.[4]

30.6 Reformist consent

Given the problems with the different forms of consent that we have examined, some theorists have tried a different tack. Because consent is an especially plausible basis for political obligations, they propose changing political circumstances to allow people expressly to consent. I will refer to these efforts as "reformist consent".

A possible mechanism would allow citizens to consent when they reach a certain age. Various political systems have had such procedures, among them ancient Greek cities. For example, in ancient Athens, at the age of 17, an individual could apply to be enrolled as a citizen and to acquire rights to the judicial and legislative privileges of adult Athenians. For instance, only citizens could take part in legal proceedings. Otherwise, one could not bring a case to court and one would have to be represented by a father or guardian in legal matters. The details may be set aside, although we should note that this process was not at all merely a formality. Under certain circumstances an individual whose application was rebuffed could be sold into slavery (for discussion, see Kraut 1984: 154–7).

A mechanism along these lines could be adapted to contemporary circumstances. According to Beran, at some point citizens would be given the option of consenting or not. If they chose not to, they would have to emigrate to a "dissenters' territory" (Beran 1987: 31–2, 109, 150). However, such a policy is obviously flawed. Forcing people to emigrate would be coercive for the reasons discussed above, and in this case would include additional stigma of forcing them to reside in a dissenters' territory.

Consider a similar mechanism that could be set up in the United States but that does not require emigration. At the age of 18, the age at which men are presently required to register for military service, they would be given the opportunity to swear an oath of allegiance to the government and/or Constitution, with advantages for taking the oath and/or penalties for not doing so. Because requiring such an oath would be coercive if non-consentors were forced to leave society, they would not be required to do this. The resultant policy would have to tread a narrow path between sanctions that were so harsh that they rendered consent coerced and others that were too weak to induce many people to take the oath and with it the responsibilities of citizenship.

One possible model would be like the Athenian system. Only people who consented would be eligible for the privileges of citizenship. Policy details could assume different forms, although all would result in dividing the population into two classes: full citizens, who had consented to the government and so assumed political obligations, and lesser citizens, who refused to consent and so were without political obligations but also without at least some privileges of full citizenship.

An ingenious account of a possible system is described by Michael Walzer, who uses resident aliens as a model for the lesser citizens (Walzer 1970). According to Walzer, individuals who consented would be full citizens and obligated to support the state's military policies. (His article was written during the Vietnam War period and is primarily concerned with military service.) "Resident aliens at home", lacking the privileges of citizenship, would have only negative obligations to obey the law and support domestic tranquility.

As a basis for political obligations, Walzer's proposal is immediately flawed. As just noted, people who refuse to consent are still required to obey the law. This of course means that some other basis for political obligations is operating. As with other possible mechanisms discussed above, Walzer's logic on this topic appears to make consent or the need for consent otiose. In addition, it is not immediately clear why people would consent if doing so required that they undertake military service, which they would not have to do if they did not consent. Are the privileges of citizenship in modern states of sufficient importance to motivate people to consent, in spite of so heavy a burden?

More importantly, a serious flaw with reformist consent proposals concerns what happens to individuals who refuse to consent (Klosko 1991). As we have repeatedly seen, it would not be acceptable to require them to leave the territory. But if they stay, they will benefit from the important public goods provided by government. Will non-consenters receive these benefits without being required to support the institutional mechanisms that provide them? If this were the implication, not consenting would seem quite a good deal and clearly unfair to consenters, whose efforts produced the benefits in question. On this plan, the benefits of non-consent could lead increasing numbers to refuse to consent, causing the full-citizens' costs in producing the public goods to rise, thereby encouraging additional people not to consent, and so leading to possible social collapse. It appears, then, that non-consentors must be required to cooperate in the provision of major public goods – however they are treated in regard to other functions of government. But this raises a problem we have repeatedly seen. If they are required so to contribute, what is the basis for such requirements? From the brief discussion here, it appears that these requirements stem from principles of reciprocity, that they should contribute to the provision of benefits they receive. But if this is the case, then once again, in regard to central political obligations, consent becomes otiose. These moral requirements would follow from other considerations, in this case the need to make appropriate return for benefits provided by the state.

30.7 Conclusion

At the beginning of this essay, I cited Hume's contention concerning the strengths and weaknesses of consent. On a theoretical level, he says, consent is not only a plausible basis for political obligations but likely the best there is. As we have noted, consent affirms liberal commitments to freedom and autonomy, and also accounts for the content-independence of political obligations and supports the self-image of the state. But as Hume notes, in regard to accounting for the political obligations of actual citizens, it does not succeed. We have surveyed a large number of attempts to ground political obligations in consent, all of which appear to come up short. In spite of these difficulties, it is likely that consent's intuitive appeal largely explains its continuing hold on public consciousness and theorists' repeated attempts to explain how, in spite of appearances to the contrary, citizens have actually consented.

To my mind, somewhat ironically, consent's theoretical advantages have had adverse consequences for dealing with problems of political obligation. Because of the features we have noted, consent has served as a model for what a successful theory of obligation should look like. A suitable theory must not only account for the obligations of actual citizens but, like consent, it should be intuitively plausible, account for content-independence, and explain obligations to obey all laws. The problem is that these are exacting standards, which it is widely believed no theory in the literature is able to meet. I believe the appeal of consent theory has contributed to current efforts to find a single moral principle that is able satisfactorily to account for all political obligations, while difficulties finding such a theory have contributed to currently widespread skepticism about the existence of political obligations in a more general sense (see esp. Simmons 1979).[5]

Notes

1 For complexities in the relationship between consent and promising, see Schnüriger (this volume, Chapter 2).

2 See Yaffe (this volume, Chapter 9).

3 See Estlund (this volume, Chapter 31).
4 An additional actual contract theory is that of Gilbert (1993, 2006), though it is central to Gilbert's position that the relevant commitments are not expressly entered into. In the absence of conscious intent to undertake them, the "joint commitments" that she discusses are too tentative and too weak to ground obligations to obey government.
5 I am grateful to Richard Dagger. Avia Pasternak, and the editors of this volume, for helpful comments on a previous version of this essay.

References

Beran, H. (1987) *The Consent Theory of Political Obligation*. London: Croom Helm.
Dworkin, R. (1977) *Taking Rights Seriously*. Cambridge, MA: Harvard University Press.
Estlund, D. (2008) *Democratic Authority: A Philosophical Framework*. Princeton, NJ: Princeton University Press.
Gilbert, M. (1993) "Group Membership and Political Obligation," *The Monist* 76: 119–31.
Gilbert, M. (2006) *A Theory of Political Obligation*. Oxford: Oxford University Press.
Green, L. (1988) *The Authority of the State*. Oxford: Oxford University Press.
Hart, H.L.A. (1955) "Are There Any Natural Rights?" *Philosophical Review* 64: 175–91.
Hart, H.L.A. (1958) "Legal and Moral Obligation," in A.I. Melden (ed.), *Essays in Moral Philosophy*. Seattle: University of Washington Press, pp. 82–107.
Hart, H.L.A. (1982) "Commands and Authoritative Legal Reasons," in *Essays on Bentham: Jurisprudence and Political Theory*. Oxford: Oxford University Press.
Hobbes, T. ([1651] 1991) *Leviathan*, edited by R. Tuck. Cambridge: Cambridge University Press, pp. 244–68.
Hume, D. ([1748] 1985) "Of the Original Contract," in E. Miller (ed.), *Essays: Moral, Political and Literary*. Revised edition. Indianapolis: Liberty Fund, pp. 465–87.
Kant, I. ([1793] 1970) "On the Current Saying: 'This May Be True in Theory, but it Does Not Apply in Practice'," in H. Reiss (ed.), *Kant's Political Writings*, trans. H. Nisbet. Cambridge: Cambridge University Press, pp. 61–92.
Klosko, G. (1991) "Reformist Consent and Political Obligation," *Political Studies* 39: 676–90.
Klosko, G. (1992) *The Principle of Fairness and Political Obligation*. Savage, MD: Rowman and Littlefield.
Klosko, G. (2011) "Political Obligation," in G. Klosko (ed.), *The Oxford Handbook of the History of Political Philosophy*. Oxford: Oxford University Press, pp. 712–24.
Kraut, R. (1984) *Socrates and the State*. Princeton, NJ: Princeton University Press.
Locke, J. ([1690] 1988) "Second Treatise on Civil Government," in P. Laslett (ed.), *Two Treatises of Government*. Cambridge: Cambridge University Press, pp. 265–428.
Plamenatz, J. (1968) *Consent, Freedom, and Political Obligation*. Second edition. Oxford: Oxford University Press.
Simmons, A.J. (1979) *Moral Principles and Political Obligations*. Princeton: Princeton University Press.
Singer, P. (1974) *Democracy and Disobedience*. Oxford: Oxford University Press.
Sreenivasan, G. (2009) "Oh But You Should Have: Estlund on Normative Consent," *Iyyun: The Jerusalem Philosophical Quarterly* 58: 62–72.
United States Elections Project. n.d. "2016 November General Election Turnout Rates," www.electproject.org/2016g (accessed August 2017).
Waldron, J. (1987) "Theoretical Foundations of Liberalism," *Philosophical Quarterly* 37: 127–50.
Walker, A.D.M. (1988) "Political Obligation and the Argument from Gratitude," *Philosophy and Public Affairs* 17: 191–211.
Walzer, M. (1970) "Political Alienation and Military Service," in *Obligations: Essays on Disobedience, War, and Citizenship*. Cambridge, MA: Harvard University Press, pp. 99–119.

Further reading

Beran, H. (1987) *The Consent Theory of Political Obligation*. London: Croom Helm. (Fullest recent defense of a consent theory of political obligation.)
Green, L. (1988) *The Authority of the State*. Oxford: Oxford University Press. (Argues that, of theories of political obligation, only consent is able to account for the authority of the state.)

Klosko, G. (1991) "Reformist Consent and Political Obligation," *Political Studies* 39: 676–90. (Critique of proposed reforms to enable widespread consent.)
Simmons, A.J. (1979) *Moral Principles and Political Obligations*, Princeton: Princeton University Press. (Now classic critique of consent and, especially, tacit consent as basis of political obligations.)

Related topics

Ch.9 Hypothetical consent
Ch.31 Normative consent and authority

31
NORMATIVE CONSENT AND AUTHORITY[1]

David Estlund

31.1 Introduction

Among our moral requirements, there might be requirements to consent to authority in certain cases. In those cases, what happens if we don't consent? Can we escape the authority in that way, by abusing our power to refuse consent? Why not say, instead, that, just as consent is sometimes null if it fails to meet certain standards, likewise, non-consent can be defective too and null as a result? The nullity of non-consent means, roughly, that the authority situation is as it would have been if the non-consent had not occurred—that is, just as if consent had occurred. The view that authority could be grounded in what would have been a requirement to consent could be formulated as a novel form of a hypothetical consent theory of authority, based on what I have called "normative consent".[2] If this view can be sustained, authority can simply befall us, whether we have consented to it or not, though the conditions under which this occurs are a separate question. In this short piece, I do not attempt to explain or defend the normative consent approach in a general way. But after a brief sketch of the approach, I go more deeply than before into the questions I refer to as "bypass objections" (which are aimed at all hypothetical consent theories) and the question of what I shall call *quasi-voluntarism*. My main thesis is that, while normative consent theory, in certain versions, might indeed be quasi-voluntarist, even if it were not it would yet have moral force on other, utterly non-voluntarist grounds. A warning: in that part of the argument we will have occasion to distinguish voluntarism, quasi-voluntarism, proto-voluntarism, pseudo-voluntarism, and anti-voluntarism. I will explain each as it arises.

31.2 Overview of normative consent

First, an overview of the idea of normative consent as a basis of authority: by *authority* I will mean the moral power to require action (borrowing a phrase from Raz) by commanding (Raz 1986).[3] To say you have authority over me on certain matters is to say that on those matters if you tell me to do something, then I am, for that reason, required to do it. It would normally be limited in scope, and also defeasible. Still, we would need to explain how an agent can ever have such a power: the fact that they command something in the relevant domain is a moral reason to do it unless it is cancelled or outweighed. This, at any rate, is the sort of moral power that I try to account for in this chapter, and I will call it "authority".

Normative consent theory rejects the actual-consent theory of authority, the view that there is no authority over a person without that person's consenting to be under that authority. Consent theory is not distinctive for holding that under the right conditions consent can establish authority. That is widely agreed. Consent theory is more controversial. Its distinctive claim is that without consent there is no authority. Consent theory, then, holds that,

> without consent there is no authority (*the libertarian[4] clause*), but unless there are certain nullifying conditions (*the nullity proviso*) consent to authority establishes authority (*the authority clause*).

The controversial nub of consent theory, then, is the libertarian clause: if A does not consent to B's authority, then, for that reason, B has no authority over A. Roughly, *no authority without consent*. As Simmons has influentially argued, if consent theory is correct then hardly anyone is under political authority. It might yet be true, of course, letting those chips fall where they may. Normative consent theory argues, however, that it is not true, that an agent's consent is not a necessary condition of their being under authority. In that important respect it is not a version of consent theory, but a competitor.

The nullity proviso in consent theory says that consent does not establish authority unless it meets certain standards, with different consent theories specifying different standards. Sometimes it is suggested that under those nullifying conditions (such as duress or coercion) there is, really, no consent after all. Other times, it is said that there is consent but that it fails to have its characteristic moral power. Either way, I want only to point out that consent theory includes an account of when (putative) consent is null or nullified. When we say that a (putative) act of consent is null or nullified, we should not assume that the resulting condition is one of non-authority. All that follows is that there is no authority *owed to that (putative) consent*. To assume that this means there is no authority would be to go beyond nullity, and illegitimately to assume the libertarian clause: that without consent there is no authority. Even where consent fails, other circumstances might establish the authority relation that is in question. So long as consent theory is held in question, null consent does not entail non-authority. It only entails that there is no authority stemming from that consent.

There is an interesting *asymmetry* of a sort in consent theory. The authority clause (stating that consent can establish authority) is limited or qualified by the nullity proviso (stating that consent is sometimes null or nullified). But the libertarian clause (stating that without consent there is no authority) is not subject to any such qualifications. Non-consent establishes non-authority, no questions asked. We can put the asymmetry this way: consent only establishes authority if it meets certain standards, whereas non-consent establishes non-authority without the need to meet any standards at all. The asymmetry by itself proves nothing, but in principle the libertarian clause could be subject to nullifying conditions too. Why couldn't non-consent be disqualified, null, in some cases?

The idea can seem foreign: what would it mean to say that *non*-consent is *null*? Recall that to say that putative consent to authority is, for some reason, null or nullified, seems to be to say that the authority situation is as if the consent had not occurred. Following that structure, the nullity of non-consent would come to this: when non-consent is nullified (if ever), the authority condition is as it would have been if the non-consent had not occurred—that is, as if there had been (non-null) consent.[5] That authority condition would then normally have been, as even consent theorists agree, the establishment of authority.

Supposed it is granted to me that if someone wrongfully refuses to consent to authority then the refusal is null, putting them under authority just as if they had exercised the power to consent. What about cases where the authority has not even been proposed, and so there has been no refusal? Call that potential objection,

> *the opportunity objection:* non-consent to authority is null only if there had been an opportunity to consent. Otherwise there is no wrongful refusal at all, and so no authority.

In reply, consider the case in which, while there was no opportunity, if there had been then refusal to consent would have been wrong. It is being granted to me that in that case the refusal would have been null. The agent lacks the power in such a case to block authority by refusing to consent to it. The opportunity objection must say, then, that even though the agent's decision whether to consent would make no difference with respect to the authority, her being bound depends on whether she is offered the chance to consent or refrain. But what moral basis would there be for thinking she escapes it if she is given no such chance? It is not as if offering her the chance to consent or not would give her a choice between being under the authority and being free of it. We are assuming that she would be under the authority whether she consented or not because non-consent would be null. The opportunity to consent or to refrain presents only a morally trivial choice: whether to consent without moral effect, or refrain without moral effect. There is no clear moral basis, then, for the opportunity objection.

It is notable that normative consent would be a particular version of hypothetical consent: even in some cases where you have not consented you are under authority just as you would have been *if you had established authority by consenting* (without its being nullified). Hypothetical consent theories are often criticized on several familiar grounds. One familiar objection claims that the appeal to the fact that one would have consented is superfluous and not at all explanatory, since the reasons that support that imaginary consent ground the authority all by themselves. This might be called the *direct authority objection*, though the issues it raises go beyond the question of authority and to hypothetical consent in other contexts, so I will discuss it under the name *bypass objection*. A second familiar objection is that hypothetical consent views seem to suggest (and sometimes assert) some connection to the agent's actual volition, where in fact there is none. We can speak of the alleged insinuation of a *quasi-voluntarism* that is supposed to be morally significant in a way akin to, but distinct from, actual voluntarism, i.e., consent. I will argue below that neither of these objections is compelling in the case of the normative consent approach to authority.

Before continuing, we should briefly acknowledge that, while the focus in this article is the explanation of authority, some of the issues we will see about hypothetical consent are, as in Thomson, not about authority but about the permission to interfere with or impose on someone in certain ways, such as subjecting them to a medical procedure, and so on. The points I make here apply equally well to both contexts, substituting (let's call it) authorized imposition, for authority. I will sometimes use the variable "A", which fits either nicely.

31.3 The bypass objection

Normative consent is meant to answer this question: What explains a command's authority?[6] In general, when we ask: "What explains x's being F?", it is not a good answer to provide just any set of features of x that entail that it is F. Someone's being a gold-medal gymnast might entail that she is strong, but it normally does not explain her being strong. Here is how some versions of the direct authority objection might seem to make this mistake. It might be pointed out that, whenever it would be reasonable or required to consent to authority, there would always be background facts, BF (moral or otherwise) that would entail (if not also explain) that the consent was required, R (by reason or morality). For this point, let the arrow stand for entailment: (BF → R). Then, if consent's being required entails that the proposed authority is genuine authority, A, (as normative consent partly says) (R → A), then, by transitivity, the background facts entail that there is genuine authority (BF → A). Since the background facts make no mention of the requirement of consent at all, that requirement R plays no role, according to this objection, in explaining the presence of authority—the entailment can bypass it. The explanation, contrary to the core claim of normative consent theory, is wholly the background facts themselves—the ones that would incidentally make it required to consent to the authority. This objection makes the mistake of supposing that any entailing set is an explaining set, and therefore fails against normative consent.

I turn next to related arguments that are focused on the question of what explains or grounds the authority. In particular, begin with the question of whether hypothetical consent is any part of the explanation, not whether it is the whole or fundamental explanation, postponing that issue for now. The main issue is familiar from discussions of the more general family of hypothetical consent views, of which normative consent is an instance. Judith Thomson puts a familiar charge against hypothetical consent theories this way: "[W]hat does the moral work in appeals to a person's hypothetical consent to a thing. . .is not that the person would consent to it, but rather whatever it is about the thing that makes it worthy of consent by the person"(Thomson 1990: 360). She argues, then, that hypothetical consent itself is no ground at all. Crucially, I will not be arguing in this particular section that it is such a ground. The issue here is the narrower one of whether Thomson's argument succeeds in showing that it is not.

There is an ambiguity in the passage from Thomson, and so I will consider the two possible interpretations in turn. Thomson refers to "whatever it is about the thing that makes it worthy of consent". On one reading, the thing's being worthy of consent is a crucial part of the explanation. What does the work is that the thing has certain features (perhaps features x, y, and z) *that make it worthy of consent*. If this is Thomson's meaning, then there is no departure from hypothetical consent theory. Consent is mentioned in this explanation, and it is not actual consent but hypothetical warranted consent.

Another reading of "whatever it is about the thing that makes it worthy of consent" would avoid my first reply by leaving the worthiness of consent out of the explanation altogether. On this reading a clearer statement would say that what does the justificatory work is not the thing's worthiness of consent, which it has in light of certain of its features, but the features themselves. Hypothetical consent and worthiness of consent both drop out completely.

Certainly, the requirement to consent must be grounded in other facts, facts that make it rational or required to consent. This, of course, is common ground. It leaves entirely open the question of whether Thomson is right that the background facts are "what does the work". She evidently means that the requirement to consent does no work—no work in morally grounding or explaining the authority. Whether or not it is the only, or the most fundamental, ground (about which nothing is decided here), the question for now is whether it is a ground at all. But observing that the requirement to consent itself has a moral ground is no argument at all that it is not itself a moral ground of—at least part of the explanation of—authority or authorized imposition.

If there is authority or authorized imposition (A) in virtue of consent's being required (R), and consent is required in virtue of the background facts (BF), then we can conclude that there is authority partly in virtue of, or partly explained by, the background facts, and moreover they might seem to be more fundamental, a deeper explanation in some sense. For simplicity, I will not inquire into whether the relevant grounding or explanation relation is generally transitive, and I grant it for the sake of argument. This appeal to transitivity is no difficulty for the position of the hypothetical consent theorist, of course, whose claim is simply granted *en route*. For example, I have claimed that there is authority in virtue of consent's being required, and this very claim of mine is the first premise of the objector's argument from transitivity:

1 A is (at least partly) in virtue of R
2 R is (at least partly) in virtue of BF
3 Therefore, by transitivity, A is (at least partly) in virtue of BF.

So there is no dispute about that according to this objection. And certainly I wouldn't deny that consent is required, when it is, in virtue of background facts. If it is asserted that, in a transitivity case, the background facts are the more fundamental explanation of the authority or authorized imposition, we would be granting the explanatory *relevance* of hypothetical consent and moving on to a new question. For what it is worth, the fundamentality claim is not, to my mind, at all obvious. But I will not take it up further here since it does not bear on this main question.

31.4 Voluntarism and quasi-voluntarism

Normative consent theory has voluntarist and non-voluntarist elements. It honors voluntary choices about what authority to subject yourself to, so long as they are not morally wrong. Within that constraint, you may accept or reject subjection to authority as you choose. In cases where you have not consented, and non-consent is permissible, the fact that you have not consented to the authority is enough to explain why you are not subject to it. In those contexts, where either consenting to authority or rejecting it is permissible, the theory is voluntaristic, congruent with actual-consent theories of political obligation. Call this the *truly voluntaristic component* of normative consent theory.

Even though normative consent, like any hypothetical consent view, is not a simply voluntaristic account of authority—one on which (as in consent theories) an agent falls under authority only voluntarily, by an exercise of her own will—normative consent might seem to retain some connection to the person's will. One might come to be under another's authority only as authorized in some way by the contents of their own will (even if not by an exercise of it—more below). This would be, as I will call it, a *quasi-voluntarist* constraint on authority. So far, though, while there is a truly voluntaristic element of the overall theory, the distinctive part—saying that you are obligated even when you do not consent so long as you would have been required to—is not yet shown to be voluntaristic at all. Now, of course, it is not supposed to be a voluntaristic theory, so the goal could at most be to explain why and how one's will must come into the account *in some way*, a weaker quasi-voluntarist condition.

Suppose it is argued that facts about what a person would have willed under counterfactual conditions are facts *about* that person's will, even if they do not invoke actual exercises of the will. That is correct, but only because it takes very little for a fact to be "about" something. Here's a fact about my will: it is not my foot. Suppose the claim is stronger: normative consent is an indication of what is supported by my will. However, the skeptic might fairly ask, is it an indication of what is supported or favored by my appetite to note that I would have eaten a sandwich if I had chosen as morally required? In some cases the appetite might play some role in choosing from within the permissible set of choices. But normative consent is a case where accepting authority would not only have been among the permissible choices, but is the only permissible choice. It is no reflection of my appetite to say, in a case where eating a sandwich is the only permissible choice for anyone in that situation, that I would have eaten a sandwich if I had done the required thing. That is much like the suggestion that normative consent invokes the subject's will. Arguably, they are both just about what is right, and are not pointing to the substance of what I will in any way.[7] A closer look at the variations available to hypothetical consent theory, however, suggests that normative consent's potential claim to quasi-voluntarism has not yet been refuted.

In a variety of contexts, it can seem to be morally significant what a certain agent who does not consent *would* consent to. Here is one familiar context:

> *Coma:*
> It is commonly believed that if a person is in a coma and cannot exercise consent to a certain risky or disfiguring medical procedure, it is morally important to do what she would have consented to if she had the chance.

Here is a very different context:

> *Social Contract:*
> Some philosophers over the centuries have argued that the burdens of state power or authority can be morally justified if, but only if, the people subject to it would have consented to it in specific circumstances.

These are very different uses of the general idea of hypothetical consent. But they have this in common: the idea of consent figures in the account, and it is not claimed to be actual consent.

Corresponding to our two examples—Coma and Social Contract—we can distinguish two uses of hypothetical consent: the former is person-specific and attitude-based. It tends to be about hypothetical consent by actual identifiable people, based on their actual attitudes. The latter kind of hypothetical consent is more familiar when the topic is a general philosophical question about duty or authority. It is typically standard-based, and person-generic (rather than attitude-based, or person-specific). That is, it tends (roughly speaking) to be about hypothetical people and what they would consent to, based on standards of morality or rationality.

> *Attitude-Based Hypothetical Consent:*
> Asks what a person would have consented to in certain real conditions if consulted, basing the answer on an inquiry into the individual's actual attitudes.

And,

> *Standard-Based Hypothetical Consent:*
> Asks what any person would have consented to if consulted, stipulating certain attitudes, and basing the answer on inquiry into the implications of a certain normative standard (such as rationality or morality).

The former person-specific, attitude-based version that is familiar in medical ethics contexts seems to me to have a strong claim to some moral significance stemming from a kind of quasi-voluntarism, while that is more doubtful in the standard-based, person-generic version, as I will explain. The quasi-voluntarism in the former case stems from its reliance on actual motives of the person in question, motives that are in a morally significant way (as I will call them) *proto-volitional:* actual beliefs and desires whose relevance is that they are of the kind that are poised to figure in the person's practical deliberation about the kind of case in question—that is, about whether or not to consent to some imposition. For example, suppose the imposition in question is a surgical procedure in which the patient's left-hand fingers will be removed, destroying his career as a saxophone player. His career could be saved, but only by allowing the spread of a disease that will make it impossible for him to sing. The relevant beliefs and desires are whichever ones are actually his, and poised to figure in his own deliberation, if only it could occur, about which procedure to choose. Their moral relevance is precisely their connection to the agent's will. On this view the question is not what is best for him, but what he has come sufficiently close to choosing. The attitudes that do the work are actual, not hypothetical, but their moral relevance is their relation to will or choice—and yet will or choice is not actual in this case. It is, then, hypothetical.

This idea of quasi-voluntarism by way of proto-volitional states is, so far, somewhat cryptic, and space prevents a fuller exploration. It will have to suffice to say only that, in the person-specific, attitude-based variety of hypothetical consent, quasi-voluntarism may have a footing. For easy reference below, call that hypothesis *proto-voluntarism*, a specific version of quasi-voluntarism. This will become important shortly. First, however, even if there is this proto-voluntarism in attitude-based and person-specific cases such as Coma, it is no case for quasi-voluntarism in the other, standard-based, person-generic version, as I will now argue.

Turning from the attitude-based variant, now consider two different standard-based hypothetical consent approaches to political authority. First,

> *Hypothetical Rational Consent*
> The hypothetical consenters are stipulated to have at least certain generic attitudes (especially ends or preferences), and then what they would consent to is derived from the normative standard of instrumental rationality, each maximizing her expected preference-satisfaction.

Call this the *rationality version* of standard-based hypothetical consent. It is one way of presenting Hobbes's social contract, for example. The next version, still standard-based, is a *morality version*:

> *Hypothetical Moral Consent*
> Hypothetical consenters are stipulated to have at least certain generic attitudes (especially ends or preferences). What they would consent to is derived not solely from instrumental rationality given their (stipulated) ends or preferences but also from the normative standard of morally permissible choice.

Rawls exemplifies this moral variant. As in the rationality version, the parties are assumed to effectively promote their own ends. But unlike certain other accounts such as that of Hobbes, their choices are rendered impartial, for moral reasons, by the imposition of the "veil of ignorance". Notably, this is formally equivalent to assuming that each chooses even without a veil, but with the moral virtue of impartiality.

Rawls explicitly suggests that such an account has (as I am calling it) a quasi-voluntarist element:

> . . . a society satisfying the principles of justice as fairness comes as close as a society can to being a voluntary scheme, for it meets the principles which free and equal persons would assent to under circumstances that are fair. In this sense its members are autonomous and the obligations they recognize self-imposed.
>
> *(Rawls 1971: 13)*

There is reason for skepticism about this quasi-voluntaristic interpretation—Rawls's own interpretation—of the original position. It is commonly suggested that an actual person, say Joe, can be placed, in an act of imagination, in the original position in order to ascertain what he would have agreed to under those conditions, and so Joe's own will plays a role. Now, *anyone* placed in those highly specific conditions would make the same choices, but that does not mean we do not learn something about Joe or his will. Joe's will might have certain features that everyone's has. If all have it then each has it. But this is not what Rawls does with the original position. If we want to say that Joe can be inserted into the original position we would have to admit in the next breath that he would be given a thorough make-over. His actual motivations are mostly ignored and replaced with the desire to maximize his bundle of stipulated "primary goods". That is quite a structured aim, with very specific components, and some of them assign—by Rawls, not by actual Joe—certain weights relative to the others. It is a motive that is probably not found in any, much less all, actual individuals.

Indeed, in Rawls's mature view, the primary goods are explicitly not meant to be attributed to people as things that everyone actually cares about (even if something closer to that is suggested in his earlier presentations). Rather, they are stipulated in an effort to devise a model of motivation in the original position, and a "political conception of the person", that would be acceptable to all reasonable comprehensive views for purposes of identifying a serviceable public conception of justice, although the details of this complicated phrase do not matter here (Rawls 1993: 1178). Insofar as the motives are stipulated rather than found, the fact that the parties would make certain choices does not signify anything in the motives or wills of the real people they represent. To be clear: I believe that the argument's purpose is to identify justice (or a viable public conception thereof), not to show that real people actually already will it, so this is not meant as an objection to the theory. The point here is only that Rawls is not persuasive that there is anything even quasi-voluntaristic about the argument from the original position.

If that moralized version of hypothetical consent lacks any connection to the will, shall we say the same about normative consent generally? There is a strong affinity between the Rawlsian moralized version of hypothetical consent, and normative consent theory, but there is this difference: normative consent theory can take either a person-specific or a person-generic form, while Rawlsian theory is solidly in the person-generic category. This might seem to position normative consent theory to have a better claim to quasi-voluntarism. Before considering that possibility, we can see that normative consent could take a person-specific form by noticing that whether a person would have been morally required to consent to some proposed authority could be held to depend partly on what else they happen to care about. Moral standards and one's own motives could be held to interact in each specific individual's case. In Rawlsian theory, by contrast, the motives of the hypothetical choosers are completely supplied by theoretical stipulation, and all parties have the same motives. For whatever reason, the standard uses of person-*specific* hypothetical consent (as in Coma) take the person's attitudes as given and project them into a hypothetical choice without the imposition of any moral standard. Moralized uses of hypothetical consent such as that of Rawls and the veil of ignorance happen to hypothesize, rather than assert or ascertain, not only the choices but also the motives of the agents, thus forfeiting the claim to quasi-voluntarism. But there is also the possibility of a version of hypothetical consent in which moral standards partly drive the result (as in, "what choice, if any, would be morally required?") and yet the actual motives of the person, rather than hypothesized or stipulated motives, bear on the answer (as in, "What would he have been morally required to do given his actual motives?").

Here is an example: suppose Len asks Jen if she will agree to do as he asks tomorrow in cleaning the garage together. And suppose that Jen had previously said that she will accept such a task on some Saturday soon, leaving the specific date to be determined by agreement. Depending on Jen's other motives, she may or may not be morally required to accept the task (and the ensuing authority) for tomorrow. If she has other significant plans, it might not be required, but if she does not, it might well be required. Jen's own aims play a determining role in whether she would be required. The truth of the normative consent claim that she is under Len's authority tomorrow because she would have been required to consent to his request depends partly on her actual motives.

In a person-specific version of normative consent, then, there does arguably remain a quasi-voluntarist element. I say "arguably" because the case for quasi-voluntarism here would be about the same as the case barely sketched above for the moral relevance of what I called proto-voluntarism in the case of person-specific (non-normative) hypothetical consent familiar in cases like Coma. There is no such case for quasi-voluntarism in Rawls's view, as we have seen, since his is person-generic, with no input from people's actual attitudes. This may or may not be an advantage for the person-specific version. I have not granted that a quasi-voluntarist element is necessary for authority. As I will argue in the next and final section, whether such an element is present or not, there is moral significance in both person-specific and person-generic versions stemming from the nullity of non-consent, which does not rely on any quasi-voluntarist claim.

31.5 The nullity of non-consent again

The argument above that there may indeed be a quasi-voluntarist element in person-specific versions of normative consent is undeveloped, but it is not needed to defend the moral significance of normative consent. To see why, for the purposes of this final section suppose it is mistaken. In that case, the interest of normative consent must lie in the moral significance of what I have called the nullity of non-consent. As I have so far argued, the prospects of that *nullity thesis*—that impermissible non-consent to authority would fail to block that authority (in at least some cases)—are not diminished by bypass arguments about hypothetical consent in general, because they fail, nor by the doubtful presence of even a quasi-voluntarist element in normative consent, since no such quasi-voluntarism is relied on by the nullity argument. I seek in this section to determine what conception of the nullity of wrongful non-consent would be required for normative consent theory.

First, though, the very idea of a requirement to consent may be unfamiliar. However, we can easily find cases that are, it seems to me, difficult to resist. Suppose your dog has settled in your neighbor's yard. To be cautious, you ask your neighbor if you may enter the yard, but your neighbor refuses. So far, the refusal might be permissible, based on reasonable considerations, such as if you were a dangerous criminal. But suppose the neighbor's aim is simply to frustrate you. The refusal of consent is morally wrong here (if this isn't obvious yet, suppose the dog will die without your immediate attention; people will die if you can't retrieve the dog, etc.) This example is not about authority (the moral power to require by commanding) for which consent is required, and so it does not matter for my purposes whether this particular wrongful non-consent nevertheless retains its force—morally prohibiting entry into the yard. Maybe; maybe not. The example is intended only to establish that consent can sometimes be morally required, and so non-consent can sometimes be morally wrong.

As we can glimpse in the example of the stranded dog owner, even when non-consent is morally wrong, it might yet retain its force. If no one is in danger, and the dog will soon relent, even wrongful refusal by the property owner might render your entering the yard morally impermissible. There are even clearer cases. In some sexual contexts it seems possible for consent to be immorally withdrawn after it had previously been given, and withdrawn for bad reasons—such as the intention simply to anger or frustrate the partner, as with the property owner's motives in the dog example. It seems difficult to deny that so withdrawing consent (obviously not *all* withdrawing of consent) might be wrongful. But it is morally effective nevertheless: the partner is still thereby forbidden to proceed with sexual contact, even if this situation might be unjust under the circumstances. The sexual context is a valuable one to consider here, since it is especially clear in such an intimate setting that the non-consent is morally effective whether or not it is morally permissible. An obstacle in the way of accepting the nullity thesis, then—which says that wrongful non-consent to authority is sometimes wrong and null as a result—is the evident fact that wrongful non-consent is not null in all contexts.

A modest but helpful point, though, is this: it does not follow from the fact that wrongful non-consent is still morally effective in some non-authority contexts that it is also effective in authority contexts. It remains open whether there is some morally relevant difference between authority contexts and non-authority contexts of wrongful non-consent that might render it effective in some cases but ineffective in others. A natural suggestion for such a distinction would be that between, on one hand, *liability to imposition*: that is, another agent's being permitted to interfere with or impose upon you, and, on the other hand, *obligation to obey*: your being morally required to act in some way as ordered by another agent. Roughly, the hypothesis would be that agents have a less weighty interest in avoiding moral obligations than they have in avoiding the permissibility of their being interfered with or imposed upon.

Now, some kinds of interference and imposition are relatively minor, and normative consent does not need it to turn out that wrongful non-consent always effectively forbids them. By the same token some cases of obligatory acts of obedience are more momentous than others, and it would be open to a normative consent theory to hold that even wrongful non-consent effectively blocks some of them—i.e., it is not null—even if it is null in the case of others. Still, there is a challenge here. A normative consent theory of political authority would presumably hope to explain such obligations (under the right procedural and other conditions) as to obey tax laws that demand a significant fraction of one's income or expenditure. Wrongful non-consent to political authority, where that includes such significant obligations, would presumably be held to be null, while wrongful non-consent to being, say, kissed or touched, even gently, retains its force.

In addition, the point is not limited to cases involving the prospect of physical or intimate contact or interaction, since the obnoxious property-owner in the dog example can be successful in prohibiting entry to his property (at least when the dog is safe and will soon move, etc.). That example stands for a broader range of property cases, of course. The hypothesis of normative consent theory, then, would include that (at least in certain social and legal contexts) one's interest in not being liable to interference with (at least some kinds of) one's property is morally weightier than one's interest in being free from moral obligations to obey, such as those of significant taxation (though leaving aside any coercive enforcement—just the obligation). What is needed is a deeper explanation of this differential moral weight. There is some plausibility to there being a weightier interest in avoiding liability—the permissibility of being imposed upon—than in avoiding obligation—an unenforced moral requirement to obey. But so far the shape of that distinction and the case for it remains out of focus. There is a challenge here for normative consent theory to explain where such a line falls and why. In my view, no absurdity or inconsistency is thereby exposed in the normative consent approach, so this falls short of a problem inherent in the approach. It is an important unanswered question—one front (no doubt there are also others) on which more work would need to be done before normative consent theory should be accepted.

What is the point of putting either of such views (Rawls's, or normative consent theory) in terms of hypothetical voluntary agreements if (as we are supposing in this section for the sake of argument) there is no prospect of tying this to the contents of individuals' wills? If there is nothing even quasi-voluntaristic about the fact that the hypothetical parties would have made certain choices, or the fact that you would have consented to certain authority if you chose rightly morally speaking, then is there any other (extra-voluntaristic) moral significance in those facts? The hypothetical consent formulation can look like a trick, a charge we might call *pseudo-voluntarism*. If nothing about my actual will is being invoked, why speak about what I would have willed?

That general line of objection can take different forms. One form would focus on the nullity of non-consent, and contend that it is a distraction to formulate that point in terms of hypothetical consent. Rather than speak of what one *would have* consented to if they did not behave wrongly, why not let the nullity point rest on the claim that it would have been *wrong* not to consent? That point, however, would still not dispense with the reference to hypothetical consent, as we can see in two steps. First, the nullity of non-consent (which is being granted as the crux in this version of the complaint) essentially refers to consent—the consent that would have been required. Second, the consent referred to is not actual; it does not actually occur. The consent referred to is in a modal context, something like this (the details won't matter here): in all possible worlds that are relevantly similar to (or "near") the actual one, and in which Joe responds permissibly to the chance to consent, Joe consents. The consent upon which the nullity account turns, then, is hypothetical: necessarily, if, in the relevant possible conditions, Joe did as required, he would have consented.[8] Call this the *modal point*.

That point, it must be granted, does not really explain why there is any explanatory value in the nullity of non-consent in the first place. It might seem like saying the explanation for my baldness is that I was powerless to prevent it. There is, on that bizarre account, reference to my preventing it, in a modal context, along with the finding that all such worlds are too distant from the actual one in certain ways, and so on. Nevertheless, my baldness is *not* plausibly explained by my powerlessness to prevent it. Similarly, what does the fact of authority over me have to do with the fact that I was powerless to prevent it—the fact that my refusal would have been null? The answer, I believe, is that in many cases, and many we are familiar with, my non-consent *is* morally effective. So it is indeed explanatory to point out that this effectiveness lapses in the case where the non-consent is wrong. This would be roughly as if I were generally capable of preventing baldness in others, but alas not my own. It would plausibly be explanatory in that case to cite the fact that my powers of baldness-prevention lapse in my own case as partly explaining why I am bald. The nullity of non-consent when it is wrong has explanatory power precisely because non-consent is so often not null. Interestingly, in that indirect way, the account relies on the moral *effectiveness* of our powers of non-consent in many cases.

One further merit of the hypothetical consent formulation is this: it is a way of exposing the fact that the actual contents of people's wills do not have as much moral weight as some seem to think. They sometimes lack moral effect—namely, when they are morally bad. We might call this the *contrapositive point:*

Another way of saying that,

A) If you'd *behaved permissibly* you would have *consented*,

is,

B) If you would <u>not</u> have *consented*, then you would <u>not</u> have *behaved permissibly*.

There is some insight in placing the emphasis not on the hypothetical choosing, as in (A), but on the impermissibility if you hadn't, as in (B), but the point is still well made in terms of a hypothetical—a conditional statement (either of them, (A) or (B); they are logically equivalent). On this way of looking at it, far from being quasi-voluntarist, the point of the distinctive part of normative consent theory—the part that is not simply congruent with actual-consent theory and so "truly voluntarist" (see above)—is not only non-voluntarist, but, in one respect, *anti*-voluntarist, emphasizing the moral nullity of certain exercises of the will—namely non-consent when it is morally wrong. Of course, this depends on bracketing the prospects of proto-voluntarism, which might vindicate normative consent's quasi-voluntarism (for what it is worth) after all.

In the original presentation of the idea of normative consent it was presented as a virtue of membership in the hypothetical consent family that it thereby retains "*some* connection to the will" (Estlund 2008: 131). This may be correct, but things now appear to be slightly more complicated:

- There may indeed be a quasi-voluntarism in the person-specific version of normative consent and the relevance there of actual proto-volitional attitudes.
- Whether or not that is so, there is the connection to the will represented in the modal point—consent is essentially mentioned, and it is hypothetical, not actual.
- However, and it would be no deficiency, unless the proto-volitional approach is sound there is no appeal to any measure of voluntarism at all, no invocation of the actual will of the person in question (as we see in the contrapositive point).
- Moreover, the distinctive part of normative consent theory—the nullity of non-consent—is, so far as it goes, *anti-voluntarist.*
- Nevertheless, normative consent theory must be seen as a hypothetical consent theory, albeit of a novel kind.

Notes

1 I received helpful comments on earlier versions of many of these ideas from participants in several settings: Workshop on "Authority" at UNC-Chapel Hill, January, 2011. Thanks especially to Paul Weithman, and to David Enoch for ensuing correspondence; Colloquium, "Political Obligation and Legitimacy of the State," Royal Netherlands Academy of Arts and Sciences, Amsterdam, June 2011, with special thanks to Geoff Sayre-McCord; my graduate seminar at Brown University, spring 2016; Conference: "Beyond Contractarianism?" Inter University Centre, Dubrovnik, Croatia, June, 2016. Thanks especially to Nic Southwood for very helpful discussion there. Finally, thanks to Andreas Müller for comments on a penultimate draft.

2 In previous work I sketched this kind of view (Estlund 2005, 2008). I have also defended the view against several critics, but I will not rehearse those exchanges here (Estlund 2009, 2010, 2011).

3 This definition of authority is not committed to Raz's important view about when and why this moral power is present.

4 It is a presumption in favor of a kind of liberty, but no further association with the family of political views known as libertarian is intended. As will emerge, authority is a limitation of one's moral liberty, not otherwise an interference or imposition on one's person or will.

5 Daniel Koltonski helpfully shows that this must mean that the authority condition is as it would have been if there had been consent *in a counterfactual world in which, while everything else relevant is the same, authority depends on consent* (Koltonski 2013). He goes on to argue that no such world is possible if authority does not depend on consent in the actual world, since two worlds can't have different moral properties unless they have different non-moral properties. But, in reply, all that is required is that each such world be logically possible, as is surely the case. The moral truth will rule one of them out as morally possible (either authority depends on consent or it doesn't, given the same non-moral properties), but that is no difficulty. Rather, it is the substantive normative position itself.

6 For an overview and assessment of the literature on "grounding", see Bliss & Trogdon (2016).
7 We observe, here, that the fact that one would have been morally required to consent does not count as any measure of voluntarism. This does not grant the Thomson charge that reference to hypothetical consent is inessential. It could yet be essential even if it does not count as any measure of voluntarism, an issue we come to below.
8 I believe this formulation avoids problems (related to the "conditional fallacy") that might arise if we were to speak of morally perfect worlds, or worlds in which Joe is a morally perfect agent.

References

Bliss, R. and K. Trogdon (2016) "Metaphysical Grounding," in E.N. Zalta (ed.), *The Stanford Encyclopedia of Philosophy*. plato.stanford.edu/archives/win2016/entries/grounding/.
Estlund, D. (2005) "Political Authority and the Tyranny of Non-Consent," *Philosophical Issues* 15: 351–67.
Estlund, D. (2008) *Democratic Authority: A Philosophical Framework*. Princeton: Princeton University Press.
Estlund, D. (2009) "Replies to Commentators," *Iyyun: The Jerusalem Philosophical Quarterly* 58: 73–88.
Estlund, D. (2010) "Replies to Commentators," *Representation* 46(1): 53–67.
Estlund, D. (2011) "Replies to Commentators," *Ethics* 121(2): 354–89.
Koltonski, D. (2013) "Normative Consent and Authority," *Journal of Moral Philosophy* 10: 255–75.
Rawls, J. (1971) *A Theory of Justice*. Cambridge, MA: Harvard University Press.
Rawls, J. (1993) *Political Liberalism*. New York: Columbia University Press.
Raz, J. (1986) *The Morality of Freedom*. Oxford: Oxford University Press.
Thomson, J.J. (1990) *The Realm of Rights*. Cambridge, MA: Harvard University Press.

Related topics

Ch.9 Hypothetical consent
Ch.30 Consent theory of political obligation

32

MORAL EDUCATION AND THE ETHICS OF CONSENT

William A. Edmundson

To consent is to exercise a moral power. It is often also to exercise a legal power, but the focus here is on the moral power. The exercise of a moral power changes the moral situation of the consenter, and that of those to whom consent is given, and perhaps that of others as well. For example, by saying "I promise to do that", *A* consents to being reproved if *A* does not do what was promised. By saying to *B*, "You may touch me there", *A* consents to *B*'s touching that place, and by consenting *A* waives the right *A* would otherwise have to object to being touched there by *B*—temporarily, and conditionally, of course.

Consenting has its typical effect only if it is freely given and given in the right circumstances. Nominal expressions of consent that are elicited under threats of serious harm are not counted as genuine consent. If *A* surrenders *A*'s wallet to *B* under *B*'s do-it-or-else threat of serious bodily harm if *A* does not comply, *A* has not consented to *B*'s possession. Nominal expressions of consent that the actor would not have given but for significant misinformation may also be discounted as invalid, especially if the benefitting party is responsible for the misinformation. For example, if *A* buys a car from *B* in reliance upon *B*'s false assurance that the car is new, *A* has not validly consented to the sale and is not bound by its terms. Nominal expressions of consent given in other nonstandard situations are invalid as well. If *B* hypnotizes *A*—with or without *A*'s consent—*A* cannot validly consent to what *B* suggests to *A* while under hypnosis. Understanding the "ethics of consent" involves understanding the conditions that must exist before expressions of consent can have their normal moral effect. It might involve more; but it at least involves this.

An important and increasingly controversial aspect of the ethics of consent has to do with moral education (MacMullen 2015). By "moral education" I mean a broad variety of practices that are meant to inculcate in the young certain dispositions and attitudes that the inculcator believes to be valuable. The objects of these dispositions and attitudes are not only platitudinous moral truths but also social roles, especially authoritative roles. Moral education brings it about that children recognize that certain things are to be done and not to be done, that certain things belong to them and others do not, and that certain people are to be believed and obeyed. In particular, the child is gotten to believe that her parents and certain other adults know better than the child what the child ought to do and to believe. To say the child is "led to believe" these things instead of "gotten to believe" is to euphemize: the child has no real say in the matter. Countering Locke's recommendation that adults reason with children, Rousseau insisted that "[c]hildhood is the sleep of reason" (Rousseau 1993 [1762]: 84).

> If children understood reason they would not need education, but by talking to them from their earliest age in a language they do not understand you accustom them to be satisfied with words . . . and whatever you think you gain from motives of reasons, you really gain from greediness, fear or vanity with which you are obliged to reinforce your reasoning.
>
> *(1993 [1762]: 63)*

Rousseau's point has been taken by liberal philosophers of education, notably John Dewey. It is unusual to find sustained dissent from the proposition that moral and civic education cannot wait upon the maturing of critical rationality, for rationality must build upon a previously instilled set of attitudes and dispositions (MacMullen 2015 cites William Galston, Eamonn Callan, Richard Dagger, Meira Levinson, Stephen Macedo. Peter Levine, Amy Gutmann, Harry Brighouse, and Warren Nord, citing only Jack Crittenden as unambiguously contra).

This necessarily non-optional process instills in the young mind beliefs about arrangements that one ought not only to go along with, but to take for granted. By the time the child reaches an "age of reason" or "age of consent", she will already have acquired a set of attitudes and dispositions regarding her employment of her moral powers. These attitudes and dispositions are ones that the child cannot have antecedently consented to be trained to acquire. Nevertheless, the conviction remains that moral education must be, and can only be, legitimated in terms of its being consented to—however circuitously—by the individual who is its subject.

32.1 The legitimation problem

It is widely acknowledged that consent is vitiated by brainwashing and other kinds of coercive indoctrination. Dystopian fiction, like *Brave New World* and *1984,* vividly depicts objectionable ways in which people can be gotten to consent to objectionable conditions. Our revulsion at such methods even in their subtler forms sits uncomfortably beside our serene acceptance of a commonplace fact: we now accept many things as more or less natural only because as children we were led to accept them by means that could not possibly secure valid consent from adults subjected to equivalent pressures. For example, a great many religious believers acquired their beliefs because they were made to attend religious services, to observe religious holidays, to listen to and to read scripture and religiously themed literature, to recite prayers at bedtime and blessings at meals. Subtler means are commonplace. Sally Haslanger describes her transition at age eight from Connecticut to Louisiana in the summer of 1963:

> I was mostly oblivious to the civil rights protests . . . . What I do remember, though, is the constant corrections and physical interventions that were attempts to retrain me to conform to the local norms of gender and race. These didn't come from my parents or siblings—they knew as little as I did about how to behave—but from teachers, neighbors, and strangers. The corrections did not come with explanations, either. Instead, I might be yanked away from a car door (I had been planning to sit in the front seat next to the Negro driver rather than in the back seat), or grabbed by the arm and scolded for my loud (and probably "know it all") tone of voice. I had learned how to be a privileged white girl in Connecticut, but this did not do in Shreveport, where Jim Crow and Southern gentility still had a hold.

> I had to relearn how to enact privilege, whiteness, and femininity. At the same time, I also had a sense, both from what I had known in my previous world and from things I overheard at home, that this new way of being wasn't quite right. I was so confused.
>
> *(Haslanger 2012: 3–4)*

It is likely that she was not the only one who was confused. Her needing those "constant corrections and physical interventions" may have surprised the local adults, but it would have dumbfounded her new classmates and contemporaries. Why had it been necessary to remind this Yankee girl of norms so natural and easy? Those other, Southern children had themselves been trained in these ways by similar means, but forgot the training even as the norms themselves became as invisibly natural as the air. Reticence and resistance by a child to pressures like these would very likely be met with stern—even astonished—parental disapproval. Set aside the content of the norms. We do not condemn these methods of indoctrinating children, in fact we use them ourselves even though we would strenuously protest the subjection of a non-consenting adult to any equivalent treatment.

The authority of parents in such matters was and still is in the protestant South and elsewhere interwoven with religious doctrines, according to which contumacious children run the risk of eternal hellfire. Liberals may disapprove of, but they will not forbid, the use of such legitimating backstories (cf. Callan 2000: 152–3). Parents, relatives, and teachers also impress the young with secular values, although typically not in explicitly eschatological terms. The school report-card is the gateway to approval and reward, or to scorn and restriction, depending on how the child performs by measures not of her choosing. Adults, too, are subject to evaluation, but within the context of a (nominally) wide freedom of occupation. The aspiration of many parents and teachers is to mold the child in such a way that his or her occupational choice, and earnest commitment to meeting the standards of performance associated with the occupational role, is guaranteed. Inculcating the right values, in the right order of priority, is the parents' central duty. If the child rebels against or rejects her parents' values, the parents may consider themselves to have failed, in some measure, even if the alternative values the child adopts are perfectly reasonable ones for any mature person to hold. Parents are aware that a plurality of (at least speciously) reasonable alternative values awaits their children at maturity. This is what gives early moral education its special urgency.

To summarize, a *principle of free consent* means that compulsory indoctrination of adults is forbidden and, where it nonetheless does occur, it negates the validity of nominal expressions of consent given under its influence (Callan & Arena 2009). But, as usually interpreted, the principle of free consent not only condones compulsory instruction of the immature, but also holds that such instruction does not negate the validity of nominal expressions of consent given under its influence. This awkward pairing underlies a good bit of the running dispute about liberal neutrality, and has been questioned in the context of specifically civic education. Civic education often involves inculcating beliefs and attitudes that incline the young to accept the legitimacy of the status quo, including the justice of the government and basic structure of society. The young are gotten to identify themselves with their nation and to experience distinctive patriotic emotions upon hearing the national anthem, and to recite a pledge of allegiance. The young are brought to accept that they have a duty to obey the laws. As Harry Brighouse has put it,

> If the state helps form the political loyalties of future citizens by inculcating belief in its own legitimacy, it will be unsurprising when citizens consent to the social

> institutions they inhabit, but it will be difficult to be confident that their consent is freely given, or would have been freely given.
>
> *(Brighouse 1998: 719)*

The supposition is that this confidence, which is so difficult to have, is needed. Why? Needed for what? Brighouse explains:

> The problem is that giving the state presumptive authority to inculcate its values in future citizens violates liberal legitimacy. If we carefully foster the virtues among those who are not yet able rationally to assess the legitimacy of the state itself, what basis do we have to think they would have freely supported it on the basis of their reason alone?
>
> *(Brighouse 1998: 723)*

Rousseau stated the underlying worry, "There is no subjection so complete as that which preserves the forms of freedom" (1993 [1762]: 100). Or, as the joke has it: When one fish asked the other, "How's the water?", the other fish answered, "What's water?" The violation of liberal legitimacy that Brighouse warns of can be understood with reference to John Rawls's Liberal Principle of Legitimacy:

> our exercise of political power is fully proper only when it is in accordance with a constitution the essentials of which all citizens as free and equal may reasonably be expected to endorse . . . .
>
> *(1996: 137)*

The problem Brighouse raises is that a liberal society, to perpetuate itself, will have to inculcate in its young a disposition to endorse—i.e., to consent to—the basic structure of society, including its political structure, in a way that seems to bypass the critical individual autonomy that liberal democracy—whether as a political or a fully "comprehensive" conception (cf. Rawls 2001: 14; Weithman 2015)—assigns a crucially high value to. In Robert Jubb's words, "If we have been made into liberals by non-transparent or coercive means and are deluded about the grounds on which liberalism rests, we face a kind of contradiction" (Jubb 2014: 922). In the direction of consent is where philosophers in the Western tradition of political philosophy typically look for logical relief, but the problem Brighouse points out suggests that the legitimacy of liberal political society cannot rest on consent "all the way down".

The question of legitimacy is distinct from the question of the justice of the state or the status quo or the basic structure of society. The question of legitimacy is also distinct from the justifiability of coercing conformity with the law or the state's directives. Legitimacy—in its most robust sense—entails a duty or obligation to comply with a certain directive, and that is a step beyond the justifiability of compelling non-obligatory compliance. It is also a step beyond the existence of reasons favoring voluntary compliance. The moral power of consent is not by itself capable of making unjust arrangements just, although it certainly negates one line of objection to them. By the same token, the justice of an arrangement does not itself assure that it is consented to—even though it ought to be. The "gap" that exists between justice and legitimacy has vexed political philosophy, and Rawls's formulation narrows it as far as Rawls thinks it could be narrowed.

> The state's authority cannot . . . be freely accepted . . . . Nevertheless we may over the course of life come freely to accept, as the outcome of reflective thought and reasoned

> judgment, the ideals, principles, and standards that specify our basic rights and liberties and effectively guide and moderate the political power to which we are subject. This is the *outer limit of our freedom.*
>
> *(2001: 94; emphasis added)*

The question Brighouse raises is whether this limit is too closed-in to circumscribe what can be properly called freedom.

32.2 Rawls's way of legitimating indoctrination

The centerpiece of Rawls's Liberal Principle of Legitimacy is not actual but hypothetical consent. It operates at two removes from actual consent. The coercive application of political power is justifiable—"fully proper"—if it conforms to a constitution. Power does not have to be consented to by the person to whom it is applied—and it may properly be applied to her over her objection. She does not have to have consented to the constitution. The Principle of Liberal Legitimacy is satisfied if she would consent to it, were she reasonable and rational, and making a choice in the right circumstances.

The fact that a just arrangement for the use of coercive power would be consented to in ideal circumstances cannot—by itself—assure that the arrangement is viable. For a just state to be viable, it "must be willingly supported by at least a substantial majority of its politically active citizens" (Rawls 2001: 34) from one generation to the next, despite what Rawls calls the "fact of reasonable pluralism" (Rawls 1996: 24)—i.e., that a just liberal democracy will inevitably comprise and generate a plurality of reasonable "comprehensive" doctrines which, from their various perspectives, may (but, then again, may not) converge upon a consensus political conception, that is, upon the "essentials of" a constitution in the most general sense. The question arises: how is this convergence to be maintained? Outright coercion is out of the question, for Rawls. Brighouse pointedly asks: how is this task of stable reproduction of political culture to be accomplished unless by (illiberally) indoctrinating the young with a liberal ideology? Some liberals, inspired by Mill, conclude that the state should not be in this business at all (Shklar 1989: 33; Flathman 1996: 15). But it is difficult to reject moral and civic education altogether, or to deny that it is a necessary safeguard against anomie and anarchy (MacMullen 2015: 6–11). The answer, Let the family do it, seems the natural response, especially if one is distrustful of the state as educator. But this merely relocates the difficulty, for now the legitimacy of parental authority comes into question (Callan 2000: 152; MacMullen 2015: 13).

Rawls was explicit that political society is not and cannot be an association that one belongs to because one consents to join it or volunteers to sign up for it (2001: 4). The issue of legitimacy turns not on actual consent, but on what it would be reasonable for one to consent to, although—as noted above—he was also explicit that society as he conceived it owes it stability to the actual willing assent of ordinary citizens to the principles governing its basic structure. Over generations, actual consent can be assured by the pervasive influence of the "political conception as educator", which presents the young "with a way of regarding themselves that otherwise they would most likely never be able to entertain" (1996: 71). Apart from the merits of the regime itself, how, precisely, does a liberal conception distinguish its methods of auto-propagation from indoctrination in some pejorative sense?

In an abstract discussion in the third part of *A Theory of Justice*, Rawls legitimated methods of persuasion by appeal to a counterfactual test: would one consent to have had one's beliefs shaped by the means at issue? If so, all is well. This is simply the application of his contractualist approach to a particular type of potentially coercive extra-rational influence. An obvious objection to this is that adults will respond to the test after, and not in advance of, their moral education as children. And so it is doubly counter-factual: "Would you, had you not been raised the way you were, have consented to being raised in that way?" As stated, it is not easy to get a handle on the question. Bear in mind that Rawls is speaking here not of parties in the original position, which are artificial devices, but of flesh-and-blood citizens. To imagine having been raised differently involves imagining the subtraction of some of the means that actually were used, and also the addition of alternative means. Eamonn Callan gives a vivid example:

> The child who is taught to believe "I must be a housewife when I grow up" and adjusts her ambitions accordingly might easily revise her belief and preference if all that sustained them were a deficit of information and skill. But if emotional inhibitions are effectively cultivated to protect the amalgam of belief and desire from future critical assessment, then knowledge of alternative careers and the skills to pursue them acquired later will do nothing to shake her sense of domestic destiny . . . [having] been manipulated to resist any reasons that challenge belief in the propriety of that role for her. Furthermore, she is also primed to resist the thought that political structures that foist that role on her and other women might not deserve their consent.
>
> *(2000: 146–7)*

To respect the principle of free consent and the values implicit in it, a legitimation of moral indoctrination has not only to invoke hypothetical consent—that is, to ask whether consent would now be given—but also to normalize the consenter. To "normalize the consenter" is to imagine how, as identifiably the same person, she *would* choose if her preferences, dispositions, and opinions had not been shaped by specified distorting influences and misinformation. The pertinent question then becomes, "Could you—regardless of whether you had been raised the way you were—*reasonably* have withheld your consent to being raised in that way?" A clear answer is unlikely to come instantly to mind.

So, Rawls's method of legitimating other kinds of indoctrination appears problematic if applied to moral education itself. It kindles a suspicion that consent has become so attenuated as to be normatively redundant. To say "You would (or could) reasonably have withheld your consent to being raised in that way just in case that way was a way in which you ought not to have been raised" seems a needlessly roundabout way of framing the question of whether that way of childrearing is wrong. "Consent" is not bearing the normative load (cf. Edmundson 2011). One way to respond would be to appeal to vicarious consent by parents or the state in loco parentis, but—as noted above—this only shifts the difficulty. Effective consent by proxy presupposes not only that the proxy not be disqualified by a conflict of interests, but also that the proxy has not been brainwashed or subjected to gross indoctrination herself. An ethics of consent thus seems to have no choice but to build upon an ethics not-of-consent (or "other-than-of-consent").

32.3 Williams's "Critical Theory" principle

The "consent of the governed" is the paradigmatic legitimation of state power. But a disposition to consent to or at least to acquiesce in the governmental status quo is already inculcated in the young, years in advance of their reaching maturity. The same is true of many other types of power differentials, such as those between genders and classes variously defined (propertied/propertyless; white/non-white; native/non-native, etc.). Whether these differentials are binding or not cannot simply come down to the question of whether they are consented to.

Sometimes people stubbornly withhold consent when it ought to be given, but they also sometimes give it when it ought to be withheld.

The significance of the consent of the advantaged party in an asymmetric relationship may be questioned, too; but the more troubling case is one in which an asymmetry is justified by appeal to the consent of those who are at a disadvantage—and who may in fact not perceive that they are disadvantaged at all. One might object to some asymmetrical relationships that they involve a disadvantage of so obnoxious a nature that they cannot be justified at all, and so a fortiori cannot be justified by consent. Many think of slavery that way. But not all disadvantages are as obnoxious as this. For example, it is widely believed that one can validly consent in the labor market to take a job that makes one a poorly paid source of wealth for superordinate others (cf. Marx and Engels 1978 [1867]: 357–8). As Bernard Williams explains, when consent to something that is not per se unjustifiable is gotten by deception or torture or gross imposition, we have a violation of

> what may be called *the critical theory principle*, that the acceptance of justification does not count if the acceptance itself is produced by the coercive power which is supposedly being justified. [This] is a sound principle: the difficulty with it, of making good on claims of false consciousness and the like, lies in deciding what counts as having been "produced by" coercive power in the relevant sense.
>
> *(2005: 6; emphasis in the original)*

The critical theory principle has both appeal and adherents; but Williams may have misidentified the real difficulty in its implementation. The difficulty lies not so much in deciding what count as legitimate and illegitimate ways of producing acceptance, as it does in deciding what is and what is not an acceptable thing to produce. If a set of attitudes toward authority is reasonable to hold—as judged from where you and I now stand—then they will be a sufficient ground for legitimating authority unless, of course, they were brought about by conspicuously wrongful methods, such as torture, "gross propaganda, and drugs" (2002: 222). Even in such cases as these, presumably the succession of generations and passage of time can legitimate an attitude toward authority that was originally brought about by conspicuously wrongful methods—if, but only if, the resulting set of attitudes is within the acceptable range (cf. Waldron 1992). Parental authority as it is recognized today, for example, might be legitimate (for fit parents), even though its historical origin lies in paternal tyranny.

Williams rejects this position and its implicit appeal to "a normatively approved list of desires" (2005: 81) or of attitudes. It is understandable why one would not want to make a normatively approved list the center of discussion. There is bound to be controversy over what does and does not belong on it. For example, Galston (1989) favors inculcating patriotic attitudes, Gutmann (1987), Macedo (1995), and Crittenden (2002) favor critical thinking, and MacMullen (2015)—with nods to Burke and Oakeshott—mounts a defense of the "status-quo bias" endemic to civic education, but restricted to an approved list of status quos. And of course the range of reasonable opinion is far wider than this.

The alternative approach Williams favors prescinds from the battle of the lists and "appeals . . . rather to some special explanations of why people do not have certain desires they might be expected to have" (2005: 81). Williams poses a hypothetical case of contented slaves. They seem to be at liberty to do whatever they wish, but that appearance owes entirely to their having been conditioned to wish for nothing inconsistent with their remaining enslaved. Even if valid consent to slavery were possible, the slavery of these slaves is not legitimated by their willingness to utter expressions of consent. In such a case, the curious "absence of a desire for freedom may be diagnosed as itself a product of [delegitimating] coercion: it is precisely because of the way they are treated, prevented from hearing other options and so on, that the state of their desires is as it is"(Williams 2005: 82). Breaking this down into its elements, Williams's "Critical Theory" test comprises the following:

(a) a presumptively normal attitudinal set *S*;
(b) coercive interference *C* blocking influences that normally foster *S*; and
(c) as a result, an abnormal ("paradoxical") attitudinal set S'.

It is not that S' is per se illegitimate—that is, too unjust to be capable of legitimating a state of affairs consistent with S' and not *S*. That is the position that Williams thinks less interesting and wants to avoid. Instead, his Critical Theory principle crucially depends upon (b), the coercive interference. It is "a genuinely universal principle, that coercion in itself cannot constitute legitimation [and] some methods of belief-formation are simply coercive" (Williams 2002: 221). Consent that is simply the expression of coercively implanted beliefs lacks the normative power to legitimate.

The application of Williams's Critical Theory test is straightforward where the objectionable coerciveness of the methods of influence is obvious to any reasonable observer. In the case of the contented slaves, Williams points to such things as enforced illiteracy and punishment for possessing reading matter. These methods can fairly be counted as coercive because nothing like them constrains adult members of the master class. The application is equally straightforward when the methods of influence cannot reasonably be objected to as coercive. For example, if the contented slaves possessed S' because of the persuasiveness of a peculiar but not absurd interpretation of stoic philosophy or Christianity. The condition of slavery should be objected to on the ground of its wrongness, rather than on the ground that the would-be slaves' consent had been coerced.

The Critical Theory principle cannot easily vindicate either parental authority or moral education. Trouble arrives from two quarters. One is that, across a range of different cultures, children are both sheltered from influences outside the family and subjected to pressures that would count as coercive outside the family or between adults. Another is that influences can themselves be the object of attitudes. Attitudinal set *S* may negatively view types of influences that S' views neutrally or even positively. "Much successful education, after all", Williams says, "is a benign form of seduction" (2002: 226). The conspicuously coercive forms having already been set aside, the problem is that determining what is and is not a *benign* form of desire-creation ("seduction") appears necessarily to involve peeking at an independently fixed, "normatively approved list of desires" (Williams 2005: 81).

The Critical Theory test could be stated in some other terms, and Williams also suggests asking:

> If they were to understand properly how they came to hold this belief [viz., in the consent-worthiness of an arrangement], would they give it up?
>
> *(2002: 227)*

This has roughly the same doubly counterfactual structure of Rawls's test: would they still consent were they properly to grasp the requisite background conditions for valid consent, and how those conditions vary from the background they had in fact been placed in? But in this form, as Williams points out, the test is either trivially satisfiable or otiose. The sticky point is the background conditions. "If we are supposing that the background is simply these people's current set of beliefs, then almost anything will pass the test. . . . If we suppose, on the other hand, an entirely external frame of reference, then nothing very distinctive is achieved by the test"(Williams 2002: 227). Nothing distinctive is achieved because the critical judgment is arrived at by striking the belief in question from the normatively approved list, and the process discredited on that basis alone.

The Critical Theory test can do its distinctive work only if it can be gotten to proceed from the inside, so to speak. "We need a schema by which we start with people's current beliefs and imagine their going through a process of criticism . . . asking a series of reflective questions about their situation" (Williams 2002: 227). If the members of the subordinated group believe that

(1) The distribution of powers and advantages in the system is basically just,

they might also come to see that

(2) They believe (1) only because members of the more powerful party (. . . the instructors) give them appropriate training.

The subordinated might see, for example, that (1) is not something otherwise discoverable. From there, it is a possible, further critical step for the subordinated to arrive at

(3) It is only if (1) is true that the instructors are in a sound position to claim that (1) is true; the basis for their authority comes from the system itself.

In other words, critical reflection might reveal that "the justice of the system, the authority of the instructors, and hence their own reasons for accepting the justice of the system all hang together" (Williams 2002: 228). From here, reflection might readily pass to

(4) There are perfectly good explanations of the instructors' belief in their own authority. This means, granted (3), that there are good explanations of their teaching (1) which do not imply that (1) is true.

The instructors might teach orthodoxy because it is in the instructors' interests, or because of their own prior indoctrination, whether or not the orthodoxy is true. Because the system is one in which the instructors enjoy advantages, "the disadvantaged will not need any very sophisticated psychological theory to accept (4)" (Williams 2002: 229). The will to power, the urge to dominate, will do.

Articulated this way, the Critical Theory test seems to undercut all asymmetrical relationships, all authority structures; but, Williams says, not so. The "power used in school to get people to learn mathematics or geography" does not fall under (4): "there is not any obvious reason why these people would teach these things unless there was at least a good chance that they were true [and] the teaching itself will have suggested, at least in outline, the ways in which people might come to know mathematical or geographical truths other than being taught them by such instructors"(Williams 2002: 229). If a pupil can go and see for herself whether the Mississippi River is indeed deep and wide, the instructor's claim to authority peels away from the truth he claims to impart, and he has little to gain by pretending to know what he can be shown to be wrong about.

Well and good. But, as one would expect, History and Civics will be tougher to handle than Geography and Mathematics. And where does this leave parental authority and the moral education that parents impart? Children believe that (1) it is just that parents have authority. (2) Children believe (1) only because their parents told them so. (3) Only if (1) is true are parents in a good position to claim (1) is true. And (4) there are perfectly good explanations of why parents teach (1) that do not imply that (1) is true. In the general case, Williams draws a drastic conclusion where (1)–(4) hold:

> [T]hese particular processes of instruction do *not* have the authority that is claimed for them. But if the disadvantaged have no reason to accept what the instructors tell them about the justice of the system, they have reason to reject it. This is not a case for mere scepticism.
>
> *(2002: 229; emphasis in the original)*

Parental authority could be distinguished from the general case, and skepticism avoided, by reference to the features of the parent/child relationship that do not disadvantage the child. It is not a mere power relationship, in which children are gotten to assent to a system in which their interests are subordinated in order to serve the interests of their elders.

This is the right thing to say about the parental case, but then the Critical Theory test turns out to be next to useless in any other case in which reflection encounters a colorable paternalistic defense of the instructors' position of relative advantage. Allowing a hearing for a paternalistic exception immediately takes us to "an entirely external frame of reference" in which "nothing very distinctive is achieved" by applying the Critical Theory test. Of course, resort to an external frame of reference is unneeded if the critical tribunal credits an equivalent to the "father knows best" story that was already internal to the parental-authority system. But it is precisely that story that the principle of free consent wanted to get critical distance from, and looked to the Critical Theory test to achieve. If the "local" legitimation story is left undisturbed by the test, then "almost anything can pass".

32.4 The road to Summerhill

We are born with an innate disposition to babble, to imitate the language of our caregivers, and to acquire their language. The legitimacy of this is beyond question. And, anyway, there is no need to threaten a child with the withdrawal of affection to get her to talk. We are also born with an innate disposition to respond to parental expressions of love and to be disturbed by the withdrawal of parental affection. A question of legitimacy does not yet arise. But we are not born with an innate disposition to accept what our parents say as authoritative. What Rawls calls "the morality of authority" (1999a: 405) is instilled in the young by the exercise of authority. Were one born with an innate disposition to consent to being molded to accept the legitimacy of one's upbringing, there might be no problem. There is a liberal problem about civic education and, more broadly, moral education only because early childhood is a period of moral nonage, in which we cannot validly consent to anything, yet the legitimacy of taking advantage of nonage as an opportunity for moral and civic education is at odds with the liberal demand for authentic, not manufactured, consent.

As Rawls tells the story of the first stage of moral development, the young child initially "experiences parental affection as unconditional" (1999a: 406), as indeed it should be: "the pleasure they [the parents] take in him [the child] is not dependent upon disciplined performances that contribute to the well-being of others" (1999a: 406). But as the child matures and begins to "launch out", her behavior will from time to time exceed the boundaries the parents will accept. The child "has no original tendency to do the things he is told to do" (1999a: 407).

The withdrawal of parental affection, and threats of its being withheld, and natural facial expressions of disapproval—Rawls is not explicit here—are normally used to exact the child's compliance and to inculcate in the child feelings of guilt when found to have disobeyed.

> The child's having a morality of authority consists in his being disposed without the prospect of [immediate or certain] reward or punishment to follow certain precepts that not only may appear to him to be largely arbitrary but which in no way appeal to his original inclinations.
>
> *(Rawls 1999a: 408)*

The precepts the child learns are not originally hers; and neither is the disposition to accept her parents' directions as authoritative. There *can* be a question about the legitimacy of this. It is conceivable that a child might arrive at the later stages of morality—the morality of association, and the morality of principle—without being put through the first stage, the morality of authority. We probably—most of us—retroactively approve of having been put through the first stage, even though we could not have consented to it at the time. We would be likelier to disapprove to the extent that the process had involved corporal punishment or other excessive harshness—as Rawls does (1999a: 408). Leave the inessential excesses aside. It is not unreasonable to suspect that our readiness retroactively to approve having been put through the (non-excessive) essentials of this process is itself an artifact of having been put through that very process.

The question of liberal legitimacy, however, is whether it would be unreasonable to dissent from this first-stage process. Practical experiments to dispense with it are not unheard-of, and the standards for judging their success are bound to be controversial (Hart 1970; MacMullen 2015). The ethics of consent arrives at a fork in the road. If the principle of free consent is interpreted strictly, to require consent all the way down, and hypothetical consent where actual consent is impossible, then it must condemn all but the most Summerhillian of moral educations as illegitimate (cf. Neill 1973). Or, if it is unwilling to accept where this leads, it must interpret the principle of free consent in a more relaxed way, and accept that social, political, and parental authority cannot be consensual all the way down, and that the legitimacy of inculcating a "shared basis for justification [to] help ensure stability from one generation to the next" (Rawls 1999b: 421) must bottom itself on something other than consent.[1]

Note

1 I thank Brian Bix, Jeremy Farris, and Peter Schaber for thoughtful criticism and suggestions.

References

Brighouse, H. (1998) "Civic Education and Liberal Legitimacy," *Ethics* 108(4): 719–45.

Callan, E. (2000) "Liberal Legitimacy, Justice, and Civic Education," *Ethics* 111(1): 141–55.

Callan, E. and D. Arena (2009) "Indoctrination," in H. Siegel (ed.), *The Oxford Handbook of Political Philosophy*. Oxford: Oxford University Press, pp. 104–21.

Crittenden, J. (2002) *Democracy's Midwife: An Education in Deliberation*. Lanham, MD: Lexington Books.

Edmundson, W. (2011) "Consent and its Cousins," *Ethics* 121: 335–53.

Flathman, R. (1996) "Liberal versus Civic, Republican, Democratic and Other Vocational Educations: Liberalism and Institutionalized Education," *Political Theory* 24(1): 4–32.

Galston, W. (1989) "Civic Education in the Liberal State," in N. Rosenblum (ed.), *Liberalism and the Moral Life*. Cambridge, MA: Harvard University Press, pp. 89–101.

Gutmann, A. (1987) "Civic Education and Social Diversity," *Ethics* 105(3): 557–79.

Hart, H. (ed.) (1970) *Summerhill: For and Against, Assessments of A.S. Neill*. New York: Hart Publishing.

Haslanger, S. (2012) *Resisting Reality: Social Construction and Social Critique*. Oxford: Oxford University Press.
Jubb, R. (2014) "Playing Kant in the Court of King Arthur," *Political Studies* 63(4): 919–34.
Macedo, S. (1995) "Liberal Civic Education and Religious Fundamentalism: The Case of *God v John Rawls*?" *Ethics* 105: 468–96.
MacMullen, I. (2015) *Civics Beyond Critics: Character Education in a Liberal Democracy*. Oxford: Oxford University Press.
Marx, K. and F. Engels (1978 [1867]) *Capital: Volume One*, in R. Tucker (ed.), *The Marx–Engels Reader*. New York: W.W. Norton, pp. 294–438.
Neill, A.S. (1973) *Neill! Neill! Orange Peel! A Personal View of Ninety Years*. London: Weidenfeld & Nicolson.
Rawls, J. (1996) *Political Liberalism*. Paperback ed. New York: Columbia University Press.
Rawls, J. (1999a) *A Theory of Justice*. Revised ed. Cambridge MA: Harvard University Press.
Rawls, J. (1999b) "The Idea of an Overlapping Consensus," in S. Freeman (ed.), *John Rawls: Collected Papers*. Cambridge, MA: Harvard University Press, pp. 421–48.
Rawls, J. (2001) *Justice as Fairness: A Restatement*. E. Kelly (ed.). Cambridge MA: Belknap/Harvard.
Rousseau, J.-J. (1993 [1762]) *Émile [ou de l'Éducation]*. B. Foxley, trans. London: Everyman.
Shklar, J. (1989) "The Liberalism of Fear," in N. Rosenblum (ed.), *Liberalism and the Moral Life*. Cambridge, MA: Harvard University Press, pp. 21–38.
Waldron, J. (1992) "Superseding Historic Injustice," *Ethics* 103(1): 4–28.
Weithman, P. (2015) "Legitimacy and the Project of *Political Liberalism*," in T. Brooks and M. Nussbaum (eds.), *Rawls's Political Liberalism*. New York: Columbia University Press, pp. 73–112.
Williams, B. (2002) *Truth and Truthfulness: An Essay in Genealogy*. Princeton, NJ: Princeton University Press.
Williams, B. (2005) *In the Beginning Was the Deed: Realism and Moralism in Political Argument*. Princeton, NJ: Princeton University Press.

Related topics

Ch.8 Valid consent
Ch.9 Hypothetical consent
Ch.19 Voluntary consent
Ch.30 Consent theory of political obligation

INDEX

For Product Safety Concerns and Information please contact our EU
representative GPSR@taylorandfrancis.com
Taylor & Francis Verlag GmbH, Kaufingerstraße 24, 80331 München, Germany

www.ingramcontent.com/pod-product-compliance
Ingram Content Group UK Ltd.
Pitfield, Milton Keynes, MK11 3LW, UK
UKHW050232200926
475702UK00020B/2983
9780367734336